Major Problems in
American History

MAJOR PROBLEMS IN AMERICAN HISTORY SERIES

GENERAL EDITOR

THOMAS G. PATERSON

Major Problems in American History

Volume I: To 1877

Documents and Essays

FOURTH EDITION

EDITED BY

ELIZABETH COBBS
Texas A&M University

EDWARD J. BLUM
San Diego State University

CENGAGE
Learning·

Australia • Brazil • Canada • Mexico • Singapore • United Kingdom • United States

CENGAGE
Learning·

Major Problems in American History, Volume I: To 1877, Documents and Essays, Fourth Edition

Elizabeth Cobbs/Edward J. Blum

Product Director: Paul R. Banks

Product Manager: Clint Attebery

Content Developer: Alison Levy

Product Assistant: Andrew Newton

Marketing Manager: Kyle Zimmerman

Senior Content Project Manager: Carol Newman

Senior Art Director: Cate Rickard Barr

Manufacturing Planner: Fola Orekoya

IP Analyst: Alexandra Ricciardi

IP Project Manager: Farah Fard

Production Service and Compositor: Lumina Datamatics, Inc.

Cover Image: SENECA FALLS MEETING, 1848. Elizabeth Cady Stanton addressing the first Women's Rights meeting at Seneca Falls, New York, on 20 June 1848. Illustration, early 20th century. Granger, NYC, All Rights Reserved.

For product information and technology assistance, contact us at **Cengage Learning Customer & Sales Support, 1-800-354-9706**

For permission to use material from this text or product, submit all requests online at **www.cengage.com/permissions** Further permissions questions can be emailed to **permissionrequest@cengage.com**

Library of Congress Control Number: 2015946494

ISBN: 978-1-305-58529-4

Cengage Learning
20 Channel Center Street
Boston, MA 02210
USA

Cengage Learning is a leading provider of customized learning solutions with employees residing in nearly 40 different countries and sales in more than 125 countries around the world. Find your local representative at **www.cengage.com**

To learn more about Cengage Learning Solutions, visit **www.cengage.com**

Purchase any of our products at your local college store or at our preferred online store **www.cengagebrain.com**

Printed at CLDPC, USA, 02-23

For our families,
especially our children

Contents

Preface

History is a matter of interpretation. Individual scholars rescue particular stories from the hubbub of human experience, analyze patterns, and offer arguments about how these events reflected or reshaped human society at a given moment. This means that other historians might select different stories, perceive different patterns, and arrive at contrasting interpretations of the same time period or even the same event. All scholars use evidence, but the choice and interpretation of evidence is to some extent an expression of professional judgment. History is not separate from historians.

The goal of *Major Problems in American History* is to place meat on this bare bones description of how the study of the past "works." Like most instructors, we want students to learn and remember important facts, yet we also want to make clear that historians sometimes disagree on what is important. And, even when historians agree on which facts are noteworthy, they often disagree on what a certain piece of evidence signifies. For example, scholars agree fifty-six men signed the Declaration of Independence in 1776, but they debate why these colonists felt compelled to take that dramatic step—and others did not.

The two volumes that comprise this book bring together primary documents and secondary sources on the major debates in American history. The primary sources give students evidence to work with. They represent a mix of the familiar and unfamiliar. Certain documents are a must in any compilation for a survey course because they had a powerful, widely noted impact on American history, such as Tom Paine's *Common Sense* (1776) or President Roosevelt's first inaugural address (1933). We have also selected pieces that evoke the personal experiences of individuals, such as letters, sermons, speeches, political cartoons, poems, and memoirs. There are accounts from European explorers, pioneer women on the frontier, immigrant workers, soldiers, eyewitnesses to the terrors of World War I, and children in rebellion against their parents during the 1960s. These documents often show conflicting points of view, from the "bottom up," the "top down," and various layers in the middle.

The secondary sources in these volumes fulfill a different goal. They expose students to basic historical debates about each broad period. Sometimes we focus on classic debates, combining very recent essays with seasoned pieces by eminent historians who set the terms of discussion for an entire generation or more. Other times we have selected essays that do not disagree openly—but show that young scholars are sometimes of different minds about the most revealing "way in" to a subject. Our purpose is to make contrasts as clear as possible for students who are just learning to distinguish interpretation from fact, and discern argument within description. In addition, the essays often make direct reference to the primary documents. This allows students to examine how the historian uses primary documents—fairly, or not. The students, therefore, can debate the use of sources and the differing historical conclusions to which they lead.

Volume I, prepared by Edward J. Blum in collaboration with Elizabeth Cobbs, begins with the collision of cultures in the late fifteenth century and ends in the Reconstruction of the United States. This volume examines how new worlds were made when Europeans, western Africans, and Native Americans interacted. It proceeds to the birth of the United States, its growth and development, and ultimately its fracture during the Civil War. Some of the main themes include: the making and unmaking of a society based on slavery; commercial development that included the emergence of cities, interlocking networks of trade, and early industrialization; the push for rights and inclusion from groups that achieved them and from groups that did not.

This book follows the same general format as other volumes in the *Major Problems in American History* series. Each chapter begins with a short introduction that orients the student. Following this, we include a section called "Questions to Think About" to help students focus their reading of the subsequent material. Next come eight to ten primary documents, followed by two essays that highlight contrasting interpretations. Headnotes at the start of the document and essay sections help readers identify key themes and debates. These headnotes also show how documents relate to each other, and how the essays differ in perspective. Each chapter concludes with a brief "Further Reading" section to tempt readers into further research. In addition, at the start of the volume, we give suggestions on how to read sources and critically analyze their content, points of view, and implications. This introduction encourages students to draw their own conclusions and use evidence to back up their reasoning.

New to the Fourth Edition

The fourth edition makes several changes to previous editions. We have retained many documents and essays that reviewers told us worked well in their survey courses, but each chapter has also been updated to reflect the latest scholarship and replace excerpts that instructors found difficult to use. The biggest change is the shift to "America in the world." We have attempted to include at least one document in every chapter that reflects globalization: the ways that the perspectives of people in other parts of the world profoundly affected the United States. Documents and essays in the fourth edition highlight the connections between American and world trends, consistent with recent initiatives in our profession to internationalize U.S. history.

All content is also available in MindTap, Cengage Learning's fully online, highly personalized learning experience. In MindTap, students will practice critical thinking skills relevant to each primary and secondary source in every chapter. Learn more at www.cengage.com.

Acknowledgments

Many friends and colleagues have contributed to these volumes. In the fourth edition we particularly wish to thank John Putman and Andrew Wiese from San Diego State University; Brian Balogh of the University of Virginia; Drew Cayton at Miami University of Ohio; Mona Domosh of Dartmouth University; Rebecca Goetz of Rice University; Paul Harvey of the University of Colorado, Colorado Springs; Eric Hinderaker at University of Utah; Anthony Kaye of Penn State University; Bruce Levine of the University of Illinois, Urbana-Champaign; Phil Morgan of Johns Hopkins; Maria Montoya of Princeton University; Bruce Schulman of Boston University; Jason Scott Smith of the University of New Mexico; James Stewart of Macalester College; Matthew Avery Sutton of Washington State University; and Ben Wright of the University of Texas at Dallas. We also wish to thank our students, who inspire and teach us.

For this edition, we received detailed and extremely helpful outside reviews from Marc Abrams, Penn State University; Robert Bionaz, Chicago State University; David Brodnax, Trinity Christian College; Cara Converse, Moorpark College; Todd Estes, Oakland University; Peter Kuryla, Belmont University; Bernard Maegi, Normandale Community College; Todd Michney, Tulane University; Stephen Rockenbach, Virginia State University; and Robert Schultz, Illinois Wesleyan University. Thomas G. Paterson, the editor of the *Major Problems* series, provided sound advice. We are obliged to our editor at Cengage Learning, Alison Levy, for her kind encouragement, insightful recommendations, and help in a pinch.

The life of the mind is exceptionally fulfilling, but it is happiest when set within the life of the family. We wish to express our deep gratitude to our families, especially our children, to whom this book is dedicated.

E. C.

E. J. B.

About the Authors

Elizabeth Cobbs, Professor and Melbern G. Glasscock Chair in American History at Texas A&M University, has won literary prizes for both history and fiction. Her books include *American Umpire* (2013), *Broken Promises: A Novel of the Civil War* (2011), *All You Need Is Love: The Peace Corps and the 1960s* (2000), and *The Rich Neighbor Policy* (1992). She has served on the jury for the Pulitzer Prize in History and on the Historical Advisory Committee of the U.S. State Department. She has received awards and fellowships from the Fulbright Commission, Woodrow Wilson International Center for Scholars, Organization of American States, and other distinguished institutions. She presently holds a Research Fellowship at Stanford University's Hoover Institution on War, Revolution, and Peace. Her essays have appeared in the *New York Times, Jerusalem Post, Los Angeles Times, Chicago Tribune, China Daily News, Washington Independent, San Diego Union,* and *Reuters.* Her current projects include a history of women soldiers in World War I and a novel on the life of Alexander Hamilton.

Edward J. Blum is professor of history at the San Diego State University. A scholar of religion and race, he is the co-author of *The Color of Christ: The Son of God and the Saga of Race in America* (2012) and the author of *W. E. B. Du Bois, American Prophet* (2007) and *Reforging the White Republic: Race, Religion, and American Nationalism, 1865–1898* (2005). An award-winning author and teacher, Blum is currently at work on a project that explores issues of radical evil during the era of the Civil War.

Introduction: How to Read Primary and Secondary Sources

College study encompasses a number of subjects. Some disciplines, such as mathematics, are aimed at establishing indisputable proofs. Students learn methods to discover the path to a correct answer. History is different. Unlike math, it is focused much more on interpretation. Historians study and analyze sources to construct arguments about the past. They generally understand there is no "right" answer, even if some arguments are more reasonable than others. They search less for absolute truth than for understanding. A historical imagination is useful in creating these interpretations. People in the past thought and acted differently than we do today. Their views of science, religion, the place of women and men—to cite only a few examples—were not the same as our views. When historians create an argument about the past, they must imagine a world unlike the one we now inhabit. They must use empathy and suspend judgment to develop understanding.

The "problems" in U.S. history on which this text focuses, then, are different from math "problems." They are a series of issues in the American past that might be addressed, discussed, and debated, but not necessarily solved. This text provides readers with two tools to grapple with these problems: primary and secondary sources. A *primary source* is a piece of evidence that has survived from the period. Primary sources may include pictures, artifacts, music, and written texts. They have survived in a number of ways. Archaeologists uncover shards of pottery and other interesting trash when digging up lost civilizations; ethnologists transcribe campfire stories; and economists numerically measure past behavior; and historians generally scrutinize surviving written sources. This volume by and large uses written texts, from political tracts to private letters to cartoons. Some of the documents, however, are transcriptions, that is, texts written by someone who noted what another person said. Sometimes the texts are memoirs, in which a person recounts an event they personally experienced long before.

On these occasions, you will see two dates: one that tells the year of the events, and a second in parentheses that tells the year in which the memoir was written.

As historians, we must treat primary sources with caution. First of all, we must consider whether a source is really from the period under consideration. You might occasionally read stories in the newspaper about paintings that had been attributed to famous artists but were later discovered to be frauds by an unknown copyist. When the fraud is discovered, the painting's value plummets. The same is true of a primary source. A letter alleged to have been written by George Washington clearly could not reveal his innermost thoughts if it was forged in 1910. But we should also be aware of the opposite: not all pieces of evidence have survived to the present. We might ask if there is a bias in the likelihood of one point of view surviving and another being lost. The experiences of slaveholders, for example, were more commonly written and published than those of slaves. Because slaves (and others, such as Native Americans) were rarely given the opportunity to publish their thoughts, they have bequeathed fewer sources and some that survived as transcriptions. As essential as transcriptions are in reconstructing the past, as historians we must be critical of them, too. Did the people writing down the spoken words accurately set them to paper or did they edit them or inject their own thoughts? In the case of memoirs, how much might current events affect memories of the past?

Once we consider the validity of sources and understand that some were more likely to survive than others, another reason to critique sources is that they are not "objective" portrayals of the past. By nature, they are points of view. Like anyone in a society, the writer of each primary source provides us with his or her viewpoint. It gives us a window through which to view the world, complete with the biases and blind spots of the author. When we read about the American Revolution, for example, we will see many different perspectives on the events leading up to the Declaration of Independence. Those who opposed independence saw events very differently from those who supported the movement. We have often read about advocates of independence who saw the British government as a threat to American freedom. They believed the thirteen colonies would be better off as one independent nation. Americans for generations have viewed this as a truly heroic episode. But others at the time did not think that independence was the correct course. A substantial minority opposed independence because they felt more secure in the British Empire. Countless members of Indian nations were suspicious of the intentions of the American "patriots" and remained loyal to the king. African American slaves were often leery of the aims of their patriot owners. The fact that people had different viewpoints allows us to grapple with multiple perspectives on the past.

When you are reading the documents in this volume, we urge you to look at each one critically. We are certain that these are valid sources, not forgeries, so your job is to ponder the implications of each document. Consider both the document and its author. Who wrote or spoke the words in the document? What was his or her reason for expressing those thoughts? Given the various authors' background and motivations, what were their perspectives and potential biases? How did they see the world differently from the way others did? And, why do *you* think these different perspectives existed? Whose viewpoint do you agree with most? Why?

It is not too much to say that the student of history is like a detective who seeks clues to reveal the lives and events of the past.

In addition to primary sources, each chapter in this volume contains two essays that represent what we call a *secondary source*. A secondary source is so named because it is one step removed from the primary source. Secondary sources are the work of historians who have conducted painstaking research in primary documents. These essays represent some of their findings about the past. You will notice that the writers do not necessarily reach similar conclusions as one another. On the contrary, they illustrate differing opinions about which events were important, why they occurred, and how they affect us today.

Hence secondary sources, like primary sources, do not provide us with un-contestable "truth," even when based on verifiable facts. Rather, historians' con-clusions vary just as your ideas about the documents might differ from those of someone else in your class. And they differ for a number of reasons. First, inter-pretations are influenced by the sources on which they depend. Occasionally, a historian might uncover a cache of primary sources heretofore unknown to other scholars, and these new sources might shed new light on a topic. Here again historians operate like detectives.

Second and more important, however, historians carry their own perspec-tives to the research. As they read secondary sources, analyze primary texts, and imagine the past, historians may develop arguments that differ in emphasis from those developed by others. As they combine their analyses with their own per-spectives, they create an argument to explain the past. Personal point of view and even society's dominant point of view may influence their thinking. If analyzing sources resembles working as a detective, writing history is similar to being a judge who attempts to construct the most consistent argument from the sources and information at hand. And historians can be sure that those who oppose their viewpoints will analyze their use of sources and the logic of their argument. Those who might disagree with them—and that might include you—will criti-cize them if they make errors of fact or logic.

The essays were selected for this text in part because they reflect differing conclusions. For example, why did the United States intervene in World War I? For decades, historians have given us a number of answers. Some have said that Woodrow Wilson foolishly broke with a tradition of non-entanglement dating back to George Washington. Others say that Wilson wisely recognized that a changed world required changes in America's international role. Or what are we to make of the 1950s? Some historians have celebrated this period as a flowering of American prosperity, unity, and democracy. Others have noted that the franchise applied only to whites and that McCarthyism suppressed free-dom of conscience and personal non-conformity. Or how do we now make sense of the Vietnam War, nearly fifty years after the first American troops landed? Was it "a terrible mistake" that undermined confidence in the United States in the words of one of its architects, or was it, in President Ronald Reagan's words, a "noble cause"?

An important question left unanswered in all of these chapters is what *you* think is the correct interpretation. In the end, you might not agree completely with any of the essayists. In fact, you might wish to create your own argument that uses primary sources found here and elsewhere and that accepts parts of one essay and parts of another. Once you do this, you become a historian, a person who attempts to analyze texts critically, and is personally engaged with the topic. If that occurs, this volume is a success.

When we discuss the discipline of history with people, we typically get one of two responses. The first is something like "I hated history in school." The other is something like "history was my favorite subject." Invariably the people who hated history cite all the boring facts that they had to memorize. Those who loved history remember a teacher or professor who brought the subject alive by imaginatively invoking the past.

As we have tried to indicate in this short overview, history is not about memorizing boring facts but rather an active enterprise of thought and interpretation. Historians are not rote learners. Instead, historians are detectives and judges, people who investigate, interpret, and reimagine what happened. They study the past to understand the world in which we live today. Facts are important, but they are building blocks in a larger enterprise of interpretation.

In sum, our intent is to show how primary and secondary sources can aid you in understanding and interpreting major problems in the American past. We also aim to keep that group of people who hate history as small as possible and enlarge that group who embrace history with passion. Frankly, the latter are more fun.

CHAPTER 1

Old Worlds Make New Ones

Tisquantum, a member of the Patuxet nation, lived a life that exemplifies the intricate connections among native peoples, European colonists, systems of labor, and new movements of people, languages, goods, and microbes. In 1605, he was kidnapped by an Englishman who was exploring the coasts of Canada and New England and was carried to England. There, he learned the English language. He eventually returned to America on another voyage of exploration in 1614, and was kidnapped again and taken to southern Spain. His abductors intended to sell him into slavery, but he was rescued by Catholic friars, with whom he lived until 1618. He returned once again to the New England coast, only to discover that his entire nation had been destroyed by disease some years before. Shortly after his return, he met a group of English colonists who called themselves Pilgrims; they were astounded when he spoke to them in English. He befriended the Pilgrims and taught them how to survive in the American wilderness—he was a participant in the first "thanksgiving"—and he became their trading partner. In late 1622, Tisquantum, whom we know today as Squanto, contracted what the English called "Indian fever" and died. Tisquantum's life, as remarkable as it was, illustrates many of the experiences of native people following contact with Europeans: travel, disease, war, enslavement, cultural exchange, and trade.

Tisquantum lived in a changing world, just as western Europeans and western Africans of the time did. Never static or uniform, these three broad cultures—Native American, western European, and western African—had profound internal differences that shifted over time. The Aztec empire, located in what is today Mexico, was characterized by its military power. It was at the peak of its strength when its people first encountered Europeans. The English, alternatively, were primarily rural, occupied an extraordinarily small piece of land, and were not only weak on the world stage, but also among European peoples.

Beginning with the landfall of Christopher Columbus and his crew in 1492, the course of world history changed dramatically. During the centuries that followed, people from Europe, the Americas, and Africa together would create a "new world." The trade for West African slaves by Portuguese explorers predated Columbus's voyages, and Africans would play a dynamic role in this new world. This creation involved both an interaction between peoples of striking differences and a brutality of remarkable proportions.

1

Perhaps at no other time did people with such different worldviews and social practices meet. Indians, West Africans, and Europeans differed not only in perceptions of physical appearance but also in such matters as work roles between women and men, notions of private property, religious belief and organizations, and governmental structures. Some of the new arrivals simply observed these differences, whereas others used them to justify conflict and savagery.

The earliest European explorers were interested in gaining riches in the Americas and from Africa. They were concerned with carrying their Christian faiths too. Once they realized the abundance of wealth that the Americas offered and the absence of Christianity, the Europeans sought to amass the wealth and convert religiously the Native Americans. Spanish conquistadors, for example, conquered the Aztec empire in 1519 and gained untold riches from it. Catholic priests and friars set about missionizing the local people. Soon, native people found themselves enslaved to provide labor for burgeoning mines and sometimes forced to bow to new gods. Between 1545 and 1660, over seven million pounds of silver were extracted from American lands by slaves for the Spanish empire. As other European states recognized the economic possibilities, they too searched for land, slaves, and riches. France, the Netherlands, Sweden, and England all attempted to build empires. These empires came into conflict with one another and in contact with indigenous peoples. This contact between Americans, Africans, and Europeans often resulted in conflict and war. The results, whether peaceably or forcefully, were always dramatic change.

Perhaps even more important than overt conflict was a mysterious and hidden exchange of disease. As native people were exposed to an array of diseases, ranging from smallpox to influenza, with which they had had little prior contact, they suffered epidemics that weakened their societies and therefore their ability to contest additional European incursions. Like Squanto, the native people became traders, but they also became slaves and victims of strange, new diseases. Their home, in effect, had become a new world for them as well as for western Europeans and Africans.

 # QUESTIONS TO THINK ABOUT

Were encounters among Native Americans, western Europeans, and western Africans defined primarily by contact, confusion, or conquest? Was the first encounter a break from older interactions or was it part of general interactions among different people groups? In what ways did Europeans of different nationalities treat Indians? What differences did Europeans focus upon between themselves, Indians, and western Africans? What role did violence play in creating the new world? Should humans be held accountable for the activities of nonhumans, such as in the case of microbes that lead to disease and death?

DOCUMENTS

The initial interactions among Indians, Africans, and Europeans involved a strange combination of terror and wonder for all those involved. Before Europeans arrived, Native American societies had been in significant flux. Document 1 is an origins tale from the Iroquois, where they relate how they were first made as a people. Pay attention to how this narrative is similar to and divergent from other creation stories with which you are familiar. Document 2 depicts how the Aztecs demanded and received gifts, such as feathers, clothing, and precious metals, from local peoples they had subjugated. Engagement with North and South America transformed how Europeans viewed the world and themselves. An image of the innovative mapmaker Gerardus Mercator is document 3. In this case, European engagement with Africa and the Americas not only compelled new visual renderings of maps and globes, but also signaled the ability of humans to be larger than the globe itself—to stand symbolically where only God had before. Decades before Columbus sailed, a Portuguese writer (document 4) chronicles one of the first expeditions to obtain slaves from West Africa. In document 5, Christopher Columbus recounts his first meeting with the people in the Caribbean and his sense of the economic possibility of the Indies. In its description of the Indians, his letter betrays an odd blending of tenderness and a brutal assessment of their potential uses. In document 6, a Spanish priest, Fray Bernardino de Sahagun, describes the conquest of the Aztecs by Spanish conquistadors in 1519. Economic and material trade was routine among the various groups, and document 7 details the give-and-take of trading. Document 8 is an engraving based on a drawing from the 1580s. It shows a Secotan village on the outer banks of North Carolina. Notice how the Secotan organized space for housing, agriculture, and religious ceremonies.

1. The Iroquois Describe the Beginning of the World, n.d.

In the Sky-World there was a man who had a wife, and the wife was expecting a child. The woman became hungry for all kinds of strange delicacies, as women do when they are with child. She kept her husband busy almost to distraction finding delicious things for her to eat....

The woman decided that she wanted some bark from one of the roots of the Great Tree—perhaps as a food or as a medicine, we don't know. She told her husband this. He didn't like the idea. He knew it was wrong. But she insisted, and he gave in. So he dug a hole among the roots of this great sky tree, and he bared some of its roots. But the floor of the Sky-World wasn't very thick, and he broke a hole through it. He was terrified, for he had never expected to find empty space underneath the world.

From "The World on the Turtle's Back," as seen in *The Great Tree and the Longhouse: The Culture of the Iroquois* by Hazel W. Hertzberg.

But his wife was filled with curiosity. He wouldn't get any of the roots for her, so she set out to do it herself. She bent over and she looked down, and she saw the ocean far below. She leaned down and stuck her head through the hole and looked all around. No one knows just what happened next. Some say she slipped. Some say that her husband, fed up with all the demands she had made on him, pushed her.

So she fell through the hole. As she fell, she frantically grabbed at its edges, but her hands slipped. However, between her fingers there clung bits of things that were growing on the floor of the Sky-World and bits of the root tips of the Great Tree. And so she began to fall toward the great ocean far below....

The great sea turtle came and agreed to receive her on his back. The birds placed her gently on the shell of the turtle, and now the turtle floated about on the huge ocean with the woman safely on his back....

One day... a man appeared. No one knows for sure who this man was. He had something to do with the gods above. Perhaps he was the West Wind. As the girl looked at him, she was filled with terror, and amazement, and warmth, and she fainted dead away. As she lay on the ground, the man reached into his quiver, and he took out two arrows, one sharp and one blunt, and he laid them across the body of the girl, and quietly went away.

When the girl awoke from her faint, she and her mother continued to walk around the earth. After a while, they knew that the girl was to bear a child. They did not know it, but the girl was to bear twins.

Within the girl's body, the twins began to argue and quarrel with one another. There could be no peace between them.

These two brothers, as they grew up, represented two ways of the world which are in all people. The Indians did not call these the right and the wrong. They called them the straight mind and the crooked mind, the upright man and the devious man, the right and the left.

The twins had creative powers. They took clay and modeled it into animals, and they gave these animals life. And in this they contended with one another. The right-handed twin made the deer, and the left-handed twin made the mountain lion which kills the deer. But the right-handed twin knew there would always be more deer than mountain lions.

And the right-handed twin made berries and fruits of other kinds for his creatures to live on. The left-handed twin made briars and poison ivy, and the poisonous plants like the baneberry and the dogberry, and the suicide root with which people kill themselves when they go out of their minds. And the left-handed twin made medicines, for good and for evil, for doctoring and for witchcraft.

2. Native Americans Pay Tithes to the Aztecs, 1541–42

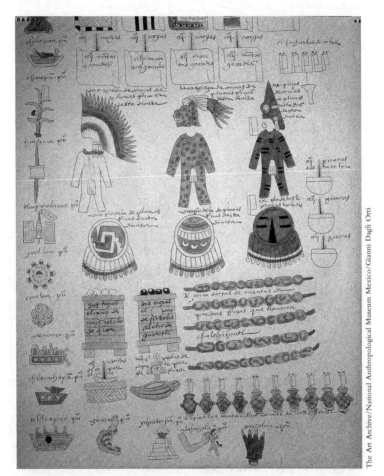

The Art Archive/National Anthropological Museum Mexico/Gianni Dagli Orti

Tithes paid to Aztecs by the peoples they conquered; feathers, jade, bags of cochineal, from modern copy of Codex Mendoza, c. 1541–52. National Anthropological Museum Mexico.

3. European Map-Makers Remake the World, 1595

Gerhard Mercator, half-length portrait, facing left, holding compass and globe, at age 62.
Library of Congress Rare Book and Special Collections Division Washington, D.C.

4. The Portuguese Lament Military Losses in Western Africa, 1448

... And when the ship had been provisioned, they made their voyage straight to Cape Verde, whereat in the past year they had captured the two Guineas of whom we have spoken in another place, and thence they passed on to the Cape of Masts....

"Of how Alvaro Fernandez returned again to the land of the Negroes...," in *Documents Illustrative of the History of the Slave Trade to America*, ed., Elizabeth Donnan (New York: Octagon Books, 1969), 1: 39–41.

And so journeying along the sea coast, in a few days they went on shore again, and came upon a village, and its inhabitants issued forth like men who showed they had a will to defend their houses, and among them came one armed with a good buckler and an assegai [spear] in his hand. And Alvaro Fernandez seeing him, and judging him to be the leader of the band, went stoutly at him, and gave him such a great wound with his lance that he fell down dead, and then he took from him his shield and assegai; and these he brought home to the Infant along with some other things, as will be related further on.

Now the Guineas, perceiving that man to be dead, paused from their fighting, and it appeared to our men to be neither the time nor the place to withdraw them from that fear. But rather they returned to their ship and on the next day landed a little way distant from there, where they espied some of the wives of those Guineas walking. And it seemeth that they were going nigh to a creek collecting shell-fish, and they captured one of them, who would be as much as thirty years of age, with a son of hers who would be of about two, and also a young girl of fourteen years, who had well-formed limbs and also a favorable presence for a Guinea; but the strength of the woman was much to be marvelled at, for not one of the three men who came upon her but would have had a great labour in attempting to get her to the boat. And so one of our men, seeing the delay they were making, during which it might be that some of the dwellers of the land would come upon them, conceived it well to take her son from her and to carry him to the boat; and love of the child compelled the mother to follow after it, without great pressure on the part of the two who were bringing her. From this place they went on further for a certain distance until they lighted upon a river, into which they entered with the boat, and in some houses that they found they captured a woman, and after they had brought her to the caravel, they returned once more to the river, intending to journey higher up in order to try and make some good booty. And as they were pursuing their voyage thus, there came upon them four or five boats of Guineas prepared like men who would defend their land, and our men in the boat were not desirous to try a combat with them, seeing the great advantage their enemies had, and especially because they feared the great peril that lay in the poison with which they shot ... their boat came so near that one of those Guineas made a shot at it and happened to hit Alvaro Fernandez with an arrow in the leg. But since he had already been warned of its poison, he drew out that arrow very quickly and had the wound washed with urine and olive oil, and then anointed it very well ... and it pleased God that it availed him, although his health was in very troublous case, for during certain days he was in the very act of passing away from life. The others on the caravel, although they saw their captain thus wounded, desisted not from voyaging forward along that coast until they arrived at a narrow strip of sand stretching in front of a great bay, and here they put out their boat and went inside to see what kind of land they would find; and when they were in sight of the beach they saw coming toward them full 120 Guineas, some with shields and assegais, others with bows. And as soon as they came near the water these began to play and dance like men far removed from any sorrow; but our men in the boat, wishful to escape from the invitation to that festival, returned to their ship.

5. Christopher Columbus Details His First Encounters with Native People, 1493

Sir,

As I know that you will have pleasure of the great victory which our Lord hath given me in my voyage, I write you this, by which you shall know that in [thirty-three] days I passed over to the Indies with the fleet which the most illustrious King and Queen, our Lords, gave me: where I found very many islands peopled with inhabitants beyond number. And, of them all, I have taken possession for their Highnesses.... Spañola is a marvel; the mountains and hills, and plains, and fields, and land, so beautiful and rich for planting and sowing, for breeding cattle of all sorts, for building of towns and villages. There could be no believing, without seeing, such harbours as are here, as well as the many and great rivers, and excellent waters, most of which contain gold. In the trees and fruits and plants, there are great differences from those of Juana [Cuba]. In [La Spañola], there are many spiceries, and great mines of gold and other metals. The people of this island, and of all the others that I have found and seen, or not seen, all go naked, men and women, just as their mothers bring them forth; although some women cover a single place with the leaf of a plant, or a cotton something which they make for that purpose. They have no iron or steel, nor any weapons; nor are they fit thereunto; not because they be not a well-formed people and of fair stature, but that they are most wondrously timorous. They have no other weapons than the stems of reeds in their seeding state, on the end of which they fix little sharpened stakes. Even these, they dare not use.... It is true that since they have become more assured, and are losing that terror, they are artless and generous with what they have, to such a degree as no one would believe but him who had seen it. Of anything they have, if it be asked for, they never say no, but do rather invite the person to accept it, and show as much lovingness as though they would give their hearts. And whether it be a thing of value, or one of little worth, they are straightways content with whatsoever trifle of whatsoever kind may be given them in return for it.... I gave gratuitously a thousand useful things that I carried, in order that they may conceive affection, and furthermore may be made Christians; for they are inclined to the love and service of their Highnesses and of all the Castilian nation, and they strive to combine in giving us things which they have in abundance, and of which we are in need. And they knew no sect, nor idolatry; save that they all believe that power and goodness are in the sky, and they believed very firmly that I, with these ships and crew, came from the sky; and in such opinion they received me at every place where I landed.... They are men of very subtle wit, who navigate all those seas, and who give a marvellously good account of everything.... As

Spanish Letter of Columbus to Luis de Sant' Angel, Escribano de Racion of the Kingdom of Aragon, Dated 15 February 1493, Reprinted in Facsimile, Translated and Edited from the Unique Copy of the Original Edition (London: 1891), 22–27. (Translator unknown; reprinted in 1891 from a copy in the possession of Bernard Quaritch.) This document can also be found in *America Firsthand*, ed. Robert Marcus and David Burner (New York: St. Martin's Press/Bedford Books, 1989), 3–8.

I have already said, they are the most timorous creatures there are in the world, so that the men who remain there are alone sufficient to destroy all that land, and the island is without personal danger for them if they know how to behave themselves. It seems to me that in all those islands, the men are all content with a single wife; and to their chief or king they give as many as twenty. The women, it appears to me, do more work than the men. Nor have I been able to learn whether they held personal property, for it seemed to me that whatever one had, they all took share of, especially of eatable things. Down to the present, I have not found in those islands any monstrous men, as many expected, but on the contrary all the people are very comely; nor are they black like those in Guinea, but have flowing hair; and they are not begotten where there is an excessive violence of the rays of the sun.... Since thus our Redeemer has given to our most illustrious King and Queen, and to their famous kingdoms, this victory in so high a matter, Christendom should take gladness therein and make great festivals, and give solemn thanks to the Holy Trinity for the great exaltation they shall have by the conversion of so many peoples to our holy faith; and next for the temporal benefit which will bring hither refreshment and profit, not only to Spain, but to all Christians. This briefly, in accordance with the facts. Dated, on the caravel, off the Canary Islands, the 15 February of the year 1493.

At your command,
THE ADMIRAL.

6. Fray Bernardino de Sahagun Relates an Aztec Chronicler's Account of the Spanish Conquest of the Aztecs, 1519

[As Cortés and his army approached Tenochtitlán, the people of the city] rose in tumult, alarmed as if by an earthquake, as if there were a constant reeling of the face of the earth.

Shocked, terrified, Moctezuma himself wept in the distress he felt for his city. Everyone was in terror; everyone was astounded, afflicted. Many huddled in groups, wept in foreboding for their own fates and those of their friends. Others, dejected, hung their heads. Some groups exchanged tearful greetings; others tried mutual encouragement. Fathers would run their hands over their small boys' hair and, smoothing it, say, "Woe, my beloved sons! How can what we fear be happening in your time?" Mothers, too: "My beloved sons, how can you live through what is in store for you?" ...

The iron of [the Spaniards'] lances ... glistened from afar; the shimmer of their swords was as of a sinuous water course. Their iron breast and back pieces, their helmets clanked. Some came completely encased in iron—as if turned to iron.... And ahead of them ... ran their dogs, panting, with foam continually dripping from their muzzles....

From an anonymous Aztec chronicler in Fray Bernardino de Sahagun, *General History of Things in New Spain* (1582).

Moctezuma's own property was then brought out … precious things like necklaces with pendants, arm bands tufted with quetzal feathers, golden arm bands, bracelets, golden anklets with shells, rulers' turquoise diadems, turquoise nose rods; no end of treasure. They took all, seized everything for themselves …

[In 1520, the Spanish occupied Tenochtitlán, took Moctezuma hostage, and finally strangled him. Then] they charged the crowd with their iron lances and hacked us with their iron swords. They slashed the backs of some…. They hacked at the shoulders of others, splitting their bodies open…. The blood of the young warriors ran like water; it gathered in pools…. And the Spaniards began to hunt them out of the administrative buildings, dragging out and killing anyone they could find … even starting to take those buildings to pieces as they searched….

[Later] there came a great sickness, a pestilence, the smallpox. It … spread over the people with great destruction of men. It caused great misery…. The brave Mexican warriors were indeed weakened by it. It was after all this had happened that the Spaniards came back.

7. An Englishman Discusses Trading with Indians on the Atlantic Coast, 1584

After thankes given to God for our safe arrivall thither, we manned our boats, and went to view the land next adjoyning, and "to take possession of the same, in the right of the Queenes most excellent Majestie, as rightfull Queene, and Princesse of the same, and after delivered the same over to your use, according to her Majesties grant, and letters patents, under her Highnesse great Seale….

We remained by the side of this Island two whole dayes before we saw any people of the Countrey: the third day we espied one small boate rowing towardes us having in it three persons: this boat came to the Island side, foure harquebuz-shot from our shippes, and there two of the people remaining, the third came along the shoreside towards us, and wee being then all within boord, he walked up and downe upon the point of the land next unto us: then the Master and the Pilot of the Admirall, Simon Ferdinando, and the Captaine Philip Amadas, my selfe, and others rowed to the land, whose comming this fellow attended, never making any shewe of feare or doubt. And after he had spoken of many things not understood by us, we brought him with his owne good liking, aboord the ships, and gave him a shirt, a hat & some other things, and made him taste of our wine, and our meat, which he liked very wel: and after having viewed both barks, he departed, and went to his owne boat againe, which hee had left in a little Cove or Creeke adjoyning: assoone as hee was two bow shoot into the water, he fell to fishing, and in lesse then halfe an houre, he had laden his boate as deepe, as it could swimme, with which hee came againe to the point of the lande, and there he devided his fish into two parts, pointing one part to

Richard Hakluyt, *The Portable Hakluyt's Voyages: The Principal Navigations, Voyages, Traffiques, and Discoveries of the English Nation* (New York: Viking, [1967, 1965]).

the ship, and the other to the pinnesse: which, after he had (as much as he might) requited the former benefites received, departed out of our sight.

The next day there came unto us divers boates, and in one of them the Kings brother, accompanied with fortie or fiftie men, very handsome and goodly people, and in their behaviour as mannerly and civill as any of Europe. His name was Granganimeo, and the king is called Wingina, the countrey Wingandacoa, and now by her Majestie Virginia.... When he came to the place, his servants spread a long matte upon the ground, on which he sate downe, and at the other ende of the matte foure others of his companie did the like, the rest of his men stood round about him, somewhat a farre off: when we came to the shore to him with our weapons, hee never mooved from his place, nor any of the other foure, nor never mistrusted any harme to be offred from us, but sitting still he beckoned us to come and sit by him, which we performed: and being set hee made all signes of joy and welcome, striking on his head and his breast and after-wardes on ours, to shewe wee were all one, smiling and making shewe the best he could of all love, and familiaritie. After hee had made a long speech unto us, wee presented him with divers things, which hee received very joyfully, and thankefully. None of the company durst speake one worde all the time: onely the foure which were at the other ende, spake one in the others eare very softly.

The King is greatly obeyed, and his brothers and children reverenced: the King himselfe in person was at our being there, sore wounded in a fight which hee had with the King of the next countrey, called Wingina, and was shot in two places through the body, and once cleane through the thigh, but yet he recovered: by reason whereof and for that hee lay at the chiefe towne of the countrey, being six dayes journey off, we saw him not at all.

After we had presented this his brother with such things as we thought he liked, wee likewise gave somewhat to the other that sat with him on the matte: but presently he arose and tooke all from them and put it into his owne basket, making signes and tokens, that all things ought to bee delivered unto him, and the rest were but his servants, and followers. A day or two after this, we fell to trading with them, exchanging some things that we had, for Chamoys, Buffe, and Deere skinnes: when we shewed him all our packet of merchandize, of all things that he sawe, a bright tinne dish most pleased him, which hee presently tooke up and clapt it before his breast, and after made a hole in the brimme thereof and hung it about his necke, making signes that it would defende him against his enemies arrowes: for those people maintaine a deadly and terrible warre, with the people and King adjoyning. We exchanged our tinne dish for twentie skinnes, woorth twentie Crownes, or twentie Nobles: and a copper kettle for fiftie skins woorth fifty Crownes. They offered us good exchange for our hatchets, and axes, and for knives, and would have given any thing for swordes: but we would not depart with any. After two or three dayes the Kings brother came aboord the shippes, and dranke wine, and eat of our meat and of our bread, and liked exceedingly thereof: and after a few dayes over passed, he brought his wife with him to the ships, his daughter and two or three children: his wife was very well favoured, of meane stature, and very bash full: shee had on her backe a long cloake of leather, with the furre side next to her body, and before her a piece of the same: about her forehead shee had a bande of white Corall, and so had her husband many times: in her eares shee had bracelets of pearles hanging downe to her middle, (whereof we delivered your worship a little bracelet) and those were of the bignes of good pease. The rest of her women of the better sort had pendants of copper hanging in either eare, and some of the children of the kings brother and other noble men, have five or sixe in either eare: he himselfe had upon his head a broad plate of golde, or copper, for being unpolished we knew not what mettal it should be, neither would he by any meanes suffer us to take it off his head, but feeling it, it would bow very easily. His apparell was as his wives, onely the women weare their haire long on both sides, and the men but on one. They are of colour yellowish, and their haire black for the most part, and yet we saw children that had very fine aburne, and chestnut coloured haire....

He was very just of his promise: for many times we delivered him merchandize upon his word, but ever he came within the day and performed his promise. He sent us every day a brase or two of fat Bucks, Conies, Hares, Fish the best of the world. He sent us divers kindes of fruites, Melons, Walnuts, Cucumbers, Gourdes, Pease, and divers rootes, and fruites very excellent good, and of their Countrey corne, which is very white, faire and well tasted, and groweth three times in five moneths: in May they sow, in July they reape, in June they sow, in August they reape: in July they sow, in September they reape: onely they cast the corne into the ground, breaking a little of the soft turfe with a wodden mattock, or pickeaxe: our selves prooved the soile, and put some of our Pease in the ground, and in tenne dayes they were of fourteene ynches high: they have also Beanes very faire of divers colours and wonderfull plentie: some growing naturally, and some in their gardens, and so have they both wheat and oates....

We were entertained with all love and kindnesse, and with as much bountie (after their maner) as they could possibly devise. We found the people most gentle, loving, and faithful, voide of all guile and treason, and such as live after the maner of the golden age. The people onely care howe to defend themselves from the cold in their short winter, and to feed themselves with such meat as the soile affoordeth: there meate is very well sodden and they make broth very sweet and savorie: their vessels are earthen pots, very large, white and sweete, their dishes are wodden platters of sweet timber: within the place where they feede was their lodging, and within that their Idoll, which they worship, of whome they speake incredible things....

They wondred marvelously when we were amongst them at the whitenes of our skins, ever coveting to touch our breasts, and to view the same. Besides they had our ships in marvelous admiration, & all things els were so strange unto them, as it appeared that none of them had ever seene the like. When we discharged any piece, were it but an hargubuz, they would tremble thereat for very feare, and for the strangenesse of the same: for the weapons which themselves use are bowes and arrowes: the arrowes are but of small canes, headed with a sharpe shell or tooth of a fish sufficient ynough to kill a naked man. Their swordes be of wood hardened: likewise they use wooden breast plates for their defence. They have besides a kinde of club, in the end whereof they fasten the sharpe hornes of a stagge, or other beast. When they goe to warres they cary about with them their idol, of whom they aske counsel, as the Romans were woont of the Oracle of Apollo. They sing songs as they march towardes the battell in stead of drummes and trumpets: their warres are very cruell and bloody, by reason whereof, and of their civill dissentions which have happened of late yeeres amongst them, the people are marvelously wasted, and in some places the countrey left desolate....

And so contenting our selves with this service at this time, which wee hope hereafter to inlarge, as occasion and assistance shalbe given, we resolved to leave the countrey, and to apply our selves to returne for England, which we did accordingly, and arrived safely in the West of England about the middest of September.

We brought home also two of the Savages being lustie men, whose names were Wanchese and Manteo.

8. English Artist John White Depicts Indian Land Use, 1619

Algonquian village on the Pamlico River estuary showing Native structures, agriculture, and spiritual life.

 ESSAYS

For centuries, historians have discussed the first engagements among Europeans, western Africans, and North and South Americans. Some scholars have wondered how the Spanish and Portuguese so easily defeated powerful indigenous empires. Others have tried to reckon with how much Native American societies were changed. The following essays question our assumptions about these momentous years. In the first, Neal Salisbury observes that the arrival of Europeans and Africans may not have altered indigenous life as much as previously assumed. Long before 1492, Native Americans had dealt with diversities of peoples, places, languages, and objects. They had made war, made peace, and crafted new alliances over time. Without doubt, Europeans posed a new and potent presence, but to claim that their advent altered everything may minimize the complexities of Native American history. The second essay, by Joyce Appleby, fixates on how the Americas helped create new worlds of imagination for Europeans. She suggests that before 1492, Europeans were an uncurious people whose minds had been circumscribed by the Catholic Church. New land masses, people, animals, and materials pushed them to reconsider the world. Studying the natural environment rose in prominence and radically transformed the West.

The Indians' Old World

NEAL SALISBURY

Scholars in history, anthropology, archaeology, and other disciplines have turned increasingly over the past two decades to the study of native peoples during the colonial period of North American history. The new work in Indian history has altered the way we think about the beginning of American history and about the era of European colonization. Historians now recognize that Europeans arrived, not in a virgin land, but in one that was teeming with several million people. Beyond filling in some of the vast blanks left by previous generations' overlooking of Indians, much of this scholarship makes clear that Indians are integral to the history of colonial North America. In short, surveys of recent textbooks and of scholarly titles suggest that Native Americans are well on their way to being "mainstreamed" by colonial historians.

Substantive as this reorientation is, it remains limited. Beyond the problems inherent in representing Indian/non-Indian interactions during the colonial era lies the challenge of contextualizing the era itself. Despite opening chapters and lectures that survey the continent's native peoples and cultures, most historians continue to represent American history as having been set in motion by the arrival of European explorers and colonizers. They have yet to recognize the existence of a North American—as opposed to English or European—background for colonial history, much less to consider the implications of such a background

Neal Salisbury, "The Indians' Old World: Native Americans and the Coming of Europeans," *William and Mary Quarterly*, 3rd Series, Vol. 53, No. 3. Reprinted by permission of William and Mary Quarterly.

for understanding the three centuries following Columbus's landfall. Yet a growing body of scholarship by archaeologists, linguists, and students of Native American expressive traditions recognizes 1492 not as a beginning but as a single
moment in a long history utterly detached from that of Europe....

... [I]ndigenous North Americans exhibited a remarkable range of languages, economies, political systems, beliefs, and material cultures. But this range
was less the result of their isolation from one another than of the widely varying
natural and social environments with which Indians had interacted over millennia. What recent scholars of pre-colonial North America have found even more
striking, given this diversity, is the extent to which native peoples' histories inter-
sected one another.

At the heart of these intersections was exchange. By exchange is meant not
only the trading of material goods but also exchanges across community lines of
marriage partners, resources, labor, ideas, techniques, and religious practices.
Longer-distance exchanges frequently crossed cultural and linguistic boundaries
as well and ranged from casual encounters to widespread alliances and networks
that were economic, political, and religious. For both individuals and communities, exchanges sealed social and political relationships. Rather than accumulate
material wealth endlessly, those who acquired it gave it away, thereby earning
prestige and placing obligations on others to reciprocate appropriately. And as
we shall see, many goods were not given away to others in this world but
were buried with individuals to accompany them to another....

By the twelfth century, agricultural production had spread over much of the
Eastern Woodlands as well as to more of the Southwest. In both regions, ... more
complex societies were emerging to dominate widespread exchange networks. In
the Mississippi Valley and the Southeast, the sudden primacy of maize horticulture
is marked archaeologically in a variety of ways—food remains, pollen profiles, studies of human bone (showing that maize accounted for 50 percent of people's diets),
and in material culture by a proliferation of chert hoes, shell-tempered pottery for
storing and cooking, and pits for storing surplus crops. These developments were
accompanied by the rise of what archaeologists term "Mississippian" societies, consisting of fortified political and ceremonial centers and outlying villages. The centers
were built around open plazas featuring platform burial mounds, temples, and elaborate residences for elite families. Evidence from burials makes clear the wide social
gulf that separated commoners from elites. Whereas the former were buried in simple graves with a few personal possessions, the latter were interred in the temples or
plazas along with many more, and more elaborate, goods such as copper ornaments,
massive sheets of shell, and ceremonial weapons. Skeletal evidence indicates that
elites ate more meat, were taller, performed less strenuous physical activity, and
were less prone to illness and accident than commoners....

The largest, most complex Mississippian center was Cahokia, located not far
from the confluence of the Mississippi and Missouri rivers, near modern East St.
Louis, Illinois, in the rich floodplain known as American Bottoms. By the
twelfth century, Cahokia probably numbered 20,000 people and contained
over 120 mounds within a five-square-mile area.... One key to Cahokia's rise
was its combination of rich soil and nearby wooded uplands, enabling inhabitants

to produce surplus crops while providing an abundance and diversity of wild food sources along with ample supplies of wood for fuel and construction. A second key was its location, affording access to the great river systems of the North American interior.

Cahokia had the most elaborate social structure yet seen in North America. Laborers used stone and wooden spades to dig soil from "borrow pits" (at least nineteen have been identified by archaeologists), which they carried in wooden buckets to mounds and palisades often more than half a mile away. The volume and concentration of craft activity in shell, copper, clay, and other materials, both local and imported, suggests that specialized artisans provided the material foundation for Cahokia's exchange ties with other peoples. Although most Cahokians were buried in mass graves outside the palisades, their rulers were given special treatment. At a prominent location in Mound 72, the largest of Cahokia's platform mounds, a man had been buried atop a platform of shell beads. Accompanying him were several group burials: fifty young women, aged 18 to 23, four men, and three men and three women, all encased in uncommonly large amounts of exotic materials. As with the Natchez Indians observed by the French in Louisiana, Cahokians appear to have sacrificed individuals to accompany their leaders in the afterlife. Cahokia was surrounded by nine smaller mound centers and several dozen villages from which it obtained much of its food and through which it conducted its waterborne commerce with other Mississippian centers in the Midwest and Southeast....

At the outset of the twelfth century, the center of production and exchange in the Southwest was in the basin of the San Juan River at Chaco Canyon in New Mexico, where Anasazi culture achieved its most elaborate expression. A twelve-mile stretch of the canyon and its rim held twelve large planned towns on the north side and 200 to 350 apparently unplanned villages on the south. The total population was probably about 15,000. The towns consisted of 200 or more contiguous, multistoried rooms, along with numerous kivas (underground ceremonial areas), constructed of veneered masonry walls and log beams imported from upland areas nearly fifty miles distant. The rooms surrounded a central plaza with a great kiva. Villages typically had ten to twenty rooms that were decidedly smaller than those in the towns. Nearly all of Chaco Canyon's turquoise, shell, and other ornaments and virtually everything imported from Mesoamerica are found in the towns rather than the villages. Whether the goods were considered communal property or were the possessions of elites is uncertain, but either way the towns clearly had primacy. Villages buried their dead near their residences, whereas town burial grounds were apparently located at greater distances, although only a very few of what must have been thousands of town burials have been located by archaeologists. Finally, and of particular importance in the arid environment of the region, the towns were located at the mouths of side canyons where they controlled the collection and distribution of water run-off....

The canyon was the core of an extensive network of at least seventy towns or "outliers," as they are termed in the archaeological literature, and 5,300 villages located as far as sixty miles from the canyon.... Facilitating the movement of people and goods through this network was a system of roads radiating outward from the canyon in perfectly straight lines, turning into stairways or footholds rather than circumventing cliffs and other obstacles....

When Europeans reached North America .... the continent's demographic and political map was in a state of profound flux. A major factor was the collapse of the great centers at Cahokia and Chaco Canyon and elsewhere in the Midwest and Southwest. Although there were significant differences between these highly centralized societies, each ran up against the capacity of the land or other resources to sustain it....

Such combinations of continuity and change, persistence and adaptability, arose from concrete historical experiences rather than a timeless tradition. The remainder of this [essay] indicates some of the ways that both the deeply rooted imperatives of reciprocity and exchange and the recent legacies of competition and upheaval informed North American history as Europeans began to make their presence felt.

Discussion of the transition from pre- to postcontact times must begin with the sixteenth century, when Indians and Europeans met and interacted in a variety of settings. When not slighting the era altogether, historians have viewed it as one of discovery or exploration, citing the achievements of notable Europeans in either anticipating or failing to anticipate the successful colonial enterprises of the seventeenth century. Recently, however, a number of scholars have been integrating information from European accounts with the findings of archaeologists to produce a much fuller picture of this critical period in North American history.

The Southeast was the scene of the most formidable attempts at colonization during the sixteenth century, primarily by Spain. Yet in spite of several expeditions to the interior and the undertaking of an ambitious colonizing and missionary effort, extending from St. Augustine over much of the Florida peninsula and north to Chesapeake Bay, the Spanish retained no permanent settlements beyond St. Augustine itself at the end of the century. Nevertheless, their explorers and missionaries opened the way for the spread of smallpox and other epidemic diseases over much of the area south of the Chesapeake and east of the Mississippi....

As in the Southeast, Spanish colonizers in the sixteenth-century Southwest launched several ambitious military and missionary efforts, hoping to extend New Spain's domain northward and to discover additional sources of wealth. The best-documented encounters of Spanish with Pueblos—most notably those of Coronado's expedition (1540–1542)—ended in violence and failure for the Spanish who, despite vows to proceed peacefully, violated Pueblo norms of reciprocity by insisting on excessive tribute or outright submission. In addition, the Spanish had acquired notoriety among the Pueblos as purveyors of epidemic diseases, religious missions, and slaving expeditions inflicted on Indians to the south, in what is now northern Mexico.

The Spanish also affected patterns of exchange throughout the Southwest. Indians resisting the spread of Spanish rule to northern Mexico stole horses and other livestock, some of which they traded to neighbors. By the end of the sixteenth century, a few Indians on the periphery of the Southwest were riding horses, anticipating the combination of theft and exchange that would spread horses to native peoples throughout the region and, still later, the Plains and the Southeast. In the meantime, some Navajos and Apaches moved near the Rio Grande Valley, strengthening ties with certain pueblos that were reinforced when inhabitants of those pueblos sought refuge among them in the face or wake of Spanish *entradas*.

Yet another variation on the theme of Indian-European contacts in the sixteenth century was played out in the Northeast, where Iroquoian-speaking villagers on the Mississippian periphery and Archaic hunter-gatherers still further removed from developments in the interior met Europeans of several nationalities. At the outset of the century, Spanish and Portuguese explorers enslaved several dozen Micmacs and other Indians from the Nova Scotia–Gulf of St. Lawrence area. Three French expeditions to the St. Lawrence itself in the 1530s and 1540s followed the Spanish pattern by alienating most Indians encountered and ending in futility. Even as these hostile contacts were taking place, fishermen, whalers, and other Europeans who visited the area regularly had begun trading with natives....

What induced Indians to go out of their way to trap beaver and trade the skins for glass beads, mirrors, copper kettles, and other goods? Throughout North America since Paleo-Indian times, exchange in the Northeast was the means by which people maintained and extended their social, cultural, and spiritual horizons as well as acquired items considered supernaturally powerful. Members of some coastal Indian groups later recalled how the first Europeans they saw, with their facial hair and strange clothes and traveling in their strange boats, seemed like supernatural figures. Although soon disabused of such notions, these Indians and many more inland placed special value on the glass beads and other trinkets offered by the newcomers. Recent scholarship on Indians' motives in this earliest stage of the trade indicates that they regarded such objects as the equivalents of the quartz, mica, shell, and other sacred substances that had formed the heart of long-distance exchange in North America for millennia and that they regarded as sources of physical and spiritual well-being, on earth and in the afterlife. Indians initially altered and wore many of the utilitarian goods they received, such as iron axe heads and copper pots, rather than use them for their intended purposes. Moreover, even though the new objects might pass through many hands, they more often than not ended up in graves, presumably for their possessors to use in the afterlife. Finally, the archaeological findings make clear that shell and native copper predominated over the new objects in sixteenth-century exchanges, indicating that European trade did not suddenly trigger a massive craving for the objects themselves. While northeastern Indians recognized Europeans as different from themselves, they interacted with them and their materials in ways that were consistent with their own customs and beliefs.

By the late sixteenth century, the effects of European trade began to overlap with the effects of earlier upheavals in the northeastern interior. Sometime between Jacques Cartier's final departure in 1543 and Samuel de Champlain's arrival in 1603, the Iroquoian-speaking inhabitants of Hochelaga and Stadacona (modern Montreal and Quebec City) abandoned their communities. The communities were crushed militarily, and the survivors dispersed among both Iroquois and

Hurons. Whether the perpetrators of these dispersals were Iroquois and Huron is a point of controversy, but either way the St. Lawrence communities appear to have been casualties of the rivalry, at least a century old, between the two confederations as each sought to position itself vis-á-vis the French. The effect, if not the cause, of the dispersals was the Iroquois practice of attacking antagonists who denied them direct access to trade goods; this is consistent with Iroquois actions during the preceding two centuries and the century that followed.

The sudden availability of many more European goods, the absorption of many refugees from the St. Lawrence, and the heightening of tensions with the Iroquois help to explain the movement of most outlying Huron communities to what is now Simcoe County area of Ontario during the 1580s. This geographic concentration strengthened their confederacy and gave it the form it had when allied with New France during the first half of the seventeenth century. Having formerly existed at the outer margins of an arena of exchange centered in Cahokia, the Hurons and Iroquois now faced a new source of goods and power to the east.

The diverse native societies encountered by Europeans as they began to settle North America permanently during the seventeenth century were not static isolates lying outside the ebb and flow of human history. Rather, they were products of a complex set of historical forces, both local and wide ranging, both deeply rooted and of recent origin. Although their lives and worldviews were shaped by long-standing traditions of reciprocity and spiritual power, the people in these communities were also accustomed—contrary to popular myths about inflexible Indians—to economic and political flux and to absorbing new peoples (both allies and antagonists), objects, and ideas, including those originating in Europe. Such combinations of tradition and innovation continued to shape Indians' relations with Europeans, even as the latter's visits became permanent.

The establishment of lasting European colonies, beginning with New Mexico in 1598, began a phase in the continent's history that eventually resulted in the displacement of Indians to the economic, political, and cultural margins of a new order. But during the interim natives and colonizers entered into numerous relationships in which they exchanged material goods and often supported one another diplomatically or militarily against common enemies. These relations combined native and European modes of exchange. While much of the scholarly literature emphasizes the subordination and dependence of Indians in these circumstances, Indians as much as Europeans dictated the form and content of their early exchanges and alliances. Much of the protocol and ritual surrounding such intercultural contacts was rooted in indigenous kinship obligations and gift exchanges, and Indian consumers exhibited decided preferences for European commodities that satisfied social, spiritual, and aesthetic values. Similarly, Indians' long-range motives and strategies in their alliances with Europeans were frequently rooted in older patterns of alliance and rivalry with regional neighbors. Such continuities can be glimpsed through a brief consideration of the early colonial-era histories of the Five Nations Iroquois in the Northeast, ... and the Rio Grande Pueblos in the Southwest.

Post-Mississippian and sixteenth-century patterns of antagonism between the Iroquois and their neighbors to the north and west persisted, albeit under altered circumstances, during the seventeenth century when France established its colony on the St. Lawrence and allied itself with Hurons and other Indians. France aimed to extract maximum profits from the fur trade, and it immediately recognized the Iroquois as the major threat to that goal. In response, the Iroquois turned to the Dutch in New Netherland for guns and other trade goods while raiding New France's Indian allies for the thicker northern pelts that brought higher prices than those in their own country (which they exhausted by midcentury) and for captives to replace those from their own ranks who had died from epidemics or in wars. During the 1640s, the Iroquois replaced raids with full-scale military assaults (the so-called Beaver Wars) on Iroquoian-speaking communities in the lower Great Lakes, absorbing most of the survivors as refugees or captives. All the while, the Iroquois elaborated a vision of their confederation, which had brought harmony within their own ranks, as bringing peace to all peoples of the region. For the remainder of the century, the Five Nations fought a grueling and costly series of wars against the French and their Indian allies in order to gain access to the pelts and French goods circulating in lands to the north and west.

Meanwhile, the Iroquois were also adapting to the growing presence of English colonists along the Atlantic seaboard.... After the English supplanted the Dutch in New York in 1664, Iroquois diplomats established relations with the proprietary governor, Sir Edmund Andros, in a treaty known as the Covenant Chain. The Covenant Chain was an elaboration of the Iroquois' earlier treaty arrangements with the Dutch, but, whereas the Iroquois had termed the Dutch relationship a chain of iron, they referred to the one with the English as a chain of silver. The shift in metaphors was appropriate, for what had been strictly an economic connection was now a political one in which the Iroquois acquired power over other New York Indians. After 1677, the Covenant Chain was expanded to include several English colonies, most notably Massachusetts and Maryland, along with those colonies' subject Indians. The upshot of these arrangements was that the Iroquois cooperated with their colonial partners in subduing and removing subject Indians who impeded settler expansion. The Mohawks in particular played a vital role in the New England colonies' suppression of the Indian uprising known as King Philip's War and in moving the Susquehannocks away from the expanding frontier of settlement in the Chesapeake after Bacon's Rebellion.

For the Iroquois, such a policy helped expand their "Tree of peace" among Indians while providing them with buffers against settler encroachment around their homelands. The major drawback in the arrangement proved to be the weakness of English military assistance against the French. This inadequacy, and the consequent suffering experienced by the Iroquois during two decades of war after 1680, finally drove the Five Nations to make peace with the French and their Indian allies in the Grand settlement of 1701. Together, the Grand Settlement and Covenant Chain provided the Iroquois with the peace and security, the access to trade goods, and the dominant role among northeastern Indians they had long sought. That these arrangements in the long run served to reinforce rather than deter English encroachment on Iroquois lands and autonomy should not obscure their pre-European roots and their importance in shaping colonial history in the Northeast....

In the Southwest, the institution of Spanish colonial rule on the Rio Grande after 1598 further affected exchange relations between Pueblo Indians and nearby Apaches and Navajos. By imposing heavy demands for tribute in the form of corn, the Spanish prevented Pueblo peoples from trading surplus produce with their non-farming neighbors. In order to obtain the produce on which they had come to depend, Apaches and Navajos staged deadly raids on some pueblos, leaving the inhabitants dependent on the Spanish for protection. In retaliation, Spanish soldiers captured Apaches and Navajos whom they sold as slaves to their countrymen to the south. From the beginning, the trading pueblos of Pecos, Picuris, and Taos most resented Spanish control and strongly resisted the proselytizing of Franciscan missionaries. From the late 1660s, drought and disease, intensified Apache and Navajo raids, and the severity of Spanish rule led more and more Indians from all pueblos to question the advantages of Christianity and to renew their ties to their indigenous religious traditions. Spanish persecution of native religious leaders and their backsliding followers precipitated the Pueblo Revolt of 1680, in which the trading Pueblos played a leading role and which was actively supported by some Navajos and Apaches.

When the Spanish reimposed their rule during the 1690s, they tolerated traditional Indian religion rather than trying to extirpate it, and they participated in interregional trade fairs at Taos and other villages. The successful incorporation of Pueblo Indians as loyal subjects proved vital to New Mexico's survival as a colony and, more generally, to Spain's imperial presence in the Southwest during the eighteenth and early nineteenth centuries.

As significant as is the divide separating pre- and post-Columbian North American history, it is not the stark gap suggested by the distinction between prehistory and history. For varying periods of time after their arrival in North America, Europeans adapted to the social and political environments they found, including the fluctuating ties of reciprocity and interdependence as well as rivalry, that characterized those environments. They had little choice but to enter in and participate if they wished to sustain their presence. Eventually, one route to success proved to be their ability to insert themselves as regional powers in new networks of exchange and alliance that arose to supplant those of the Mississippians, Anasazis, and others.

To assert such continuities does not minimize the radical transformations entailed in Europeans' colonization of the continent and its indigenous peoples. Arising in Cahokia's wake, new centers at Montreal, Fort Orange/Albany, Charleston, and elsewhere permanently altered the primary patterns of exchange in eastern North America. The riverine system that channeled exchange in the interior of the continent gave way to one in which growing quantities of goods arrived from, and were directed to, coastal peripheries and ultimately Europe. In the Southwest, the Spanish revived Anasazi links with Mesoamerica at some cost to newer ties between the Rio Grande Pueblos and recently arrived, nonfarming Athapaskan speakers. More generally, European colonizers brought a complex of demographic and ecological advantages, most notably epidemic diseases and their own immunity to them, that utterly devastated Indian communities; ideologies and beliefs in their cultural and spiritual superiority to native peoples and their entitlement to natives' lands; and economic, political, and military systems organized for the engrossment of Indian lands and the subordination or suppression of Indian peoples.

Europeans were anything but uniformly successful in realizing their goals, but the combination of demographic and ecological advantages and imperial intentions, along with the Anglo-Iroquois Covenant Chain, enabled land-hungry colonists from New England to the Chesapeake to break entirely free of ties of dependence on Indians before the end of the seventeenth century. Their successes proved to be only the beginning of a new phase of Indian-European relations. By the mid-eighteenth century, the rapid expansion of land-based settlement in the English colonies had sundered older ties of exchange and alliance linking natives and colonizers nearly everywhere east of the Appalachians, driving many Indians west and reducing those who remained to a scattering of politically powerless enclaves in which Indian identities were nurtured in isolation. Meanwhile, the colonizers threatened to extend this new mode of Indian relations across the Appalachians. An old world, rooted in indigenous exchange, was giving way to one in which Native Americans had no certain place.

The Europeans' New World

JOYCE APPLEBY

When Christopher Columbus returned from the Western Hemisphere in the spring of 1493, he came with news that would decisively change Europe. No consequence would be more portentous than the conversation his discoveries prompted about the natural world, for he made the subject of nature suddenly interesting with all the odd things he brought home. Sailing back to Spain on the *Niña,* he packed the little caravel to the gunwales with fantastic objects from the Caribbean islands he visited. Six Taino natives, out of a dozen, survived the return trip, giving vivid proof that people lived in what geographers called the antipodes. Birds from the West Indies survived the trip better than the Tainos. Columbus had plucked flowers even more colorful than the brilliant parrots he found in the tropical rain forests. He showed his sponsors, King Ferdinand and Queen Isabella, a bit of gold that some natives had given him, thinking that it would guarantee funding for subsequent voyages—and he was right.

Over the course of the next three centuries, a succession of amateur investigators laid the foundation for the modern life sciences even though before the end of the fifteenth century, Europeans had been an incurious people. Finding these masses of land filled with mysterious people, unfamiliar plants, weird animals, and striking topography produced the kind of shock essential to shaking free of the church's venerable injunction against asking questions about nature. Men and women in China and Muslim Spain's Córdoba had demonstrated a much stronger inquisitive spirit. In Europe, isolation and religious disapproval had curtailed curiosity for over a millennium.

Today, plying incessant questions to nature is one of the strongest features of the modern West. The stirring of Europeans' interest in the physical world began at the end of the fifteenth century with the discovery of two continents lying between them and the Orient. Like most profound cultural changes, there were layers of habits and convictions to work through before Europeans could engage fully with the natural world. They had to break with the church's prohibition of intrusive questioning about God's domain—the phenomena of his created universe. The assumption that they already knew everything worth knowing had erected another barrier to the investigative spirit, as well as the predisposition to look backward to biblical or classical times for guidance and knowledge. The designation New World suggests the dimension of their surprise....

The Catholic Church had succeeded for a thousand years in keeping curiosity in check out of fear of probing questions about cosmic events like eclipses and comets. Such inquiries were deemed vain, a petty challenge to God's all-encompassing knowledge. Of course the church couldn't suppress all curiosity, certainly not a child's endless queries about what and why. But even the spirits of children will be dulled if the answers they hear are always "because God willed it so." The campaign against curiosity began with Augustine, who lived when Christianity was becoming the dominant religion in Europe....

A very powerful and pervasive institution, the church claimed the authority to discriminate between legitimate and illicit knowledge, between permitted and prohibited questions, even between accepted and forbidden methods of acquiring knowledge. After the Reformation, Protestant leaders revived the attack on curiosity in the sixteenth century. John Calvin associated it with the deadliest of deadly sins: pride. King James I of England pointed to Eve for evidence of how curiosity could harm someone.

Europeans were little exposed to the larger world through travel. Religion had stirred crusades to the Holy Lands in the tenth, eleventh, and twelfth centuries, but after that, the crusaders' descendants stayed put. Overland trade with Asia was cut off for decades at a time. Still, there were some venturous souls. Merchants in Genoa and Majorca began visiting the islands off Africa. The Vivaldi brothers of Genoa set sail west to India, but were never heard from again.

When that most celebrated traveler, Marco Polo, returned to Europe in 1294, he landed in a Genoese prison. Fortunately for thousands of future readers, his cell mate happened to be a writer. To him, Polo recounted the details of his Venetian merchant family's twenty years in the Orient and how his father met Kublai Khan, the grandson of Genghis Kahn. He described their encounters as diplomats and traders at the great Mongol court at Karakorum and the high drama of their escape from their possessive host in a perilous two-year voyage. Most Europeans got their first impression of China, India, and Japan from this travel journal.

Henry the Navigator, a Portuguese prince, spent his considerable fortune sending expeditions down the west coast of Africa in the middle decades of the fifteenth century. He was determined to find out what lay south of Cape Bojador at the 24th parallel, which marked the farthest that Europeans had sailed down the west coast of Africa, but he dispatched others there, preferring to stay at home himself.

Henry was fired by the desire to wrest the Canary Islands from Spain and to find a coastal source for the gold and slaves traded in the interior of the African continent. Where he differed from his predecessors was in recognizing the importance of improving navigation. While fighting for Portugal against the Arabs in Morocco, he took stock of what their mariners knew about commercial linkages and the level of their sailing skills. He familiarized himself with Arab map-making. Never going to sea himself, Henry was content with gathering around him in his academy at Sagres a cadre of expert navigators, shipwrights, astronomers, pilots, and cartographers, both Christian and Jewish. He was mindful of fears that the southern waters were filled with monsters and wrapped in deadly fog, but he calmly stated, "You cannot find a peril so great that the hope of reward will not be greater." Like Columbus a half century later, ambition fueled his many navigational projects.

The ships that plied the Mediterranean were far too slow and large for oceanic travel. Venturing out in this unknown stretch of the Atlantic demanded new techniques and new equipment, accrued through trial and error. Arab navigators in the southern Mediterranean had introduced triangular sails, fore and aft, called lateen sails. They also added a small foremast, the mizzen, that improved steering. Henry incorporated these Arab inventions into his light, fast caravel, rigged for sailing close to the wind. From his estate perched on the rocky promontory jutting into the Atlantic in the southwest corner of Portugal, he sent pairs of these caravels to chart the winds and waters along the bulge of Africa.

From the 1420s until his death in 1460, Henry's expeditions got ever larger; they located successful routes and found safe harbors for provisioning. Slowly, after many failed endeavors, they solved the problems of navigation in the South Atlantic. Once they brought back gold and slaves, the voyages became remunerative. Within a century, Africans composed a tenth of the population of Lisbon, a city still underpopulated from the Black Death of the previous century.

Henry died before Bartolomeu Dias rounded the Cape of Good Hope in 1487, but by that time explorations down the coast of Africa had found other royal patrons. When the Portuguese mariners got below the equator, the North Star was no longer in the heavens, which meant that they had to develop new celestial navigation with the Southern Cross, the constellation visible in the Southern Hemisphere almost any time of the year.

Adding to the pressure to find a sea route to the Indies was the fall in 1453 of Constantinople to the Ottoman Turks, who closed off trade with Europe. Bringing in cinnamon, cloves, nutmeg, and pepper on overland routes became more costly and more fraught with peril. Going by water to the fabulous islands could cut out the Arab merchants who acted as middlemen. Having discovered the winds that would carry ships around the tip of the continent, Dias opened the way for others to reach the East Indies. A generation of sailors from the ports of Italy and the Iberian Peninsula could now follow where the geographic pioneering of Henry had pointed.

With prospects for great success, the Portuguese king had no compunctions about rejecting appeals for support from a Genoan named Christopher Columbus, who had a different idea about reaching the Indies. Discouraged, Columbus turned to Spain, where Queen Isabella and King Ferdinand had just joined their kingdoms to form a united monarchy in Spain. As rivals of Portugal, they sought a different route to the fabled riches of the Orient and offered to sponsor Columbus's expedition. Even more important to the devout queen than catching up with the Portuguese was the possibility of extending the realm of Christendom in Asia. Columbus shared this goal. He extracted promises from them to receive 10 percent of all the goods found in the lands. His son wryly noted years later when the family was fighting over what they thought was due their father that the monarchs had probably not expected him to get back alive. But he did, after a seven-month round trip to the Caribbean.

News of the discoveries in the Western Hemisphere arrived when Europeans were still absorbing the philosophy of ancient Greece and Rome. After being cut off from these stores of knowledge and wisdom for a millennium, scholars acquired access to them through the libraries of the Muslims in Córdoba. The rebirth in the term "Renaissance" refers to the flowering of art and literature in response to this recovery of classical texts. After the Turks took Constantinople, many Greek scholars moved to Italy, bringing with them a thorough understanding of the Greco-Roman writers whose worldly perspective was so different from the spiritual otherworldliness of medieval Europe....

Ancient writings brought in a questioning attitude that startled with its intellectual insouciance. They bristled with inquiries, hypotheses, and stratagems for proof. To read them was to reassess what one thought one knew. The freshness of this engagement has to be measured against the medieval obsession with doctrine, form, and faithfulness to sacred texts. An appreciation of the Greek and Roman philosophers, like news of the voyages of discovery, moved from the fifteenth-century preserve of classicists to a wider group of educated readers with the publication of translations of the texts....

Europeans began studying the recovered works of Ptolemy, the first-century Greek who had collected in one volume all the geographic knowledge that had been acquired in his Greco-Roman world, just as the discovery of the New World was making more salient than ever how little they actually knew about the planet they lived on. With an old text and a new map, they began delving into just those subjects that Augustine had excoriated, Even Spanish churchmen who followed in the wake of the explorers became curious. They justified this new intellectual trait on the grounds that none of their authorities—biblical or ancient—knew anything about these strange continents accidentally discovered on the way to the Orient.

An avid appreciation for ancient philosophers created a whole new category—that of the humanists, who cultivated classical ideas and styles through

a rigorous study of Greek and Latin. Greek and Roman thinkers had been famously curious, asking a myriad of questions about the heavens, the planets,
and earth's human inhabitants. Reading their works couldn't but nurture an investigative spirit. Responding to this, the humanists formed clubs to talk about
the knowledge gleaned from the recovered texts. Their growing numbers signaled a discontent with the inward, logical reasoning of the Scholastics, who
were the principal interpreters of the Christian dogma that had dominated thinking since Augustine's time.

The new focus on the classics was not like sailing off into the Western
Hemisphere, but studying Greek philosophy prepared some to ponder the puz-
zles that the discoveries turned up. Especially startling was Europe's new location
on the globe, no longer joined to the Middle East and Asia through a vast land
bridge, but separated from Asia by two huge oceans and the linked continents of
North and South America. Maps had to be redrawn and redrawn again as successive explorers returned with new sightings. Ironically, the fact that the existence of the New World was unknown to the ancient writers dented their
reputation a bit. Greek geographers had planted serious doubts about there being
life near the equator. Desiderius Erasmus, the great Dutch humanist, wondered
in what other ways the ancients might be in error. This attitude of questioning, if
pressed too far, led to conflicts with the Scholastics.

Turning toward this world, as ancient learning encouraged the humanists to
do, meant attending to the objects people encountered every day—the animals,
rocks, mountains, trees, and stars—not to mention fellow human beings. Leo-
nardo da Vinci's many anatomical drawings exemplified this new fascination
with the here and now. His accurate depictions of the human body merged art
into scientific inquiry. Not until the nineteenth century did philosophers, math-
ematicians, artists, and scientists go their separate ways. For three centuries, gifted
amateurs in all these fields took the lead in examining natural objects, both domestic and foreign.

Printing with movable type, introduced in the second half of the fifteenth
century, made the reproduction of writings and illustrations much less expensive
than the written manuscripts that had preserved texts before. During these same
decades, the reading public expanded with the switch from Latin to vernacular
languages. Publishing and literacy enhanced one another as the catch basin for
communication widened. The divergence of Greek learning from Christian cosmology added to the intellectual turmoil from the discovery of the New World.
More and more men and women had to cope with the intrusion of novelty, but
it would be a mistake to exaggerate the immediate impact. Still, there was a momentum going for new initiatives in exploration.

Greeks had long pointed to the Pillars of Hercules, the promontories
flanking the Mediterranean's opening to the ocean, with the warning *ne plus
ultra*—go no farther. Portugal and Spain, facing the Atlantic, became the obvious
kingdoms to reject this advice. During the 1580s and '90s the Portuguese had
been building victualing stations on African islands and for their commercial
fleets en route to the trading centers in the East Indies. Meanwhile, a French
navigator, Jean de Bethencourt, sailing for Castile in 1402, conquered the

Canaries, which lay some 1,200 miles from Cadiz, winning for the Spanish a key station in the Atlantic. From the Canaries Spanish sailors could catch the best winds to carry them west. By the end of the fifteenth century, monarchs and financiers were ready to open up their purses to expeditions that would explore the world by sea.

Like Prince Henry, Columbus studied navigation. He made maps to depict his conjectures of what the globe really looked like. He also got in touch with Paolo de Pozzo Toscanelli, a Florentine astronomer and geographer of note, who had come into contact with writings long lost to Western Europe. Lorenzo the Magnificent had summoned an ecumenical council in 1439. The thirty-one Greek bishops who attended this extraordinary gathering brought with them the knowledge of ancient philosophy that had been preserved in the Byzantine Empire. They knew the speculations and experiments of the inquisitive Greeks. Toscanelli talked to these bishops in Florence, reigniting his zeal to figure out the shape of the earth.

It was one thing to know that the world was not flat and another to have an accurate idea of its size and shape. Europeans had neither. Worse, their heads were full of hideous pictures of what lay beyond the waters that lapped at their shores. Only with the great persuasive powers of a prince of the realm had Henry the Navigator got his sailors to press farther down the west coast of Africa. Most people believed that fantastic creatures inhabited the Ocean Sea, as they called the Atlantic. Others were sure that the bottom teemed with sinners who were burning in a molten mass that could suck in vessels that sailed out too far. Access to the writings of Strabo, a first-century Greek, dissuaded Toscanelli of the existence of these terrors. Strabo insisted that there was one world and it was habitable and its landmasses were joined by the Ocean Sea. Toscanelli went further and said that it would be possible to sail from Europe to India along the same parallel.

Men with grand visions like those of Columbus had existed before; he succeeded in implementing his plans because financiers, merchants, and monarchs—usually given to caution—responded positively to his outsized ambition. Columbus's plan contained two errors: he calculated that Japan was 2,400 nautical miles from the Canaries when it was actually over 10,000. As problematically, he did not anticipate there being a landmass between Europe and Asia! With the confidence of ignorance, he departed in August 1492 with some 120 men dispersed among two little caravels, the *Niña* and the *Pinta,* and the larger *Santa Maria.*

Ardor for heroic adventures may have helped suppress the fear of Columbus's seamen for what lay beyond the coastal waters. His sailors were lucky that Columbus knew about the clockwise circular wind patterns of the Atlantic, which would get them back home before exhausting their food supply. Elated by his success in making a landfall after nine weeks, Columbus sailed home convinced that he had found a landmass not far away from Asia whose store of riches he had read about in his favorite text, *The Travels of Marco Polo.*

In 1497 the king of Portugal commissioned Pedro Álvares Cabral to strengthen contacts with Asian merchants, sending him off with a fleet of thirteen ships. Blown off course in a storm, Cabral landed in Brazil and forthwith claimed it for Portugal before pushing on to India. Eager to tamp down the already disruptive competition between the two Catholic countries of the Iberian Peninsula, Pope Alexander VI had divided the globe between Portugal and Spain. Now he had to make a large jag in the established line (longitudes were then guessed at) to honor Portugal's new possession.

Columbus's discoveries were extraordinary enough to batter at the wall of inhibitions that surrounded questioning of Christian cosmology. There was no place in the European system of knowledge to fit in the plants, animals, minerals, and humans he brought back. They challenged settled opinions and provoked unbidden questions; they tugged at the roots of faith. The voyages of discovery proved to be the catalysts for breaching the church's curbs on curiosity, but it took time.

The intellectual consequences of Spain's venture across the Atlantic long outlasted its empire. Slowly the age-old concern with acquiring wisdom through contemplation was pushed aside in the pell-mell search for mundane details about the earth and its contents. Old ways of knowing were turned upside down. A passion for collecting information through observation, measurement, and description of new phenomena grew stronger, though it took successive generations to generate hypotheses about their meaning. This new form of pursuing information opened up the doors of inquiry to less educated amateurs, once excluded from the closed circles of the Scholastics and humanists who had to master ancient languages.

The engagement with natural phenomena involved Europeans in an inquiry about sex and sexuality. The nude bodies of the Amerindians provoked questions about the meaning of nakedness. Innocence and barbarity competed as answers. When explorers encountered willing sexual partners in the New World, their reports led to a new discourse about sexuality. Nor were sexual questions confined to humans. Botanists would use reproductive organs to categorize plants, and the sexual exclusivity among animals became the way naturalists defined species. Reproduction and the incorporation of new traits in the lineage of living things would form the basis of Darwin's explosive explanation of human origins, bringing to a climax the four-century examination of natural phenomena that the discoveries of the world outside of Europe provoked.

No one had any idea of what would happen if ships sailed west across the Atlantic. Columbus's sponsors certainly did not expect the most significant unintended consequences of all: the breaking open of the closed world of Christianity. A civilization marked by a reverence for sacred texts so deep that it disallowed questions about natural phenomena became the trailblazer in inquiries about nature. The Church Fathers had been correct. Curiosity was dangerous. Passing from amateur passions to sober investigations of biology, geology, and astronomy, it upended the grand Christian narrative of the origins of life and the place of our planet in the universe. Over the course of four hundred years the research spawned by Columbus's discovery of the New World set Europe apart from any other society on the globe, and, even more, from its own past.

FURTHER READING

Joyce Appleby, *Shores of Knowledge: New World Discoveries and the Scientific Imagination* (2013).

James Axtell, *The Invasion Within: The Contest of Cultures in Colonial North America* (1986).

Alfred W. Crosby, *The Columbian Exchange: Biological and Cultural Consequences of 1492* (1972).

Felipe Fernández-Armesto, *1492: The Year the World Began* (2009).

Francis Jennings, *The Founders of America: From the Earliest Migrations to the Present* (1993).

Alvin M. Josephy, Jr., *America in 1492: The World of Indian Peoples before the Arrival of Columbus* (1992).

Karen O. Kupperman, *Settling with the Indians: The Meeting of English and Indian Cultures in America, 1580–1640* (1980).

Charles C. Mann, *1491: New Revelations of the Americas before Columbus* (2005).

Anthony Pagden, *Lords of All the World: Ideologies of Empire in Spain, Britain, and France, c. 1500–c. 1800* (1995).

William and Carla Phillips, *The Worlds of Christopher Columbus* (1992).

Daniel K. Richter, *Facing East from Indian Country: A Native History of Early America* (2003).

David J. Weber, *The Spanish Frontier in North America* (1993).

Additional critical thinking activities and content are available in MindTap.

 **MindTap** is a fully online, highly personalized learning experience built upon Cengage Learning content. MindTap combines student learning tools—readings, multimedia, activities, and assessments—into a singular Learning Path that guides students through the course.

CHAPTER 2

Colonial Settlements and Conflicts, 1600–1690

The English trailed the Spanish, Portuguese, and the French in exploring and colonizing the Americas. After earlier engagements with the Atlantic slave trade and attempts at colonization, the English established their first permanent colony in 1607 at Jamestown, Virginia. They had attempted to form colonies beginning in the sixteenth century in locations as varied as present-day Maine and Virginia, but all had failed. Jamestown probably would have failed as well but for some fortunate circumstances.

Following the establishment of Jamestown, English colonists slowly populated areas to the north and the south. In 1620, a group boarded the Mayflower and set sail for Virginia. These dissenters from the Church of England called themselves Pilgrims. They missed their mark and landed hundreds of miles north near Cape Cod. Ten years later, another group in search of religious freedom, known as Puritans, arrived in Massachusetts. To the south, English colonists occupied islands in the Caribbean. At each location, the English encountered hostile and friendly natives, Spaniards, and French adventurers.

On the continent, Virginia and Massachusetts became the most successful English colonies, but for very different reasons. After several years of starvation and disease in Virginia, the almost exclusively male colonists began planting West Indian tobacco in 1611. Within two decades, tobacco exports grew to 1.5 million pounds. A demanding crop, tobacco rapidly depleted the soil, which increased the demand for land. Tobacco, like sugar in the Caribbean, required intensive labor, which led to the importation of unfree workers. Colonists, including former indentured servants, increasingly looked to the land controlled by Indians, leading to conflict between the two groups. This was the basis of the demands in Bacon's Rebellion in 1676. Although the bound laborers tended to be European indentured servants in the early years, African slaves later began to replace them. Legal distinctions between servants and slaves at first were imprecise, but over time the status of African slaves in relation to English servants deteriorated. This decline in status coincided with an increase in the slave population. By 1690, the Chesapeake area contained more African slaves than European servants.

Massachusetts fared well, in part, because of the winter and the immigration of family units. Cold temperatures and snow killed many of the microbes that wreaked havoc in North and South America, while the emphasis on establishing new societies in the Americas—building a "city upon a hill"—had New Englanders committed to communities that could last. Although the number of slaves in New England did not match that of the developing colonies in the South, levels of unfree labor defined social life there as well.

A series of other colonies in the South followed the Virginia pattern. Maryland (founded in 1634), the Carolinas (1669), and Georgia (1732) joined profitable British colonies in the Caribbean. South Carolina and Georgia relied on indigo, a purple dye, and on rice, whereas the Caribbean colonies produced sugar. Which crops were grown profoundly influenced the workers' lives. Sugar production was particularly toilsome, and rice demanded different rhythms of labor. In all of these colonies, however, the slave population grew until the Caribbean colonies and South Carolina had an African majority. In most regions of the South, colonies with slaves ultimately became slave colonies.

Between Virginia and Massachusetts, small colonies of Dutch and Swedish settlers, who were particularly interested in trading with the Indians, gained toeholds. Although England eventually seized both New Netherlands and New Sweden, the ethnic diversity brought by these early colonization efforts would endure. In 1681, King Charles II granted William Penn a huge tract of land, which became known as Pennsylvania, or "Penn's woods." Pennsylvania too would become a site of religious and ethnic diversity. From these modest beginnings, the colonial regions of New England (the colonies of Massachusetts, Connecticut, Rhode Island, and New Hampshire) and the Middle Colonies (New York, Pennsylvania, Delaware, and New Jersey) would grow to power and influence.

 ## QUESTIONS TO THINK ABOUT

Historians have tended to separate the English colonies by geography, religious values, gender structures, and labor forms. How different do the colonies seem? How did settlement differences, such as Virginia being comprised of male adventurers, while Massachusetts was settled mostly by English families, impact colonial development? What hopes or goals did the participants share? What were their main concerns and fears? How were various groups set against one another? How did they rely upon one another?

 ## DOCUMENTS

Document 1 reports on an Indian attack on English colonists in 1622 and argues that the English now have a right to destroy their Indian adversaries. The life of an English indentured servant could be difficult, as document 2 indicates. In this letter to his parents, Richard Frethorne recounts the trials of living in seventeenth-century Virginia and pleads to return to England. Written by Governor John Winthrop in 1630, document 3, *A Model of Christian Charity*, asks the people to work together to create a godly society. South of Virginia and

Massachusetts, planters in Barbados made it into a hub of sugarcane growth. Document 4 illustrates that transformation. Document 5 is a poem written in 1656 by Anne Bradstreet, one of the original Puritan settlers. In it she discusses her feelings for her children and their activities. We see within it the mobility and instability of colonial society. The English were never alone in the wilderness, and document 6 contains a French missionary's encounters with the Iroquois. A contrast to Frethorne's letter, in document 7, George Alsop contends that the indentured servants enjoy good fortune. You might wish to consider why these two accounts differ so much. On rare occasion, slaves and servants enter the record with their own words. During the Salem witchcraft trials, however, one named Tituba was examined by the court for her insights into the dark realms. Unlike many others in the colonies, she survived the ordeal.

1. Edward Waterhouse, a British Official, Recounts an Indian Attack on Early Virginia Settlement, 1622

The houses generally set open to the Savages, who were always friendly entertained at the tables of the English, and commonly lodged in their bed-chambers....

Yea, such was the treacherous dissimulation of that people who then had contrived our destruction, that even two days before the massacre, some of our men were guided through the woods by them in safety.... Yea, they borrowed our own boats to convey themselves across the river (on the banks of both sides whereof all our plantations were) to consult of the devilish murder that ensued, and of our utter extirpation, which God of his mercy (by the means of some of themselves converted to Christianity) prevented.... On Friday morning (the fatal day) the 22 of March, as also in the evening, as in other days before, they came unarmed into our houses, without bows or arrows, or other weapons, with deer, turkey, fish, furs, and other provisions, to sell, and truck with us, for glass, beads, and other trifles: yea in some places, sat down at breakfast with our people at their tables.... And by this means that fatal Friday morning, there fell under the bloody and barbarous hands of that perfidious and inhumane people, contrary to all laws of God and men, of nature and nations, 347 men, women, and children, most by their own weapons; and not being content with taking away life alone, they fell after again upon the dead, making as well as they could, a fresh murder, defacing, dragging, and mangling the dead carkasses into many pieces, carrying some parts away in derision....

Our hands which before were tied with gentleness and fair usage, are now set at library by the treacherous violence of the savages ... that we, who hitherto have had possession of no more ground then their waste, and our purchase at a valuable consideration to their own contentment, gained; may now by right of war, and law of nations, invade the country, and destroy them who sought to destroy us: whereby wee shall enjoy their cultivated places.... Now their cleared grounds in

Susan Myra Kingsbury, ed., *The Records of the Virginia Company of London*, III (Washington, D.C.: U.S. Government Printing Office, 1933), 550–551, 556–557.

all their villages (which are situate in the fruitfullest places of the land) shall be inhabited by us, whereas heretofore the grubbing of woods was the greatest labor.

2. Indentured Servant Richard Frethorne Laments His Condition in Virginia, 1623

Loving and kind father and mother, my most humble duty remembered to you hoping in God of your good health, as I my self am at the making hereof, this is to let you understand that I your Child am in a most heavy Case by reason of the nature of the Country is such that it Causeth much sickness, as the scurvy and the bloody flux [dysentery], and divers other diseases, which maketh the body very poor, and Weak, and when we are sick there is nothing to Comfort us; for since I came out of the ship, I never ate any thing but peas and loblollie (that is water gruel) as for deer or venison I never saw any since I came into this land, there is indeed some fowl, but We are not allowed to go and get it, but must Work hard both early and late for a mess of water gruel, and a mouthful of bread, and beef, a mouthful of bread for a penny loaf must serve for 4 men which is most pitiful if you did know as much as I, when people cry out day, and night, Oh that they were in England without their limbs and would not care to lose any limb to be in England again, yea though they beg from door to door, for we live in fear of the Enemy every hour, yet we have had a Combat with them on the Sunday before Shrovetide, and we took two alive, and make slaves of them.... [W]e are fain to get other men to plant with us, and yet we are but 32 to fight against 3000 if they should Come, and the nighest help that We have is ten miles of us, and when the rogues overcame this place last, they slew 80 persons. How then shall we doe for we lie even in their teeth, they may easily take us but that God is merciful, and can save with few as well as with many; as he showed to Gilead and like Gilead's soldiers if they lapped water, we drink water which is but Weak, and I have nothing to Comfort me, nor there is nothing to be gotten here but sickness, and death, except that one had money to lay out in some things for profit; But I have nothing at all, no not a shirt to my backe, but two Rags nor no Clothes, but one poor suit, nor but one pair of shoes, but one pair of stockings, but one Cap, but two bands, my Cloak is stolen by one of my own fellows.... I am not half a quarter so strong as I was in England, and all is for want of victuals, for I do protest unto you, that I have eaten more in a day at home than I have allowed me here for a Week. You have given more than my day's allowance to a beggar at the door.... [I]f you love me you will redeem me suddenly, for which I do entreat and beg, and if you cannot get the merchants to redeem me for some little money then for God's sake get a gathering or entreat some good folks to lay out some little sum of money, in meal, and Cheese and butter, and beef, any eating meat will yield great profit, ... and look whatsoever you send me be it never so much,

Richard Frethorne to his mother and father, March–April, 1623, in *The Records of the Virginia Company*, ed. Susan M. Kingsbury, IV (Washington, D.C.: U.S. Government Printing Office, 1935), 58–62.

look what I make of it. I will deal truly with you. I will send it over, and beg the profit to redeem me, and if I die before it Come I have entreated Goodman Jackson to send you the worth of it, who hath promised he will. If you send you must direct your letter to Goodman Jackson, at James Town, a Gunsmith.... Good Father do not forget me, but have mercy and pity my miserable Case. I know if you did but see me you would weep to see me, for I have but one suit, but it is a strange one, it is very well guarded, wherefore for God's sake pity me. I pray you to remember my love to all my friends, and kindred, I hope all my Brothers and sisters are in good health, and as for my part I have set down my resolution that certainly Will be, that is, that the Answer of this letter will be life or death to me, there good Father send as soon as you can, and if you send me any thing let this be the mark.

Richard Frethorne
Martin's Hundred

3. Puritan Leader John Winthrop Provides a Model of Christian Charity, 1630

1. For the persons, we are a Company professing ourselves fellow members of Christ....
2. For the work we have in hand, it is by a mutual consent through a special overruling providence, and a more than an ordinary approbation of the Churches of Christ to seek out a place of Cohabitation and Consortship under a due form of Government both civil and ecclesiastical....
3. The end is to improve our lives to do more service to the Lord the comfort and increase of the body of christ whereof we are members that ourselves and posterity may be the better preserved from the Common corruptions of this evil world....
4. For the means whereby this must be effected, they are 2fold, a Conformity with the work and end we aim at, these we see are extraordinary, therefore we must not content ourselves with usual ordinary means whatsoever we did or ought to have done when we lived in England, the same must we do and more also where we go: That which the most in their Churches maintain as a truth in profession only, we must bring into familiar and constant practice, as in this duty of love we must love brotherly without dissimulation, we must love one another with a pure heart fervently we must bear one another's burdens, we must not look only on our own things, but also on the things of our brethren, neither must we think that the lord will

John Winthrop, "A Model of Christian Charity" (1630), in *Collections*, Massachusetts Historical Society, 3d ser., VII (1838), 3–48; reprinted in *Winthrop Papers*, Massachusetts Historical Society, II (Boston: Massachusetts Historical Society, 1931), 282–295.

bear with such failings at our hands as he doth from those among whom we have lived....

... [F]or we must Consider that we shall be as a City upon a Hill, the eyes of all people are upon us; so that if we shall deal falsely with out god in this work we have undertaken and so cause him to withdraw his present help from us, we shall be made a story and a by-word through the world, we shall open the mouths of enemies to speak evil of the ways of god and all professors for God's sake; we shall shame the faces of many of gods worthy servants, and cause their prayers to be turned into Curses upon us till we be consumed out of the good land whether we are going.

4. Sugar Planters Transform Barbados, 1647–1650

Now for the Masters, I have yet said but little, nor am able to say half of what they deserve. They are men of great abilities and parts, otherwise they could not go through, with such great works as they undertake; the managing of one of their Plantations, being a work of such a latitude, as will require a very good head-peece, to put in order, and continue it so.

I can name a Planter there, that feeds daily two hundred mouths, and keeps them in such order, as there are no mutinies amongst them; and yet of several nations. All these are to be employed in their several abilities, so as no one be idle. The first work to be considered, is Weeding, for unless that be done, all else (and the Planter too) will be undone, and if that be neglected but a little time, it will be a hard matter to recover it again, so fast will the weeds grow there. But the ground being kept clean, 'tis fit to bear any thing that Country will afford. After weeding comes Planting, and they account two seasons in the year best, and that is, *May* and *November*; but Canes are to be planted at all times, that they may come in, one field after another; otherwise, the work will stand still. And commonly they have in a field that is planted together, at one time, ten or a dozen acres. This work of planting and weeding, the Master himself is to see done; unless he have a very trusty and able Overseer; and without such a one, he will have too much to do. The next thing he is to consider, is the Ingenio, and what belongs to that; as, the Ingenio it self, which is the *Primum Mobile* of the whole work, the Boyling-house, with the Coppers and Furnaces, the Filling room, the Still-house, and Cureing-house; and in all these, there are great casualties. If any thing in the Rollers, as the Goudges, Sockets, Sweeps, Cogs, or Braytrees, be at fault, the whole work stands still; or in the Boyling-house, if the Frame which holds the Coppers, (and is made of Clinkers, fastned with plaister of *Paris*) if by the violence of the heat from the Furnaces, these Frames crack or break, there is a stop in the work, till that be mended. Or if any of the Coppers have a mischance, and be burnt, a new one must presently be had, or there is a stay in the work. Or if the mouths of the Furnaces, (which are made of a sort

---

Richard Ligon, "A True and Exact History of the Island of Barbadoes (1673)," pp. 55–57, 85–86.

of stone, which we have from *England*, and we call it there, high gate stone) if that, by the violence of the fire, be softned, that it moulder away, there must new be provided, and laid in with much art, or it will not be. Or if the bars of Iron, which are in the floor of the Furnace, when they are red hot (as continually they are) the fire-man, throw great shides of wood in the mouths of the Furnaces, hard and carelesly, the weight of those logs, will bend or break those bars, (though strongly made) and there is no repairing them, without the work stand still; for all these depend upon one another, as wheels in a Clock. Or if the Stills be at fault, the *kill-devil* cannot be made. But the main impediment and stop of all, is the loss of our Cattle, and amongst them, there are such diseases, as I have known in one Plantation, thirty that have dyed in two dayes. And I have heard, that a Planter, an eminent man there, that clear'd a dozen acres of ground, and rail'd it about for pasture, with intention, as soon as the grass was grown to a great height, to put in his working Oxen; which accordingly he did, and in one night fifty of them dyed; so that such a loss as this, is able to undo a Planter, that is not very well grounded. What it is that breeds these diseases, we cannot find, unless some of the Plants have a poysonous quality; nor have we yet found out cures for these diseases; Chickens guts being the best remedy was then known, and those being chop'd or minc'd, and given them in a horn, with some liquor mixt to moisten it, was thought the best remedy: yet it recovered very few. Our Horses too have killing diseases amongst them, and some of them have been recovered by Glisters, which we give them in pipes, or large Seringes made of wood, for the same purpose. For, the common diseases, both of Cattle and Horses, are obstructions and bindings in their bowels; and so lingring a disease it is, to those that recover, as they are almost worn to nothing before they get well. So that if any of these stops continue long, or the Cattle cannot be recruited in a reasonable time, the work is at a stand; and by that means, the Canes grow over ripe, and will in a very short time have their juice dryed up, and will not be worth the grinding.

Now to recruit these Cattle, Horses, Camels, and Assinigos, who are all liable to these mischances and decayes, Merchants must be consulted, ships provided, and a competent Cargo of goods adventured, to make new voyages to forraign parts, to supply those losses; and when that is done, the casualties at Sea are to be considered, and those happen several wayes, either by shipwrack, piracy, or fire. A Master of a ship, and a man accounted both able, stout, and honest, having transported goods of several kinds, from *England* to a part of *Africa*, the River of *Gambra*, and had there exchanged his Commodities for *Negroes*, which was that he intended to make his voyage of, caused them all to be ship'd, and did not, as the manner is, shakle one to another, and make them sure, but having an opinion of their honesty and faithfulness to him, as they had promised; and he being a credulous man, and himself good natur'd and merciful, suffered them to go loose, and they being double the number of those in the Ship, found their advantages, got weapons in their hands, and fell upon the Saylers, knocking them on the heads, and cutting their throats so fast, as the Master found they were all lost, out of any possibility of saving; and so went down into the Hold, and blew all up with himself; and this was before they got out of the River. These, and several other wayes there will happen, that extreamly retard the work of Sugar-making.

Now let us consider how many things there are to be thought on, that go to the actuating this great work, and how many cares to prevent the mischances, that are incident to the retarding, if not the frustrating of the whole work; and you will find them wise and provident men, that go on and prosper in a work, that depends upon so many contingents.

This I say, to stop those mens mouths, that lye here at home, and expect great profit in their adventures, and never consider, through what difficulty, industry and pains it is acquired. And thus much I thought good to say, of the abilities of the Planters....

At the time we landed on this Island, which was in the beginning of *September*, 1647. we were informed, partly by those Planters we found there, and partly by our own observations, that the great work of Sugar-making, was but newly practiced by the inhabitants there. Some of the most industrious men, having gotten Plants from *Fernambock*, a place in *Brasil*, and made tryal of them at the *Barbadoes*; and finding them to grow, they planted more and more, as they grew and multiplyed on the place, till they had such a considerable number, as they were worth the while to set up a very small Ingenio, and so make tryal what Sugar could be made upon that soyl. But, the secrets of the work being not well understood, the Sugars they made were very inconsiderable, and little worth, for two or three years. But they finding their errours by their daily practice, began a little to mend; and, by new directions from *Brasil*, sometimes by strangers, and now and then by their own people, (who being covetous of the knowledge of a thing, which so much concerned them in their particulars, and for the general good of the whole Island) were content sometimes to make a voyage thither, to improve their knowledge in a thing they so much desired. Being now made much abler to make their queries, of the secrets of that mystery, by how much their often failings, had put them to often stops and nonplusses in the work. And so returning with most Plants, and better Knowledge, they went on upon fresh hopes, but still short, of what they should be more skilful in: for, at our arrival there, we found them ignorant in three main points, that much conduced to the work; *viz.* The manner of Planting, the time of Gathering, and the right placing of their Coppers in their Furnaces; as also, the true way of covering their Rollers, with plates or Bars of Iron: All which being rightly done, advance much in the performance of the main work. At the time of our arrival there, we found many Sugar-works set up, and at work; but yet the Sugars they made, were but bare Muscavadoes, and few of them Merchantable commodities; so moist, and full of molosses, and so ill cur'd, as they were hardly worth the bringing home for *England*. But about the time I left the Island, which was in 1650. they were much better'd; for then they had the skill to know when the Canes were ripe, which was not, till they were fifteen months old; and before, they gathered them at twelve, which was a main disadvantage to the making good Sugar; for, the liquor wanting of the sweetness it ought to have, caused the Sugars to be lean, and unfit to keep. Besides, they were grown

greater proficients, both in boyling and curing them, and had learnt the knowledge of making them white, such as you call Lump Sugars here in *England*; but
not so excellent as those they make in *Brasil*, nor is there any likelyhood they can
ever make such: the land there being better, and lying in a Continent, must
needs have constanter and steadier weather, and the Aire much drier and purer,
than it can be in so small an Iland, and that of *Barbadoes*. And now, seeing this
commodity, Sugar, hath gotten so much the start of all the rest of those, that
were held the staple Commodities of the Iland, and so much over-top't them, as
they are for the most part slighted and neglected. And, for that few in *England*
know the trouble and care of making it, I think it convenient, in the first place, to
acquaint you, as far as my memory will serve, with the whole process of the work of
Sugar-making, which is now grown the soul of Trade in this Iland. And leaving to
trouble you and my self, with relating the errours our Predecessors so long wandred
in, I will in brief set down the right and best way they practiced, when I left the
Island, which, I think, will admit of no greater or farther improvement.

But, before I will begin with that, I will let you see, how much the land there
hath been advanc'd in the profit, since the work of Sugar began, to the time of
our landing there, which was not above five or six years: For, before the work
began, this Plantation of Major *Hilliards*, of five hundred acres, could have been
purchased for four hundred pound sterling; and now the halfe this Plantation,
with the halfe of the Stock upon it was sold for seven thousand pound sterling.
And it is evident, that all the land there, which has been imployed to that work,
hath found the like improvement. And I believe, when the small Plantations in
poor mens hands, of ten, twenty, or thirty acres, which are too small to lay to
that work, be bought up by great men, and put together, into Plantations of
five, six, or seven hundred acres, that two thirds of the Iland will be fit for Plantations of Sugar, which will make it one of the richest Spots of earth under the Sun.

5. Anne Bradstreet Discusses Her Children in the Colonies, 1656

I had eight birds hatcht in one nest,

Four Cocks were there, and Hens the rest.

I nurst them up with pain and care,

No cost nor labour did I spare

Till at the last they felt their wing,

Mounted the Trees and learned to sing.

Chief of the Brood then took his flight

To Regions far and left me quite.

My mournful chirps I after send

Anne Bradstreet, "In Reference to Her Children," (1656) in *The Poems of Mrs. Anne Bradstreet (1612–1672)* (1897), 275–279.

Till he return, or I do end....

My second bird did take her flight

And with her mate flew out of sight.

Southward they both their course did bend,

And Seasons twain they there did spend,

Till after blown by Southern gales

They Norward steer'd with filled sails....

One to the Academy flew

To chat among that learned crew.

Ambition moves still in his breast

That he might chant above the rest,

Striving for more than to do well,

That nightingales he might excel....

If birds could weep, then would my tears

Let others know what are my fears

Lest this my brood some harm should catch

And be surpris'd for want of watch

Whilst pecking corn and void of care

They fall un'wares in Fowler's snare; ...

6. A French Missionary Describes the Iroquois, 1659–1660

... The Ocean which separates us from France sees, on its eastern side, only rejoicing, splendor, and bonfires; but, on its western, nothing but war, slaughter, and conflagrations....

What consoles us is our full assurance that people do not regard us merely as do those who, being themselves in port or on the shore, contemplate with some compassion the wreck of a poor vessel shattered by the storm, and even shed some tears over it. But we promise ourselves much more, knowing the vows, the prayers, the penances, and all sorts of good works, which are being performed almost everywhere for the conversion of our Savages; and learning of the good purposes with which God has inspired many persons of merit, for accomplishing the destruction of the Iroquois. That means, to open a door, high and wide, for proclaiming the Faith and giving the Preachers of the Gospel access to peoples of great extent, in regard to both the territories which they occupy, and the diversity of Nations composing them—all of whom are four or five hundred leagues distant from us in the forests, shunning the common enemy. Were

"The Jesuit Relations and Allied Documents, 1610–1791," Vol. 45, *Relation of 1659–1660*, ed. Reuben Gold Thwaites. Also found at http://puffin.creighton.edu/jesuit/relations/relations_45. html (accessed 7/23/13).

it not for the latter, they would come and enrich this country with their furs, and we should visit them to enrich Heaven with the glorious spoils that we should wrest from the powers of Hell....

We know ... that there are tribes of the same language, both stationary and wandering, as far as the North sea, on whose shores these nations border; and that there are others, very recently discovered, extending as far as the South sea. They stretch out their arms to us, and we ours to them, but on both sides they are too short to unite across such a distance; and when, finally, we are on the point of embracing each other, the Iroquois steps in between and showers blows upon both of us.

We know that very far beyond the great Lake of the Hurons,—among whom the Faith was so flourishing some years ago, when the Iroquois did not molest our Missions, and before he had expelled us from them by the murder of our Fathers and the pillage of those nascent Churches,—we know that some remnants of the wreck of that Nation rallied in considerable numbers beyond the lakes and mountains frequented by their enemies, and that but recently they sent a deputation hither to ask back again their dear old Pastors. But these good Pastors are slain on the way by the Iroquois, their guides are captured and burned, and all the roads are rendered impassable. We even know that among the Iroquois the Faith is in a vigorous condition, although they do not possess it in their own persons, but in those of numerous captives. These only long to have us with them, or to be themselves with us....

Finally, we know that, whithersoever we go in our forests, we find some fugitive Church, or else some infant one; everywhere we find children to send to Heaven, everywhere sick people to baptize, and adults to instruct, But everywhere, too, we find the Iroquois, who, like an obtrusive phantom, besets us in all places....

They prevent the tribes from five or six hundred leagues about us, from coming down hither, laden with furs that would make this country overflow with immense riches—as was done in a single journey which some of those Nations undertook this year—although secretly, and, as it were, by stealth, from fear of their foes....

What gives the enemy this advantage over us is, that all the rural settlements outside of Québec are without defense, and are distant from one another as much as eight or ten leagues on the banks of the great River. In each house there are only two, three, or four men, and often only one, alone with his wife and a number of children, who may all be killed or carried off without any one's knowing aught about it in the nearest house.

I say nothing of the losses that France would suffer if these vast regions should pass from her control. The foreigner would reap, a great advantage, to the detriment of French navigation." ...

They come like foxes through the woods, ... They attack like lions ... They take flight like birds, disappearing before they have really appeared.... Of the five tribes constituting the entire Iroquois nation, that which we call the Agnieronnons has been so many times at both the top and the bottom of the wheel, within less than sixty years, that we find in history few examples of similar revolutions.... We cannot go back very far in our researches in their past history, as they have no Libraries other than the memory of their old men; and perhaps we should find nothing worthy of publication. What we learn then from these living books is that, toward the end of the last century, the Agnieronnons were reduced so low by the Algonkins that there seemed to be scarcely any more of them left on the earth. Nevertheless, this scanty remnant, like a noble germ, so increased in a few years as to reduce the Algonquins in turn to the same condition as its own. But this condition did not last long; for the Andastogehronnons waged such energetic warfare against them during ten years that they were overthrown for the second time and their nation rendered almost extinct, or at least so humiliated that the mere name Algonkin made them tremble, and his shadow seemed to pursue them to their very firesides.

That was at the time when the Dutch took possession of these regions and conceived a fondness for the beavers of the natives, some thirty years ago; and in order to secure them in greater number they furnished those people with fire-arms, with which it was easy for them to conquer their conquerors, whom they put to rout, and filled with terror at the mere sound of their guns. And that is what has rendered them formidable everywhere, and victorious over all the N'ations with whom they have been at war; it has also put into their heads that idea of sovereign sway to which they aspire, mere barbarians although they are, with an ambition so lofty that they think and say that their own destruction cannot occur without bringing in its train the downfall of the whole earth.

But what is more astonishing is, that they actually hold dominion for five hundred leagues around, although their numbers are very small; for, of the five Nations constituting the Iroquois, the Agnieronnons do not exceed five hundred men able to bear arms, who occupy three or four wretched Villages. ... [I]t is beyond doubt that, if the Agnieronnons were defeated by the French, the other Iroquois Nations would be glad to compromise with us, and give us their chil-dren as hostages of their good faith. Then those fair Missions would be revived at Onnontagué, at Oiogoen, and in all the other remaining Iroquois Nations, among whom we have already sown the first seeds of the faith. These have been so well received by the common people that we may not, without distrust-ing the divine Providence, despair of one day reaping therefrom very abundant fruits. Moreover, the great door would be open for so many old and new mis-sions toward the tribes of the North, and toward those newly discovered ones of the West, all of whom we embrace under the general name of Algonquins.

7. George Alsop, a Resident of Maryland, Argues That Servants in Maryland Profit from Life in the Colonies, 1666

The necessariness of Servitude proved, with the common usage of Servants in Mary-Land, together with their Priviledges.

... There is no truer Emblem of Confusion either in Monarchy or Domestick Governments, then when either the Subject, or the Servant, strives for the upper

---

George Alsop, "A Character of the Province of Maryland, 1666," in *Narratives of Early Maryland*, ed. C. C. Hall (New York: Charles Scribner's Sons, 1910; copyright renewed Barnes and Noble, 1946), 354–360.

hand of his Prince, or Master, and to be equal with him, from whom he receives his present subsistance: Why then, if Servitude be so necessary that no place can be governed in order, nor people live without it, this may serve to tell those which prick up their ears and bray against it, That they are none but Asses, and deserve the Bridle of a strict commanding power to rein them in: For I'me certainly confident, that there are several Thousands in most Kingdoms of Christendom, that could not at all live and subsist, unless they had served some prefixed time, to learn either some Trade, Art, or Science, and by either of them to extract their present livelihood.

Then methinks this may stop the mouths of those that will undiscreetly compassionate them that dwell under necessary Servitudes....

... [L]et such, where Providence hath ordained to life as Servants, either in England or beyond Sea, endure the pre-fixed yoak of their limited time with patience, and then in a small computation of years, by an industrious endeavour, they may become Masters and Mistresses of Families themselves. And let this be spoke to the deserved praise of Mary-Land. That the four years I served there were not to me so slavish, as a two years Servitude of a Handicraft Apprenticeship was here in London....

They whose abilities cannot extend to purchase their own transportation over into Mary-Land, (and surely he that cannot command so small a sum for so great a matter, his life must needs be mighty low and dejected) I say they may for the debarment of a four years sordid liberty, go over into this Province and there live plentiously well. And what's a four years Servitude to advantage a man all the remainder of his dayes, making his predecessors happy in his sufficient abilities, which he attained to partly by the restrainment of so small a time? ...

The Merchant commonly before they go aboard the Ship, or set themselves in any forwardness for their Voyage, has Conditions of Agreements drawn between him and those that by a voluntary consent become his Servants, to serve him, his Heirs or Assigns, according as they in their primitive acquaintance have made their bargain, some two, some three, some four years; and whatever the Master or Servant tyes himself up to here in England by Condition, the Laws of the Province will force a performance of when they come there: Yet here is this Priviledge in it when they arrive. If they dwell not with the Merchant they made their first agreement withall, they may choose whom they will serve their prefixed time with; and after their curiosity has pitcht on one whom they think fit for their turn, and that they may live well withall, the Merchant makes an Assignment of the Indenture over to him whom they of their free will have chosen to be their Master, in the same nature as we here in England (and no otherwise) turn over Covenant Servants or Apprentices from one Master to another. Then let those whose chaps are always breathing forth those filthy dregs of abusive exclamations, ... against this Country of Mary-Land, saying, That those which are transported over thither, are sold in open Market for Slaves, and draw in Carts like Horses; which is so damnable as untruth, that if they should search to the very Center of Hell, and enquire for a Lye of the most antient and damned stamp, I confidently believe they could not find one to parallel this: For know, That the Servants here in Mary-Land of all Colonies, distant or remote Plantations, have the least cause to complain, either for strictness of Servitude, want of Provisions, or need of Apparel: Five dayes and a half in the Summer weeks is the alotted time that they work in; and for two months, when the Sun predominates in the highest pitch of his heat, they claim an antient and customary Priviledge, to repose themselves three hours in the day within the house, and this is undeniably granted to them that work in the Fields....

... He that lives in the nature of a Servant in this Province, must serve but four years by the Custom of the Country; and when the expiration of his time speaks him a Freeman, there's a Law in the Province, that enjoyns his Master whom he hath served to give him Fifty Acres of Land, Corn to serve him a whole year, three Sutes of Apparel, with things necessary to them, and Tools to work withall; so that they are no sooner free, but they are ready to set up for themselves, and when once entered, they live passingly well.

The Women that go over into this Province as Servants, have the best luck here as in any place of the world besides; for they are no sooner on shoar, but they are courted into a Copulative Matrimony, which some of them (for aught I know) had they not come to such a Market with their Virginity might have kept it by them until it had been mouldy....

In short, touching the Servants of this Province, they live well in the time of their Service, and by their restrainment in that time, they are made capable of living much better when they come to be free; which in several other parts of the world I have observed, That after some servants have brought their indented and limited time to a just and legal period by Servitude, they have been much more incapable of supporting themselves from sinking into the Gulf of a slavish, poor, fettered, and intangled life, then all the fastness of their pre-fixed time did involve them in before.

8. Tituba, a Servant-Slave in Salem, Massachusetts, Answers Questions About the Devil, 1692

Salem Village, March 1, 1692

Tituba an Indian woman brought before us by Constable Joseph Herrick of Salem upon suspicion of witchcraft by her committed according to the complaint of Joseph Hutcheson and Thomas Putnam, etc. of Salem Village as appears per warrant granted Salem 29 February 1691/2. Tituba upon examination and after some denial acknowledged the matter of fact according to her examination

Salem Witchcraft Papers: Verbatim Transcripts of the Legal Documents, ed. Paul Boyer and Stephen Nissenbaum (New York: Da Capo, 1977), 3:1747–49.

given in more fully will appear and who also charged Sarah Good and Sarah Osborne with the same....

John Hathorne and Jonathan Corwin, Assistants

(HATHORNE:) Titibe what evil spirit have you familiarity with?

    (TITUBA:) None.

      (H:) Why do you hurt these children?

      (T:) I do not hurt them.

      (H:) Who is it then?

      (T:) The devil for ought I know.

      (H:) Did you never see the devil?

      (T:) The devil came to me and bid me serve him....

      (H:) Who have you seen?

      (T:) Four women sometimes hurt the children.

      (H:) Who were they?

      (T:) Goody Osborne and Sarah Good and I do not know who the other were. Sarah Good and Osborne would have me hurt the children but I would not....

      (H:) When did you see them?

      (T:) Last night at Boston.

      (H:) What did they say to you?

      (T:) They said hurt the children,...

      (H:) What is this appearance you see?

      (T:) Sometimes it is like a hog and sometimes like a great dog.

      (H.) What did it say to you?

      (T:) The black dog said serve me but I said I am afraid. He said if I did not he would do worse to me.

      (H:) What did you say to it?

      (T:) I will serve you no longer. Then he said he would hurt me and then he looks like a man and threatens to hurt me.... and he told me he had more pretty things that he would give me if I would serve him.

      (H:) What were these pretty things?

      (T:) He did not show me them.

      (H:) What else have you seen?

      (T:) Two rats, a red rat and a black rat....

      (H:) Do you see who it is that torments these children now?

      (T:) Yes, it is Goody Good. She hurts them in her own shape.

      (H:) And who is it that hurts them now?

      (T:) I am blind now, I cannot see....

 ESSAYS

The making of "New England" ushered in a new world along the east coast of North America. New people, new beliefs, new social structures, new languages, and new materials from Europe were matched by new social relations, political dynamics, alliances, and discords. How did people of the age experience it? Was successful English colonization inevitable, surprising, or a fluke of history? These two essays examine how different groups made and reacted to those changes. In the first, James H. Merrell argues that a "new world" was created for Indians when they encountered Europeans and Africans in the Carolinas and Virginia. Merrell stresses that the vast changes that contact brought about created a new order not unlike that encountered by the Europeans and Africans who crossed the ocean. While Merrell emphasizes the abundant newness of changes, Rachel B. Herrmann looks at the dynamic role of supposed scarcity in colonial Virginia. Analyzing discussions of food and cannibalism before, during, and after the so-called Starving Time of early Jamestown, Herrmann suggests that reports of scarcity and laziness were reworked into a founding myth of and advertisement for British immigration to the new world: that hard work would lead to plenty of food.

The Indians' New World

JAMES H. MERRELL

In August 1608 John Smith and his band of explorers captured an Indian named Amoroleck during a skirmish along the Rappahannock River. Asked why his men—a hunting party from towns upstream—had attacked the English, Amoroleck replied that they had heard the strangers "were a people come from under the world, to take their world from them." Smith's prisoner grasped a simple yet important truth that students of colonial America have overlooked: after 1492 native Americans lived in a world every bit as new as that confronting transplanted Africans or Europeans.

The failure to explore the Indians' new world helps explain why, despite many excellent studies of the native American past, colonial history often remains "a history of those men and women—English, European, and African— who transformed America from a geographical expression into a new nation." One reason Indians generally are left out may be the apparent inability to fit them into the new world theme, a theme that exerts a powerful hold on our historical imagination and runs throughout our efforts to interpret American development.... [S]cholars have analyzed encounters between peoples from the Old World and conditions in the New, studying the complex interplay between European or African cultural patterns and the American environment. Indians

James H. Merrell, "The Indians' New World: The Catawba Experience," *William and Mary Quarterly*, 3rd Series, Vol. 41, No. 4 (October 1984). Reprinted by permission of William and Mary Quarterly.

crossed no ocean, peopled no faraway land. It might seem logical to exclude them.

The natives' segregation persists, in no small degree, because historians still tend to think only of the new world as the New World, a geographic entity bounded by the Atlantic Ocean on the one side and the Pacific on the other. Recent research suggests that process was as important as place. Many settlers in New England recreated familiar forms with such success that they did not really face an alien environment until long after their arrival. Africans, on the other hand, were struck by the shock of the new at the moment of their enslavement, well before they stepped on board ship or set foot on American soil. If the Atlantic was not a barrier between one world and another, if what happened to people was more a matter of subtle cultural processes than mere physical displacements, perhaps we should set aside the maps and think instead of a "world" as the physical and cultural milieu demanding basic changes in ways of life. Considered in these terms, the experience of natives was more closely akin to that of immigrants and slaves, and the idea of an encounter between worlds can—indeed, must—include the aboriginal inhabitants of America.

For American Indians a new order arrived in three distinct yet overlapping stages. First, alien microbes killed vast numbers of natives, sometimes before the victims had seen a white or black face. Next came traders who exchanged European technology for Indian products and brought natives into the developing world market. In time traders gave way to settlers eager to develop the land according to their own lights. These three intrusions combined to transform native existence, disrupting established cultural habits and requiring creative responses to drastically altered conditions. Like their new neighbors, then, Indians were forced to blend old and new in ways that would permit them to survive in the present without forsaking their past. By the close of the colonial era, native Americans as well as whites and blacks had created new societies, each similar to, yet very different from, its parent culture.

The range of native societies produced by this mingling of ingredients probably exceeded the variety of social forms Europeans and Africans developed. Rather than survey the broad spectrum of Indian adaptations, this [essay] considers in some depth the response of natives in one area, the southern piedmont.... Avoiding extinction and eschewing retreat, the Indians of the piedmont have been in continuous contact with the invaders from across the sea almost since the beginning of the colonial period....

... [T]hese groups [the piedmont peoples] shared a single history once Europeans and Africans arrived on the scene. Drawn together by their cultural affinities and their common plight, after 1700 they migrated to the Catawba Nation, a cluster of villages along the border between the Carolinas that became the focus of native life in the region. Tracing the experience of these upland communities both before and after they joined the Catawbas can illustrate the consequences of contact and illuminate the process by which natives learned to survive in their own new world.

For centuries, ancestors of the Catawbas had lived astride important aboriginal trade routes and straddled the boundary between two cultural traditions, a position that involved them in a far-flung network of contacts and affected everything from potting techniques to burial practices. Nonetheless, Africans and Europeans were utterly unlike any earlier foreign visitors to the piedmont. Their arrival meant more than merely another encounter with outsiders; it marked an important turning point in Indian history. Once these newcomers disembarked and began to feel their way across the continent, they forever altered the course and pace of native development.

Bacteria brought the most profound disturbances to upcountry villages. When Hernando de Soto led the first Europeans into the area in 1540, he found large towns already "grown up in grass" because "there had been a pest in the land" two years before, a malady probably brought inland by natives who had visited distant Spanish posts. The sources are silent about other "pests" over the next century, but soon after the English began colonizing Carolina in 1670 the disease pattern became all too clear. Major epidemics struck the region at least once every generation—in 1698, 1718, 1738, and 1759—and a variety of less virulent illnesses almost never left native settlements.

Indians were not the only inhabitants of colonial America living—and dying—in a new disease environment. The swamps and lowlands of the Chesapeake were a deathtrap for Europeans, and sickness obliged colonists to discard or rearrange many of the social forms brought from England. Among native peoples long isolated from the rest of the world and therefore lacking immunity to pathogens introduced by the intruders, the devastation was even more severe....

Survivors of these horrors were thrust into a situation no less alien than what European immigrants and African slaves found. The collected wisdom of generations could vanish in a matter of days if sickness struck older members of a community who kept sacred traditions and taught special skills. When many of the elders succumbed at once, the deep pools of collective memory grew shallow, and some dried up altogether. In 1710, Indians near Charleston told a settler that "they have forgot most of their traditions since the Establishment of this Colony, they keep their Festivals and can tell but little of the reasons: their Old Men are dead." Impoverishment of a rich cultural heritage followed the spread of disease. Nearly a century later, a South Carolinian exaggerated but captured the general trend when he noted that Catawbas "have forgotten their ancient rites, ceremonies, and manufactures."

The same diseases that robbed a piedmont town of some of its most precious resources also stripped it of the population necessary to maintain an independent existence. In order to survive, groups were compelled to construct new societies from the splintered remnants of the old. The result was a kaleidoscopic array of migrations from ancient territories and mergers with nearby peoples. While such behavior was not unheard of in aboriginal times, population levels fell so precipitously after contact that survivors endured disruptions unlike anything previously known....

No mere catalog of migrations and mergers can begin to convey how profoundly unsettling this experience was for those swept up in it. While upcountry Indians did not sail away to some distant land, they, too, were among the uprooted, leaving their ancestral homes to try to make a new life elsewhere. A village and its surrounding territory were important elements of personal and collective identity, physical links in a chain binding a group to its past and making a locality sacred....

The toll could be physical as well as spiritual, for even the most uneventful of moves interrupted the established cycle of subsistence. Belongings had to be packed and unpacked, dwellings constructed, palisades raised. Once migrants had completed the business of settling in, the still more arduous task of exploiting new terrain awaited them. Living in one place year after year endowed a people with intimate knowledge of the area. The richest soils, the best hunting grounds, the choicest sites for gathering nuts or berries—none could be learned without years of experience, tested by time and passed down from one generation to the next. Small wonder that Carolina Indians worried about being "driven to some unknown Country, to live, hunt, and get our Bread in."

Some displaced groups tried to leave "unknown Country" behind and make their way back home. In 1716 Enos asked Virginia's permission to settle at "Enoe Town" on the North Carolina frontier, their location in Lawson's day. Seventeen years later William Byrd II came upon an abandoned Cheraw village on a tributary of the upper Roanoke River and remarked how "it must have been a great misfortune to them to be obliged to abandon so beautiful a dwelling." The Indians apparently agreed: in 1717 the Virginia Council received "Divers applications" from the Cheraws (now living along the Pee Dee River) "for Liberty to Seat themselves on the head of Roanoke River." Few natives managed to return permanently to their homelands. But their efforts to retrace their steps hint at a profound sense of loss and testify to the powerful hold of ancient sites.

Compounding the trauma of leaving familiar territories was the necessity of abandoning customary relationships. Casting their lot with others traditionally considered foreign compelled Indians to rearrange basic ways of ordering their existence. Despite frequent contacts among peoples, native life had always centered in kin and town. The consequences of this deep-seated localism were evident even to a newcomer like John Lawson, who in 1701 found striking differences in language, dress, and physical appearance among Carolina Indians living only a few miles apart. Rules governing behavior also drew sharp distinctions between outsiders and one's own "Country-Folks." Indians were "very kind, and charitable to one another," Lawson reported, "but more especially to those of their own Nation." A visitor desiring a liaison with a local woman was required to approach her relatives and the village headman. On the other hand, "if it be an *Indian* of their own Town or Neighbourhood, that wants a Mistress, he comes to none but the Girl." Lawson seemed unperturbed by this barrier until he discovered that a "Thief [is] held in Disgrace, that steals from any of his Country-Folks," "but to steal from the *English* [or any other foreigners] they reckon no Harm."

Communities unable to continue on their own had to revise these rules and reweave the social fabric into new designs. What language would be spoken? How would fields be laid out, hunting territories divided, houses built? How would decisions be reached, offenders punished, ceremonies performed? When Lawson remarked that "now adays" the Indians must seek mates "amongst Strangers," he unwittingly characterized life in native Carolina. Those who managed to withstand the ravages of disease had to redefine the meaning of the term *stranger* and transform outsiders into insiders....

Muskets and kettles came to the piedmont more slowly than smallpox and measles. Spanish explorers distributed a few gifts to local headmen, but inhabitants of the interior did not enjoy their first real taste of the fruits of European technology until Englishmen began venturing inland after 1650. Indians these traders met in upcountry towns were glad to barter for the more efficient tools, more lethal weapons, and more durable clothing that colonists offered. Spurred on by eager natives, men from Virginia and Carolina quickly flooded the region with the material trappings of European culture. In 1701 John Lawson considered the Wateree Chickanees "very poor in *English* Effects" because a few of them lacked muskets.

Slower to arrive, trade goods were also less obvious agents of change. The Indians' ability to absorb foreign artifacts into established modes of existence hid the revolutionary consequences of trade for some time. Natives leaped the technological gulf with ease in part because they were discriminating shoppers. If hoes were too small, beads too large, or cloth the wrong color, Indian traders refused them. Items they did select fit smoothly into existing ways. Waxhaws tied horse bells around their ankles at ceremonial dances, and some of the traditional stone pipes passed among the spectators at these dances had been shaped by metal files. Those who could not afford a European weapon fashioned arrows from broken glass. Those who could went to great lengths to "set [a new musket] streight, sometimes shooting away above 100 Loads of Ammunition, before they bring the Gun to shoot according to their Mind."

Not every piece of merchandise hauled into the upcountry on a trader's packhorse could be "set streight" so easily. Liquor, for example, proved both impossible to resist and extraordinarily destructive. Indians "have no Power to refrain this Enemy," Lawson observed, "though sensible how many of them (are by it) hurry'd into the other World before their Time." And yet even here, natives aware of the risks sought to control alcohol by incorporating it into their ceremonial life as a device for achieving a different level of consciousness. Consumption was usually restricted to men, who "go as solemnly about it, as if it were part of their Religion," preferring to drink only at night and only in quantities sufficient to stupefy them. When ritual could not confine liquor to safe channels, Indians went still further and excused the excesses of overindulgence by refusing to hold an intoxicated person responsible for his actions. "They never call any Man to account for what he did, when he was drunk," wrote Lawson, "but say, it was the Drink that caused his Misbehaviour, therefore he ought to be forgiven."

Working to absorb even the most dangerous commodities acquired from their new neighbors, aboriginal inhabitants of the uplands, like African slaves in the lowlands, made themselves at home in a different technological environment. Indians became convinced that "Guns, and Ammunition, besides a great many other Necessaries, … are helpful to Man" and eagerly searched for the key that would unlock the secret of their production. At first many were confident that the "*Quera*, or good spirit," would teach them to make these commodities "when that good Spirit sees fit." Later they decided to help their deity along by approaching the colonists. In 1757, Catawbas asked Gov. Arthur Dobbs of North Carolina "to send us Smiths and other Tradesmen to teach our Children."

It was not the new products themselves but the Indians' failure to learn the mysteries of manufacture from either Dobbs or the *Quera* that marked the real revolution wrought by trade. During the seventeenth and eighteenth centuries, everyone in eastern North America—masters and slaves, farmers near the coast and Indians near the mountains—became producers of raw materials for foreign markets and found themselves caught up in an international economic network....

By forcing Indians to look beyond their own territories for certain indispensable products, Anglo-American traders inserted new variables into the aboriginal equation of exchange. Colonists sought two commodities from Indians—human beings and deerskins—and both undermined established relationships among native groups. While the demand for slaves encouraged piedmont peoples to expand their traditional warfare, the demand for peltry may have fostered conflicts over hunting territories. Those who did not fight each other for slaves or deerskins fought each other for the European products these could bring. As firearms, cloth, and other items became increasingly important to native existence, competition replaced comity at the foundation of trade encounters as villages scrambled for the cargoes of merchandise....

… The mask [of the natives' control of their own destiny] came off when, in 1715, the traders—and the trade goods—suddenly disappeared during the Yamassee War.

The conflict's origins lay in a growing colonial awareness of the Indians' need for regular supplies of European merchandise. In 1701 Lawson pronounced the Santees "very tractable" because of their close connections with South Carolina. Eight years later he was convinced that the colonial officials in Charleston "are absolute Masters over the *Indians* … within the Circle of their Trade." Carolina traders who shared this conviction quite naturally felt less and less constrained to obey native rules governing proper behavior. Abuses against Indians mounted until some men were literally getting away with murder. When repeated appeals to colonial officials failed, natives throughout Carolina began to consider war. Persuaded by Yamassee ambassadors that the conspiracy was widespread and convinced by years of ruthless commercial competition between Virginia and Carolina that an attack on one colony would not affect relations with the other, in the spring of 1715 Catawbas and their neighbors joined the invasion of South Carolina.

The decision to fight was disastrous. Colonists everywhere shut off the flow of goods to the interior, and after some initial successes Carolina's native enemies soon plumed the depths of their dependence. In a matter of months, refugees holed up in Charleston noticed that "the Indians want ammunition and are not able to mend their Arms." The peace negotiations that ensued revealed a desperate thirst for fresh supplies of European wares. Ambassadors from piedmont towns invariably spoke in a single breath of restoring "a Peace and a free Trade," and one delegation even admitted that its people "cannot live without the assistance of the English." ...

By the end of the colonial period delicate negotiations across cultural boundaries were as familiar to Catawbas as the strouds they wore and the muskets they carried. But no matter how shrewdly the headmen loosened provincial purse strings to extract vital merchandise, they could not escape the simple fact that they no longer held the purse containing everything needed for their daily existence. In the space of a century the Indians had become thoroughly embedded in an alien economy, denizens of a new material world. The ancient self-sufficiency was only a dim memory in the minds of the Nation's elders.

The Catawba peoples were veterans of countless campaigns against disease and masters of the arts of trade long before the third major element of their new world, white planters, became an integral part of their life. Settlement of the Carolina uplands did not begin until the 1730s, but once underway it spread with frightening speed. In November 1752, concerned Catawbas reminded South Carolina governor James Glen how they had "complained already ... that the White People were settled too near us." Two years later five hundred families lived within thirty miles of the Nation and surveyors were running their lines into the middle of native towns. "[T]hose Indians are now in a fair way to be surrounded by White People," one observer concluded.

Settlers' attitudes were as alarming as their numbers. Unlike traders who profited from them or colonial officials who deployed them as allies, ordinary colonists had little use for Indians. Natives made poor servants and worse slaves; they obstructed settlement; they attracted enemy warriors to the area. Even men who respected Indians and earned a living by trading with them admitted that they made unpleasant neighbors. "We may observe of them as of the fire," wrote the South Carolina trader James Adair after considering the Catawbas' situation on the eve of the American Revolution, " 'it is safe and useful, cherished at proper distance; but if too near us, it becomes dangerous, and will scorch if not consume us.' "

A common fondness for alcohol increased the likelihood of intercultural hostilities. Catawba leaders acknowledged that the Indians "get very Drunk with [liquor] this is the Very Cause that they oftentimes Commit those Crimes that is offencive to You and us." Colonists were equally prone to bouts of drunkenness. In the 1760s the itinerant Anglican minister, Charles Woodmason, was shocked to find the citizens of one South Carolina upcountry community "continually drunk." ...

Even when sober, natives and newcomers found many reasons to quarrel. Catawbas were outraged if colonists built farms on the Indians' doorstep or tramped across ancient burial grounds. Planters, ignorant of (or indifferent to) native rules of hospitality, considered Indians who requested food nothing more than beggars and angrily drove them away. Other disputes arose when the Nation's young men went looking for trouble. As hunting, warfare, and other traditional avenues for achieving status narrowed, Catawba youths transferred older patterns of behavior into a new arena by raiding nearby farms and hunting cattle or horses.

Contrasting images of the piedmont landscape quite unintentionally generated still more friction. Colonists determined to tame what they considered a wilderness were in fact erasing a native signature on the land and scrawling their own. Bridges, buildings, fences, roads, crops, and other "improvements" made the area comfortable and familiar to colonists but uncomfortable and unfamiliar to Indians. "The Country side wear[s] a New face," proclaimed Woodmason proudly; to the original inhabitants, it was a grim face indeed. "His Land was spoiled," one Catawba headman told British officials in 1763. "They have spoiled him 100 Miles every way." Under these circumstances, even a settler with no wish to fight Indians met opposition to his fences, his outbuildings, his very presence. Similarly, a Catawba on a routine foray into traditional hunting territories had his weapon destroyed, his goods confiscated, his life threatened by men with different notions of the proper use of the land.

To make matters worse, the importance both cultures attached to personal independence hampered efforts by authorities on either side to resolve conflicts. Piedmont settlers along the border between the Carolinas were "people of desperate fortune," a frightened North Carolina official reported after visiting the area. "[N]o officer of Justice from either Province dare meddle with them." Woodmason, who spent even more time in the region, came to the same conclusion. "We are without any Law, or Order," he complained; the inhabitants' "Impudence is so very high, as to be past bearing." Catawba leaders could have sympathized. Headmen informed colonists that the Nation's people "are oftentimes Cautioned from … ill Doings altho' to no purpose for we Cannot be present at all times to Look after them." "What they have done I could not prevent," one chief explained….

The Indians would have to find some way to get along with these unpleasant neighbors if the Nation was to survive. As Catawba population fell below five hundred after the smallpox epidemic of 1759 and the number of colonists continued to climb, natives gradually came to recognize the futility of violent resistance. During the last decades of the eighteenth century they drew on years of experience in dealing with Europeans at a distance and sought to overturn the common conviction that Indian neighbors were frightening and useless….

Catawbas took one of the first steps along the road to accommodation in the early 1760s, when they used their influence with colonial officials to acquire a reservation encompassing the heart of their ancient territories. This grant gave the Indians a land base, grounded in Anglo-American law, that prevented farmers from shouldering them aside. Equally important, Catawbas now had a commodity to exchange with nearby settlers. These men wanted land, the natives had plenty, and shortly before the Revolution the Nation was renting tracts to planters for cash, livestock, and manufactured goods.

Important as it was, land was not the only item Catawbas began trading to their neighbors. Some Indians put their skills as hunters and woodsmen to a different use, picking up stray horses and escaped slaves for a reward. Others bartered their pottery, baskets, and table mats. Still others traveled through the upcountry, demonstrating their prowess with the bow and arrow before appreciative audiences. The exchange of these goods and services for European merchandise marked an important adjustment to the settlers' arrival. In the past, natives had acquired essential items by trading peltry and slaves or requesting gifts from representatives of the Crown. But piedmont planters frowned on hunting and warfare, while provincial authorities—finding Catawbas less useful as the Nation's population declined and the French threat disappeared—discouraged formal visits and handed out fewer presents. Hence the Indians had to develop new avenues of exchange that would enable them to obtain goods in ways less objectionable to their neighbors. Pots, baskets, and acres proved harmless substitutes for earlier methods of earning an income.

Quite apart from its economic benefits, trade had a profound impact on the character of Catawba-settler relations. Through countless repetitions of the same simple procedure at homesteads scattered across the Carolinas, a new form of intercourse arose, based not on suspicion and an expectation of conflict but on trust and a measure of friendship. When a farmer looked out his window and saw Indians approaching, his reaction more commonly became to pick up money or a jug of whiskey rather than a musket or an axe. The natives now appeared, the settler knew, not to plunder or kill but to peddle their wares or collect their rents....

On that August day in 1608 when Amoroleck feared the loss of his world, John Smith assured him that the English "came to them in peace, and to seeke their loves." Event soon proved Amoroleck right and his captor wrong. Over the course of the next three centuries not only Amoroleck and other piedmont Indians but natives throughout North America had their world stolen and another put in its place. Though this occurred at different times and in different ways, no Indians escaped the explosive mixture of deadly bacteria, material riches, and alien peoples that was the invasion of America. Those in the southern piedmont who survived the onslaught were ensconced in their new world by the end of the eighteenth century. Population levels stabilized as the Catawba peoples developed immunities to once lethal diseases. Rents, sales of pottery, and other economic activities proved adequate to support the Nation at a stable (if low) level of material life. Finally, the Indians' image as "inoffensive" neighbors gave them a place in South Carolina society and continues to sustain them today.

Vast differences separated Catawbas and other natives from their colonial contemporaries. Europeans were the colonizers, Africans the enslaved, Indians the dispossessed; from these distinct positions came distinct histories. Yet once we acknowledge the differences, instructive similarities remain that help to integrate natives more thoroughly into the story of early America. By carving a niche for themselves in response to drastically different conditions, the people who composed the Catawba Nation shared in the most fundamental of American experiences. Like Afro-Americans, these Indians were compelled to accept a subordinate position in American life yet did not altogether lose their cultural integrity. Like settlers of the Chesapeake, aboriginal inhabitants of the uplands adjusted to appalling mortality rates and wrestled with the difficult task of "living with death." Like inhabitants of the Middle Colonies, piedmont groups learned to cope with unprecedented ethnic diversity by balancing the pull of traditional loyalties with the demands of a new social order. Like Puritans in New England, Catawbas found that a new world did not arrive all at once and that localism, self-sufficiency, and the power of old ways were only gradually eroded by conditions in colonial America.

Cannibalism and Abundance in Colonial Jamestown

RACHEL B. HERRMANN

When historians write about early colonial Virginia, they often mention cannibalism to illustrate the severity of the Starving Time during the winter of 1609–10. According to a college-level U.S. history textbook published in 2009, "A few desperate colonists were driven to cannibalism, an ironic situation since early explorers had assumed that only Native Americans would eat human flesh." In his canonical *American Slavery, American Freedom*, Edmund S. Morgan notes that the Starving Time offers "the only authentic examples of cannibalism witnessed in Virginia. One provident man chops up his wife and salts down the pieces. Others dig up graves to eat corpses. By spring only sixty are left alive."...

Historians generally take the case of cannibalism in Jamestown for granted; they usually assume that colonists practiced man-eating during that winter, and then they move ahead quickly to tobacco planting, sometimes pausing to discuss the Powhatan-English wars of the 1610s and 1620s. In fact the existence of cannibalism in Virginia is not easily verifiable. Early writers in colonial Virginia wrote about that winter with varying degrees of horror, remorse, and amusement, and they were influenced as well by their own fluctuating levels of personal interest in the colony's success. For too long historians have taken these writers at their word, without considering their motivations for publication. Cannibalism may or may not have taken place during 1609–10; some evidence exists to suggest that it did, whereas other accounts might be cited to argue that it did not. Ultimately, there is no way to answer this particular question definitively, nor is it the intent of this essay to do so. What historians can do is consider the various accounts together and acknowledge that cannibalism should no longer be stated as a bare fact in the

Excerpt, Rachel B. H. Herrmann, "The 'tragicall historie': Cannibalism and Abundance in Colonial Jamestown," *The William and Mary Quarterly* 68, no. 1 (January 2011): 47–74). Reprinted with permission.

chronology of early Jamestown.... The reports of that fateful winter reinforced—yet also modified—the concept of abundance in America, an idea
that became ubiquitous in an emerging American mythology and persisted
into the twenty-first century. Before the Starving Time, writers depicted
America as an Edenic paradise where food was plentiful and required little labor. But the new, postlapsarian Virginia demanded hard work and persever-
ance to realize the land's bounty. Thus, in the 1610s and 1620s, colonial
leaders enacted new laws about food production and consumption, in part because of the concomitant appearance of Starving Time accounts. Memories of
the winter of 1609–10 acted as indispensable cautionary tales that shaped Virginia's future governance as well as settlers' sense of themselves and their colony. Jamestown became America's first real creation myth, which was a
mixture of truth and fiction that chronicled Virginia's failures as well as its
eventual triumphs. Fears about repeat periods of dearth and starvation created
powerful motivations for developing a successful colony that would become
the prototype for all other English "projects" in America....

When historians mention the Starving Time in Jamestown, they traditionally cite Captain John Smith's and George Percy's familiar accounts of cannibalism during that difficult winter of 1609–10. Three other English narratives
survive from the first quarter of the seventeenth century: Thomas Gates's *A
True declaration of the estate of the Colonie in Virginia*, the Virginia Assembly's
"The Tragical Relation of the Virginia Assembly," and William Strachey's *A
True Reportory*. Gates's 1610 refutation of cannibalism published for the Virginia Council came first, preceding the others by fourteen years. Gates became
governor of Virginia after Percy's rule, but, delayed by a shipwreck in Bermuda, he did not set foot in the colony until May 1610. He arrived in the
colony after the Starving Time when the worst of the winter was over and
decided that returning to England was the only way to feed himself, his shipwrecked crew, and the original Jamestown colonists. On June 7, 1610, as the
colonists were on their way down the James River, they ran into a longboat
belonging to Thomas West's fleet, which had ample new supplies and an influx
of men. The colony was saved, and West officially assumed rule of Virginia,
leaving Gates free to return in July to England, where he published *A True
Declaration*. Since scholars have long acknowledged *A True Declaration's* influence on William Shakespeare's *The Tempest*, initially performed in 1611 and
finally published in 1623, Gates's account presumably achieved wide circulation by the early 1610s. It would regain attention in 1625, when it was included in William Strachey's *A True Reportory*.

It is illuminating and important to recognize that all five accounts appeared
and circulated during 1624–25....

Before the Starving Time of 1609–10, writers portrayed Virginia as a food-
filled paradise where people did not have to labor to produce things to eat. That
winter marked a turning point at which the characterization of New World
abundance shifted from limitless to attainable only via hard work and strict regulations enforcing industrious behavior. The rumors of the Starving Time circulated by the pirates in Thomas Gates's account, by John Smith after his return to

England, and by the Spanish served to increase investors' worries about the colony. These stories provoked changes in laws pertaining to food supply and, consequently, Virginia's security....

Early explorers and writers described the New World as a paradise where food was readily available for virtually no work. These descriptions usually began with a listing of the land's merchantable or edible commodities. As early as the fourteenth century, Sir John Mandeville had promised abundance from new lands, and Richard Hakluyt was the first to do so specifically for English readers. One of the stories he quoted in his 1582 *Divers Voyages* promised spices such as cinnamon, cloves, mace, and nutmeg. The New World, he wrote, was "abounding in hony, venison, wilde foule, forests, [and] woods of all sortes." Abundance became one of the most useful and convincing keywords to describe the Americas.

Later travelers wrote glowing accounts of the country to prove that Virginia was a hospitable, fruitful, and boundless land. Writing in 1589, Arthur Barlowe observed, "The earth bringeth foorth all things in abundance, as in the first creation, without toile or labour." Barlowe compared Virginia with the garden in Genesis, where Adam and Eve lived without having to work. He also compared the Virginia coast with other places, arguing, "in all the world the like abundance is not to be founde: and my selfe having seene those partes of Europe that most abound, finde such difference, as were incredible to be written." Virginia was exceptional, paradisaical; Europe offered no comparison with the ease of living in the New World.

Once Englishmen arrived in the Chesapeake, they quickly recited these earlier literary tropes and assumptions. One can almost picture early colonists wandering around the New World coast, putting various items into their mouths and rushing home to write about it. Smith wrote of rivers in the lands around Jamestown "so covered with swans, geese, duckes, and cranes, that we daily feasted with good bread, Virginia pease, pumpions, and putchamins, fish, fowle, and diverse sorts of wild beasts as fat as we could eate them." Smith noted the "great abundance" of birds, as well as numerous types of fish. Agriculture seldom played a role in these early accounts by colonial writers; rather, colonists ambled about, plucking game from the forests and fish from the sea.

Following the Starving Time, perceptions of abundance changed drastically. The early 1610s witnessed a spate of writing that referred to the colony's tribulations and acknowledged that optimistic appraisals of the country had led to disaster. Though some of these writers went so far as to call the Starving Time stories false or slanderous, they all agreed that the tales had injured Virginia's reputation. In 1611 Deputy Governor Thomas Dale, in a letter to Robert Cecil, 1st Earl of Salisbury, referred to Virginia's early history, noting "some former slaunders yet upon itt (not removed)." In Alexander Whitaker's 1613 *Good Newes from Virginia*, the dedication by William Crashawe—an anti-Catholic preacher and investor in the Virginia Company—ridiculed "these idle and slanderous surmises" as well as "the calumnies and slanders, raised upon our Colonies, and the Countrey it selfe." When men mentioned these slanders, they probably referred to the cannibalism accusations spread by rumormongers. In Crashawe's opinion these stories were "blowen abroad by Papists, Players and such like, till they have filled the vulgar eares." Crashawe, then, attributed the rumors to the Spanish (the Papists) and, it would seem, to early enactments of William Shakespeare's *The Tempest*, in other words, to the literary iteration of the Gates account. In 1615 Ralph Hamor, who sat on the Virginia Council and served as its secretary in 1611, published *A True Discourse of the Present State of Virginia*. He referred to the cannibalism stories by citing the "manifould imputations, & disgraces, which Virginia hath innocently undergon." All these writers observed the damage that rumors of famine and cannibalism had done to the Virginia enterprise. They had their work cut out for them as they sought to turn the tide of public opinion.

Though historians have ascribed early failures in Virginia to any number of factors—exceptionally harsh winters, "unprecedented drought," poor planning with regard to food supplies, disease, or salt poisoning—English observers at the time concluded that the causes of starvation boiled down to laziness, selfishness, and poor governance. As rumors about cannibalism during the winter of 1609–10 reached the metropole, colonial leaders in Jamestown began to fling accusations at each other and at the colonists. Leaders blamed each other for hoarding food. Such criticisms implied that there might have been enough food in Virginia, as Gates had suggested, but that leaders had allotted it unevenly, precipitating a Starving Time severe enough to prompt cannibalism rumors. The problem of greedy leaders went back to the colony's first weeks. Smith did not hesitate to name names, citing President Edward Maria Wingfield as one of the guilty who ate from his private stores of "Oatmeale, Sacke, Oyle, Aquavitæ, Beefe, [and] Egges" while the rank and file starved during some of Smith's earliest days in Virginia. For this reason Smith and other members of the council deposed Wingfield on September 10, 1607, and replaced him with John Ratcliffe. Even these actions, however, did not remedy food problems in a way sufficient to prevent famine in 1609–10.

Critics also decried the laziness of early colonists. In doing so writers implied that the problem was not Virginia but the people living there; in contrast, industrious men would prosper in the New World. Crashawe described the "base and idle lubbers, that come from thence." Hamor suggested that if there had been a famine, it had resulted from indolence. He noted that he would "deterre all lasie, impotent, and ill livers from addressing themselves thither, as being a Country too worthy for them, and altogeather disconsonant to their natures." By claiming that only the most hardworking men deserved the New World, such writers reserved Virginia for the virtuous and blamed the earlier misery and death on the failings of indolent and selfish colonists as well as on the inadequate leadership of early governors. These writers argued that it was possible for investors and settlers to recoup their losses and start over; idleness was an easily remedied sin. By leveling these charges, writers suggested that the colony could still have a bright future.

New laws implemented in the second decade of the seventeenth century suggest that stories about cannibalism during the Starving Time functioned as a turning point in how colonists understood foodways in Virginia. In 1612 William Strachey published the *Lawes Divine, Morall and Martiall*, a compendium of regulations for the colony first envisioned by Gates in May 1610, approved by Thomas West in June, and enlarged by Dale in 1611. Significantly, three of the men connected to cannibalism stories during the Starving Time—Gates and Strachey, in refuting rumors, and West, by virtue of having a brother responsible for the storytelling pirates—involved themselves directly in the lawmaking process undertaken to prevent starvation in the future. Even as they denied stories of cannibalism and famine, these men constructed regulations to control food supply and consumption.

Lawes Divine, Morall and Martiall contained numerous rules dictating access to and control of food, manifesting a singular preoccupation with such matters. In fact, of the first thirty-seven articles, more than one-quarter dictated how people would eat: seven referred directly to food and three to provisions trading. Punishments for stealing and hoarding food were draconian. One would face execution if caught robbing provisions from the common store, "by water or land, out of boate, house, or knapsack." Those daring to "spoile and wast or steale the same, or robbe any vineyard, or gather up the grapes, or steale any eares of the corne growing" would also "be punished with death." Laws warned that bakers who employed weights to make their loaves heavier or used less flour or meal (presumably siphoning it off to hoard) would lose their ears for a first offense, be confined for "a yeare [in] the Gallies" for a second, and spend three years in prison for a third. Even colonists who owned their animals had to ask permission from those in charge before butchering them, perhaps to prevent colonists who did not own domesticated animals from killing those belonging to others. Those guilty of this crime "in the Principall" would die; those "in the accessary" would have their hands burned and ears lopped off, and those concealing the aforesaid crime would be whipped....

Not incidental to these rules about food and eating were warnings about gluttony as well as elements that might refer to the cannibalism stories. One of Strachey's final observations for the common soldier cautioned, "He must not set his minde over-greedily upon his belly, and continuall feeding, but rest himselfe contented with such provisions as may bee conveniently provided, his owne labour purchase, or his meanes reach unto." Though Lawes Divine, Morall and Martiall did not explicitly mention cannibalism, it instituted new laws against murder, except in self-defense. Perhaps Dale, Gates, Strachey, and West were thinking back to the case of the wife killer and hoped to forestall such excuses in the future.

At the same time, Lawes Divine, Morall and Martiall more directly implied that anthropophagy would be punished severely, even in desperate circumstances. Strachey took special care to warn against the especially heinous crime of a man committing murder "to satisfie his owne pleasure and appetite." By 1612 "appetite" certainly connoted a desire for food, and a meaning propounded as early as 1366 indicated that the desire for food was natural. Lawmakers acknowledged that the need to feed oneself, even in the face of starvation, was a natural desire but indicated that cannibalism was still unacceptable. Given the prevalence of rumors about cannibalism, Strachey's use of the word appetite must have given men pause; they were not to kill because they were hungry.

Men employing the starvation defense would be punished the same as those who killed in anger. Colonists contemplating such actions would do well to remember that "the life of a souldier, or a laborer, belongs to none to take away, but to the Lord Generall, Lieftenent General, Marshal, or their deputy or deputies." One who killed a man to eat him would pay with his life. Colonial leaders may not have been willing to face the issue of cannibalism in overt terms or to answer the question of whether it had actually occurred, but they took extraordinary measures to prevent instances of man-eating in the future. By publishing *Lawes Divine, Morall and Martiall* in London, they did more than publicly pronounce new policies; they also offered reassurance....

After the implementation of William Strachey's *Lawes Divine, Morall and Martiall*, post–Starving Time accounts of the colony ensured that cannibalism would remain etched in colonial memory for a long time. These memories served two purposes in the 1610s and 1620s. They allowed colonists to see the Starving Time, even in all its gruesomeness, as a moment when colonists continued to observe English foodways. More importantly, they enabled writers to posit a sense of optimism about the future that, though more measured than Richard Hakluyt's early accounts, still fostered a sense of unity and possibility regarding the colony's development.

Memories of the Starving Time explained how colonists understood cannibalism within the cultural context of the Old and New World. Preconceived notions about Indian cannibalism as well as Indian methods of obtaining food shaped these perceptions. Long before English colonization began, fantasies of cannibals infused textual and visual representations of the New World. Travelers coming to America expected to encounter the practice because they had seen cannibals depicted on New World maps and read about cannibals in ancient mythology, in Sir John Mandeville's writings, and in more recent accounts of Spanish voyages by Christopher Columbus, writer-lawyer Hakluyt, and his cousin, Richard Hakluyt the Younger. Only years before, witch-hunters in Europe—especially in Germany—had accused suspected women of killing and eating babies. But the English were not averse to making use of human bodies for medical purposes. Doctors recorded treatments for epilepsy, vertigo, and other "lunatisms" that recommended eating dried placenta and powdered human skull, and these medical recipes, or receipts, made their way from pharmacopoeias into contemporary cookbooks. These examples are not to suggest that recipes reflect what everyone was eating or that medicinal cannibalism shocked patients in the same way as Hakluyt's account of European travelers shamefully admitting they had broiled and eaten meat "of such a mans buttocke"; rather, cannibalism could at times titillate and at other times represent conventional practices.

When the English arrived in Virginia, they were astonished to find that the Powhatans were not man-eaters. Robert Appelbaum has suggested that the English, finding the Indians were not cannibals, claimed cannibalism for themselves. In remembering cannibalism during the Starving Time, George Percy and John Smith portrayed it as a deliberately non-Indian practice that otherwise followed English foodways. Unlike Chesapeake Indians who, according to incorrect European perceptions, adhered to a fast-and-feast cycle of eating, preferred their food raw, and did not preserve food, Englishmen refused to allow the natural absence of food to determine whether they would be allowed to eat. Once they acquired food, the eaters were restrained in their consumption; in Smith's account, the colonists took the time to prepare the body with roots and herbs, and Percy and Smith recorded the colonists eating only part of the corpses at once. The eaters employed salting to preserve what was left of the bodies, indicating a continuing concern with obtaining food. Such moves implied adherence to English foodways: even when starving, the English stored their food and ate it in moderation, allowing them to survive and maintain their Englishness in the most desperate of circumstances....

Memories of the Starving Time combined with the continued belief that cannibalism had occurred played important roles in creating the colonists' collective sense of themselves as hardworking laborers in the first half of the seventeenth century. Remembering the Starving Time fostered a growing sense of optimism that such tragedy would not occur again. Ralph Hamor asked in 1615, "why should any man (if he be industrious) mistrust starving?" In 1617 John Rolfe observed that the colony was "plentifully stoored with food and other commodities" and wondered incredulously whether it was possibly "the same still it was, when men pined with famyne?" His point was like that of the other writers: Virginia had not changed but its colonists supposedly had.

A quarter century later, cannibalism still lingered in Virginians' memory. In 1650 writer Edward Williams noted that "the incomparable Virgin hath raised her dejected head, cleared her enclouded reputation, and now like the Eldest Daughter of Nature expresseth a priority in her Dowry ... her unwounded wombe full of all those Treasuries which indeere Provinces to respect of glory." He used the metaphor of a woman who had not yet given birth, which drew readers' attention to the potential inherent in Virginia. After a second Starving Time, colonial leaders had fought off rumors of laziness, squashed stories of cannibalism, and instituted stricter laws. And the colony was finally prospering, though from tobacco instead of any sort of food....

Cannibalism captured the early colonial imagination. The reiterations of tales describing cannibalism served as a turning point in Virginia's history. They enabled colonists to shift from envisioning the New World as a place of boundless abundance to one of more realistic and measured possibility. The Starving Time functioned as a fortunate fall that allowed leaders to reassert control over unruly settlers and to impose laws controlling food production, dissemination, and consumption. Tales from the time also dictated refined rules for future English settlement. Men settling in other parts of the New World would take note of Virginians' experiences. Unlike men in Jamestown, Plymouth settlers knew not to permit food hoarding. And though they also experienced a period of dearth, it was shorter than Jamestown's, and no one was accused of eating anyone else. Plymouth colonists agreed before departing England that for seven years "all profits and benefits that are got by trade, traffic, trucking, working, fishing or any other means of any person or persons, remain still in the common stock." After Jamestown future colonists instituted preventative measures to guard against famine, most likely because accounts of the Starving Time had already served their purpose, warning of dangers involved in settling the New World.

The circulation of Starving Time accounts raised awareness about the possibility of famine and justified stringent measures for preventing repeat occurrences. Once the Starving Time was long enough past, it allowed colonists to reflect on how far they had come. The stories of that winter helped to create one of the first myths in American history: the myth of Jamestown's creation through the absence of food and settlers' efforts to overcome starvation. Whether people believed early colonials practiced cannibalism, the failures of the Starving Time enabled Virginians to realize that they could try again, that future starvation was not inevitable, and that the possibilities for future colonial endeavors were, in fact, abundant.

 # FURTHER READING

Elaine G. Breslaw, *Tituba, Reluctant Witch of Salem: Devilish Indians and Puritan Fantasies* (1997).

Trevor Burnard, *Mastery, Tyranny, and Desire: Thomas Thistlewood and His Slaves in the Anglo-Jamaican World* (2004).

Kirsten Fischer, *Suspect Relations: Sex, Race, and Resistance in Colonial New England* (2002).

Alison Games, *Migration and the Origins of the English Atlantic World* (1999).

Joyce Goodfriend, *Before the Melting Pot: Society and Culture in Colonial New York City, 1664–1730* (1992).

Jill Lepore, *The Name of War: King Philip's War and the Origins of American Identity* (1999).

Daniel C. Littlefield, *Rice and Slaves: Ethnicity and the Slave Trade in Colonial South Carolina* (1981).

Sidney Mintz, *Sweetness and Power: The Place of Sugar in Modern History* (1985).

Anthony S. Parent, Jr., *Foul Means: The Formation of a Slave Society in Virginia, 1660–1740* (2003).

Richard White, *The Middle Ground: Indians, Empires, and Republics in the Great Lakes Region, 1650–1815* (1991).

Additional critical thinking activities and content are available in MindTap.

   **MindTap** is a fully online, highly personalized learning experience built upon Cengage Learning content. MindTap combines student learning tools—readings, multimedia, activities, and assessments—into a singular Learning Path that guides students through the course.

CHAPTER 3

British Colonial Development,
1690–1770

So much changed for the British from their first permanent settlement of Jamestown to the eve of the American Revolution in the 1770s. "The United Kingdom of Great Britain," in fact, became an entity in 1707 when England and Scotland banded together in an "Act of Union." As Great Britain grew into a naval and commercial empire that stretched throughout the world, its colonies in North America grew as well. In 1700, there were about 260,000 settlers. By 1770, there were more than 2 million. The number of slaves grew rapidly as well. By 1720, slaves comprised 30% of Virginia's population. In South Carolina, that number was about 70 percent. By the time of the American Revolution, Virginia alone had 175,000 enslaved individuals. Together, those held in bondage and the colonists produced more and more tobacco, timber, naval stores, and rice. Most of these goods were shipped from the colonies to Britain, while an array of goods were sent to the colonists for purchase. Geographically, the colonists moved inland and to the North and the South. As they moved, they met Native Americans, along with French and Spanish traders, missionaries, and settlements.

Colonial development generated new and broader conflicts. At first, local movements created small skirmishes and wars between colonists and Native Americans. Over time, however, as the colonies expanded, their battles enveloped the British in bigger conflicts. By the 1750s, when British colonists initiated wars with Native Americans and the French near the Appalachian Mountains, it sparked a worldwide conflict that became known as the "Seven Years' War." British victory largely vanquished the French from the continent and left the British with massive holdings. But the war had been costly and British officials worried that the colonists would precipitate more conflict with Native Americans. In response, the British reworked their approach to the colonies. The British government endeavored to tighten its control over the colonies. For the colonists, who knew what "enslavement" looked like and who had created the social and political means for it, the treatment they received from the British government felt increasingly like they were being reduced to slavery. All of this inexorably led to political and military conflict between the colonists and the British.

Amid these developments and fractures, Native Americans had to choose sides as well. Politically, militarily, and even religiously, Native Americans could no longer simply "walk away" to avoid the European presence. Alliances—whether to the French or the British, whether to the Christian God or to new cross-tribal religious forms—entailed new possibilities and new perils. Being on the losing side often meant devastation, while being on the winning side was no guarantee of good treatment.

In many ways, the subsequent American Revolution was a product of the success of colonial development. The British colonists prospered. They knew what it meant to have rights that they held from others. They became too big for the British to ignore, but also too big to control. The subsequent war would not only change North America; it would alter the course of the world.

QUESTIONS TO THINK ABOUT

After years of slow growth, the British colonies developed rapidly during the eighteenth century. What accounted for this change? Was it the control of individuals and communities through slavery? Was it the mistreatment of the original inhabitants? Was it optimism and hard work? Was it God's will? Was it a factor of broader European, and in particular British, economic growth? Pay attention not only to how the colonies changed materially and legally, but also the costs and benefits, drawbacks and gains.

DOCUMENTS

The first four documents emphasize the role of African explorations and slavery and in British and colonial developments. Document 1 recounts the journey of an Englishman and his crew into western Africa and how they encountered diverse people, animals, and societies. Document 2 follows the flow of how chattel slavery was created from other forms of unfree labor. This selection of Virginia laws from 1660 to 1705 illustrate the ways in which the position of African slaves hardened when compared with that of English servants. Document 3, the secret diary of William Byrd, a wealthy slaveholder in Virginia, illustrates a strange blend of devotion to God and learning with cruelty to slaves. "Slaves Stringing and Rolling Tobacco" is illustrated in Document 4. It shows African men, women, and children working hard in the southern colonies. The next two documents detail economic development in the northern colonies. Document 5 is from a diary by a Scottish traveler named Alexander Hamilton, who noted in 1744 that northerners were increasingly buying material goods and displaying these goods in their homes. In Document 6, a German immigrant named Gottlieb Mittelberger tells how Germans coming to America often faced a frightful journey and then had to serve terms as unfree laborers to pay off the costs of their passage. The final documents examine how colonial developments influenced those near and far. In Document 7, Samson Occom describes his life religiously as he is surrounded by British colonial growth. Document 8 comes from the defining work of Adam Smith, *The Wealth of Nations*. In it, where Smith outlines his theories for capitalism, he pays close attention to colonial economic growth and how it has and will change the world materially.

1. An Englishman Recounts His Travels into Western Africa, 1623

To speak of the Country, and the inhabitants, I take my beginning from the mouth of the River, where at our first entrance, we find the Black men called *Mandingos*, and that they do continue amongst themselves, still one and the selfe same language: Those of them who are inhabiting, or dwelling in the mouth of the River, or within certain leagues of the first enterance, are very fearefull to speake with any shipping, except they have perfect knowledge of them, in regard they have beene many times, by severall nations, suprized, taken and carried away; but upon some knowledge they wil resort to the shore neare unto us, and bring with them Beeves, Goates, Hennes, and aboundance of Bonanos, in the West Indies called Plantanos, a most excellent good, and wholesome fruit; likewise of their Country pease, and other graine, and in way of Trade some hides: ... I must breake of a while from them, and acquainte you first, of another sort of people we finde dwelling, or rather lukring, amongst these *Maudingos*, onely some certaine way up the River.

And these are, as they call themselves, *Portingales*, and some few of them seeme the same; others of them are *Molatoes*, betweene blacke and white, but the most part as blacke, as the naturall inhabitants: they are scattered, some two or three dwellers in a place, and are all married, or rather keepe with them the country blacke-women, of whom they beget children, howbeit they have amongest them, neither Church, nor Frier, nor any other religious order. It doth manifestly appeare, that they are such, as have beene banished, or fled away, from forth either of *Portingall*, or the Iles belonging unto that government, they doe generally imploy themselves in buying such commodities the country affords, wherein especially they covet the country people, who are sold unto them, when they commit offences, as you shall reade where I write of the generall government: all which things they are ready to vent, unto such as come into the river, but the blacke people are bought away by their owne nation, and by them either carried, or solde unto the Spaniard, for him to carry into the West *Indies*, to remain as slaves, either in their Mines, or in any other servile uses, they in those countries put them to.

2. Virginia's Statutes Illustrate the Declining Status of African American Slaves, 1660–1705

1660–1661, Act XXII.

English running away with negroes.

BEE itt enacted That in case any English servant shall run away in company with any negroes who are incapable of makeing satisfaction by addition of time,

Richard Jobson, *The Golden Trade* (1623). Reprint, edited by Charles G. Kingsley (Teignmouth: E. E. Speight and R. H. Walpole, 1904), 34–35.

William Waller Hening, ed., "The Statutes at Large: Being a Collection of all the Laws of Virginia," from the First Session of the Legislature, in the Year 1619, I, II, III, © 1823.

Bee itt enacted that the English so running away in company with them shall serve for the time of the said negroes absence as they are to do for their owne by a former act.

1662, Act XII.

Negro womens children to serve according to the condition of the mother.

WHEREAS some doubts have arrisen whether children got by any Englishman upon a negro woman should be slave or ffree, *Be it therefore enacted and declared by this present grand assembly,* that all children borne in this country shalbe held bond or free only according to the condition of the mother, *And* that if any christian shall commit fornication with a negro man or woman, hee or shee soe offending shall pay double the ffines imposed by the former act.

1705, Chap. XLIX.

IV. *And also be it enacted, by the authority aforesaid, and it is hereby enacted,* That all servants imported and brought into this country, by sea or land, who were not christians in their native country, (expect Turks and Moors in amity with her majesty, and others that can make due proof of their being free in England, or any other christian country, before they were shipped, in order to transportation hither) shall be accounted and be slaves, and as such be here bought and sold notwithstanding a conversion to christianity afterwards....

VII. *And also be it enacted, by the authority aforesaid, and it is hereby enacted,* That all masters and owners of servants, shall find and provide for their servants, wholesome and competent diet, clothing, and lodging, by the discretion of the county courts and shall not, at any time, give immoderate corrections neither shall, at any time, whip a christian white naked, without an order from a justice of the peace....

X. *And be it also enacted,* That all servants, whether, by importation, indenture, or hire here, as well feme coverts, as others, shall, in like manner, as is provided, upon complaints of misusage, have their petitions received in court, for their wages and freedom....

XI. And for a further christian care and usage of all christian servants, *Be it also enacted, by the authority aforesaid, and it is hereby enacted,* That no negroes, mulattos, or Indians, although christians, or Jews, Moors, Mahometans, or other infidels, shall, at any time, purchase any christian servant, nor any other, except of their own complexion, or such as are declared slaves by this act....

XV. *And also be it enacted, by the authority aforesaid, and it is hereby enacted,* That no person whatsoever shall buy, sell, or receive of, to, or from, any servant, or slave, any coin or commodity whatsoever, without the leave, licence, or consent of the master or owner of the said servant, or slave....

XVII. *And also be it enacted, by the authority aforesaid, and it is hereby enacted, and declared,* That in all cases of penal laws, whereby persons free are punishable by fine, servants shall be punished by whipping, after the rate of twenty lashes for every five hundred pounds of tobacco, or fifty shillings current money, unless the servant so culpable, can and will procure some person or persons to pay the fine....

XVIII. And if any women servant shall be delivered of a bastard child within the time of her service aforesaid, *Be it enacted, by the authority aforesaid, and it is hereby enacted,* That in recompense of the loss and trouble occasioned her master or mistress thereby, she shall for every such offence, serve her said master or owner one whole year after her time by indenture, custom, and former order of court, shall be expired; or pay her said master or owner, one thousand pounds of tobacco; and the reputed father, if free, shall give security to the church-wardens of the parish where that child shall be, to maintain the child, and keep the parish indemnified; or be compelled thereto by order of the county court, upon the said church-wardens complaint....

And if any woman servant shall be got with child by her master, neither the said master, nor his executors administrators, nor assigns, shall have any claim of service against her, for or by reason of such child; but she shall, when her time due to her said master, by indenture, custom or order of court, shall be expired, be sold by the church-wardens, for the time being, of the parish wherein such child shall be born, for one year, or pay one thousand pounds of tobacco; and the said one thousand pounds of tobacco, or whatever she shall be sold for, shall be emploied, by the vestry, to the use of the said parish. And if any woman servant shall have a bastard child by a negro, or mulatto, over and above the years service due to her master or owner, she shall immediately, upon the expiration of her time to her then present master or owner, pay down to the church-wardens of the parish wherein such child shall be born, for the use of the said parish, fifteen pounds current money of Virginia, or be by them sold for five years, to the use aforesaid: And if a free christian white woman shall have such bastard child, by a negro, or mulatto, for every such offence, she shall, within one month after her delivery of such bastard child, pay to the church-wardens for the time being, of the parish wherein such child shall be born, for the use of the said parish fifteen pounds current money of Virginia, or be by them sold for five years to the use aforesaid: And in both the said cases, the church-wardens shall bind the said child to be a servant, until it shall be of thirty one years of age.

XIX. And for a further prevention of that abominable mixture and spurious issue, which hereafter may increase in this her majesty's colony and dominion, as well by English, and other white men and women intermarrying with negros or mulattos, as by their unlawful coition with them, *Be it enacted, by the authority aforesaid, and it is hereby enacted,* That whatsoever English, or other white man or woman, being free, shall intermarry with a negro or mulatto man or woman, bond or free, shall, by judgment of the county court, be committed to prison, and there remain, during the space of six months, without bail or mainprize, and shall forfeit and pay ten pounds current money of Virginia, to the use of the parish, as aforesaid.

XX. *And be it further enacted,* That no minister of the church of England, or other minister, or person whatsoever, within this colony and dominion, shall hereafter wittingly presume to marry a white man with a negro or mulatto woman; or to marry a white woman with a negro or mulatto man, upon pain of forfeiting and paying, for every such marriage the sum of ten thousand pounds of tobacco.

3. Southern Planter William Byrd Describes His Views Toward Learning and His Slaves, 1709–1710

[February 22, 1709] I rose at 7 o'clock and read a chapter in Hebrew and 200 verses in Homer's Odyssey. I said my prayers and ate milk for breakfast. I threatened Anaka with a whipping if she did not confess the intrigues between Daniel and Nurse, but she prevented by a confession. I chided Nurse severely about it, but she denied, with an impudent face, protesting that Daniel only lay on the bed for the sake of the child. I ate nothing but beef for dinner....

[June 10, 1709] I rose at 5 o'clock this morning but could not read anything because of Captain Keeling, but I played at billiards with him and won half a crown of him and the Doctor. George B-th brought home my boy Eugene.... In the evening I took a walk about the plantation. Eugene was whipped for running away and had the [bit] put on him. I said my prayers and had good health, good thought, and good humor, thanks be to God Almighty....

[September 6, 1709] ... About one o'clock this morning my wife was happily delivered of a son, thanks be to God Almighty. I was awake in a blink and rose and my cousin Harrison met me on the stairs and told me it was a boy. We drank some French wine and went to bed again and rose at 7 o'clock. I read a chapter in Hebrew and then drank chocolate with the women for breakfast. I returned God humble thanks for so great a blessing and recommended my young son to His Divine protection.

[October 6, 1709] I rose at 6 o'clock and said my prayers and ate milk for breakfast. Then I proceeded to Williamsburg, where I found all well. I went to the capitol where I sent for the wench to clean my room and when I came I kissed her and felt her, for which God forgive me. Then I went to see the President, whom I found indisposed in his ears. I dined with ... on beef. Then we went to his house and played at piquet where Mr. Clayton came to us. We had much to do to get a bottle of French wine. About 10 o'clock I went to my lodgings. I had good health but wicked thoughts, God forgive me....

[December 1, 1709] I rose at 4 o'clock and read two chapters in Hebrew and some Greek in Cassius. I said my prayers and ate milk for breakfast. I danced my dance. Eugene was whipped again for pissing in bed and Jenny for concealing it....

[December 3, 1709] I rose at 5 o'clock and read two chapters in Hebrew and some Greek in Cassius. I said my prayers and ate milk for breakfast. I danced

Louis B. Wright and Marion Tinling, eds., *The Secret Diary of William Byrd of Westover, 1709–1712* (Richmond, Va.: Dietz Press, 1941), 7, 46, 79–80, 90–91, 113, 159, 192.

my dance. Eugene pissed abed again for which I made him drink a pint of piss. I settled some accounts and read some news.…

[March 31, 1710] I rose at 7 o'clock and read some Greek in bed. I said my prayers and ate milk for breakfast. Then about 8 o'clock we got a-horseback and rode to Mr. Harrison's and found him very ill but sensible.… In the morning early I returned home and went to bed. It is remarkable that Mrs. Burwell dreamed this night that she saw a person that with money scales weighed time and declared that there was no more than 18 pennies worth of time to come, which seems to be a dream with some significance either concerning the world or a sick person. In my letters from England I learned that the Bishop of Worcester was of opinion that in the year 1715 the city of Rome would be burned to the ground, that before the year 1745 the popish religion would be routed out of the world, that before the year 1790 the Jews and Gentiles would be converted to the Christianity and then would begin the millennium.

[June 17, 1710] … I set my closet right. I ate tongue and chicken for dinner. In the afternoon I caused L-s-n to be whipped for beating his wife and Jenny was whipped for being his whore. In the evening the sloop came from Appomattox with tobacco. I took a walk about the plantation. I said my prayers and drank some new milk from the cow.…

4. Enslaved Workers Cultivate Tobacco, 1738

Scene on an American tobacco plantation From A. Pomet, *A Compleat History of Drugs* (London, 1725).

5. Dr. Alexander Hamilton Depicts the Material Acquisitions of Northern Colonists, 1744

New York

Saturday, June 16th....

I found the city less in extent, but by the stir and frequency upon the streets, more populous than Philadelphia. I saw more shipping in the harbour. The houses are more compact and regular, and in general higher built, most of them after the Dutch model, with their gavell ends fronting the street. There are a few built of stone; more of wood, but the greatest number of brick, and a great many covered with pantile and glazed tile with the year of God when built figured out with plates of iron, upon the fronts of several of them. The streets in general are but narrow, and not regularly disposed. The best of them run parallel to the river, for the city is built all along the water, in general.

This city has more of an urban appearance than Philadelphia. Their wharfs are mostly built with logs of wood piled upon a stone foundation. In the city are several large public buildings. There is a spacious church, belonging to the English congregation, with a pretty high, but heavy, clumsy steeple, built of freestone....

Schenectady

... In the city are about 4,000 inhabitants, mostly Dutch or of Dutch extract.

The Dutch here keep their houses very neat and clean, both without and within. Their chamber floors are generally laid with rough plank, which in time, by constant rubbing and scrubbing, becomes as smooth as if it had been planed. Their chambers and rooms are large and handsome. They have their beds generally in alcoves, so that you may go thro' all the rooms of a great house and see never a bed. They affect pictures much, particularly scripture history, with which they adorn their rooms. They set out their cabinets and *buffets* much with china. Their kitchens are likewise very clean, and there they hang earthen or delft plates and dishes all round the walls, in manner of pictures, having a hole drilled thro' the edge of the plate or dish, and a loop of ribbon put into it to hang it by; but notwithstanding all this nicety and cleanliness in their houses they are in their persons slovenly and dirty. They live here very frugally and plain, for the chief merit among them seems to be riches, which they spare no pains or trouble to acquire, but are a civil and hospitable people in their way, but at best rustic and unpolished....

Nantucket Fall...

While I waited for the chocolate which I had ordered for breakfast, Angell gave me an account of his religion and opinions, which I found were as much out of

---

Dr. Alexander Hamilton, *Hamilton's Itinerarium; Being a Narrative of a journey... from May to September, 1744,* ed. Albert Bushnell Hart (St. Louis, Mo.: The De Vinne Press, 1907), 51, 87–88, 182–183, 197.

the common road as the man himself. I observed a paper pasted upon the wall, which was a rabble of dull controversy betwixt two learned divines, of as great consequence to the publick as *The Story of the King and the Cobbler* or *The Celebrated History of the Wise Men of Gotham.* This controversy was intituled *Cannons to batter the Tower of Babel.* Among the rest of the chamber furniture were several elegant pictures, finely illuminated and coloured, being the famous piece of *The Battle for the Breeches, The Twelve Golden Rules,* taken from King Charles I's study, of blessed memory (as he is very judiciously styled), *The Christian Coat of Arms,* &c., &c., &c., in which pieces are set forth divine attitudes and elegant passions all sold by Overton, that inimitable ale-house designer at the White Horse without Newgate....

New London...

I went home at six o'clock, and Deacon Green's son came to see me. He entertained me with the history of the behaviour of one Davenport, a fanatick preacher there, who told his flock in one of his enthusiastic rhapsodies, that in order to be saved they ought to burn all their idols. They began this conflagration with a pile of books in the publick street, among which were Tillotson's *Sermons,* Beveridge's *Thoughts,* Drillincourt on *Death,* Sherlock, and many other excellent authors, and sang psalms and hymns over the pile while it was a-burning. They did not stop here, but the women made up a lofty pile of hoop petticoats, silk gowns, short cloaks, cambrick caps, red-heeled shoes, fans, necklaces, gloves, and other such apparel, and, what was merry enough, Davenport's own idol, with which he topped the pile, was a pair of old wore-out plush breeches.

6. Gottlieb Mittelberger, a German Immigrant, Portrays the Difficulties of Immigration, 1750

When the ships have for the last time weighed their anchors near the city of Kaupp in Old England, the real misery begins with the long voyage. For from there the ships, unless they have good wind, must often sail 8, 9, 10 to 12 weeks before they reach Philadelphia. But even with the best wind the voyage lasts 7 weeks.

But during the voyage there is on board these ships terrible misery, stench, fumes, horror, vomiting, many kinds of sea-sickness, fever, dysentery, headache, heat, constipation, boils, scurvy, cancer, mouth-rot, and the like all of which come from old and sharply salted food and meat, also from very bad and foul water, so that many die miserably.

Add to this want of provisions, hunger, thirst, frost, heat, dampness, anxiety, want, afflictions and lamentations, together with other trouble, as *c.v.* the lice abound so frightfully, especially on sick people, that they can be scraped off

Gottlieb Mittelberger, *Gottlieb Mittelberger's Journey to Pennsylvania in the Year 1750 and Return to Germany in the Year 1754,* trans. by Carl Theodore Eben, 1898. https://archive.org/details/gottliebmittelbe00mitte.

the body. The misery reaches the climax when a gale rages for 2 or 3 nights and days, so that every one believes that the ship will go to the bottom with all human beings on board. In such a visitation the people cry and pray most piteously.

When in such a gale the sea rages and surges, so that the waves rise often like high mountains one above the other, and often tumble over the ship, so that one fears to go down with the ship; when the ship is constantly tossed from side to side by the storm and waves, so that no one can either walk, or sit, or lie, and the closely packed people in the berths are thereby tumbled over each other, both the sick and the well—it will be readily understood that many of these people, none of whom had been prepared for hardships, suffer so terribly from them that they do not survive it.

I myself had to pass through a severe illness at sea, and I best know how I felt at the time. These poor people often long for consolation, and I often entertained and comforted them with singing, praying and exhorting; and when-ever it was possible and the winds and waves permitted it, I kept daily prayer-meetings with them on deck. Besides, I baptized five children in distress, because we had no ordained minister on board. I also held divine service every Sunday by reading sermons to the people; and when the dead were sunk in the water, I commended them and our souls to the mercy of God....

No one can have an idea of the sufferings which women in confinement have to bear with their innocent children on board these ships. Few of this class escape with their lives; many a mother is cast into the water with her child as soon as she is dead. One day, just as we had a heavy gale, a woman in our ship, who was to give birth and could not give birth under the circumstances, was pushed through a loop-hole [port-hole] in the ship and dropped into the sea, because she was far in the rear of the ship and could not be brought forward.

Children from 1 to 7 years rarely survive the voyage; and many a time parents are compelled to see their children miserably suffer and die from hunger, thirst and sickness, and then to see them cast into the water, I witnessed such misery in no less than 32 children in our ship, all of whom were thrown into the sea. The parents grieve all the more since their children find no resting-place in the earth, but are devoured by the monsters of the sea. It is a notable fact that children, who have not yet had the measles or small-pocks, generally get them on board the ship, and mostly die of them.

Often a father is separated by death from his wife and children, or mothers from their little children, or even both parents from their children; and sometimes whole families die in quick succession; so that often many dead persons lie in the berths beside the living ones, especially when contagious diseases have broken out on board the ship....

Toward the end we were compelled to eat the ship's biscuit which had been spoiled long ago; though in a whole biscuit there was scarcely a piece the size of a dollar that had not been full of red worms and spiders' nests. Great hunger and thirst force us to eat and drink everything; but many a one does so at the risk of his life....

When the ships have landed at Philadelphia after their long voyage, no one is permitted to leave them except those who pay for their passage or can give good security; the others, who cannot pay, must remain on board the ships till they are purchased, and are released from the ships by their purchasers. The sick always fare the worst, for the healthy are naturally preferred and purchased first; and so the sick and wretched must often remain on board in front of the city for 2 or 3 weeks, and frequently die, whereas many a one, if he could pay his debt and were permitted to leave the ship immediately, might recover and remain alive....

The sale of human beings in the market on board the ship is carried on thus: Every day Englishmen, Dutchmen and High-German people come from the city of Philadelphia and other places, in part from a great distance, say 20, 30, or 40 hours away, and go on board the newly arrived ship that has brought and offers for sale passengers from Europe, and select among the healthy persons such as they deem suitable for their business, and bargain with them how long they will serve for their passage-money, which most of them are still in debt for. When they have come to an agreement, it happens that adult persons bind themselves in writing to serve 3, 4, 5 or 6 years for the amount due by them, according to their age and strength. But very young people, from 10 to 15 years, must serve till they are 21 years old.

Many parents must sell and trade away their children like so many head of cattle; for if their children take the debt upon themselves, the parents can leave the ship free and unrestrained; but as the parents often do not know where and to what people their children are going, it often happens that such parents and children, after leaving the ship, do not see each other again for many years, perhaps no more in all their lives....

7. Samson Occom (Mohegan) Gives a Short Narrative of His Life, 1768

From my Birth till I received the Christian Religion

I was Born a Heathen and Brought up In Heathenism, till I was between 16 & 17 years of age, at a Place Calld Mohegan, in New London, Connecticut, in New England. My Parents Livd a wandering life, for did all the Indians at Mohegan, they Chiefly Depended upon Hunting, Fishing, & Fowling for their Living and had no Connection with the English, excepting to Traffic with them in their small Trifles; and they Strictly maintained and followed their Heathenish Ways, Customs & Religion, though there was Some Preaching among them. Once a Fortnight, in ye Summer Season, a Minister from New London used to come up, and the Indians to attend; not that they regarded the Christian Religion, but they had Blankets given to them every Fall of the Year and for these

Typescript found in Baker Library Special Collections, Dartmouth College, Hanover, N.H. and Colin G. Calloway, ed, *The World Turned Upside Down: Indian Voices from Early America* (Boston: Bedford Books, 1994).

things they would attend and there was a Sort of School kept, when I was quite young, but I believe there never was one that ever Learnt to read any thing,— and when I was about 10 Years of age there was a man who went about among the Indian Wigwams, and wherever he Could find the Indian Children, would make them read; but the Children Used to take Care to keep out of his way;— and he used to Catch me Some times and make me Say over my Letters; and I believe I learnt Some of them. But this was Soon over too; and all this Time there was not one amongst us, that made a Profession of Christianity—Neither did we Cultivate our Land, nor kept any Sort of Creatures except Dogs, which we used in Hunting; and we Dwelt in Wigwams. These are a Sort of Tents, Covered with Matts, made of Flags. And to this Time we were unaquainted with the English Tongue in general though there were a few, who understood a little of it.

From the Time of our Reformation till I left Mr. Wheelocks

When I was 16 years of age, we heard a Strange Rumor among the English, that there were Extraordinary Ministers Preaching from Place to Place and a Strange Concern among the White People. This was in the Spring of the Year. But we Saw nothing of these things, till Some Time in the Summer, when Some Ministers began to visit us and Preach the Word of God; and the Common People all Came frequently and exhorted us to the things of God, which it pleased the Lord, as I humbly hope, to Bless and accompany with Divine Influence to the Conviction and Saving Conversion of a Number of us; amongst whom I was one that was Imprest with the things we had heard. These Preachers did not only come to us, but we frequently went to their meetings and Churches. After I was awakened & converted, I went to all the meetings, I could come at; & Continued under Trouble of Mind about 6 months; at which time I began to Learn the English Letters; got me a Primer, and used to go to my English Neighbours frequently for Assistance in Reading, but went to no School. And when I was 17 years of age, I had, as I trust, a Discovery of the way of Salvation through Jesus Christ, and was enabl'd to put my trust in him alone for Life & Salvation. From this Time the Distress and Burden of my mind was removed, and I found Serenity and Pleasure of Soul, in Serving God. By this time I just began to Read in the New Testament without Spelling,—and I had a Stronger Desire Still to Learn to read the Word of God, and at the Same Time had an uncommon Pity and Compassion to my Poor Brethren According to the Flesh. I used to wish I was capable of Instructing my poor Kindred. I used to think, if I Could once Learn to Read I would Instruct the poor Children in Reading,— and used frequently to talk with our Indians Concerning Religion. This continued till I was in my 19th year: by this Time I Could Read a little in the Bible. At this Time my Poor Mother was going to Lebanon, and having had Some Knowledge of Mr. Wheelock and hearing he had a Number of English youth under his Tuition, I had a great Inclination to go to him and be with him a week or a Fortnight, and Desired my Mother to Ask Mr. Wheelock whether he would take me a little while to Instruct me in Reading. Mother did so; and when She Came Back, She Said Mr. Wheelock wanted to See me as Soon as possible. So I went up, thinking I Should be back again in a Few Days; when I got up there, he received me With kindness and Compassion and in Stead of Staying a Fortnight or 3 Weeks, I Spent 4 Years with him.—After I had been with him Some Time, he began to acquaint his Friends of my being with him, and of his Intentions of Educating me, and my Circumstances. And the good People began to give Some Assistance to Mr. Wheelock, and gave me Some old and Some New Clothes. Then he represented the Case to the Honorable Commissioners at Boston, who were Commission'd by the Honorable Society in London for Propagating the gospel among the Indians in New England and parts adjacent, and they allowed him 60 £ in old Tender, which was about 6 £ Sterling, and they Continu'd it 2 or 3 years, I can't tell exactly.—While I was at Mr. Wheelock's, I was very weakly and my Health much impaired, and at the End of 4 Years, I over Strained my Eyes to such a Degree, I Could not peruse my Studies any Longer; and out of these 4 years I Lost Just about one year;— And was obliged to quit my Studies.

8. Adam Smith Analyzes the British Colonies in Terms of the Wealth of Nations, 1776

PART II—*Causes of the Prosperity of new colonies.*—The colony of a civilized nation which takes possession either of a waste country, or of one so thinly inhabited that the natives easily give place to the new settlers, advances, more rapidly to wealth and greatness than any other human society.

The colonists carry out with them a knowledge of agriculture and of other useful arts, superior to what can grow up of its own accord in the course of many centuries among savage and barbarous nations. They carry out with them, too, the habit of subordination, some notion of the regular government, which takes place in their own country, of the system of laws, which supports it, and of a regular administration of justice and they naturally establish something of the same kind in a new settlement. But among savage and barbarous nations the natural progress of law and government is still slower than the natural progress of arts, after law and government have been so far established as is necessary for their protection. Every colonist gets more land than he can possibly cultivate. He has no rent and scarce any taxes to pay. No landlord shares with him in its produce, and the share of the sovereign is commonly but a trifle. He has every motive to render as great as possible a produce which is thus to be almost entirely his own. But his land is commonly so extensive that, with all his own industry, and with all the industry of other people whom he can get to employ, he can seldom make it produce the tenth part of what it is capable of producing. He is eager, therefore, to collect labourers from all quarters, and to reward them with the most liberal wages. But those liberal wages joined to the plenty and cheapness of land, soon make those labourers leave him, in order to become

"Wealth of Nations", Adam Smith, London, George Routledge an Son, Limited, 1900.

landlords themselves, and to reward, with equal liberality, other labourers, who soon leave them for the same reason that they left their first master. The liberal reward of labour encourages marriage. The children, during the tender years of infancy, are well fed and properly taken care of, and when they are grown up the value of their labour greatly overpays their maintenance. When arrived at maturity, the high price of labour and the low price of land enable them to establish themselves in the same manner as their fathers did before them.

In other countries, rent and profit eat up wages, and the two superior orders of people oppress the inferior one. But in new colonies the interest of the two superior orders obliges them to treat the inferior one with more generosity and humanity, at least where that inferior one is not in a state of slavery. Waste lands of the greatest natural fertility are to be had for a trifle. The increase of revenue which the proprietor, who is always the undertaker, expects from their improvement constitutes his profit; which in these circumstances is commonly very great. But this great profit cannot be made without employing the labour of other people in clearing and cultivating the land; and the disproportion between the great extent of the land and the small number of the people, which commonly takes place in new colonies, makes it difficult for him to get this labour. He does not, therefore, dispute about wages, but is willing to employ labour at any price. The high wages of labour encourage population. The cheapness and plenty of good land encourage improvement, and enable the proprietor to pay those high wages. In those wages consists almost the whole price of the land; and though they are high, considered as the wages of labour, they are low considered as the price of what is so very valuable. What encourages the progress of population and improvement encourages that of real wealth and greatness.

In the plenty of good land, the European colonies established in America and the West Indies resemble, and even greatly surpass, those of ancient Greece. In their dependency upon the mother state, they resemble those of ancient Rome; but their great distance from Europe has in all of them alleviated more or less the effects of this dependency. Their situation has placed them less in the view and less in the power of their mother country. In pursuing their interest their own way, their conduct has upon many occasions been overlooked, either because of known or not understood in Europe; and upon some occasions it has been fairly suffered and submitted to, because their distance rendered it difficult to restrain it. Even the violent and arbitrary government of Spain has upon many occasions been obliged to recall or soften the orders which had been given for the government of her colonies, for fear of a general insurrection. The progress of all the European colonies in wealth, population, and improvement has accordingly been very great.

But there are no colonies of which the progress has been more rapid than that of the English in North America.

Plenty of good land, and liberty to manage their own affairs their own way, seem to be the two great causes of the prosperity of all new colonies. In the plenty of good land the English colonies of North America, though no doubt very abundantly provided, are inferior to those of the Spaniards and Portuguese, and not superior to some of those possessed by the French before the late war. But the political institutions of the English colonies have been more favourable to the improvement and cultivation of this land than those of any of the other three nations.

III. The labour of the English colonists is not only likely to afford a greater and more valuable produce, but, in consequence of the moderation of their taxes, a greater proportion of this produce belongs to themselves, which they may store up and employ in putting into motion a still greater quantity of labour. The English colonists have never yet contributed anything toward the defence of the mother country, or towards the support of its civil government. They themselves, on the contrary, have hitherto been defended almost entirely at the expense of the mother country. But the expense of fleets and armies is out of all proportion greater than the necessary expense of civil government. The expense of their own civil government has always been very moderate. It has generally been confined to what was necessary for paying competent salaries to the governor, to the judges, and to some other officers of police, and for maintaining a few of the most useful public works.

 ESSAYS

Historians debate the relationship between religion and economic interests in colonial America. These two essays show distinct angles of the era. The first, by David D. Hall, focuses upon the religious views of the colonists in the seventeenth century. Their worlds, Hall contends, were defined by wonder and sacred judgment, and they sought to make spiritual sense of their confusing world. In contrast, T. H. Breen, observes that colonial Americans were increasingly concerned with becoming part of an "empire of goods" in the eighteenth century. Americans were consumers, and in order to consume, they needed to accumulate wealth. Breen argues that Americans' patterns of consumption fostered identities that not only tied them to the British empire, but enabled them to perceive common bonds with other colonists. Both Hall and Breen focus on the ways colonists linked themselves to broader worlds spiritually and materially.

Worlds of Wonder in the Northern Colonies

DAVID D. HALL

The People of seventeenth-century New England lived in an enchanted universe. Theirs was a world of wonders. Ghosts came to people in the night, and trumpets blared, though no one saw the trumpeters. Nor could people see the lines of force that made a "long staff dance up and down in the chimney" of William Morse's house in Newbury. In this enchanted world, the sky on a "clear day" could fill with "many companies of armed men in the air, clothed in light-colored garments, and the commander in sad [somber]." The townsfolk of New Haven saw a phantom ship sail regally into the harbor. An old man in Lynn espied

> a strange black cloud in which after some space he saw a man in arms complete standing with his legs straddling and having a pike in his hands which he held across his breast.... After a while the man vanished in whose room appeared a spacious ship seeming under sail though she kept the same station.

Voices spoke from heaven and children from their cradles.

All of these events were "wonders" to the colonists, events betokening the presence of the supernatural. Some wonders were like miracles in being demonstrations of God's power to suspend or interrupt the laws of nature. The providence of God was "wonder-working" in making manifest the reach of his sovereignty; such acts of "special providence" represented God's clearer and more explicit than usual intervention into the affairs of man. But he was not alone in having supernatural power. The events that Cotton Mather described in *Wonders of the Invisible World* were the handiwork of Satan and his minions. A wonder was also any event people perceived as disrupting the normal order of things—a deformity of nature such as a "monster" birth, a storm or devastating fire. Always, wonders evidenced the will of God.

Many of the colonists experienced such wonders. Many also read about or were told stories of them. There was nothing odd about this practice. Everywhere in Europe people were observing the same kinds of portents and telling the same kinds of stories. Everywhere these stories drew upon a lore of wonders rooted in the Bible and antiquity. Chaucer used this lore in *The Canterbury Tales*, as did the fourteenth-century author of *The Golden Legend*, a collection of saints' lives. Whenever the colonists spoke or wrote of wonders, they relied on an old tradition; theirs was a borrowed language.

The transmitters of this language were the London printers and booksellers, who churned out tales of wonders in abundance. Portents and prodigies were the stuff of scores of English printed broadsides. "Strange news from Brotherton," announced a broadside ballad of 1648 that told of wheat that rained down from the sky. "A wonder of wonders" of 1663 concerned an invisible drummer boy who banged his drum about the streets of Tidworth. In "Strange and true news from Westmoreland," a tale of murder ended with the Devil pointing out the guilty person. Newssheets, which began appearing with some regularity in the 1620s, carried tales of other marvels. Pamphlets contained reports of children speaking preternaturally and offered *Strange and wonderful News... of certain dreadful Apparitions*. The yearly almanacs weighed in with their accounts of mystic forces emanating from the stars and planets.

The same events occur repeatedly. Tales of witchcraft and the Devil, of comets, hailstorms, monster births, and apparitions—these were some of the most commonplace. "Murder will out," as supernatural forces intervened to indicate the guilty. The earth could open up and swallow persons who told lies. "Many are the wonders which have lately happened," declared the man who compiled *A Miracle, of Miracles,*

> as of sodaine and strange death upon perjured persons, strange sights in the Ayre, strange births on the Earth, Earthquakes, Commets, and fierie Impressions, with the execution of God himselfe from his holy fire in heaven, on the wretched man and his wife, at Holnhurst....

A single ballad spoke of blazing stars, monstrous births, a rainstorm of blood, lightning, rainbows, and the sound of great guns. Others told of dreams and prophecies that bore upon the future of kings and countries. Almanacs and other astrological compendia reported similar events: comets, eclipses, joined fetuses, infants speaking....

Much of this great mass of materials was compounded out of four main systems of ideas—apocalypticism, astrology, natural history, and the meteorology of the Greeks. Each of these systems was in decay or disrepute by the middle of the seventeenth century, under challenge either from an alternative, more up-to-date science or from a growing disenchantment with prophetic visionaries. But even in decay these systems continued to give meaning to the wonder tales....

The meaning of the wonder owed much to these four structures of ideas. But the most crucial framework was the doctrine of God's providence. That doctrine antedated Luther and Calvin. Chaucer's Knight had spoken of "Destiny, that Minister-General/Who executed on earth and over all/That Providence which God has long foreseen," and the Psalmist sang of a God who stretched out his protection to the ends of the earth. Nonetheless, the doctrine gained fresh importance in the sixteenth century. Calvin gave providence a position of prominence in the *Institutes,* contrasting it with Stoic fatalism and mere chance. In the wake of Calvin, Thomas Beard assured his readers that God was immediately and actively present in the world, the ultimate force behind everything that happened: "Is there any substance in this world that hath no cause of his subsisting?... Doth not every thunderclap constraine you to tremble at the blast of his voyce?" Nothing in the world occurred according to contingency or "blind chance." The "all-surpassing power of God's will" was manifested in a regularity that Beard thought of as "marvellous," though never to be counted on completely since God retained the power to interrupt the laws of nature. The providence of God was as manifest in the unexpected or surprising as in the "constant" order of the world.

And Providence revealed an angry God. Portents and prodigies arose within a world besmirched with sin, a world of men and women who failed to heed his laws. The murderer, the mocking cavalier, the liar, the sabbath-breaker—all these and many others could expect that someday, somehow, their violation of the moral order would provoke awful warnings or more awful judgments. Behind the logic of this theory lay a long tradition, far older than the Reformation, of foreseeing order collapse into chaos or peace give way to violence. Strife and violence abound in the wonder tales, whether caused by man, the Devil, or an avenging God....

This attentiveness to prodigies and portents bespoke deep feelings about communal danger and security. The men who interlaced the Dorchester and Roxbury church records with providential events were consciously performing a public function. So were Winthrop and Bradford in their journal histories, and Edward Johnson in *The Wonder-Working Providence of Sions Saviour*. To chronicle the wonder was to chart the zones of danger through which a community must pass. In early modern Europe, every community had its good times and its bad. The good times were when rain came at the right moment and the harvest was abundant, when neighbors lived in peace and landlords were not greedy, when servants obeyed their masters. The hard times were when food ran low and famine threatened, when disease was epidemic, or when peace gave way to conflict. In many European villages, a craving for protection was satisfied by "miracles" or extraordinary events that promised the return of peace, health, and prosperity. Thus, when epidemics threatened, villagers in late-medieval Spain—young girls, shepherds, old men—had visions of the Virgin Mary in which she demanded that the village build a chapel or renew its vows of faith. In thirteenth-century Burgundy, women washed newborn or ailing infants in water from a well associated with a miracle.

Women were still bringing infants to the well of St. Guinefort in Burgundy when the colonists departed for New England. In the towns from which these people came, many of the customs that once addressed the dangers of everyday life had lapsed into disuse. Once past their own "starving time," these people found themselves becoming prosperous—owners of their land, blessed with healthy children, reaping ample harvests. Yet all of the first generation had risked the dangers of the sea in coming to New England. Then as well as later, the wilderness that lay around them contained hostile Indians and their Catholic allies from French Canada. Back in England, the government (except when Puritans had reigned) regarded them with disfavor. And, as they discovered, there were enemies within—those who lied, cursed, or profaned the Sabbath, old women who allied themselves with Satan, children who grew up rebellious, neighbors who disputed each stray pig and cow, and, increasingly, merchants who lived ostentatiously. Danger pressed as much upon the godly in their new home as in England.

Responding to these dangers, the colonists employed an old language of interpretation in which the key words were "sin" and "judgment." That language reached them via Beard and the ballad writers, and also via poems like *Pestilence* (1625), a narrative of epidemic illness that painted it as God's response to man's indifference. What enriched and made this language relevant was the colonists' assumption that they lived in covenant with God. For them the covenant transformed the body social into a moral order, a "Theocratie" erected on the basis of the laws of God. It was the wonder that made visible this fusion of the social and the moral, at once manifesting God's protection and—more frequently—warning of God's anger at their carelessness.

John Winthrop kept his journal not out of private curiosity but in order to record the flow of "providences" betokening the situation of a covenanted people. "It is useful to observe, as we go along," Winthrop wrote in 1635, "such especial providences of God as were manifested for the good of these plantations." What he meant by "good" was the safety of the whole, and the general welfare. Anyone who put self-interest ahead of the welfare of the whole was likely to become an example of God's judgments—to drown in a shipwreck, die in an explosion ("wherein the judgment of God appeared, for the master and company were many of them profane scoffers at us"), lose some of his property. Perhaps because he sacrificed so much of his own estate, Winthrop was especially attracted to cases of the rich and covetous becoming poor. "Divers homes were burnt this year," he noted in 1642, "by drying flax. Among others, one Briscoe, of Watertown, a rich man, a tanner, who had refused to let his neighbor have leather for corn, saying he had corn enough...." Servants and sea captains who were suddenly enriched at the expense of others often suffered bad dreams or psychological distress, or simply lost their money as rapidly as it had been acquired. Winthrop's conception of the general good extended to those standbys of the Puritan program, Sabbatarianism and temperance. He told of drunkards who drowned and of people who died after having worked on the Sabbath—in one case, after carting dung. He was much relieved when murderers and thieves were detected by special acts of providence; reporting two examples, he summed up their meaning as "show[ing] the presence and power of God in his ordinances, and his blessing upon his people, while they endeavor to walk before him with uprightness." Always portents reaffirmed the rightness of a moral order.

Meanwhile there were constant "plots" spawned by the Devil to "disturb our peace, and to raise up instruments one after another." The "old serpent" tried his hand at "sowing jealousies and differences between us and our friends at Connecticut." But God sent tokens to reveal that he stood by the colonists. Perhaps the most impressive of these tokens for the men and women who came in the 1630s was their safe passage of the ocean. A folklore emerged from the fact that every ship but one (the *Angel Gabriel*) had reached New England safely: "wherein" (as William Hibbins told the Boston congregation in 1642) "it was very observable what care the Lord had of them." Citing Hibbins in the journal, Winthrop added that "indeed such preservations and deliverances have been so frequent, to such ships as have carried those of the Lord's family between the two Englands, as would fill a perfect volume to report them all." A more confusing token was the snake that crawled into Cambridge meetinghouse while a synod of the ministers was listening to a sermon. There was panic before "Mr. Thomson, one of the elders of Braintree, (a man of much faith) trode upon the head of it." Interpretation followed, the ministers agreeing that the snake was Satan attempting "their disturbance and dissolution": "This being so remarkable, and nothing falling out but by divine providence, it is out of doubt, the Lord discovered somewhat of his mind in it." Mixed in with events Winthrop knew how to interpret were others that remained mysterious. It was not clear why "one James Everell... saw a great light in the night at Muddy River," or why "a voice was heard upon the water between Boston and Dorchester, calling out in a most dreadful manner, boy, boy, come away, come away," or why at

Ipswich in 1646 "there was a calf brought forth with one head, and three mouths, three noses, and six eyes": "What these prodigies portended the Lord only knows, which in his due time he will manifest."…

Thus it was that men and women in New England learned to analyze the inward workings of the Holy Spirit and to recognize the larger structure of God's providence. For some, this recognition was confined to a diary. John Hull thus undertook to write down "Some Passages of God's Providence about myself and in relation to myself; penned down that I may be the more mindful of, and thankful for, all God's dispensations Towards men." Michael Metcalfe of Dedham, a weaver back in England but a farmer here, left but a single page of private text in which he commemorated the mercy of God that enabled him to escape the "ceremonies" of the English church. Recalling how he suffered "many times much affliction, for the sake of religion" in old England, Metcalfe remembered vividly the "many dangers, troubles, vexations and sore afflictions" that complicated his first attempt to transport all his family to New England. Succeeding on a second try, he asked that "Glory be given to God, for all his mercies to me." Edward Johnson expanded on these themes in a published book, *The Wonder-Working Providence of Sions Saviour.* Selectman, town clerk, church member, and captain of the citizens' militia in Woburn, Johnson employed several of the metaphors that pervade Foxe's *Book of Martyrs:* the colonists as "Soldiers" in Christ's "Army," the "wilderness" as the place where the colonists would "re-build the most glorious Edifice of Mount Sion." Like the writers of wonder lore, Johnson relished the surprising inversion that Christ performed in bringing "sudden, and unexpected destruction" on opponents of the Puritans. For him the overriding theme, as indicated by his running title, was the providence of God.

Mary Rowlandson, wife of the minister in Lancaster, drew on the providence tradition in describing the weeks she passed as captive of the Indians in 1676. Her tale was rich in pathos, as in her account of the moaning of the "wounded babe" she carried in her arms, and his death some ten days into their captivity. She told of being famished, and of faltering from exhaustion as she struggled through rough country with her captors. There came easily to her a sense that her "doleful" suffering had its parallel in the lives of Jacob and Lot's wife. Thus, too, she compared herself to the Prodigal Son confessing, "Father, I have sinned against heaven, and in thy sight" (Luke 15:21). There came easily to her also a way of writing that conflated her "wilderness" experience with events in Scripture. The smoke that rose above the burning houses of Lancaster was "ascending to heaven," like the smoke that rose above embattled cities in the Old Testament (see Joshua 8:20–21; Judges 20:38) or that which "ascendeth up for ever and ever" from those who suffer in hell (Revelation 14:10–11). When she was restored to the English settlements and had "bread again," the real food she craved was the "honey" that comes "out of the rock," or God's blessing. Like the martyrs she had surely read about, she praised a God who worked the most amazing inversions—turning victory into defeat or defeat into victory, and delivering the weak and helpless from the proud and mighty: "and though they had made a pit, in their own imaginations, as deep as hell for the Christians that summer, yet the Lord hurled themselves into it." "Victory and deliverance"—these were the work of a "wonderful power" that sustained the faithful.

In such narratives, a pattern emerged out of the relationship between individual experience and the providential history of God's people over time. When other men and women wrote or talked about their lives, as in testifying of the "work of grace" before a body of church members, the frame of reference was the "strait and narrow way" that few would find—the way that led to Christ, the moment of "election" to salvation. Hence the questions Roger Clap remembered people asking of each other in the 1630s: "How shall we go to Heaven? Have I true Grace wrought in my Heart? Have I Christ or no?" Hundreds gave their answers to these questions as part of the process of becoming a church member. Early on, the procedure was established in most congregations that those who wished to become members must "make their faith & holynes visible" by something more emphatic than taking part in the rite of baptism. That extra something included evidence of "a civille restrained life and some religious duties performed," as the founders of the church in Dedham put it. But the more significant task was to make visible the "inward worke of faith and grace." Thus it happened that some decades before Bunyan wrote his tale *Pilgrim's Progress*, the colonists were standing up in church to describe how God worked on their hearts.

The starting point for most of those who testified was how they learned to see themselves as sinners worthy of damnation. William Manning told the Cambridge church of feeling "loathe and ashamed to make my condition... known" because he realized he was a "gross" sinner. William Andrews and Jane Winship were convinced of their "guilt" as sinners. John Fessenden acknowledged having "lived in sin." The people testifying in John Fiske's congregation spoke similarly of "unworthiness." The wife of Phineas Fiske thought of herself as in a "worse condition than any toad" by reason of the sins she had committed. She named specific failures, as did Mary Goldsmith, who recalled "the discovery of her sin of disobedience to them over her and her unfaithfulness in her particular calling." The first sentence of Francis Moore's confession in Cambridge sums up what all these people said about themselves: "The Lord revealed his estate to him that he was miserable."

Some people generalized about their sinfulness, as Mary Goldsmith did in reporting the "discovery of her accursed condition in the state of nature." Thereby she voiced a fundamental doctrine of Christianity, that everyone participated in the fall of Adam. "In Adam's Fall/We sinn'd all," ran a couplet in the *New England Primer,* and New England catechisms taught the same fundamental principle. Few people in their testimonies referred specifically to Adam or to the doctrine by name, though Brother Jackson's maid "saw my original corruption." Edward Kemp of Wenham was "convinced of his evil condition by nature," Joan White had "heard of original sin," and Sister Batchelor, perhaps responding to a question about "the doctrine of original sin," spoke of being convinced of it "from Isaiah 44:22."...

When the house of Brother Crackbone and his wife caught fire and burned down, she prayed that the "fire" of the Holy Spirit would burn her as well:

"And as my spirit was fiery so to burn all I had, and hence prayed Lord would send fire of word, baptize me with fire."

Another woman who watched as her house burned to the ground turned the experience into poetry. Anne Bradstreet was more gifted as a writer than Brother Crackbone's wife, but her technique was the same, as was the moral that it taught. Sorrowing, Bradstreet shifted from complaint to recognizing it "was just" that God deprived her of so much:

> Then streight I gin my heart to chide,
> And did thy wealth on earth abide?
> Didst fix thy hope on mouldring dust,
> The arm of flesh didst make thy trust?
> Raise up thy thoughts above the skye
> That dunghill mists away may flie.

Bradstreet saw her poems as exercises in the disciplining of the self. In one poem she dramatized the tension between "The Flesh and the Spirit." In another, she fused her emotions about death with the figure of the pilgrim:

> A pilgrim I, on earth, perplext
> with sinns with cares and sorrows vext
> By age and paines brought to decay
> and my Clay house mouldring away
> Oh how I long to be at rest
> and soare on high among the blest.

The struggle to subdue the self and remain conscious of God's presence infused the prose "meditations" she wrote out and willed to her children. In them she taught how to see God's purpose even in the humble act of keeping a house clean: "That house which is not often swept, makes the cleanly inhabitant soone loath it, and that heart which is not continually purifieing itself, is no fit temple for the spirit of god to dwell in." Meditation was recurrent and unending if the "pilgrim" was to remain steadfast on his journey.

The technique of turning pain into a blessing was at the heart of the prose masterpiece in which Mary Rowlandson described her captivity during King Philip's War. One evening, as she sensed herself about to faint, she found "sweet cordial" in a verse (Jeremiah 31:16) to which she returned "many and many a time" in the classic manner of devotional practice. This facility enabled Rowlandson to perceive her captivity as a time of spiritual self-searching and renewal. The outward history of "removes"—her name for changes of location—became a tale of deepening humiliation as she realized her dependence on God's mercy.

> I then remembered how careless I had been of God's holy time, how
> many Sabbaths I had lost and misspent, and how evilly I had walked
> in God's sight; which lay so close unto my spirit, that it was easy for me
> to see how righteous it was with God to cut off the thread of my life,
> and cast me out of his presence forever.

She remembered too that living "in prosperity, having the comforts of the world about me, my relations by me, my heart cheerful," she took "little care for anything." Knowing she had sinned, Mary Rowlandson acknowledged God was justified in causing her to suffer. Quoting Psalms 119:71 on the blessing of affliction—"It is good for me that I have been afflicted"—she affirmed the lesson of the *vanitas* tradition:

> The Lord hath showed me the vanity of these outward things. That
> they are the vanity of vanities, and vexation of spirit; that they are but
> a shadow, a blast, a bubble, and our whole dependence must be upon
> Him....

A more consequential event was the collapse of witch-hunting in the aftermath of the witch craze of 1692. Witch-hunting, or the process of identifying witches and imposing proper punishment, involved fasting, execution, and confession. One of its motifs was heresy, for like Baptists and the Quakers, witches were accused of joining with the Devil to subvert Christ's kingdom. Another was the theme of murder, for people often blamed a "witch" for unexpected deaths of children. Men and women testified of seeing apparitions of dead people who demanded that their murder be revenged. There was even more to witchcraft and witch-hunting. As a "hidden Work of Darkness," witchcraft was something that godly men must struggle to make visible. Witchcraft was a mighty "Judgment," a sign from God of sins that must be purged. These sins included the longstanding, much-lamented problem of anger between people; witches seemed especially discontented and disruptive of the Christian ethic. In using witch-hunts to purge witches, the colonists were resorting to familiar instruments, the fast day and the public execution, to cleanse their land of sin. But what if those who died as witches were innocent, not guilty?

In telling whether someone was a witch, the colonists counted on confession as the surest of the several kinds of evidence. Confession had a singular importance for two reasons: it made visible the hidden (no one actually saw the occult lines of force that witches were supposed to use), and it confirmed that the root of witchcraft was a compact with the Devil. Hence it happened that, interrogating men and women charged by neighbors with the crime of witchcraft, magistrates and ministers inquired of them if they had entered into such a compact. Some said yes. Mary Johnson, a servant girl in Wethersfield, Connecticut, admitted to "Familiarity with the Devil"; furthermore, she confessed that "she was guilty of the Murder of a Child, and that she had been guilty of Uncleanness with Men and Devils." A Springfield woman told a Massachusetts court in 1651 that she had "entred into covenant with Satan and became a witch." As though she could not resist the unfolding of the ritual, she went on (apparently) to confess the crime of infanticide. A Hartford woman, Rebecca Greensmith, confessed in 1662 that "she... had had familiarity with the Devil. Being asked whether she had made an express covenant with him, she answered, she had not, only as she promised to go with him when he called...."

Where confession blossomed was in hearings and court trials arising out of presumed witchcraft in a farming village attached to the town of Salem. Tituba, a servant in the household of the Salem Village minister, confessed to entering into compact with the Devil; as one eyewitness reported afterward, she added a description of "the times when & places where they met, with many other circumstances to be seen at large." William Barker confessed that he signed a "design" to "destroy the Church of God, and to set up Satans Kingdom, and then all will be well." In all, some fifty persons, most of them from Andover, confessed in 1692 to covenanting with the Devil, and to taking part in counter-rituals deep within the woods. Almost simultaneously, a man in Fairfield, Connecticut, acknowledged having "made a Contract with the devell five years senc with his heart and signed... the devells book and then seald it with his bloud...."

The crime to which these people confessed was making Satan master of their souls in place of God. But in several of these cases, and especially in the testimony neighbors offered of their suffering from suspected witches, it was said that witches used occult powers to cause death or sickness. The minister of Springfield blamed Mary Parsons for the sickness of his children, she in turn accused her husband of bewitching a young child to death, and neighbors testified of other children's deaths that seemed connected to her threats. When a Newbury woman "was ill, she would often cry out and complaine" that Elizabeth Morse "had bewitched her." A daughter testified that once when Goodwife Morse came to the house, "my Mother Cryed out, that wicked Woman would kill her, be the Death of her, she could not beare it, and fell into a grievous Fitt...." Another neighbor declared that after Morse had "stroakt Goodwife Ordway['s] child over the Head, when it was sick... the Child dyed."

The evidence assembled in the Salem trials included apparitions of the dead returning to seek vengeance; thus, Ann Putnam saw "a man in a Winding Sheet; who told her that Giles Corey had Murdered him, by pressing him to Death with his Feet." Her tale had credibility because it prompted people to remember that a man who lived with Corey many years before had died inexplicably. The same Ann Putnam had seen apparitions of two former wives of George Burroughs, who came to her and declared "that their blood did crie for vengeance against him." The murderer himself had told her he had killed several persons! Susannah Sheldon testified that she had seen the apparition of Bridget Bishop, another accused witch, and "immediately" thereafter "t[w]o little children" who "said that they ware Thomas Greens two twins and tould Bridget Bishop to hir face that she had murthered them in setting them into fits wher of they dyed." On the stories flowed, stories mainly rooted in the suffering of bewildered people who watched children or their spouses die or suffer agonizing fits—thus William Brown of Salisbury, who blamed the "miserabl[e]" condition of his wife (her "strang kind of distemper & frensy uncapible of any reasional action") on Susannah Martin, and the man who traced the "grevious fitts" of his child ("who promised as much health & understanding both by Countenance and actions as any other Children of his years") to Bridget Bishop. It was the illness of his wife that moved Joseph Ballard to ride from Andover to Salem Village, a step that rapidly engulfed his town in witchcraft accusations and confessions.

How else did witches violate the order of God's people? Neighbors described those accused of witchcraft as contentious, angry people, or else (as Martha Corey said) as "idle sloathfull persons [who] minded nothing that was good." Many were the stories of a quarrel over animals that strayed into another person's garden or over work and how it was not fully performed, of requests for help that went unanswered, of bargains gone astray. Apparently because the Morses complained of an uncompleted task, their next-door neighbor described Elizabeth Morse as having "Malice and Envy [in her] Heart." Several persons described the "threatninge" manner of Hugh Parsons when they protested about the quality of his brickmaking of some business matters. A man linked the death of a calf to "a bargaine about" cattle he was engaged in with Thomas Disbrough; "they not agreeing... sd Disbroughs wife was very angry and many hard words pased..." A New Haven woman, not accused of witchcraft though "suspitious" on that poynt," was described in court as someone who made, "discord among neighbors," and who uttered "filthy & uncleane speeches." Someone's speech was often used against him: curses, in particular, betokened antisocial anger that was felt as threatening by townspeople. Rebecca Eames, accused in 1692 of witchcraft and of promising her son Daniel to Satan, acknowledged that she feared Daniel was a witch "becaus he used dredfull bad words when he was angry: and bad wishes...." Often, accused witches had been refused loans or gifts by neighbors who subsequently suffered illness or an accident. Summing up these kinds of social interaction, John Hale noted in his retrospective history of New England witchcraft that "in many of these cases there had been antecedent personal quarrels, and so occasions of revenge...."

Revenge! Associated with the wonder, a motif of the ritual of martyrdom, a favored curse of apparitions representing murdered souls, revenge was central to witchcraft and witch-hunting as these people understood them. What were witches but malicious people bent on harming Christians, in imitation of their wicked master? Rebecca Eames, confessing she had covenanted with the Devil, explained that he had "promised her... [the] powr to avenge her selfe on them that offended her." What was witch-hunting but a process of returning blow for blow, of defeating Satan's "plot" against New England? Hugh Parsons, soon to die because of his wife's testimony, came home one day and told her that he hoped "that God will find out all such wicked Persons and purge New England of all Witches...." Such cleansing of the land from witches was acted out in public executions....

A third ritual intruded in witch-hunting, the practice of confession. Not only were confessions the best evidence of witchcraft; they also were a means of reconciling with the covenanted community, of reenacting (or restoring) someone's passage out of bondage into grace. The men and women who confessed to being witches were acknowledging the power of a rite that promised them redemption if they brought all hidden sins to light. Mary Parsons had not really killed anyone, but she fell into confession because other sins (or guilt) weighed upon her. Elizabeth Knapp, a possessed girl who nearly was accused of witchcraft, had likewise to confess her "many sins, disobedience to parents, neglect of attendance upon ordinances, attempts to murder herself and others." At Salem, people had what seem like modest sins to admit; for most, it was a matter of acknowledging indifference to the ordinances or their wish to have more property. Yet upon listening to a minister insist that only by confessing could they save their souls, some fantasized of covenanting with the Devil. Poor Martha Tyler did so after being told by her minister, "Well I see you will not confess! Well, I will now leave you, and then you are undone, body and soul, for ever."

Most striking, in the records, is the exchange between Ann Foster, her daughter Mary Lacey, and her granddaughter, Mary Lacey (Jr.), and four of the magistrates:

> Q. [By the magistrates] Are you willing your daughter should make a full and free confession? A. Yes. Q. Are you willing to do so too? A. Yes. Q. you cannot expect peace of conscience without a free confession. A. If I knew any thing more, I would speak it to the utmost.—

The next voice is that of Mary Lacey, Sr.:

> Oh! mother! how do you do? We have left Christ, and the devil hath gat hold of us. How shall I get rid of this evil one? I desire God to break my rocky heart that I may get the victory this time.

Worlds of Goods in the Northern Colonies

T. H. BREEN

Just before Christmas 1721 William Moore, described in court records as "a Pedler or Petty Chapman," arrived in the frontier community of Berwick, Maine. Had Moore bothered to purchase a peddler's license, we would probably know nothing of his visit. He was undone by success. His illicit sales drew the attention of local authorities, and they confiscated Moore's "bagg or pack of goods." From various witnesses the magistrates learned that the man came to Berwick with "sundry goods and Merchandizes for Saile & that he has Travelled from town to town Exposeing said Goods to Sale and has Sold to Sundry persons."

The people of Berwick welcomed Moore to their isolated community. One can almost imagine the villagers, most of them humble farmers, rushing to Phillip Hubbard's house to examine the manufactured goods that the peddler had transported from Boston. Daniel Goodwin, for example, purchased "a yard and halfe of Stuff for handcarchiefs." Sarah Gooding could not forgo the opportunity to buy some muslin, fine thread, and black silk. She also bought "a yard and Quarter of Lase for a Cap." Patience Hubbard saw many things that she wanted, but in the end she settled for a "pare of garters." Her neighbor, Sarah Stone, took home a bundle of "smole trifles." None of the purchases amounted to more than a few pennies.

Colonial American historians have understandably overlooked such trifling transactions. They have concentrated instead on the structure of specific communities, and though they have taught us much about the people who lived in villages such as Berwick, they have generally ignored the social and economic ties that connected colonists to men and women who happened to dwell in other places. But Moore's visit reminds us that Berwick was part of an empire—an empire of goods. This unfortunate peddler brought the settlers into contact with a vast market economy that linked them to the merchants of Boston and London, to the manufacturers of England, to an exploding Atlantic economy that was changing the material culture not only of the well-to-do but also of average folk like Sarah Stone and Patience Hubbard....

... [A] major obstacle to fresh analysis of the Anglo-American empire of the eighteenth century is the almost unshakable conviction that the colonists were economically self-sufficient. Modern historians who do not agree on other points of interpretation have found themselves defending this hardy perennial. Before World War II, it was common to encounter in the scholarly literature the resourceful yeoman, an independent, Jeffersonian figure who carved a farm out of the wilderness and managed by the sweat of his brow to feed and clothe his family. This is the theme of patriotic mythology. These were men and women who possessed the "right stuff."

In recent years this self-sufficient yeoman has recruited some enthusiastic new support. James A. Henretta, in an influential essay entitled "Families and Farms," offered perhaps the most coherent argument for this position. These colonial farmers, he insisted, were not agrarian entrepreneurs who focused their energies on maximizing profit. To the contrary, they represented a "precapitalist" way of life. They saw themselves not so much as individuals as members of lineal families or of little communities. Since their primary goals were to provide for the welfare of dependents, to pass productive land on to future generations, and to achieve economic security, these colonial farmers studiously avoided the risks associated with the market economy. They rejected innovation in favor of tradition. They were deaf to market incentives. Within their households they attempted to satisfy as many of their material needs as possible, and when they required something they could not produce, they preferred to deal with neighbors rather than outside merchants. In other words, from this perspective, subsistence was not the result of personal failure or physical isolation. It was a positive expression of precapitalist values, a *mentalité*, that was slowly and painfully being eroded by the advance of commercial capitalism. If this is correct, we might as well forget about the consumer society. It hardly seems likely that a few imported English baubles would have turned the heads of such militantly self-sufficient farmers.

This thesis struck a responsive chord among some American historians. They saw the essay as an important statement in a much larger critique of capitalism in the United States, and they claim to have discovered this precapitalist mentality throughout American history, in urban as well as rural situations, in the South as well as the North. For them, colonial yeoman become "cultural heroes," warriors in what James T. Lemon has ironically termed "a desperate rear-guard action" against the encroachment of capitalism....

Though these embattled precapitalist farmers flourish in the pages of learned journals, they have proved remarkably difficult to find in the historical record.

Colonial historians who have gone in search of precapitalist colonial America have discovered instead entrepreneurial types, men and women shamelessly thrusting themselves into the market economy. Joyce Appleby reviewed this literature and announced that "evidence mounts that prerevolutionary America witnessed a steady commercialization of economic life: trades of all kinds increased; frontier communities quickly integrated themselves into market networks; large and small farmers changed crops in response to commercial incentives; new consuming tastes and borrowing practices proliferated." James T. Lemon experienced no better luck than did Appleby in discovering a precapitalist mentality. This careful student of Pennsylvania agriculture stated that, "far from being opposed to the market, 'independent' farmers eagerly sought English manufactured goods and in other ways acted as agents of capitalism."...

The argument for self-sufficiency encounters other problems as well. Henretta originally posed his interpretation as a dichotomous proposition: either colonial Americans toiled to preserve the "lineal family," or they strove to participate fully in the market economy. But, surely, there is some middle ground. No one seriously maintains that the people who settled New England and the Middle Colonies were unconcerned about the well-being of family members. They knew how difficult it was to survive a hard winter. They planned ahead as best they could. They also worried about their children's futures, about providing education, about dowries for daughters and land for sons. Such human concerns would hardly seem to be the monopoly of precapitalists. Love of family certainly did not cool the enthusiasm of Pennsylvania farmers for commercial agriculture, nor for that matter did the sale of wheat on the world market unloose an outpouring of corrosive economic individualism....

Having liberated ourselves from the myth of self-sufficiency, we can return with fresh appreciation to the world of consumption. Between 1700 and 1770, the population of the mainland colonies rose approximately eightfold, from roughly 275,000 to 2,210,000. During the decade of the 1760s, it jumped almost 40 percent. Such extraordinarily rapid growth must have strained economic and political institutions. At any given time the majority of this population consisted of young people, boys and girls who were consumers but not yet full producers in this agricultural economy. And yet, contrary to Malthusian expectations, the eighteenth-century colonists were remarkably prosperous. They managed to raise the value of their exports to the mother country by some 500 percent during this period. The importation of British goods rose at an even faster rate. In 1700 the average American annually purchased British imports valued at just under a pound sterling. By 1700 the per capita figure had jumped to £1.20, a rise made all the more impressive when set against the population explosion. What this meant is each succeeding generation of colonial American farmers possessed more British imports than their fathers had. Gloria L. Main discovered that even in New England, the poorest region of the continent, "parents of each generation succeeded in raising their children in material circumstances no worse and possibly a little better than that enjoyed by themselves."

These numbers alone reveal why British merchants and manufacturers were increasingly drawn to this robust American market. Over the course of the eighteenth century, the center of Britain's commercial gravity shifted west, away from traditional linkages to the Continent to new ports such as Liverpool and Glasgow that catered to the colonial consumer demand. In other words, as the American buyers became more dependent on British suppliers, the British business community became more dependent on the colonial market. "It was thus hard facts," explains Jacob M. Price, "and not imagination that made British manufacturers so sensitive to the opening and closing of the North American market at the time of the nonimportation agreements of the 1760's and 1770's."

The Americans were only slowly integrated into the British consumer economy. The key decade in this commercial process appears to be the 1740s. Before that time, colonial demand for imports rose, but not very rapidly....

During the 1740s, the American market suddenly took off. British goods flooded the colonies, and though war occasionally disrupted trade, business always rebounded. Journals carried more and more advertisements for consumer goods. Stores popped up in little New England country villages and along the rivers of the Chesapeake. Carolinians demanded consumer goods; so too did the wheat farmers and the Indian traders of the Middle Colonies. Everywhere the pace of business picked up. By 1772 the Americans were importing British manufactures in record volume. As in the mother country, this market was driven largely by demand. To pay for these goods the colonists produced more and more tobacco, rice, indigo, wheat, fish, tar—indeed, anything that would supply the income necessary to purchase additional imports. The Staple Colonies maintained direct trade links with England and Scotland, but in New England and the Middle Colonies the consumer challenge forced merchants to peddle local products wherever there was a market. Pennsylvania merchants carried ever larger amounts of wheat and flour to southern Europe. New Englanders relied on the West Indian trade to help pay the bill for British manufactures. As one New Yorker explained in 1762, "Our importation of dry goods from England is so vastly great, that we are obliged to betake ourselves to all possible arts to make remittances to the British merchants. It is for this purpose we import cotton from St. Thomas's and Surinam; lime-juice and Nicaragua wood from Curacoa [sic]; and logwood from the bay, &c. and yet it drains us of all the silver and gold we can collect."

This consumer revolution affected the lives of all Americans. To be sure, the social effect was uneven, and the British imports initially flowed into the households of the well-to-do. These are the goods that catch our eyes in modern museums and restored colonial homes. Not surprisingly, we know a good deal about the buying habits of the gentry. Their lives were often well documented, and the fine pieces of china and silver that came into their possession are more apt to have survived to the present than were the more ordinary items that found their way into modest households. The general pattern of cultural diffusion seems clear enough. Poorer colonists aped their social betters, just as wealthy Americans mimicked English gentlemen. However slowly these new tastes may have been communicated, they eventually reached even the lowest levels of society. In her study of colonial Maryland, for example, Lorena Walsh discovered that, "by the 1750s, even the poorer sorts were finding a wide variety of non-essentials increasingly desirable. At the lowest levels of wealth this meant acquiring more of the ordinary amenities families had so long foregone—tables, chairs, bed steads, individual knives and forks, bed and table linens, and now-inexpensive ceramic tableware." A similar transformation of material culture was occurring in other regions.

Perhaps the central item in this rapidly changing consumer society was tea. In the early decades of the eighteenth century, tea began to appear in the homes of wealthier Americans. It may have replaced stronger drinks such as the popular rum punch, and by the 1740s proper ladies and gentlemen regularly socialized over tea. Taking tea became a recognized ritual requiring the correct cups and saucers, sugar bowls, and a collection of pots. By mid-century lesser sorts insisted on drinking tea, and though their tea services may not have been as costly as those of the local gentry, they performed the ritual as best they could. Even the poor wanted tea. One historian found that, during a confrontation with city officials that occurred in 1766, the residents of the Philadelphia poor house demanded Bohea tea. For all these Americans, drinking tea required cups that could hold extremely hot liquids and that, in turn, forced them to import the technically advanced ceramics that originated in Staffordshire. Not until well after the Revolution were American potters able to produce cups of such high quality at competitive prices. What catches our attention is how colonial Americans were increasingly drawn into the marketplace. A decision to buy tea led to other purchases. English glasses held imported wines. English cloth fashioned into dresses and coats looked better with imported metal buttons. One had to serve imported sugar in the appropriate imported pewter or silver bowl.

The consumer revolution also introduced choice into the lives of many Americans. With each passing generation the number of imported goods available to the colonists expanded almost exponentially. In the 1720s, for example, the newspapers carried advertisements for at most a score of British manufactures. Usually, these were listed in general categories, such as dry goods, and one has the impression that even urban merchants carried a basic and familiar stock. But after the 1740s American shoppers came to expect a much larger selection, and merchants had to maintain ever larger inventories. When Gottlieb Mittelberger, a German minister, traveled through Pennsylvania in the early 1750s, he could not believe how many imported items he saw for sale: wine, spices, sugar, tea, coffee, rice, rum, fine china, Dutch and English cloth, leather, linen cloth, fabrics, silks, damask, and velvet. "Already," Mittelberger declared, "it is really possible to obtain all the things one can get in Europe in Pennsylvania, since so many merchant ships arrive there every year." Individual merchants placed journal advertisements during the 1760s announcing the arrival from the mother country of hundreds of items. During some busy months, more than 4,000 separate goods appeared in the newspaper columns. Advertisers now broke down general merchandise groups by color and design. The consumer revolution exposed the colonists not only to a proliferation of goods but also to an ever escalating descriptive language. No doubt, as time passed, colonial buyers became more discerning, demanding increasingly better quality and wider variety.

For many consumers—particularly for women—the exercise of choice in the marketplace may have been a liberating experience, for with choice went a measure of economic power. One could literally take one's business elsewhere. We have come to think of consumerism as a negative term, as a kind of mindless mass behavior, but for the colonists of the mid-eighteenth century, shopping must have heightened their sense of self-importance. It was an arena in which they could ask questions, express individuality, and make demands. One could plausibly argue that, by exposing colonists to this world of consumer choice, the British reinforced the Americans' already strong conviction of their own personal independence....

These colonial stores, wherever they appeared, provided an important link between the common people of America and the mother country. Unfortunately, we do not know much about these scattered places of business. Most were probably small, no larger than a garage in a home today. Such certainly was the store operated by Jonathan Trumbull in rural Connecticut. But despite their modest size, these buildings—sometimes a room in the merchant's home— held an amazing variety of goods. As Glenn Weaver, Trumbull's biographer, explains, a sampling of the merchant's ledger books during the 1730s and 1740s reveals an amazingly full stock of imports: "Pepper, lace, gloves, gunpowder, flints, molasses, rum, *Watts' Psalms,* mohair, drugs, tiles, paper, garlix (a kind of cloth), pots, pans, 'manna,' cord, pails, needles, knives, indigo, logwood, earthenware, raisins, thimbles, buckles, allspice, tea, buttons, mace, combs, butter, spectacles, soap, brimstone, nails, shot, sewing silk, sugar, wire, looking glasses, tape, 'Italian crape,' 'allam,' pewter dishes, etc." One wonders what items were hidden in Weaver's "etc." He seems already to have listed just about everything that a Connecticut farm family might have desired....

Along the roads of mid-eighteenth-century America also traveled the peddlers, the chapmen, and the hawkers, figures celebrated in folklore but ignored almost completely by serious historians. The failure to explore the world of these itinerant salesmen is unfortunate, for they seem to have accounted for a considerable volume of trade. The peddlers made up a sizable percentage of James Beckman's customers, and he was one of the most successful import merchants in New York City. In Boston Thomas Hancock took good care of his "country chaps," making certain British merchants and manufacturers supplied them with the items that the colonists actually wanted to buy. These travelers seem to have hawked their goods along city streets as well as country highways. Men as well as women peddled their wares. A New York law setting conditions for this sort of business specifically mentioned "he" and "she," indicating that in this colony at least people of both sexes carried consumer goods from town to town.

But whatever their gender, itinerants sometimes traveled far, popping up everywhere, ubiquitous denizens of village taverns. When Alexander Hamilton journeyed through the northern colonies in 1744, for example, he regularly encountered peddlers. "I dined att William's att Stonington[, Connecticut] with a Boston merchant name Gardiner and one Boyd, a Scotch Irish pedlar," Hamilton scribbled. "The pedlar seemed to understand his business to a hair. He sold some dear bargains to Mrs. Williams, and while he smoothed her up with palaber, the Bostoner amused her with religious cant. This pedlar told me he had been some time agoe att Annapolis[Maryland]." In Bristol, Rhode Island, Hamilton and his black servant were taken for peddlers because they carried large "portmanteaux," and the local residents rushed out into the street to inspect their goods. The number of peddlers on the road appears to have been a function of the general prosperity of the colonial economy. In other words, they do not seem to have represented a crude or transitional form of merchandising. As the number of stores increased, so too did the number of peddlers. In fact, the two groups often came into conflict, for the peddlers operating with little overhead could easily undercut the established merchant's price. Shopkeepers petitioned the various colonial legislatures about this allegedly unfair competition. In turn, the lawmakers warned the peddlers to purchase licenses, some at substantial fees, but judging from the repetition of these regulations in the statutes, one concludes that the peddlers more than held their own against the rural merchants....

One can only speculate about the motivation of the colonial buyer. The psychology of eighteenth-century consumption was complex, and each person entered the market for slightly different reasons. Some men and women wanted to save money and time. After all, producing one's own garments—a linen shirt, for example—was a lengthy, tedious process, and the purchase of imported cloth may have been more cost effective than was turning out homespun. Beauty also figured into the calculus of consumption. An imported Staffordshire plate or a piece of ribbon brought color into an otherwise drab environment. Contemporary merchants certainly understood that aesthetics played a major role in winning customers. In 1756, for example, one frustrated English supplier wrote to the Philadelphia merchant John Reynall, "There is no way to send goods with any certainty of sale but by sending Patterns of the several colours in vogue with you." No doubt, some Americans realized that ceramic plates and serving dishes were more sanitary to use than were the older wooden trenchers. In addition, consumer goods provided socially mobile Americans with boundary markers, an increasingly recognized way to distinguish betters from their inferiors, for though the rural farmer may have owned a tea cup, he could not often afford real china. In whatever group one traveled, however, one knew that consumer goods mediated social status. Their possession gave off messages full of meanings that modern historians have been slow to comprehend. Finally, just as it is today, shopping in colonial times was entertaining. Consumer goods became topics of conversation, the source of a new vocabulary, the spark of a new kind of social discourse.

...British imports provided white Americans with a common framework of experience. Consumption drew the colonists together even when they themselves were unaware of what was happening. Men and women living in different parts of the continent purchased a similar range of goods. The items that appeared in New England households also turned up in the Carolinas. The rice planters of Charleston probably did not know that northern farmers demanded the same kinds of imports. They may not have even cared. But however tenuous communication between mid-eighteenth-century colonists may have been, there could be no denying that British manufacturers were standardizing the material culture of the American colonies. Without too much exaggeration, Staffordshire pottery might be seen as the Coca-Cola of the eighteenth century. It was a product of the metropolitan economy that touched the lives of people living on the frontier of settlement, eroding seventeenth-century folkways and bringing scattered planters and farmers into dependence on a vast world market that they did not yet quite comprehend.

Herein lies a paradox[:] ... The road to Americanization ran through Anglicization. In other words, before these widely dispersed colonists could develop a sense of their own common cultural identity, they had first to be integrated fully into the British empire. Royal government in colonial America was never large enough to effect Anglicization. Nor could force of arms have brought about this cultural redefinition. Such a vast shift in how Americans viewed the mother country and each other required a flood of consumer goods, little manufactured items that found their way into gentry homes as well as frontier cabins....

The extent of this imperialism of goods amazed even contemporaries. In 1771, William Eddis, an Englishman living in Maryland, wrote home that "the quick importation of fashions from the mother country is really astonishing. I am almost inclined to believe that a new fashion is adopted earlier by the polished and affluent American than by many opulent persons in the great metropolis.... In short, very little difference is, in reality, observable in the manners of the wealthy colonist and the wealthy Briton." Eddis may have exaggerated, but probably not much. Students of the book trade, for example, have discovered that the colonists demanded volumes printed in England. Indeed, so deep was the Anglicization of American readers that "a false London imprint could seem an effective way to sell a local publication." Newspaper advertisements announced that merchants carried the "latest English goods." By the mid-eighteenth century, these imported items had clearly taken on symbolic value. Put simply, pride of ownership translated into pride of being part of the empire, a sentiment that was reinforced but not created by the victory of the British army over the French in the Seven Years' War.

So long as the king of England ruled over an empire of goods, his task was relatively easy. The spread of the consumer society, at least before the Stamp Act Crisis, tied the colonists ever closer to the mother country. This is what Benjamin Franklin tried to communicate to the House of Commons. He observed that before 1763 the Americans had "submitted willingly to the government of the Crown, and paid, in all their courts, obedience to acts of parliament." It cost Parliament almost nothing, Franklin explained, to maintain the loyalty of this rapidly growing population across the Atlantic. The colonists "were governed by this country at the expense only of a little pen, ink, and paper. They were led by a thread. They had not only a respect, but an affection, for Great Britain, for its laws, its customs and manners, and even a fondness for its fashions, that greatly increased the commerce." No American, of course, had a greater fondness for cosmopolitan fashion than did Franklin. And in 1763 he could not comprehend why anyone would want to upset a system that seemed to operate so well.

 # FURTHER READING

T. H. Breen, *The Marketplace of Revolution: How Consumer Politics Shaped American Independence* (2005).

T. H. Breen and Timothy D. Hall, *Colonial America in an Atlantic World* (2003).

Kathleen M. Brown, *Good Wives, Nasty Wenches, and Anxious Patriarchs: Gender, Race, and Power in Colonial Virginia* (1996).

Richard Bushman, *The Refinement of America: Persons, Houses, Cities* (1992).

Jon Butler, *Becoming American: The Revolution Before 1776* (2001).

Jack P. Greene, *Pursuits of Happiness: The Social Development of Early Modern British Colonies and the Formation of American Culture* (1988).

David D. Hall, *Worlds of Wonder, Days of Judgment: Popular Religious Belief in Early England* (1990).

Brendan McConville, *The King's Three Faces: The Rise and Fall of Royal America, 1688–1776* (2006).

Gary B. Nash, *The Urban Crucible: Social Change, Political Consciousness, and the Origins of the American Revolution* (1979).

Sharon V. Salinger, *"To Serve Well and Faithfully": Labor and Indentured Servitude in Pennsylvania, 1682–1800* (1987).

Additional critical thinking activities and content are available in MindTap.

MindTap

MindTap is a fully online, highly personalized learning experience built upon Cengage Learning content. MindTap combines student learning tools—readings, multimedia, activities, and assessments—into a singular Learning Path that guides students through the course.

CHAPTER 4

The American Revolution

When the French and Indian War concluded with the Treaty of Paris in 1763, the map of North America was radically redrawn. Because France lost the war, it was forced to relinquish vast territories in Canada to Britain. France's Indian allies faced defeat as well. For years, Indian nations had successfully played off the English and the French. When the French were removed, this strategy was no longer feasible. Pontiac, an Ottawa chief, realized this fact shortly after the war's conclusion. He forged an alliance with neighboring Indian nations and laid siege to Fort Detroit. When Pontiac was defeated, his people's situation became, if anything, worse than before.

The winners seemingly were the British empire and its American subjects. The empire had expanded, and white Americans thirsted after the opportunities for trade, farming, and land speculation promised by the new acquisitions of land. As one Bostonian put it, the "garden of the world [with] all things necessary for the conveniency and delight of life" awaited. Thirteen years after the Treaty of Paris, however, enough people within thirteen of the colonies were so disgusted with their position within the British empire that they decided to declare their independence. How this could have happened is one of the most important questions in American history.

The first step in the journey to separation was the British response following the end of the French and Indian War. The war had been expensive—the national debt had doubled during the war—and British officials were determined to recoup some of their losses through a reorganization of the empire. Accordingly, they enacted a series of measures that attempted to regulate settlement and trade and to increase the tax burden of the colonists. The Proclamation of 1763, for example, forbade colonists to live west of a line drawn at the crest of the Appalachian Mountains. The Sugar Act of 1764 was the first in a series of acts that attempted to enforce more rigorously the rules of trade within the British empire. And the Stamp Act of 1765 levied direct taxes on a variety of items ranging from newspapers to legal documents.

If British officials felt that these were just actions made necessary by the costs of empire, many Americans perceived this reorganization in a very different light. They saw the Proclamation of 1763 as an effort to restrict economic growth and the Stamp Act as the first step in imposing direct taxation on the colonies. The response of many was to protest in the streets and to speak out in political assemblies. As early as 1765, a secret organization *called the Sons of Liberty was formed to resist British initiatives. Though the British ultimately repealed the Stamp Act, they still felt the need to increase revenue from and control over their American colonies. A series of additional acts, including the Townshend Acts (1767), the Tea Act (1773), and the "Intolerable Acts" (1774), were passed, and the colonial response continued to bewilder British officials. Legislation was followed by protest, which often resulted in more legislation. Colonial rhetoric grew more heated, and events like the Boston Massacre in 1770, which followed the quartering of troops in Boston, and the Boston Tea Party in 1773, which followed the Tea Act, only served to ratchet up the tension between the mother country and its unruly colonies. By 1774, King George III had concluded that "blows must decide." When independence was declared in 1776, the colonists had already engaged in battles with the British.*

American leaders differed in their views of the reorganization of the empire. Many focused on the ways their rights as English people were being ignored. If they had no direct representation in Parliament, were not these efforts at direct taxation intolerable? If they had no say in the levels of taxation, was not this patently unjust? Even more serious was the argument that imperial policy was only part of a larger plot to deny the liberties not only of colonists but of all English people. From this perspective, their protests were attempts to restore the constitution of English society before this conspiracy was put in place. Although colonists looked backward to a time when the empire was operating properly, they increasingly looked forward to the possibilities of an independent America. Many Americans were taken with the idea that they could best control the "garden of the world" that lay to the west. The Revolution and especially the Declaration of Independence, moreover, encouraged and continue to encourage people in other nations to articulate their rights and be willing to turn to militant measures to assert them.

QUESTIONS TO THINK ABOUT

The Revolution affected virtually everyone in American society. How did it alter the lives of various groups—men and women; Indians and slaves; loyalists and patriots—in different ways? Do the British measures leading up to the Revolution in retrospect look reasonable? If so, how can one explain the American response to them? Would you characterize the Revolution as a conflict that looked forward or backward? How did it impact the rest of the world?

DOCUMENTS

These documents illustrate how the American colonists moved toward independence and offer questions about how radical the Revolution was. Document 1 is the Resolutions of the Stamp Act Congress, which was convened in 1765 and which argued that no taxes could be imposed on the colonists without their consent. Document 2 is a selection from Thomas Paine's powerful pamphlet *Common Sense*. Published in 1776, it was among the most popular tracts advocating American independence and a republican system of government. The power and limits of revolution are shown in documents 3, 4, and 5, which provide insights from a woman, a Native American, and enslaved African Americans. In document 3, Abigail Adams reminds her husband, John Adams, to "remember the ladies," and John responds by mocking her. In document 4, Joseph Brant depicts the loyalty of many Indians to the king of England. This loyalty, as Brant points out, hurt his Mohawk nation because it brought them into further opposition with the rebelling colonists. Document 5 is a poem from the war, encouraging the people to "[t]ake up our arms and go with speed." In document 6, African Americans use revolutionary ideology and biblical ideals to petition for liberty. Document 7 shows George Washington's concern about the state of his army and the need for its adequate funding, while document 8 comes from decades after the Revolution. This Declaration of Independence from Venezuela follows and differs from that of the American colonists.

1. Congress Condemns the Stamp Act, 1765

The members of this Congress, sincerely devoted with the warmest sentiments of affection and duty to His Majesty's person and Government, inviolably attached to the present happy establishment of the Protestant succession, and with minds deeply impressed by a sense of the present and impending misfortunes of the British colonies on this continent: having considered as maturely as time will permit the circumstances of the said colonies esteem it our indispensable duty to make the following declarations of our humble opinion respecting the most essential rights and liberties of the colonists, and of the grievances under which they labour, by reason of several late Acts of Parliament.

I. That His Majesty's subjects in these colonies owe the same aliegiance to the Crown of Great Britain that is owing from his subjects born within the realm, and all due subordination to that august body the Parliament of Great Britain.

II. That His Majesty's liege subjects in these colonies are intitled to all the inherent rights and liberties of his natural born subjects within the kingdom of Great Britain.

III. That it is inseparably essential to the freedom of a people and the undoubted right of Englishmen, that no taxes be imposed on them but with their own consent, given personally or by their representatives.

IV. That the people of these colonies are not, and from their local circumstances cannot be, represented in the House of Commons in Great Britain.

V. That the only representatives of the people of these colonies are persons chosen therein by themselves and that no taxes ever have been, or can be constitutionally imposed on them, but by their legislatures.

VI. That all supplies to the Crown being free gifts of the people it is unreasonable and inconsistent with the principles and spirit of the British

"Resolutions," October 19, 1765, in *Collection of Interesting, Authentic Papers Relative to the Dispute Between Great Britain and North America*, ed. John Almon (London: 1777), 27.

Constitution, for the people of Great Britain to grant to His Majesty the property of the colonists.

VII.   That trial by jury is the inherent and invaluable right of every British subject in these colonies.

VIII. That the late Act of Parliament, entitled *An Act for granting and applying certain stamp duties, and other duties, in the British colonies and plantations in America, etc.*, by imposing taxes on the inhabitants of these colonies; and the said Act, and several other Acts, by extending the jurisdiction of the courts of Admiralty beyond its ancient limits, have a manifest tendency to subvert the rights and liberties of the colonists.

IX.   That the duties imposed by several late Acts of Parliament, from the peculiar circumstances of these colonies, will be extremely burthensome and grievous; and from the scarcity of specie, the payment of them absolutely impracticable.

X.   That as the profits of the trade of these colonies ultimately center in Great Britain, to pay for the manufactures which they are obliged to take from thence, they eventually contribute very largely to all supplies granted there to the Crown.

XI.   That the restrictions imposed by several late Acts of Parliament on the trade of these colonies will render them unable to purchase the manufactures of Great Britain.

XII.   That the increase, prosperity, and happiness of these colonies depend on the full and free enjoyments of their rights and liberties, and an intercourse with Great Britain mutually affectionate and advantageous.

XIII. That it is the right of the British subjects in these colonies to petition the King or either House of Parliament.

Lastly, That it is the indispensable duty of these colonies to the best of sovereigns, to the mother country, and to themselves, to endeavour by a loyal and dutiful address to His Majesty, and humble applications to both Houses of Parliament, to procure the repeal of the Act for granting and applying certain stamp duties ... and of the other late Acts for the restriction of American commerce.

2. Pamphleteer Thomas Paine Advocates the "Common Sense" of Independence, 1776

In the following pages I offer nothing more than simple facts, plain arguments, and common sense; and have no other preliminaries to settle with the reader, than that he will divest himself of prejudice and prepossession, and suffer his reason and his feelings to determine for themselves; that he will put *on*, or rather that he will not put *off* the true character of a man, and generously enlarge his views beyond the present day....

Thomas Paine, *The Essential Thomas Paine* (London: Penguin Books, 1986), 36–40, 43–45, 48–49, 54–57, 59.

... Now is the seed-time of continental union, faith and honor. The least fracture now will be like a name engraved with the point of a pin on the tender rind of a young oak; the wound will enlarge with the tree, and posterity read it in full grown characters....

As much hath been said of the advantages of reconciliation, which, like an agreeable dream, hath passed away and left us as we were, it is but right, that we should examine the contrary side of the argument, and inquire into some of the many material injuries which these colonies sustain, and always will sustain, by being connected with, and dependant on Great-Britain....

I have heard it asserted by some, that as America hath flourished under her former connexion with Great-Britain, that the same connexion is necessary to-wards her future happiness, and will always have the same effect. Nothing can be more fallacious than this kind of argument. We may as well assert that because a child has thrived upon milk, that it is never to have meat, or that the fires twenty years of our lives is to become a precedent for the next twenty. But even this is admitting more than is true, for I answer roundly, that America would have flourished as much, and probably much more, had no European power had any thing to do with her. The commerce, by which she hath enriched herself, are the necessaries of life, and will always have a market while eating is the cus-tom of Europe....

It has lately been asserted in parliament, that the colonies have no relation to each other but through the parent country, i.e. that Pennsylvania and the Jerseys, and so on for the rest, are sister colonies by the way of England; this is certainly a very round-about way of proving relationship, but it is the nearest and only true way of proving enemyship, if I may so call it. France and Spain never were, nor perhaps ever will be our enemies as *Americans*, but as our being the *subjects of Great-Britain*.

But Britain is the parent country, say some. Then the more shame upon her conduct. Even brutes do not devour their young, nor savages make war upon their families; wherefore the assertion, if true, turns to her reproach; but it hap-pens not to be true, or only partly so, and the phrase *parent* or *mother country* hath been jesuitically adopted by the king and his parasites, with a low papistical design of gaining an unfair bias on the credulous weakness of our minds. Europe, and not England, is the parent country of America. This new world hath been the asylum for the persecuted lovers of civil and religious liberty from *every part* of Europe. Hither have they fled, not from the tender embraces of the mother, but from the cruelty of monster; and it is so far true of England, that the same tyranny which drove the first emigrants from home, pursues their descendants still....

... Not one third of the inhabitants, even of this province, are of English descent. Wherefore I reprobate the phrase of parent or mother country applied to England only, as being false, selfish, narrow and ungenerous....

... Our plan is commerce, and that, well attended to, will secure us the peace and friendship of all Europe; because, it is the interest of all Europe to have America a *free port*. Her trade will always be a protection, and her barren-ness of gold and silver secure her from invaders....

... It is the true interest of America to steer clear of European contentions, which she never can do, while by her dependance on Britain, she is made the make-weight in the scale of British politics....

As to government matters, it is not in the power of Britain to do this continent justice: The business of it will soon be too weighty, and intricate, to be managed with any tolerable degree of convenience, by a power so distant from us, and so very ignorant of us; for if they cannot conquer us, they cannot govern us....

Small islands not capable of protecting themselves, are the proper objects for kingdoms to take under their care; but there is something very absurd, in supposing a continent to be perpetually governed by an island. In no instance hath nature made the satellite larger than its primary planet, and as England and America, with respect to each other, reverses the common order of nature, it is evident they belong to different systems; England to Europe, America to itself....

... No man was a warmer wisher for reconciliation than myself, before the fatal nineteenth of April 1775, but the moment the event of that day was made known, I rejected the hardened, sullen tempered Pharaoh of England for ever; and disdain the wretch, that with the pretended title of FATHER OF HIS PEOPLE can unfeelingly hear of their slaughter, and composedly sleep with their blood upon his soul.

But admitting that matters were now made up, what would be the event? I answer, the ruin of the continent. And that for several reasons.

First, The powers of governing still remaining in the hands of the king, he will have a negative over the whole legislation of this continent. And as he hath shewn himself such an inveterate enemy to liberty, and discovered such a thirst for arbitrary power, is he, or is he not, a proper man to say to these colonies, *"You shall make no laws but what I please."* And is there any inhabitant in America so ignorant, as not to know, that according to what is called the *present constitution,* that this continent can make no laws but what the king gives leave to; and is there any man so unwise, as not to see, that (considering what has happened) he will suffer no law to be made here, but such as suit *his* purpose. We may be as effectually enslaved by the want of laws in America as by submitting to laws made for us in England....

But where, says some, is the King of America? I'll tell you. Friend, he reigns above, and doth not make havoc of mankind like the Royal Brute of Britain. Yet that we may not appear to be defective even in earthly honors, let a day be solemnly set apart for proclaiming the charter; let it be brought forth placed on the divine law, the word of God; let a crown be placed thereon, by which the world may know, that so far we approve of monarchy, that in America THE LAW IS KING....

Some, perhaps, will say, that after we have made it up with Britain, she will protect us. Can we be so unwise as to mean, that she shall keep a navy in our harbours for that purpose? Common sense will tell us, that the power which hath endeavoured to subdue us, is of all others the most improper to defend us....

Another reason why the present time is preferable to all others, is, that the fewer our numbers are, the more land there is yet unoccupied, which instead of being lavished by the king on his worthless dependants, may be hereafter applied, not only to the discharge of the present debt, but to the constant support of government. No nation under heaven hath such an advantage at this....

As to religion, I hold it to be the indispensable duty of all government, to protect all conscientious professors thereof, and I know of no other business which government hath to do therewith, Let a man throw aside that narrowness of soul, that selfishness of principle, which the niggards of all professions are so unwilling to part with, and he will be at once delivered of his fears on that head. Suspicion is the companion of mean souls, and the bane of all good society. For myself, I fully and conscientiously believe, that it is the will of the Almighty, that there should be diversity of religious opinions among us: It affords a large field for our Christian kindness. Were we all of one way of thinking, our religious dispositions would want matter for probation; and on this liberal principle, I look on the various denominations among us, to be like children of the same family, differing only, in what is called, their Christian names....

These proceedings may at first appear strange and difficult; but, like all other steps which we have already passed over, will in a little time become familiar and agreeable; and, until an independence is declared, the Continent will feel itself like a man who continues putting off some unpleasant business from day to day, yet knows it must be done, hates to set about it, wishes it over, and is continually haunted with the thoughts of its necessity.

3. Abigail and John Adams Debate Women's Rights, 1776

Braintree March 31 1776

I wish you would ever write me a Letter half as long as I write you; and tell me if you may where your Fleet are gone? What sort of Defence Virginia can make against our common Enemy? Whether it is so situated as to make an able Defence? Are not the Gentery Lords and the common people vassals, are they not like the uncivilized Natives Brittain represents us to be? I hope their Riffel Men who have shewen themselves very savage and even Blood thirsty; are not a specimen of the Generality of the people....

I have sometimes been ready to think that the passion for Liberty cannot be Eaquelly Strong in the Breasts of those who have been accustomed to deprive their fellow Creatures of theirs. Of this I am certain that it is not founded upon that generous and christian principal of doing to others as we would that others should do unto us....

The Town in General is left in a better state than we expected, more oweing to a precipitate flight than any Regard to the inhabitants, tho some

Charles Frances Adams, ed., from *Letters of John Adams and His Wife Abigail Adams* (1875) in *Adams Family Correspondence*, I (Cambridge, Mass.: Harvard University Press, 1963), 369–370.

individuals discovered a sense of honour and justice and have left the rent of the Houses in which they were, for the owners and the furniture unhurt, or if damaged sufficent to make it good.

Others have committed abominable Ravages. The Mansion House of your President is safe and the furniture unhurt whilst both the House and Furniture of the Solisiter General have fallen a prey to their own merciless party....

I feel very differently at the approach of spring to what I did a month ago. We knew not then whether we could plant or sow with safety, whether when we had toild we could reap the fruits of our own industery, whether we could rest in our own Cottages, or whether we should not be driven from the sea coasts to seek shelter in the wilderness, but now we feel as if we might sit under our own vine and eat the good of the land....

... I long to hear that you have declared in independancy—and by the way in the new Code of Laws which I suppose it will be necessary for you to make I desire you would Remember the Ladies, and be more generous and favourable to them than your ancestors. Do not put such unlimited power into the hands of the Husbands. Remember all Men would be tyrants if they could. If perticuliar care and attention is not paid to the Laidies we are determined to foment a Rebelion, and will not hold ourselves bound by any Laws in which we have no voice, or Representation.

That your Sex are Naturally Tyrannical is a Truth so thoroughly established as to admit of no dispute, but such of you as wish to be happy willingly give up the harsh title of Master for the more tender and endearing one of Friend. Why then, not put it out of the power of the vicious and the Lawless to use us with cruelty and indignity with impunity. Men of Sense in all Ages abhor those customs which treat us only as the vassals of your Sex. Regard us then as Beings placed by providence under your protection and in immitation of the Supreem Being make use of that power only for our happiness.

John Adams Responds

As to your extraordinary code of laws, I cannot but laugh. We have been told that our struggle has loosened the bonds of government everywhere; that children and apprentices were disobedient; that schools and colleges were grown turbulent; that Indians slighted their guardians, and negroes grew insolent to their masters. But your letter was the first intimation that another tribe, more numerous and powerful than all the rest, were grown discontented. This is rather too coarse a Compliment but you are so saucy, I won't blot it out.

Depend upon it, we know better than to repeal our masculine systems. Although they are in full force, you know they are little more than theory. We dare not exert our power in its full latitude. We are obliged to go fair and softly, and, in practice, you know we are the subjects. We have only the name of masters, and rather than give up this, which would completely subject us to the despotism of the petticoat, I hope General Washington and all our brave heroes would fight; I am sure every good politician would plot, as long as he would against despotism, empire, monarchy, aristocracy, oligarchy, or ochlocracy.

4. Mohawk Leader Joseph Brant Commits the Loyalty of His People to Britain, 1776

Brother Gorah [British Secretary of State Lord Germain]:

We have cross'd the great Lake and come to this kingdom with our Superintendant Col. Johnson from our Confederacy the Six Nations and their Allies, that we might see our Father the Great King, and joyn in informing him, his Councillors and wise men, of the good intentions of the Indians our bretheren, and of their attachment to His Majesty and his Government.

Brother: The Disturbances in America give great trouble to all our Nations, as many strange stories have been told to us by the people in that country. The Six Nations who alwayes loved the King, sent a number of their Chiefs and Warriors with their Superintendant to Canada last summer, where they engaged their allies to joyn with them in the defence of that country, and when it was invaded by the New England people, they alone defeated them.

Brother: In that engagement we had several of our best Warriors killed and wounded, and the Indians think it very hard they should have been so deceived by the White people in that country, the enemy returning in great numbers, and no White people supporting the Indians, they were oblidged to retire to their vilages and sit still. We now Brother hope to see these bad children chastised, and that we may be enabled to tell the Indians, who have always been faithfull and ready to assist the King, what His Majesty intends.

Brother: The Mohocks our particular Nation, have on all occasions shewn their zeal and loyalty to the Great King; yet they have been very badly treated by his people in that country, the City of Albany laying an unjust claim to the lands on which our Lower Castle is built.... We have been often assured by our late great friend Sr William Johnson who never deceived us, and we know he was told so that the King and wise men here would do us justice; but this notwithstanding all our applications has never been done, and it makes us very uneasie.... We have only therefore to request that his Majesty will attend to this matter: it troubles our Nation & they cannot sleep easie in their beds. Indeed it is very hard when we have let the Kings subjects have so much of our lands for so little value, they should want to cheat us in this manner of the small spots we have left for our women and children to live on. We are tired out in making complaints & getting no redress. We therefore hope that the Assurances now given us by the Superintendant may take place, and that he may have it in his power to procure us justice.

Brother: We shall truly report all that we hear from you, to the Six Nations at our return. We are well informed there has been many Indians in this Country who came without any authority, from their own, and gave much trouble. We desire Brother to tell you this is not our case. We are warriors known to all the Nations, and are now here by approbation of many of them, whose sentiments we speak.

Brother: We hope these things will be considered and that the King or his great men will give us such an answer as will make our hearts light and glad

---

E. B. O'Callaghan, ed., *Documents Relative to the Colonial History of the State of New York*, VIII (Albany, N.Y.: Weed, Parsons, 1853–1887), 670–671.

before we go, and strengthen our hands, so that we may joyn our Superintendant Col. Johnson in giving satisfaction to all our Nations, when we report to them, on our return; for which purpose we hope soon to be accomodated with a passage.

Dictated by the Indians and taken down by

Jo: CHEW, Secy

5. A New Song Inspires Revolutionaries, 1776

WAR SONG.

HARK, hark the sound of war is heard,
And we must all attend;
Take up our arms and go with speed,
Our country to defend.

Our parent state has turned our foe,
Which fills our land with pain;
Her gallant ships, manned out for war,
Come thundering o'er the main.

There's Carleton, Howe, and Clinton too.
And many thousands more,
May cross the sea, but all in vain,
Our rights we'll ne'er give o'er.

Our pleasant homes they do invade,
Our property devour;
And all because we won't submit
To their despotic power.

Then let us go against our foe,
We'd better die than yield;
We and our sons are all undone,
If Britain wins the field.

Tories may dream of future joys,
But I am bold to say,
They'll find themselves bound fast in chains,
If Britain wins the day.

Husbands must leave their loving wives,
And sprightly youths attend,
Leave their sweethearts and risk their lives,
Their country to defend.

Songs and Ballads of the American Revolution (1905), 94–96.

May they be heroes in the field,
Have heroes' fame in store;
We pray the Lord to be their shield,
Where thundering cannons roar.

6. African Americans Petition for Freedom, 1777

To the Honorable Counsel & House of [Representa]tives for the State of Massachusitte Bay in General Court assembled, Jan. 13, 1777.

The petition of A Great Number of Blackes detained in a State of slavery in the Bowels of a free & Christian Country Humbly shuwith that your Petitioners apprehend that thay have in Common with all other men a Natural and Unaliable Right to that freedom which the Grat Parent of the Unavers hath Bestowed equalley on all menkind and which they have Never forfuted by any Compact or agreement whatever—but thay wher Unjustly Dragged by the hand of cruel Power from their Derest friends and sum of them Even torn from the Embraces of their tender Parents—from A populous Pleasant and plentiful contry and in violation of Laws of Nature and off Nations and in defiance of all the tender feelings of humanity Brough[t] hear Either to Be sold Like Beast of Burthen & Like them Condemnd to Slavery for Life—Among A People Profesing the mild Religion of Jesus A people Not Insensible of the Secrets of Rationable Being Nor without spirit to Resent the unjust endeavours of others to Reduce them to a state of Bondage and Subjection your honouer Need not to be informed that A Life of Slavery Like that of your petitioners Deprived of Every social privilege of Every thing Requiset to Render Life Tolable is far worse then Nonexistance.

[In imitat]ion of the Lawdable Example of the Good People of these States your petiononers have Long and Patiently waited the Evnt of petition after petition By them presented to the Legislative Body of this state and cannot but with Grief Reflect that their Success hath ben but too similar they Cannot but express their Astonishment that It has Never Bin Consirdered that Every Principle from which Amarica has Acted in the Cours of their unhappy Deficultes with Great Briton Pleads Stronger than A thousand arguments in favowrs of your petioners they therfor humble Beseech your honours to give this peti[ti]on its due weight & consideration and cause an act of the Legislatur to be past Wherby they may Be Restored to the Enjoyments of that which is the Naturel Right of all men—and their Children who wher Born in this Land of Liberty may not be heald as Slaves after they arive at the age of Twenty one years so may the Inhabitance of thes Stats No longer chargeable with the inconsistancey of acting themselves the part which they condem and oppose in others Be prospered in their present Glorious struggle for Liberty and have those Blessing to them, &c.

Prince Hall, Lancaster Hill, Peter Bess, Brister Slenser, Jack Pierpont, Nero Funelo, Newport Sumner, Job Look, "Slave Petition for Freedom to the Massachusetts Legislature", Massachusetts Bay in General Court, January 13th, 1777.

7. General Washington Argues for Greater Military Funding by Portraying the Plight of Soldiers at Valley Forge, 1778

I am pleased to find, that you expect the proposed establishment of the Army will succeed; though it is a painful consideration, that matters of such pressing importance and obvious necessity meet with so much difficulty and delay. Be assured the success of the measure is a matter of the most serious moment, and that it ought to be brought to a conclusion, as speedily as possible. The spirit of resigning Commissions has been long at an alarming height, and increases daily....

The necessity of putting the Army upon a respectable footing, both as to numbers and constitution, is now become more essential than ever. The Enemy are beginning to play a Game more dangerous than their efforts by Arms, tho' these will not be remitted in the smallest degree, and which threatens a fatal blow to American Independence, and to her liberties of course: They are endeavouring to ensnare the people by specious allurements of Peace. It is not improbable they have had such abundant cause to be tired of the War, that they may be sincere, in the terms they offer, which, though far short of our pretensions, will be extremely flattering to Minds that do not penetrate far into political consequences: But, whether they are sincere or not, they may be equally destructive; for, to discerning Men, nothing can be more evident, than that a Peace on the principles of dependance, however limited, after what has happened, would be to the last degree dishonourable and ruinous. It is, however, much to be apprehended, that the Idea of such an event will have a very powerful effect upon the Country, and, if not combated with the greatest address, will serve, at least, to produce supineness and dis-union. Men are naturally fond of Peace, and there are Symptoms which may authorize an Opinion, that the people of America are pretty generally weary of the present War....

Among Individuals, the most certain way to make a Man your Enemy, is to tell him, you esteem him such; so with public bodies, and the very jealousy, which the narrow politics of some may affect to entertain of the Army, in order to a due subordination to the supreme Civil Authority, is a likely mean to produce a contrary effect; to incline it to the pursuit of those measures which that may wish it to avoid. It is unjust, because no Order of Men in the thirteen States have paid a more sanctimonious regard to their proceedings than the Army; and, indeed, it may be questioned, whether there has been that scrupulous adherence had to them by any other, [for without arrogance, or the smallest deviation from truth it may be said, that no history, now extant, can furnish an instance of an Army's suffering such uncommon hardships as ours have done, and bearing them with the same patience and Fortitude. To see Men without Cloathes to cover their nakedness, without Blankets to lay on, without Shoes, by which their Marches might be traced by the Blood from their feet, and almost as often without provisions

The George Washington Papers at the Library of Congress, 1741–1799.

as with; Marching through frost and Snow, and at Christmas taking up their Winter Quarters within a day's March of the enemy, without a House or Hurt to cover them till they could be built and submitting to it without a murmur, is a mark of patience and obedience which in my opinion can scarce be a parallel'd.]

8. Venezuela Declares Independence, 1810

Act of Independence

In the name of the All-powerful God,

WE the Representatives of the united Provinces of CARACAS, CUMANA, VARINAS, MARGARITA, BARCELONA, MERIDA, and TRUXILLO, forming the American Confederation of Venezuela, in the South Continent, in Congress assembled, considering the full and absolute possession of our Rights, which we recovered justly and legally from the 19th of April, 1810, in consequence of the occurrences in Bayona, and the occupation of the Spanish Throne by conquest, and the succession of a new Dynasty, constituted without our consent: are desirous, before we make use of those Rights, of which we have been deprived by force for more than three ages, but now restored to us by the political order of human events, to make known to the world the reasons which have emanated from these same occurrences, and which authorise us in the free use we are now about to make of our own Sovereignty.

We do not wish, nevertheless, to begin by alledging the rights inherent in every conquered country, to recover its state of property and independence; we generously forget the long series of ills, injuries, and privations, which the sad right of conquest has indistinctly caused, to all the descendants of the Discoverers, Conquerors, and Settlers of these Countries, plunged into a worse state by the very same cause that ought to have favoured them; and, drawing a veil over the 300 years of Spanish dominion in America, we will now only present to view the authentic and well-known facts, which ought to have wrested from one world, the right over the other, by the inversion, disorder, and conquest, that have already dissolved the Spanish Nation....

Notwithstanding our protests, our moderation, generosity, and the inviolability of our principles, contrary to the wishes of our brethren in Europe, we were declared in a state of rebellion; we were blockaded; war was declared against us; agents were sent amongst us, to excite us one against the other, endeavouring to take away our credit with the other Nations of Europe, by imploring their assistance to oppress us.

Without taking the least notice of our reasons, without presenting them to the impartial judgment of the, world, and without any other judges than our own enemies, we are condemned to a mournful incommunication with our brethren; and, to add contempt to calumny, empowered agents are named for

London, Printed for Longman and Co. [etc.] https://archive.org/details/interestingoffi00venegoog

us, against our own express will, that in their Cortes they may arbitrarily dispose of our interests, under the influence and force of our enemies....

But we, who glory in grounding our proceedings on better principles, and not wishing to establish our felicity on the misfortunes of our fellow-beings, do consider and declare as friends, companions of our fate, and participators of our felicity, those who, united to us by the ties of blood, language, and religion, have suffered the same evils in the anterior order of things, provided they acknowledge our *absolute independence* of the same, and of any other foreign power whatever; that they aid us to sustain it with their lives, fortune, and sentiments; declaring and acknowledging them (as well, as to every other nation,) in war enemies, and in peace friends, brothers and co-patriots....

In consequence whereof, considering, by the reasons thus alledged, that we have satisfied the respect which we owe to the opinions of the human race, and the dignity of other nations, in the number of whom we are about to enter, and on whose communication and friendship we rely: We, the Representatives of the United Provinces of Venezuela, calling on the SUPREME BEING to witness the justice of our proceedings and the rectitude of our intentions, do implore his divine and celestial help; and ratifying, at the moment in which we are born to the dignity which his Providence restores to us, the desire we have of living and dying free, and of believing and defending the holy Catholic and Apostolic Religion of Jesus Christ. We, therefore, in the name and by the will and authority which we hold from the virtuous People of Venezuela, DO declare solemnly to the world, that its united Provinces are; and ought to be, from this day, by act and right; Free, Sovereign, and Independent States.

 # ESSAYS

Historians have for decades debated the origins and meaning of the Revolution for American society. They have argued over the reasons for rebellion and the outcomes. Was it a fight for "home rule" (whether the colonies should be independent of Britain) or over "who should rule at home" (who should direct and control life in English America)? Scholars have also disputed the degree to which the Revolution altered life in the Americas. Was it a conservative affair that left little unchanged for most people or was it a radical departure from the past?

More recently, historians have discussed the impact of the Revolution on the broader world. The two essays here emphasize the broad implications of the Revolution but do so from very different perspectives. In the first essay, Christopher Paul Magra focuses upon the terrain between Britain and the colonies—the sea. Magra suggests that commercial interests of maritime trade drove the Revolution and that the war provided significant economic opportunities everyday fishermen. The second essay by David Armitage looks at the impact of the Declaration of Independence and its ideals in a global perspective. Armitage shows how these American ideas traveled outward in space and time to influence anti-colonial movements throughout the nineteenth and twentieth centuries.

Maritime Dimensions of the American Revolution

CHRISTOPHER PAUL MAGRA

After a long transatlantic journey, which included a sailing time of approximately eight weeks, the brig *Pitt Packet* was homeward bound on April 22, 1769. A rising April sun would have melted fog and warmed chilled hands in the early spring morning as the brig's crew made preparations to enter the harbor at Marblehead, Massachusetts. Thomas Power, the *Pitt Packet's* master, probably shouted orders for tack and sheet lines to be hauled in and secured as the brig angled toward the harbor mouth. A chorus of barefoot seamen would then sing pulling songs, or sea chanties, in order to lend a cadence to barehanded tacking labors. Singing and working, anticipating long-absent family and friends, the *Pitt Packet's* crew prepared to come home.

The brig belonged to Robert "King" Hooper, proprietor of one of the largest fish merchant houses in Marblehead, which was then the principal commercial fishing port in New England in terms of capital investment, number of vessels, and manpower. The *Pitt Packet's* crew had transported their dried, salted cod to overseas markets in Spain, as did a smaller percentage of other colonial crews in the eighteenth century. There, the processed fish was sold to merchants in ports such as Bilbao and Cadiz. Typically, crews returned with fruits, loads of salt, lines of credit, and manufactured goods from England. On this particular voyage, the *Pitt Packet* was returning directly from Cadiz with salt for Marblehead's commercial fishing industry.

The brig did not immediately reach Marblehead's harbor that chilly April morning, however. Dawn's early light also illuminated bent backs and busy hands on board the British naval frigate *Rose*, which was patrolling Atlantic waters along New England's coastline. The *Rose's* Captain, Benjamin Caldwell, sent Lieutenant Henry Gibson Panton with several aimed men to board the *Pitt Packet* early Saturday morning on the pretext of searching for contraband. But, Caldwell's real intent was to press men into naval service. With its sails trimmed in preparation for homecoming, the Marblehead brig could not evade the *Rose* and its press gang.

The crew-members on board the *Pitt Packet*, however, were not willing to surrender once Panton and the press gang boarded the brig. Michael Corbet, Pierce Fenning, John Ryan, and William Conner, Irishmen who called Marblehead home, picked up "fish gig, musket, hatchet, and harpoon" and stood ready to forcibly resist impressment. It is likely that the brig served double duty in Hooper's employ as a fishing vessel and a trading vessel, and the work tools

Excerpt from Christopher Paul Magra, *The Fisherman's Cause: Atlantic Commerce and Maritime Dimensions of the American Revolution* (Cambridge: Cambridge University Press, 2009). Reprinted with the permission of Cambridge University Press.

had simply been left on board during the trade voyage. In any case, the four common seamen, those directly in danger of being impressed, armed themselves with fishing implements and retreated inside the brig.

The resistance quickly escalated. After a tense standoff amidst piles of salt in the forepeak, Corbet drew a line on the floor using handfuls of the preservative and dared the press gang to cross it. Panton unwisely took up this challenge, stepped over the salt line, and advanced toward "the Ship's People." Corbet then launched the harpoon he had been holding, which struck Panton in the neck, severing his jugular vein. The British lieutenant fell, his men carried him to the main deck, and he bled to death. During the ensuing mêlée, two Marblehead mariners were shot and severely wounded. The colonial laborers were then arrested and tried for murder. Their trial gained notoriety throughout the colonies. In the end, the maritime laborers' defense attorney, who was none other than John Adams, was able to get the men acquitted on the basis that Panton's death occurred as a result of justifiable homicide in self-defense.

The *Pitt Packet* affair, colonial fish merchants, and those who labored in the colonial fishing industry are not typically part of the American independence story. The British North American mainland colonies that became the United States of America have been portrayed as being fundamentally rural and agrarian, with inconsequential port cities. Farmers and farming tend to dominate accounts of European settlement and economic development in North America. Political and economic issues surrounding the ability to buy and sell borderlands between British settlement and Indian country have been shown to have influenced the decision of colonial land speculators and agriculturalists to resist British authority during the late eighteenth century imperial crisis. In the words of one notable early American historian, the American Revolution should be seen "as a consequence of the forty-year-long effort to subject the Ohio Country, and with it the rest of the Transappalachian west, to imperial control." Other colonial farmers remained relatively isolated from the outside world in rural communities and only reluctantly agreed to fight for American independence when the British Army was on their doorsteps and town meetings were banned. Farmers then became minutemen, filled the ranks of the Continental Army under George Washington, and heroically fought against a powerful British military to defend their liberties and livelihoods in the face of tyranny. In this interpretation, the Atlantic Ocean represents nothing more than a large liminal space separating lands where history unfolded. The maritime dimensions of the American Revolution fade to black.

Farmers played formative roles in the origins and progress of the American Revolution; yet, the *Pitt Packet* affair serves as a stark reminder that colonial resistance to British authority during the Revolutionary Era cannot be fully explained without investigating why those who made their living from the sea participated in this resistance. Similarly, the progress of this formative event cannot be completely understood without coming to terms with how those tied to the sea contributed to the war for independence. In, the case of New

England, it was both an epicenter of revolutionary fervor and the headquarters of commercial fishing in colonial America.

It is widely acknowledged that New Englanders played important roles in bringing about the imperial crisis that separated the colonies from the mother country at the end of the eighteenth century. Riots directed against the sovereignty of the British government were particularly prevalent in New England throughout the 1760s and early 1770s. In these mob activities, effigies and customs vessels were burned; customs officials and royal governors were forced to watch their property being destroyed; monopolized tea became flotsam and jetsam; and British soldiers were harassed to the point at which they were willing to shoot into a crowd of unarmed colonists. Moreover, the idea to boycott British manufactured goods and use consumer power as a political weapon began in Massachusetts; militia units were formed here with the intention of resisting British authority at a minute's notice; elites in this region established the first committees of correspondence to unite colonists in opposition; and the "shot heard around the world" was fired here.

Furthermore, men from New England were exceptionally active during the American Revolutionary War. Communities in this area supplied more manpower to the war effort on a consistent yearly basis for the duration of the conflict than any other region. In any given year, no colony/state ever provided more men for service in the Continental Army than Massachusetts. In addition, three of the four major generals who served under George Washington at the start of the war were from New England, and seven of the eight brigadier generals hailed from this region. Also, four of the seven members of the first Naval Committee appointed by the Continental Congress in 1775 were New Englanders. It is no coincidence that these revolutionaries lived and worked in a region that was the center of commercial fishing in colonial America.

The cod fishing industry, in particular, was one of the most valuable extractive industries in all of colonial America, and it was the single most lucrative export business in New England. On the eve of the American Revolution, between 1768 and 1772, colonial merchants sold fish overseas valued at £152,155, which represented thirty-five per cent of the region's total export revenue. Moreover, the cod fisheries employed a significant portion of colonial New England's population. Of the 581,100 people living in this region in 1770, an estimated 10,000 men found employment in this sector of the economy. These 10,000 men represented eight per cent of the adult male working population. Such levels of labor and capital impressed overseas observers such as Adam Smith, who penned the following at the start of the American Revolutionary War: "[T]he New England fishery in particular was, before the late disturbances, one of the most important, perhaps, in the world."

Massachusetts was the site of the principal fishing ports and shipping centers in New England throughout the colonial period. By themselves, Marblehead and Gloucester, Massachusetts, accounted for sixty per cent of all the fish caught annually in the entire New England region. Coastal communities in this colony were responsible for shipping nearly 100 per cent of the total quintals (112 pounds dry weight; pronounced "kentals") of cod exported from New England to Southern Europe between 1771 and 1772. The same ports were responsible for shipping forty-five per cent of the total quintals of cod to the West Indies during this period. Combined, these coastal communities shipped eighty-five per cent of all the fish caught in the colonies in the early 1770s. Although there were certainly commercial fisheries in other colonies, none were as extensive or commercially viable as those in Massachusetts....

It is becoming increasingly clear, however, that the Atlantic Ocean connected colonists in North America to a wider world beyond imperial borders. This "ocean-centered" insight is changing the way historians write about the Revolution. Whereas town histories have focused on local, domestic factors that influenced colonists' decisions to resist British authority, and imperial historians emphasized transatlantic causes of the Revolution that were particular to an Anglo-American context, Atlantic historians focus on supra-imperial forces that pressurized the British Empire until it cracked. Whereas previous scholars have used the nation-state as the fundamental framework of analysis, Atlantic academics highlight those processes that crossed political borders but remained primarily within the geographic limits of the regions intimately connected to the Atlantic Ocean....

[This essay] defends a two-fold argument pertaining to the why and how of the American Revolution. The British government's efforts to control and command colonists' commercial use of the Atlantic Ocean stimulated colonial resistance to British authority. The colonists then used the ocean to achieve their independence by mobilizing maritime commercial assets for war. Simply put, the origins and progress of the American Revolution cannot be fully understood without coming to terms with its maritime dimensions.

Parliament's Restraining Act made commercial fishing on the Atlantic Ocean illegal for colonial fishermen such as skipper Joshua Burnham and the crew of the schooner *Polly*. The maritime laborers from Ipswich, Massachusetts, did not sit idle, however. They were able to find alternate means of employment. They enlisted with the Continental Navy shortly after Congress signed the Declaration of Independence. The navy offered jobs, wages, and the promise of prize shares, which held out hope to poorer fishing families. Three of the *Polly's* crew joined Burnham on December 7, 1776, in agreeing to "ship ourselves" and "Follow all the regulations of the American Congress & be under such regulations as is Customary for Seamen & Mariners." These men were not the first, nor were they the last, to make the transition from commercial fishing to military service.

In addition to fish, fishing vessels, and overseas commercial connections, American fishermen were mobilized for war. The British government's efforts to control colonists' use of the sea disaffected laborers formerly employed in the chief engine of maritime commerce in New England. Fishermen then flooded the decks of America's fighting vessels and filled the ranks of the Continental Army. They fought at sea and on land in every capacity, and their military service was invaluable to the American war effort....

Other fishermen chose to fight in Massachusetts's navy. Eleven states had their own flotillas during the war. Massachusetts began arming vessels in 1775 and formally established its own fleet in February 1776. The wages for the officers and men in the Massachusetts Navy were as follows: Captains earned £4 each month; 1st Lieutenants made £3 per month; 2nd Lieutenants and Surgeons each earned £2.10.0 per month; Masters earned £2; Boatswains, Carpenters, Gunners, Pilots, Quartermasters, Stewards, Master-at-Arms all earned £1.10.0 each month; while "Foremast Men" made £1.4.0 per month. In. addition to these wages, and for "further Encouragement to the said Officers and Seamen," crews were to receive "one Third the Proceeds of all Captures." Such prize shares provided a lucrative incentive over-and-above wages that were already attractive for unemployed fishermen. While a Captain in the state navy could have earned £48 per year, common seamen only earned £14.8.0 for the same length of service. Such compensation by itself did not compare favorably to peace-time annual earnings in the fishing industry. Prize shares, however, held out the potential for extra earnings that are difficult to quantify because of their variability....

To promote the "Activity, and Courage" of her crew, George Washington spelled out the distribution of prize money the crew of the Marblehead schooner *Hannah* would receive "over and above your Pay." First, prizes were to be sent "to the nearest and safest Port," and the commander-in-chief was to be informed "immediately of such Capture, with all Particulars and there to way my further Direction." As of yet, no Admiralty courts had been established for the adjudication of legal prizes. In effect, Washington told the *Hannah's* crew that he would be their ultimate judge. In the event that a prize was judged legitimate, meaning that it was neither a re-capture nor a vessel belonging to a patriot merchant, the crew would earn one-third of the value of whatever cargo was taken on a prize ship, except "military and naval stores." These stores, along with the "vessels and apparel" were "reserved for public service." In addition, the Continental Congress, which had paid for the conversion of the fishing schooner, and Washington, as their commander-in-chief, received two-thirds of the cargo's remaining value. Washington then divided the crew's one-third share in the following manner: the Captain earned six shares of the one-third; the 1st Lieutenant earned five shares; the 2nd lieutenant four; the "Ship's Master" 3; the steward 2; the mate 1.5; the gunner 1.5; the boatswain 1.5; the gunner's mate and the Sergeant each earned 1.5; and the Privates earned a singe share.

Such prize shares could amount to a princely sum for unemployed workers. In 1777, the armed schooner *Franklin* and its crew captured the powder ship *Hope*. The *Hope's* precious cargo was valued at £54,075.17.2, one third of which amounted to £18,025.5.8. A single lowly Private's share for this prize, taken from the one third, was worth £487.3.4. This figure, which represents the low end of the prize shares, would have been equivalent to six-and-a-half years of work in the commercial fishing industry for even the most experienced, highest paid skippers/masters. In this way, the potential for large sums of money might be offered as an incentive for unemployed, poorer working men to go to sea to capture British military supply vessels and smaller warships....

Fishermen also engaged in privateering during the American Revolution. William Le Craw was born into a (French, most likely of Jersey Island) fishing family in Marblehead on May 26, 1736. Two other Le Craws can be found listed in probate records as having worked as fishermen in Marblehead, including Phillip Le Craw, who worked as a sharesman and skipper for William Knight on board the schooner *Molly* in the 1760s. Like Phillip, William probably became a skipper before the war's outbreak. Unfortunately, the records of William's career in the fishing industry beyond his probate record have not survived. However, he commanded two Marblehead privateers during the war: the schooner *Necessity* (1776) and the brig *Black Snake* (1777). Fish merchants and vessel owners such as John Selman and Joshua Orne, who owned *Necessity*, would not have trusted their property and their enterprise to someone with little experience. As captain of these privateers, Le Craw would have earned the highest share among the crew of any prizes taken, but no wages.

While it might be expected that fishermen would fight at sea, it is perhaps less obvious that such maritime laborers would also fight on land. Yet, Marblehead fishermen who fought in the war participated on one occasion or another in some military service on *terra firma*. The local militia regiments that formed at the start of the conflict provided the first means by which Massachusetts's fishermen could supplement or replace the earnings they had lost as a result of the Restraining Act. Such local regiments then became part of the first American Army once Washington assumed command. These men earned wages on top of bounties that they qualified for through their enlistment in the Continental Army....

The Declaration of Independence in World Context

DAVID ARMITAGE

Where better to begin internationalizing the history of the United States than at the beginning, with the Declaration of Independence? No document is as familiar to students or so deeply entwined with what it means to be an American. The "self-evident truths" it proclaimed to "life, liberty, and the pursuit of happiness" have guaranteed it a sacrosanct place as "American scripture," a testament to the special qualities of a chosen people. Little wonder, then, that it stands as a cornerstone of Americans' sense of their own uniqueness. If a document so indelibly American as the Declaration of Independence can be put successfully into a world context, then surely almost any subject in U.S. history can be internationalized. This can be done for the Declaration by showing that it was the product of a pressing international context in 1776, by examining the host of imitations it spawned and the many analogous documents that have been issued from 1790 to 1988, and by comparing the starkly different histories of its reception within and beyond the United States. Accordingly, this essay will deal with the immediate motivations that led to the Declaration in 1776. with the first fifty

Republished with permission of the University of Illinois Press, from David Armitage, "The Declaration of Independence in World Context". In *America on the World Stage: A Global Approach to US History*, ed. Gary Reichard and Ted Dickson. Chicago: University of Illinois Press, pp. 17–28, copyright 2008; permission conveyed through Copyright Clearance Center, Inc.

years of reactions to it, at home and abroad, and with the subsequent history of declaring independence across the world, from Venezuela to New Zealand. It will then conclude with some reflections on what the Declaration's afterlife can tell us about the broader modern history of rights, both individual and collective.

To ask just what the Declaration declared is to see that, first and foremost, it announced the entry of the United States into international history. The very term "United States of America" had not been used publicly before its appearance in the Declaration. As the opening paragraph stated, the representatives of the states were laying before "the opinions of mankind" the reasons "one people" had chosen "to assume among the powers of the earth, the separate and equal station to which the Laws of Nature and of Nature's God entitle them." Those "powers of the earth"—meaning other sovereign states—were the immediate international audience for the Declaration. The United States intended to join them on an equal footing "as Free and Independent States" that "have full Power to levy War, conclude Peace, contract Alliances, establish Commerce, and to do all other Acts and Things which independent States may of right do." With that statement from the concluding paragraph of the Declaration, the United States announced that they had left the transnational community of the British Empire to join instead the international community of sovereign states.

The Declaration of Independence was therefore a declaration of interdependence. Its primary intention was to turn a civil war among Britons, and within the British Empire, into a legitimate war between states under the law of nations. In August 1775, George III had already turned the American colonists into rebels by proclaiming them to be outside his protection. To transform themselves from outlaws into legitimate belligerents, the colonists needed international recognition for their cause and foreign allies to support it. Thomas Paine's best-selling pamphlet *Common Sense* made this motivation clear. In February 1776, Paine argued in the closing pages of the first edition of *Common Sense* that the "custom of nations" demanded a declaration of American independence, if any European power were even to mediate a peace between the Americans and Great Britain. France and Spain in particular could not be expected to aid those they considered rebels against another monarch. Foreign courts needed to have American grievances laid before them persuasively in a "manifesto" that could also reassure them that the Americans would be reliable trading partners. Without a declaration, Paine concluded, "[t]he custom of all courts is against us, and will be so, until, by an independence, we take rank with other nations."

The records of the Continental Congress confirm that the need for a declaration of independence was intimately linked with the demands of international relations. When on June 7, 1776, Richard Henry Lee tabled a resolution before the Continental Congress declaring the colonies independent, he also urged Congress to resolve "to take the most effectual measures for forming foreign Alliances" and to prepare a plan of confederation for the newly independent states. Congress formally adopted the resolution on July 2, 1776, but only after creating three overlapping committees to draft the Declaration, a model treaty, and the Articles of Confederation. The Declaration announced the states' entry into the international system; the model treaty was designed to establish amity and commerce with other states; and the Articles of Confederation, which established "a firm league" among the thirteen free and independent states, constituted an international agreement to set up central institutions for the conduct of vital domestic and foreign affairs. To grasp the original meaning of the Declaration, it should be read alongside the Franco-American treaty of 1778 and the Articles of Confederation as one of a trio of international documents produced in sequence by the Continental Congress.

The Declaration's primary meaning in 1776 was to affirm before world opinion the rights of a group of states to enter the international realm as equals with other such states. John Adams, writing in 1781, called the Declaration of Independence "that memorable Act, by which [the United States] assumed an equal Station among the Nations." John C. Calhoun concurred a generation later: "The act was, in fact, but a formal and solemn announcement to the world, that the colonies had ceased to be dependent communities, and had become free and independent States." For almost fifty years after 1776, the Declaration's meaning for Americans lay in its opening and closing paragraphs, not in the self-evident truths that "all men are created equal" with unalienable rights to life, liberty, and the pursuit of happiness. Even Abraham Lincoln saw those truths as strictly surplus to requirements in 1776: "The assertion that 'all men are created equal' was of no practical use in effecting our separation from Great Britain; and it was placed in the Declaration, not for that, but for future use." The history of the responses to the Declaration, and the imitations of it, prove that Lincoln's point held true not only in the American context but also in a world context.

The rapid transmission and translation of the Declaration around the Atlantic world and across Europe indicated the systems of communication and the common arguments that bound together the late-eighteenth-century international community. It appeared in London newspapers in mid-August 1776, had reached Florence and Warsaw by mid-September, and a German translation appeared in Switzerland by October. The Spanish-American authorities actively banned its distribution, but other obstacles (not least that it was written in English) stood in the way of its circulation. The first copy of the Declaration sent to France—the most likely and sought-after ally for the new United States—went astray; a second copy arrived only in November 1776, when American independence was already old news throughout Europe. By that time, too, the British government of Lord North had commissioned an anonymous rebuttal of the Declaration by a young conservative pamphleteer and lawyer, John Lind, and his friend, the even younger philosopher, Jeremy Bentham. Bentham's blistering attack on the "contemptible and extravagant" "opinions of the Americans on Government" in his "Short Review of the Declaration" foreshadowed his later criticisms of the "nonsense upon stilts" he found in the French Declaration of the Rights of Man and the Citizen. The Declaration thereby became a primary document in a larger international debate over the origins, the scope, and the limits of rights, both collective and individual.

The Franco-American Treaty was signed only in February 1778 but it helped ensure ultimate American victory over British forces. However, if the

United States had been soundly defeated at the battle of Saratoga or York-town, the American rebellion might be only as famous today as the other failed independence movements of the late eighteenth century, in Corsica, Montenegro, Greece, or the Crimea, for example. The Declaration of Independence might then be just another historical curiosity, known only to scholars and a dwindling band of hard-core nationalists keeping the flame of independence alive.

The recognition by Britain of the colonies' independence by the Peace of Paris in 1783 indisputably confirmed what the Declaration had contentiously affirmed: that the colonies were free and independent states, not just de facto but de jure, too. Its immediate purpose having been served, the opening and closing paragraphs of the Declaration fell into oblivion in the United States, except when they were recalled by southern proponents of states' rights like Calhoun. The second paragraph did not immediately rise to prominence in the first generation after American independence. Its claims to natural rights and a right of revolution sounded suspiciously like the "jacobinical" tenets of the French Revolution and were tainted with Jeffersonian republicanism in an age of partisan strife. Only in the aftermath of the War of 1812, once all suspicion had been removed that the Declaration was anti-British, pro-French, and an incitement to insurrection, could the second paragraph of the Declaration begin its progress toward becoming the presumed heart of the Declaration's true meaning in the United States.

Yet if the assertion that the united colonies were "free and independent States" was not long remembered in the United States, it would frequently be recalled as the inspiration for other anti-imperial and anticolonial secession movements over the next two centuries. There have been three major periods of declaring independence: the years from 1776 to the revolutions of 1848 in Europe; the immediate aftermath of the First World War (and the break-up of the Ottoman, Romanov, and Austro-Hungarian Empires); and the decades from to 1945 to 1979, when seventy newly independent states emerged from the wreckage of the European colonial empires. During the first great age of declaring independence, other declarations generally alluded to the opening and closing paragraphs of the American Declaration, as did the earliest known imitation, which came from Flanders in 1790 when rebels in the Austrian Netherlands declared that their province "EST & a droit d'æTRE un *Etat libre & indépendant*" ("is, and of right ought to be, a Free and Independent State") in words taken directly from the American Declaration. Two decades later, the Venezuelan Congress proclaimed on July 5, 1811, (having just missed the anniversary of the American Declaration) that the "United Provinces" of Venezuela now stood "among the sovereign nations of the earth the rank which the Supreme Being and nature has assigned us" as "Free, Sovereign and Independent States." Likewise, the Texas Declaration of Independence (1836) affirmed the necessity of "severing our political connection with the Mexican people, and assuming an independent attitude among the nations of the earth." In this early period, the Liberian Declaration of Independence (1847), composed by the Virginia-born African American Hilary Teague, alone enshrined the recognition of "certain inalienable rights; among these are life, liberty, and the right to acquire, possess, enjoy, and defend property"; it, too, began with a declaration that the Republic of Liberia was "a free, sovereign, and independent state."

It was only in the mid-twentieth century that the second paragraph of the Declaration would be used in other declarations of independence. Two such examples, each of which heralded one of the later heydays of declaring independence, were the Declaration of Independence of the Czechoslovak Nation (1918) and the Vietnamese Declaration of Independence (1945). The Czechoslovak Declaration was drafted in Washington, D.C., by, among others, Gutzon Borglum, the sculptor of Mount Rushmore. It placed the American Declaration within a lineage stretching from the proto-Protestantism of Jan Hus in the fifteenth century all the way to the Wilsonian promise of self-determination in the early twentieth. Likewise, Ho Chi Minh's Declaration opened with quotations from the second paragraph of the American Declaration and the French Declaration of the Rights of Man. Ho Chi Minh, long an admirer of George Washington, thereby placed the Vietnamese revolution into a longer revolutionary tradition while also making a shrewd, albeit unsuccessful, bid for American support for Vietnamese independence. However, even these examples were not typical in their respect for the Declaration's "self-evident truths." More characteristic of the century before the Universal Declaration of Human Rights (1948) was the British foreign secretary Arthur Balfour's response at the Versailles conference in 1919 to a proposal that the covenant of the League of Nations include a racial equality clause "commencing with the proposition taken from the Declaration of Independence, that all men are created equal. Mr. Balfour said that was an eighteenth century proposition which he did not believe was true. He believed it was true in a certain sense that all men of a particular nation were created equal, but not that a man in Central Africa was created equal to a European."

Active resistance of the rights to life, liberty, and the pursuit of happiness helped turn the Declaration of Independence into a blueprint for white settler revolt. Thus, the South Carolina Declaration of Secession (December 20, 1860) asserted that "South Carolina has resumed her position among the nations of the world, as a separate and independent State; with full power to levy war, conclude peace, contract alliances, establish commerce, and to do all the other acts and things which independent States may of right do." Even more closely modeled on the form, and even the purpose, of the American Declaration was the Unilateral Declaration of Independence issued by the embattled white minority government of southern Rhodesia (November 11, 1965). In conscious imitation of the 1776 Declaration, it opened with the words, "Whereas in the course of human affairs history has shown that it may become necessary for a people to resolve the political affiliations which have connected them with another people and to assume among other nations the separate and equal status to which they are entitled." Two years earlier, in 1963, the British government had prepared military contingency plans against the possibility of just such a unilateral declaration: the ominous title of the secret file containing them was "Boston Tea Party."

The great majority of the unilateral declarations of independence issued after 1776 made no direct reference to the American Declaration. For example, the Haitian Declaration of January 1, 1804, the first declaration of independence in the Western Hemisphere after 1776, ignored the American Declaration altogether, and with good reason in light of Thomas Jefferson's policy not to recognize the legitimacy of the Haitian Revolution. "To draw up the act of independence," wrote Louis Boisrond Tonnerre, the author of the Haitian declaration, "we need the skin of a white man for parchment, his skull for an inkwell, his blood for ink, and a bayonet for a pen!" His declaration, unlike the American, marked a wholly new beginning for the first black republic in the Western Hemisphere and made no concessions to the former colonial masters. Many later declarations would be more pragmatic, even as others, like the declaration issued by the Palestinian National Council in November 1988, catalogued unresolved grievances and unfulfilled aspirations to statehood.

This brief global history of the Declaration of Independence since 1776 should be contrasted with Gordon Wood's recent judgment that it "set forth a philosophy of human rights that could be applied not only to Americans, but also to peoples everywhere. It was essential in giving the American Revolution a universal appeal." Rather, it is more the story of the rights of states than of individuals or groups. Indeed, the history of the Declaration of Independence in world context is above all an account of how our world of states emerged from an earlier world of multinational empires. The transition from one to the other did not necessarily benefit equally all those who had been the subjects of empires. Thus, declarations of independence by indigenous peoples are historically rare. The most notable instance—the "Declaration of the Independence of New Zealand" (1835)—is in fact a counterexample because it preceded the imposition of colonial authority, and made such authority possible by constituting the Maori chiefs as a sovereign body with which the British could then conclude the Treaty of Waitangi in 1840. Successful examples of declarations of independence by ethnic minorities within independent nation-states are just as rare. It seems to be a historical rule that once states have established their right to external self-determination, they become resistant to further internal challenges to their autonomy or integrity.

The Declaration of Independence possessed meanings as varied for international audiences as it did for different American publics. Its status however, as a charter of individual rights has never been as prominent on the world stage as it has been within the United States. To examine the Declaration's reception in world history since 1776 is to discover just how relatively recent and persistently fragile is the prominence of talk about the rights of non-state groups and individuals in international affairs. Perhaps the only self-evident lesson to be learned from this global history of the Declaration of Independence is that the protection of those rights demands constant vigilance against the powers of the earth, not least because the individual rights to "life, liberty, and the pursuit of happiness" have not always been easily reconciled with "all the other Acts and Things which independent States may of right do."

 FURTHER READING

Fred Anderson, *Crucible of War: The Seven Years' War and the Fate of Empire in British North America, 1754–1766* (2001).

T. H. Breen, *The Marketplace of Revolution: How Consumer Politics Shaped American Independence* (2004).

Sylvia Frey, *Water from the Rock: Black Resistance in a Revolutionary Age* (1991).

Linda K. Kerber, *Women of the Republic: Intellect and Ideology in Revolutionary America* (1997).

Pauline Maier, *American Scripture: Making the Declaration of Independence* (1998).

Robert Middlekauff, *The Glorious Cause: The American Revolution, 1763–1789* (1982).

Gary B. Nash, *The Unknown American Revolution: The Unruly Birth of Democracy and the Struggle to Create America* (2006).

Ray Raphael, *A People's History of the American Revolution* (2002).

Charles Royster, *A Revolutionary People at War: The Continental Army and American Character, 1775–1783* (1996).

Gordon S. Wood, *The Radicalism of the American Revolution* (1993).

Additional critical thinking activities and content are available in MindTap.

MindTap

MindTap is a fully online, highly personalized learning experience built upon Cengage Learning content. MindTap combines student learning tools—readings, multimedia, activities, and assessments—into a singular Learning Path that guides students through the course.

CHAPTER 5

From Confederation to Constitution

In late May 1787, George Washington called to order a convention of fifty-five delegates in Philadelphia. Throughout a hot, steamy summer, this group deliberated and argued until it arrived at a plan to restructure the government of the United States. The Constitution, as it was called, was a controversial reform, and it was not ratified by the nine states necessary for it to take effect until the summer of 1788. Yet the Constitution continues to be the framework of the United States, one of the oldest frameworks of government still in place in the twenty-first century. Many Americans at the time, however, were not convinced of the wisdom of the Constitution or optimistic about its meaning for the future of the United States.

The Constitution was not the first framework of government for the country; the Articles of Confederation, which offered a less centralized government than the Constitution proposed, had been ratified in 1781. The central government under the Articles had limited powers: it had no power to tax, it could not compel the states to contribute to financing its operations, and it could not enforce a uniform commercial policy. Its structure was weak as well. It had no executive branch and no separate judiciary; instead, it relied on a legislature in which each state had equal representation. Given the U.S.'s recent experiences with a monarchy, many Americans were satisfied with a decentralized government. And the Articles period was not without its successes. Perhaps its most notable achievement was the Northwest Ordinance, which laid the groundwork for the method by which new states would enter the Union. Still many Americans soon concluded that the government was inadequate to meet the country's needs.

The shortcomings of the Articles were exacerbated by the crises that the new nation encountered. An economic depression wracked the nation shortly after the conclusion of war in 1781, and this was accompanied by a monetary crisis as the value of paper money declined. The phrase "not worth a Continental" came into usage, indicating the declining value of the new nation's currency. These difficulties were compounded by diplomatic and commercial failures. The British continued to occupy western forts on American territory, and Congress could not establish a national commercial policy because federal tariffs could be passed only if all the states agreed to them. As the postwar depression worsened, Americans began to pressure their government for relief. In western Massachusetts, farmers pleaded for lower taxes and a larger supply of money. When the state government rejected all of their requests in 1786, a group of farmers began forcibly closing down the courts in which debtors were tried. Under the leadership of Daniel Shays, this rebellion spread throughout western Massachusetts, and it was ended only by calling out the state militia. Once Shays's Rebellion was put down, John Adams, who years before had led his own revolution, called these rebels "ignorant, restless, desperadoes, without conscience or principles." Many Americans concluded that the limited government under the Articles was a failure.

Given these concerns, the members of the Constitutional Convention sought to restructure the national government. Their deliberations resulted in a government with three branches, including an executive and a judiciary, as well as a legislature. The legislative branch was bicameral, with one house providing equal representation to all states and the other providing proportional representation based on population. The president was elected by the Electoral College, in which the number of electors from each state was equal to the number of that state's senators and representatives. Perhaps most controversial was the three-fifths compromise, which included three-fifths of the slave population in a state's headcount; this increased the power of the states in which slavery existed.

The framers provided that the Constitution had to be ratified by nine of thirteen state conventions before it would become the law of the land. The national debate quickly divided the Federalists, who favored ratification, from the Antifederalists, who did not. The latter group argued that the Constitution was an exercise in elitism that would lead to rule by a wealthy, unrepresentative minority. They lauded the Revolution that had just been won and warned that the Constitution might lead to a return to "despotism" and "tyranny," pointing to the absence of a Bill of Rights to support their claim. In contrast, the Federalists, most brilliantly represented by Alexander Hamilton, James Madison, and John Jay in The Federalist Papers, argued that the United States was in crisis and that the Constitution would preserve the republic and promote economic prosperity. When Jay and Hamilton pledged to support a Bill of Rights should the Constitution be ratified, they undercut much of the Antifederalist argument. By 1788, ratification was complete and the course of the United States changed yet again.

QUESTIONS TO THINK ABOUT

Would the United States have survived as a nation if the Articles of Confederation had remained the framework of government? How would government and society have differed if the Articles had not been replaced by the Constitution? Was the framing and ratification of the Constitution "counterrevolutionary"? Compare and contrast the focus upon religious freedom and physical enslavement. How did the United States justify slavery but accept freedom of religion? Also, how radical were the changes in the United States versus other nations, such as France, who also had revolutions during this era?

DOCUMENTS

Document 1, an abridgement of the Articles of Confederation, illustrates the power of states and the weakness of the national government. Pivotal questions, ranging from the place of religion in the republic to the status of slavery, had to be decided by the new nation, as the next four documents illustrate. Document 2 is a petition from Cato, "a poor negro," to the Pennsylvania Assembly, urging it to reject conservative attempts to repeal a law that set in motion an end to slavery. Just as the new nation and new states had to determine the place of slaves, they also had to interact in new ways with Native Americans. Document 3 is a treaty made between the young United States and the Iroquois. In document 4, slaveholders in Virginia seek to protect slavery. With petitions, they urge the retention of slavery. Document 5 is a proposal authored by Thomas Jefferson that provides for the formal protection of religious freedom in Virginia. Document 6 describes Shays's Rebellion in 1787 when the militia was called out to put down an uprising of farmers. The next two documents explore the debates surrounding the Constitution. Document 7 includes excerpts from *The Federalist Papers*, a series of 85 essays written by James Madison, Alexander Hamilton, and John Jay in 1787 and 1788 to explain and defend the Constitution. Finally, for comparison's sake, document 8 is the plan to change the calendar in France after its revolution.

1. The Articles of Confederation Stress the Rights of States, 1781

Preamble

To all to whom these Presents shall come, we the undersigned Delegates of the States affixed to our Names send greeting.

Articles of Confederation and perpetual Union between the States of New Hampshire, Massachusetts bay, Rhode Island and Providence Plantations, Connecticut, New York, New Jersey, Pennsylvania, Delaware, Maryland, Virginia, North Carolina, South Carolina, and Georgia.

Article I. The Stile of this Confederacy shall be "The United States of America."

Article II. Each state retains its sovereignty, freedom, and independence, and every power, jurisdiction, and right, which is not by this Confederation expressly delegated to the United States, in Congress assembled.

Article III. The said States hereby severally enter into a firm league of friendship with each other, for their common defense, the security of their liberties, and their mutual and general welfare, binding themselves to assist each other, against all force offered to, or attacks made upon them, or any of them, on account of religion, sovereignty, trade, or any other pretense whatever.

Article V. For the most convenient management of the general interests of the United States, delegates shall be annually appointed in such manner as the legislatures of each State shall direct, to meet in Congress on the first Monday in November, in every year, with a power reserved to each State to recall its

The Articles of Confederation (1777, ratified and in force 1781).

delegates, or any of them, at any time within the year, and to send others in their stead for the remainder of the year....

In determining questions in the United States in Congress assembled, each State shall have one vote....

Article VIII. All charges of war, and all other expenses that shall be incurred for the common defense or general welfare, and allowed by the United States in Congress assembled, shall be defrayed out of a common treasury, which shall be supplied by the several States in proportion to the value of all land within each State, granted or surveyed for any person, as such land and the buildings and improvements thereon shall be estimated according to such mode as the United States in Congress assembled, shall from time to time direct and appoint.

The taxes for paying that proportion shall be laid and levied by the authority and direction of the legislatures of the several States within the time agreed upon by the United States in Congress assembled.

Article IX....The United States in Congress assembled shall never engage in a war, nor grant letters of marque or reprisal in time of peace, nor enter into any treaties or alliances, nor coin money, nor regulate the value thereof, nor ascertain the sums and expenses necessary for the defense and welfare of the United States, or any of them, nor emit bills, nor borrow money on the credit of the United States, nor appropriate money, nor agree upon the number of vessels of war, to be built or purchased, or the number of land or sea forces to be raised, nor appoint a commander in chief of the army or navy, unless nine States assent to the same: nor shall a question on any other point, except for adjourning from day to day be determined, unless by the votes of the majority of the United States in Congress assembled.

2. Cato, an African American, Pleads for the Abolition of Slavery in Pennsylvania, 1781

Mr. PRINTER.

I AM a poor negro, who with myself and children have had the good fortune to get my freedom, by means of an act of assembly passed on the first of March 1780, and should now with my family be as happy a set of people as any on the face of the earth; but I am told the assembly are going to pass a law to send us all back to our masters. Why dear Mr. Printer, this would be the cruellest act that ever a sett of worthy good gentlemen could be guilty of. To make a law to hang us all, would be *merciful,* when compared with this law.... I have read the act which made me free, and I always read it with joy—and I always dwell with particular pleasure on the following words, spoken by the assembly in the top of the said law. "We esteem it a particular blessing granted to us, that we are enabled this day to add one more step to universal civilization, by removing as much as possible the sorrows of those, who have lived in *undeserved* bondage, and from which, by the assumed authority of the kings of Great

From collections of the *Historical Society of Pennsylvania.* Obtained from http://www.pbs.org/wgbh/aia/part2/2h73t.html.

Britain, no effectual legal relief could be obtained." See it was the king of Great Britain that kept us in slavery before.—Now surely, after saying so, it cannot be possible for them to make slaves of us again—nobody, but the king of England can do it—and I sincerely pray, that he may never have it in his power.... [W]hat is most serious than all, what will our great father think of such doings? But I pray that he may be pleased to tern the hearts of the honour-able assembly from this cruel law; and that he will be pleased to make us poor blacks deserving of his mercies.

CATO.

3. The Iroquois and the U.S. Make the Treaty of Fort Stanwix, 1784

Articles

Concluded at Fort Stanwix, on the twenty-second day of October, one thousand seven hundred and eighty-four, between Oliver Wolcott, Richard Butler, and Arthur Lee, Commissioners Plenipotentiary from the United States, in Congress assembled, on the one Part, and the Sachems and Warriors of the Six Nations, on the other.

The United States of America give peace to the Senecas, Mohawks, Onondagas and Cayugas, and receive them into their protection upon the following conditions:

Article I. Six hostages shall be immediately delivered to the commissioners by the said nations, to remain in possession of the United States, till all the prisoners, white and black, which were taken by the said Senecas, Mohawks, Onondagas and Cayugas, or by any of them, in the late war, from among the people of the United States, shall be delivered up.

Article II. The Oneida and Tuscarora nations shall be secured in the possession of the lands on which they are settled.

Article III. A line shall be drawn, beginning at the mouth of a creek about four miles east of Niagara, called Oyonwayea, or Johnston's Landing-Place, upon the lake named by the Indians Oswego, and by us Ontario; from thence southerly in a direction always four miles east of the carrying-path, between Lake Erie and Ontario, to the mouth of Tehoseroron or Buffaloe Creek on Lake Erie; thence south to the north boundary of the state of Pennsylvania; thence west to the end of the said north boundary; thence south along the west boundary of the said state, to the river Ohio; the said line from the mouth of the Oyonwayea to the Ohio, shall be the western boundary of the lands of the Six Nations, so that the Six Nations shall and do yield to the United States, all claims to the country west of the said boundary, and then they shall be secured in the peaceful possession of the lands they inhabit east and north of the same, reserving only six miles square round the fort of Oswego, to the United States, for the support of the same.

In Wilcomb E. Washington, comp., *The American Indian and the United States: A Documentary History*, Vol. IV (Westport, CT: Greenwood Press, 1973), 2267–2271.

Article IV. The Commissioners of the United States, in consideration of the present circumstances of the Six Nations, and in execution of the humane and liberal views of the United States upon the signing of the above articles, will order goods to be delivered to the said Six Nations for their use and comfort.

4. Slaveholders in Virginia Argue Against the Abolition of Slavery, 1784–1785

Gentlemen,

When the British parliament usurped a Right to dispose of our Property without our consent we dissolved the Union with our parent country and established a ... government of our own. We risked our Lives and Fortunes, and waded through Seas of Blood ... we understand a very subtle and daring attempt is made to dispossess us of a very important Part of our Property ... TO WREST US FROM OUR SLAVES, by an act of Legislature for general emancipation.

It is unsupported by Scripture. For we find in the Old Testament... slavery was permitted by the Deity himself....It is also exceedingly impolitic. For it involves in it, and is productive of Want, Poverty, Distress, and Ruin to FREE citizens, Neglect, Famine and Death to the black Infant.... The Horrors of all Rapes, Murders, and Outrages which a vast multitude of unprincipled unpropertied, revengeful and remorseless Banditti are capable of perpetrating ... sure and final Ruin to this now flourishing free and happy Country.

We solemnly adjure and humbly pray that you will discountenance and utterly reject every motion and proposal for emancipating our slaves....

Some men of considerable weight to wrestle from us, by an Act of the legislature, the most valuable and indispensable Article of our Property, our SLAVES by general emancipation of them.... Such a scheme indeed consists very well with the principles and designs of the North, whose Finger is sufficiently visible in it.... No language can express our indignation, Contempt and Detestation of the apostate wretches....It therefore cannot be admitted that any man had a right ... to divest us of our known rights to property which are so clearly defined.... To an unequivocal Construction therefore of this Bill of rights we now appeal and claim the utmost benefits of... in whatever may tend... to preserve our rights ... secure to us the Blessings of the free....

And we shall ever Pray....

5. Thomas Jefferson Proposes the Protection of Religious Freedom in Virginia, 1786

Whereas, Almighty God has created the mind free; that all attempts to influence it by temporal punishment, or burthens, or by civil incapacitations, tend

---

Petitions submitted in several Virginia counties in 1784 with almost 300 signatures and in Lundenburg County in 1785 with 161 signatures, from collections of the Library of Virginia. Obtained from http://www.pbs.org/wgbh/aia/part2/2h65.html.

Thomas Jefferson, *The Virginia Statute for Religious Freedom* (1786).

only to beget habits of hypocrisy and meanness, and are a departure from the plan of the Holy Author of our religion, who, being Lord both of body and mind, yet chose not to propagate it by coercions on either, as was in his Almighty power to do; that the impious presumption of legislators and rulers, civil as well as ecclesiastical, who, being themselves but fallible and uninspired men, have assumed dominion over the faith of others, setting up their own opinions and modes of thinking as the only true and infallible and as such endeavoring to impose them on others, have established and maintained false religions over the greatest part of the world, and through all time; that to compel a man to furnish contributions of money for the propagation of opinions which he disbelieves, is sinful and tyrannical, and even the forcing him to support this or that teacher of his own religious persuasion, is depriving him of the comfortable liberty of giving his contributions to the particular pastor whose morals he would make his pattern, and whose powers he feels most persuasive to righteousness, and is withdrawing from the ministry those temporary rewards which, proceeding from an approbation of their personal conduct, are an additional incitement to earnest and unremitting labors, for the instruction of mankind; that our civil rights have no dependence on our religious opinions any more than our opinions in physics or geometry; that therefore the proscribing any citizen as unworthy of the public confidence by laying upon him an incapacity of being called to offices of trust and emolument, unless he profess or renounce this or that religious opinion, is depriving him injuriously of those privileges and advantages to which, in common with his fellow citizens, he has a natural right; that it tends only to corrupt the principles of that religion it is meant to encourage, by bribing, with a monopoly of worldly honors and emoluments, those who will externally profess and conform to it; that though indeed, those are criminal who do not withstand such temptation, yet, neither are those innocent who lay the bait in their way; that to suffer the civil magistrate to intrude his powers into the field of opinion, and to restrain the profession or propagation of principles on supposition of their ill tendency, is a dangerous fallacy, which at once destroys all religious liberty, because he, being of course judge of that tendency, will make his opinions the rules of judgment, and approve or condemn the sentiments of others only as they shall square with or differ from his own; that it is time enough for the rightful purposes of civil government, for its officers to interfere, when principles break out into overt acts against peace and good order; and finally, that truth is great and will prevail, if left to herself; that she is the proper and sufficient antagonist to error, and has nothing to fear from the conflict, unless by human interposition disarmed of her natural weapons, free argument and debate; errors ceasing to be dangerous when it is permitted freely to contradict them:

Be it enacted by the General Assembly, that no man shall be compelled to frequent or support any religious worship, place or ministry whatsoever, nor shall he otherwise suffer on account of his religious opinions or belief; but that all men shall be free to profess, and by argument to maintain, their opinions in matters of religion, and that the same shall in no wise diminish, enlarge or affect their civil capacities.

And though we well know that this Assembly, elected by the people for the ordinary purposes of legislation only, have no power to restrain the acts of succeeding assemblies constituted with powers equal to our own, and that, therefore, to declare this act to be irrevocable would be of no effect in law; yet we are free to declare, and do declare, that the rights hereby asserted are of the natural rights of mankind; and that if any act shall be hereafter passed to repeal the present, or to narrow its operation, such act will be an infringement of natural right.

6. Daniel Shays and Followers Declare Their Intent to Protect Themselves Against "Tyranny," 1787

Pelham, January 15th, 1787.

Sir,

According to undoubted intelligence received from various parts of this Commonwealth, it is determined by the Governour and his adherents, not only to support the Court of Common Please and General Sessions of the Peace, to be holden at Worcester next week, by point of sword, but to crush the power of the people at one bold stroke, and render them incapable of ever opposing the cruel power, Tyranny, hereafter, by bringing those who have stepped forth to ward off the evil that threatens the people with immediate ruin, to an unconditional submission, and their leaders with an infamous punishment. Notwithstanding it is thought prudent, by a number of officers and others, convened at Pelham on the 15th Jan.... to consult on the exigencies of the present times, that the people of the country of Hampshire immediately assemble in arms, to support and maintain, not only the rights and liberties of the people, since our opponents, by their hasty movement, refuse to give opportunity to wait the effect of their prayers and petitions. This is therefore to desire you to assemble the company under your command, well armed and equipped, with ten days provision, and march there in season, to be at or near Dr. Hind's in Pelham, by Friday the 19th instant, there to receive further orders.

(Signed)

D. Shays
J. Powers
R. Dickinson
J. Bordwell
J. Billings

The Worchester Magazine (1787)
http://www.nps.gov/spar/historyculture/shays-reb-regulator-and-mil-docs.htm

7. *The Federalist Papers* Illustrate the Advantages of Ratification of the Constitution, 1787–1788

Factions and Their Remedy (James Madison, No. 10)

To the People of the State of New York:

Among the numerous advantages promised by a well constructed Union, none deserves to be more accurately developed than its tendency to break and control the violence of faction. The friend of popular governments, never finds himself so much alarmed for their character and fate, as when he contemplates their propensity to this dangerous vice....

By a faction I understand a number of citizens, whether amounting to a majority or minority of the whole, who are united and actuated by some common impulse of passion, or of interest, adverse to the rights of other citizens, or to the permanent and aggregate interests of the community....

The latent causes of faction are thus sown in the nature of man, and we see them every where brought into different degrees of activity, according to the different circumstances of civil society. A zeal for different opinions concerning religion, concerning Government and many other points, as well of speculation as of practice; an attachment to different leaders ambitiously contending for pre-eminence and power; or to persons of other descriptions whose fortunes have been interesting to the human passions, have in turn divided mankind into parties, inflamed them with mutual animosity, and rendered them much more disposed to vex and oppress each other, than to co-operate for their common good. So strong is this propensity of mankind to fall into mutual animosities, that where no substantial occasion presents itself, the most frivolous and fanciful distinctions have been sufficient to kindle their unfriendly passions, and excite their most violent conflicts. But the most common and durable source of factions, has been the various and unequal distribution of property.... The regulation of these various and interfering interests forms the principal task of modern Legislation, and involves the spirit of party and faction in the necessary and ordinary operations of Government....

... [A] pure Democracy, by which I mean, a Society, consisting of a small number of citizens, who assemble and administer the Government in person, can admit of no cure for the mischiefs of faction. A common passion or interest will, in almost every case, be felt by a majority of the whole; a communication and concert results from the form of Government itself; and there is nothing to check the inducements to sacrifice the weaker party, or an obnoxious individual....

A Republic, by which I mean a Government in which the scheme of representation takes place, opens a different prospect, and promises the cure for which we are seeking....

Alexander Hamilton, John Jay, and James Madison, *The Federalist Papers* (New York: Random House, 1961), Nos. 10, 51, and 69.

The two great points of difference between a Democracy and a Republic are, first, the delegation of the Government, in the latter, to a small number of citizens elected by the rest: secondly, the greater number of citizens, and greater sphere of country, over which the latter may be extended.

The effect of the first difference is, on the one hand to refine and enlarge the public views, by passing them through the medium of a chosen body of citizens, whose wisdom may best discern the true interest of their country, and whose patriotism and love of justice, will be least likely to sacrifice it to temporary or partial considerations....

... [T]he same advantage, which a Republic has over a Democracy, in controling the effects of faction, is enjoyed by a large over a small Republic —is enjoyed by the Union over the States composing it. Does this advantage consist in the substitution of Representatives, whose enlightened views and virtuous sentiments render them superior to local prejudices, and to schemes of injustice? It will not be denied, that the Representation of the Union will be most likely to possess these requisite endowments. Does it consist in the greater security afforded by a greater variety of parties, against the event of any one party being able to outnumber and oppress the rest? In an equal degree does the encreased variety of parties, comprised within the Union, encrease this security. Does it, in fine, consist in the greater obstacles opposed to the concert and accomplishment of the secret wishes of an unjust and interested majority? Here, again, the extent of the Union gives it the most palpable advantage....

In the extent and proper structure of the Union, therefore, we behold a Republican remedy for the diseases most incident to Republican Government.

The System of Checks and Balances (Alexander Hamilton or James Madison, No. 51)

To the People of the State of New York:

To what expedient, then, shall we finally resort, for maintaining in practice the necessary partition of power among the several departments, as laid down in the Constitution? The only answer that can be given is, that as all these exterior provisions are found to be inadequate, the defect must be supplied, by so contriving the interior structure of the government as that its several constituent parts may, by their mutual relations, be the means of keeping each other in their proper places....

... [T]he great security against a gradual concentration of the several powers in the same department, consists in giving to those who administer each department the necessary constitutional means and personal motives to resist encroachments of the others. The provision for defence must in this, as in all other cases, be made commensurate to the danger of attack. Ambition must be made to counteract ambition. The interest of the man must be connected with the constitutional rights of the place. It may be a reflection on human nature, that such devices should be necessary to control the abuses of government. But what is government itself, but the greatest of all reflections on human nature? If men were angels, no government would be necessary. If angels were to govern men, neither external nor internal controls on government would be necessary....

But it is not possible to give to each department an equal power of self-defence. In republican government, the legislative authority necessarily predominates. The remedy for this inconveniency is to divide the legislature into different branches.... As the weight of the legislative authority requires that it should be thus divided, the weakness of the executive may require, on the other hand, that it should be fortified....

A Defense of the Presidency (Alexander Hamilton, No. 69)

To the People of the State of New York:

I proceed now to trace the real characters of the proposed executive as they are marked out in the plan of the Convention. This will serve to place in a strong light the unfairness of the representations which have been made in regard to it....

The President of the United States would be an officer elected by the people for *four* years. The King of Great-Britain is a perpetual and *hereditary* prince. The one would be amenable to personal punishment and disgrace: The person of the other is sacred and inviolable. The one would have a *qualified* negative upon the acts of the legislative body: The other has an *absolute* negative. The one would have a right to command the military and naval forces of the nation: The other in addition to this right, possesses that of *declaring* war, and of *raising* and *regulating* fleets and armies by his own authority. The one would have a concurrent power with a branch of the Legislature in the formation of treaties: The other is the *sole possessor* of the power of making treaties. The one would have a like concurrent authority in appointing to offices: The other is the sole author of all appointments. The one can infer no privileges whatever: The other can make denizens of aliens, noblemen of commoners, can erect corporations with all the rights incident to corporate bodies. The one can prescribe no rules concerning the commerce or currency of the nation: The other is in several respects the arbiter of commerce, and in this capacity can establish markets and fairs, can regulate weights and measures, can lay embargoes for a limited time, can coin money, can authorise or prohibit the circulation of foreign coin. The one has no particle of spiritual jurisdiction: The other is the supreme head and Governor of the national church!—What answer shall we give to those who would persuade us that things so unlike resemble each other?—The same that ought to be given to those who tell us, that a government, the whole power of which would be in the hands of the elective and periodical servants of the people, is an aristocracy, a monarchy, and a despotism.

8. France Devises a New Republican Calendar, 1793

The NEW FRENCH CALENDAR for the present Year, commencing Sept. 22.

MONTHS.	ENGLISH.	AUTUMN.	TERM.		
Vindemaire	Vintage Month	from	Sept.	22 to	Oct. 21
Brumaire	Fog Month	—	Oct.	22 to	Nov. 20
Frumaire	Sleet Month	—	Nov.	21 to	Dec. 20

WINTER.

Nivos	Snow Month	—	Dec.	21 to	Jan. 19
Pluvios	Rain Month	—	Jan.	20 to	Feb. 18
Ventos	Wind Month	—	Feb.	19 to	March 20

SPRING.

Germinal	Sprouts Month	—	March	21 to	April 19
Floreal	Flowers Month	—	April	20 to	May 19
Priareal	Pasture Month	—	May	20 to	June 18

SUMMER.

Messidor	Harvest Month	—	June	19 to	July 18
Fervidor	Hot Month	—	July	19 to	Aug. 17
Fructidor	Fruit Month	—	Aug.	18 to	Sept. 16

Sans Culotides, as Feasts dedicated to

Les Vertus	The Virtues	Sept. 17.
Le Genie	Genius	Sept. 18.
Le Travail	Labour	Sept. 19.
L'Opinion	Opinion	Sept. 20.
Les Recompenses	Rewards	Sept. 21

ESSAYS

What were the main reasons for the shift from the Confederation to the Constitution? The following two essays offer differing perspectives. Alfred F. Young suggests that the push for liberty was so strong among common people and that they were seeking to enter public politics so forcefully that the constitutional framers were forced to create a stronger government but with some accommodations to "the people." Elizabeth Cobbs Hoffman views the formation of the Constitution as an early act of "foreign policy." Unsure of the relationship between the individual states and the central government, the Constitution became a template for how differing government systems could work separately and together. She believes that this was the beginning of the shift from older models of empire to a newer model of the nation as an "umpire."

An Impartial History of the Late Revolution in France (Boston, 1794), p. 496.

The Pressure of the People on the Framers
of the Constitution

ALFRED F. YOUNG

On June 18, 1787, about three weeks into the Constitutional Convention at Philadelphia, Alexander Hamilton delivered a six-hour address that was easily the longest and most conservative the Convention would hear. Gouverneur Morris, a delegate from Pennsylvania, thought it was "the most able and impressive he had ever heard."

Beginning with the premise that "all communities divide themselves into the few and the many," "the wealthy well born" and "the people," Hamilton added the corollary that the "people are turbulent and changing; they seldom judge or determine right." Moving through history, the delegate from New York developed his ideal for a national government that would protect the few from "the imprudence of democracy" and guarantee "stability and permanence": a president and senate indirectly elected for life ("to serve during good behavior") to balance a house directly elected by a popular vote every three years. This "elective monarch" would have an absolute veto over laws passed by Congress. And the national government would appoint the governors of the states, who in turn would have the power to veto any laws by the state legislatures.

If others quickly saw a resemblance in all of this to the King, House of Lords and House of Commons of Great Britain, with the states reduced to colonies ruled by royal governors, they were not mistaken. The British constitution, in Hamilton's view, remained "the best model the world has ever produced."

Three days later a delegate reported that Hamilton's proposals "had been praised by everybody," but "he has been supported by none." Acknowledging that his plan "went beyond the ideas of most members," Hamilton said he had brought it forward not "as a thing attainable by us, but as a model which we ought to approach as near as possible." When he signed the Constitution the framers finally agreed to on September 17, 1787, Hamilton could accurately say, "no plan was more remote from his own."

Why did the framers reject a plan so many admired? To ask this question is to go down a dark path into the heart of the Constitution few of its celebrants care to take. We have heard so much in our elementary and high school civics books about the "great compromises" within the Convention—between the large states and the small states, between the slaveholders and non-slaveholders, between North and South—that we have missed the much larger accommodation that was taking place between the delegates as a whole at the Convention and what they called "the people out of doors."

The Convention was unmistakably an elite body. The official exhibit for the bicentennial, "Miracle at Philadelphia," opens appropriately enough with a large

---

Alfred F. Young, "Framers of the Constitution and the 'Genius' of the People." *In These Times*, September 9–15, 1987. Reprinted by permission of In These Times.

oil portrait of Robert Morris, a delegate from Philadelphia, one of the richest merchants in America, and points out elsewhere that 11 out of 55 delegates were business associates of Morris'. The 55 were weighted with merchants, slaveholding planters and "monied men" who loaned money at interest. Among them were numerous lawyers and college graduates in a country where most men and only a few women had the rudiments of a formal education. They were far from a cross section of the four million or so Americans of that day, most of whom were farmers or artisans, fishermen or seamen, indentured servants or laborers, half of whom were women and about 600,000 of whom were African-American slaves.

I. The First Accommodation

Why did this elite reject Hamilton's plan that many of them praised? James Madison, the Constitution's chief architect, had the nub of the matter. The Constitution was "intended for the ages." To last it had to conform to the "genius" of the American people. "Genius" was a word eighteenth-century political thinkers used to mean spirit: we might say character or underlying values.

James Wilson, second only to Madison in his influence at Philadelphia, elaborated on the idea. "The British government cannot be our model. We have no materials for a similar one. Our manners, our law, the abolition of entail and primogeniture," which made for a more equal distribution of property among sons, "the whole genius of the people, are opposed to it."

This was long-range political philosophy. There was a short-range political problem that moved other realistic delegates in the same direction. Called together to revise the old Articles of Confederation, the delegates instead decided to scrap it and frame an entirely new constitution. It would have to be submitted to the people for ratification, most likely to conventions elected especially for the purpose. Repeatedly, conservatives recoiled from extreme proposals for which they knew they could not win popular support.

In response to a proposal to extend the federal judiciary into the states, Pierce Butler, a South Carolina planter, argued, "the people will not bear such innovations. The states will revolt at such encroachments." His assumption was "we must follow the example of Solomon, who gave the Athenians not the best government he could devise but the best they would receive."

The suffrage debate epitomized this line of thinking. Gouverneur Morris, Hamilton's admirer, proposed that the national government limit voting for the House to men who owned a freehold, i.e. a substantial farm, or its equivalent. "Give the vote to people who have no property and they will sell them to the rich who will be able to buy them," he said with some prescience. George Mason, author of Virginia's Bill of Rights, was aghast. "Eight or nine states have extended the right of suffrage beyond the freeholders. What will people there say if they should be disfranchised?"

Benjamin Franklin, the patriarch, speaking for one of the few times in the convention, paid tribute to "the lower class of freemen" who should not be disfranchised. James Wilson explained, "it would be very hard and disagreeable for the same person" who could vote for representatives for the state legislatures "to be excluded from a vote for this in the national legislature." Nathaniel Gorham, a Boston merchant, returned to the guiding principle: "the people will never allow" existing rights to suffrage to be abridged. "We must consult their rooted prejudices if we expect their concurrence in our propositions."

The result? Morris' proposal was defeated and the convention decided that whoever each state allowed to vote for its own assembly could vote for the House. It was a compromise that left the door open and in a matter of decades allowed states to introduce universal white male suffrage.

II. Ghosts of Years Past

Clearly there was a process of accommodation at work here. The popular movements of the Revolutionary Era were a presence at the Philadelphia Convention even if they were not present. The delegates, one might say, were haunted by ghosts, symbols of the broadly based movements elites had confronted in the making of the Revolution from 1765 to 1775, in waging the war from 1775 to 1781 and in the years since 1781 within their own states.

The first was the ghost of Thomas Paine, the most influential radical democrat of the Revolutionary Era. In 1776 Paine's pamphlet *Common Sense* (which sold at least 150,000 copies), in arguing for independence, rejected not only King George III but the principle of monarchy and the so-called checks and balances of the unwritten English constitution. In its place he offered a vision of a democratic government in which a single legislature would be supreme, the executive minimal, and representatives would be elected from small districts by a broad electorate for short terms so they could "return and mix again with the voters." John Adams considered *Common Sense* too "democratical," without even an attempt at "mixed government" that would balance "democracy" with "aristocracy."

The second ghost was that of Abraham Yates, a member of the state senate of New York typical of the new men who had risen to power in the 1780s in the state legislatures. We have forgotten him; Hamilton, who was very conscious of him, called him "an old Booby." He had begun as a shoemaker and was a self-taught lawyer and warm foe of the landlord aristocracy of the Hudson Valley which Hamilton had married into. As James Madison identified the "vices of the political system of the United States" in a memorandum in 1787, the Abraham Yateses were the number-one problem. The state legislatures had "an itch for paper money" laws, laws that prevented foreclosure on farm mortgages, and tax laws that soaked the rich. As Madison saw it, this meant that "debtors defrauded their creditors" and "the landed interest has borne hard on the mercantile interest." This, too, is what Hamilton had in mind when he spoke of the "depredations which the democratic spirit is apt to make on property" and what others meant by the "excess of democracy" in the states.

The third ghost was a very fresh one—Daniel Shays. In 1786 Shays, a captain in the Revolution, led a rebellion of debtor farmers in western

Massachusetts which the state quelled with its own somewhat unreliable militia. There were "combustibles in every state," as George Washington put it, raising the specter of "Shaysism." This Madison enumerated among the "vices" of the system as "a want of guaranty to the states against internal violence." Worse still, Shaysites in many slates were turning to the political system to elect their own kind. If they succeeded they would produce legal Shaysism, a danger for which the elites had no remedy.

The fourth ghost we can name [is] the ghost of Thomas Peters, although he had a thousand other names. In 1775, Peters, a Virginia slave, responded to a plea by the British to fight in their army and win their freedom. He served in an "Ethiopian Regiment," some of whose members bore the emblem "Liberty to Slaves" on their uniforms. After the war the British transported Peters and several thousand escaped slaves to Nova Scotia from whence Peters eventually led a group to return to Africa and the colony of Sierra Leone, a long odyssey to freedom. Eighteenth-century slaveholders, with no illusions about happy or contented slaves, were haunted by the specter of slaves in arms.

III. Elite Divisions

During the Revolutionary Era elites divided in response to these varied threats from below. One group, out of fear of "the mob" and then "the rabble in arms," embraced the British and became active Loyalists. After the war most of them went into exile. Another group who became patriots never lost their obsession with coercing popular movements.

"The mob begins to think and reason," Gouverneur Morris observed in 1774. "Poor reptiles, they bask in the sunshine and ere long they will bite." A snake had to be scotched. Other thought of the people as a horse that had to be whipped. This was coercion.

Far more important, however, were those patriot leaders who adopted a strategy of "swimming with a stream which it is impossible to stem." This was the metaphor of Robert R. Livingston, Jr., like Morris, a gentleman with a large tenanted estate in New York. Men of his class had to learn to "yield to the torrent if they hoped to direct its course."

Livingston and his group were able to shape New York's constitution, which some called a perfect blend of "aristocracy" and "democracy." John Hancock, the richest merchant in New England, had mastered this kind of politics and emerged as the most popular politician in Massachusetts. In Maryland Charles Carroll, a wealthy planter, instructed his anxious father about the need to "submit to partial losses" because "no great revolution can happen in a state without revolutions or mutations of private property. If we can save a third of our personal estate and all of our lands and Negroes, I shall think ourselves well off."

The major leaders at the Constitutional Convention in 1787 were heirs to both traditions: coercion and accommodation—Hamilton and Gouverneur Morris to the former, James Madison and James Wilson much more to the latter.

They all agreed on coercion to slay the ghosts of Daniel Shays and Thomas Peters. The Constitution gave the national government the power to "suppress insurrections" and protect the states from "domestic violence." There would be a national army under the command of the president, and authority to national-ize the state militias and suspend the right of habeas corpus in "cases of rebellion or invasion." In 1794 Hamilton, as secretary of the treasury, would exercise such powers fully (and needlessly) to suppress the Whiskey Rebellion in western Pennsylvania.

Southern slaveholders correctly interpreted the same powers as available to shackle the ghost of Thomas Peters. As it turned out, Virginia would not need a federal army to deal with Gabriel Prosser's insurrection in 1800 or Nat Turner's rebellion in 1830, but a federal army would capture John Brown after his raid at Harpers Ferry in 1859.

But how to deal with the ghosts of Thomas Paine and Abraham Yates? Here Madison and Wilson blended coercion with accommodation. They had three solutions to the threat of democratic majorities in the states.

Their first was clearly coercive. Like Hamilton, Madison wanted some kind of national veto over the state legislatures. He got several very specific curbs on the states written into fundamental law: no state could "emit" paper money or pass "laws impairing the obligation of contracts." Wilson was so overjoyed with these two clauses that he argued that if they alone "were inserted in the Consti-tution I think they would be worth our adoption."

But Madison considered the overall mechanism adopted to curb the states "short of the mark." The Constitution, laws and treaties were the "su-preme law of the land" and ultimately a federal court could declare state laws unconstitutional. But this, Madison lamented, would only catch "mischiefs" after the fact. Thus they had clipped the wings of Abraham Yates but he could still fly.

The second solution to the problem of the states was decidedly democratic. They wanted to do an end-run around the state legislatures. The Articles of Confederation, said Madison, rested on "the pillars" of the state legislatures who elected delegates to Congress. The "great fabric to be raised would be more stable and durable if it should rest on the solid grounds of the people themselves"; hence, there would be popular elections to the House.

Wilson altered only the metaphor. He was for "raising the federal pyramid to a considerable altitude and for that reason wanted to give it as broad a base as possible." They would slay the ghost of Abraham Yates with the ghost of Thomas Paine.

This was risky business. They would reduce the risk by keeping the House of Representatives small. Under a ratio of one representative for every 30,000 people, the first house would have only 65 members; in 1776 Thomas Paine had suggested 390. But still, the House would be elected every two years, and with each state allowed to determine its own qualifications for voting, there was no telling who might end up in Congress.

There was also a risk in Madison's third solution to the problem of protect-ing propertied interests from democratic majorities: "extending the sphere" of government. Prevailing wisdom held that a republic could only succeed in a small geographic area; to rule an "extensive" country, some kind of despotism was considered inevitable.

Madison turned this idea on its head in his since famous *Federalist* essay No. 10. In a small republic, he argued, it was relatively easy for a majority to gang up on a particular "interest." "Extend the sphere," he wrote, and "you take in a greater variety of parties and interests." Then it would be more difficult for a majority "to discover their own strength and to act in unison with each other."

This was a prescription for a non-colonial empire that would expand across the continent, taking in new states as it dispossessed the Indians. The risk was there was no telling how far the "democratic" or "leveling" spirit might go in such likely would-be states as frontier Vermont, Kentucky and Tennessee.

IV. Democratic Divisions

In the spectrum of state constitutions adopted in the Revolutionary era, the federal Constitution of 1787 was, like New York's, somewhere between "aristocracy" and "democracy." It therefore should not surprise us—although it has eluded many modern critics of the Constitution—that in the contest over ratification in 1787–88, the democratic minded were divided.

Among agrarian democrats there was a gut feeling that the Constitution was the work of an old class enemy. "These lawyers and men of learning and monied men," argued Amos Singletary, a working farmer at the Massachusetts ratifying convention, "expect to be managers of this Constitution and get all the power and all the money into their own hands and then will swallow up all of us little folks ... just as the whale swallowed up Jonah."

Democratic leaders like Melancton Smith of New York focused on the small size of the proposed House. Arguing from Paine's premise that the members of the legislature should "resemble those they represent," Smith feared that "a substantial yeoman of sense and discernment will hardly ever be chosen" and the government "will fall into the hands of the few and the great." Urban democrats, on the other hand, including a majority of the mechanics and tradesmen of the major cities who in the Revolution had been a bulwark of Paineite radicalism, were generally enthusiastic about the Constitution. They were impelled by their urgent stake in a stronger national government that would advance ocean-going commerce and protect American manufacturers from competition. But they would not have been as ardent about the new frame of government without its saving graces. It clearly preserved their rights to suffrage. And the process of ratification, like the Constitution itself, guaranteed them a voice. As early as 1776 the New York Committee of Mechanics held it as "a right which God has given them in common with all men to judge whether it be consistent with their interest to accept or reject a constitution."

Mechanics turned out en masse in the parades celebrating ratification, marching trade by trade. The slogans and symbols they carried expressed their political ideals. In New York the upholsterers had a float with an elegant

"Federal Chair of State" flanked by the symbols of Liberty and Justice that they identified with the Constitution. In Philadelphia the bricklayers put on their banner "Both buildings and rulers are the work of our hands."

Democrats who were skeptical found it easier to come over because of the Constitution's redeeming features. Thomas Paine, off in Paris, considered the Constitution "a copy, though not quite as base as the original, of the form of the British government." He had always opposed a single executive and he objected to the "long duration of the Senate." But he was so convinced of "the absolute necessity" of a stronger federal government that "I would have voted for it myself had I been in America or even for a worse, rather than have none." It was crucial to Paine that there was an amending process, the means of "remedying its defects by the same appeal to the people by which it was to be established."

V. The Second Accommodation

In drafting the Constitution in 1787 the framers, self-styled Federalists, made their first accommodation with the "genius" of the people. In campaigning for its ratification in 1788 they made their second. At the outset, the conventions in the key states—Massachusetts, New York and Virginia—either had an anti-Federalist majority or were closely divided. To swing over a small group of "antis" in each state, Federalists had to promise that they would consider amendments. This was enough to secure ratification by narrow margins in Massachusetts, 187 to 168; in New York, 30 to 27; and in Virginia, 89 to 79.

What the anti-Federalists wanted were dozens of changes in the structure of the government that would cut back national power over the states, curb the powers of the presidency as well as protect individual liberties. What they got was far less. But in the first Congress in 1789, James Madison, true to his pledge, considered all the amendments and shepherded 12 amendments through both houses. The first two of these failed in the states; one would have enlarged the House. The 10 that were ratified by December 1791 were what we have since called the Bill of Rights, protecting freedom of expression and the rights of the accused before the law. Abraham Yates considered them "trivial and unimportant." But other democrats looked on them much more favorably. In time the limited meaning of freedom of speech in the First Amendment was broadened far beyond the framers' original intent. Later popular movements thought or the Bill of Rights as an essential part of the "constitutional" and "republican" rights that belonged to the people.

VI. The "Losers'" Role

There is a cautionary tale here that surely goes beyond the process of framing and adopting the Constitution and Bill of Rights from 1787 to 1791. The Constitution was as democratic as it was because of the influence of popular movements that were a presence, even if not present. The losers helped shape the results. We owe the Bill of Rights to the opponents of the Constitution, as we do many other features in the Constitution put in to anticipate opposition.

In American history popular movements often shaped elites, especially in times of crisis when elites were concerned with the "system." Elites have often divided in response to such threats and according to their perception of the "genius" of the people. Some have turned in coercion, others to accommodation. We run serious risk if we ignore this distinction. Would that we had fewer Gouverneur Morrises and Alexander Hamiltons and more James Madison, and James Wilsons to respond to the "genius" of the people.

Making an American Umpire in the Presence of European Empires

ELIZABETH COBBS HOFFMAN

In a peculiar way, Americans' first foreign alliances—and thus their first foreign relations—were with one another. After the colonies collectively declared independence, each wrote and adopted a separate constitution. They knew they would have to stick together to resist Britain's fearsome opposition, so they also passed the Articles of Confederation. This document created a permanent body to replace the emergency assemblies that had been called in 1774 and 1775 as the First and Second Continental Congresses. The resulting federation could make recommendations to the sovereign states but had no power over them or their citizens. It could not impose one penny in taxes, or regulate one item of commerce. It had no executive or judiciary. Any change to its charter required the unanimous approval of the member states. They were more like thirteen countries than one.

It took seven bloody years for the thirteen states to achieve their independence. But once the revolutionaries climbed that peak they saw another range of obstacles stretching out before them. Within a few short years, the states combined forces even more firmly and placed what they called a "general government" over their heads. To achieve this they wrestled with age-old tensions between nation and empire how to maintain state autonomy while reaping the advantages of belonging to a larger confederacy.

In 1789, they cobbled together the valuable traits they saw in both nations and empires, creating a hybrid. They fashioned a republic of republics. At the top was an elected government that could act, when necessary, as an "umpire" between political contestants and "compel acquiescence"—to use their terms. It was not an empire for the reason that participant states joined voluntarily and ruled collaboratively. They were not victors or victims of conquest. This atypical, often awkward arrangement gave Americans experience with the notion that one might have dual citizenship in both the state and nation, and that one government could yield to a more powerful one above it without losing dignity. The prerogatives that the federal government ultimately assumed—to reach across state borders to punish or protect individuals, and even to overrule the laws of states themselves—were the subject of ongoing controversy. They evolved gradually. Some of the founders did not get as powerful a central government as they initially wished for (and later regretted, in the case of James Madison). But passage of the Constitution propelled the federal government down the road toward "umpire."

Europe then had nothing comparable. No higher authority could discipline the governments of, say, England or France, or arrest its citizens for a crime. Indeed, for more than a century, since 1648, Europeans had emphatically rejected any authority superior to the nation-state. Consequently, Americans developed a different feel for sovereignty from that of their cousins across the Atlantic. They became willing to grant at least some powers to an overarching government. Interventionism across state borders, in extremis became acceptable. Each generation became more accustomed to the arrangement. By the end of the first century, they even spoke of themselves differently: as *the* United States, not *these* United States.

The American constitutional experiment was a fork in the road. In the far future, this path led to the United Nations and the European Union. But to a greater extent than the nations that joined these later bodies, perhaps because of their longer historical experience with dual sovereignty, Americans came to accept the exercise of a higher power as sometimes "necessary and proper." They recognized the importance of an umpire, first for themselves in their domestic arrangements, and then in their international relationships.

Although it is natural to fix U.S. history on a grid marked by milestones like the founding of Jamestown or the Revolution, this can be like walking into the middle of a conversation. As historian Daniel Rodgers observes: "Every serious reader of the past instinctively knows … that nations lie enmeshed in each others' history. Even the most isolated of nation-states is a semipermeable container, washed over by forces originating far beyond its shores."…

Once independence was achieved, the challenges of acting cooperatively became even greater. The states soon found that the provisions governing their relations were too loose for effective coordination. Like European countries, their economic and political interests frequently clashed. They were thirteen different republics, each with its own constitution, administration, and militia. Any and all decisions concerning their common affairs, from the mundane to the extraordinary, had to pass through a fractious, unicameral Congress that in theory could adjourn at any time, for up to six months each year. Every state had the power to recall its delegation at will, though none did.

Meanwhile, bilateral relations among the states were equally tortured. State governments relied on tariffs for revenue. Within a couple of years of independence, each was slapping taxes on goods that crossed state borders. Mercantile New York was a principal offender, as was Connecticut, which placed a 5 percent duty on numerous items "imported" from its neighbors. Massachusetts,

New Jersey, Rhode Island, and Vermont reacted angrily to taxes against which they had little power of retaliation and that made their products more expensive and thus harder to sell. By 1785, most tariffs within the confederation were aimed not at external competitors like Great Britain, but at rival sister states.

The problems were evident to no one more than George Washington, the retired military leader who had given the colonies their victory. He had planned to enjoy his remaining years at his pastoral overlook on the broad Potomac. The troops had sent him off with tears and huzzahs. He had said good-bye to governing anything but his own plantation. But the failings of the Confederacy—which proved unable to collect revenue, pay its foreign debt, or resolve tariff feuds—were apparent even from his rural retreat. Washington's generation had made a revolution, but not a government. "We are either a united people under one head, and for federal purposes; or we are thirteen independent sovereignties, eternally counteracting each other," Washington wrote in 1785 to James McHenry, a Scotch-Irish physician who had served in the general's small so-called family of adjutants during the war. How could the United States effectively defend or represent itself in the world, the general worried, when "we are one nation today, & thirteen tomorrow"? The new country needed some kind of higher authority to settle the states' competing claims. It needed an umpire.

The defeated British gloated over the Confederation's incompetence. They treated U.S. minister John Adams with ill-disguised contempt. "An ambassador from America! Good heavens what a sound!" sneered one London newspaper. The London government refused to appoint an opposite number to America, eschewing normal diplomatic reciprocity. As one wag queried, should Whitehall send one minister to the Continental Congress, or thirteen? Meanwhile, brazen Redcoats continued to occupy seven of their old forts on U.S. land in the northwest. Four years had flown by since victory at Yorktown, and yet the British still had not withdrawn their troops from American soil. And who was going to make them leave? The Continental Congress did not have a functional army, most of its men having gone into retirement along with George Washington. When Minister John Adams asked the British government to evacuate American territory, the letter he mailed—just across London—went unanswered for three months, after which the request was simply denied. If the United States could not defend its/their Westphalian sovereignty, it/they would not enjoy the perquisites. Was the United States a singular entity, or a plural one?

The Spanish Empire also bullied the United States with little fear for the consequences. In 1784 Spain closed the mouth of the Mississippi River to American ships. The United States had no recourse. What navy or army would enforce American claims to the right of passage on an international waterway? The cash-poor Congress had sold its last naval ship to a private buyer in 1785. The army had shrunk to 700 soldiers. States that did not border the Mississippi were hardly eager to hazard their militias or spend their own limited funds to liberate the river for the benefit of other governments. New Yorker John Jay, asked by Congress to reason with Spain, found that the best deal he could wangle was the right to trade in Spanish colonial ports, if Americans promised to stay off the Mississippi. To those looking or heading west, Jay's willingness to even entertain such an insulting offer was treachery. Others were willing to grant Jay's good intentions but feared that such a compromise would lead westerners to secede from the union. And who, Thomas Jefferson asked rhetorically, would be willing to "cut the throats of their own brothers and sons" to make them stay?...

The [constitutional] proceedings were confidential, to minimize outside interference and protect the delegates' freedom to speak candidly. But the demand for transparency was becoming engrained and assuming a life of its own. To those not invited, confidentiality seemed a cloak for conspiracy. Meetings of the Continental Congress before, during, and after the Revolutionary War had also occurred behind closed doors, yet their proceedings were published monthly, while decision making was still in progress. The reticence in 1787 to air the debates of the Philadelphia convention prior to revealing its finished product now seemed unreasonable. Mercy Otis Warren, a well-known playwright and close friend of John Adams, noted from a firsthand perspective that "it was thought by some, who had been recently informed of the secret transactions of the convention at Philadelphia, that the greatest happiness of the greatest number was not the principal object of their contemplations, when they ordered their doors to be locked, their members inhibited from all communication abroad, and when proposals were made that their journals should be burnt, lest their consultations and debates should be viewed by the scrutinizing eye of a free people."

Yet as controversial as the proceedings were, and as rickety as the Confederation had become, what is most remarkable is the degree of cooperation that the revolutionaries were willing to consider. After the Peace of Westphalia, European governments rejected *any* limits on their internal freedom of action, and they competed constantly for territory. In contrast, despite contentious discussions over how much sovereignty to cede, representatives to the convention in 1787 drafted a constitution for a "general" or "federal" government. They entertained proposals for a type of "umpire" to guide compromise.

This was not an easy process. Rhode Island had refused to send a representative to the Constitutional Convention, so opposed was it to giving Congress any additional powers. Other states sent delegates who felt much the same. New York's representatives (with the singular exception of Alexander Hamilton) objected to any proposal that led to "the consolidation of the United States into one government"—revealing that in their eyes the United States was not a single country, but merely a coalition (a "they" rather than an "it"). Across the long, hot, humid Philadelphia summer, the delegates debated the future structure of a general government that not everyone agreed ought to exist.

Diminutive, bookish James Madison, often called the Father of the Constitution, was one of the participants most ambitious for its powers (at least until he became leader of the opposition during George Washington's first administration). Madison hoped that the new government would have a blanket veto: "A negative *in all cases whatsoever* on the legislative acts of the States, as heretofore exercised by the Kingly prerogative." Madison was not arguing for a king, but for what he explicitly called a "dispassionate umpire in disputes"—a higher government to which the states would send representatives and that would, in an ambiguous sense, rule over them. Here Madison was wrestling with the conflict between post-Westphalian autonomy and imperial-level coordination. America needed parts of Roman government and parts of Tudor government. The "individual independence of the States is utterly irreconcilable" with their functionality as "an aggregate sovereignty," he wrote George Washington at Mount Vernon, but neither did anyone want "consolidation of the whole into one simple republic." So, as he explained to both Washington and Edmund Randolph, "I have sought some middle ground."

Other delegates at the Constitutional Convention in Philadelphia thought even this middle ground was too close to tyranny, and they voted seven states to three against Madison's proposal to create a veto. However, they did devise a Supreme Court, which left the door open for judicial review of state laws to ensure compliance with the national constitution. In essence, the court would exercise a veto over state laws when necessary. In the end, after a seventeen-week marathon, the weary delegates placed their signatures on a document that also provided for an elected chief executive (the president) and a bicameral legislature. The Senate would give equal representation to every state (preserving the Westphalian principle that *all sovereign states are equal*), while the House of Representatives would give local delegations greater or lesser weight in relation to population size. If passed, the proposal would bind the separate states more tightly than ever before, inexorably diminishing their sovereignty in order to elevate the national authority....

Federalists painted a benevolent face on the hoped-for higher government. James Madison used the term "compound republic," and emphasized a division of powers balanced against one another to prevent tyranny. Tellingly, the founders sometimes called the proposed general government an umpire, other times an empire.

Then as now, "empire" was an elusive term. The founding generation used it casually, but always to indicate the thirteen states acting cooperatively. When George Washington retired at the end of the Revolutionary War, the citizens of Richmond welcomed him back to the bosom of his "native country" (Virginia) while thanking him for his exertions on behalf of the "Empire" (the United States). In conversations about where to establish a permanent capital, General Washington called the proposed home of congress the "seat of Empire." Before the Constitutional Convention, when it seemed John Jay was willing to exchange the use of the Mississippi for access to Spain's colonial ports, James Madison was outraged that the New Yorker would barter away "the interests of one part of the empire" to serve the interests of yet another.

But whenever the founders used the term "empire," they clearly viewed their experimental union as different in kind from all preceding empires. It would borrow from Rome in that it would coordinate and protect, but its members would join voluntarily and rule democratically. It would have no hereditary aristocracy, nor any subjects who were not also full citizens. (Of course, they conveniently ignored the hypocrisy in their treatment of slaves, Indians, and women, who obtained full civil rights only much later.) It would differ from Rome by eschewing conquest. Under the Northwest Ordinance of 1787, the original thirteen had already declined to keep any superior voting privileges for themselves if joined by new members. They again rejected special privileges for themselves at the Constitutional Convention. Unlike empires of old, the American union would defend the rights and integrity of individual states, rather than robbing them. Yet, akin to Henry VIII's England, America would also be, in some ways, one country—an "empire unto itself." As Alexander Hamilton averred, it would be "an empire in many respects the most interesting in the world." The revolutionary United States was not alone in thinking of itself this way. When Hairi declared independence from France just a few years later, the new Caribbean nation also described itself as an "empire of liberty."…

The founders also freely used the term "umpire," found in the writings of Washington, Jefferson, Madison, Hamilton, Jay, and others with reference to the proposed federal government. Although the traditional English sport of cricket then employed umpires, what the founders meant was a decisive power in politics. The term dated to the Middle Ages, from the Middle French word *nonper,* meaning without *(non)* peer *(per).* An umpire was someone with the power to resolve disputes between contending parties. An umpire stood apart and was supposed to be an impartial higher authority with no stake in the outcome—an odd man out, so to speak. Umpires could even be coercive. In 1718, English poet Nicholas Rowe lyrically wrote that, in battle, "The Sword is now the Umpire to decide." But James Madison's allusion was more typical: what better "umpires could be desired by two violent factions," he wrote, than peaceful representatives in congress from states "not heated by the local flame?" Empire and umpire thus had overlapping meanings, as a metaphor for a supreme decision-making power above sovereign states.…

Americans muddled "empire," "umpire," "state," and "nation" so that they could have government both ways: sovereignty at the state level to maintain their freedom from distant rulers, combined with a superior sovereign to compel peaceable coordination. It was not a program for future expansion but one to deal with expansion retroactively. James Madison and Thomas Jefferson would be among the first to challenge the authority of the United States government in following years. The Civil War would try the full extent of its power. Yet the founders did not mean "empire" in the way it is sometimes employed today in reference to the founders' vision. They aimed at *internal* coherence, not at dominance over populations beyond America's political boundaries.

Although it is easily forgotten centuries later, the original thirteen states were most internationalistic not with respect to foreign countries but with respect to relations among themselves. The trust they gradually and grudgingly extended to one another was extraordinary. It was soon sorely tested.

 FURTHER READING

Akhil Reed Amar, *America's Constitution: A Biography* (2005).

Richard Beeman, *Plain, Honest Men: The Making of the American Constitution* (2009).

Richard Beeman et al., *Beyond Confederation: Origins of the Constitution and American National Identity* (1987).

George Athan Billias, *American Constitutionalism Heard round the World, 1776–1989: A Global Perspective* (2009).

Catherine Drinker Bowen, *Miracle at Philadelphia: The Story of the Constitutional Convention* (1986).

Saul Cornell, *The Other Founders: Anti-Federalism and the Dissenting Tradition in America, 1788–1828* (1999).

Woody Holton, *Unruly Americans and the Origins of the Constitution* (2008).

Forrest McDonald, *Novus Ordo Seclorum: The Intellectual Origins of the Constitution* (1985).

Jack Rakove, *Original Meanings: Politics and Ideas in the Making of the Constitution* (1996).

Additional critical thinking activities and content are available in MindTap.

MindTap

MindTap is a fully online, highly personalized learning experience built upon Cengage Learning content. MindTap combines student learning tools—readings, multimedia, activities, and assessments—into a singular Learning Path that guides students through the course.

CHAPTER 6

Nation Among Nations

The first president, by unanimous vote in the electoral college, was George Washington, war hero and patriot. Washington's inauguration, which evoked among the people a feeling of pride in the nation's revolutionary past and hope for its future, ushered in a brief period of political unity. The nationalist spirit was evident in the first session of Congress, which succeeded in passing a series of key measures. The Constitution had not defined the structure of the federal judiciary, but Congress acted quickly, passing the Judiciary Act of 1789, which established judicial procedures and lower federal courts. Next, Congress imposed a tariff on imported goods to provide the federal government with revenue. Finally, as promised during the ratification debate, Congress passed the Bill of Rights, ten constitutional amendments that were sent to the states for ratification. Following ratification, Americans were guaranteed freedoms of speech and religion and given rights to bear arms and avoid "cruel and unusual punishments."

Yet the unity was short-lived. Within a few years, the national government was divided into two political factions with different visions for the future of the United States. The two principal protagonists of these visions were Thomas Jefferson and Alexander Hamilton, both of whom served in Washington's cabinet. Hamilton dreamed of transforming the United States into a manufacturing giant like Britain. America, he was fond of saying, was "a Hercules in the cradle." Hamilton was also suspicious of the people—he considered the masses "turbulent and changing"—and believed the government would be strong if it won the favor of the financial elite. In contrast, Jefferson feared the growth of manufacturing because he sensed that it would decrease the citizenry's independence. His vision focused on a nation of commercial agriculture and independent farmers; virtue, he argued, was best maintained by those "who labor in the earth."

The divisions between Jefferson and Hamilton deepened when the United States was pulled into a European conflict in the 1790s. After the French Revolution unraveled into unparalleled bloodshed, France declared war on Britain, Spain, and Holland. Whereas Jefferson and his followers saw the French Revolution as heir to the American War for Independence, the people who shared Hamilton's views watched it with horror as the revolution spun out of control. Out of these differences, political groups began to coalesce. Those sympathetic to the French and fearful of Hamilton's vision formed Democratic-Republican societies. In response, another group, led by Hamilton, Washington, and John Adams, united under the Federalist banner. Acrimonious political battles and vitriolic debate became commonplace in the late 1790s. After John Adams was elected to succeed Washington, the divisions deepened as the United States became further embroiled in European conflicts and nearly went to war against France.

At the same time, these factions-becoming-parties had to contend with and articulate their relationship to Native American nations and empires. Alliances and struggles with European powers not only carried Americans to problems across the Atlantic Ocean, but also into contests on the North American interior. There, the United States and its citizens ran up against newly powerful Native American "empires," such as the Comanche.

Adams's failures as president almost guaranteed a Democratic-Republican victory in 1800, and Jefferson heralded his election as the "revolution of 1800." Although this was undoubtedly an overstatement, his ascension to the presidency is noteworthy because the Federalists peacefully handed over their power to a hated rival. Never again would the Federalist Party control the presidency or Congress. Nonetheless, the Federalist vision endured particularly in the judiciary. The competing visions of national development, moreover, would continue to divide American society as Americans puzzled over the future of their young nation.

QUESTIONS TO THINK ABOUT

Whose vision of America's future, Jefferson's or Hamilton's, is most appealing to you? Whose vision was most fully realized? What places emerged for women in this new nation? Was the United States active in building itself or reactive in response to other nations and peoples? How did Federalists and Democratic-Republicans represent and misrepresent one another?

DOCUMENTS

Document 1 details the overthrow of Spanish rule by the Comanche before the American Revolution. As Americans moved west, it would be this empire they would encounter. In document 2, Thomas Jefferson argues that the future of the United States is best left in the hands of the yeoman farmers, who will retain their virtue and industry. Judith Sargent Murray calls for "the Equality of the Sexes" in document 3. A friend of Abigail Adams's, Murray hoped that gender equality could be a part of the new republic. Alexander Hamilton provides his vision of national development in document 4, which is in marked contrast to that of Jefferson's. Hamilton hopes to create an American economy that would look like Great Britain's, one based on manufacturing. The next four documents illustrate the factional conflict that resulted from these very different visions of the direction of national development. In document 5, "A Peep into the Antifederal Club," a Federalist cartoonist depicts the Democratic-Republicans as unruly and pompous. Their charter reads, "The People are All/and we are the People." Document 6 is a resolution secretly written by Jefferson for the state of Kentucky in response to a series of laws known as the Alien and Sedition Acts. In this resolution, Jefferson argues that the states have the right to say when Congress has exceeded its powers. Document 7 is the ruling by Chief Justice John Marshall that states that the Constitution is paramount law. The victory of Thomas Jefferson in the presidential election of 1800 is the subject of document 8. In it, Jefferson's supporters trumpet their reasons for voting for him.

1. A Spanish Soldier Describes the Comanche Destruction of the San Saba Mission in Texas, 1758

… The Sergeant was asked then why he had not tried to reach the Mission by some other route, instead of the one occupied by the hostile Indians. He said: There is a canyon between the hillsides and the river, and his party was caught in it when the enemy opened fire. The squadron became disorganized, and only one soldier, Joseph Vázquez, was able to slip through the barbarians to the shelter of the woods along the river bank, and he made his way as best he could by unobstructed paths. The witness declared that he and his soldiers would have put up a stronger resistance if the enemy had been armed only with bows and arrows, for the Spaniards were accustomed to fighting Indians armed with less powerful weapons [than muskets] and were able to protect themselves against arrows by means of their leather jerkins and shields, but they were helpless against the accurate musket fire of the Indian barbarians. The Sergeant expressed regret that there was no force in the Presidio able to prevail against a strong body of the enemy equipped with the same weapons as ours, and very cunning and treacherous besides. He was asked whether, in his 30 years in the King's service, in the presidios and on the frontiers, he had ever before seen so many hostile Indians equipped with firearms and so skilled in their use as those he encountered on his way to the Mission. He replied that he had never seen or heard of hostile Indians attacking our forces in such numbers and so fully armed. Formerly the barbarians had fought with arrows, pikes, hatchets, and similar weapons, against which the officers and soldiers of the presidios had held the advantage and had won many victories: at the Presidio of San Antonio del Río Grande, for example, and elsewhere. At the same time our forces had endured much suffering and many deaths at the hands of the savage barbarians, who did not spare the lives of the religious, or those of the women and children. Nor did they spare the buildings and workshops, which they burned to the ground.

In Leslie Byrd Simpson, ed., *The San Saba Papers: A Documentary Account of the Founding and Destruction of the San Saba Mission* (San Francisco: John Howell Books, 1959), 52–3.

2. Republican Thomas Jefferson Celebrates the Virtue of the Yeoman Farmer, 1785

In Europe the lands are either cultivated, or locked up against the cultivator. Manufacture must therefore be resorted to of necessity not of choice, to support the surplus of their people. But we have an immensity of land courting the industry of the husbandman. Is it best then that all our citizens should be employed in its improvement, or that one half should be called off from that to exercise manufactures and handicraft arts for the other? Those who labor in the earth are the chosen people of God, if ever He had a chosen people, whose breasts He has made His peculiar deposit for substantial and genuine virtue. It is the focus in which he keeps alive that sacred fire, which otherwise might escape from the face of the earth. Corruption of morals in the mass of cultivators is a phenomenon of which no age nor nation has furnished an example. It is the mark set on those, who, not looking up to heaven, to their own soil and industry, as does the husbandman, for their subsistence, depend for it on casualties and caprice of customers. Dependence begets subservience and venality, suffocates the germ of virtue, and prepares fit tools for the designs of ambition. This, the natural progress and consequence of the arts, has sometimes perhaps been retarded by accidental circumstances; but, generally speaking, the proportion which the aggregate of the other classes of citizens bears in any State to that of its husbandmen, is the proportion of its unsound to its healthy parts, and is a good enough barometer whereby to measure its degree of corruption. While we have land to labor then, let us never wish to see our citizens occupied at a workbench, or twirling a distaff. Carpenters, masons, smiths, are wanting in husbandry; but, for the general operations of manufacture, let our workshops remain in Europe. It is better to carry provisions and materials to workmen there, than bring them to the provisions and materials, and with them their manners and principles. The loss by the transportation of commodities across the Atlantic will be made up in happiness and permanence of government. The mobs of great cities add just so much to the support of pure government, as sores do to the strength of the human body.

3. Judith Sargent Murray Argues for the "Equality of the Sexes," 1790

Is it upon mature consideration we adopt the idea, that nature is thus partial in her distributions? Is it indeed a fact, that she hath yielded to one half of the human species so unquestionable a mental superiority? I know that to both sexes elevated understandings, and the reverse, are common. But, suffer me to ask, in what the minds of females are so notoriously deficient, or unequal. May not the

Thomas Jefferson, "Notes on the State of Virginia" (1785), in *The Life and Selected Writings of Thomas Jefferson*, eds. Adrienne Koch and William Peden (New York: Library of America, 1984), 280.

Judith Sargent Murray, *On the Equality of the Sexes*. http://digital.library.upenn.edu/women/murray/equality/equality.html.

intellectual powers be ranged under these four heads—imagination, reason, memory, and judgment. The province of imagination hath long since been surrendered to us, and we have been crowned and undoubted sovereigns of the regions of fancy. Invention is perhaps the most arduous effort of the mind; this branch of imagination hath been particularly ceded to us, and we have been time out of mind invested with that creative faculty. Observe the variety of fashions (here I bar the contemptuous smile) which distinguish and adorn the female world: how continually are they changing, insomuch that they almost render the wise man's assertion problematical, and we are ready to say, *there is something new under the sun....* Perhaps it will be asked if I furnish these facts as instances of excellency in our sex. Certainly not; but as proofs of a creative faculty, of a lively imagination. Assuredly great activity of mind is thereby discovered, and was this activity properly directed, what beneficial effects would follow. Is the needle and kitchen sufficient to employ the operations of a soul thus organized? I should conceive not, Nay, it is a truth that those very departments leave the intelligent principle vacant, and at liberty for speculation....

Meantimes she herself is most unhappy; she feels the want of a cultivated mind. Is she single, she in vain seeks to fill up time from sexual employments or amusements. Is she united to a person whose soul nature made equal to her own, education hath set him so far above her, that in those entertainments which are productive of such rational felicity, she is not qualified to accompany him. She experiences a mortifying consciousness of inferiority, which embitters every enjoyment. Doth the person to whom her adverse fate hath consigned her, possess a mind incapable of improvement, she is equally wretched, in being so closely connected with an individual whom she cannot but despise.

Now, was she permitted the same instructors as her brother, (with an eye however to their particular departments) for the employment of a rational mind an ample field would be opened. In astronomy she might catch a glimpse of the immensity of the Deity, and thence she would form amazing conceptions of the august and supreme Intelligence. In geography she would admire Jehovah in the midst of his benevolence; thus adapting this globe to the various wants and amusements of its inhabitants. In natural philosophy she would adore the infinite majesty of heaven, clothed in condescension; and as she traversed the reptile world, she would hail the goodness of a creating God. A mind, thus filled, would have little room for the trifles with which our sex are, with too much justice, accused of amusing themselves, and they would thus be rendered fit companions for those, who should one day wear them as their crown....

Yes, ye lordly, ye haughty sex, our souls are by nature *equal* to yours; the same breath of God animates, enlivens, and invigorates us; and that we are not fallen lower than yourselves, let those witness who have greatly towered above the various discouragements by which they have been so heavily oppressed; and though I am unacquainted with the list of celebrated characters on either side, yet from the observations I have made in the contracted circle in which I have moved, I dare confidently believe, that from the commencement of time to the present day, there hath been as many females, as males, who, by the *mere force of natural powers*, have merited the crown of applause; who, *thus unassisted*, have seized the wreath of fame....

AND now assist me, O thou genius of my sex, while I undertake the arduous task of endeavouring to combat that vulgar, that almost universal errour.... The superiority of your sex hath, I grant, been time out of mind esteemed a truth incontrovertible; in consequence of which persuasion, every plan of education hath been calculated to establish this favourite tenet....

4. Federalist Alexander Hamilton Envisions a Developed American Economy, 1791

It is now proper to proceed a step further, and to enumerate the principal circumstances, from which it may be inferred—That manufacturing establishments not only occasion a positive augmentation of the Produce and Revenue of the Society, but that they contribute essentially to rendering them greater than they could possibly be, without such establishments. These circumstances are—

1. The division of Labour.
2. An extension of the use of Machinery.
3. Additional employment to classes of the community not ordinarily engaged in the business.
4. The promoting of emigration from foreign Countries.
5. The furnishing greater scope for the diversity of talents and dispositions which discriminate men from each other.
6. The affording a more ample and various field for enterprize.
7. The creating in some instances a new, and securing in all, a more certain and steady demand for the surplus produce of the soil.

Each of these circumstances has a considerable influence upon the total mass of industrious effort in a community. Together, they add to it a degree of energy and effect, which are not easily conceived. Some comments upon each of them, in the order in which they have been stated, may serve to explain their importance.

I. As to the Division of Labour.

It has justly been observed, that there is scarcely any thing of greater moment in the economy of a nation, than the proper division of labour. The separation of occupations causes each to be carried to a much greater perfection, than it could possible acquire, if they were blended. This arises principally from three circumstances.

1st—The greater skill and dexterity naturally resulting from a constant and undivided application to a single object....

2nd. The economy of time—by avoiding the loss of it, incident to a frequent transition from one operation to another of a different nature....

3rd. An extension of the use of Machinery. A man occupied on a single object will have it more in his power, and will be more naturally led to exert his imagination in devising methods to facilitate and abrige labour, than if he were perplexed by a variety of independent and dissimilar operations....

Alexander Hamilton, "Report on Manufactures" (1791), in *Alexander Hamilton's Papers on Public Credit, Commerce and Finance*, ed. Samuel McKee, Jr. (New York: The Liberal Arts Press, 1934), 190–192, 195–199.

II. As to an extension of the use of Machinery a point which though partly anticipated requires to be placed in one or two additional lights.

The employment of Machinery forms an item of great importance in the general mass of national industry. 'Tis an artificial force brought in aid of the natural force of man; and, to all the purposes of labour, is an increase of hands; an accession of strength, *unincumbered too by the expence of maintaining the laborer.* May it not therefore be fairly inferred, that those occupations, which give greatest scope to the use of this auxiliary, contribute most to the general Stock of industrious effort, and, in consequence, to the general product of industry?...

If there be anything in a remark often to be met with—namely that there is, in the genius of the people of this country, a peculiar aptitude for mechanic improvements, it would operate as a forcible reason for giving opportunities to the exercise of that species of talent, by the propagation of manufactures.

VI. As to the affording a more ample and various field for enterprise.

...To cherish and stimulate the activity of the human mind, by multiplying the objects of enterprise, is not among the least considerable of the expedients, by which the wealth of a nation may be promoted. Even things in themselves not positively advantageous, sometimes become so, by their tendency to provoke exertion. Every new scene, which is opened to the busy nature of man to rouse and exert itself, is the addition of a new energy to the general stock of effort.

The spirit of enterprise, useful and prolific as it is, must necessarily be contracted or expanded in proportion to the simplicity or variety of the occupations and productions, which are to be found in a Society. It must be less in a nation of mere cultivators, than in a nation of cultivators and merchants; less in a nation of cultivators and merchants, than in a nation of cultivators, artificers and merchants.

VII. As to the creating, in some instances, a new, and securing in all a more certain and steady demand, for the surplus produce of the soil....

To secure such a market, there is no other expedient, than to promote manufacturing establishments. Manufacturers who constitute the most numerous class, after the Cultivators of land, are for that reason the principal consumers of the surplus of their labour.

This idea of an extensive domestic market for the surplus produce of the soil is of the first consequence. It is of all things, that which most effectually conduces to a flourishing state of Agriculture. If the effect of manufactories should be to detatch a portion of the hands, which would otherwise be engaged in Tillage, it might possibly cause a smaller quantity of lands to be under cultivation but by their tendency to procure a more certain demand for the surplus produce of the soil, they would, at the same time, cause the lands which were in cultivation to be better improved and more productive. And while, by their influence, the condition of each individual farmer would be meliorated, the total mass of Agricultural production would probably be increased. For this must evidently depend as much, if not more, upon the degree of improvement; than upon the number of acres under culture.

It merits particular observation, that the multiplication of manufactories not only furnishes a Market for those articles, which have been accustomed to be produced in abundance, in a country; but it likewise creates a demand for such as were either unknown or produced in inconsiderable quantities. The bowels as well as the surface of the earth are ransacked for articles which were before neglected. Animals, Plants and Minerals acquire an utility and value, which were before unexplored.

The foregoing considerations seem sufficient to establish, as general propositions, That it is the interest of nations to diversify the industrious pursuits of the individuals, who compose them—That the establishment of manufactures is calculated not only to increase the general stock of useful and productive labour; but even to improve the state of Agriculture in particular; certainly to advance the interests of those who are engaged in it.

5. A Cartoonist Attacks the Degenerate French Over the XYZ Affair, 1798

"Cinque-Tetes, or the Paris Monster," a Federalist cartoon on the XYZ affair in 1798. The French government, headed by a five-man consortium known as the Directory, demands "Money, Money, Money!!" from the three American commissioners sent by President John Adams to try to end American hostilities with France. News of the affair inflamed pro-war and pro-administration opinion in America. Note the depiction on the right of the French as a bloodthirsty, poor, and degraded radical people, who would give a black man—perhaps one of the ex-slaves freed by the French republic—a place at the table for their "Civic Feast."

6. Thomas Jefferson Advances the Power of the States, 1798

1. *Resolved,* That the several States composing the United States of America, are not united on the principle of unlimited submission to their general government; but that, by a compact under the style and title of a Constitution for

Thomas Jefferson, *The Kentucky Resolutions of 1798.* Obtained from http://www.constitution.org/cons/kent/1798.htm Also available in *The Virginia and Kentucky Resolutions, with the Alien Sedition and Other Acts, 1798–1799* (New York: A. Lovell, 1894).

the United States, and of amendments thereto, they constituted a general government for special purposes—delegated to that government certain definite powers, reserving, each State to itself, the residuary mass of right to their own self-government; and that whensoever the general government assumes undelegated powers, its acts are unauthoritative, void, and of no force: that to this compact each State acceded as a State, and is an integral part, its co-States forming, as to itself, the other party: that the government created by this compact was not made the exclusive or final judge of the extent of the powers delegated to itself; since that would have made its discretion, and not the Constitution, the measure of its powers; but that, as in all other cases of compact among powers having no common judge, each party has an equal right to judge for itself, as well of infractions as of the mode and measure of redress.

2. *Resolved,* That the Constitution of the United States, having delegated to Congress a power to punish treason, counterfeiting the securities and current coin of the United States, piracies, and felonies committed on the high seas, and offenses against the law of nations, and no other crimes, whatsoever; and it being true as a general principle, and one of the amendments to the Constitution having also declared, that "the powers not delegated to the United States by the Constitution, not prohibited by it to the States, are reserved to the States respectively, or to the people," therefore the act of Congress, passed on the 14th day of July, 1798, and intituled "An Act in addition to the act intituled An Act for the punishment of certain crimes against the United States," as also the act passed by them on the—day of June, 1798, intituled "An Act to punish frauds committed on the bank of the Untied States," (and all their other acts which assume to create, define, or punish crimes, other than those so enumerated in the Constitution,) are altogether void, and of no force; and that the power to create, define, and punish such other crimes is reserved, and, of right, appertains solely and exclusively to the respective States, each within its own territory.

3. *Resolved,* That it is true as a general principle, and is also expressly declared by one of the amendments to the Constitution, that "the powers not delegated to the United States by the Constitution, nor prohibited by it to the States, are reserved to the States respectively, or to the people"; and that no power over the freedom of religion, freedom of speech, or freedom of the press being delegated to the United States by the Constitution, nor prohibited by it to the States, all lawful powers respecting the same did of right remain, and were reserved to the States or the people: that thus was manifested their determination to retain to themselves the right of judging how far the licentiousness of speech and of the press may be abridged without lessening their useful freedom, and how far those abuses which cannot be separated from their use should be tolerated, rather than the use be destroyed. And thus also they guarded against all abridgment by the United States of the freedom of religious opinions and exercises, and retained to themselves the right of protecting the same, as this State, by a law passed on the general demand of its citizens, had already protected them from all human restraint or interference.

And that in addition to this general principle and express declaration, another and more special provision has been made by one of the amendments to the Constitution, which expressly declares, that "Congress shall make no law respecting an establishment of religion, or prohibiting the free exercise thereof, or abridging the freedom of speech or of the press": thereby guarding in the same sentence, and under the same words, the freedom of religion, of speech, and of the press: insomuch, that whatever violated either, throws down the sanctuary which covers the others, and that libels, falsehood, and defamation, equally with heresy and false religion, are withheld from the cognizance of federal tribunals. That, therefore, the act of Congress of the United States, passed on the 14th day of July, 1798, intituled "An Act in addition to the act intituled An Act for the punishment of certain crimes against the United States," which does abridge the freedom of the press, is not law, but is altogether void, and of no force.

4. *Resolved,* That alien friends are under the jurisdiction and protection of the laws of the State wherein they are: that no power over them has been delegated to the United States, nor prohibited to the individual States, distinct from their power over citizens. And it being true as a general principle, and one of the amendments to the Constitution having also declared, that "the powers not delegated to the United States by the Constitution, nor prohibited by it to the States, are reserved to the States respectively, or to the people," the act of the Congress of the United States, passed on the—day of July, 1798, intituled "An Act concerning aliens," which assumes powers over alien friends, not delegated by the Constitution, is not law, but is altogether void, and of no force.

5. *Resolved,* That in addition to the general principle, as well as the express declaration, that powers not delegated are reserved, another and more special provision, inserted in the Constitution from abundant caution, has declared that "the migration or importation of such persons as any of the States now existing shall think proper to admit, shall not be prohibited by the Congress prior to the year 1808" that this commonwealth does admit the migration of alien friends, described as the subject of the said act concerning aliens: that a provision against prohibiting their migration, is a provision against all acts equivalent thereto, or it would be nugatory: that to remove them when migrated, is equivalent to a prohibition of their migration, and is, therefore, contrary to the said provision of the Constitution, and void.

7. Chief Justice John Marshall Argues for the Primacy of the Federal Government, 1803

The question whether an act repugnant to the constitution can become the law of the land, is a question deeply interesting to the United States.... That the people have an original right to establish for their future government such

John Marshall, Opinion in *Marbury v. Madison* (1803), in *United States Supreme Court Reporters,* V, 137.

principles as, in their opinion, shall most conduce to their own happiness, is the basis on which the whole American fabric has been erected....

This original and supreme will organizes the government, and assigns to different departments their respective powers. It may either stop here or establish limits not to be transcended by those departments.

The government of the United States is of the latter description. The powers of the legislature are defined and limited; and that those limits may not be mistaken or forgotten, the constitution is written.... The distinction between a government with limited and unlimited powers is abolished if those limits do not confine the persons on whom they are imposed and if acts prohibited and acts allowed are of equal obligation. It is a proposition too plain to be contested, that the constitution controls any legislative act repugnant to it; or, that the legislature may alter the constitution by an ordinary act. Between these alternatives there is no middle ground....

Certainly all those who have framed written constitutions contemplate them as forming the fundamental and paramount law of the nation, and consequently the theory of every such government must be that an act of the legislature repugnant to the Constitution is void.

This theory is essentially attached to a written constitution, and is consequently to be considered, by this court as one of the fundamental principles of our society....

The Constitution is either a superior, paramount law, unchangeable by ordinary means, or it is on a level with ordinary legislative acts, and, like other acts, is alterable when the legislature shall please to alter it.

If the former part of the alternative be true, then a legislative act contrary to the Constitution is not law: if the latter part be true, then written Constitutions are absurd attempts, on the part of the people, to limit a power in its own nature illimitable....

It is emphatically the province and duty of the judicial department to say what the law is. Those who apply the rule to particular cases, must of necessity expound and interpret that rule. If two laws conflict with each other, the courts must decide on the operation of each....

If, then, the courts are to regard the Constitution, and the Constitution is superior to any ordinary act of the legislature, the Constitution, and not such ordinary act, must govern the case to which they both apply.

8. Thomas Jefferson's Supporters Sing of His Victory, ca. 1801

Jefferson and Liberty

The gloomy night before us lies,
The reign of terror now is o'er;
Its gags, inquisitors and spies,

Jefferson and Liberty, *Thomas Jefferson's Supporters Sing of His Victory*, ca. 1801.

Its hordes of harpies are no more
    Rejoice, Columbia's sons, rejoice
    To tyrants never bend the knee
    But join with heart, and soul and voice
  For Jefferson and Liberty....

Within its hallow'd walls immense
No hireling band shall e'er arise;
Array'd in tyranny's defence,
To hear an injur'd people's cries.
    Rejoice etc.

No lordling here with gorging jaws.
Shall wring from industry its food;
No fiery bigot's holy laws,
Lay waste our fields and streets in blood.
    Rejoice etc.

Here strangers from a thousand shores
Compell'd by tyranny to roam;
Shall find, amidst abundant stores,
A nobler and a happier home.
    Rejoice etc....

From Europe's wants and woes remote
A dreary waste of waves between;
Here plenty cheers the humble cot,
And smiles on every village green.
    Rejoice etc.

Here, free as air's expanded space,
To every soul and sect shall be;
That sacred privilege of our race,
The worship of the Deity.
    Rejoice etc.

These gifts, great Liberty, are thine,
Ten thousand more we owe to thee;
Immortal may their mem'ries shine,
Who fought and died for Liberty.
    Rejoice etc.

Let foes to freedom dread the name,
But should they touch the sacred tree
Twice fifty thousand swords would flame,
For Jefferson and Liberty.
    Rejoice etc....

 ESSAYS

It is difficult for us today to understand how fragile a republic the United States was in the late eighteenth and early nineteenth centuries. Political divisions and economic weaknesses plagued the new nation, and many European powers doubted whether the United States as a nation would survive. Moreover, it is difficult to underestimate how uncertain the powers of the new nation were. The first essay by Pekka Hämäläinen emphasizes that the United States was not the only expanding nation in North America. To the West, the Comanche had overthrown Spanish authority and were creating their own economic and military empire. In this period, it was not certain which group would dominate the future. The second essay by David Waldstreicher looks not so much at what nations do but rather how they create organizing myths and rituals about themselves in order to instill a sense of nationalism. How Americans came to believe themselves as part of a "nation" and what defined that nation, Waldstreicher suggests, was just as political, partisan, and regional as were struggles over finances, federal powers, and national expansion. Together, these essays ask you to determine just how powerful and unique the young United States was and to examine the myths, symbols, and rituals of nations to see what they reveal and what they hide.

The Comanche Empire

PEKKA HÄMÄLÄINEN

Viewed broadly, the Southwest under the Comanche regime becomes a case study of alternative frontier history. From a Comanche point of view, in fact, there were no frontiers. Where contemporary Euro-Americans (as well as later historians) saw or imagined solid imperial demarcations, Comanches saw multiple opportunities for commerce, gift exchanges, pillaging, slave raiding, ransoming, adoption, tribute extracting, and alliance making. By refusing to accept the Western notion of sovereign, undivided colonial realms, they shredded Euro-American frontiers into their component parts—colonial towns, presidios, missions, ranches, haciendas, Native villages—and dealt with each isolated unit separately, often pitting their interests against one another. In the colonial Southwest, it was Comanches, not Euro-Americans, who mastered the policies of divide and rule.

Similarly, Comanches' assertive and aggressive policies toward Euro-Americans were only secondarily a borderland product. Comanches certainly benefited from their location between competing colonial regimes, but they had little in common with the Indians found in most borderland histories. Rather than marginalized people balancing between rival colonial regimes to enact minor

Excerpt from Pekka Hämäläinen, *The Comanche Empire* (New Haven: Yale University Press, 2008). Reprinted with permission from Yale University Press.

alleviations in imperial policies, Comanches were key players who often forced the would-be colonizers to compete for *their* military support and goodwill and navigate *their* initiatives and intentions. In character and logic, the eighteenth- and early nineteenth-century Southwest was unequivocally a Comanche creation, an indigenous world where intercolonial rivalries were often mere surface disturbances on the deeper, stronger undercurrent of Comanche imperialism....

Contrary to Spanish hopes, the 1762 treaty [which granted the Spanish nominal rights to the middle section of North America] did not stop Comanche expansion. At the time Comanches solidified their dominance over the grasslands east of New Mexico in the 1762 accord, the next—the third—distinctive phase of their expansion was already well on its way. In the early 1750s, with the wars of the previous expansionist phase still raging on the Llano Estacado, several Kotsoteka bands plunged south, crossing the vast table of the Edwards Plateau to the Balcones Escarpment, where the high plains dissolve into the lowlands of Texas. It was one of the most explosive territorial conquests in North American history. In less than a decade, the entire Texas plains—a huge spread of undulating hill country and plains stretching from the Pecos River in the west to the Cross Timbers in the east and from the Red River in the north to the Balcones Escarpment in the south—became a Comanche dominion. This expansionist burst turned the Comanches into a territorial superpower. The Comanchería that emerged covered some quarter of a million square miles, casting a long shadow on European imperial designs in the continent's center.

The Comanche conquest of the Texas plains was fueled by several factors. In part, it was a repeat of the familiar dynamic. A need to expand their horse-and-bison economy had driven the Comanches to grasslands around 1700 and now, half a century later, the same need pushed them into the Texas plains. By the 1750s Comanches had completed their shift to mounted hunting and nomadism and in the process drastically simplified their economy. The mounted chase became the foundation of their economy, overshadowing other subsistence strategies. Gathering decreased, eating fish became a taboo, and fowl was reduced to an emergency food eaten only when other provisions failed. But now everything hinged on their ability to keep their horse herds large and growing, and it was this imperative that drew them south. Spanish Texas was dotted with horse-rich but often poorly manned missions, presidios, and civilian ranches, which were a reasonably easy prey for mounted guerrilla attacks. An even greater incentive were innumerable wild horses roaming in the hill country just north of the Texas frontier, perhaps more than one million in all, ready to be seized and tamed.

The invasion may have also been motivated by changing geopolitics. The late 1740s witnessed the emergence of yet another anti-Comanche coalition—this time between Spanish Texas and Lipan Apaches. Since the founding of first permanent Spanish colonial settlements in San Antonio and Los Adaes in the late 1710s, Spaniards had been struggling with the

Lipans who raided Texas for the European technology they could no longer acquire from New Mexican markets. It was a consuming on-and-off raiding war, characterized by Lipan livestock poaching, Spanish reprisals, and mutual captive seizing. But in 1749, after several aborted efforts, the two sides made peace in San Antonio in a three-day ceremony, which climaxed in a ritual burial of weapons, a live horse, and the war itself. The accord was prompted by the rising Comanche threat. Lipans, who had recently incorporated large numbers of Jicarilla refugees from the north, stated during the peace talks that they wanted Spanish support and weapons to fend off the Comanche war bands that had started to infringe upon their lands. Equally alarmed by Comanche expansion, Spanish officials seized the opportunity. By arming the Lipans, they reasoned, it would be possible to create a barrier between their young colony and the expansionist Comanches. Comanches, whose hunting and scouting parties had frequented the Texas plains since the early 1740s, were probably aware of the new threat from the outset.

Finally, the Comanche sweep into the Texas plains may have been a response to a changing commercial geography. The expulsion of their Taovaya allies from the Arkansas to the Red River in the 1750s under Osage pressure prompted French traders to refocus their operations from the Arkansas channel to the lower Red River, where an important trading satellite, Fort St. Jean Baptiste aux Natchitoches, had been established in 1716. This sudden shift in commercial gravity must have been a strong incentive for Comanches to relocate south as well, for they had grown heavily dependent on the French-Taovaya trade axis, their principal source of maize, guns, and metal.

The Comanche invasion of the Texas plains unfolded on two levels—diplomatic and military. When they arrived in the Red River valley, Comanches first integrated themselves into the region's alliance network. They reestablished their trade relationship with the Taovayas, who then brought them in touch with the Tonkawas, a multiethnic group of nomadic hunters between the Colorado and Trinity rivers. Comanches also forged tentative ties with the Hasinai confederacy, the westernmost extension of Caddo people, who lived in large urban communities between the Ouachita and Neches rivers and made annual hunting excursions to the southern plains. This emerging coalition, which Spaniards would come to label as *Norteños*, was founded on shared foreign political interests. Taovayas, Tonkawas, and Hasinais—like Comanches—were alarmed by the Lipan-Spanish pact, which threatened to exclude them from Texas markets and leave them vulnerable against the Apaches. Taovayas and Hasinais were also engaged in a losing war with Lipans over hunting ranges and were eager to enlist the support of the formidable Comanches. Although Spanish officials would later blame French agents for promoting an anti-Spanish Norteño coalition, the immediate motivation for the Comanche-Taovaya-Tonkawa-Hasinai alliance was Spain's decision to ally with the Lipans at the exclusion of the other Native groups.

Thus strengthened by new allies and arms, Comanches launched in the early 1750s a systematic offensive against the Lipans. It was a near repeat of the previous Comanche-Apache wars. Like their northern relatives, Lipans had gradually taken up small-scale riverside farming, which now undermined their ability to confront the wide-ranging Comanche war parties. Fixed to their fields and short of horses—a severe drought had devastated their herds in the 1740s—the Lipans were powerless to halt the Comanche advance. In 1755 they invited the Comanches to peace talks along the Guadalupe River. The two groups "sang together and touched weapons in token of friendship," but the peace did not last. Lipans then turned to Spaniards for military support, vowing to accept Christianity, give up their nomadic ways, and take on full-time farming. The offer was received excitedly by the colonists who, after decades of frustrating missionary efforts, could finally start fulfilling their assigned role within Spain's imperial system: turning nomads to neophytes and building a buffer zone of pacified Indian farmers to protect the silver mines of northern Mexico against foreign invasion. The construction of a new mission-presidio complex began in the spring of 1757 in the San Sabá valley.

The San Sabá scheme epitomized in microcosm the kind of strategic miscalculations that had encumbered Spain's North American ventures from the outset. The first miscalculation involved the site itself, which at first glance seemed an auspicious choice. The San Sabá valley had a broad, irrigable bottom that was suitable for farming, and it had prospects of mining. Separated from the principal political and population center, San Antonio, by 135 miles, San Sabá also could have become a protective bastion for Texas deep on the interior plains. But that middle distance also meant that the mission-presidio complex would be an isolated outpost at the edge of Comanche range, where it stood defenseless in a conflict its very presence provoked. (Lipans, it seems, were fully aware of this: in June 1757 a massive party of some three thousand visited the construction site, but in the end only a few families stayed with the Franciscans; the rest, leaving, protested that the site was too close to Comanche territory.) San Sabá was also poorly designed for defense. To prevent sexual interaction and cohabitation between Spanish soldiers and Indian women, the friars had insisted that the presidio be built three miles upriver from the mission complex, which thus lay utterly exposed to attack. But perhaps the most serious miscalculation was financial. Although the mission was funded privately by a mining magnate, the presidio, designed to lodge four hundred people, absorbed men and funds that would have been needed elsewhere in poverty-stricken Texas. In the San Sabá scheme, then, Texas tied its limited resources in an improbable venture that virtually invited enemy assault.

That assault came in March 16, 1758, when an estimated two thousand allied Comanches, Taovayas, Tonkawas, and Hasinais appeared at the gates of the

San Sabá mission, announcing that "they had come with intention of killing the Apaches." The bulk of the force broke into the mission compound and began looting it and searching for Apaches, while the rest approached the presidio. When the presidial soldiers opened fire, the Indians retreated and gathered in and around the mission. Their faces "smeared with black and red paint," equipped with lances, cutlasses, helmets, metal breastplates, and "at least 1,000" French muskets, and led by a Comanche chief clad in a French officer's uniform, they set fire to the buildings—"so quickly that it seems probable that they were prepared in advance to do so," one soldier recalled—and gunned down those who failed to find shelter. The body count, made by the presidial soldiers who had been too terrified to confront the overwhelming Indian force, revealed eight casualties.

If the loss of life was limited, the psychological aftermath was enormous. The attack was a military operation aimed at eliminating an enemy encroachment, but it was also a symbolic act laden with political messages. The attackers openly declared their nationality, perhaps to stake territorial claims or perhaps to proclaim that they were not afraid of Spanish reprisals, and their French weapons, by all accounts manifestly displayed, bespoke of far-reaching commercial and political connections. The violence itself, it seems, was staged for maximum impact. The attackers slaughtered oxen and other animals, destroyed church ornaments and sacred jewels and pictures, and overturned and beheaded the effigy of Saint Francis. They left behind stripped, scalped, eyeless bodies and placed the beheaded body of a friar on the church altar. If the intention was to use strategic violence to coerce the Spaniards to cut off their support to the Apaches, it worked. "Intent as they are on robbery and blunder," Father Manuel de Molina testified, "they will not desist from such activities, nor cease to carry out their diabolic schemes. Therefore I consider it impossible to reduce and settle these Apache Indians along the San Sabá, or for many leagues roundabout, even with the aid of the King's forces." The bare facts of the assault—the size of the coalition, its abundant French weaponry, its apparent organizational capacity—sent shock waves across Spanish Texas. The Indians were so superior "in firearms as well as in numbers," one officer declared, "that our destruction seems probable."…

In February 1763 the world's greatest powers gathered in Paris to untangle a global chaos they had created. The summit was convened to terminate the virulent Seven Years' War that had raged for eight years over three continents, but it became an imperial reordering of unparalleled scale. Humbled by a series of defeats, France ceded all its possessions in North America and saw its American empire reduced to a few sugar islands in the Lesser Antilles, tiny fishing bases off Newfoundland, and a foothold in Guyana. Britain, whose army and fleet had scored victories from Manila to Montreal, won Canada, Grenada, and Senegal, emerging as the world's paramount colonial empire. Spain, a late arrival to the war, had suffered one humiliating loss after another as France's ally, but two interlinked transactions allowed it to actually expand its imperial presence in North America. It ceded Florida to Britain in Paris but balanced that loss with the 1762 Treaty of Fontainebleau in which Spain gained Louisiana from Louis XV, who was eager to get rid of the money-draining colony. And so, with a few casual incisions of diplomatic surgery, North America received a new imperial face. New France was stamped out, British dominion expanded to the north, south, and west, and the Spanish frontier leaped eastward. The complex colonial collage of old was replaced with a symmetrical division into British East and Spanish West along the Mississippi watershed.

The Treaty of Paris reconfigured the global balance of power and streamlined colonial North America, but its makers suffered from a striking tunnel vision. Acknowledging only claims to land of European nation-states, they utterly ignored the realities of indigenous power on the ground. The Indian nations in the Great Lakes region and the Ohio Country bitterly objected to the new order, insisting that the French had no right to give Britain lands that were under Indian control. The British then provoked a massive pan-Indian uprising, Pontiac's War, by claiming possession to the entire eastern half of North America, by treating Indians as conquered subjects, and by building unauthorized forts on their lands.

A similar neglect and disregard of Native presence and power took place in the Southwest, where Spain won vast paper claims to the interior. At the same time that Britain and France had won and lost enormous colonial claims across North America during the French and Indian War, Comanches had completed their own sweeping campaign of conquest, which by the early 1760s made them the masters of the entire western Great Plains south of the Arkansas River. When Louis XV surrendered Louisiana to Carlos III in 1762, the transfer was, in effect, imaginary. By European reasoning, the treaty gave Spain all lands between the Mississippi valley and the Rio Grande, but the real Spanish possessions formed a mere edging to a much larger geopolitical entity, Comanchería, which stretched six hundred miles north of Texas and four hundred miles east of New Mexico.

Ignoring that reality—as well as the warnings marqués de Rubí and other frontier officials had made about the rising Comanche power—Spanish policymakers set out to create a cohesive colonial domain out of their suddenly swollen North American possessions. Embellishing their frontier policy with French-styled strategies, they moved to pacify and ultimately absorb the *indios bárbaros* of the interior plains through treaties and trade. But because Spanish officials failed to take cognizance of the Comanche ascendancy, their attempts were destined to fail. Ignored and massively underestimated, Comanches continued their decades-long expansion, but with a new set of ambitions. If earlier their aim had been to colonize the game-rich grasslands of the southern Great Plains, they now moved to bend the bordering regions —New Mexico, Texas, the lower Mississippi valley, and the northern Great Plains—to their own uses. By the late 1770s, less than two decades after the Treaty of Paris, Spain's imperial system in North America had become hollow. Rather than New Spain absorbing the southern plains into its imperial body, Comanches had reduced the Spanish borderlands to a hinterland for an imperial system of their own....

Before long, in fact, western Comanches accumulated such quantities of guns and other manufactured goods that they could start exporting them. Domingo Cabelloy Robles, governor of Texas, reported in the 1780s that western Comanches sold guns, powder, balls, lances, cloth, pans, and large knives to their eastern relatives on the Texas plains, who in turn supplied western Comanches with horses and mules, some of which were then traded to Wichitas, Pawnees, Cheyennes, Kiowas, Kansas, and Iowas. Moreover, in a reversal of the typical roles of colonial trade, western Comanches started to sell guns and other manufactures to Spanish New Mexico. Such a trade was first mentioned in 1760 by Bishop Pedro Tamarón y Romeral who wrote that Comanches sold muskets, shotguns, munitions, and knives at Taos. Fifteen years later the trade had become a routine. When visiting the town's summer fair in 1776, Fray Francisco Atanasio Domínguez was struck by Comanches' export stock, which included tin pots, hatchets, shot, powder, pistols, and "good guns." The gun trade, Domíguez noted, had become established enough to be based on fixed rates: "If they sell a pistol, its price is a bridle." In exchange for the precious manufactured items, Comanches received special equestrian and hunting gear, such as bridles and *belduques*, broad butchering knives, which were available only in New Mexico. Western Comanches, it seems, were creating a multilevel commodity flow that furnished them with imported staples, such as maize and horses, as well as with more specialized manufactured products....

Meanwhile, horses proliferated in Comanchería. In the 1770s and 1780s, many western Comanche rancherías possessed more than two horses per capita, which indicates a substantial surplus, since plains nomads needed only an average of one horse per capita for basic hunting and transportation needs. For example, a western Comanche family of eight needed one or two running horses for hunting and warfare, three to five riding animals for women and children, and two or three pack horses to move the tipi and other belongings. Such a family was likely to have possessed approximately eight extra animals that could be traded away at anytime.

The burgeoning horse wealth enhanced western Comanches' trading power, but it also gave them yet another reason to raid New Mexico—captive seizure. The rapidly growing horse herds, together with probable negative demographic effects of the drought years, increased the demand for imported labor in Comanchería. Since most Apache villages had retreated below the Río Grande and beyond easy reach from Comanchería, Comanches turned on New Mexico. The Comanche–New Mexico border became a slaving frontier. In many of their recorded attacks on New Mexico, Comanches took or tried to take captives, usually women and children working in fields or tending livestock. Some of these captives were returned to New Mexico for ransom—Spanish bureaucracy established in 1780 a formal *limosna* (alms) fund to facilitate such rescues—and some were sold to the Wichitas, Pawnees, and French. But Comanches also absorbed large numbers of captives into their workforce as horse herders and hide processors, thereby initiating a process that in the early nineteenth century would see the emergence of a large-scale slave economy in Comanchería.

By the late 1770s, New Mexico began disintegrating under the weight of Comanche violence. The combined effect of raids and drought sapped the colony's energy, pushing it into a steep decline. In 1766 Nicolás de Lafora, the engineer of the marqués de Rubí expedition, had envisioned New Mexico as an "impenetrable barrier" against hostile Indians, but only a decade later this strongest of Spain's North American colonies had been reduced to a captive territory, where horseless troops watched in passive frustration as Comanche raiders destroyed towns and drained ranches, and where impoverished settlers subsisted on roasted hides, old shoes, and "the vellum from the saddletrees." Age-old settlement patterns broke down as violence and horror uprooted families and entire communities. In 1776, with Comanches storming into the colony "by all routes," New Mexicans lived "in such a state of terror that they sow their lands like transients and keep going and coming to the place where they can live in less fear." But finding such places was virtually impossible amidst the shifting coordinates of terror: in 1777 and 1778 alone, Comanches killed or captured almost two hundred New Mexicans....

The decline of Spanish power in Texas and its borderlands was astoundingly precipitous. As late as 1778 Spaniards were still dreaming of a great imperial future for Texas. Commanding General Croix proposed that Texas build a series of outposts among the Taovayas on the Red River, which would mark the northern limit of effective Spanish rule in the continent's center. "This new line would be the palladium of war," he envisioned, "but from it to the interior of our now distant frontier there would be no enemies, and the provinces which now suffer hostilities would experience prosperity." Even the usually cautious [Athanase] de Mézières [an officer for the French and then the Spanish] had been widely optimistic about the prospects of colonizing the Taovaya country. "It is certain that if this place comes to be settled," he predicted, "it will be one of the most important [Spanish colonial outposts], both at present and in the future, because it is the master-key of the north, where the friendly nations will be dealt with through their [Taovayas'] mediation, the unfriendly, such as the Comanches and the Osages, will be won over, or, with the help of the friendly nations, conquered." A Spanish colony on the middle Red River, he believed, could also be turned into a buffer "where any new enterprise or invasion of the neighboring English will be prevented" and an interimperial nerve center "where prompt and easy communication will be had with Natchitoches, Ilinoeses, New Mexico, and Bejar."

Only a few years later, however, an almost diametrically contrasting geopolitical pattern had emerged. Texas was sliding into political and economic paralysis, and it was the Comanches who extended their sphere of authority to the coveted Red River valley and among the Taovayas. They usurped much of the

Wichita commerce along the Red and Brazos rivers and extended their camping and hunting grounds south toward the lower Brazos valley. They incorporated large numbers of Taovaya warriors into their raiding parties, which sent Spanish officials into speculating that the Comanches had spawned a large anti-Spanish coalition that could obliterate the entire colony. By the early 1780s, the terror of Comanche assaults had become so entrenched on the Texas frontier that when a smallpox epidemic brought about a sudden hiatus in violence in late 1781, it stirred greater anxiety than the actual attacks. The years 1782 and 1783 passed in Texas with relative peace on the frontier—and rampant rumors of an imminent Comanche invasion....

On February 25, 1786, Juan Bautista de Anza, lieutenant colonel in the Spanish Army and the governor of New Mexico, stood in front of his palace, preparing himself for the ceremony. He had waited for this moment too long, ever since the glorious day on the llanos [plains] seven years ago when he held the green-horned headdress in his hands. The memory of his triumph was already growing faint, making his gubernatorial tenure seem like a failure, but now there was hope again. He examined his subjects—*hispanos, indios, genízaros,* men, women, children—who swarmed in the dirt plaza, filling it with nervous expectation. Then the crowd shivered, erupting into shrieks and yells, and Anza saw him. Ecueracapa, the *capitan general* of the western Comanches, emerged at the end of a corridor of shouting people. The Indian rode slowly toward him, flanked by three adjutants and escorted by a column of Spanish soldiers and Santa Fe's most prominent citizens. He calmly crossed the square, dismounted in front of Anza, and gently embraced him. It was there, in the arms of the man he could think of only as a savage, that Anza knew there would be peace.

The embrace brought together two men and two nations, and it saved New Mexico. The meeting of Anza and Ecueracapa put an end to a century of on-and-off warfare, which in the 1770s had nearly broken the kingdom of New Mexico. For the remaining Spanish tenure in the Americas, the western Comanches maintained an uninterrupted peace with the Spaniards, allowing New Mexico to heal and even prosper. A similar and simultaneous development took place in Texas, where the eastern Comanches and Spaniards forged a separate peace treaty, ending thirty years of nearly constant bloodshed.

But if Anza and Ecueracapa's encounter is one of the cardinal moments of the colonial Southwest, it is also one of the most enigmatic. What made the Comanches give up their lucrative raiding-and-trading policy which brought them unforeseen prosperity and gave them such power over New Mexico? And why did the Spaniards, who had fought, feared, and despised the Comanches for generations, suddenly welcome their embrace?...

Engulfed in war, Comanches were also struck by severe economic and commercial reversals. Not only did western Comanches see their long-standing trade links with Kiowas and Pawnees disintegrate into bloodshed, but they also lost their connections with Kansas and Iowas, whose trading power was undercut by overhunting and Osage attempts to monopolize Spanish fur trade from St. Louis. Eastern Comanches faced a similar commercial crisis. In the late 1770s, after a protracted rivalry, they had finally replaced Wichitas as the trade gateway to the lower Mississippi valley—only to see how changing imperial geopolitics smothered the eastern markets. The first blow came in 1779, when Spain joined the thirteen rebelling colonies against Great Britain and seized the eastern bank of the lower Mississippi valley, thus preventing British traders from slipping into Comanchería. Then Franco-Spanish traders of Louisiana withdrew from the plains in order to reap profits from the war that raged up and down the Mississippi and along the Gulf Coast. By the early 1780s the westbound trade from the lower Mississippi valley had all but dried up, rendering eastern Comanches' victory over Wichitas meaningless: they were a trade gateway without trade.

But such military and economic setbacks pale in significance to the demographic disaster that fell upon the Comanches. In 1780 or 1781 a sprawling continent-wide smallpox epidemic descended into Comanchería, causing unforeseen destruction among its nomadic population that had not yet been exposed to the disease and thus formed a virgin soil for the virus to spread and kill. The epidemic, raging from Mexico City to Hudson Bay and the war-ravaged East to the Northwest Coast, struck New Orleans in the winter of 1779–80. It then moved up the Red River to a cluster of newly established Wichita villages north of the Red River and leaped into Comanchería. The devastation was unfathomable. Eastern Comanches stated that they lost two-thirds of their population, perhaps as many as sixteen thousand people. The epidemic also hit New Mexico, but it failed to spread among the nearby western Comanches,... But even with half of the Comanche nation spared, waves of horror and despair reverberated across Comanchería.

It was in the aftermath of this catastrophe that Comanches finally began to reassess their policies toward the Spaniards. With Native enemies edging into their domain, with their trade network in shambles, and with the eastern rancherías decimated by alien microbes, they found it practical and perhaps necessary to seek closer diplomatic and commercial ties with Spanish colonies. Eastern Comanches cut back their raiding into Texas in the winter of 1781–82, and in 1783 western Comanches opened peace talks in Santa Fe.

Fortunately for Comanches, their desire for peace coincided with a parallel process of political reevaluation on the Spanish side. That reassessment was brought about by the mixed consequences of the American Revolution for Spain. In the treaty accords signed in Paris in 1783, Britain returned the Floridas to Spain, but it also granted the new United States a generous southern boundary on the thirty-first parallel. This outraged Spanish officials who insisted that their West Florida province extended in the north all the way to the Tennessee valley and the confluence of the Ohio and Mississippi rivers. Eager to secure access to the Mississippi frontage and southeastern fur trade, Americans refused to negotiate for a compromise, and so the Spaniards found themselves embroiled in a bitter border dispute with a republic of "a new and vigorous people, hostile to all subjection, advancing and multiplying." The Treaty of Paris thus created an unexpected predicament for the Spaniards. The acquisition of the Floridas fulfilled their long-standing dream of a continuous transcontinental empire in North America, and yet their position felt more threatened than ever.

Spain's simultaneously strong and susceptible position spawned several drastic foreign political schemes. Spanish officials closed the lower Mississippi to American shipping in order to isolate the settler-farmers in Kentucky and Tennessee from transportation and market outlets, but opened Louisiana and the Floridas for American emigrants who promised to become Catholics and the king's vassals. But this policy of confining and co-opting the Americans was a mere emergency measure: Spain's chief tactic in checking the expansionist United States was a new secularized Indian policy.

Lacking the demographic and military power to restrain the Americans, Spanish officials set out to build extensive barriers of loyal Indians on both sides of the Mississippi valley to block the seemingly imminent American expansion to the Great Plains and northern Mexico. Instead of conversion and coercion, the traditional cornerstones of Spain's Indian policy, the agents were now instructed to rely on treaties, trade, and gifts to win Indians' allegiance. East of the Mississippi, the officials negotiated by 1784 agreements with Creeks, Alabamas, Choctaws, Chickasaws, and Seminoles, creating an extensive Indian-alliance network that covered much of the area under dispute with the United States. Carlos III then appointed Bernardo de Gálvez, Louisiana's celebrated governor during the American Revolution and nephew of José de Gálvez, as the viceroy of New Spain. Gálvez's jurisdiction was extended over the Interior Provinces, Louisiana, the Floridas, and Cuba in the hope that the energetic young officer could organize those wide-ranging dominions into a unified front against the United States....

The Making of American Nationalism

DAVID WALDSTREICHER

Nationalism in America hasn't been a great idea that has waxed and waned, something that people truly had or did not have. It has been a set of practices that empowered Americans to fight over the legacy of their national Revolution and to protest their exclusion from that Revolution's fruits. It is not inherently reactionary or progressive; like other nationalisms, its political meanings are multiple, even contradictory, and can be shown to have changed radically over time. Thus, it will be instructive, first, to see how, by stressing the ideological nature instead of examining the everyday practice, we have misunderstood American nationalism....

From *In The Midst of Perpetual Fetes: The Making of American Nationalism, 1776–1820* by David Waldstreicher. Published for the Omohundro Institute of Early American History and Culture. Copyright © 1997 by the University of North Carolina Press. Used by permission of the publisher. www.uncpress.unc.edu.

The particular strategies of early American nationalists derived from a particular moment in world history. Older approaches to that nationalism tended to ignore the international trends of "the age of the democratic revolutions" (perhaps better termed the age of the nationalist democratic revolutions). Newer scholarship stresses that the invention of modern democracy in the late eighteenth century was inextricably tied to the creation of newly coherent national peoplehoods whose will, it was believed, ought to be expressed in national political institutions. A "dramatically new political culture" emerged in both France and England during this era, despite these nations' very different political histories. [Petitions, huge outdoor meetings, committees of correspondence, and innovative uses of the press energized older customs like ritualized crowd actions. The new reality of the age was much more than the idea of the nation: it was the new political practices justified in the name of the nation and its people.]

The rites of nationhood are best understood in the context of this broad range of popular activities, often festive or celebratory, that constituted political action between elections. Too often, an anthropological understanding of such ritual has led scholars to view American holidays in isolation both from the customary and innovative behavior of early modern crowds and from the ritualized rhetoric and behaviors that made up an expanding sphere of politics. From its beginning, the Fourth of July—itself the model for an expanding calendar of post-Revolutionary festivals—drew upon these traditions and innovations. Much as the Fourth improvised upon the old holiday of the King's Birthday, the new American nationals demonstrated their joy or sorrow in a wide range of political events and anniversaries. These nationalist celebrations consisted of far more than parades: there were orations, celebratory dinners at which politically rousing toasts were given, and printed commentary on all of these, in their wake. Such rituals might have aspired to a unity beyond political division, but, because of their origins and the political needs of various groups, they did not and could not merely reflect ideological consensus. Instead, they engendered both nationalism and political action.

This irony has been lost on even the most prescient students of American culture. Perhaps because our expectations of nationalist ritual have been formed by the relentlessly (but really only seemingly) depoliticized celebrations of a later day, scholars still recoil at the inescapably partisan parades of the early Republic. In a work otherwise sensitive to the value of conflicts over the meanings of patriotism and national memory, Michael Kammen writes: "Perhaps the most notable aspect of Independence day in our early history was *not* that it became an occasion for consensus, but rather that for a while memory frequently fell victim to fierce factional disputes. Partisanship and mutual recriminations became the order of the nation's natal day, rather than reciprocal congratulations based upon shared legends." Politicization here victimizes "memory," which must be completely shared and consensual in order to be truly national; as a result, a familiar dichotomy recurs: parades are really something other than politics.

This study argues nearly the opposite: that relentless politicization gave nationalist rituals their most important meanings. Conflict produced "the nation" as contestants tried to claim true American nationality and the legacy of the Revolution....

New England as America

By the end of the eighteenth century, New Englanders had a long tradition of national regionalism. From the Puritans of the 1630s to the Boston rebels of the 1760s, even when New Englanders did not see themselves as America writ small, they at least defined themselves as its saving remnant. The myth of the errand into the wilderness persisted. Into the nineteenth century, latter-day Puritans could still see the emergence of an American empire as a direct continuation of their original project.

Yet by the mid-1790s it had become clear that New England was losing political power in the nation as a whole. Eastern areas remained nearly stable in population while the natural and imported increase was forging southward and westward into less densely settled regions. The increase in the number of states was decreasing the proportion of senators and representatives who championed New England interests in Philadelphia and then Washington. Thanks to the Napoleonic Wars, Yankee farmers and merchants flourished during the decade after ratification; but international conflict also led to controversies over national policy, like Jefferson's embargo, that highlighted the distinctiveness of Yankee political economy. Nationally, New England Federalists were on the defensive after 1800, when a series of Virginia Republicans occupied the presidency, and they found themselves increasingly challenged by "democrats" at home.

Tellingly, the rearticulation of New England regionalism began in an attack upon southern distinctiveness. New England Federalists projected the growing internal opposition to their political dominance at home into the nether regions, making the southern planter the emblem of a national threat: hypocritical support for democracy and the French Revolution. Who were those "feudal barons, who reign over a thousand negroes," to talk of aristocracy in government? The partisan critique of southern slavery meshed with rising antislavery activity in the North, but Federalists held no patent on antislavery notions in New England. The critique in this instance was part of a strategy to conflate party and region: to symbolically place all the nation's sins (including the Republican opposition) "mostly in the southern and middle states." Actually, such expressions made only a limited contribution to antislavery, because they were not meant to end slavery: they were meant to discredit southern Jeffersonians and their allies. The New England attack on southern slaveholding often centered on the three-fifths clause of the Constitution (by which 60 percent of slaves were counted in apportionment of presidential electors and seats in the House of Representatives, increasing white southern power in the federal government). Nothing in their pronouncements suggests that Federalists thought that southern slaves—or, for that matter, free blacks north or south—should exercise the vote. Thus the participants at a Forefathers' Day feast in Boston toasted, "Our Sister

Virginia—when she changes three fifths of her Ethiopian skin we will respect her as the head of our White family."

If the rise of the Republicans fearsomely paralleled the demographic growth of the South, the acquisition of the Louisiana Territory in 1803 threatened to further reduce New England's power in the nation. Orators wasted little time in blaming the South, and Virginia in particular, for a scheme that would lead to New England's subjection and, eventually, western secession. George Washington Stanley insisted that any "inhabitants of New England" who celebrated such an event could no longer be "in principle New-Englandmen." On the Fourth of July prominent Federalists accused Virginia of "trying to divide the northern from the southern states" and seeking to "increase the number of her *slaves* among the *freemen* of New England." In 1804, a profusion of toasts urged New Englanders to "resist the encroachment of Southern despotism." Campaigns to alter the three-fifths clause or delay the admittance of new states to the union were said to illuminate the Constitution by a "steady Northern light."...

For the next decade, New England Federalists cultivated a vision of a loyal but aggrieved northern America. The geographical contours of this region remained purposefully ambiguous, as these Federalists hoped to bring eastern or seaport areas, particularly New York, into their northern or eastern political fold. The image of the feudal landlord or aristocratic tyrant, surrounded by his real (black) and political (Republican) servants, helped opponents of Jefferson to rewrite the "Revolution of 1800" as the first act of an era that they hoped would conclude with their own second American Revolution. "The People of the Northern States" were toasted by the Connecticut Cincinnati in 1804: "Descended from Freemen, they will never be governed by Southern Slaves."

The Embargo controversy helped the Federalists to flesh out this picture with an international dimension. Southerners were "Frenchified enemies to commerce," and New England Republicans mere functionaries of the French interest. In this atmosphere, disunion, unspeakable to nationalists, could be openly discussed or even proposed, because its cause was always the actions of the conspiring, foreign-influenced other party. Disunion was really a defense of New England (and America) against narrow regionalists who cloaked their southern agenda in nationalism. Republican papers carried article after article on the "Essex Junto," who favored a northern confederacy. Federalists replied with exposes of the "Virginia Junto," who caused the bad blood in the first place.

Although the machinations of real Essex secessionists amounted to little, northeastern Massachusetts emerged nonetheless as the mythic center of New England, if only because it revived the celebration of the Pilgrims' landing at Plymouth and Puritan Forefathers' Day in Boston. On these occasions, similar in form to General Election Day rites, Federalist preachers reminded all who came of the superior virtues of New England's founding generation. If the "myth of New England exclusiveness" developed and disseminated through these festivals was a provincial myth, it also asserted its righteous Americanness

and for this reason served New England's Federalists well. It helped them relocate declension geopolitically, justifying their resistance to the federal government as the godly actions of a saving remnant.

When the Republican-dominated Congress, led by southern and western
War Hawks, voted to commence hostilities against England in 1812, Massachusetts
governor Caleb Strong lost little time in declaring a statewide fast for July 23. In
his official message Strong beseeched God to "inspire the President and Congress,
and the Government of Great Britain, with just and pacific sentiments," Pointing
to England as the "bulwark of [our] religion" and the source of American patri-
mony, Strong asked every citizen to pray against an American alliance with the
infidel, France.

This fast on July 23, also observed in Connecticut, set the tone for the
remarkably sectional dissent of the New England Federalists during the War
of 1812. Seizing upon the form of the fast day as avidly as they had in the
late 1790s, sacred and secular officials alike described a true New England
that resisted the war effort out of tradition and a belief in their region's
superior Christianity. "The Puritans of New England must not, will not,
cannot be dragged into this execrable war," intoned Elijah Parish in the
best-known of the 1812 fast sermons. "You must change the radical traits
of your character, you must cease to be New England men, before you can
exhibit this tame, African, slavish deportment." Throughout the war, these
Federalists portrayed Republicans not only as southern and western in orien-
tation and as morally and racially contaminated by a slavish dependence on
slaves but also as Frenchified "infidels." "Fast Day, appointed by our excellent Governor Strong," wrote a leading citizen of Brookline in his diary:
"that the People may atone for their sins in electing over them rulers, without Honesty or Knowledge, men neither fearing God or who have any love
for their country."

Federalist leaders combined this revival of New England Christian identity
with a claim to the heritage of the American Revolution. A widely published
song of 1812 presents the New England "fathers" as the planters of liberty in
America. Their eighteenth-century sons defended these liberties against the
British and the French; this tradition gave Americans the right to stay out of
Europe's interminable wars. But then the Madison administration had dropped
the country back into the "quicksand" of imperial struggles:

> They might know, witless dunces, the method at once, is
>   To give up the helm to *New-England*—
>
> ....
>
> Our true Northern notions would settle commotions,
>   And teach them respect to *New-England*.

In 1812 Federalists still hoped for an electoral solution to the problem of
the war; this preelection song rallied the faithful to the polls. Yet the "them"
here seems intentionally ambiguous: is it Europe, or the floundering Republican administration, that must learn "respect to *New England*"? In the next

stanza, the Republican rulers themselves are again the culprits. Having left the northern coasts unprotected, they seem to revel in the decline of New England and in its possible invasion by the enemy. Nevertheless, "these buckskins will find, the Yankee's inclin'd / To stick to the RIGHTS OF NEW ENGLAND." After this defense of ancient, local liberties that antedate yet inform the American national Revolution, the song concludes with a promise to join loyally in wartime defense:

> But since War is declar'd, let us all be prepar'd,
> For the dangers that threaten our dear land;
> With a STRONG to parade us, who'er may invade us,
> We'll fight for the RIGHTS of *New-England*—
>   We'll die or live free in *New-England*—
>   In the shade of the TREE of *New-England*—
> And the NATION shall know, who is truly their foe,
> Is also the foe of NEW ENGLAND!

"Our dear land," it turns out, may suffer "dangers" from any number of invaders, perhaps including the federal government. New England must be defended, but can be only from within New England itself, under the original liberty tree. Although it is finally admitted the "the nation" is more than New England, the last appeal is one of self-definition through opposition. The real enemies of America are those who oppose New England's "RIGHTS."

Placing themselves simultaneously in the lineage of the Puritans and the founding fathers, New England Federalists constructed a mythic South and West that possessed no real claims to the legacy of the Revolution. It should be stressed, though, that the Federalists did so in a manner no less authentic than the Republicans' own version of the War of 1812 as a struggle to reestablish the (once again unstable) "national character." Theirs was the conservative American Revolution, the one limited to the restoration of ancient (British) rights and privileges. The Massachusetts Federalists consistently stressed New England's British heritage, ethnic homogeneity, and leadership of the Revolution. On the floor of the House of Representatives and in an often reprinted Washington Benevolent Society oration, Josiah Quincy charged that the "original compact" of the nation had been abridged by the extension of equal representation to "Frenchmen, Spaniards ... Creoles and Negroes." In a truly reactionary derivation of political citizenship, intellectuals and politicians like Quincy traced American rights, not to nature, but to genealogy, prefiguring a century of racial Anglo-Saxonism that would continue to validate its intellectual pedigree in New England. "Our adversaries accuse us of foreign partiality, we love no country like our own, "insisted Benjamin Whitwell in Boston's official July Fourth oration in 1814.

> We are attached to the union, being all members of one body, of which Virginia assumes to be the head, but we know that NEW-ENGLAND is the heart; their sons have no certificates of French citizenship to divide their

love. She has no patriots by adoption.... Her sons trace their descent from ancestors, whose institutions they preserve and whose memory they venerate. She requires no mixture of the best nations on earth in her political composition, let the head, and the heart, and the arm be purely American.

"Ancestors," in these New England festivals of national memory, meant Puritans and revolutionaries. Latter-day patriots did not have to resist Old England at all, since the new tyrants lay among the partisans of the new France.

The isolation of New England during the war only strengthened the ideological link between the defense of liberty and New England tradition. Federalists in other states gladly lauded Massachusetts as the leader of this latter-day rebellion in toasts like one given at Fairhaven, Vermont, on July 4, 1813: "The Commonwealth of Massachusetts—The cradle of American liberty; she still nurses its defenders." Those Massachusetts legislators who supported attempts to foil the enlistment of federal troops in New England "evinced a spirit worthy of *Freemen*, but dreadful to tyrants." Resistance to war was defense of the Revolution, and Federalists who sang celebratory odes participated in national renewal:

Rouse to action every power,
Now's the dire, decisive hour,
True to freedom's high command,
Independence bids you stand.

Indeed, the "clamorous patriots of Virginia, Kentucky and Tennessee," according to one orator, not only had no real interest in the maritime issues that had supposedly led to war; they were also the authors of the Whiskey Rebellion and the Virginia and Kentucky Resolutions of 1799. When the national capital was in the hands of truly disloyal men, it could not be disloyal to protest those who would ruin the Atlantic trade and expose the seaports to attack in order to augment territories more than a thousand miles away. The New Englanders who toasted four of their fellow Yankee states went on to raise their glass to "The state of Louisiana—The fifth wheel of a Waggon!" No expansive union worthy of the name could depend on the patriotism of these southern and western former rebels and their supporters. Active opposition to the war would ultimately "convince your rulers, that there exists, at least in New England, a redeeming spirit, able and willing to save the country."...

 # FURTHER READING

Joyce Oldham Appleby, *Inheriting the Revolution: The First Generation of Americans* (2000).

Ron Chernow, *Alexander Hamilton* (2004).

Stanley Elkins and Eric McKitrick, *The Age of Federalism, 1788–1800* (1993).

Joseph J. Ellis, *American Sphinx: The Character of Thomas Jefferson* (1998).

Joanne B. Freeman, *Affairs of Honor: National Politics in the New Republic* (2002).

Pekka Hämäläinen, *The Comanche Empire* (2008).

Linda K. Kerber, *Women of the Republic: Intellect and Ideology in Republican America* (1980).

David McCullough, *John Adams* (2002).

James Roger Sharp, *American Politics in the Early Republic: The New Nation in Crisis* (1993).

David Waldstreicher, *In the Midst of Perpetual Fetes: The Making of American Nationalism, 1776–1820* (1997).

Gordon Wood, *Empire of Liberty* (2011).

Philipp Ziesche, *Cosmopolitan Patriots: Americans in Paris in the Age of Revolution* (2009).

Additional critical thinking activities and content are available in MindTap.

MindTap

MindTap is a fully online, highly personalized learning experience built upon Cengage Learning content. MindTap combines student learning tools—readings, multimedia, activities, and assessments—into a singular Learning Path that guides students through the course.

CHAPTER 7

Foreign Policy, Western
Movement, and Indian Removal

American foreign policy in the early national period looked both east and west. The United States continued to maintain and develop relationships with European nations, and this interaction had a profound impact on American development. For example, France sold the Louisiana territory to the United States in 1803, doubling the latter's size with the stroke of a pen, which made the United States one of the largest nations in the world. Less advantageous for the United States was its weak standing in relation to the European powers. British and French warships harassed American ships in the early nineteenth century, and the hostile posture of the British became particularly galling for many Americans. Struggles with France and Britain caused economic problems for Americans, as they sought to protect their economy from foreign goods while still wishing to sell goods abroad. The Embargo Act of 1807, which forbade international trade to and from American ports, was largely a failure of Jefferson's administration to respond to international war and economics.

By 1812, the United States, led by a group of young and aggressive legislators known as "Warhawks," declared war on Britain. After a series of battles that put the future of the United States in danger—including the British attacks on Washington and Baltimore— the war turned into a stalemate. An inconclusive war finally culminated in the Treaty of Ghent in 1815. The War of 1812 had two profound consequences. First, American leaders became increasingly leery of what President Washington had called "entangling alliances" with European nations. Second, many white Americans turned their attention westward to regions peopled by members of Indian nations.

As American foreign policy became focused on relationships with Indian nations, the challenges for Indian people multiplied. Indian-white interaction had existed for centuries and native people accepted some aspects of Euro-American society and rejected others. The accelerated growth in the early nineteenth century, however, only made more urgent the Native American response. Some elements of Indian cultures fostered movements of revitalization that attempted to reclaim aspects of culture that had been lost due to Indian interaction. On occasion, these revitalization movements were powerful forces in nurturing efforts by Indians to band together and contest white society.

The most notable movement began in 1805 when a Shawnee man named Lalawathika seemingly returned from death. He told of meeting the Master of Life who showed him the way to lead his people out of degradation. Known to Americans as the Prophet, he adopted the name Tenskwatawa and he began to preach a message that advocated a return to a traditional lifestyle. By 1807, he began to suggest that Indian groups unite to resist white expansion. Just prior to the War of 1812, Tenskwatawa and his brother Tecumseh had built a confederacy of Indian nations to challenge American military aims in present-day Indiana. The movement ended in bloody conflict, the most notable battle being the Battle of Tippecanoe, when the American army aided by frontiersmen defeated the Indian coalition.

An alternative strategy in resisting the westward migration was a selective acceptance of certain aspects of white society. In particular, people from the Creek and Cherokee nations were active in embracing aspects of white society varying from written language, farming, and even slavery. By 1827, the Cherokee drafted and ratified a constitution and began publishing their own newspaper one year later. Unfortunately for them, these innovations were dismissed by the state of Georgia. In 1828, the Cherokee constitution was annulled by the Georgia legislature. Despite—perhaps because of—legal appeals to the U.S. Supreme Court, the hostility toward the Cherokee increased. Between 1830 and 1835, Indian nations in the southeastern United States, Cherokees and Creeks included, were forced to move to "Indian territory" in present-day Oklahoma.

 ## QUESTIONS TO THINK ABOUT

What advantages might the United States have gained from its policies toward Europe ranging from President Washington's Farewell Address to the Monroe Doctrine? How could white–Indian interaction reflect a combination of cooperation and savagery? Which strategy used by Indians—resistance or acculturation—was more successful in grappling with the westward migration of white Americans?

 ## DOCUMENTS

The documents in this chapter alternatively focus upon American approaches to and interactions with Europeans and Native Americans. President George Washington, in document 1, worries about entering into alliances with other nations in his Farewell Address in 1796. Document 2 moves to the frontier, where William Clark—one of the leaders of the Lewis and Clark journey to the Pacific Ocean—writes about his diplomatic engagements with native peoples. In a letter written in 1806 to a white man who has offered assistance in dealing with the Indians, Clark includes a speech that he delivered to the Yellowstone Indians. Document 3 is an address by Sagoyewatha, also known as Red Jacket, to a Massachusetts missionary. A member of the Seneca nation, Sagoyewatha chides the missionary for his attempt to convert the Indians to Christianity. William Cullen Bryant, who would become one of the most famous American poets, satirizes the Embargo Act in document 4 with a poem he wrote at only thirteen years old. The next two documents illustrate the conflicts between Indians and the U.S. government that developed around the time of the War of 1812. In document 5, Tecumseh, in a speech delivered to Governor William H. Harrison in 1810, recounts the misdeeds of whites and expresses his belief that the only way to stop "this evil" is for all Indians to unite. Documents 6 and 7 turn our attention back to American foreign policy with Europeans. Document 6 is a report on the burning of Washington, D.C. by the British, while Document 7, less than ten years later, has President James Monroe declaring that the entire Western Hemisphere is closed to further European colonization. Document 8 pushes back to the interior and highlights the continuing ravages of disease and epidemic. Although Europeans had arrived hundreds of years earlier, the devastating sharing of microbes continued to wreak havoc.

1. President George Washington Warns Against "Entangling Alliances," 1796

As avenues to foreign influence in innumerable ways, such attachments are particularly alarming to the truly enlightened and independent patriot. How many opportunities do they afford to tamper with domestic factions, to practice the arts of seduction, to mislead public opinion, to influence or awe the public councils! Such an attachment of a small or weak towards a great and powerful nation dooms the former to be the satellite of the latter.

Against the insidious wiles of foreign influence (I conjure you to believe me, fellow citizens) the jealousy of a free people ought to be constantly awake, since history and experience prove that foreign influence is one of the most baneful foes of republican government. But that jealousy to be useful must be impartial; else it becomes the instrument of the very influence to be avoided, instead of a defense against it. Excessive partiality for one foreign nation and excessive dislike of another cause those whom they actuate to see danger only on one side, and serve to veil and even second the arts of influence on the other. Real patriots, who may resist the intrigues of the favorite, are liable to become suspected and odious, while its tools and dupes usurp the applause and confidence of the people to surrender their interests.

The great rule of conduct for us in regard to foreign nations is, in extending our commercial relations, to have with them as little political connection as possible. So far as we have already formed engagements, let them be fulfilled with perfect good faith. Here let us stop.

Washington's Farewell Address (1796). Reprinted in *Washington's Farewell Address to the People of the United States*, Senate Publication No. 108-21 (Washington, 2004), 25–28.

Europe has a set of primary interests, which to us have none or a very remote relation. Hence she must be engaged in frequent controversies, the cause of which are essentially foreign to our concerns. Hence therefore it must be unwise in us to implicate ourselves, by artificial ties, in the ordinary vicissitudes of her politics or the ordinary combinations and collisions of her friendships or enmities.

Our detached and distant situation invites and enables us to pursue a different course. If we remain one people under an efficient government, the period is not far off when we may defy material injury from external annoyance; when we may take such an attitude as will cause the neutrality we may at any time resolve upon to be scrupulously respected; when belligerent nations, under the impossibility of making acquisitions upon us, will not lightly hazard the giving us provocation; when we may choose peace or war, as our interest guided by justice shall counsel.

Why forgo the advantages of so peculiar a situation? Why quit our own to stand upon foreign ground? Why, by interweaving our destiny with that of any part of Europe, entangle our peace and prosperity in the toils of European ambition, rivalship, interest, humor, or caprice?

It is our true policy to steer clear of permanent alliances with any portion of the foreign world—so far, I mean, as we are now at liberty to do it, for let me not be understood as capable of patronizing infidelity to existing engagements (I hold the maxim no less applicable to public than to private affairs, that honesty is always the best policy)—I repeat it therefore, let those engagements be observed in their genuine sense. But in my opinion it is unnecessary and would be unwise to extend them.

2. William Clark of the Lewis and Clark Expedition Enters into Diplomacy with Native People, 1806

SIR   In the winter of 1805, you were so obliging as to express a disposition to assist us in the execution of any measure relative to the Savages with whome you were conversant, or that you would lend your aid in furthering the friendly views of our government in relation to the Same, no object as we then informed you did at that time present itself to our view, which we conceived worthy of your attention, at present we have a commission to charge you with, which if executed, we have no doubt will tend to advance your private interest, while it will also promote those of the U. States in relation to the intercourse of her citizens with the Indian nations in the interior of North America. It is that of provailing on some of the most influencial Chiefs of those bands of Sioux who usially resort the borders of the Missouri to visit the Seat of our Government, and to accompany them there yourself with us. The Tetons of the burnt woods, Teton Ockandandas, and other bands of Tetons, Cisitons, and yanktons of the

Letter to Hugh Henney and speech prepared for Yellowstone Indians, in *The Journals of Lewis and Clark*, Meriwether Lewis and William Clark, V (1806), in *Original Journals of the Lewis and Clark Expedition, 1804–1806*, ed, Reuben Gold Thwaites (New York: Dodd, Mead, 1905), 282–283, 285–286, 299–301.

Plains are the Objects of our attention on this occasion, Particularly the Bands of Tetons; those untill some effectual measures be taken to render them pacific, will always prove a serious source of inconveniance to the free navigation of the Missouri, or at least to it's upper branches, from whence the richest portion of it's fur trade is to be derived.

The ardent wish of our government has ever been to conciliate the esteem and secure the friendship of all the Savage nations within their territory by the exercise of every consistent and pacific measure in her power, applying those of coercion only in the last resort; certain we are that her disposition towards the native inhabitants of her newly acquired Territory of Louisiana is not less friendly; but we are also positive that she will not long suffer her citizens to be deprived of the free navigation of the Missouri by a few comparatively feeble bands of Savages who may be so illy advised as to refuse her proffered friendship and continue their depridation on her citizens who may in future assend or decend that river.

We believe that the sureest guarantee of savage fidility to any nation is a thorough conviction on their minds that their government possesses the power of punishing promptly every act of aggression committed on their part against the person or property of their citizens; to produce this conviction without the use of violence, is the wish of our government; and to effect it, we cannot devise a more expedient method than that of takeing some of the best informed and most influential Chiefs with us to the U. States, where they will have an ample view of our population and resources, become convinced themselves, and on their return convince their nations of the futility of an attempt to oppose the Will of our government, particularly when they shall find, that their acquies-cence will be productive of greater advantages to their nation than their most sanguine hopes could lead them to expect from oppersition.

We have before mentioned to you the intentions of our government to form tradeing establishments on the Missouri with a view to secure the attach-ments of the nativs and emeliorate their sufferings by furnishing them with such articles as are necessary for their comfort on the most moderate terms in ex-change for their peltries and furs.... an Indian *Agent* will of course be necessary at that post, your long acquaintance and influence with those people necessary places your protentions to that appointment on the fairest Ground, and should you think proper to under take the commission now proposed, it will still fur-ther advance those pretentions....

In your communication with the *Sioux,* in addition to other considerations which may suggest themselves to your mind, you will be pleased to assure them of the friendly views of our government towards them, their power and resources, their intention of establishing trading houses in their neighborhood and the objects of those establishments, inform them that the mouth of all the rivers through [which] traders convey Merchindize to their country are now in possession of the United States, who can at pleasure cut off all communication between themselves and their accustomed traders, and consequently the inter-est they have in cultivateing our friendship. You may also promis them in the event of their going on with us, that they shall receive from our government a

considerable present in Merchindize, which will be conveyed at the public expence with them to their nation on their return, urge them also to go imediately,
on the ground, that their doing so will haisten the establishment of the tradeing
house in contemplation.

[Speech prepared for Yellowstone Indians]

Children   The Great Spirit has given a fair and bright day for us to meet together in his View that he may inspect us in this all we say and do.

Children   I take you all by the hand as the children of your Great father the
President of the U. States of America who is the great chief of all the white
people towards the riseing sun.

Children   This Great Chief who is Benevolent, just, wise & bountifull has
sent me and one other of his chiefs (who is at this time in the country of the
Blackfoot Indians) to all his read children on the Missourei and its waters quite
to the great lake of the West where the land ends and the [sun] sets on the face
of the great water, to know their wants and inform him of them on our return....

Children   The object of my comeing to see you is not to do you injurey but
to do you good   the Great Chief of all the white people who has more goods at
his command than could be piled up in the circle of your camp, wishing that all
his read children should be happy has sent me here to know your wants that he
may supply them.

Children   Your great father the Chief of the white people intends to build a
house and fill it with such things as you may want and exchange with you for
your skins & furs at a very low price. & has derected me [to] enquire of you, at
what place would be most convenient for to build this house. and what articles
you are in want of that he might send them imediately on my return

Children   The people in my country is like the grass in your plains noumer-
ous they are also rich and bountifull. and love their read brethren who inhabit
the waters of the Missoure

Children   I have been out from my country two winters, I am pore necked
and nothing to keep of [f] the rain.   when I set out from my country I had a
plenty but have given it all to my read children whome I have seen on my way
to the Great Lake of the West. and have now nothing....

Children   The red children of your great father who live near him and have
opened their ears to his counsels are rich and hapy have plenty of horses cows &
Hogs fowls bread &c. &c. live in good houses, and sleep sound. and all those of
his red children who inhabit the waters of the Missouri who open their ears to
what I say and follow the counsels of their great father the President of the
United States, will in a fiew years be a[s] hapy as those mentioned &c.

Children   It is the wish of your Great father the Chief of all the white people that some 2 of the principal Chiefs of this [blank space in diary.] Nation
should Visit him at his great city and receive from his own mouth. his good
counsels, and from his own hands his abundant gifts,   Those of his red children
who visit him do not return with empty hands, he [will] send them to their
nation loaded with presents

Children   If any one two or 3 of your great chiefs wishes to visit your great father and will go with me, he will send you back next Summer loaded with presents and some goods for the nation. You will then see with your own eyes and here with your own years what the white people can do for you. they do not speak with two tongues nor promis what they can't perform

Children   Consult together and give me an answer as soon as possible   your great father is anxious to here from (& see his red children who wish to visit him) I cannot stay but must proceed on & inform him &c.

3. Iroquois Chief Red Jacket Decries the Day When Whites Arrived, 1805

"Brother; Listen to what we say.

"There was a time when our forefathers owned this great island. Their seats extended from the rising to the setting sun. The Great Spirit had made it for the use of Indians. He had created the buffalo, the deer, and other animals for food. He had made the bear and the beaver. Their skins served us for clothing. He had scattered them over the country, and taught us how to take them. He had caused the earth to produce corn for bread. All this He had done for his red children, because He loved them. If we had some disputes about our hunting ground, they were generally settled without the shedding of much blood. But an evil day came upon us. Your forefathers crossed the great water, and landed on this island. Their numbers were small. They found friends and not enemies. They told us they had fled from their own country for fear of wicked men, and had come here to enjoy their religion. They asked for a small seat. We took pity on them, granted their request: and they sat down amongst us. We gave them corn and meat, they gave us poison (alluding, it is supposed, to ardent spirits) in return.

"The white people had now found our country, Tidings were carried back, and more came amongst us. Yet we did not fear them. We took them to be friends. They called us brothers. We believed them, and gave them a larger seat. At length their numbers had greatly increased. They wanted more land: they wanted our country. Our eyes were opened, and our minds became uneasy. Wars took place, Indians were hired to fight against Indians, and many of our people were destroyed. They also brought strong liquor amongst us. It was strong and powerful, and has slain thousands.

"Brother; Our seats were once large and yours were small. You have now become a great people, and we have scarcely a place left to spread our blankets. You have got our country, but are not satisfied; you want to force your religion upon us.

"Brother; Continue to listen.

Red Jacket's Reply to Reverend Cram (1805), first published in *Monthly Anthology and Boston Review* 6 (April 1809): 221–224. This document can also be found in *Red Jacket: Iroquois Diplomat and Orator*, Christopher Densmore (Syracuse, N.Y. Syracuse University Press, 1999), 135–140.

"You say that you are sent to instruct us how to worship the Great Spirit agreeably to his mind, and, if we do not take hold of the religion which you white people teach, we shall be unhappy hereafter. You say that you are right and we are lost. How do we know this to be true? We understand that your religion is written in a book. If it was intended for us as well as you, why has not the Great Spirit given to us, and not only to us, but why did he not give to our forefathers the knowledge of that book, with the means of understanding it rightly? We only know what you tell us about it. How shall we know when to believe, being so often deceived by the white people?

"Brother; You say there is but one way to worship and serve the Great Spirit. If there is but one religion; why do you white people differ so much about it? Why not all agreed, as you can all read the book?

"Brother; We do not understand these things.

"We are told that your religion was given to your forefathers, and has been handed down from father to son. We also have a religion, which was given to our forefathers, and has been handed down to us their children. We worship in that way. It teaches us to be thankful for all the favors we receive; to love each other, and to be united. We never quarrel about religion.

"Brother; The Great Spirit has made us all, but he has made a great difference between his white and red children. He has given us different complexions and different customs. To you He has given the arts. To these He has not opened our eyes. We know these things to be true. Since He has made so great a difference between us in other things; why may we not conclude that He has given us a different religion according to our understanding? The Great Spirit does right. He knows what is best for his children; we are satisfied.

"Brother; we do not wish to destroy your religion or take it from you. We only want to enjoy our own.

"Brother; We are told that you have been preaching to white people in this place. These people are our neighbors. We are acquainted with them. We will wait a little while, and see what effect your preaching has upon them. If we find it does them good, makes them honest, and less disposed to cheat Indians; we will then consider again of what you have said.

"Brother; you have now heard our answer to your talk, and this is all we have to say at present.

"As we are going to part, we will come and take you by the hand, and hope the Great Spirit will protect you on your journey, and return you safe to your friends."

As the Indians began to approach the missionary, he rose hastily from his seat and replied, that he could not take them by the hand; that there was no fellowship between the religion of God and the works of the devil.

This being interpreted to the Indians, they smiled, and retired in a peaceable manner.

It being afterwards suggested to the missionary that his reply to the Indians was rather indiscreet; he observed, that he supposed the ceremony of shaking hands would be received by them as a token that he assented to what was said. Being otherwise informed, he said he was very sorry for the expressions.

4. William Cullen Bryant Satirizes the Embargo Act, 1808

… WAKE Muse of Satire, in the cause of trade,
Thou scourge of miscreants who the laws evade!
Dart thy keen glances, knit thy threat'ning brows,
And hurl thine arrows at fair Commerce's foes!

MUCH injur'd Commerce! 'tis thy falling cause,
Which, from obscurity, a stripling draws;
And were his powers but equal to his zeal,
Thy dastard foes his keen reproach should feel.
Curse of our Nation, source of countless woes,
From whole dark womb unreckon'd misery flows;
Th' embargo rages like a sweeping wind,
Fear low'rs before, and famine stalks behind.
What words, oh, Muse! can paint the mournful scene,
The saddening street, the desolated green;
How hungry labourers leave their toil and sigh,
And sorrow droops in each desponding eye!

SEE the bold sailor from the ocean torn,
His element, sink friendless and forlorn!
His suffering spouse the tear of anguish shed,
His starving children cry in vain for bread!

THE farmer, since supporting trade is fled,
Leaves the rude joke, and cheerless hangs his head;
Misfortunes fall, an unremitting shower,
Debts follow debts, on taxes, taxes pour.
See in his stores his hoarded produce rot,
Or sheriff sales his profits bring to naught;
Disheartening cares in thronging myriads flow,
Till down he sinks to poverty and woe!

OH, ye bright pair, the blessing of mankind!
Whom time has sanction'd, and whom fate has join'd,
COMMERCE, that bears the trident of the main,
And AGRICULTURE, empress of the plain;

William Cullen Bryant, *The Embargo, or Sketches of the Times* (1808).

Who, hand in hand, and heav'n - directed, go
Diffusing gladness through the world below;
Whoe'er the wretch, would hurl the flaming brand,
Of dire disunion, palsied be his hand! ...

WHEN shall this land, some courteous angel say,
Throw off a weak, and erring ruler's sway?
Rife, injur'd people, vindicate your cause!
And prove your love of Liberty and laws;
Oh wrest, sole refuge of a sinking land,
The sceptre from the slave's imbecile hand!
Oh ne'er consent, obsequious, to advance
The *willing vassal* of imperious France!
Correct that suffrage you misus'd before,
And lift your voice above a Congress' roar? ...
Go, *wretch*, resign the presidential chair,
Disclose thy secret measures foul or fair,
Go, search, with curious eye, for horned frogs,
'Mongst the wild wastes of Louisianian bogs;
Or where Ohio rolls his turbid stream,
Dig for huge bones, thy glory and thy theme; ...

5. Shawnee Chief Tecumseh Recounts the Misdeeds of Whites and Calls for Indian Unity, 1810

Brother, I wish you to give me close attention, because I think you do not clearly understand. I want to speak to you about promises that the Americans have made.

You recall the time when the Jesus Indians of the Delawares lived near the Americans, and had confidence in their promises of friendship, and thought they were secure, yet the Americans murdered all the men, women, and children, even as they prayed to Jesus?

The same promises were given to the Shawnee one time. It was at Fort Finney, where some of my people were forced to make a treaty. Flags were given to my people, and they were told they were now the children of the Americans. We were told, if any white people mean to harm you, hold up these flags and you will then be safe from all danger. We did this in good faith. But what happened? Our beloved chief Moluntha stood with the American flag in

---

Speech to William Harrison, governor of the Indian Territory (August 11, 1810). http://injesus.com/messages/content/45035.

front of him and that very peace treaty in his hand, but his head was chopped by an American officer, and that American officer was never punished.

Brother, after such bitter events, can you blame me for placing little confidence in the promises of Americans? ...

It is you, the Americans, by such bad deeds, who push the red men to do mischief. You do not want unity among the tribes, and you destroy it. You try to make differences between them. We, their leaders, wish them to unite and consider their land the common property of all, but you try to keep them from this. You separate the tribes and deal with them that way, one by one, and advise them not to come into this union. Your states have set an example of forming a union among all the Fires, why should you censure the Indians for following that example?

But, brother, I mean to bring all the tribes together, in spite of you, and until I have finished, I will not go to visit your president. Maybe I will when I have finished, maybe. The reason I tell you this, you want, by making your distinctions of Indian tribes and allotting to each a particular tract of land, to set them against each other, and thus to weaken us....

The only way to stop this evil is for all the red men to unite in claiming an equal right in the land. That is how it was at first, and should be still, for the land never was divided, but was for the use of everyone. Any tribe could go to an empty land and make a home there. And if they left, another tribe could come there and make a home. No groups among us have a right to sell, even to one another, and surely not to outsiders who want all, and will not do with less.

Sell a country! Why not sell the air, the clouds, and the Great Sea, as well as the earth? Did not the Great Good Spirit make them all for the use of his children?

Brother, I was glad to hear what you told us. you said that if we could prove that the land was sold by people who had no right to sell it, you would restore it. I will prove that those who did sell did not own it. Did they have a deed? A title? No! You say those prove someone owns land. Those chiefs only spoke a claim, and so you pretended to believe their claim, only because you wanted the land. But the many tribes with me will not agree with those claims. They have never had a title to sell, and we agree this proves you could not buy it from them. If the land is not given back to us, you will see, when we return to our homes from here, how it will be settled. It will be like this:

We shall have a great council, at which all tribes will be present. We shall show to those who sold that they had no rights to the claim they set up, and we shall see what will be done to those chiefs who did sell the land to you. I am not alone in this determination, it is the determination of all the warriors and red people who listen to me. Brother, I now wish you to listen to me. If you do not wipe out that treaty, it will seem that you wish me to kill all the chiefs who sold the land! I tell you so because I am authorized by all tribes to do so! I am the head of them all! All my warriors will meet together with me in two or three moons from now. Then I will call for those chiefs who sold you this land, and we shall know what to do with them. If you do not restore the land, you will have had a hand in killing them!

I am Shawnee! I am a warrior! My forefathers were warriors. From them I took only my birth into this world. From my tribe I take nothing. I am the maker of my own destiny! And of that I might make the destiny of my red people, of our nation, as great as I conceive to in my mind, when I think of We-shemoneto, who rules this universe! I would not then have to come to Governor Harrison and ask him to tear up this treaty and wipe away the marks upon the land. No! I would say to him, "Sir, you may return to your own country!" The being within me hears the voice of the ages, which tells me that once, always, and until lately, there were no white men on all this island, that it then belonged to the red men, children of the same parents, placed on it by the Great Good Spirit who made them, to keep it, to traverse it, to enjoy its yield, and to people it with the same race. Once they were a happy race! Now they are made miserable by the white people, who are never contented but are always coming in! You do this always, after promising not to anyone, yet you ask us to have confidence in your promises. How can we have confidence in the white people? When Jesus Christ came upon the earth, you killed him, the son of your own God, you nailed him up! You thought he was dead, but you were mistaken. And only after you thought you killed him did you worship him, and start killing those who would not worship him. What kind of a people is this for us to trust?

Now, Brother, everything I have said to you is the truth, as Weshemoneto has inspired me to speak only truth to you. I have declared myself freely to you about my intentions. And I want to know your intentions. I want to know what you are going to do about the taking of our land. I want to hear you say that you understand now, and will wipe out that pretended treaty, so that the tribes can be at peace with each other, as you pretend you want them to be. Tell me, brother. I want to know now.

6. A Newspaper Reports on the Burning of Washington, D.C., 1814

I arrived at Washington on Sunday, the 21st.... At that time, the officers of government and the citizens were very apprehensive of an attack from the British, who had landed a force on the Patuxent. Their numbers had not been ascertained, but reports were various, stating them from 4000 to 16,000.... [T]he public officers were all engaged in packing and sending off their books and the citizens their furniture. On Monday, this business was continued with great industry, and many families left the city. The specie was removed from all the Banks in the district....

[T]he battle commenced, and was contested ... with great spirit and gallantry, until it appeared useless for so small a force, very badly supported, to stand against *six thousand regulars*.... [R]etreat was ordered, when the President, who had been on horseback with the army the whole day, retired from the mortifying scene and left the city on horseback....

When we remarked, in our paper of yesterday, that private property had in general been scrupulously respected by the enemy during his late incursion, we spoke what we believed, from a hasty survey, and perhaps without sufficient inquiry. Greater respect was certainly paid to private property than has usually been exhibited by the enemy in his marauding parties. No houses were half as

A Newspaper Reports on the Burning of Washington, D.C., 1814.

much *plundered* by the enemy as by the knavish wretches about the town who profited from the general distress. There were, however, several private buildings wantonly destroyed, and some of those persons who remained in the city were scandalously maltreated....

The enemy was conducted through the city by a former resident, who, with other detected traitors, is now in confinement.

[The British commanding officer] Cockburn was quite a mountebank in the city, exhibiting in the streets a gross levity of manner, displaying sundry articles of trifling value of which he had robbed the President's house, and repeating ... coarse jests and vulgar slang ... respecting the chief magistrate and others....

7. President James Monroe Declares That European Powers May Not Interfere in the Americas, 1823

... [A]s a principle in which the rights and interests of the United States are involved, that the American continents, by the free and independent condition which they have assumed and maintain, are henceforth not to be considered as subjects for future colonization by any European powers.

... Of events in that quarter of the globe, with which we have so much intercourse, and from which we derive our origin, we have always been anxious and interested spectators. The citizens of the United States cherish sentiments the most friendly, in favor of the liberty and happiness of their fellow men on that side of the Atlantic. In the wars of the European powers, in matters relating to themselves, we have never taken any part, nor does it comport with our policy so to do. It is only when our rights are invaded, or seriously menaced, that we resent injuries, or make preparation for our defense. With the movements in this hemisphere, we are, of necessity, more immediately connected, and by causes which must be obvious to all enlightened and impartial observers. The political system of the allied powers is essentially different, in this respect, from that of America. This difference proceeds from that which exists in their respective governments. And to the defence of our own, which has been achieved by the loss of so much blood and treasure, and matured by the wisdom of their most enlightened citizens, and under which we have enjoyed unexampled felicity, this whole nation is devoted. We owe it, therefore, to candor, and to the amicable relations existing between the United States and those powers, to declare, that we should consider any attempt on their part to extend their system to any portion of this hemisphere, as dangerous to our peace and safety. With the existing colonies or dependencies of any European power, we have not interfered, and shall not interfere. But, with the governments who have declared their independence and maintained it, and whose independence we have, on great consideration and on just principles, acknowledged, we could not view any interposition for the purpose of oppressing them, or controlling, in any other manner, their destiny, by any European power, in any other light than as the manifestation of

James Monroe, *The Monroe Doctrine* (1823).

an unfriendly disposition towards the United States. In the war between these new governments and Spain, we declared our neutrality at the time of their recognition, and to this we have adhered, and shall continue to adhere, provided no change shall occur, which, in the judgment of the competent authorities of this government, shall make a corresponding change, on the part of the United States, indispensable to their security.

...Our policy, in regard to Europe, which was adopted at an early stage of the wars which have so long agitated that quarter of the globe, nevertheless remains the same, which is, not to interfere in the internal concerns of any of its powers; to consider the government de facto as the legitimate government for us; to cultivate friendly relations with it, and to preserve those relations by a frank, firm, and manly policy, meeting, in all instances, the just claims of every power, submitting to injuries from none. But, in regard to those continents, circumstances are eminently and conspicuously different.

It is impossible that the allied powers should extend their political system to any portion of either continent, without endangering our peace and happiness; nor can any one believe that our Southern Brethren, if left to themselves, would adopt it of their own accord. It is equally impossible, therefore, that we should behold such interposition, in any form, with indifference. If we look to the comparative strength and resources of Spain and those new governments, and their distance from each other, it must be obvious that she can never subdue them. It is still the true policy of the United States, to leave the parties to themselves, in the hope that other powers will pursue the same course.

8. Francis Chardon Bemoans the Destruction of the Arikaras and Mandans by Smallpox, 1837

[July] *Wednesday 26*, The Rees [Arikaras] And Mandans all arrived to Day Well loaded With Meat, Mitchel also arrived with 15 pieces, The 4 Bears (Mandan) has caught the small pox, and got crazy, and has disappeared from camp—he arrived here in the afternoon—The Indians of the Little Village all arrived in the evening Well loaded—With dried Meat—the small Pox has broke Out among them, several has died,

Thursday 27, Indians all Out after berries, No News from Any quarter, the small pox is Killing them of at the Village, four died to day—

Friday 28, Rain in the Morning—This day was very Near being my last—a young Mandan came to the Fort with his gun cocked, And secreted under his robe, With the intention of Killing Me, after hunting Me in 3 or 4 of the houses he at last found Me, the door being shut, he waited some time for Me to come Out, just as I Was in the Act of going Out, Mitchel caught him, and gave him in the hands of two Indians Who Conducted him to the Village, had Not Mitchel perceived him the instant he did, I would Not be at the trouble of Makeing this statement—I am upon my guard, the Rees are Out rageous against the Mandans,

---

Francis Chardon, *Journal*, July 26, 1837 to September 1837.

they say that the first Mandan that Kills a White, they Will exterminate the whole race, I have got 100 Guns ready And 1000 Powder, ready to hand Out to them when the fun Commences—The War Party of Rees that left here the 7th inst came back to day—With five horses, that they stole from the Sioux—a lodge that was encamped at the Little Missr they attacked it in the Night, after fireing several shots they departed takeing with them all the Horses they think to have Killed 3 or 4 in the lodge—The Mandans & Rees gave us two splendid dances, they say they dance, on account of their Not haveing a long time to live, as they expect to all die of the Small Pox—and as long as they Are alive, They Will take it Out in danceing.

Saturday 29, Several More Mandans died last night. Two GrosVentres arrived from their dried Meat camp, it appears that it has Not broke Out Among them as yet—

Sunday 30, An other report from the GrosVentres to day say, they are Arrived at their Village, and that 10 or 15 of them have died, two big fish Among them, they threaten Death And Distruction to us all at this Place, saying that I was the Cause of the small pox Makeing its appearance in this Country— One of Our best friends of the Village (The Four Bears) died today, regretted by all Who Knew him,

Monday 31, Mandans are getting worse Nothing Will do them except revenge. Three of the War party that left here the 26th of last Month Arrived to day. With each of them One horse, that they stole from the Yanctons on White River,

Killed 61 Rats this Month—total 1778

August 31 Days—1837

Tuesday 1st, The three horses that the war party brought in yesterday they say that they belong to the Compy that they were stole on the Island below the Little Missr the Soldiers was takeing them from them, but I told them to Waite untill the Arrival of Lachapelle Who I expect to Arrive in 4 or 5 days—

The Mandans Are Makeing their Medicine for rain, As their Corn is all drying up—to day we had several light showers—

Wednesday 2nd, Yesterday an Indian that was Out after berris discovered a band of Cows, all hands Out to run them, they all Arrived in the Afternoon Well laden With fresh meat haveing ran three Bands—

Thursday 3rd, All quiet, No News from Any quarter the GrosVentres Not yet Arrived from their Dried Meat excursion—

Friday 4th, Same As Yesterday—Nothing New, Only two deaths today— sprinkled with rain in the Morning—

Saturday 5th, Portrá a half breed from the North started to day—alone, for Red River, Indians Out after berries, others Out After Meat—News from the GrosVentres, they say that they are encamped this side of Turtle Mountain, And that a great Many of them have died of the Small Pox—several chiefs Among them, they swear vengence Against all the Whites, As they say the small Pox Was brought here by the S. B. [Steamboat].

Sunday 6, One More Ree died last Night—To day we had a tremendous storm of rain, hale, And Wind, which Continued for ½ hour With great Violence, the Fort came very Near blowing down, 40 or 50 Loads of hay that I have Out is Much damaged

Monday 7, Six More died to day—several Rees left the Mandan Village and pitched their Lodges Out in the Prairies—rain all day—report from the Gros-Ventres say they will be at their Village tomorrow—

Tuesday 8, Four More died to day—the two thirds of the Village are sick, to day I gave six pounds of Epsom salts in doses to Men, Women, and children the small Pox has broke Out at the Little Mandan Village. three died yesterday, two chiefs—

Wednesday 9, Seven More died to day—the Men came back from the hay at full speed haveing saw enemies, all hands out for the fight, False alarm,

Thursday 10, All the Rees that were encamped in the Mandan lodges, except a few that are sick, Moved down to the Island hoping to get rid of the small Pox—the Mandans talk of Moveing to the other side of the river, 12 or 15 died to day—

Friday 11, Sent old Charboneau up to the GrosVentres with some tobacco; and a bag full of good talk, as yesterday they sent a very severe threat to Me, Mandans all crossed to the other Side of the river to encamp—leaveing all that were sick in the Village, I Keep No A/c of the dead, as they die so fast that it is impossible—

Saturday 12, Cool And pleasant Weather, one of My best friends of the Little Village died to day—(Le Fort)—News of a War party of GrosVentres And Rees (70) being used up by the Saons [Sioux], quicker Work than the small Pox.

Sunday 13, Several reports from the GrosVentres that they are bent on the distruction of us all, As yet I do Not place Much confidence in what report says, Charboneau Will bring us the strait News—The Mandan are dying 8 and 10 every day—an Old fellow who has lost the whole of his family to the Number of 14, harrangued to day, that it was time to begin to Kill the Whites, as it was them that brought the small Pox in the Country—

Tuesday 22, Cool pleasant Weather, The disease still Keeps ahead 8 and 10 die off daily, thirty five Mandans (Men) have died, the Women and Children I keep No Account of—Several Mandans have come back to remain in the Village, One of My Soldiers a (Ree) died to day—Two Young Mandans shot themselves this Morning—News from the Little Village, that the disease is getting worse and worse every day. It is now two months that it broke Out—A Ree that has the small Pox, And thinking that he was going to die, approached Near his Wife, a Young Woman of 19—And struck her in the head With his tommahawk, With the intent to Kill her, that she Might go With him in the Other World—she is badly Wounded a few Minutes after he cut his throat, a report is in Circulation, that they intend to fire the Fort, Stationed guards in the Bastion

Wednesday 23, May and Charboneau arrived late last night from the Gros-Ventres all appears to be quiet in that quarter. The little Sioux a *Mandan* died last night, We had three allerts to day—all hands under Arms, all false reports Several Rees Arrived from their camp at the GrosVentres

Thursday 24, Seven More died at the Village last Night, and Many More at the Ree camp at the point of Woolds below The fellow that we Killed on the 17th all his band Came to day to smoke With us and Make Peace, how long it will last I Cannot tell, however We Must put up With it, good or bad—

Friday 25, May And Charboneau started last Night for the GrosVentres sent a few pounds of powder & Ball to the GrosVentres And Rees—An other Mandan chief died to day—(The long fingers) total Number of Men that has died—50, I have turned Out to be a first rate doctor St Grado, an Indian that has been bleeding at the Nose all day, I gave him a decoction of all sorts of ingredients Mixed together, enough to Kill a Buffaloe Bull of the largest size, and stopped the effusion of Blood, the decoction of Medicine, Was, a little Magnisia, peppermint, sugar lead, all Mixed together in a phial, filled With Indian grog—and the Patient snuffing up his nose three or four times—I done it out of experiment And Am Content to say, that it proved effectual, the Confidence that an Indian has in the Medicine of the whites, is half the Cure,

Saturday 26, The Indians all started Out on the North side in quest of Buffaloe, As they have Nothing to eat A Young Ree, the Nephew of Garreau, died at the Village last Night, Much regretted by us all, As he was one of the foresmost in aideing to Kill the dog on the 17th inst & A Mandan of the Little Village Came to the Fort to day to Sing his Medicine Song, got paid for his trouble, and Went off—glad to get clear of him—A young Ree that has the Small Pox, told his Mother to go and dig his grave, she accordingly did so—after the grave Was dug, he walked With the help of his Father to the Grave, I Went Out With the Interpreter to try to pursuade him to return back to the village— but he would not, Saying for the reason that all his young friends Were gone, And that he wished to follow them, torwards evening he died—

Sunday 27, Strong east Wind, rain in the Morning, The Indians Came back from the *Cerne* Well loaded With fresh Meat, report Cattle in abundance 20 Miles off—News from the GrosVentres of the disease breaking Out amongst them,

Monday 28, Wind from the North, rain, disagreeable Weather, several More Indians Arrived With fresh Meat—from the North Side gave us a small quantity which we found very good—Three More fell sick in the Fort to day—My interpreter for one, if I loose him I shall be badly off, the bad Weather continued all day—and no Prospects of Clearing off—

Tuesday 29, Last Night I Was taken Very Sick With the Fever, there is Six of us in the Fort that has the Fever, and One the Small Pox—An Indian Vacinated his child, by Cutting two small pieces of flesh Out of her Arms, and two on the belly—and then takeing a Scab from One, that Was getting Well of the disease, and rubbing it on the Wounded part, three days after, it took effect, and the child is perfectly Well—

Wednesday 30, All those that I thought had the small Pox turned out to be true, the fever left them yesterday, and the disease showed itself, I Am perfectly Well, as last Night, I took a hot Whiskey Punch, Which Made Me sweat all last Night, this Morning I took My daily Bitters as usual, Indians Arrived with fresh Meat, report Cattle in abundance opposite the Little Lake below—

Thursday 31, A Young Mandan that died 4 days ago, his Wife haveing the disease also Killed her two Children. One a fine Boy of eight years, and the other six, to complete the affair she hung herself.

Month of August I bid you farewell With all My heart, after running twenty hair breadth escapes, threatened every instant to be all Murdered, however it is the Wish of [your] humble Servant that the Month of September Will be More Favorable. The Number of Deaths up to the present is Very Near five hundred The Mandans are all Cut off except 23 young and Old Men

Killed 89 Rats this Month Total 1867—

September 30 Days—1837

Friday 1, This Morning two dead bodies wrapped in a White skin, and laid on a raft passed by the Forks on their way to the regions below. May success attend them. The Rees that are encamped in the Point of Woods below, Are Moveing up to encamp at the Mandans Corn fields No doubt with the intention of takeing all from them, as what few Mandans are left are Not able to Contend with the Rees—Mitchels squaw fell to day.

Saturday 2, Being Out of wood, risqued the Men—to the point of Woods below hauled eight loads. Several Indians Arrived With fresh Meat, out 2 days, but one death to day, although several are sick, those that catch the disease at Present, seldom die. One Fellow I saw on horseback to day— he looked More like a gohst than a [human] being—

Sunday 3, A Young Mandan came to pay us a Visit from the Little Village, he informes us, that they are all Most all used up, and that it is his opinion that before the disease stops, that there will not One be left, except 8 or 10 that has Weathered Out the Sickness—....

[*December*] *Sunday 31*, Sent a Man down to the Ree camp to collect some News—Caught three foxes last Night—Charboneau Arrived from the GrosVentre camp. he was accompanied by 2 Mandan and one GrosVentre, he is encamped with only Ten Lodges, the rest of the Lodges are scattered, on the Little Misso he has had No News of them, for two Months, in all Probability they Are all Dead, the last News that he had from them was, that 117 had died, and the disease was still rageing—

Killed 85 Rats this Month— total 2294

▙ ESSAYS

As the United States grew into a nation, it struggled with its relationship to Great Britain. At times, revolutionaries and political leaders like Thomas Jefferson endeavored to forge stronger relationships with the French, especially since they had helped in the War for Independence and had their own overthrow of a monarch. Others, like Alexander Hamilton, hoped not only for close economic ties with the British but also to emulate their material prosperity. These two essays show Americans at odds with the British and in favor of following them. Alan Taylor looks at the final days of the War of 1812, as Americans battled the British and their Native American allies from the northeast to the southern city of New Orleans. Alternately, Emily Conroy-Krutz focuses on the movement of American Protestant missionaries from the United States to places throughout the world. These missionaries consciously imitated British missionaries and often found themselves protected by the British government. The War of 1812, however, strained these alliances and compelled the question of what the relationship would look like between the onetime colony and its former ruler.

The War of 1812 as a Borderland War

ALAN TAYLOR

In the fall of 1812, Ned Myers, nineteen years old, marched across New York State with a party of fellow sailors bound for Lake Ontario, where the American navy was building warships for an invasion of British Canada. But Myers felt the enemy long before he reached the Canadian border. In northern New York, the sailors came to a village where the inhabitants bitterly opposed the war. On a trumped-up charge, the villagers arrested the officers in command of Myers's party but released them when the sailors threatened to burn the village. Moving on to Oswego Falls, the sailors got caught in a downpour, and sought refuge in a large barn. That night, as Myers recalled, they "caught the owner coming about with a lantern to set fire to the barn, and we carried him down to a boat, and lashed him there until morning, letting the rain wash all the combustible matter out of him." In the War of 1812 Myers had to fight against Americans as well as Britons.

During the following summer on Lake Ontario, a British warship captured the schooner that Myers served on. As a prisoner, Myers dreaded the discovery of his secret: that he had been born a British subject in Quebec in 1793. Abandoned by his father, a German officer serving in the British army, Myers had grown up in Halifax, the capital of Nova Scotia, another British colony. At age eleven he ran away to New York City to become a sailor. Rejecting his birthright as a British subject, Myers *chose* to become an American citizen: "America was, and ever has been, the country of my choice, and while yet a child I may say I decided for myself to sail under the American flag; and if my father had a right to make an Englishman of me by taking service under the English crown, I think I had a right to make myself what I pleased when he left me."

But the British insisted that every "natural-born subject" remained so for life. Before the war, Myers had repeatedly and narrowly dodged the Royal Navy press-gangs, which stopped and boarded American ships in search of any mariner who seemed British. And once the war began, British officers treated former subjects as traitors if they were captured while fighting in the American service. As a British prisoner, Myers feared for his life.

In September at Quebec, a press-gang boarded his prison ship to seize Myers and seven other prisoners. Myers insisted that five of them were Americans by birth, but a British naval officer "pronounced us all Englishmen" obliged to serve in the Royal Navy or face trial and hanging as traitors. All eight refused to serve on a warship, but consented to work on an unarmed transport vessel. They sailed for Bermuda, where naval officers again impressed them to serve on a warship, which threatened "to swallow us all in the enormous maw of the British navy." Refusing again, the captives hazarded a court-martial. Unable to prove that the sailors were subjects, the British transferred them to a prison at Halifax, where Myers worried that the locals would remember and recognize him.

The War of 1812 pivoted on the contentious boundary between the king's subject and the republic's citizen. In the republic, an immigrant chose citizenship— in stark contrast to a British subject, whose status remained defined by birth. That distinction derived from the American Revolution, when the rebelling colonists became republican citizens by rejecting their past as subjects. An immigrant re-enacted that revolution by seeking citizenship and forsaking the status of a monarch's subject. But the British denied that the Americans could convert a subject into a citizen by naturalization. By seizing supposed subjects from merchant ships, the Royal Navy threatened to reduce American sailors and commerce to a quasi-colonial status, for every British impressment was an act of counterrevolution. By resisting impressment and declaring war, the Americans defended their revolution.

War raised the stakes in the conflict over subjects and citizens. By converting prisoners or hanging a few as deserters, the British bolstered their contention that any natural born subject owed allegiance for life, no matter where he went or what nation pretended to naturalize him. Returning the favor, the republic's officers sought to entice captive Britons to enter the American service, thereby reenacting the revolution on an individual scale. Because the line between citizen and subject was so contested, rival commanders promoted the desertion of enemy soldiers, the defection of prisoners, and the subversion of civilians in occupied regions. As much as on any battlefield, the British and the Americans waged the War of 1812 in the hearts and minds of Ned Myers and his fellow soldiers and sailors on both sides.

In the American Revolution the victorious Patriots forsook the mixed constitution of Great Britain, where a monarch and aristocrats dominated the common people—then the norm throughout the world. In a radical gamble, the Patriots created a republic premised on the sovereignty of the collective people, rather than of a monarch and his parliament Meant to protect and promote the liberty, property, and social mobility of ordinary white men, the republic bred a suspicion of government's power as a tool for aristocrats to live as parasites on the labor of the people. But that republic for white men hastened the dispossession of Indians and prolonged the enslavement of African-Americans in the southern states. And the British despised the new republic as a dangerous folly, for they celebrated their mixed constitution as more stable, just, and powerful. Where Americans sought to disperse and reduce the power of government, the British sustained an empire with the coercive "energy" to regulate liberty, particularly that of their colonists and the sailors needed for the Royal Navy.

After the revolution, the British empire and the American republic remained uneasy neighbors in North America. In addition to spawning the republic, the revolution led the British to build a counterrevolutionary regime in Canada, beginning with 38,000 American Loyalists expelled by the Patriot victory. In Upper Canada they developed a Loyalist America meant to set an example of superior stability and prosperity that eventually would entice the rebel Americans to forsake their republican experiment Loyalists did not believe that their empire had permanently lost the fight against the republican revolution.

Neither Britons nor Americans thought that their rival political systems could coexist for long on a shared continent Britons predicted that the republic inevitably would collapse into anarchy and civil war. Surely repentant Americans would then beg for readmission into the empire. With equal conviction, Americans insisted that nature destined their republic to dominate the continent. Eventually, they predicted, the Canadians would join the United States by rejecting the artificial rule of a foreign empire. Created by the revolution, the border between the republic and the empire seemed tenuous and temporary, destined to shift either north or south as one or the other regime collapsed, Paradoxically, until 1812, the parallel convictions of providential inevitability kept relations tense but short of war, for why risk blood and treasure on an invasion when the rival's collapse would come naturally in due time?

Partisan divisions within the republic helped to provoke the war. After 1801, the dominant Republican party challenged the British maritime policies as a threat to American sovereignty. But the minority Federalist party sympathised with Britain's global struggle against the French empire led by the despot Napoleon Bonaparte. The Federalists also despised the Republicans as demagogues who pandered to the common people by weakening the national government. By 1812, the Republicans believed that the Federalists in New England were conspiring with the British to break up the union. And the Republicans accused the Loyalists in Canada of covertly assisting Indian attacks on frontier settlements. By invading Canada and defeating the British, the Republicans hoped to unite and save the republic from a menacing convergence of internal and external enemies. Instead, the war alienated the Federalists, who preferred to smuggle with the British rather than to fight them.

Ned Myers fought in a civil war between kindred peoples, recently and incompletely divided by the revolution. In September 1813, a British lieutenant, John Le Couteur, visited an American army camp, where he marveled upon meeting the enemy officers: "Strange indeed did it appear to me to find so many names, 'familiar household words,' as enemies—the very names of Officers in our own army. How uncomfortably like a civil war." Le Couteur bantered with an

American officer, just returned from shooting birds. "Much pleasanter Sport, isn't it, than shooting one's own kindred and language." The American replied, "Indeed, Lieutenant, it is so, I assure you. Believe me when I tell you it so grieves my heart to fire my Guns on your people that I have asked leave to return to Virginia or to serve elsewhere." But a month later, an atrocity by American troops led Le Couteur to denounce them as deserving no mercy in battle: "The rascals, they are worse than Frenchmen." So said the British officer with a French name.

In July 1812 William K. Beall of Kentucky was a prisoner held by the British at Amherstburg, in the Western District of Upper Canada, Beall "was amused in contrasting the [tavern] signs with those in our Country. Instead of Washington, Green[e] and others might be seen George III, the Lion, the Crown, the King's Bake house, etc." But the allegiance of people was less clear. Beall lodged at "the sign of the harp of Erin," with a landlord named Boyle who had left Ireland for America, where he had served in the republic's army during the early 1790s. Deserting to the British, he had settled at Amherstburg, but in 1812 Boyle fell under official suspicion for expressing sympathy for the Americans. Allegiance was slippery and suspect where so many people had crossed boundaries in geography and identity.

Beall also met William Elliott, a former American officer from Maryland. A Federalist, Elliott had lost his commission in a Republican political purge in 1802. Disgusted with the republic, Elliott moved to Upper Canada, where he swore allegiance to the king, which secured him land and appointment as a captain in the militia. Across the river at Detroit, one of Elliott's brothers served in the American army poised to attack Amherstburg in 1812.

In this North American civil war, brother fought brother in a borderland of mixed peoples. At Kingston, Le Couteur lodged with a Mrs. Elizabeth Robinson: "They are a Yankee family, and have several relatives in the American army and navy." Another British officer, William Dunlop, reported that a Canadian soldier of the Glengarry Light Infantry shot an American rifleman and plundered his corpse, when "he discovered that it was his own brother," and coldly remarked "that it 'served him right for fighting for the rebels, when all the rest of his family fought for King George.'" Like so many on both sides, this Canadian thought of the war as continuing the revolutionary struggle between Loyalists and rebels. Dunlop concluded, "Such is the virulence of political rancour, that it can overcome all the ties of nature."

As Myers found on his march to the front, the war also divided the Americans within the United States. Beall noted that the British "depend more upon parry divisions and disturbances among our people than they do on their own strength." Major Daniel McFarland, an Irish-American, insisted that the British were "engaged in the hellish project of creating a civil war" by promoting disaffection within the United States. The British exploited the polarized politics of the republic, where Federalists denounced a war declared by the governing Republicans. A New Yorker concluded, "between the two parties, a hostility existed little short of civil war."

To call the War of 1812 a "civil war" now seems jarring because hindsight has distorted our perspective on the past. Given the later power and prosperity of the United States, we underestimate the fluid uncertainty of the postrevolutionary generation, when the new republic was so precarious and so embattled. We also imagine that the revolution effected a clean break between Americans and Britons as distinct peoples. In fact, the republic and the empire competed for the allegiance of the peoples in North America—native, settler, and immigrant. Americans and Britons spoke the same language and conducted more trade with one another than with other nations, but their overlapping migrations and commerce generated the friction of competition. A British diplomat noted the paradox: "the similarity of habits, language, and manners, between the inhabitants of the two Countries is productive ... of complaint and regret."

The revolution had divided Americans by creating a new boundary between the victors in the United States and the Loyalists in Canada. And, within the republic, bitter partisan politics led the Republicans to cast the Federalists as crypto-Loyalists. In 1812, a newspaper writer explained that ideology rather than nationality distinguished the North American republican from a Loyalist:

> As much as the people of the two nations resemble each other in face, it is notoriously evident that there are some in America whose souls are perfectly British, and it is believed that there are some in Britain who are Americans at heart.... It is not where a man was born, or who he looks like, but what he thinks, which ought at this day to constitute the difference between an American [citizen] and a British subject.

The ideological competition between the republic and the empire blurred the national boundaries and political identities in North America.

After the revolution, the overlap of Britons and Americans became more complicated despite the new border in North America. Thousands of British emigrants poured into American seaports. Primarily from restive Ireland, the newcomers fled from British rule to seek economic opportunity and political liberty in the republic. At the same time (1792–1812), about 30,000 Americans left the republic to seek land in Upper Canada. Euphemistically called "Late Loyalists," these newcomers became the majority in that colony by the eve of war. Invited by the British to help develop Upper Canada, the settlers took an oath of allegiance and received grants of Crown land, the prerogatives of subjects. In return, they were supposed to defend tie colony against any American invasion. But if it was treason for natural-born subjects to fight against the empire, how could the regime expect natural-born citizens to fight against American invaders?.

By insisting that the subject was permanent but the citizen fungible, the British asserted the superiority of their empire over the new republic. They implicitly treated Americans as residual or potential subjects, which hedged American independence. But that assertion of power masked the British weakness as a small island running a big empire, 125 times larger than their little homeland. In 1810 a Briton likened the empire to "an oak planted in a flower-pot." To defend that overstretched empire, the British desperately needed every subject who could serve in the British army or Royal Navy. So they insisted on their right to reclaim any subject found on the high seas *and* to make subjects of foreign-born sailors and of American settlers in Canada. This doable policy angered Americans hypersensitive to any erosion of their new independence.

The two migration streams—of the Irish to America and of Americans to Canada—collided in the civil war of 1812. Becoming staunch Republicans, the Irish-Americans sought revenge on the empire for dominating Ireland and for treating them as runaway subjects when found on American ships. Irish-Americans served in disproportionate numbers in the armies that invaded Upper Canada, where they sought support from the Late Loyalist majority. But that support withered as the American troops proved more adept at looting than at fighting. Defeats cast scores of Irish-Americans into British prisons, where they had to enlist in the royal forces or face trial as traitors. To save them, the American government threatened to execute a captured Briton for every soldier hanged by the British. In an escalating spiral, most of the prisoners on both sides became hostages for the fate of the Irish-American soldiers threatened with British trial.

The civil war had four overlapping dimensions. In the first, Loyalists and Americans battled for control of Upper Canada. Second, the bitter partisanship within the United States threatened to become a civil war, as many Federalists served the British as spies and smugglers, while their leaders in New England flirted with secession. Third, Irish republicans waged a civil war within the British empire, renewing in Canada their rebellion, which the British had suppressed in Ireland in 1798, Invading Canada, Irish-American soldiers faced British regiments primarily recruited in Ireland, for thousands of Irishmen had fled from poverty by enlisting in the royal forces. Fourth, the war embroiled and divided native peoples. In the Great Lakes country, the Indians allied with the British to roll back American expansion. By intimidating and defeating the invaders, the native warriors obliged the Americans to seek their own Indian allies from reservations within the United States. The fighting especially divided the Shawnee and the Haudenosaunee nations. In the North American civil war of 1812, Americans fought Americans, Irish battled Irish, and Indians attacked one another. They struggled to extend, or to contain, the republicanism spawned by the American Revolution....

In early 1815 news traveled slowly across the Atlantic, at the creeping pace of a sailing ship buffeted by head winds and winter gales. On February 11, six weeks after the signing at Ghent, an official copy of the treaty reached New York City and then passed overland to the national capital two days later. Madison promptly sent the treaty to the Senate with his endorsement, and the Senate unanimously approved on February 16. The next day, the war formally ended when Monroe exchanged ratified copies of the treaty with a newly arrived British diplomat, Anthony St. John Baker.

Reports of peace reached Upper Canada and northern New York in late February. Recent enemies, the officers of both sides could now exchange friendly visits. At Kingston on February 25 Lieutenant John Le Couteur reported, "Several American officers came over from Sackets Harbour with the news. We received them very well, gave them a dinner, and made our Band play 'Yankee Doodle' on drinking the President's health, which gave them great pleasure." The officers of both sides could indulge in a professional solidarity as military men, no longer divided by national and ideological enmity. Le Couteur celebrated the end of "a hot and unnatural war between kindred people. Thank God!"

A stunning and pleasant surprise, the treaty saved the republic from division, doubts, and financial ruin. Welcoming "the heartily cheering intelligence," a Philadelphia merchant, Thomas Cope, confided, "a continuation of the war must have ended in our political dissolution." Giddy with relief, Americans celebrated with parades, fireworks, illuminations, toasts, and ringing bells. "The public manifestations of joy are almost unbounded," Cope noted. In Salem, Massachusetts, a Federalist noted, "Our Town was frantic with joy at the news of Peace. It has come just in season to save our Country from destruction."

Noting the treaty's silence on the causes of the war, most Federalists detected another national disgrace that, they hoped, would at last discredit the Republican party. But one savvy Federalist aptly predicted that the Republicans would downplay the failed invasion of Canada and, instead, portray "a war on our part of pure self defence against the designs of the British to reduce us again to subjection." Indeed, Madison extolled the treaty as "an event which is highly honorable to the nation, and terminates, with peculiar felicity, a campaign signalised by the most brilliant successes." A Federalist complained, "it is attempted to make us believe that all the objects of the war have been obtained, when every thing, for which it was declared has been abandoned."

Having failed to conquer Canada or compel British maritime concessions, the Republicans redefined national survival as victory. Monroe assured the Senate that "our Union has gained strength, our troops honor, and the nation character, by the contest." He concluded, "By the war we have acquired a character and a rank among other nations, which we did not enjoy before." By emphasizing honor rather than territory as the measure of victory, Republicans took their cue from General Jacob Brown, who had developed that theme during his 1814 campaign on the Niagara front. In return, the Republican spin on the peace treaty imparted a rosier glow in memory to Brown's futile campaign.

In early February the myth of the glorious war got a boost with the arrival, on the East Coast, of dramatic news that American troops had won a sensational victory near New Orleans. On January 8, in the war's most lopsided battle, General Andrew Jackson's army had routed six thousand British regulars. At a cost of only thirty minutes and seventy-one casualties, the Americans had killed 290 Britons, wounded 1,262, and captured 484. Before dying in the battle, the overconfident British commander had marched his men across open ground in a frontal assault on entrenched Americans who merely had to blast away at the exposed attackers.

The battle of New Orleans nicely fit the cherished stereotype of bungling Britons unsuited for war in North America, so it became celebrated in American story and song. In fact, the battle was exceptional. Most of the war had been fought in the northern borderland, where Britons and their Indians had been more resourceful and victorious. And at New Orleans the victory primarily belonged to the artillery of the regular army rather than to the celebrated riflemen from the frontier.

A different legend dismisses the battle as inconsequential because it was waged two weeks after the signing of the peace treaty. In fact, the peace did not become official until the exchange of ratifications on February 17, more than a month after the battle of New Orleans. And the battle had an enormous impact on a generation of British officers and officials, who balked at again invading the United

States. New Orleans confirmed the lesson of Saratoga and Yorktown from the previous war: that invaders risked destruction within the United States. Thereafter, British restraint gave the Americans a free hand to dispossess Indians. The victory at New Orleans had enduring and massive consequences.

At Dartmoor, news of Jackson's triumph thrilled the American prisoners because it humbled their jailers:

> Nothing now is thought of or talked of, but *New Orleans* and *Jackson*, and *Jackson* and *New Orleans*. We already perceive that we are treated with more respect, and our country spoken of in honorable terms. The language now is—we are all one of the same people. You have all English blood in your veins, and it is no wonder that you fight bravely.

An enormous psychological victory for the Americans, the battle of New Orleans helped to reconcile the British to the peace treaty. In effect, the victory enabled the United States to turn the ambiguous treaty into an advantage in subsequent dealings with the British.

In mid-February news of the great victory merged with the ratification of peace to shape the American memory of the war. Because most Americans learned of New Orleans shortly before hearing of the peace treaty, they believed that their one big victory on land had forced the British to abandon the war. The news from New Orleans and Ghent also coincided with the arrival in Washington of a delegation of New England Federalists bearing the demands of the Hartford Convention. Unlucky in their timing, the delegates were roundly mocked by Republicans as defeatist fools and crypto-traitors. Ignored by Congress and the president, the delegates returned home in a disgrace inflicted by the unanticipated events at New Orleans and Ghent. Thereafter, the Hartford Convention became a synonym for treason, hurled at the Federalists during every election.

Most voters preferred the comforting myth of a glorious war confirmed by an honorable peace, so the Federalists crumbled at the polls, even in New England. In the election of 1816 James Monroe easily won the presidency, and the Federalists lost a third of their seats in Congress, and they would lose half of the rest two years later. "Never was there a more glorious opportunity," Joseph Story boasted, "for the Republican party to place themselves permanently in power."

International Missions and Tenuous Anglo-American Relations

EMILY CONROY-KRUTZ

In December of 1812, American missionary Samuel Newell sat down to write a letter home. His wife Harriet and their newborn baby had just died, and he wanted to send word to her family in Massachusetts. Yet getting this news

Excerpt from Emily Conroy-Krutz, "Engaged in the Same Glorious Cause:' Anglo-American Connections in the American Missionary Entrance into India, 1790–1815." *Journal of the Early Republic*, Vol. 34, No.1 (Spring 2014). Reprinted with permission of the University of Pennsylvania Press.

from the Isle of France (Mauritius), where Newell was exiled, back to Salem proved difficult, as there were no ships traveling between the two. As Newell wrote, the War of 1812 was in its seventh month, and he along with his missionary brethren had been arrested in India and threatened with deportation either back to the United States or to England as prisoners of war. The first American foreign mission had arrived in Asia at a particularly inauspicious time. Disconnected from his friends, his missionary board, and his country, Samuel Newell turned to Joseph Hardcastle, a leader of the London Missionary Society (LMS), for help. It was Hardcastle who would deliver the news of the death of the first martyr to the American missionary movement, which was a fitting testament to the relationship between British and American evangelicals in the early nineteenth century. Even as the nations that the two groups represented waged war, missionaries and their supporters relied on trans-Atlantic networks for survival and information. The American evangelical connection to Britain inspired and sustained the American foreign mission movement in its first years. As Newell and his brethren discovered during their time in India during the War of 1812, however much they identified as part of a shared Anglo–American Christian project, their national identity mattered, too. As American missionaries in the British Empire during an Anglo–American war, these missionaries provide a window on American national identity during the early republic.

The story of the American entry into foreign mission work does not have significance only to the religious historian. It reveals the continued links between Americans and the British in the early republic. During this era of American national identity formation, global connections were incredibly important for some Americans. Historians have typically portrayed the early national era as one of isolationist or protectionist foreign relations. Embargo and non-intercourse defined the period immediately before the War of 1812, when American evangelicals began to fashion their proposals for the conversion of the world. Yet this was also a time in which Americans throughout the country were working out what it meant to be former British colonies. Not yet sure of what it meant to be "American," many Americans of this era joined the missionaries in focusing on British example for definitions of "civilization" and culture. For many Americans of the time, and particularly the inhabitants of port cities Salem and Boston who were such important figures in the early history of American missions, however, the late eighteenth and early nineteenth centuries were years of continued connection across the Atlantic and increasing ambition for national (or at least regional) prominence abroad. Evangelical Christians expressed this ambition through their participation in the foreign mission movement. Building upon a long tradition of trans-Atlantic networks, supporters of the American Board asserted their equality with Britain in representing the embodiment of "true religion" and the ability to spread that Christianity abroad. As they would discover in India, however, this equality had little basis in reality. In highlighting the Anglo–American connections in the early foreign mission movement, this article reorients our attention to the ways that Americans of the early republic created their national identity within a global context.

The creation of the American Board of Commissioners for Foreign Missions (ABCFM) in 1810 marked a new stage in American Protestant evangelization. In the aftermath of the American Revolution, American Christians had formed new missionary societies in Connecticut, Massachusetts, New York, and Pennsylvania. Their missionaries had focused on converting Native Americans within state boundaries. At first, American missionaries did not seem to think that they could or even should attempt to evangelize outside of these territorial limits. American missionary societies saw as their own territory the "large tracts of country still unsettled" within the United States. They expected that even within these boundaries "the field for missionary labors will therefore be extending itself for many years, if not ages," as the domain of the United States expanded likewise. Yet by 1810, these same individuals insisted that Providence directed American Christians to work in and alongside the expanding British Empire.

In the first decade of the century, American evangelicals shifted their attention abroad, and began to include foreign fields in their ideas about the proper sphere of labor for American missionaries. This transition happened quite quickly. In 1805, the Connecticut Missionary Society insisted that it could not send missionaries to Canada because not only was there not enough money, but it was a British territory. They feared that it would seem improper to both U.S. and Canadian authorities to have Connecticut missionaries operating there. Canada should be the concern of the British missionaries. In 1810, however, many of these same supporters of the Massachusetts, Connecticut, and London Missionary Societies within the United States had formed the ABCFM. It no longer seemed to be a problem for American missionaries to operate within territories governed by another nation.

This shift can be explained in part as a new development out of the long-standing connections between American and British evangelicals. American Christians had been eager consumers of the news of British missionary progress. Dispatches from British missionaries in Tahiti, South Africa, and India were shared frequently enough across the Atlantic that the *Christian Observer*, a publication of the American Episcopal Church, informed its readers that by the time the annual report from the LMS reached its desk in 1805, "the greatest part of the information which it contains, respecting the progress of their missions, has already been communicated to our readers." In spite of the differences in scope of their operations in the 1790s and 1800s, the directors of American and British mission societies corresponded across the Atlantic, elected each other honorary directors, and generally considered themselves "engaged in the same glorious cause": the conversion of the whole world to an Anglo–American model of Protestant Christianity.

In the midst of this trans-Atlantic cooperation, one group seemed to be having much more success than the other and to be making a more significant impact in the global work of conversion. Americans frequently noted that British missionaries were more successful than their own, and that the so-called "heathen" of other parts of the world seemed more ready for evangelization than those in North America. At this time, missions to Native Americans were showing little sign of success. The Connecticut Missionary Society, for example, described the "heathen on our borders" as "in many respects more unfavorable to the reception of the Gospel, than ... the inhabitants of the South Sea" with whom British missionaries were working. With limited funds, the northeastern missionary societies were able to accomplish little along the lines of permanent missionary institutions or conversions. In 1811, Samuel Worcester, Corresponding Secretary of the ABCFM, addressed those in England who "may wonder" at Americans' entry into global mission work. He explained that though the Board was aware of the needs of many on "our own Continent," the attempts to evangelize to them had been "attended with so many discouragements, and South America is yet in such a state, that the opinion very generally prevails, that for the Pagans on this Continent, but little can immediately be done." Instead, he wrote, "the eastern world is thought to present a more promising field."

Worcester and others had come to this conclusion because of the news of British missionary success around the world. The expansion of the British Empire had allowed missionaries to reach new places, and they reported great success throughout the world. The longstanding connections between American and British missionary societies meant that Americans eventually wanted to join the British in the more fruitful parts of the globe. In addition to private and published correspondence, Americans had access to published sermons by East India Company chaplains like Claudius Buchanan, as well as missionary treatises by William Carey. These made specific reference to India and to the Christian community's perceived responsibility to the subcontinent. Adoniram Judson, one of the first ABCFM missionaries, credited Buchanan's sermon "A Star in the East" with having first inspired his calling to mission. This was Buchanan's goal; the sermon sought to convince Christians in England and America that the time had come "for diffusing our religion in the east." Sending the Bible to Asia would give "light and knowledge" and lead to "the conversion of the heart." Buchanan cited recent converts and efforts to translate the scriptures to give a sense of this as a moment of great promise. Americans in particular, he wrote, ought to take this opportunity to "be an instrument of good in the world."

Given the rich Anglo–American evangelical network and the participation of northeastern merchants in trade with Asia, it was only a matter of time before Americans, too, embraced the British theological reading of Empire. For many British evangelicals, the presence of an Empire demanded a religious response. The British Empire was a sign that the time had come to engage in mission work; it was God's way of opening the world to the spread of the Gospel. Americans, too, saw Providential signs in the expansion of the British Empire, the possibility of passage on American ships to Asia, and the new knowledge of the world obtained by explorers.

Inspired by these factors and moved by a deep sense of calling, four students at Andover Seminary in Massachusetts approached some local ministers in 1810 with their proposal to dedicate their lives to overseas mission work. The ABCFM was founded out of that meeting. It was the first American overseas mission organization, composed of Presbyterians, Congregationalists, and Dutch Reformed Christians with an evangelical fervor to convert the whole world. In spite of its denominational boundaries and its New England base, the Board envisioned itself as nationally representative within the work of world mission. The Board's missionaries, for example, were always defined simply as Americans, and almost never by their denominational backgrounds. The Board's Prudential Committee planned to spend the year following its creation gathering information about the "unevangelized nations" of the world to learn where they ought to direct their work. Such research involved contact with American commercial networks as well as extensive correspondence with British mission boards, continuing the tradition of cooperation and consultation across the Atlantic, Once the Americans had formed their own missionary society, however, this correspondence took on a new tone. In American eyes, they were now joining the British as partners. That partnership, as they would find, was hardly one of equals.

Aside from any geopolitical issue, it was unclear in 1810 whether the American public would be able to financially support such a project. In light of the previous connections between American mission supporters and the LMS, the Board sent Adoniram Judson, one of its missionaries, to London to ask if these connections might be formalized. In his letter to the Society, Board Secretary Samuel Worcester expressed his hopes that "Great Britain and these States, may 'always be one, united by one language and religion, and by mutual interest.'" The Board hoped that the British would sponsor the American missionaries, while still allowing the ABGFM to retain control over where they went and what they did. This attempt on the part of the Board to balance financial and governing insecurities revealed the American missionary dependence on the British even as they attempted to assert an independent presence in the work of worldwide benevolent reform.

Americans saw the move into overseas mission work as representing a shift in Anglo–American relations. Just as the United States was, in the political and economic spheres, attempting to assert its national strength in relation to Europe, so too were American Christians claiming a role for themselves equal to that of the British. "If all the circumstances of the case are considered," the ABCFM reminded its supporters in America, "we are more able to take an active part in evangelizing the heathen, than any other people on the globe, With the exception of Great Britain, indeed, no nation but our own has the inclination, or the ability, to make great exertions in the prosecution of this design." In making these claims, the Board shifted the emphasis in the long tradition of Anglo–American evangelical connections from the eighteenth century. Before, the two groups were evangelicals from metropole and colony of a shared empire, and Americans were the lesser party. Now, they were separate nations, linked by a common tradition but distinct in political affairs, and the Americans felt that they had raised their rank enough to proclaim themselves, along with Britain, as the sole country that could send appropriate missions out into the world. As the Board continued this address, it asserted the importance of American missionary exertions, perhaps even beyond what England could accomplish, At the time, the British were at war with France and this, according to the Board, distracted them from the full realization of their religious duty. Americans, free from European imperial struggles, were thus better positioned than the British to take on the mantle of evangelists to the world....

By February 1812, the Board had received sufficient donations to send out missionaries [to India] under its own care. Judson, Hall, Newell, Nott, and Luther Rice were ordained as missionaries and instructed to establish an American mission in South Asia that would transform Asia into part of God's "civilized" and Protestant kingdom through education, preaching, and distribution of sacred texts. American supporters saw the hand of Providence in these events, indicating God's pleasure in their entry into foreign missions. Yet the American identity of these missionaries would prove challenging within a few months, when the United States declared war on Britain. The Board and its supporters opposed the "deplorable war," which interrupted their contact with the missionaries in India and challenged the logic supporting the American missionary endeavor as a whole. Even in the year before, the Board had described the "aspect of our national affairs" as "gloomy." Wartime brought a bleaker outlook. Practically speaking, the war made it even more difficult for the Board to send instructions, funds, and goods to its missionaries in India; their correspondence would need to be directed through England. Ships to India were harder than ever to come by, and the Board noted in its Annual Report of 1812 that had the missionaries not left when they did, they would not likely have been able to establish a mission until the war's conclusion.

The Board had more philosophical points of opposition, too. Like the mission movement itself, the war was at least in part a statement about the supposed place of the United States in the world relative to England. Yet they were very different statements. If the mission movement claimed that the United States was the equal of England and could accordingly be its partner in world mission, the current international conflict between the two nations challenged this partnership. Further, the Board had argued that Americans should begin mission work partly because the British were distracted by their war with France. The beginning of an American war with Britain belied this logic. The directors of the Board were very concerned that the war might distract both the American public and the missionaries themselves from the needs of the "heathen." Quickly changing their argument, the Board began to praise Britain for maintaining "a liberality, a zeal, and a spirit of enterprise" in its mission work despite having been embroiled in many years of war. In this time of war, "America should be provoked to emulation" and not "faint or be discouraged," They went on to suggest that to allow charitable exertions to flag would add "immeasurably to all the necessary evils of war," and would in fact constitute "a return to the ages of barbarism." One of the Board's primary critiques of the war, then, was that it would potentially counter the effects of the missionary awakening that had just begun within the United States. Importantly, the most direct statements about the war's effect on missionary activities were confined to personal correspondence and excluded from the public writings of the Board.

In his first letter to the missionaries after the war began, the Board's Corresponding Secretary Samuel Worcester reminded the missionaries that the war made it essential that both the missionaries and the Board be sure to cooperate with the British in India. Political affairs, he insisted, were not their concern. Instead, he wrote, "The kingdom, to whose interests you are devoted, is not of this world. It is the kingdom of grace and truth, of righteousness and peace." Nonetheless, the war might require the missionaries to choose a location "without the limits of the British empire." Worcester's letter suggested the tensions that the war created for the American missionaries. They did not see themselves as being particularly defined by their nationality. Their concern was not earthly politics; they sought to expand God's kingdom, and to fight what they called the *"terrible empire"* of Satan. Yet the war forced them to be aware of national differences. By the time the missionaries received this letter, they had experienced first-hand the effects of the war on their work....

As the missionaries asserted their right to work in India, they relied on a few different points of argumentation. First, and most important, was the importance of their work, which transcended national differences. Their goals were simply to do the work of God through translation, education, and preaching. Accordingly, the missionaries' claims were decidedly not nationalistic. They stressed their educational work, particularly among European children, which would not even excite the religious concerns of the native population. They emphasized the Anglo–American nature of their project when they presented their letters from George Burder [an English minister] to prove that they had British support. If Americans had not provided them with funding, they "should at the same time have come to this country as English Missionaries with the same object in view as at the present moment." The "only difference between us and English Missionaries," they went on to explain, was who paid them....

The news of the war's end reached the missionaries in 1815, and they, along with the ABCFM in Boston, offered their "perpetual thanks" to God for this peace. For the Board, peace meant greater ease of contact with its missionaries and expanded opportunities for establishing new missions overseas. It meant a restoration of order and a reestablishment of regular trans-Atlantic correspondence with British evangelicals. Only a week after Evarts wrote to the missionaries, Oliver Smith in Philadelphia wrote to the LMS—the first opportunity to write since the war began, and the first chance to share a report of students in Smith's school reading letters from the British missionaries on board the Harmony, which "drew tears from the eyes of almost all present." In August, the New York Missionary Society renewed its correspondence with London, and by the fall, the LMS was writing back to America, sending publications, news of translation progress abroad, and funds to support efforts to evangelize the Native Americans. The conclusion of the war, then, allowed many aspects of the Anglo–American missionary network to return to normal, with one important difference: Now, the American missionaries were secure in their position in South Asia, and the reopening of trade meant that the Board could dispatch more missionaries to support the Bombay station and establish a new mission at Ceylon. Future correspondence between the ABCFM and LMS would be marked by occasional conflicts over the division of the territories across the globe, as American missionaries really did come to take full part in the global work of world mission.

 FURTHER READING

Stephen E. Ambrose, *Undaunted Courage: Meriwether Lewis, Thomas Jefferson, and the Opening of the American West* (1997).

Stephen Aron, *How the West Was Lost: The Transformation of Kentucky from Daniel Boone to Henry Clay* (1996).

Gregory Evans Dowd, *War under Heaven: Pontiac, the Indian Nations, and the British Empire* (2002).

John Mack Faragher, *Daniel Boone: The Life and Legend of an American Pioneer* (1992).

Matthew Mason, *Slavery and Politics in the Early American Republic* (2006).

Gretchen Murphy and Donald E. Pease, *Hemispheric Imaginations: The Monroe Doctrine and Narratives of U.S. Empire* (2006).

Peter S. Onuf, *Jefferson's Empire: The Language of American Nationhood* (2000).

Greg Russell, *John Quincy Adams and the Public Virtues of Diplomacy* (1995).

Christina Snyder, *Slavery in Indian Country* (2012).

J. C. A. Stagg, *Mr. Madison's War: Politics, Diplomacy and Warfare in the Early Republic* (1983).

John Sugden, *Tecumseh: A Life* (1997).

Additional critical thinking activities and content are available in MindTap.

MindTap   **MindTap** is a fully online, highly personalized learning experience built upon Cengage Learning content. MindTap combines student learning tools—readings, multimedia, activities, and assessments—into a singular Learning Path that guides students through the course.

CHAPTER 8

Market and Transportation Revolutions

The early nineteenth century witnessed vast changes in American society that irrevocably altered the lives of most Americans. These changes were so momentous that historians have strained to find the right name. Some call it a "market revolution." Others call it a "transportation" or "communication" or "information" revolution. All seem to agree that 1850 was quite distinct from 1750.

These changes were nurtured by specific efforts of leaders in government and business. In the years following the War of 1812, a group of American statesmen envisioned a national economic policy that would foster economic development. Known as the "American System," this plan called for a national bank, protective tariffs, and improved transportation and communication. The American System would not be enacted in its entirety, but beginning with the Wilderness Road in 1795, some 4,000 miles of turnpikes were constructed by 1821. Roads were complemented by the construction of canals. Most remarkable was the Erie Canal, completed in 1825, that linked New York City to the American interior. In the next 15 years, the Erie Canal was supplemented by some 3,300 miles of canals that crisscrossed the nation.

When steam power was harnessed, steamboats and railroads were built to ply goods on rivers and rails. Information traveled wider and faster too. In 1780, the United States had about thirty newspapers. By 1820, that number had ballooned to more than five hundred. Then with the patenting of the electric telegraph in the 1840s, information could travel faster than ships, wagons, or horseback. In less than twenty years, telegraph lines connected not only much of the United States but also the nation to Europe. The costs of the transport of bulky goods fell 95 percent between 1825 and 1855, the speed of transport increased fivefold, and information could be relayed instantly and widely.

Technological changes and altered business practices proceeded apace as well. By 1850, some one thousand patents were issued by the U.S. Patent Office to inventors. And the corporation became an increasingly powerful business practice that pooled capital and distributed profits. The Supreme Court facilitated these practices when it issued a series of decisions that aided business and fostered economic development. Contracts, the Court held, were secure from the meddling of state and local officials and Congress was supreme in dealing with interstate commerce.

These changes laid the foundation for a market revolution that irreversibly altered the daily activities of people and changed the economic landscape of the nation. Before improvements in transportation and communication, people had produced much of what they ate and wore at home or in their local communities. As late as 1820, no more than one-quarter of the harvests on American farms were exported from the local community. As the market revolution progressed, people now increasingly produced commodities for sale and used the income they earned to purchase goods produced by others. Most notably, the production of cotton in the South exploded. In 1820, for example, not only had the output of cotton become over one hundred times greater than it had been thirty years before, but it now accounted from over one-half of all agricultural exports from the United States. Because regions of the nation—such as the South—possessed certain natural advantages, a national market economy developed. People in the South specialized in producing crops for export; those in the Northwest produced food to feed people in the East and the South who were specializing in export agriculture, commerce, or manufacturing.

These changes wrought opportunities and challenges alike for Americans living in the North and the South, and working in the factory and on the farm. It is true that people increasingly lived and worked in the city. In 1820, only 6 percent lived in towns of more than 2,500 people. By 1860, the figure was 20 percent. And whereas over 80 percent of Americans labored on plantations and farms in 1800, the proportion had dropped to 50 percent by 1860. Whether they toiled in the city or in rural locales, however, the cadence of their work, the use of their produce, and the structure of their families and communities were forever changed.

QUESTIONS TO THINK ABOUT

In what ways did the transportation, communication, and market revolutions change the everyday lives of Americans? Were there winners and losers in the outcome of the market revolution? On balance, was it a beneficial development? Were the South and the North on opposite ends of this development or connected? Do you think a "national market economy," in which regions of the nation specialized in certain goods for trade with other regions, would link the nation together or pull it apart?

DOCUMENTS

This set of documents illustrates efforts by Americans to facilitate a market revolution and the impact of the revolution itself on the ways in which people lived their lives. Document 1 is an early account of the forced migration of slaves from eastern states to the regions of burgeoning cotton production in the South. In document 2, President John Quincy Adams, in his first annual message to Congress in 1825, urged a group of internal improvement projects including exploring the West and fostering scientific research. Documents 3 and 5 illustrate farm life and the changes wrought by the various revolutions. Document 4 is a memoir written by Harriet Hanson Robinson, a woman who did not labor on a farm but instead toiled in the textile mills in Lowell, Massachusetts, in the early 1830s. Despite assurances from the mill owners that the mills were safe and respectable, Robinson focuses instead on the harsh conditions and labor unrest. In document 6, Charles Dickens, the prominent English author, provides a vivid description of the frenzy of riding on a train in the early days of railroad travel. Document 7 depicts the growing significance of the mother as the center of the middle-class family, a family in which the significance of the mother in instructing her children is highlighted. Document 8 showcases how southern cotton was influential in northern and national development as well. This advertisement from a northern business not only sells the "southern" product but does so with the growing "southern" ideology of states' rights that would help undo the nation as these market forces tied them together.

1. Slave Charles Ball Mourns the Growth of Cotton Culture and "Sale Down the River," c. 1800

After we were all chained and handcuffed together, we sat down upon the ground; and here reflecting upon the sad reverse of fortune that had so suddenly overtaken me, I became weary of life, and bitterly execrated the day I was born. It seemed that I was destined by fate to drink the cup of sorrow to the very dregs, and that I should find no respite from misery but in the grave. I longed to die, and escape from the hands of my tormentors; but even the wretched privilege of destroying myself was denied me, for I could not shake off my chains, nor move a yard without the consent of my master....

Our master ordered a pot of mush to be made for our supper; after despatching which we all lay down on the naked floor to sleep in our handcuffs and chains. The women, my fellow-slaves, lay on one side of the room; and the men who were chained with me, occupied the other. I slept but little this night, which I passed in thinking of my wife and little children, whom I could not hope ever to see again. I also thought of my grandfather, and of the long nights I had passed with him, listening to his narratives of the scenes through which he had passed in Africa. I at length fell asleep, but was distressed by painful dreams....

We left this place early in the morning, and directed our course toward the south-west; our master riding beside us, and hastening our march, sometimes by words of encouragement, and sometimes by threats of punishment. The women took their place in the rear of our line. We halted about nine o'clock for breakfast,

Charles Ball, *Fifty Years in Chains: Or the Life of an American Slave* (New York: Dayton, and Indianapolis, Ind.: Asher and Company, 1860), 30–31, 33–35.

and received as much corn-bread as we could eat, together with a plate of boiled herrings, and about three pounds of pork amongst us. Before we left this place, I was removed from near the middle of the chain, and placed at the front end of it; so that I now became the leader of the file, and held this post of honor until our irons were taken from us, near the town of Columbia in South Carolina....

We continued our course up the country westward for a few days and then turned South, crossed James river above Richmond, as I heard at the time. After more than four weeks of travel we entered South Carolina near Camden, and for the first time I saw a field of cotton in bloom.

As we approached the Yadkin river the tobacco disappeared from the fields and the cotton plant took its place as an article of general culture.

I was now a slave in South Carolina, and had no hope of ever again seeing my wife and children. I had at times serious thoughts of suicide so great was my anguish. If I could have got a rope I should have hanged myself at Lancaster. The thought of my wife and children I had been torn from in Maryland, and the dreadful undefined future which was before me, came near driving me mad.

2. President John Quincy Adams Urges Internal Improvements, 1825

In assuming her station among the civilized nations of the earth it would seem that our country had contracted the engagement to contribute her share of mind, of labor, and of expense to the improvement of those and of expense to the improvement of those parts of knowledge which lie beyond the reach of individual acquisition, and particularly to geographical and astronomical science. Looking back to the history only of the half century since the declaration of our independence, and observing the generous emulation with which the Governments of France, Great Britain, and Russia have devoted the genius, the intelligence, the treasures of their respective nations to the common improvement of the species in these branches of science, is it not incumbent upon us to inquire whether we are not bound by obligations of a high and honorable character to contribute our portion of energy and exertion to the common stock? The voyages of discovery prosecuted in the course of that time at the expense of those nations have not only redounded to their glory, but to the improvement of human knowledge. We have been partakers of that improvement and owe for it a sacred debt, not only of gratitude, but of equal or proportional exertion in the same common cause....

In inviting the attention of Congress to the subject of internal improvements upon a view thus enlarged it is not my design to recommend the equipment of an expedition for circumnavigating the globe for purposes of scientific research and inquiry. We have objects of useful investigation nearer home, and to which our

John Quincy Adams, (Annual Message to Congress) (1825), in *The Selected Writings of John and John Quincy Adams*, ed. Adrienne Koch and William Peden (New York: Alfred A. Knopf, 1946), 361–364.

cares may be more beneficially applied. The interior of our own territories has been imperfectly explored. Our coasts along many degrees of latitude upon the shores of the Pacific ocean, though much frequented by our spirited commercial navigators, have been barely visited by our public ships. The River of the West, first fully discovered and navigated by a countryman of our own, still bears the name of the ship in which he ascended its waters, and claims the protection of our armed national flag at its mouth. With the establishment of a military post there or at some other point of that coast, recommended by my predecessor and already matured in the deliberations of the last Congress, I would suggest the expediency of connecting the equipment of a public ship for the exploration of the whole northwest coast of this continent.

The establishment of an uniform standard of weights and measures was one of the specific objects contemplated in the formation of our Constitution, and to fix that standard was one of the powers delegated by express terms in that instrument to Congress....

Connected with the establishment of an university, or separate from it, might be undertaken the erection of an astronomical observatory, with provision for the support of an astronomer, to be in constant attendance of observation upon the phenomena of the heavens, and for the periodical publication of his observations....

And while scarcely a year passes over our heads without bringing some new astronomical discovery to light, which we must fain receive at second hand from Europe, are we not cutting ourselves off from the means of returning light for light while we have neither observatory nor observer upon our half of the globe and the earth revolves in perpetual darkness to our unsearching eyes?

3. A Family in Illinois Struggles with Marketing Their Crops, 1831

Having thrashed and winnowed our wheat ..., our next consideration was how we were to sell it. The produce of the three acres might be about eighty bushels, one-fourth of which was but imperfectly cleared of cheat [a troublesome weed that grows in wheat], and was therefore unsaleable. We had only five sacks, ... but these even we did not require, as we subsequently learnt the store-keepers were accustomed to furnish the settlers with bags for their corn. My husband took a specimen of wheat, which as it had been sown too sparingly on the ground was a fine sample. Mr. Varley offered half a dollar per bushel in money, or a few cents more in barter. We borrowed a waggon and a yoke of oxen of one of our neighbours, and carried to the store fifty bushels. The first thing we did was to settle our meal account; we next bought two pairs of shoes for self and husband, which by this time we wanted as we did

Rebecca and Edward Burlend, in *A True Picture of Emigration*, ed. Milo Milton Quaife (Secaucus, N.J.: The Citadel Press, 1968), 107–109.

other articles of apparel, which we knew we could conveniently procure. The truth is, we had intended to have a little more clothing, but finding the prices so extravagant, we felt compelled to abandon that intention. For a yard of common printed calico, they asked half a dollar, or a bushel of wheat, and proportionate prices for other goods. We gave ten bushels of wheat for the shoes.... Our next purchase was a plough, bought in hopes that we should, at some time, have cattle to draw it, as we were tired of the hoeing system. We also bought two tin milk bowls; these and the plough cost about twenty bushels. We obtained further a few pounds of coffee, and a little meal; the coffee cost us at the rate of a dollar for four pounds; and thus we laid out the greater part of our first crop of wheat. We had only reserved about twenty bushels for seed, besides a quantity imperfectly cleared of cheat, which unfit either for sale or making bread. On balancing our account with Mr. Varley, we found we had to take about five dollars, which we received in paper money, specie being exceedingly scarce in Illinois.

4. Harriet Hanson Robinson, a "Lowell Girl," Describes Her Labor in a Textile Mill, 1831

In 1831, under the shadow of a great sorrow, which had made her four children fatherless,—the oldest but seven years of age,—my mother was left to struggle alone; and, although she tried hard to earn bread enough to fill our hungry mouths, she could not do it, even with the help of kind friends....

Shortly after this my mother's widowed sister, Mrs. Angeline Cudworth, who kept a factory boarding-house in Lowell, advised her to come to that city.

I had been to school constantly until I was about ten years of age, when my mother, feeling obliged to have help in her work besides what I could give, and also needing the money which I could earn, allowed me, at my urgent request (for I wanted to earn *money* like the other little girls), to go to work in the mill. I worked first in the spinning-room as a "doffer." The doffers were the very youngest girls, whose work was to doff, or take off, the full bobbins, and replace them with the empty ones....

... When not doffing, we were often allowed to go home, for a time, and thus we were able to help our mothers in their housework. We were paid two dollars a week; and how proud I was when my turn came to stand up on the bobbin-box, and write my name in the paymaster's book, and how indignant I was when he asked me if I could "write." "Of course I can," said I, and he smiled as he looked down on me.

The working-hours of all the girls extended from five o'clock in the morning until seven in the evening, with one-half hour for breakfast and for dinner. Even the doffers were forced to be on duty nearly fourteen hours a day, and this was the greatest hardship in the lives of these children....

Harriet Hanson Robinson, *Loom and Spindle or Life Among the Early Mill Girls* (New York: T. Y. Crowell, 1898; reprinted, Press Pacifica, 1976), 16–22, 37–43, 51–53.

I do not recall any particular hardship connected with this life, except getting up so early in the morning, and to this habit, I never was, and never shall be, reconciled, for it has taken nearly a lifetime for me to make up the sleep lost at that early age. But in every other respect it was a pleasant life. We were not hurried any more than was for our good, and no more work was required of us than we were able easily to do.

Most of us children lived at home, and we were well fed, drinking both tea and coffee, and eating substantial meals (besides luncheons) three times a day. We had very happy hours with the older girls, many of whom treated us like babies, or talked in a motherly way, and so had a good influence over us....

I cannot tell how it happened that some of us knew about the English factory children, who, it was said, were treated so badly, and were even whipped by their cruel overseers....

In contrast with this sad picture, we thought of ourselves as well off, in our cosey corner of the mill, enjoying ourselves in our own way, with our good mothers and our warm suppers awaiting us when the going-out bell should ring.

When I look back into the factory life of fifty or sixty years ago, I do not see what is called "a call" of young men and women going to and from their daily work, like so many ants that cannot be distinguished one from another; I see them as individuals, with personalities of their own. This one has about her the atmosphere of her early home. That one is impelled by a strong and noble purpose. The other,—what she is, has been an influence for good to me and to all womankind.

Yet they were a class of factory operatives, and were spoken of (as the same class is spoken of now) as a set of persons who earned their daily bread, whose condition was fixed, and who must continue to spin and to weave to the end of their natural existence. Nothing but this was expected of them, and they were not supposed to be capable of social or mental improvement....

In 1831 Lowell was little more than a factory village. Several corporations were started, and the cotton-mills belonging to them were building. Help was in great demand; and stories were told all over the country of the new factory town, and the high wages that were offered to all classes of work-people,—stories that reached the ears of mechanics' and farmers' sons, and gave new life to lonely and dependent women in distant towns and farmhouses....

But the early factory girls were not all country girls. There were others also, who had been taught that "work is no disgrace." There were some who came to Lowell solely on account of the social or literary advantages to be found there. They lived in secluded parts of New England, where books were scarce, and there was no cultivated society. They had comfortable homes, and did not perhaps need the *money* they would earn; but they longed to see this new "City of Spindles." ...

It must be remembered that at this date woman had no property rights. A widow could be left without her share of her husband's (or the family) property, a legal "incumbrance" to his estate. A father could make his will without reference to his daughter's share of the inheritance....

The law took no cognizance of woman as a money-spender. She was a ward, an appendage, a relict. Thus it happened, that if a woman did not choose to marry, or, when left a widow, to re-marry, she had no choice but to enter one of the few employments open to her, or to become a burden on the charity of some relative.

In almost every New England home could be found one or more of these women, sometimes welcome, more often unwelcome, and leading joyless, and in many instances unsatisfactory, lives. The cotton-factory was a great opening to these lonely and dependent women. From a condition approaching pauperism they were at once placed above want; they could earn money, and spend it as they pleased; and could gratify their tastes and desires without restraint, and without rendering an account to anybody....

One of the first strikes of cotton-factory operatives that ever took place in this country was that in Lowell, in October, 1836. When it was announced that the wages were to be cut down, great indignation was felt, and it was decided to strike, *en masse*....

One of the girls stood on a pump, and gave vent to the feelings of her companions in a neat speech, declaring that it was their duty to resist all attempts at cutting down the wages. This was the first time a woman had spoken in public in Lowell, and the event caused surprise and consternation among her audience.

Cutting down the wages was not their only grievance, nor the only cause of this strike. Hitherto the corporations had paid twenty-five cents a week towards the board of each operative, and now it was their purpose to have the girls pay the sum; and this, in addition to the cut in wages, would make a difference of at least one dollar a week. It was estimated that as many as twelve or fifteen hundred girls turned out, and walked in procession through the streets....

It is hardly necessary to say that so far as results were concerned this strike did no good. The dissatisfaction of the operatives subsided, or burned itself out, and though the authorities did not accede to their demands, the majority returned to their work, and the corporation went on cutting down the wages.

And after a time, as the wages became more and more reduced, the best portion of the girls left and went to their homes, or to the other employments that were fast opening to women, until there were very few of the old guard left; and thus the *status* of the factory population of New England gradually became what we know it to be to-day.

5. Mary Graham Describes Life on a Commercializing Farm, 1835–1844

Buckland, April 6th 1835

Near and very dear friends,

I believe I shant wait in silence any longer for a letter. We have traveled too and from the Post Office for weeks, in vain. I now sit down to inquire the

From Edwards Family Correspondence, Manuscripts Collection, Trustees' Room, Forbes Library, Northampton, MA.

cause—is it sickness of death, or have you removed to the far west, to seek the goodly land, or did you during the extreme cold weather last winter freeze up and have not yet thawed out. If this be the cause do write and let us know and we will try to render you some assistance.... Will tell you something about our own family. Here we are all in comfortable health. L and myself have had to work as hard as we have been able, and a good deal harder than we wanted to. We are very much confined at home. I have not visited an afternoon in the town of B[uckland] for more than a year except at N's twice or three times. I have shoes a plenty to bind, from six to eight and twelve pairs in a week—and with all the rest have got four as dirty, noisy, ragged children to take care of as any other woman, they look as though they would do to put out in the cornfields in about six or eight weeks to keep away the crows....

Buckland Feb. 5, 1837

Dear Friends at Northampton ...

Hardly know what to say about ourselves, but will say this we have plenty of hard work and poor keeping and money at interest, and are always like to have. I can hardly feel reconciled to not visiting you this winter, but so much to do and so much money at interest that we cant get enough to bear our expences down there back again. Of course we must stay at home....

Buckland Feb. 12, 1839

Dear Brother and Sister ...

I now seat myself to acknowledge the reception of a few lines from you some weeks since. Probably you have expected an answer before this, which I allow to be reasonable, but by way of apology will just say that I work in the shop most of the time. We have been unusually [crowded?] with work, have been obliged to be in the shop early and late. Of course not much time to write.... We received a letter from Clark and Caroline a few weeks since, they were in Indianna, New Albany, Floyd County. She has had a son and lost it. They were in comfortable health when they wrote.... We have had a terrible freshet and from accounts think it did considerable damage in your region. The bridge at the Falls barely escaped, one shop was washed away and several dwelling houses were in danger. Cousin G's was among the number....
PS Perhaps you may wonder what I do in the shop so much. I do the pegging, hammer the leather and considerable of the fitting....

Buckland March 3, 1844

Dear Brother and Sister,

I suppose I must answer your letter whether I want to or not. To tell the truth, I don't want to, for I don't feel like writing to anyone. You wanted all the news. I have some that is not very pleasant to me. In the first place, Lucius has sold us out of house and home with the [privilege] of staying here until the first of June. If he can rake and scrape enough after paying his debts to set his family down in Wisconsin he is determined to go. So you wonder that I feel sad. Nothing but poor health and poverty to begin with in a new country looks dark to me. But I can't help it, go we must I suppose if the means can be raised. Don't know as I shall be permitted to visit you, expect he will think that every dollar must be saved to go to the far West. Do come and see us *once more* for I can't endure that I shall never see you again....

6. Author Charles Dickens Describes Travel on an Early Railroad Train, 1842

Before leaving Boston, I devoted one day to an excursion to Lowell....

I made acquaintance with an American railroad, on this occasion, for the first time. As these works are pretty much alike all through the States, their general characteristics are easily described.

There are no first and second class carriages as with us; but there is a gentlemen's car and a ladies' car: the main distinction between which is that in the first, everybody smokes; and in the second, nobody does. As a black man never travels with a white one, there is also a negro car; which is a great, blundering, clumsy chest, such as Gulliver put to sea in, from the kingdom of Brobdingnag [a land where everything is huge]. There is a great deal of jolting, a great deal of noise, a great deal of wall, not much window, a locomotive engine, a shriek, and a bell.

The cars are like shabby omnibuses, but larger: holding thirty, forty, fifty, people. The seats, instead of stretching from end to end, are places crosswise. Each seat holds two persons. There is a long row of them on each side of the caravan, a narrow passage up the middle, and a door at both ends. In the centre of the carriage there is usually a stove, fed with charcoal or anthracite coal; which is for the most part red-hot. It is insufferably close; and you see the hot air fluttering between yourself and any other object you may happen to look at, like the ghost of smoke....

Except when a branch road joins the main one, there is seldom more than one track of rails; so that the road is very narrow, and the view, where there is a deep cutting, by no means extensive. When there is not, the character of the scenery is always the same. Mile after mile of stunted trees: some hewn down by the axe, some blown down by the wind, some half fallen and resting on their neighbours, many mere logs half hidden in the swamp, others mouldered away to spongy chips. The very soil of the earth is made up of minute fragments such as these; each pool of stagnant water has its crust of vegetable rottenness; on every side there are the boughs, and trunks, and stumps of trees, in every possible stage of decay, decomposition, and neglect. Now you emerge for a few brief minutes on an open country, glittering with some bright lake or pool, broad as many as English river, but so small here that it scarcely has a name; now catch hasty glimpses of a distant town, with its clean white houses and their cool piazzas, its prim New England church and schoolhouse; when whir-r-r-r! almost

Charles Dickens, *American Notes for General Circulation* (New York: Harper & Brothers, 1842; reprinted Harmondsworth, Eng.: Penguin, 1972), 111–113.

before you have seen them, comes the same dark screen: the stunted trees, the stumps, the logs, the stagnant water—all so like the last that you seem to have been transported back again by magic.

The train calls at stations in the woods, where the wild impossibility of anybody having the smallest reason to get out, is only to be equalled by the apparently desperate hopelessness of there being anybody to get in. It rushes across the turnpike road, where there is not gate, no policeman, no signal: nothing but a rough wooden arch, on which is paint "WHEN THE BELL RINGS, LOOK OUT FOR THE LOCOMOTIVE." On it whirls headlong, dives through the woods again, emerges in the light, clatters over frail arches, rumbles upon the heavy ground, shoots beneath a wooden bridge which intercepts the light for a second like a wink, suddenly awakens all the slumbering echoes in the main street of a large town, and dashes on haphazard, pell-mell, neck-or-nothing, down the middle of the road. There—with mechanics working at their trades, and people leaning from their doors and windows, and boys flying kites and playing marbles, and men smoking, and women talking, and children crawling, and pigs burrowing, and unaccustomed horses plunging and rearing, close to the very rails—there—on, on, on—tears the mad dragon of an engine with its train of cars; scattering in all directions a shower of burning sparks from its wood fire; screeching, hissing, yelling, panting; until at last the thirsty monster stops beneath a covered way to drink, the people cluster round, and you have time to breathe again.

7. A Guidebook Instructs Women on the Role of Mother, 1845

It takes a long time for the world to grow wise. Men have been busying themselves these six thousand years nearly to improve society. They have framed systems of philosophy and government, and conferred on their own sex all the advantages which power, wealth and knowledge could bestow. They have founded colleges and institutions of learning without number, and provided themselves teachers of every art and science; and, after all, the mass of mankind are very ignorant and very wicked. Wherefore is this? Because the *mother,* whom God constituted the first teacher of every human being, has been degraded by men from her high office; or, what is the same thing, been denied those privileges of education which only can enable her to discharge her duty to her children with discretion and effect. God created the woman as a *help-meet* for man in every situation; and while he, in his pride, rejects her assistance in his intellectual and moral career, he never will succeed to improve his nature and reach that perfection in knowledge, virtue and happiness, which his faculties are constituted to attain.

If half the effort and expense had been directed to enlighten and improve the minds of females which have been lavished on the other sex, we should now have a very different state of society. Wherever a woman is found excelling in judgment and knowledge, either by natural genius or from better

"Maternal Instruction," *Godey's Lady's Book* (1845).

opportunities, do we not see her children also excel? Search the records of history, and see if it can be found that a great and wise man ever descended from a weak and foolish mother. So sure and apparent is this maternal influence, that it has passed into an axiom of philosophy, it is acknowledged by the greatest and wisest of men; and yet, strange to say, the inference which ought to follow, namely, that in attempting to improve society, the first, most careful and continued efforts should be to raise the standard of female education, and qualify woman to become the educator of her children, has never yet been acted upon by any legislators, or acknowledged and tested by any philanthropists.

What is true of the maternal influence respecting sons is, perhaps, more important in the training of daughters. The fashionable schools are a poor substitute for such example and instruction as a thoroughly educated and right principled mother would bestow on her daughters. The best schools in the world will not, in and of themselves, make fine women. The tone of *family education* and of society needs to be raised. This can never be done till greater value is set on the cultivated female intellect. Young ladies must be inspired with high moral principles, noble aims, and a spirit of self-improvement to become what they ought to be. Maternal instruction is the purest and safest means of opening the fountain of knowledge to the young mind.

8. A Northern Advertisement Sells "Southerner Rights Segars," 1859

Library of Congress Prints and Photographs Division[LC-USZC4-12488]

 ESSAYS

These revolutions modified patterns of everyday life in the United States. In these two essays, we observe the transformation of several important aspects of life. Nancy F. Cott focuses on the profound adjustments within the rural family—with particular reference to the modification in the roles of women—that resulted from a burgeoning market economy. Not only did patterns of labor change, but the meaning of work and the responsibilities within the home were transformed as well. Daniel Walker Howe examines the role of cotton, transportation, and communication in creating these economic changes. Although the market revolution is typically seen originating in northern cities, Howe demonstrates the critical role of slavery and southern agrarian life in transforming America. Moreover, he suggests that changes to infrastructure and communication technology were more important than changes in labor practices and business. Although both Cott and Howe find dramatic changes occurring in the United States, they disagree about the primary locations of those changes and what altered most.

The Market Revolution and the Changes in Women's Work

NANCY F. COTT

"A woman's work is never done," Martha Moore Ballard wrote in her journal one November midnight in 1795, having been busy preparing wool for spinning until that time, "and happy she whos[e] strength holds out to the end of the [sun's] rays." Ballard was sixty years old that year—a grandmother several times over—though she still had at home her youngest child of sixteen. Housekeeper and domestic manufacturer for a working farm where she baked and brewed, pickled and preserved, spun and sewed, made soap and dipped candles, she also was a trusted healer and midwife for the pioneer community of Augusta, Maine. During a quarter-century of practice continuing past her seventieth year, she delivered more than a thousand babies. The very processes of her work engaged her in community social life. In her medical work she became acquainted with her neighbors as she provided services for them, and domestic crafts, such as quilting and spinning, also involved her in both cooperative and remunerative social relationships. The pattern of her life was not atypical for the matron of a farm household, particularly in a frontier community, in the late eighteenth century....

The basic developments hastening economic productivity and rationalizing economic organization in New England between 1780 and 1835 were extension of the size of the market, increases in agriculture efficiency, reduction in transportation costs, and consequent specialization of economic function, division of labor, and concentration of industry. In late eighteenth-century towns, subsistence farming and household production for family use prevailed, supplemented

From Nancy F. Cott, *The Bonds of Womanhood: "Woman's Sphere" in New England,* 1780–1935, 2nd ed., pp. 19, 23–27, 36–46, 57–58, 61–62. Copyright © 1997. Reprinted by permission of Yale University Press.

by individual craftsmen (cobblers, coopers, blacksmiths, tailors, weavers, etc.) who were established or itinerant depending on density of population in their locale, and by small industrial establishments such as sawmills, gristmills, fulling mills, ironworks, and brickyards. The Revolutionary War stimulated some forms of household production (such as "homespun"), and so did the disruption of the international market during the Napoleonic wars, but more continuous lines of change moved the New England economy from its agricultural and household-production base and gave it a commercial and then industrial emphasis by 1835.

Merchant capitalism was a primary force in this transformation. Merchant capitalists took risks, supplied capital, searched out markets, and attempted to maximize profits by producing standardized goods at the least cost, thus organizing production on a larger scale than had previously been typical. Their actions commanded a shift away from home production for family use, and from local craftsmen's production of custom or "bespoke" work for known individuals, toward more standardized production for a wider market. Mercantile capitalism flourished during the enormous expansion of New England's carrying trade and re-export business that occurred from 1793 to 1807 because of the confusion of European shipping during the Napoleonic wars. This burst of shipping energy also caused subsidiary economic activities, such as shipbuilding, and complementary businesses, such as brokerage, marine insurance, warehousing, and banking, to grow. Under the brunt of the national embargo in 1807 and the subsequent war with England this blooming of the American carrying and re-export trade faded, but since much of the capital involved was transferred to manufacturing activity overall economic productivity did not diminish greatly.

The shift to market-oriented production under merchant capitalists prepared the way for the development of manufacturing and the factory system. Under the demand of the merchant capitalist for widely distributable goods, the craftsman's shop became a larger and more specialized unit, for production only rather than (as formerly) for production and retail sale. The master craftsman became the "boss" of a larger number of journeymen and apprentices. In New England another production system, limited mainly to shoes and textiles, also preceded and overlapped with industrial manufacture. This was the "putting-out" or "given-out" system, in which a merchant or master craftsman distributed materials to individuals to work on in their homes at piece-work rates, and collected and sold the finished goods. As the given-out system developed, the individuals (often women) it employed at home performed more and more specialized and fragmentary handicrafts. Indeed, the hallmarks of economic development in this period were functional specialization and division of labor. Where there had been "jacks-of-all-trades" there came specialized laborers; where there had been eclectic merchants there came importers and exporters, wholesalers and jobbers and retailers. Farmers who had produced only for subsistence trained their eyes on, and diverted some of their energies to, the market for commercial produce. New specialists appeared in fields from insurance to banking to transportation, as incorporations of businesses multiplied and turnpikes and bridges replaced wooden paths. In order to understand shifts in women's work during these years, rapid changes of this type must be kept in mind. Whether a woman lived toward the beginning or toward the end of this half-century may have informed the character of her work as much as, or more than, her geographical location, wealth, or marital status, which were other significant factors. Comparison of the kinds of work recorded in women's diaries in the earlier and later years makes that clear.

During the late eighteenth century both unmarried and married women did their primary work in households, in families. Unmarried daughters might be called upon to help their fathers in a store or shop connected to the house: Sally Ripley, a tradesman's daughter in Greenfield. Massachusetts, more than once recorded in her diary, "This morning my Father departed for Boston, & I am again entrusted with the charge of the Store." But daughters' assistance in the housewife's realm of food preparation and preservation, dairying, gardening, cleaning, laundering, soap making, candle making, knitting, and textile and clothing manufacture was the more usual case. Mothers and daughters shared these labors. The continual and time-consuming work of spinning was the most readily delegated to the younger generation, it seems. Hannah Hickok Smith of Glastonbury, Connecticut, managed to avoid spinning, because she had five daughters at home. "The girls ... have been very busy spinning this spring," she reported to their grandmother in 1800, "and have spun enough for about seventy yards besides almost enough for another carpet." Spinning must have taken precedence in the daughters' work, for when they had "no spinning to do for any consequence" then Mrs. Smith admitted that she "lived very easy, as the girls have done every thing."...

The first "manufactories" in the United States were places of business established in major cities in the 1760s to collect yarn spun and cloth woven by women in their homes by traditional hand methods. Some merchants soon put spinning wheels and looms on the premises of their manufactories, and hired women and children to work them there; but in general they employed a much larger proportion of women working in their own homes than on the manufactory premises. After Samuel Slater introduced industrial spinning machinery to New England in 1789, and other entrepreneurs established spinning mills, employing women to work the machinery, the proportions working at home and on the premises were reversed. The early mills (between 1790 and 1815) produced only yarn, which was distributed to domestic weavers like Samantha Barrett to be made into cloth. The power loom did not appear in New England until 1814. That year the Boston Manufacturing Company introduced it at Waltham, Massachusetts, uniting under one factory roof all the operations necessary to turn raw fiber into finished cloth. Factories mass-producing cotton cloth multiplied during the 1820s.

By 1830, industrial manufacture had largely superseded home spinning and weaving in New England by producing cloth more cheaply. This changed women's work more than any other single factor, and likely had more emphatic impact on unmarried women than on mothers of families. Industrialization of textiles disrupted daughters' predictable role in the household first. Mothers' lives continued to be defined by household management and child rearing. Daughters, however, often had to earn wages to replace their contribution to family sustenance. Textile mill operatives, who were almost all between the ages of fifteen and thirty, were young women who followed their traditional occupation to a new location, the factory. New England textile factories from the start employed a vastly greater proportion of women than men.

The economic and social change of the period injected uncertainty, variety, and mobility into young women's lives—into none more dramatically than the early mill operatives'. Mary Hall began industrial employment after her academy schooling and experience in schoolteaching. In November 1830 she started folding books at a shop in Exeter, New Hampshire, not happy to be removed from her family. "Yes, I shall probably be obliged to call this, to me a land of strangers, home for the present," she wrote in her dairy. "But home sweet home can never be transfer'd in the affections of Me.... How often this day amidst its cares and business have I been in imagination under the paternal roof seeing, hearing and conversing with its lov'd inhabitants." She was twenty-four years old. After seven months she returned home, because several family members were ill. In September 1831, she went to Lowell, Massachusetts, for employment as a cotton-mill operative. She worked in Lowell for the next five years, except for returns home to Concord for more than a year between 1832 and 1833, for the summer in 1834, for weeks in November and December 1834 (because of deaths in her family), and in November 1835 and June 1836. During her years in Lowell she worked for at least three different corporations.

Emily Chubbuck, whose family was probably poorer than Mary Hall's, had a more disjointed employment history. The fifth child in a New Hampshire family transplanted to upstate New York, she went to work in 1828, at the age of eleven, splicing rolls in a woolen factory. Her parents allowed her to keep her weekly wage of $1.25. When the factory closed in January 1829 she began attending a district school, to supplement the education she had received from an older sister. Two months later the factory reopened and she resumed work there. During the next three years, as her family moved several times in attempts to make a living, she intermittently worked for a Scottish weaver twisting thread, attended an academy, washed and ironed for her family's boarders, sewed for a mantuamaker, and attended a district school. At fourteen, despite her mother's advice to apprentice herself to a milliner, she lied about her age to obtain a schoolteaching job. Her wages were only 75 cents a week plus board. She knew that she "could earn as much with the milliner, and far more at twisting thread," but she hoped for a future in literary pursuits rather than manual employment.

There was a large class of young women who would have spun at home in early decades but whose families' incomes or priorities made factory work unlikely for them. Their work too became variable and sporadic, shifting among the options of schoolteaching, needlework, domestic work, and given-out industry. None of these was really a full-time, year-round occupation. Women tended to combine them. Rachel Stearns, under pressure of necessity, became willing to intersperse sewing in another household with her schoolteaching, although earlier she had "thought it quite too degrading to go to Uncle F's and sew." Nancy Flynt, a single woman of Connecticut, wrote to her married sister around 1810, "[I am] a tugging and a toiling day and night to get a maintenance, denying myself the pleasure of calling on my nearest neighbors.... I would tell you how much work I have dispatched since I saw you, I have a great deal of sewing on hand now." The twenty-five-year-old daughter of the minister in Hawley, Massachusetts, decided she should learn to support herself "by the needle" and therefore began to learn the milliner's trade, but her health failed, preventing her from continuing. "Perhaps [I] flattered myself too much with the idea of being able to bear my own expenses," she reflected somewhat bitterly.

Given-out industry, which constituted a significant stage in the industrial development of New England, enabled women to earn money while staying at home. Two kinds of production organized this way drew heavily on women's labor: the stitching and binding of boots and shoes (concentrated in eastern Massachusetts) and the braiding, or plaiting, of straw bonnets. The latter was a handicraft designed before 1800 by New England women who used native rye straw for the material. By 1830 thousands carried it on in the employ of entrepreneurs who imported palm leaves from Cuba and distributed them to farmhouses to be made up into hats. Eliza Chaplin and her sister Caroline of Salem, Massachusetts, made and sold bonnets during the 1820s, the same years that they taught school. Julia Pierce taught school in the summer and had "plenty of work" to do in the winter, she said: "I have braided more than 100 hats and the other girls as many more." The working life of Amanda Elliot of Guilford, Connecticut, exemplifies the variety of this transitional period. Within six months in 1816–17 she devoted considerable time to splitting straw and braiding hats; noted five new boarders; taught school; and mentioned binding shoes, in addition to usual domestic needlework, knitting, washing, and ironing. For some fortunate young women, of course, the diminution of household manufacture for the family meant greater leisure and opportunity for education. Hannah Hickok Smith's letters after 1800 revealed that spinning gradually dwindled in importance in her daughters' occupations. "As we have had much leisure time this winter," she wrote in 1816, "the girls have employed themselves chiefly in reading writing and studying French Latin and Greek."

While economic modernization changed young unmarried women's work more conspicuously than their mothers' at first, the disruption of the integral relation between the household and the business of society was bound to rede-fine matrons' occupations too. Wife-and-motherhood in a rural household of the eighteenth century implied responsibility for the well-being of all the family. Upon marriage a woman took on "the Cares of the world," Elizabeth Bowen admitted as she recounted her past life, at mid-century. Fond as Esther Edwards Burr was of improving her mind, she declined an opportunity to take French lessons in the 1750s with the forceful comment, "The married woman has some-thing else to care about besides lerning [sic] French!" Sarah Snell Bryant's daily diary reported in straightforward fashion her matronly duties in an educated, respectable, but impecunious farm family in western Massachusetts. During the 1790s and early 1800s she bore and nursed six children (usually returning to household cares within a few days after childbirth), and taught them all to read the Bible before sending them to school. Generally she occupied every day in making cloth and clothing—from the "hatcheling" of flax and "breaking" of wool to the sewing of shirts, gowns, and coats—knitting gloves and stockings, baking, brewing, preserving food, churning butter, gardening, nursing the sick, making candles or soap, washing, ironing, scouring, quilting with neighbors, and even entertaining visitors. During a summer when her husband was traveling, she also taught school. Contemporaries of Sarah Snell Bryant who lived in more densely populated and commercial locations might have less labor to perform, especially if their husbands' wealth allowed their families to purchase goods and services. Martha Church Challoner, who lived in Newport, a lively Rhode Island port, in the 1760s, was able to buy various fabrics, shoes, and some basic foods. She had two black women in her house as servants (or slaves, possibly), and hired others to do washing, mending, spinning, carding, sewing, nursing. Still, she herself made candles, knit stockings, sold butter and eggs, and sewed household linens, while supervising the household....

Well into the middle decades of the nineteenth century married women's work remained centered on household management and family care, although the growing ramifications of the market economy diminished the importance of household manufacture and enlarged families' reliance on money to purchase basic commodities. Greater population density, commercial expansion, technological advances in transportation and communication, specialization in agriculture, and involvement of rural residents in given-out industry all contributed to the demise of the self-contained household economy. "There is no way of living in this town without cash," Abigail Lyman reported from Boston in 1797, and smaller towns rapidly manifested the same commercial spirit and need. Hannah Hickok Smith's account book for the years 1821–24 points out the extent to which a prosperous farm matron in an "urban"-sized commercial town— Glastonbury, Connecticut—was involved in commercial transaction. She recorded the purchase of edibles and baking supplies (spices, plums, currants, raisins, sugar, molasses, salt, wine, coffee, tea); of household items (teacups, platters, chest, jug, box, coffeepot, tinware, pins) and construction materials (pine boards, nails, steel); of writing accoutrements (paper, pen-knife, spelling book), nursing supplies (camphor, plaister) and soap, and some luxuries (snuff, tobacco, shell combs, parasol). Furthermore, she purchased at least eleven different kinds of fabric (such as dimity, brown holland, "factory cloth"), four kinds of yarn and thread, leather, and buttons; bought silk shawls, bonnets, dresses, stockings, and kid gloves, and also paid for people's services in making clothing. The farm produced the marketable commodities of grain (oats, rye, corn) and timber, animals (calves, turkeys, fowl) and animal products (eggs, hens' feathers, quills, wool, pork), and other farm produce which required more human labor, such as butter, cider, lard, and tallow....

The growing availability of goods and services for purchase might spare a married woman from considerable drudgery, if her husband's income sufficed for a comfortable living. It also heightened her role in "shoping," as Abigail Brackett Lyman spelled it (her consumer role), although that was subject to her husband's authority over financial resources. In colonial America husbands, as "providers," typically were responsible for purchasing goods—including household goods, furniture, and food staples, if they were to be bought—but in commercial towns of the late eighteenth and early nineteenth century wives more frequently became shoppers, especially for articles of dress and food. The increasing importance of monetary exchange bore hard on those who needed to replace their former economic contribution of household manufacture with income-producing employment, while meeting their domestic obligations. Taking in boarders was one alternative. Betsey Graves Johnson did that while she brought up the five children born to her between 1819 and 1830. Otherwise, married women had the same options for wage earning as single women who wished to stay at home: to take in sewing, or work in given-out industry. Schoolteaching, a slight possibility for wives, was a likelier one for widows whose children had reached school age. One widow's "cares," as described by her sister in 1841, were "enough to occupy all her time and thoughts almost.... [She] is teaching from 16 to 20 sholars [*sic*] boarding a young lady, and doing the housework, taking care of her children, &c."

These constants—"doing the housework, taking care of her children"— persisted in married women's lives. Child care required their presence at home. This responsibility revealed itself as the heart of women's domestic duties when household production declined. After four years of marriage Sarah Ripley Stearns regretfully attributed her neglect of church attendance and devotional reading not to household duties but to "the Care of my Babes, which takes up so large a portion of my time of my time [*sic*] & attention." More than ever before in New England history, the care of children appeared to be mothers' sole work and the work of mothers alone. The expansion of nonagricultural occupations drew men and grown children away from the household, abbreviating their presence in the family and their roles in child rearing. Mothers and young children were left in the household together just when educational and religious dicta both newly emphasized the malleability of young minds. Enlightenment psychology drew tighter the connection between early influence on the child, and his or her eventual character, just as mothers' influence on young children appeared more salient....

While changes in economy and society made young women's work more social, more various and mobile, the same developments reduced the social engagement, variety, and mobility in the work of wives and mothers. Housekeeping and child care continued to require married women's presence at home, while the household diminished in population, kinds of business, and range of contacts. In an intriguing development in language usage in the early nineteenth century, "home" became synonymous with "retirement" or "retreat" from the world at large. Mary Tucker quoted approvingly in 1802 an author's assertion that "a woman's noblest station is retreat." On a cousin's approaching marriage she remarked, "Sally has passed her days in the shade of *retirement* but even there many virtues and graces have ripened to perfection, she has every quality necessary for a *good wife*." Salome Lincoln's marriage to a fellow preacher in 1835 virtually ended her extradomestic pursuits; she subsequently used her preaching talents only on occasional travels with her husband. The shifting emphasis among married women's occupations emerges clearly in the comparison of Lydia Hill

Almy's occupations in 1797–99 with Mary Hurlbut's in the 1830s. The former not only kept house but let rooms, collected firewood, attended to livestock, and arranged to sell tanned skins; she considered her two children "grown out of the way" and "very little troble [sic]" when the younger was not yet weaned. Mary Hurlbut, in contrast, appeared solely concerned with her children's lives and prospects.

Married women's work at home distinguished itself most visibly from men's work, especially as the latter began to depart from the household/farm/craftshop to separate shops, offices, and factories. The rhythms of adult men's and women's work diverged even as did their places of work. During the eighteenth century, in agricultural towns, men and women had largely shared similar work patterns; their work, tied to the land, was seasonal and discontinuous. It was conditioned by tradition, family position, and legal obligation as well as by economic incentive. E. P. Thompson has called the dominant characteristic of work in such an agricultural/artisanal economy its "task-orientation," in contrast to the "time-discipline" required under industrial capitalism. Task-orientation implies that the worker's own sense of customary need and order dictates the performance of work. Intensification or delay occurs as a response to perceived necessity: in farming, for instance, the former occurs in harvest time, or the latter during stormy weather. Irregular work patterns typically result. "Social intercourse and labour are intermingled," Thompson also has pointed out, "the working-day lengthens or contracts according to the task—and there is no great sense of conflict between labour and 'passing the time of day.'" Persons accustomed to time-discipline, however, may consider task-oriented work patterns "wasteful and lacking in urgency." Thompson's analysis derived from his study of eighteenth-century English farmers, artisans, and laborers but can be applied to their contemporaries in New England. Even eighteenth-century colonial merchants, who, as risk-taking capitalists, might be expected to initiate disciplined work habits, structured their work lives in what Thompson would denote "preindustrial" ways, intermingling their work with recreation and with the conduct of their households. "The Founding Fathers, after all, lived in a preindustrial, not simply an 'agrarian' society," as Herbert Gutman has remarked, "and the prevalence of premodern work habits among their contemporaries was natural."

The social transformation from 1780 to 1835 signalled a transition from pre-industrial to modern industrial work patterns. The replacement of family production for direct use with wage earning, the institution of time-discipline and machine regularity in place of natural rhythms, the separation of workplaces from the home, and the division of "work" from "life" were overlapping layers of the same phenomenon....

Despite the changes in its social context adult women's work, for the most part, kept the traditional mode and location which both sexes had earlier shared. Men who had to accept time-discipline and specialized occupations may have begun to observe differences between their own work and that of their wives. Perhaps they focused on the remaining "premodern" aspects of women's household work: it was reassuringly comprehensible, because it responded to immediate needs; it represented not strictly "work" but "life," a way of being; and it also looked unsystematized, inefficient, nonurgent. Increasingly men did distinguish women's work from their own, in the early nineteenth century, by calling it women's "sphere," a "separate" sphere.

Women's sphere was "separate" not only because it was at home, but also because it seemed to elude rationalization and the cash nexus, and to integrate labor with life. The home and occupations in it represented an alternative to the emerging pace and division of labor. Symbol and remnant of preindustrial work, perhaps the home commanded men's deepest loyalties, but these were loyalties that conflicted with "modern" forms of employment. To be idealized, yet rejected by men—the object of yearning, and yet of scorn—was the fate of the home-as-workplace. Women's work (indeed women's very character, viewed as essentially conditioned by the home) shared in that simultaneous glorification and devaluation.

The Changes Wrought by Cotton, Transportation, and Communication

DANIEL WALKER HOWE

On the twenty-fourth of May 1844, Professor Samuel F. B. Morse, seated amidst a hushed gathering of distinguished national leaders in the chambers of the United States Supreme Court in Washington, tapped out a message on a device of cogs and coiled wires:

What Hath God Wrought

Forty miles away, in Baltimore, Morse's associate Alfred Vail received the electric signals and sent the message back. The invention they had demonstrated was destined to change the world. For thousands of years messages had been limited by the speed with which messengers could travel and the distance at which eyes could see signals such as flags or smoke. Neither Alexander the Great nor Benjamin Franklin (America's first postmaster general) two thousand years later knew anything faster than a galloping horse. Now, instant long-distance communication became a practical reality. The commercial application of Morse's invention followed quickly. American farmers and planters—and most Americans then earned a living through agriculture—increasingly produced food and fiber for distant markets. Their merchants and bankers welcomed the chance to get news of distant prices and credit....

The invention of electric telegraphy ... represented a climactic moment in a widespread revolution of communications. Other features of this revolution included improvements in printing and paper manufacturing; the multiplication of newspapers, magazines, and books; and the expansion of the postal system (which mostly carried newspapers and commercial business, not personal letters).

What Hath God Wrought: The Transformation of America 1818–1848 by Howe (2009) pp. 1–2, 4–7, 125–126, 128–129, 131–134, 213–214, 216, 222–223, 227, 242. By permission of Oxford University Press, USA.

Closely related to these developments occurred a simultaneous revolution in transportation: the introduction of steamboats, canals, turnpikes, and railroads, shortening travel times and dramatically lowering shipping costs.... Their consequences certainly rivaled, and probably exceeded in importance, those of the revolutionary "information highway" of our own lifetimes....

The most common name for the years ... is "Jacksonian America." I avoid the term because it suggests that Jacksonianism describes Americans as a whole, whereas in fact Andrew Jackson was a controversial figure and his political movement bitterly divided the American people....

Another term that has sometimes been applied to this period—more by historians than by the general public—is "the market revolution." I avoid this expression also. Those historians who used it have argued that a drastic change occurred during these years, from farm families raising food for their own use to producing it for distant markets. However, more and more evidence has accumulated in recent years that a market economy already existed in the eighteenth-century American colonies. To be sure, markets expanded vastly in the years after the end of the War of 1812, but their expansion partook more of the nature of a continuing evolution than a sudden revolution. Furthermore, their expansion did not occur in the face of resistance from any substantial group of people preferring subsistence farming to market participation. Most American family farmers welcomed the chance to buy and sell in larger markets. They did not have to be coerced into seizing the opportunities the market economy presented.

Accordingly, I provide an alternative interpretation of the early nineteenth century as a time of a "communications revolution." This, rather than the continued growth of the market economy, impressed contemporary Americans as a startling innovation. During the thirty-three years that began in 1815, there would be greater strides in the improvement of communication than had taken place in all previous centuries. This revolution, with its attendant political and economic consequences, would be a driving force in the history of the era....

More than any other discussion, the debate over the future of human slavery in an empire dedicated to liberty threatened to tear the country apart. The communications revolution gave a new urgency to social criticism and to the slavery controversy in particular. No longer could slave-holders afford to shrug off the commentary of outsiders. Critics of slavery seized upon the new opportunities for disseminating ideas to challenge the institution in the South itself. Alarmed, the defenders of slavery erected barricades against the intrusion of unwelcome expression. Better communication did not necessarily foster harmony....

The World That Cotton Made

The end of the War of 1812 precipitated one of the great migrations of American history. White settlers eagerly took advantage of Andrew Jackson's expropriation of 14 million acres from the Creeks. Shortly after signing the Treaty of Fort Jackson, the general sent his topographical engineer to report on the condition of the Alabama River valley. Along his route, Major Howell Tatum could observe farms with all their improvements that had been abandoned by the dispossessed natives (many of whom, ironically, had been Jackson's allies in the war). The officer concluded in his report that the land was "capable of producing, in great abundance, every article necessary to the sustenance of man or beast." Jackson encouraged white squatters to move onto the lands immediately, without waiting for survey or legal authorization. In December 1815, President Madison ordered them evicted, but his proclamation proved impossible to enforce. When the army moved people off, they came back again as soon as the soldiers had left....

Seldom in human history has so large a territory been settled so rapidly. Between 1810 and 1820, Alabama's population increased twelvefold to 128,000; Mississippi's doubled to 75,000 even though the Choctaw and Chickasaw Indian tribes still owned the northern two-thirds of the state. The population of Louisiana also doubled to 153,000, as an influx of white American southerners arrived to rival the old multicultural society of colonial New Orleans. Fittingly, when the ambitious settlers of Mississippi established a capital for their state, they called the new little settlement Jackson....

What made migration into this hazardous environment so attractive was the high price of cotton. The difficulties in processing short-staple greenseed cotton into textiles had earlier been surmounted through a series of technological innovations culminating in the development of the "saw" cotton gin ("gin" being short for "engine"). The contribution of the Connecticut Yankee Eli Whitney to this long process has been much exaggerated. But the Napoleonic Wars had inhibited international commerce and delayed the mass marketing of cotton for nearly a generation. Now, within a year of the end of hostilities in Europe and North America, the price of raw cotton doubled on the New Orleans market, reaching twenty-seven cents a pound. Wherever the soil was suitable and the farmer could count on two hundred frost-free days in the year, short-staple cotton suddenly became an economically attractive crop. The virgin earth of the New Southwest seemed ideal: While backcountry South Carolina yielded three hundred pounds of cotton per acre, the Alabama black belt could yield eight hundred or even a thousand pounds per acre. In response to an apparently insatiable world demand for textiles, U.S. cotton production soared from seventy-three thousand bales in 1800 to ten times that in 1820—the year the United States surpassed India, long the leading cotton producer. Cotton, fueling an expansion of transatlantic industrial capitalism, enormously enhanced the importance of the United States in the world economy. In 1801, 9 percent of the world's cotton came from the USA and 60 percent from Asia. Half a century later, the United States provided 68 percent of a total world production three times as large. The American South was to be the most favored place for the production of a raw material of global significance, as the Caribbean sugar islands had been in the eighteenth century or as the oil-rich Middle East would become in the twentieth.

Cotton cultivation required labor-intensive application, but chattel slavery remained legal in the states where the climate was favorable to cotton. The new marketability of short-staple cotton prompted the expansion of slave-plantation agriculture far beyond the areas that would have sustained the traditional export crops, tobacco, rice, and indigo. The spread of cotton cultivation entailed not only the westward migration of free farmers but also the massive forced migration of enslaved workers into the newly acquired lands. Not all cotton planters in the Southwest were self-made pioneers, for some already wealthy men hastened to the area and purchased large holdings, clearing the forest and draining the swamps with slave labor. Whether he owned many slaves or few, a master might bring his bondsmen with him, but sometimes he would go out and select the lands to buy first, returning (or sending agents) later to buy a workforce suited to the property. Most often, the southwestern planter bought slaves who had been transported to that region by a trader. Because the importation of slaves from overseas had been illegal since 1808, the trader's human merchandise could only come from the seaboard slave states. Contemporaries typically observed the transit of a slave coffle with disgust and shame: "a wretched cavalcade ... marching half naked women, and men loaded with chains, without being charged with any crime but that of being black, from one section of the United States to another, hundreds of miles." Such a procession could number anywhere from a dozen to over a hundred souls, who were expected to walk up to twenty-five miles a day and sleep on the ground. The long trek overland from Virginia to Mississippi or Louisiana would consume six to eight weeks and was usually undertaken in winter, when agricultural labor could best be spared. Coastal vessels, more expensive, absorbed some of the traffic when the great slave marketplace in New Orleans was the destination. Only later, after Kentucky and Tennessee acquired surpluses of slaves and began exporting them, did the phrase "sold down the river" come into common use. The slave traders favored people in the prime of life—late teens or early twenties—since they could withstand the rigors of the march and bring a good price as field hands and (in the case of the women) breeders. Small children accompanying their mothers were placed in the supply wagon. The interstate slave trade was big business; the Chesapeake Bay region alone exported 124,000 enslaved workers, mostly across the Appalachians, during the decade following 1810....

The rapid rise of "the Cotton Kingdom" wrought a momentous transformation. Cotton became a driving force in expanding and transforming the economy not only of the South but of the United States as a whole—indeed of the world. While the growing of cotton came to dominate economic life in the Lower South, the manufacture of cotton textiles was fueling the industrial revolution on both sides of the Atlantic. Most of the exported American cotton went to Britain, in particular to the port of Liverpool, convenient to the textile mills of Lancashire. During the immediate postwar years of 1816 to 1820, cotton constituted 39 percent of U.S. exports; twenty years later the proportion had increased to 59 percent, and the value of the cotton sold overseas in 1836 exceeded $71 million. By giving the United States its leading export staple, the workers in the cotton fields enabled the country not only to buy manufactured goods from Europe but also to pay interest on its foreign debt and continue to import more capital to invest in transportation and industry. Much of the Atlantic civilization in the nineteenth century was built on the back of the enslaved field hand....

The same short-staple cotton that spread plantation agriculture all over the South gave rise to textile mills. In New England, the War of 1812 climaxed a series of interruptions playing havoc with the maritime trade and fishing that had been the mainstays of the regional economy. American commerce was driven from the seas. Watching their ships rot in port, Yankee investors hit upon a solution. As southern planters solved the problem of worn-out lands and low tobacco prices by shifting their workforce to the new cotton fields, New England merchants solved their own problem by shifting capital from shipping to manufacturing. What they started to manufacture was inexpensive cloth, made from local wool and southern cotton....

Farm women had long supplemented the family income by weaving woolen yarn and cloth, using spinning wheels and hand looms at home. Now cotton from the South provided raw material much more plentiful than local sheep. So young women left home, recruited by company-owned boardinghouses in Lowell. There they put in long hours under unhealthy conditions and contracted not to leave until they had worked at least a year. But twelve to fourteen dollars a month was a good wage, and the new town had attractive shops, social activities, churches, lending libraries, and evening lectures. The "mill girls," as they called themselves, wrote and published a magazine, the *Lowell Offering*. Americans had feared industrialization, lest it create an oppressed, depraved, and turbulent proletariat. But because these women typically worked for only a few years prior to marriage, and did so in a morally protected environment, they did not seem to constitute a permanent separate working class. To observers, the community looked like an industrial utopia, more successful than the Scottish models that Francis Lowell and Nathan Appleton had toured years before. Lowell, Massachusetts, boasted the largest concentration of industry in the United States before the Civil War....

Overthrowing the Tyranny of Distance

People throughout the United States recognized the need for a better transportation system. The Great Migration had increased the number of agricultural producers wanting to get their crops from the interior to national or international markets. While some people moved westward, others were migrating to the coastal cities to work in the merchant marine and its many ancillary occupations, from shipbuilding to insurance. These city people had a need to be fed even more urgent than that of the farmers to market their crops. Pressure for improvements in transportation came at least as much from cities eager to buy as from farmers seeking to sell. Urban merchants hoped to funnel as much farm produce as possible from as large a hinterland as possible into their own market, either for consumption or transshipment elsewhere. Technology, new or newly applied, made available improvements in transportation, but constructing "internal improvements" posed problems not only physical but also economic, legal, and political....

The invention of the steamboat enhanced the comparative advantages of water transportation. In 1787, John Fitch had built the first American steamer, but he could not obtain financial backing and died in obscurity. The first commercially successful steamboat, Robert Fulton's *Clermont,* plied the Hudson River starting in 1807. Steamboats proved most valuable for trips upstream on rivers with powerful currents, of which the Mississippi was the ultimate example. In 1817, a twenty-five day steamer trip up the Mississippi from New Orleans to Louisville set a record; by 1826, the time had been cut to eight days. Pre-steamboat traffic on the Mississippi had been mostly one-way downstream; at New Orleans, boatmen broke up their barges to sell for lumber and *walked* back home to Kentucky or Tennessee along the Natchez Trace road....

For all their utility, nineteenth-century steamboats were dangerous. Between 1825 and 1830 alone, forty-two exploding boilers killed 273 people. Commenting on steamboat accidents, Philip Hone of New York City, one of the great diarists of the period, observed in 1837. "We have become the most careless, reckless, headlong people on the face of the earth. 'Go ahead' is our maxim and pass-word, and we do go ahead with a vengeance, regardless of consequences and indifferent to the value of human life." In 1838, an enormous boiler explosion in Charleston took 140 lives....

Canals further extended the advantages of water transport. Canals might connect two natural waterways or parallel a single stream so as to avoid waterfalls, rapids, or obstructions. Locks raised or lowered the water level. Horses or mules walking along a towpath moved barges through the canal; an animal that could pull a wagon weighing two tons on a paved road could pull fifty tons on the towpath of a canal. In Europe, canals had been around a long time; the Languedoc Canal connected the Mediterranean with the Bay of Biscay in 1681. In North America, canal construction had been delayed by the great distances, sparse population, and (embarrassing as it was to admit) lack of engineering and management expertise. During the years after 1815, a society eager for transportation and open to innovation finally surmounted these difficulties. Because canals cost more to construct than turnpikes, public funding proved even more important in raising the capital for them. Energy and flexibility at the state level got canal construction under way when doubts about constitutional propriety made the federal government hesitate. Many canals were built entirely by state governments, including the most famous, economically important, and financially successful of them all, the Erie Canal in New York....

As part of the celebration of the Erie Canal's completion, cannons were placed within earshot of each other the entire length of its route and down the Hudson. When Governor Clinton's boat departed from Buffalo that October morning in 1825, the first cannon of the "Grand Salute" was fired and the signal relayed from gun to gun, all the way to Sandy Hook on the Atlantic coast and back again. Three hours and twenty minutes later, the booming signal returned to Buffalo. Except for elaborately staged events such as this, communication in early nineteenth-century America usually required the transportation of a physical object from one place to another—such as a letter, a newspaper, or even a message attached to the leg of a homing pigeon. This was how it had been since time immemorial. But as transportation improved, so did communications, and improved communications set powerful cultural changes in motion....

From New York City, information dispersed around the country and appeared in local newspapers. In 1817, news could get from New York to Philadelphia in just over a day, traveling as far as New Brunswick, New Jersey, by steamer. To Boston from New York took more than two days, with the aid of steamboats in Long Island Sound. To Richmond the news took five days; to Charleston, ten. These travel times represented a great improvement over the pre-steamboat 1790s, when Boston and Richmond had each been ten days away from New York, but they would continue to improve during the coming generation. For the most important news of all, relay express riders were employed. In 1830, these riders set a record: They carried the presidential State of the Union message from Washington to New York in fifteen and a half hours.

Communications profoundly affected American business. For merchants eagerly awaiting word of crop prices and security fluctuations in European cities, the advantage of being one of the first to know such information was crucial. New Yorkers benefited because so many ships came to their port first, even though Boston and Halifax, Nova Scotia, were actually closer to Europe. The extra days of delay in receiving European news handicapped merchants based in Charleston, Savannah, or New Orleans. The availability of information affected investors of all kinds, not only commodity traders. No longer did people with money to invest feel they needed to deal only with their relatives or others they knew personally. Through the New York Stock Exchange, one could buy shares in enterprises one had never seen. Capital flowed more easily to places where it was needed. Information facilitated doing business at a distance; for example, insurance companies could better assess risks. Credit rating agencies opened to facilitate borrowing and lending; the first one, the Mercantile Agency, was established by the Tappan brothers, who also created the New York *Journal of Commerce* and bankrolled much of the abolitionist movement. In colonial times, Americans had needed messages from London to provide commercially relevant news. Now, they could get their news from New York and get it faster. Improved communications stimulated economic growth....

As early as 1822, the United States had more newspaper readers than any other country, regardless of population. This market was highly fragmented; no one paper had a circulation of over four thousand. New York City alone had 66 newspapers in 1810 and 161 by 1828, including *Freedom's Journal,* the first to be published by and for African Americans.

The expansion of newspaper publishing resulted in part from technological innovations in printing and papermaking. Only modest improvements had been made in the printing press since the time of Gutenberg until a German named Friedrich Koenig invented a cylinder press driven by a steam engine in 1811. The first American newspaper to obtain such a press was the *New York Daily Advertiser* in 1825; it could print two thousand papers in an hour. In 1816, Thomas Gilpin discovered how to produce paper on a continuous roll instead of in separate sheets that were slower to feed into the printing press. The making of paper from rags gradually became mechanized, facilitating the production of books and magazines as well as newspapers; papermaking from wood pulp did not become practical until the 1860s. Compositors still set type by hand, picking up type one letter at a time from a case and placing it into a handheld "stick." Until the 1830s, one man sometimes put out a newspaper all by himself, the editor setting his own type. The invention of stereotyping enabled an inexpensive metal copy to be made of set type; the copy could be retained, and if a second printing of the job seemed warranted (such as a second edition of a book), the type did not have to be laboriously reset. More important than innovations in the production of printed matter, however, were the improvements in transportation that facilitated the supply of paper to presses and then the distribution of what they printed. After about 1830, these improvements had reached the point where a national market for published material existed....

Late in 1833, a twenty-seven-year-old French engineer named Michel Chevalier arrived in the United States. American canals, bridges, steamboats, and railroads fascinated him. During his two-year tour of the country, he concluded that improvements in transportation had democratic implications. In former times, he remarked, with roads rough and dangerous, travel required "a long train of luggage, provisions, servants, and guards," making it rare and expensive. "The great bulk of mankind, slaves in fact and in name," had been "chained to the soil" not only by their legal and social status but also "by the difficulty of locomotion." Freedom to travel, the ability to leave home, was essential to the modern world and as democratic as universal suffrage, Chevalier explained:

> To improve the means of communication, then, is to promote a real, positive, and practical liberty; it is to extend to all the members of the human family the power of traversing and turning to account the globe, which has been given to them as their patrimony; it is to increase the rights and privileges of the greatest number, as truly and as amply as could be done by electoral laws. The effect of the most perfect system of transportation is to reduce the distance not only between different places, but between different classes.

As Chevalier realized, improved transportation and communications facilitated not only the movement of goods and ideas but personal, individual freedom as well. Americans, a mobile and venturesome people, empowered by literacy and technological proficiency, did not hesitate to take advantage of the opportunity provided (as he put it) to turn the globe to their account.

In traditional society, the only items worth transporting long distances had been luxury goods, and information about the outside world had been one of the most precious luxuries of all. The transportation and communications revolutions made both goods and information broadly accessible. In doing so, they laid a foundation not only for widespread economic betterment and wider intellectual horizons but also for political democracy; in newspapers and magazines, in post offices, in nationwide movements to influence public opinion, and in mass political parties.

FURTHER READING

Edward J. Balleisen, *Navigating Failure: Bankruptcy and Commercial Society in Antebellum America* (2001).

Ruth S. Cowan, *A Social History of American Technology* (1997).

Daniel Walker Howe, *What Hath God Wrought: The Transformation of America, 1815–1846* (2007).

Richard R. John, *Spreading the News: The American Postal System from Franklin to Morse* (1996).

Walter Johnson, *River of Dark Dreams: Slavery and Empire in the Cotton Kingdom* (2013).

John Lauritz Larson, *Internal Improvement: National Public Works and the Promise of Popular Government in the Early United States* (2001).

Marla R. Miller, *The Needle's Eye: Women and Work in the Age of Revolution* (2006).

David Reynolds, *Waking Giant: America in the Age of Jackson* (2008).

Charles Sellers, *The Market Revolution: Jacksonian America, 1815–1846* (1991).

Gavin Wright, *Slavery and American Economic Development* (2006).

Additional critical thinking activities and content are available in MindTap.

   **MindTap** is a fully online, highly personalized learning experience built upon Cengage Learning content. MindTap combines student learning tools—readings, multimedia, activities, and assessments—into a singular Learning Path that guides students through the course.

CHAPTER 9

Nationalism and Sectionalism

When Frenchman Michel Chevalier witnessed a parade in New York City in 1834, he was dazzled: it was a mile-long procession lit by hundreds of torches, and it included banners, portraits of political leaders, and even a live eagle mounted on a pole (see document 7 in this chapter). "These scenes belong to history," he later wrote. "They are the episodes of a wondrous epic which will bequeath a lasting memory to posterity, that of the coming of democracy." For this visitor, the political world in the United States differed radically from that of his European home. Americans were enjoying the burgeoning of a democracy that was likely to reverberate throughout the world. Historians have found reason to substantiate these claims. In the early nineteenth century, ballot restrictions were eased so that all white men, even those who owned no property, could vote. By 1840, those Americans who could vote did so in record numbers. Politics became a pageant, filling the streets with demonstrations and parades. Andrew Jackson, elected in 1828, was heralded by his supporters as a man of the people.

However, other historians have considered these developments in a different light. Not only was universal suffrage restricted to white men, but free black men were losing their voting rights in a number of states during this period. In this purported era of democracy, Indian removal, as we saw in Chapter 7, was accelerating. The United States, many historians argue, was not a paragon of democracy but rather "a white man's republic." Still other historians contend that the level of democracy even among white voters is overstated. Politics might have appeared as pageantry, but this was really a façade. Elections decided less than voters believed.

Whether politics represented the flowering of democracy or was a sham, political organization and behavior changed beginning in 1824. The second party system, as it is called, developed in large part in reaction to the political career of Andrew Jackson. Defeated by John Quincy Adams in 1824, Jackson vowed revenge in the next presidential election. Following his resounding victory in 1828 as leader of the Democratic Party, he set about creating a federal bureaucracy that would be loyal to him and his party. The adage "to the victor belong the spoils" was cited to defend the appointment of loyal Democrats to government jobs. A series of divisive political battles over such issues as a national bank followed. By 1834, a group of politicians who opposed Jackson's initiatives formed an alternative party, which they called the Whigs, in opposition to "King Andrew." For the next twenty years, national elections were closely contested, eligible voters participated in large numbers, and professional politicians vied for votes and rewarded their followers with patronage if they were victorious. Whereas politicians at one time had disdained campaigning for office, the second party system fostered raucous campaigns and ambitious politicians.

In this new political environment, politicians addressed issues that would continue to plague the United States in the years to come. Perhaps the most ominous was the question of states' rights and national power. In 1832, Congress passed a tariff that seemed excessive to southern political leaders. Because the southern economy continued to be based on agriculture, the South benefited less from tariffs than did the North. Senator John C. Calhoun from South Carolina responded to this "tariff of abominations" by arguing that a state had the right to "nullify" laws with which it disagreed. Jackson responded as a nationalist and declared nullification illegal. The difference even punctuated dinner conversation. On one occasion, President Jackson toasted to the "Federal Union: it must be preserved." Calhoun, the vice president at the time, responded, "The Union: next to our liberty the most dear." Ultimately a compromise was reached, but certainly there were aspects of the debate that were not settled. Historians have considered this crisis a prelude to the Civil War.

One area in which most politicians and voters could agree, however, was the urgency of expanding westward. Westward migration, so the argument went, would not only increase national power but also bring benefits to those who were conquered. By 1845, this impulse was encoded in an ideology known as "manifest destiny." According to journalist John L. O'Sullivan, it was "the fulfillment of our manifest destiny to overspread the continent." Armed with a rhetoric that knit westward expansion with national fulfillment, Americans in the 1840s pushed for annexation of western lands. The United States annexed Texas in 1845, gained Oregon in a treaty with Great Britain, and conquered regions of Mexico following the Mexican-American War, which began in 1846. As of 1848, the United States, which now comprised nearly three million square miles, had tripled in size in seventy-some years. This "white man's republic" seemingly had fulfilled its destiny. Yet storm clouds were on the horizon, as we shall see, precisely because of the territories in the West.

QUESTIONS TO THINK ABOUT

To what degree was this a period of increasing democracy? How were notions about "the people" or "the common man" used to celebrate the potential of the United States? How were these celebrations linked to expansion and "manifest destiny"? How was the issue of nullification ominous for American nationalists? Were loyalties primarily given to localities or to the nation? Is it possible for them to work together, or will these forces tend toward division?

DOCUMENTS

The first five documents illustrate the issues of nationalism and sectionalism during the presidency of Andrew Jackson. Document 1 records a popular song that promoted the presidential aspirations of Andrew Jackson. In document 2, Senator John C. Calhoun of South Carolina argues against the "tariff of abominations" and for an open market. Document 3 focuses upon the western borderlands with a description of the area just before Texans and Americans would wage war with Mexico. In document 4, Senator Daniel Webster of Massachusetts argues that the people have ratified a Constitution that has made the national government the supreme law of the land. In document 5, President Andrew Jackson responds to the action of South Carolina in calling for the nullification of a federal law. Jackson agrees with Webster, arguing that no state can declare a law void because the Constitution has formed a government in which all the people are represented. Document 6 gives us a view of the battle at the Alamo in 1836 from the point of view of a Mexican colonel. Document 7 is an observation by Michel Chevalier who marvels at a procession of Democrats in New York City in 1839. Document 8 from Frederick Douglass, a former slave who achieved freedom and fame before the Civil War, connects western movement and war to the issue of slavery. Douglass's speech, given in Ireland, shows how American conflicts were brought to the broader world.

1. A New Song Endeavors to Put Andrew Jackson in the White House, c. 1820s

Huzza! for General Jackson.

Come all who are our country's friends,
And unto these few lines attend,
Perhaps before you reach the end
You'll find something for to mend, ...

Our opposition party say,
If Jackson should but gain the day,
There will be war without delay,
And proselytes they gain this way,
To build their fed'ral faction.
But all who are for liberty,
Their deepest plans can sometimes see,
But always let our motto be,
"We're determin'd to be free,"
Huzza! for Gen'ral Jackson.

We have great numbers on our side,
Old vet'rans who have been well tried,
And never yet have turn'd aside,
All opposition still outride,
Who scorn the fed'ral faction.

America Singing: Nineteenth-Century Song Sheets. American Memory, Library of Congress.

And when they're call'd for to defend,
Their country's rights they will attend,
And all that's in their power they'll spend,
And will stand by their old tried friend,
General Andrew Jackson....

If Jackson should be president,
We'll borrow guns of Government,
And you may load and I'll tend vent,
Then touch her off and let her vent,
With huzza! for Andrew Jackson.
And when the people hear the gun,
The men and boys they all will run,
Expecting for to see the fun,
When they get there will all as one,
Huzza! for Andrew Jackson. ...

There's some who at our party rail,
Call us the rag-tag and bob-tail,
But we have one within our pale,
Who we are sure will never fail,
To vote for General Jackson.
The Jackson Ticket they do say,
Is blood and carnage, by the way
Of slander, yet we hope we may
Join with our southern friends and say,
Huzza! for Andrew Jackson.

2. Vice President John C. Calhoun Argues That Tariffs Disadvantage the South, 1828

The Committee do not propose to enter into an elaborate, or refined argument on the question of the Constitutionality of the Tariff System. The Gen[era]l Government is one of specifick powers, and it can rightfully exercise only the powers expressly granted, and those that may be necessary and proper to carry them into effect, all others being reserved expressly to the States, or the people. It results necessarily, that those who claim to exercise power under the Constitution, are bound to show, that it is expressly granted, or that it is necessary and proper as a means to some of the granted powers. The advocates of the Tariff have offered no such proof....

So partial are the effects of the system, that its burdens are exclusively on one side, and the benefits on the other. It imposes on the agricultural interest of the south, including the South west, with that portion of our commerce and

The Papers of John C. Calhoun, ed. Clyde N. Wilson and W. Edwin Hemphill, X (Columbia: University of South Carolina Press, 1959), 444–532.

navigation engaged in foreign trade, the burden not only of sustaining the system itself, but that also of the Government....

That the manufacturing States, even in their own opinion, bear no share of the burden of the Tariff in reality, we may infer with the greatest certainty from their conduct. The fact that they urgently demand an increase, and consider any addition as a blessing, and a failure to obtain one, a curse, is the strongest confession, that whatever burden it imposes in reality, falls, not on them but on others. Men ask not for burdens, but benefits. The tax paid by the duties on impost [*sic*] by which, with the exception of the receipts in the sale of publick land and a few incidental items, the Government is wholly supported, and which in its gross amount annually equals about $23,000,000 is then in truth no tax on them. Whatever portion of it they advance, as consumers of the articles on which it is imposed, returns to them ... with usurious interest through an artfully contrived system. That such are the facts, the Committee will proceed to demonstrate by other arguments, besides the confession of the party interested through their acts, as conclusive as that ought to be considered....

We cultivate certain great staples for the supply of the general market of the world; they manufacture almost exclusively for the home market. Their object in the Tariff is to keep down foreign competition, in order to obtain a monopoly of the domestick market. The effect on us is to compel us to purchase at a higher price, both what we purchase from them and from others, without receiving a correspondent increase in the price, of what we sell....

We are told by those who pretend to understand our interest better than we do, that the excess of production, and not the Tariff, is the evil which afflicts us, and that our true remedy is a reduction of the quantity of cotton, rice and tobacco which we raise, and not a repeal of the Tariff. They assert that low prices are the necessary consequence of excess of supply, and that the only proper correction is in diminishing the quantity.... Our market is the world, and as we cannot imitate their example by enlarging it for our products through the exclusion of others, we must decline to their advice, which instead of alleviating would increase our embarrassment. We have no monopoly in the supply of our products. One half of the globe may produce them. Should we reduce our production, others stand ready by increasing theirs to take our place, and instead of raising prices, we would only diminish our share of the supply. We are thus compelled to produce on the penalty of loosing our hold on the general market. Once lost it may be lost forever; and lose it we must, if we continue to be compelled as we now are, on the one hand by general competition of the world to sell low, and on the other by the Tariff to buy high. We cannot withstand this double action. Our ruin must follow. In fact our only permanent and safe remedy is not the rise in the price of what we sell in which we can receive but little aid from our Government, but a reduction in that which we buy which is prevented by the interference of the Government. Give us a free and open competition in our own market, and we fear not to encounter like competition in the general market of the world. If under all of our discouragement by the acts of our Government, we are still able to contend there against the world, can it be doubted, if this impediment were removed, we would force out all competitors; and thus also enlarge our market, not by the oppression of our fellow citizens of other States, but by our industry, enterprize [*sic*] and natural advantages.

3. A Mexican General Describes the Borderland, 1828, 1829

... As one covers the distance from Béjar to this town [Nacogdoches], he will note that Mexican influence is proportionately diminished until on arriving in this place he will see that it is almost nothing. And indeed, whence could such influence come? Hardly from superior numbers in population, since the ratio of Mexicans to foreigners is one to ten; certainly not from the superior character of the Mexican population, for exactly the opposite is true, the Mexicans of this town comprising what in all countries is called the lowest class—the very poor and very ignorant. The naturalized North Americans in the town maintain an English school, and send their children north for further education; the poor Mexicans not only do not have sufficient means to establish schools, but they are not of the type that take any thought for the improvement of its public institutions or the betterment of its degraded condition. Neither are there civil authorities or magistrates; one insignificant little man—not to say more—who is called an alcalde [magistrate], and an ayuntamiento [council] that does not convene once in a lifetime is the most that we have here at this important point on our frontier; yet, wherever I have looked, in the short time that I have been here, I have witnessed grave occurrences, both political and judicial. It would cause you the same chagrin that it has caused me to see the opinion that is held of our nation by these foreign colonists, since, with the exception of some few who have journeyed to our capital, they know no other Mexicans than the inhabitants about here, and excepting the authorities necessary to any form of society, the said inhabitants are the most ignorant of Negroes and Indians, among whom I pass for a man of culture. Thus, I tell myself that it could not be otherwise than that from such a state of affairs should arise an antagonism between the Mexicans and foreigners, which is not the least of the smoldering fires which I have discovered. Therefore, I am warning you to take timely measures. Texas could throw the whole nation into revolution.

The colonists murmur against the political disorganization of the frontier, and the Mexicans complain of the superiority and better education of the colonists; the colonists find it unendurable that they must go three hundred leagues to lodge a complaint against the petty pickpocketing that they suffer from a venal and ignorant alcalde, and the Mexicans with no knowledge of the laws of their own country nor those regulating colonization, set themselves against the foreigners, deliberately setting nets to deprive them of the right of franchise and to exclude them from the ayuntamiento. Meanwhile, the incoming stream of

---

General Manuel Mier y Terán, quoted in Alleine Howren, "Causes and Origin of the Decree of April 6, 1830," *Southwestern Historical Quarterly* 16 (1913), 95–98.

new settlers is unceasing; the first news of these comes by discovering them on land already under cultivation, where they have been located for many months; the old inhabitants set up a claim to the property, basing their titles of doubtful priority, and for which there are no records, on a law of the Spanish government; and thus arises a lawsuit in which the alcalde has a chance to come out with some money. In this state of affairs, the town where there are no magistrates is the one in which lawsuits abound, and it is at once evident that in Nacogdoches and its vicinity, being most distant from the seat of the general government, the primitive order of things should take its course, which is to say that this section is being settled up without the consent of anybody....

In spite of the enmity that usually exists between the Mexicans and the foreigners, there is a most evident uniformity of opinion on one point, namely the separation of Texas from Coahuila and its organization into a territory of the federal government. The idea, which was conceived by some of the colonists who are above the average, has become general among the people and does not fail to cause considerable discussion. In explaining the reasons assigned by them for this demand, I shall do no more than relate what I have heard with no addition of my own conclusions, and I frankly state that I have been commissioned by some of the colonists to explain to you their motives, notwithstanding the fact that I should have done so anyway in the fulfillment of my duty.

They claim that Texas in its present condition of a colony is an expense, since it is not a sufficiently prosperous section to contribute to the revenues of the state administration; and since it is such a charge it ought not to be imposed upon a state as poor as Coahuila, which has not the means of defraying the expenses of the corps of political and judicial officers necessary for the maintenance of peace and order. Furthermore, it is impracticable that recourse in all matters should be had to a state capital so distant and separated from this section by deserts infected by hostile savages. Again, their interests are very different from those of the other sections, and because of this they should be governed by a separate territorial government, having learned by experience that the mixing of their affairs with those of Coahuila brings about friction. The native inhabitants of Texas add to the above other reasons which indicate an aversion for the inhabitants of Coahuila; also the authority of the comandante and the collection of taxes is disputed....

The whole population here is a mixture of strange and incoherent parts without parallel in our federation: numerous tribes of Indians, now at peace, but armed and at any moment ready for war, whose steps toward civilization should be taken under the close supervision of a strong and intelligent government; colonists of another people, more progressive and better informed than the Mexican inhabitants, but also more shrewd and unruly; among these foreigners are fugitives from justice, honest laborers, vagabonds and criminals, but honorable and dishonorable alike travel with their political constitution in their pockets, demanding the privileges, authority and officers which such a constitution guarantees.

4. Senator Daniel Webster Lays Out
His Nationalist Vision, 1830

Sir, let me recur to pleasing recollections; let me indulge in refreshing remembrance of the past; let me remind you that, in early times, no States cherished greater harmony, both of principle and feeling, than Massachusetts and South Carolina. Would to God that harmony might again return! ...

I understand the honorable gentleman from South Carolina to maintain, that it is a right of the State legislatures to interfere, whenever, in their judgment, this government transcends its constitutional limits, and to arrest the operation of its laws.

I understand him to maintain this right, as a right existing *under* the Constitution, not as a right to overthrow it on the ground of extreme necessity, such as would justify violent revolution.

I understand him to maintain an authority, on the part of the States, thus to interfere, for the purpose of correcting the exercise of power by the general government, of checking it, and of compelling it to conform to their opinion of the extent of its powers.

I understand him to maintain, that the ultimate power of judging of the constitutional extent of its own authority is not lodged exclusively in the general government, or any branch of it: but that, on the contrary, the States may lawfully decide for themselves, and each State for itself, whether, in a given case, the act of the general government transcends its power.

I understand him to insist, that, if the exigency of the case, in the opinion of any State government, require it, such State government may, by its own sovereign authority, annul an act of the general government which it deems plainly and palpably unconstitutional.

This is the sum of what I understand from him to be the South Carolina doctrine, and the doctrine which he maintains. I propose to consider it, and compare it with the Constitution....

This leads us to inquire into the origin of this government and the source of its power. Whose agent is it? Is it the creature of the State legislatures, or the creature of the people? If the government of the United States be the agent of the State governments, then they may control it, provided they can agree in the manner of controlling it; if it be the agent of the people, then the people alone can control it, restrain it, modify, or reform it. It is observable enough, that the doctrine for which the honorable gentleman contends leads him to the necessity of maintaining, not only that this general government is the creature of the States, but that it is the creature of each of the States severally, so that each may assert the power for itself of determining whether it acts within the limits of its authority. It is the servant of four-and-twenty masters of different wills and different

Second reply to Hayne (January 26–27, 1830), in *Speeches and Formal Writings*, I, Daniel Webster, 285–348, as reprinted in *Daniel Webster: The Completest Man*, ed. Kenneth E. Shewmaker (Hanover, N.H.: University Press of New England, 1990), 113–120.

purposes and yet bound to obey all. This absurdity (for it seems no less) arises from a misconception as to the origin of this government and its true character. It is, Sir, the people's Constitution, the people's government, made for the people, made by the people, and answerable to the people. The people of the United States have declared that the Constitution shall be the supreme law. We must either admit the proposition, or dispute their authority. The States are, unquestionably, sovereign, so far as their sovereignty is not affected by this supreme law. But the State legislatures, as political bodies, however sovereign, are yet not sovereign over the people. So far as the people have given power to the general government, so far the grant is unquestionably good, and the government holds of the people, and not of the State governments. We are all agents of the same supreme power, the people. The general government and the State governments derive their authority from the same source. Neither can, in relation to the other, be called primary, though one is definite and restricted, and the other general and residuary. The national government possesses those powers which it can be shown the people have conferred on it, and no more. All the rest belongs to the State governments, or to the people themselves. So far as the people have restrained State sovereignty, by the expression of their will, in the Constitution of the United States, so far, it must be admitted, State sovereignty is effectually controlled. I do not contend that it is, or ought to be, controlled farther. The sentiment to which I have referred propounds that State sovereignty is only to be controlled by its own "feeling of justice": that is to say, it is not to be controlled at all, for one who is to follow his own feelings is under no legal control. Now, however men may think this ought to be, the fact is, that the people of the United States have chosen to impose control on State sovereignties. There are those, doubtless, who wish they had been left without restraint; but the Constitution has ordered the matter differently. To make war, for instance, is an exercise of sovereignty; but the Constitution declares that no State shall make war. To coin money is another exercise of sovereign power, but no State is at liberty to coin money. Again, the Constitution says that no sovereign State shall be so sovereign as to make a treaty. These prohibitions, it must be confessed, are a control on the State sovereignty of South Carolina, as well as of the other States, which does not arise "from her own feelings of honorable justice." The opinion referred to, therefore, is in defiance of the plainest provisions of the Constitution....

... I hold [this government] to be a popular government, erected by the people; those who administer it, responsible to the people; and itself capable of being amended and modified, just as the people may choose it should be. It is as popular, just as truly emanating from the people, as the State governments. It is created for one purpose; the State governments for another. It has its own powers; they have theirs. There is no more authority with them to arrest the operation of a law of Congress, than with Congress to arrest the operation of their laws.... The States cannot now make war; they cannot contract alliances; they cannot make, each for itself, separate regulations of commerce; they cannot lay imposts; they cannot coin money. If this Constitution, Sir, be the creature of

State legislatures, it must be admitted that it has obtained a strange control over the volitions of its creators....

... Sir, the people have wisely provided, in the Constitution itself, a proper, suitable mode and tribunal for settling questions of constitutional law. There are in the Constitution grants of powers to Congress, and restrictions on these powers. There are, also, prohibitions on the States. Some authority must, therefore, necessarily exist, having the ultimate jurisdiction to fix and ascertain the interpretation of these grants, restrictions, and prohibitions. The Constitution has itself pointed out, ordained, and established that authority. How has it accomplished this great and essential end? By declaring, Sir, that *"the Constitution, and the laws of the United States made in pursuance thereof, shall be the supreme law of the land, any thing in the constitution or laws of any State to the contrary notwithstanding."*

This, Sir, was the first great step. By this the supremacy of the Constitution and laws of the United States is declared. The people so will it. No State law is to be valid which comes in conflict with the Constitution, or any law of the United States passed in pursuance of it. But who shall decide this question of interference? To whom lies the last appeal? This, Sir, the Constitution itself decides also, by declaring, *"that the judicial power shall extend to all cases arising under the Constitution and laws of the United States."* These two provisions cover the whole ground. They are, in truth, the keystone of the arch! With these it is a government; without them it is a confederation.... Congress established, at its very first session, in the judicial act, a mode for carrying them into full effect, and for bringing all questions of constitutional power to the final decision of the Supreme Court. It then, Sir, became a government. It then had the means of self-protection; and but for this, it would, in all probability, have been now among things which are past. Having constituted the government, and declared its powers, the people have further said, that, since somebody must decide on the extent of these powers, the government shall itself decide; subject, always, like other popular governments, to the responsibility to the people.

—Liberty *and* Union, now and for ever, one and inseparable!

5. President Andrew Jackson Condemns the Rights of "Nullification" and Secession, 1832

To preserve this bond of our political existence from destruction, to maintain inviolate this state of national honor and prosperity, and to justify the confidence my fellow-citizens have reposed in me, I, Andrew Jackson, President of the United States, have thought proper to issue this my proclamation, stating my views of the Constitution and laws applicable to the measures adopted by the convention of South Carolina and to the reasons they have put forth to sustain them, declaring the course which duty will require me to pursue, and, appealing to the understanding and patriotism of the people, warn them of the

Andrew Jackson, "Proclamation to the People of South Carolina, December 10, 1832."

consequences that must inevitably result from an observance of the dictates of the convention.

The ordinance is founded, not on the indefeasible right of resisting acts which are plainly unconstitutional and too oppressive to be endured, but on the strange position that any one State may not only declare an act of Congress void, but prohibit its execution; that they may do this consistently with the Constitution; that the true construction of that instrument permits a State to retain its place in the Union and yet be bound by no other of its laws than those it may choose to consider as constitutional. It is true, they add, that to justify this abrogation of a law it must be palpably contrary to the Constitution; but it is evident that to give the right of resisting laws of that description, coupled with the uncontrolled right to decide what laws deserve that character, is to give the power of resisting all laws; for as by the theory there is no appeal, the reasons alleged by the State, good or bad, must prevail....

This right to secede is deduced from the nature of the Constitution, which, they say, is a compact between sovereign States who have preserved their whole sovereignty and therefore are subject to no superior; that because they made the compact they can break it when in their opinion it has been departed from by the other States. Fallacious as this course of reasoning is, it enlists State pride and finds advocates in the honest prejudices of those who have not studied the nature of our Government sufficiently to see the radical error on which it rests.

The people of the United States formed the Constitution, acting through the State legislatures in making the compact, to meet and discuss its provisions, and acting in separate conventions when they ratified those provisions; but the terms used in its construction show it to be a Government in which the people of all the States, collectively, are represented. We are *one people* in the choice of President and Vice-President. Here the States have no other agency than to direct the mode in which the votes shall be given. The candidates having the majority of all the votes are chosen. The electors of a majority of States may have given their votes for one candidate, and yet another may be chosen. The people, then, and not the States, are represented in the executive branch.

In the House of Representatives there is this difference, that the people of one State do not, as in the case of President and Vice-President, all vote for the same officers. The people of all the States do not vote for all the members, each State electing only its own representatives. But this creates no material distinction. When chosen, they are all representatives of the United States, not representatives of the particular State from which they come. They are paid by the United States, not by the State; nor are they accountable to it for any act done in the performance of their legislative functions; and however they may in practice, as it is their duty to do, consult and prefer the interests of their particular constituents when they come in conflict with any other partial or local interest, yet it is their first and highest duty, as representatives of the United States, to promote the general good.

The Constitution of the United States ... forms a *government,* not a league; and whether it be formed by compact between the States or in any other manner, its character is the same. It is a Government in which all the people are represented, which operates directly on the people individually, not upon the States; they retained all the power they did not grant. But each State, having expressly parted with so many powers as to constitute, jointly with the other States, a single nation, can not, from that period, possess any right to secede, because such secession does not break a league, but destroys the unity of a nation....

Fellow-citizens of my native State, let me not only admonish you, as the First Magistrate of our common country, not to incur the penalty of its laws, but use the influence that a father would over his children whom he saw rushing to certain ruin. In that paternal language, with that paternal feeling, let me tell you, my countrymen, that you are deluded by men who are either deceived themselves or wish to deceive you.... They are not champions of liberty, emulating the fame of our Revolutionary fathers, nor are you an oppressed people, contending, as they repeat to you, against worse than colonial vassalage. You are free members of a flourishing and happy Union. There is no settled design to oppress you.

6. Lieutenant-Colonel José Enrique de la Peña Defends Mexico's Actions Against the Texans, 1836

The insults lavished upon the nation as represented by the customs officials and commanders of military detachments, the disregard for laws, and the attitudes with which the colonists looked upon those who had given them a country were more than sufficient causes to justify war on our part. They were the aggressors and we the attacked, they the ingrates, we the benefactors. When they were in want we had given them sustenance, yet as soon as they gained strength they used it to destroy us.

On the 17th of February the commander in chief had proclaimed to the army: "Comrades in arms," he said, "our most sacred duties have brought us to these uninhabited lands and demand our engaging in combat against a rabble of wretched adventurers to whom our authorities have unwisely given benefits that even Mexicans did not enjoy, and who have taken possession of this vast and fertile area, convinced that our own unfortunate internal divisions have rendered us incapable of defending our soil. Wretches!"

This address was received enthusiastically, but the army needed no incitement; knowing that it was about to engage in the defense of the country and to avenge less fortunate comrades was enough for its ardor to become as great as the noble and just cause it was about to defend.... For their part, the enemy leaders had addressed their own men in terms not unlike those of our commander. They said that we were a bunch of mercenaries, blind instruments of tyranny; that without any right we were about to invade their territory; that

José Enrique de la Peña, *With Santa Anna in Texas: A Personal Narrative of the Revolution*, trans. Carmen Perry (College Station: Texas A&M University Press, 1975), 4–5, 40–52.

we would bring desolation and death to their peaceful homes and would seize their possessions; that we were savage men who would rape their women, decapitate their children, destroy everything, and render into ashes the fruits of their industry and their efforts. Unfortunately they did partially foresee what would happen, but they also committed atrocities that we did not commit, and in this rivalry of evil and extermination, I do not dare to venture who had the ignominious advantage, they or we! ...

Among the defenders [of the Alamo] there were thirty or more colonists; the rest were pirates, used to defying danger and to disdaining death, and who for that reason fought courageously; their courage, to my way of thinking, merited them the mercy for which, toward the last, some of them pleaded; others not knowing the language, were unable to do so.... The order had been given to spare no one but the women and this was carried out.

7. Michel Chevelier, a French Visitor, Marvels at the Pageantry of Politics, 1839

But this entry of the hickory [that is, the entrance of Andrew Jackson] was but a bymatter compared with the procession I witnessed in New York. It was in the night after the closing of the polls, when victory had pronounced in favour of the democratic party.... The procession was nearly a mile long; the democrats marched in good order to the glare of torches; the banners were more numerous than I had ever seen them in any religious festival; all were in transparency, on account of the darkness. On some were inscribed the names of the democratic societies or sections; *Democratic young men of the ninth* or *eleventh ward;* others bore imprecations against the Bank of the United States; *Nick Biddle* and *Old Nick* here figured largely, and formed the pendant of our *libera nos a malo*. Then came portraits of General Jackson afoot and on horseback; there was one in the uniform of a general, and another in the person of the Tennessee farmer, with the famous hickory cane in his hand. Those of Washington and Jefferson, surrounded with democratic mottoes, were mingled with emblems in all tastes and of all colours. Among these figured an eagle, not a painting, but a real live eagle, tied by the legs, surrounded by a wreath of leaves, and hoisted upon a pole, after the manner of the Roman standards. The imperial bird was carried by a stout sailor, more pleased than ever was a sergeant permitted to hold one of the strings of the canopy, in a catholic ceremony. From further than the eye could reach, came marching on the democrats. I was struck with the resemblance of their air to the train that escorts the *viaticum* in Mexico or Puebla. The American standard-bearers were as grave as the Mexican Indians who bore the sacred tapers. The democratic procession, also, like the Catholic procession, had its halting places; it stopped before the houses of the Jackson men to fill the air with cheers, and halted at the doors of the leaders of the Opposition, to give three,

Michel Chevelier, *Society, Manners, and Politics in the United States* (Boston: Weeks, Jordan and Company, 1839), 318–319.

six, or nine groans. If these scenes were to find a painter, they would be admired at a distance, not less than the triumphs and sacrificial pomps, which the ancients have left us delineated in marble and brass; for they are not mere grotesques after the manner of Rembrandt, they belong to history, they partake of the grand; they are the episodes of a wondrous epic which will bequeath a lasting memory to posterity; that of the coming of democracy.

8. Frederick Douglass Addresses Texas and Slavery While Speaking in Ireland, 1846

Belfast *News Letter*, January 6, 1846.

Mr. Frederick Douglass rose—his coming forward upon the platform was greeted with applause which lasted more than a minute. He said—Mr. Chairman, Ladies and Gentlemen, according to the notice that has been given to this highly respectable and intelligent audience, I rise for the purpose of calling your attention to the subject of the Annexation of Texas to the United States. A question may rise in your minds as to what the Annexation of Texas to the States has to do with Slavery in America. This question I think I shall be able to answer during the remarks I shall have to make this evening.

I regret my inability to give you in one short lecture the history of the various circumstances leading to the consummation of the Annexation of Texas. If I were able to do so, you would see that it was a conspiracy from beginning to end—a most deep and skilfully devised conspiracy—for the purpose of upholding and sustaining one of the darkest and foulest crimes ever committed by man. But I will not attempt to give you a minute history of the incidents and occurrences which have led to the present position of the question.

Texas is that part of Mexico, north [south] of Arkansas and extending from the Gulf of Mexico to the Rio Del Norte. The extent of this country is almost equal to that of France, and its fertility is such that it is estimated as being able to support not less than twenty millions of souls. In 1820 this vast territory, as well as all the rest of Mexico, was subject to the Spanish Government. The history of the settlement of Texas by its present population is briefly as follows: In the year just mentioned, Moses Austin, of the State of Tennessee—a slave holding State—obtained a grant from the Royal Government of Spain to settle in that territory 300 families, on the condition that they should be industrious, sober, upright men, and professors—mark this—of the Roman Catholic religion. Austin obtained by this grant, great advantages to himself, and when he died his son Stephen Austin became the legal representative of his father, and prosecuted the work of settling the 300 families, for whom his father had obtained the large grants of land, with vigour, stimulating many who would not have otherwise thought of leaving their homes to go into this beautiful

Frederick Douglass Addresses Texas and Slavery While Speaking in Ireland, 1846, Frederick Douglass, "Texas, Slavery, and American Prosperity: An Address Delivered in Belfast, Ireland, on January 2, 1846." Belfast News Letter, January 6, 1846.

country, that they might enrich themselves, and lay the foundations of wealth for their children. During the prosecution of this design, however, the revolution broke out in Mexico, by which that country was severed from the Spanish government, and this event rendered the original contract of settlement null and void, so that Austin applied for and obtained a similar grant from Mexico, by which he succeeded in completing the number of families intended to be settled in Texas.

The settlers soon spread abroad reports of the fertility and salubrity of the country, and these reports induced a general spirit of speculation, and thus a way was opened for the practice of the grossest hypocrisy. Many persons were induced, from the love of gold, to pretend the profession of the Roman Catholic religion, thus obtaining large quantities of land. This spirit of speculation was entered into by the people of different nations, including many from England, Ireland, and Scotland. I have the names of several persons even from this town who took part in the settlement of Texas, but the territory was chiefly settled by the citizens of the United States—of the slaveholding states—of America. It was early seen by them that this would be a delightful spot to curse with slavery. They accordingly took their families and slaves to Texas, from the blighted and blasted fields of Virginia— fields once fertile as any under Heaven—(hear)—and which would have still remained so had they not been cursed by the infernal spirit of slavery.

We do not hear of much confusion in Texas, until 1828 or 1829, when Mexico after having erected herself into a separate government and declared herself free, with a consistency which puts to the blush the boasted "land of freedom," proclaimed the deliverance of every captive on her soil. Unlike the boasted republic of America, she did this at an immense cost to her own slaveholders—not proclaiming liberty with her lips, while she fastened chains on the slave—not securing liberty for her own children but also for the degraded bondsman of Africa. (Cheers.) This act of the Mexican government was resisted at once by the settlers who had carried their slaves into Texas, though they were bound by a solemn agreement to submit to the laws of Mexico. They remonstrated with the government. They said their slaves were too ignorant and degraded to be emancipated. The Mexican government, desirous to treat amicably with those whom it had welcomed to its bosom, listened to this remonstrance, and consented that the Texian slaves should be only gradually emancipated under a system of indentured apprenticeship. Even this restriction was evaded by the Texians, making the indentures binding for 99 years. In fact they showed themselves to be a set of swindlers. Well, Mexico attempted an enforcement of her law, making it impossible for any man to hold an apprentice more than ten years. This was resisted on the plea that the slaves would not be fit for freedom even then. One would think ten years long enough to teach them the value of liberty, but these wise Americans could not understand how that could be the case.

The Texians still persisted in holding their slaves, contrary to the express declaration of their legislature—contrary to the law of the land—to drive them before the biting lash to their hard tasks, day after day, without wages. Again, the Mexican Government attempted to enforce its law, but then Texas revolts—defies the law—and calls upon the people of the United States to aid her in, what they termed their struggle for religious liberty! (Hear.) Yes, they said they could not worship God according to the dictates of their conscience, alluding to the contract entered into by them as professing Roman Catholics. I am not prepared to say whether that contract was a righteous one or not, but, I do say, that after possessing themselves of the land, on the faith of their being Roman Catholics, they should be the last to complain on that score. If they had been honest, they would have said, in regard to their religious opinions, "We have changed our minds; we feel we cannot longer belong to the Church of Rome; we cannot, according to our contract, worship God as our conscience dictates; many of us are Methodists—many are Presbyterians; if you will allow us to worship God as we think right, we will stay in the soil; if not, we feel compelled to abandon it, and seek some other place." (Cheers.) That is the way that common honesty would force them to act, but the people of the United States—and here is one of the darkest acts of their whole history—understanding the terms upon which the Texians had obtained the territory, and well-knowing the exact nature of the contract—offered them the means of successfully resisting Mexico—afforded them arms and ammunition, and even the men who at San Jacinto, wrested the territory from the rightful owners. Here was an act of national robbery perpetrated, and for what? For the re-establishment of slavery on a soil which had been washed pure from its polluting influence by the generous act of a "semibarbarous" people! (Hear.)

The man who goes into your ship on the high seas, puts out the captain, takes down the ensign and declares himself the owner—is no greater robber than the people of the United States. And what are their excuses, their apologies, their reasons—for they always give reasons for what they do? One of them is, that Mexico is unable to defend her territory, and that therefore they have a right to take it! What do you think of a great heavy-fisted fellow pouncing on every little man he meets, and giving as his reason that the little man is unable to take care of himself? (Cheers.) We don't see this pretext made use of in the case of Canada. (Hear.) Mexico, nevertheless, is a sister republic, which has taken that of the United States for a model. But Mexico is a weak government, and that is the reason America falls on her—the British territories are safe because England is strong. (Hear.)

Oh, how superlatively base—how mean—how dastardly—do the American people appear in the light of justice—of reason—of liberty—when this particular point of her conduct is exposed! But here there was a double point to be gained—on the part of the Southern planters to establish and cultivate large plantations in the South—and on that of the Northern ones, to support what Daniel O'Connell says should not be called the internal, but the infernal, slave-trade, which is said to be worse than the foreign slave-trade, for it allows men to seize upon those who have sported with them on the hills, and played with them at school, and are associated with them in so many ways and under so many interesting circumstances. This is more horrible still than to prowl along the African shore and carry off thence men with whose faces at least we are unfamiliar, and to whose characters we are strangers. Still the chief object of the Annexation of Texas was the quickening of the foreign slave-trade, which is the very jugular vein of slavery, and of which, if kept within narrow limits, we would soon be rid. But the cry of slavery is ever "Give, give, give!" That cry is heard from New England to Virginia. It goes on, leaving a blighted soil behind—leaving the fields which it found fertile and luxuriant, covered with stunted pines. From Virginia it has gone to North Carolina, and from that to South Carolina, leaving ruin in its train, and now it seizes on the fertile regions of Texas, where it had been previously abolished by a people whom we are wont to call semi-civilized. They say they only want to increase their commerce, and add to their security. Oh what a reason to give for plunder! (Hear.) The pirate of the high seas might make the same excuse.

Mankind thinks that whatever is prosperous is right. Henry Clay said that what the law has made property is property, and that 200 years of legislation has made the negro slave property. With a *sang froid* more like that of a demon than a man he added, "It will be asked will not slavery come to an end? Why, that question has been asked fifty years ago, and answered by fifty years of prosperity." Prosperity is the rule of conduct. Justice is nothing—humanity is nothing—Christianity is nothing—but prosperity is everything. (Hear.) I was some time since, on the same principle, spoken to by a member of the church, who told me I was mistaken in my views and laboring against the will and wisdom of God, in this manner—"Don't you see," said he, "that we have been adding to our numbers, lengthening our cords and strengthening our stakes—don't you see the church growing in the favor of the world." This element of character is peculiar to the Americans; all they ask is prosperity, and therefore we see their bony fingers pointing towards the Pacific, threatening to overwhelm and destroy every other power which may dispute their claims. I am sorry that England, on this occasion, did not act with that high spirit of justice which led her to emancipate 800,000 of her own slaves elsewhere. I am sorry that she stepped forward with almost indecent haste to recognise the Texian banditti as an independent Republic. (Hear.) Oh, the love of money! rightly has it been called the root of all evil—with this lust for gold has England too been contaminated, and hence the result we witness.

Two years ago, I had hoped that there was morality enough, Christian-mindedness enough, love of liberty enough, burning in the bosoms of the American people, to lead them to reject for ever the unholy alliance in which they have bound themselves to Texas. When I first heard of this event, at a meeting in Massachusetts, I was covered with confusion of face, for I believed we had religion enough among us to have prevented the horrid consummation. That event threw a gloom over the hearts of the struggling abolitionists, and led them to feel that the powers of darkness had prevailed against them. I hung my head, and felt that I was deceived in the people among whom I lived, and that they were hurrying their own destruction by dipping their hands in the blood of millions of slaves. However, I recovered when I remembered that ours was not a ca[u]se in which the human arm was the only agent—when I remembered that God was God still, I took courage again, and resolved to continue to pray to that God who has the destinies of nations in his hand to change their hearts.

We are still, however, strong, for the last intelligence I had from the United States was, that 40,000 good men and true, in Massachusetts, had petitioned the Government not to allow Texas to be received as a State until she had abolished slavery. (Cheers.) What will be the immediate result, I know not, but Texas in the Union or out of it—slavery upheld or slavery abolished—one thing I do know—that the true words now spoken, in Massachusetts, will create a resistance to this damning measure, which will go on under the smiles of an approving God, augmenting in power till slavery in the United States will be abolished. (Hear.) I know not how that consummation will be achieved. It may be in a manner not altogether agreeable to my own feelings. I do not know but the spirit of rapine and plunder, so rampant in America, will hurry her on to her own destruction. I hope it will not, for although America has done all that a nation could do to crush me— although I am a stranger among you—a refugee abroad, an outlaw at home—yet, I trust in God, no ill may befall her. I hope she will yet see that it will be her duty to emancipate the slaves. The friends of emancipation are determined to do all they can—

Weapons of war we have cast from the battle,—
Truth is our armour, our watchword is love;
Hushed be the sword and the musketry's rattle,
All our equipments are drawn from above.

Let no one accuse me of attempting to stir up a spirit of war. You may accuse me of being an impostor, or trying to make money—you may accuse me of what you please—but not of stirring up a war against that land which has done me and my race so much injury. For, though, If ever a man had cause to curse the region in which he was born, I am he—though my back is scarred with the lash of the driver—nature, law, and Christianity bind me to the United States of America.

Mr. Douglass then alluded to the charges which had been made against him, and which are fully disposed of in the letter in reply to "Civis," already alluded to. He then spoke of 36 ministers of Belfast having signed a resolution to the effect that slave-holders should not be admitted as members of the Christian Church. That circumstance had cheered his heart, and he would re-member the 2d of Jan. 1846, as a most glorious day, inasmuch as with the recollections of that day would always be associated what 36 Christian minis-ters of Belfast had done in furtherance of the great cause he advocated. Their protest would cross the Atlantic, and fall as a bomb-shell amongst the slave-holders, filling their souls with terror and dismay.

Mr. Douglass then alluded to the many kind friends he had met with In Belfast, and said they would always be dear to his heart wherever his lot might be cast. Their Christian and fatherly advice would never be forgotten; and he would take care so to walk, that they would never hear that he had by any con-duct of his retarded the progress of the holy cause of which he was the humble advocate, or that he had acted a part unbecommg an humble follower of the Lord Jesus. He then resumed his seat amid the warmest and most enthusiastic demonstrations of applause.

ESSAYS

Historians have long marveled at how the United States grew powerfully in the first fifty years of the nineteenth century and how it fractured. The nation became stronger, yet so too did the sections. In the essays that follow, historians Sean Wilentz and Susan-Mary Grant examine the powerful role of sectional constructions during this time of national expansion and development. Wilentz fixates on the rise of Andrew Jackson, the first president from the "West," and how Texas and the Southwest promised both possibility and peril for the United States. Western lands, which were seen as central to national development and the expansion of slavery and cotton, unnerved many northerners who saw in it the growth of slavery. Susan-Mary Grant focuses less on politics and more on sensibilities. She examines how "the South" went from a land and location of esteem and intrigue for northerners to one of backwardness and frustration. For Grant, the creation of a northern sectionalism was just as important, albeit less often noted, as was southern sectionalism or western expansion.

The Rise of Andrew Jackson, the Annexation of Texas, and the Perils and Possibilities of Nationalism and Sectionalism

SEAN WILENTZ

On pleasant evenings in the middle of the 1830s, Noah Webster, nearing his eighties, would return home from his daily walk around New Haven, sit in his front-porch rocker, pick up his newspaper, and moan. The latest political dispatches told Webster that the republic he had loved and fought for had gone to the devil, a democratic devil in the shape of Andrew Jackson, and the future looked bleak. Webster's wife, upon hearing his sighs, knew what was coming: a monologue on mob rule, the death of Christian virtue, and the savagery of strange doctrines and slogans ("rotation in office," "the rich oppress the poor," "*the spoils belong to the victors*") that had taken the country by storm. Later in the evening, a few of Webster's professor friends from Yale might stop by to listen and nod their heads, forming a mutually admiring circle of dyspeptic learned men. On these occasions, Webster would brighten momentarily. But many of his companions, like himself, had grown old, and the number of Americans like them was too small, Webster feared, to save the republic now.

When the professors did not appear, Webster would rouse himself, scratch down his opinions, and mail them to a few agreeable editors and elected officials. He was still a well-known figure, a veteran political controversialist, die-hard nationalist, and self-made man, a Founding Father of sorts. Although the great dictionary he had published years earlier had not yet found its market, his blue-backed speller had been a rousing success, and trustworthy critics had hailed him as the man who had literally defined the American language. Perhaps his countrymen would heed his wisdom after all. And so he composed his didactic letters, denouncing President Jackson and Jackson's fanatical democratic principles. Webster devised a plan to check the egalitarian tide by raising the voting age to forty-five, dividing the electorate into two classes according to age and wealth, and letting each class choose one house of Congress—an Americanized gerontocratic version of the British Lords and Commons. But his ideas impressed few readers and caused many to snicker, and the old man sank into acrid reveries about his days as a boy soldier during the American Revolution. Had he foreseen what would follow, he told an associate, he never would have enlisted in the patriot cause.

Webster was a political relic in the 1830s, yet around the country, other Americans were also pessimistic. In the summer of 1837, James Kent, the nation's most distinguished legal commentator, journeyed to the spa at Saratoga Springs and joined other gentlemen in discussing the destructiveness of what Kent called "the democracy of numbers and radicalism." In Manhattan, the affluent parvenu and former mayor of New York, Philip Hone, recoiled with horror from the unkempt Jacksonian supporters who ran wild in the streets on election days, and who on one dismal occasion besieged him in his own house with catcalls. Further south, slaveholding planters and officeholders who thought Jackson a turncoat despaired at his popularity with the plain people and voters. "The old Warrior Chief has kicked up a h-ll of a dust throughout the nation," a Tennessean wrote to a North Carolina planter, in 1834, adding that while "most of our friends of N. Carolina are against [Jackson's] 'experiments,' I should suppose that the people of the State were for him." Other southerners despaired that the masses of farmers and the anti-Jacksonians were like aliens in blood.

Andrew Jackson and his political supporters read President Adams's ambitious first annual message with indignant disbelief. As they saw it, a president whose election lacked democratic legitimacy had brazenly bid the Congress to disregard the will of the electorate, expand its own powers, and legislate on behalf of the favored few at the expense of the many. "When I view the splendor & magnificence of the government" that Adams proposed, Jackson wrote, "together with the declaration that it would be criminal for the agents of our government to be palsied by the will of their constituents, I shudder for the consequence—if not checked by the voice of the people, it must end in consolidation & then in despotism."

Jackson, already looking to a rematch in the 1828 elections, was confident that "the intelligence, and virtue, of the great body of the American people" would defeat Adams's plans. Instead of extravagant programs enlarging the federal government's authority, Jackson proposed that Congress should pay off the national debt and apportion whatever surplus remained to the states for the education of the poor. At such moments, when he stressed retrenchment, Jackson sounded much like his old foe William Crawford and the other state-rights southern Radicals. Although they had some things in common, Jackson's evolving politics were more complex. And although Jackson would welcome, indeed court, the state-rights Radicals, including Crawford, he knew that they provided an insufficient political base for a national victory.

The fragmented results of 1824 had shown clearly that success at the national level required building disparate coalitions that cut across the lines of class and section. To defeat Adams, Jackson needed to find a message that conveyed his thinking above and beyond state rights, and build a winning national combination. He needed, in particular, to expand beyond his connections to William Duane and Steven Simpson and impress city and country democrats who had not backed him in 1824. That would not be simple. Conceptions of American democracy were, as ever, in flux in the late 1820s, appearing in new variations to suit altered social circumstances. And by 1828, democratic movements were forming new minor parties and raising new issues about equality, the Constitution, and economic justice.

Although he looked like a distinguished old warrior, with flashing blue eyes and a shock of whitening steely gray hair, Andrew Jackson was by now a physical wreck. Years of ingesting calomel and watered gin to combat his chronic dysentery had left him almost toothless. (In 1828, he obtained an ill-fitting set of dentures, but he often refused to wear them). An irritation of his lungs, caused by a bullet he had caught in one of his early duels, had developed into bronchiectasis, a rare condition causing violent coughing spells that would bring up what he called "great quantities of slime." The bullet itself remained lodged in his chest, and another was lodged in his left arm, where it accelerated the onset of osteomyelitis. Rheumatism afflicted his joints, and his head often ached, the effect of a lifetime of chewing and smoking tobacco. He had survived near-total collapse of his health in 1822 and 1825, but for the rest of his life, he enjoyed few days completely free of agony. His outbursts of irascible fury, which sometimes shocked even his old friends and allies, owed partly to his suffering and to his efforts to suppress it. But after the debacle of 1825, they also owed to his determination to vindicate not just his own honor but that of the American people. For Jackson and his admirers, the two had become identical.

Willfulness did not mean rashness. In preparing to wreak his vengeance on Adams (whom he respected) and Clay (whom he despised), Jackson took care not to violate the accepted etiquette of presidential campaigning and appeal directly for the job. He was available to serve his country once more, but to look or sound less elevated than that would have been dishonorable (as well as onerous, given the state of his health). Jackson made only one major public appearance over the months before the election, at a public festivity in New Orleans on January 8, commemorating his great victory thirteen years earlier—an invitation, issued by the Louisiana legislature, that he could not refuse without seeming churlish. Yet while he stuck close to the Hermitage, Jackson threw himself into the fray as no other previous presidential candidate before him had, making himself available for visiting delegations of congressmen, giving interviews to interested parties, and writing letters for newspaper publication. When personal attacks on his character began, he became even more active, his sense of honor on the line. Some of his chief supporters, including Van Buren, asked that "we be let alone" and that Jackson "be *still*," but Jackson would command this campaign just as surely as he had any of his military exploits.

While Jackson and his closest advisors refined this message and called the shots from Nashville, his supporters built a sophisticated campaign apparatus unlike any previously organized in a presidential election, a combination so effective that it obviated the need for either a congressional caucus nomination or a national convention. At the top, Jackson's most capable Tennessee operatives, including John Overton, William Lewis, and John Eaton, concentrated their efforts in a central committee headquarters established in Nashville, where decisions about strategy and tactics could be taken efficiently, in rapid response to continuing events and with Jackson's approval. (A similar, smaller Jackson committee headquarters was established in Washington, to work closely with the pro-Jackson caucus in Congress that met regularly under Van Buren's aegis.) The central committee in turn dispatched its messages to (and received intelligence from) Jackson campaign committees established in each state. Finally, the Jacksonians responded to the reforms in presidential voting around the country—reforms that, by 1828, had included, in all but two states, giving the power to choose presidential electors directly to the voters—by coordinating activities at the local level. The state pro-Jackson committees linked up with local Jackson committees, sometimes called Hickory Clubs, that stirred up enthusiasm with rallies and parades and made sure that their supporters arrived at the polls.

Even more extraordinary than the campaign committees was the dense network of pro-Jackson newspapers that seemed to arise out of nowhere beginning in the spring of 1827. Early in the campaign, Jackson's congressional supporters had caucused and pledged to establish "a chain of newspaper posts, from the New England States to Louisiana, and branching off through Lexington to the Western States." In North Carolina alone, nine new Jacksonian papers had appeared by the middle of 1827, while in Ohio, eighteen new papers supplemented the five already in existence in 1824. In each state, the Jackson forces arranged for one newspaper to serve as the official organ of their respective state committees, refining the broadcast of an authoritative message while promoting a cadre of prominent loyal editors, including Ritchie at the *Enquirer*, Amos Kendall at the *Argus of Western America*, Edwin Croswell at the *Albany Argus*, Isaac Hill at the New Hampshire *Patriot*, and, above all, in Washington, Calhoun's friend Duff Green at the anti-administration *United States Telegraph*....

Texas annexation had long been a taboo subject for Whigs and Democrats alike. Ever since the formation of the independent Lone Star Republic in 1836, its new government had expressed interest in joining the United States. The newly elected Texas president, Sam Houston, backed the idea in his inaugural address in October, and in August 1837, a proposal favoring Texas annexation was laid before Congress. But the idea instantly ran into trouble in Washington. Although Jackson had been happy to recognize the new Texas Republic, annexing it as a state could well lead to war with Mexico, which both Jackson and Van Buren wanted to avoid. Moreover, northern antislavery opinion, riveted by Benjamin Lundy's account of the Texas revolution as a slaveholders' uprising, saw annexation as the latest southern subterfuge to augment slavery's control of the federal government "[T]he whole people of the United States," John Quincy Adams told the House, have "a deep, deep, deep interest in the matter." Adams was convinced that a very large portion of the citizenry, "dearly as they loved the Union, would prefer its total dissolution to the act of annexation of Texas." He proceeded to filibuster the annexation resolution for more than three weeks. In late August 1837, Secretary of State John Forsyth informed Texas officials that the effort would fail.

Under Houston's successor, the Georgia émigré Mirabeau Buonaparte Lamar, Texas renounced annexation and turned inward, removing Indians by force, planning a state education system, and raising hopes that one day the Lone Star Republic would extend to the Pacific—all while its treasury virtually collapsed. There the annexation issue rested (even after Houston's return as president) until 1843, when rumors began feeding fears that the British government had designs on the floundering republic. "I anticipate an important movement in regard to Texas," [John] Upshur wrote, months before he took over from Webster. Texas also had become ripe for reconquest by Mexico, which had never conceded its loss. The British, so the stories ran, would be happy to step in and prevent it, and get Mexico at last to recognize Texas's independence—so long as the Texans, respectful of the authority of Her Majesty's government, freed their slaves. From one angle, Upshur and other Tidewater conservatives reasoned, the British interference might be beneficial if it prevented the further draining away of eastern slaves westward and thereby helped the old-line eastern patricians to rebuild their former glory. But from another angle, the prospect of establishing a huge free territory (and potential haven for runaway slaves) on the borders of Louisiana and Arkansas was frightening.

For Upshur, raising the specter of slavery besieged looked like the best way to break through the demagogy of low political party managers and initiate the great southern-led state-rights party. Prodded by word from Calhoun's right-hand man Duff Green, and then from Calhoun himself, that the British government, with assistance of British abolitionists, was on the verge of striking a deal with the Texans, Upshur pressed Tyler to secure the only practical check on Britain's ambitions, Texas annexation. By September, administration officials were engaged in secret talks with Sam Houston. On October 16, Upshur met with the Texas chargé d'affaires Isaac Van Zandt and began preliminary discussions toward negotiating an annexation treaty.

The pursuit of Texas was bound to cause some sectional disagreements among the Whigs ... Since 1836, most old-guard and new-school northern Whigs had opposed annexation, some fearing a further expansion of slavery and southern power, others fearing that the nation was expanding too quickly ahead of the civilizing hand of moral progress and the American System, and still others hoping to make life more complicated for Webster's rival Clay. (Pro-expansionist Democrats added charges that pro-business Whigs opposed westward expansion in order to create a glut in the eastern labor market and suppress workers' wages.) Although some influential northern Whigs, above all Tyler's minister to England, Edward Everett, strongly backed annexation, they were in the decided minority. And if state-rights southern Whigs were more receptive to Tyler's plans, a significant number of Whig planters, mainly in the older southeastern states, opposed them in order to halt the diffusion of the slave population—and what they feared was their imminent abandonment to their depleted land and unpaid debts. Annexation's impact on the Democracy would be even more complicated. Southern Democrats, as expected, generally lined up with the administration, but the northern Democracy was deeply divided. Some leading New York Radicals took a dim view of annexation. Other northern Democrats loudly supported it, shouting new slogans about Manifest Destiny.

The Manifest Destiny impulse fed off a mixture of crassness, truculence, and high idealism. Without question, there were those who proclaimed America's providential mission to expand as a eulogistic cover for speculation in land and paper. But those were hardly the motives of John L. O'Sullivan, the writer who coined the term, or the other writers, loosely referred to as Young America, in and around O'Sullivan's *Democratic Review* (which had relocated from Washington to Manhattan over the winter of 1840–41). For O'Sullivan and his allies, the expansionist imperative was essentially democratic—not simply in the old Jeffersonian tradition of enlarging the empire of liberty, but in a supercharged moral sense, stressing America's duties to spread democratic values and institutions to a world still dominated by monarchs and deformed by ignorant superstition. The grand national mission, O'Sullivan wrote as early as 1839, was to spread four great freedoms around the globe: freedom of conscience, freedom of person, freedom of trade, and what he called "universality of freedom and equality." The mission was even more precise closer to home, where, O'Sullivan claimed six years later, America enjoyed "the right of our manifest destiny to overspread and to possess the whole of the continent which Providence has given us for the ... great experiment of liberty."

In retrospect this posturing can look like the most arrogant form of imperial bullying. Certainly it was arrogant, and Mexicans, including Mexican liberals, had ample reason to consider it imperialist But there was a deeply idealistic democratic side to Manifest Destiny that, to be understood, requires an appreciation for the situation facing democrats around the world, and especially in Britain and Europe, in the early 1840s. That situation was terrible. In Britain, the Reform Bill of 1832 had left the vast majority of urban and rural workingmen disenfranchised. Radicals from William Cobbett (who wrote an admiring brief biography of Jackson) to the Chartists were struggling through one setback after another, on the road to Chartism's collapse in 1848. In France, the hopeful revolution of 1830 had produced a stockjobber monarchy that hesitated not at all to repress popular republican stirrings in blood—and that inspired, in Paris, Honoré Daumier's brilliant pictorial satires and indictments. In Ireland, Daniel O'Connell's nonviolent mass movement for repeal of the union with Britain was stirring great crowds, but getting nowhere fast against the obdurate ministry of Sir Robert Peel. Across the face of Europe, nationalist as well as democratic aspirations remained stifled by Metternichian reaction. In all of these places, but especially in England and Ireland, intellectuals and agitators looked to the United States for practical as well as spiritual inspiration—and, when the repression at home got too great, looked to the United States for asylum.

Manifest Destiny was rooted in its proponents' allegiance to the beleaguered forces of democracy outside the United States. The name ascribed to and then embraced by the O'Sullivan circle, Young America, had been borrowed from the insurgent liberals of Giuseppe Mazzini's Young Italy, initiated in the 1830s. (There were, in time, many others in the international movement, including Young Germany, Young England. Young Ireland, Young France, Young Poland—and even, one writer tried to claim during the Dorr Rebellion, a Young Rhode Island.) Democracy, the expansionists asserted, was a universal value that should—and could—rule the world. "Why should not England be republican?" the *Democratic Review* queried in a typical article on the Chartists. "Are her lower classes unfit for the burden of government?" And what of Ireland, her lifeblood drained for centuries by the British monarchy: "[I]s Ireland incapable of entering upon (he simple task of self government, because for so long she has been unused to it?" What of the French, the Hungarians, the Italians, the much-abused Greeks?

There were, of course, large omissions from this expansionist idealism: black slaves along with, as ever, displaced Indians. O'Sullivan and his admirers sharply denied that their intentions were pro-slavery. (On the Texas question, O'Sullivan agreed with southerners, most prominently Senator Robert J. Walker of Mississippi, who argued that annexation would lead to a dispersal of the slave population through the West and into Latin America, hasten slavery's demise, and leave behind an all-white United States—a rehashing of the old Jeffersonian "diffusion" idea.) But neither were they capable of expanding their democratic radicalism to endorse antislavery. Like the centrist mainstream of their party, the Manifest Destiny Democrats took an agnostic position on slavery. With regard to race, they candidly but clumsily evaded even considering the possibilities of equality between blacks and whites. "Strong as are our sympathies in behalf of liberty, universal liberty, in all applications of the principle not forbidden by great and manifest evils," O'Sullivan wrote in the *Democratic Review*, "we confess ourselves not prepared with any satisfactory solution of the great problem of which these questions present various aspects." After 1845, this moral indifference about slavery and race would leave the Young America movement and the slogans of Manifest Destiny vulnerable to capture by pro-slavery ideologues. But until then, Young America could electrify masses of northern Democrats, for whom enlarging on what O'Sullivan called the "gigantic boldness" of the American Revolution was the greatest idea in the world.

O'Sullivan and Young America won support from a diverse collection of northern Radicals, Hunkers, and Calhounites, including Churchill Cambreleng and Mike Walsh. But there were other Democrats, including the flickering taper that was once Andrew Jackson, who desired Texas for defensive reasons, to block the unending treachery of Great Britain. For Jackson, the Texas maneuverings created the imminent danger of a British reconquest of America. With a base in Texas, Jackson predicted, the British would gather up hordes of Indians as well as slaves to attack the nation's borders, then send in their own troops to march on New Orleans and seize control of both the lower Mississippi Valley and the Gulf of Mexico. Reversing that course, even if successful, would spill oceans of American blood and cost untold fortunes. Texas, Jackson told Francis Blair in 1844, was "the important key to our future safety—take and lock the door against all danger of foreign influence."

Contrary to both Young America and Jackson, however, a significant portion of the northern Democracy strongly objected to Texas annexation. Theodore Sedgwick III, the party's leading anti-annexation voice, had been writing antislavery Democratic pieces for the *Evening Post* for several years. In 1840—while he was working on the *Amistad* case and putting through the press a two-volume posthumous edition of William Leggett's collected writings—he sustained Leggett's Jacksonian abolitionism in terms that spoke directly to the Democracy: "Give us the real issue," he bellowed. "*Is Slavery a good or an evil to the free citizens of these States?*" Three years later, Sedgwick composed a fresh series of articles (which he eventually collected under the disarmingly calm title *Thoughts on the Proposed Annexation of Texas*) laying out the case that the admission of Texas to the Union was just "another name for '*the perpetuity of slavery*,'" which threatened the dignity of northern labor and thus democracy itself. Sedgwick's articles caused a stir among the New York Barnburners, which in turn reinforced Democratic antislavery opinion elsewhere. Silas Wright came out strongly against annexation, as did Wright's protégé, the one-time radical Jacksonian hotspur and now congressman from St. Lawrence County Preston King, They were joined by Marcus Morton of Massachusetts and another hard-money Radical Democrat, New Hampshire Senator John Parker Hale.

Antislavery Democrats had long been a submerged element within the party, harassed by party officials and, in some cases, subdued by their own self-censorship in order to keep up a united front against the Whigs. By 1844, some had finally defected in disgust to the Liberty Party. Others had either died, fallen by the political wayside, or, like Nat Turner's defender George Henry Evans, embarked on the strange journey that took them temporarily into Calhounism. The fight over Texas, however, revived the antislavery intellectual strain with the Democracy, and it gave antislavery a new and potentially disruptive political urgency among party leaders. It was one thing for Sedgwick's Manhattan friends (including William Cullen Bryant) to oppose Texas annexation; it was quite another when the opposition came to include Silas Wright. Once Wright and other Radical worthies joined the anti-annexationists, questions inevitably arose about their boss and mentor, the Democracy's prospective presidential nominee, Martin Van Buren. Would Texas annexation enter into the campaign of 1844? If it did, how would the preternaturally cautious Van Buren handle it? And no matter how Van Buren acted, could a Democratic Party that included pro-slavery southerners, Manifest Destiny enthusiasts, and anti-annexationist northerners possibly unite as long as the Texas question was on everybody's mind?

Secretary of State Upshur was intent on forcing the issue, and he was not alone. At the end of 1843, Calhounites all across the South began exploiting Texas annexation to revive their man's fading presidential chances. Only "the immediate calling up of the Texas question," Calhoun's Maryland friend Virgil Maxcy wrote in December, could unite the South, weaken Henry Clay, and bring a true southern candidate to power. (Maxcy was already plotting with the South Carolina extremist Robert Barnwell Rhett on how to kill Van Buren's chances at the Democratic convention.) Upshur had a different script in mind: the South should nominate Calhoun as a third-party presidential candidate on a pro-annexation platform; that candidacy would throw the election into the House of Representatives; and the southern members, by refusing to vote for Van Buren, would at the very least hold the balance of power in selecting the next administration. Calhoun dampened speculation when he formally abandoned his quest for the Democratic nomination in January 1844, but he remained open to using Texas as a political bludgeon on behalf of the South and did not rule out a third-party presidential run. President Tyler, meanwhile, hoping to become the South's tribune, tried with his usual ineptness to get Van Buren out of the way by offering him a seat on the Supreme Court. Tyler's messenger brought back the derisive reply that Van Buren's nomination to the Court would give the nation "a broader, deeper, heartier, laugh than it ever had."

On the diplomatic front, Upshur's steady labor was proving, tortuously, successful. He was well aware that gaining the two-thirds' majority in the Senate necessary to ratify any annexation treaty with Texas would be an uphill fight. The quicker he could conclude the treaty itself, the quicker he and his friends could go to work convincing Anglophilic southerners that the English emancipation threat had become an emergency. The southerners could then force the northern congressional Democrats to heel—or, failing in that, could form their own party along the lines Upshur favored and elect either Tyler or, even better, Calhoun as president. But getting a treaty out of the Texans proved difficult. President Sam Houston truly was interested in the British option and was pursuing it vigorously and openly. Only by applying all of the political pressure on Houston it could think of—including a plea from his old friend, Andrew Jackson—did the administration finally get him to come around. Finally, late in February 1844, Houston gave way. But by the time news of Houston's agreement arrived in Washington, on March 5, Secretary Upshur was dead.

Six days earlier, Upshur had joined a large presidential party aboard the battleship USS *Princeton,* anchored in the Potomac. The *Princeton* was the pride of the fleet, carrying the largest naval gun ever built, called "The Peacemaker." The day's highlight was to be a demonstration firing of the massive weapon, but something went terribly wrong and instead it exploded, blasting the dignitaries and sailors on deck to pieces. Tyler's life was spared, but Upshur, along with Secretary of the Navy Thomas Gilmer, Calhoun's close friend Virgil Maxcy, and five others were killed, and nine persons, including Senator Thomas Hart Benton, were injured. The president, although stunned and grief-stricken, acted swiftly to shore up his shaken government. At his Fort Hill plantation, in the same mail that carried an eyewitness description of the tragedy from his son Patrick (who was nearly killed himself), John C. Calhoun received word that Tyler would nominate him as Upshur's successor. Suddenly, the southern sectionalists' hero, who had figured so greatly in the plotting over Texas annexation, would be back in Washington as the chief officer of the cabinet, overseeing the entire Texas matter.

Northerners Begin to the See "the South" as the Problem

SUSAN-MARY GRANT

[T]here is no sectionalism to be found in any part of the country except what is generated by Nationalism. The feeling of loyalty and fidelity to the Union is strong and all pervading. Calhoun and his legatees were and are sectionalists. They call themselves State-rights men, but it was an assumed living to subserve sectional ends, and their constant efforts were to engender strife and hostility between the North and the South.
— Gideon Welles to General Houston, 22 July 1855

"Liberty *and* Union, now and forever, one and inseparable," was the ringing injunction with which Daniel Webster concluded his second reply to Robert Hayne in the Senate of the United States on 27 January 1830. Webster's speech sold over 40,000 copies in three months and was reprinted in many newspapers. In pamphlet form it exceeded 100,000 copies. It was, according to [historian] Merrill Peterson, "the triumph of an idea: the supremacy and permanency of the Union." It "raised the idea of Union above contract or expediency and enshrined it in the American heart. Liberty was identified with the Union, the Union with Liberty; together they defined American nationhood."

Even Daniel Webster, however, defined American nationhood from what was essentially a sectional perspective. His speech was one "in which the virtues of New England life and character were pitted against those of the South." Seldom, [historian] William Taylor argued, "had the complexities of the national character been so interestingly and so publicly expressed." Whereas Hayne "cast himself as a passionate Cavalier and slipped frequently into military terminology," Webster "was the transcendent Yankee, peaceable, cool and deliberate." In his Senate speech, Webster stressed the importance of union in the face of Hayne's essentially sectional rhetoric. More than that, he portrayed New England and the North as being more strongly devoted to union than the South. The southern outlook, declared Webster, was narrow in contrast

Excerpt from Susan-Mary Grant, *North Over South: Northern Nationalism and American Identity in the Antebellum Era* (Lawrence: University Press of Kansas, 2000).]

to the national outlook of the North. "[W]e narrow-minded people of New England do not reason thus," Webster asserted.

> Our notion of things is entirely different. We look upon the states, not as separated, but as united. We love to dwell on that Union, and on the mutual happiness which it has so much prompted, and the common renown which it has so greatly contributed to acquire. In our contemplation, Carolina and Ohio are parts of the same country—states united under the same general government, having interests common, associated, intermingled.... We do not impose geographical limits to our patriotic feeling or regard; we do not follow rivers, and mountains, and lines of latitude, to find boundaries beyond which public improvements do not benefit us.

Clearly Webster was a man who knew his audience. If he attributed national sentiments to the North and sectional sentiments to the South, there must have been many in Congress and beyond who would have concurred with him.

The sectional theme in American national construction always found its clearest and most destructive expression via the U.S. Congress. The eventual emergence of a northern sectional party—the Republicans—brought together a plethora of northern concerns about the South and focused these in a dangerously partisan way, giving them a momentum they would not otherwise have had. Specifically, although the idea of the "slave power" had emerged outside Congress, it was predicated on the behavior of southern representatives and senators in the U.S. legislature. The belief that southerners had always enjoyed, and continued to hold, a disproportionate share of power in the federal government contributed to northern fears of the slave power conspiracy, and the violent behavior of several individual southern representatives in Washington in the 1850s reinforced these fears.

The South had, of course, through the agency of the Democratic Party, been able to exploit the divisions between the factions in the North, so northern concerns in this regard were not wholly unfounded. The basis of the South's power was deemed to derive from the fact that the region's various interest groups, unlike those in the North, were able to act in a coherent, united manner. The institution of slavery was the main reason for the South's apparent unity, but it was not the only one. Northerners were generally unable to see the South as a diverse region. Increasingly, they saw it, and reacted to it, as a single entity. This not only led some northerners to make sweeping generalizations about the South's exclusively sectional outlook but also encouraged them in their belief that a united South might very well be a threat to the free-labor society of the North. Consequently, when the slave power idea became more prevalent, as it did in the later antebellum period, it found an audience that was already primed to believe in it.

As Webster's speech made clear, as early as 1830 there was a tendency for northerners to sectionalize the nation's problems. Not only did the antebellum North attempt to wash its hands of the glaring moral dilemma posed by slavery, but by doing so, it was able to portray itself as the section that adhered most closely to American national ideals as set out in the Declaration of Independence. Webster had declared liberty and union to be one and inseparable, yet liberty, as antebellum northerners continually reminded themselves, was not a national institution. Slavery was not a national institution either, but it was, arguably, a national problem, even though many in the North refused to see it this way. Some northerners tended to take refuge behind a conveniently placed sectional barrier of their own construction, while at the same time attacking the South for being, in their view, too narrowly sectional. But to what extent was Webster playing to the gallery when he chose to juxtapose the exclusive sectionalism of the South with the inclusive nationalism of the North? To answer this question, it is productive to go back a few years and consider how previous generations approached the question of sectionalism in general and the South in particular.

Long before the notion of the slave power was introduced in the North, both northern and southern congressmen had been preconditioned to think and behave in a sectional way. The terms "section" and "sectional" had, since the third quarter of the eighteenth century, been favored by American congressmen and politicians, even when the rest of the country was still using terms such as "department," "part," and "quarter." Whichever term was used, however, the impulse to "think sectionally" had been reinforced as early as the revolutionary era, when the Atlantic communities were always listed from north to south in the political arena. In the first meeting of Congress on 5 September 1774, the roll call ran from New Hampshire, Massachusetts, Rhode Island, Connecticut, and so on down the eastern seaboard. Listing the colonies geographically had the effect of reinforcing a sectional awareness that had been present even at the outset of the new nation's life.

The Founding Fathers had been aware of the existence of sectional forces. George Washington sought to direct Americans toward the path of successful nationhood in his Farewell Address of 1796. He encouraged them to avoid sectional disagreement and to strive for national unity. Washington's emphasis on Americans as a people bonded not by ethnic or historical ties but by political inclusiveness and through choice found a resonant echo in Abraham Lincoln's invocation of the Declaration of Independence as the only viable means to nationhood for a people comprising so many different ethnicities and histories. During the Constitutional Convention of 1787, George Mason expressed his concern that the government be composed of representatives from the northern, middle, and southern states "to quiet the minds of the people and convince them that there will be proper attention paid to their respective concerns." Similarly, James Madison believed that the greatest danger to the new government lay in "the great southern and northern interests of the continent being opposed to each other. Look to the votes in Congress," Madison urged, "and most of them stand divided by the geography of the country, not according to the size of the states." As the years went by, Madison's fears were confirmed. Gradually the terms "section" and "sectional" became more common in both legislative and popular usage.

By the time of the Missouri Compromise debate, some northerners were not optimistic about the future of the Union. In 1820, Harrison Gray Otis had expressed views on the South, and on the behavior of southerners, that would become standard observations some thirty years later. "In the South," he declared, "party and local interests are combined in one, which is made indissoluble by the common tie of property in slaves," whereas the North was divided between local and party interests. "Thus have we been always governed and controlled by the South," he concluded; "while Pennsylvania, New York and the Eastern States are agitated by feuds which appear to be of deadly malignity … the South moves in phalanx upon all great occasions and leaves us to our brawls … to their infinite sport and adventure." Three years after Webster's reply to Hayne, Otis repeated his concerns to Theodore Sedgwick, writing that Sedgwick's father had "belonged to a party who forty years ago, well understood that the negro holders when they ceased to govern us, would cease to be governed by us. As yet the contingency has not happened. They govern us effectually thus far, and I believe will effectually blast the prosperity of N. England this very Anno Domini." Two months later, Otis received a letter from George Harrison, who observed despondently, "[i]f I have a few years longer … I shall witness the dissolution of our Union & I am not one who will deplore it. I would willingly and cheerfully let the South go."

For northern congressmen, the very fact that they were in Washington representing their states gave them a stronger regional awareness than existed in northern society as a whole. On the one hand, as defenders of their section's interests—most notably in the debates over the Missouri Compromise and later the tariff debates—they had more cause, on a daily basis, to work up anger against representatives of interests that were opposite and hostile to their own. The Gag Rule (the 21st rule), which prevented discussion of anti-slavery petitions in Congress between 1835 and 1844, also had an effect, since it shaped northern ideas concerning free speech and civil liberties and was not regarded as a purely slavery-related issue. On the other hand, northern representatives and senators also had more opportunities to get to know southerners personally, to cultivate friendships, and, given Washington's location, to visit the South with relative ease. Many of them did so, visiting the homes of southern representatives they had befriended. In short, along with the opportunities for intersectional hostility, there were also at least some chances for intersectional understanding and an opportunity to dispel some of the myths and false images of the South.

Yet when northern representatives described the South in their letters home and in their speeches, the same images and themes appeared. Some representatives, especially in the 1820s and 1830s, argued that the South was not to blame for its peculiar institution and were positive about the black experience under slavery. In 1822, Caleb Cushing, for example, defended the South from its critics. He argued that southern planters were "wholly blameless" in the crime of slavery, since the institution was merely their inheritance from the previous generation. Cushing stressed that blacks were happier on southern plantations than they could hope to be elsewhere. And in his opinion, slaves had easier lives than the mass of European peasants. Too many northerners, Cushing averred, were guilty of "misplaced sentimentality" on the subject of slavery.

The image of the aggressive and aristocratic southerner was also standard, even in the letters of those who were essentially supportive of the South. "I am sensible," wrote one of Cushing's correspondents, "that the southern members are violent & too dictatorial, but great allowance is to be made, assailed as they are by the frantic abolitionists & standing as it seems on the crater of a Volcano. I think therefore it is the duty of the northern members to [stamp] upon all attempts at immediate emancipation—indeed at present nothing can be done on the subject except to assert our constitutional principles & these certainly are not to be yielded." Some thought that the North had already yielded too much. One correspondent argued that "[f]it only for *Slaves* are those persons who can sit calmly by their fire-sides in a state of inaction and lethargy, while their dearest rights are trampled underfoot.... Tell the haughty Southerners," he advised Cushing, "that they shall not ride roughshod over the necks of New England men—that the spirit which brought the Puritans to the rock of Plymouth, and animated our fathers at Bunker Hill, yet glows ... in the bosom of their descendants." Still others thought that Cushing had already done much to support the North against southern aggression and wrote to thank him for "the very manly and honorable stand which most of the delegation from Massachusetts ... have taken in maintaining the rights of the North, and the pure principles of liberty as designed by the formation of our government."

Cushing's correspondents touched on a theme that was prevalent both in and out of Congress throughout the 1830s: southern dominance versus northern submission and the South's use of the Union for its own ends. One northern minister, for example, advised his congregation that northerners were not safe in the southern states and were frequently attacked. He argued that the power of the southerner in Congress only served to diminish the authority of the North. He suggested, too, that southerners generally hated northerners, and whereas the "inhabitants of the non-slaveholding States are generally disposed to be quiet and civil," southerners were rowdy, violent, and sought only to dominate the rest of the nation. As one northern representative put it in 1832, "[w]e of the North and West ... are tributary—'hewers of wood and drawers of water' for the South. But with all this they are not content; we must be degraded to the condition of abject slaves; and if we object, they will dissolve the Union! Sir, it is the South, and not the North, that is most benefited by the Union." The biblical allusion to the "hewers of wood and drawers of water" was a common one, used by the press, in pamphlets, and in political speeches. Taken from the Book of Joshua, the phrase referred to the punishment inflicted on the inhabitants of Gideon for attempting to deceive the children of Israel. The fact that northerners used it on a fairly regular basis to invoke their relationship with the South spoke volumes—as it was doubtless intended to.

This is not to suggest that southerners were always portrayed in a negative light, but their arrogance and aristocratic bearing were considered detrimental to the North's representatives and to the North as a whole. When serving in Congress, Nathan Appleton received a letter from Amos Lawrence about the ongoing debates over the protective tariff—which Appleton had helped frame—in which Lawrence portrayed southerners as chivalrous bullies. Lawrence was not overtly critical, but he objected to what he saw as the South's superior tone.[14] Even a cursory study of the *Register of Debates* reveals repeated evidence of this theme in both the House and the Senate, particularly when it came to the issue of the tariff. Senator Dickerson of New Jersey argued, "If the cotton planters of the South would, with candid and liberal feelings, consider the immense advantages they enjoy over the North, in consequence of this Union, their deadly hostility to our protective system would cease." Senator Holmes of Maine summed up the prevalent view of the North-South divide when he observed, "Sir, it is not the democracy, it is the aristocracy of the country that is complaining [about the tariff]."

The shortcomings of the South also concerned northerners in the 1830s and 1840s in other ways. They were especially worried about how the existence of slavery was regarded abroad and what it said about their republican experiment. As William Cullen Bryant noted, Americans were particularly sensitive to foreign criticism. "They have this in common with other nations," he observed, "but they have another habit which shows that, with all their national vanity, they are not so confident of their own greatness, or of their own capacity to estimate it properly.... They are perpetually asking, what do you think of us in Europe? How are we regarded abroad?" In a letter to Robert Winthrop, William Channing proved Bryant's point. Channing reported a conversation with an Englishman who had been critical of slavery. "How painful and humbling," Channing wrote, "that our country, boasting of its attachment to freedom, should come in conflict with another, because the latter declares that whoever touches her soil is free." Americans, Channing argued, had good reason to be ashamed of their country, and its poor reputation throughout Europe was well deserved. "I fear," he concluded, "that we are to plunge into deeper infamy, are to array ourselves against the principles of justice and humanity which other nations have adopted,—are to throw ourselves in the way of the advancing civilization and Christianity of our age. The free States have been so accustomed to succumb to the arrogance of the South on the subject of slavery that I cannot but fear."

Throughout the 1830s and 1840s, events conspired to persuade a growing number of northerners that the South was not merely an affront to national pride but also a direct and growing threat to the northern states. The expulsion from South Carolina of Massachusetts' emissary Samuel Hoar—who had gone to Charleston to protest the fact that northern African American seamen were routinely imprisoned there while their ships were in dock—provoked intense outrage in Massachusetts and prompted the state senate to inquire hotly whether the "Constitution of the United States [has] the least practical validity or binding force in South Carolina, excepting where she thinks its operation favorable to her? ... Are the other States of the Union to be regarded as the conquered Provinces of South Carolina?" Ralph Waldo Emerson was equally angered by what he saw as South Carolina's high-handedness, but he was opposed to retaliation. This, he felt, would only bring New England down to South Carolina's level, something he could not envisage. New England culture, Emerson declared, "is not so low. Ours is not a brutal people, but intellectual and mild. Our land is not a jail." In the future, Emerson concluded, northerners should go to South Carolina "in disguise and with pistols in our pockets, leaving our pocketbooks at home, making our wills before we go." He saw the whole event as typical, and it offered further proof that North and South were separated by more than slavery. "It is the inevitable effect of culture to dissolve the animal ties of brute strength, to insulate, to make a country of men; not one strong officer, but a thousand strong men… . In all South Carolina there is but one opinion, but one man—Mr. Calhoun. Its citizens are but little Calhouns. In Massachusetts there are many opinions, many men."

Emerson was not alone in his assessment of either South Carolina or John C. Calhoun. As Merrill Peterson noted, Calhoun eventually attained "on a symbolic level the sectional ascendancy he could never attain politically. Among anti-slavery men in the North he already appeared as the evil genius of the Slave Power." Actually, Calhoun, along with the state he represented, had a fairly poor reputation even among moderate northerners. Philip Hone, for example, the famous New York diarist and close friend of William H. Seward, Daniel Webster, Henry Clay, and John Pendleton Kennedy, remained as critical of extremists in the North as he was of those in the South. But even he thought that the South had gone too far over issues such as the Gag Rule and the restrictions placed on mail to the South, which sought to limit if not wholly prevent the dissemination of abolitionist literature south of the Mason-Dixon line. The general tone of southerners in Congress upset him. Like Emerson, he advocated moderation, since in his view, "the remedy [was] worse than the disease." South Carolina, however, worked him up to such an extent that he described South Carolinians as "the most clannish, selfish people in America. They have no affection for anything except South Carolina." South Carolina personified had much the same effect on Hone as it had on Emerson. "I am a Northern man, and a New Yorker," Hone declared, and as such "I can never consent to be ruled by one whose paramount object is one of opposition to the interests and prosperity of this part of the Union. Mr. Calhoun has talents of a superior order. So much the worse, for his enmity is the more effective. The canker of envy, hatred and malice against the Northern and eastern States lies deep in his heart." Hone was not alone in his antipathy for South Carolina. George Templeton Strong, another New York diarist, consistently expressed similar sentiments. South Carolina was described by Strong in 1850 as a "preposterous little state … utterly below the city of New York or Boston or Philadelphia in resources, civilization, importance, and everything else." He repeated this view even more strongly later in the decade, after events in Congress had confirmed his earlier assessment.

For many northerners, the threat presented by southern views on the tariff and the Gag Rule and irrational acts such as Hoar's unceremonious expulsion from South Carolina was nothing compared with the threat presented by the annexation of Texas and the Mexican War that broke out as a result. As Edward Everett wrote in dismay to Robert Winthrop, "[w]e have sprung up at once into a nation of Conquerors. Heaven preserve us from the heroes." The historical assessment of the Mexican War has tended to stress its national, rather than its sectional, impact. In his assessment of the war's influence on the American imagination, Robert Johannsen argued strongly that it had the effect of papering over sectional differences and reinvigorating the patriotic sense of the American people. A sufficiently large number of Americans supported the war, Johannsen argued, "to give credence to the popular perception of the war as an important episode in the American quest for national identity." However, when one assesses the response to the Mexican War in the context of northern images of the South, it is clear that both those who supported it and those who opposed it were prompted to reconsider their ideas concerning American patriotism. Ultimately, the Mexican War could be said to have reinforced American patriotism but undermined *national* identity. For many northerners, the patriotism they took into the conflict was not quite the same as the sense of national identity they took away from it.

There is a wealth of evidence that some felt that during the Mexican War the country actually grew closer together. The war was not cited as the cause of this, however. "There is a steady growth of nationality among our people," the *American Review* declared, "a feeling that the States are merged in the Nation, and owe their power, importance and dignity in the eyes of the world to the Union and the General Government." The journal put this down to a general expansion of industry and a reduced reliance on southern products, which "must make the South less peculiar in its interests, less separate in its position, more inclined to compromise or co-operate with the other portions of the Union.... To industrial change, bringing about a great community of labor and production," it concluded, "do we confidently look for the gradual dissipation of all sectional prejudices, in every part of the Union, and the growth in their stead of a lasting community of interest and regard." Two years later, the journal was still optimistic concerning the "manners and customs and habits of thought" of Americans, which it believed were "generally alike throughout our country; so much so that it may be said with truth, we think, that a native of any Southern State would scarcely be distinguished ... the very first day he should be transplanted from his native region to a residence in Boston." There is also, however, a wealth of evidence showing exactly the opposite. As one northern representative declared:

> If there were a defect more prominent than any other in the national character of these United States, it was the very want of nationality. A spirit of common loyalty has not been as successfully cultivated here as among some other nations.... A nation derives strength as well as pride from the recollection of its heroic ancestry. It ever looks through the era of achievement, and glories in the simplicity of the dawning of its common origin.... What has the rock of Plymouth or the settlement of Jamestown ... to do with Texas or the Rio del Norte? ... The effect of annexation in any shape is at variance with the constitution.

The war that resulted in the following year concerned many northerners for several reasons. Many clearly thought that the war was intended to expand the slaveholding states, which would thereby increase the South's power in

Congress. However, many also saw it as a watershed in American development as a whole. The South, by pushing for the war, was seeking not only the domination of new lands but also the domination and transformation of America's republican experiment. Concern over this aspect of southern behavior can be traced to the start of the annexation debate, when the *Pittsburgh Daily Gazette* warned, somewhat lyrically, that when "this nation goes to war, its cause should be such as Angels might espouse.... When Liberty draws the sword, Honor should hold the scabbard. The people should be more concerned at the sacrifice of truth than at the approach of an army with banners. Foreign invaders may be repulsed but what can wipe off a stain upon the character of the nation?" For northern radicals such as John Gorham Palfrey, the war offered further evidence—if any were needed—that North and South were worlds apart in outlook. "Every person in the United States is the subject of two governments," Palfrey asserted. "We, of this Commonwealth, considered as the people of Massachusetts, are free citizens of an excellently constituted republic. Considered as people of the United States, we, with the rest of the so-called free people, both of the free and of the slave States ... are subjects of an oligarchy of the most odious possible description; an oligarchy composed of about one hundred thousand owners of men ... [who] administer our affairs."

For Horace Bushnell, too, the war represented nothing less than "the influence of slavery, as it enters into our American social state, and imparts its moral type of barbarism, through emigration to the new west ... which has its beginning and birth in what I have called the bowie-knife style of civilization—a war in the nineteenth century, which, if it was not purposely begun, many are visibly determined shall be, a war for the extension of slavery." Bushnell was not alone in his views. All over New England, ministers took it upon themselves to warn their congregations of the dangers posed to American democracy by the annexation of Texas and the designs of the slave power. The Reverend George Allen, for one, declared that the annexation of Texas was designed specifically to "fortify, extend and perpetuate the slave-holding power" and could have only a bad effect on the nation. The *New York Tribune* concurred with such views, especially once the war had broken out. "We do not believe it possible," the paper argued, "that our country *can* be prosperous in such a War as this. It may be victorious; it may acquire immense accessions of territory; but these victories, these acquisitions, will prove fearful calamities, by sapping the morals of our people, inflating them with pride and corrupting them with the lust of conquest and of gold."

The Mexican War had the effect of forcing northerners, in particular, to reconsider the foundations of their nation's success as well as its future direction. Again, the past played a role in northern assessments of the nation's future. Greek democracy and the early, virtuous Roman republic rather than the later Rome of the Caesars held a continued fascination for antebellum Americans, representing, as they did, the basis of so much American political theory. The Mexican War, however, brought the country uncomfortably closer to the Rome of the Caesars than it had ever expected to go. The *New York Tribune* did not allow its readers to ignore this fact. "The analogy between the character of the Roman

Republic and our own becomes more striking each day of our national existence," the paper warned, "[as] wars of conquest and colonization vex us now
as formerly them; we equally 'annex' whole countries and extend to the conquered population full citizenship, in servile imitation of Roman example."
The *Tribune* ended by reminding its readers that the "analogy may become still
more complete, and more fatal," since slavery had been the real source of the
Roman Empire's downfall.

For northerners opposed to the war, its outbreak represented the culmination of a series of events that offered proof positive that the South constituted a
tangible threat to American national success and stability and, indeed, to American national character. Under slavery, one northern minister argued, "pride is
engendered, indolence is encouraged, and profligacy, intemperance, licentiousness, cruelty, revenge, murder, assassination, and all manner of evils are very
prevalent." In editorials that covered the history of the previous decade and beyond, the northern press emphasized that the South had dominated, was dominating, and would doubtless continue to dominate the affairs of the nation. The
New York Tribune was the most outspoken of all the northern papers but was not
alone in its sentiments. For years, the *Tribune* declared, "a spirit has been rampant
in our public affairs, styling itself 'the South,' and demanding that the whole nation should fall down and worship whatever graven images it chooses to set up."
Citing the tariff debates, internal improvements, the use of public funds, the Gag
Rule, and the annexation of Texas as evidence, the paper concluded, "in short,
'the South' must be allowed to do everything they please, and make the North
do likewise." A few months later, the paper asked, "how can any man who pre-
tends to be a Republican ... look on these proceedings without apprehension
and abhorrence... . Who does not see that they are undermining all the settled
and salutary standards of popular judgement—exalting Might above Right—and
teaching our Youth to look to superior force rather than to Law as the guide of
their aspiring steps? Has the world ever known a Republic which extended its
boundaries by the subjugation of diverse and hostile races without undermining
thereby its own liberties?"

One of the most outspoken opponents of the war was William Jay, who
argued that in light of "the bitter sectional feelings already engendered by the
question respecting the extension of slavery over these regions ... and the perpetual struggle for mastery which must prevail between a powerful yeomanry,
depending on their own industry, and a landed aristocracy supported by some
millions of serfs, surely we have cause to apprehend much irritation, civil dissensions, and the ultimate disruption of the Union."... Jay's criticism of the
aristocracy of the South, the threat he saw in that section, the military spirit
that attended it, and the dangers this posed to American democracy were familiar themes for Americans in the 1840s. His criticism of the Mexican War, indeed, summed up the concerns of many in the North and went straight to the
heart of how northerners understood their national identity in this period.
Patriotism is not something that can only be created and defended in a positive

way. Indeed, it is more likely to be successfully defined against opposition, either to a military opponent or to those within the same culture holding alternative views.

By its actions with regard to Texas annexation and the resultant conflict, many northerners believed that the nation had betrayed, not confirmed, its revolutionary past. This did not mean that they felt less patriotic toward the nation, however. If anything, it intensified their belief in and support for the American republican experiment. Northerners would not have expressed concern over the fact that the Mexican War had, in their view, "dyed the garments of the Nation in blood" if they had not felt a strong sense of attachment to that nation. Unfortunately for American national stability, the fact that opposition to and support for the war were frequently couched in sectional terms meant that although many northerners came away from the conflict with a heightened sense of obligation to the nation, it was an obligation that expressed itself in opposition to the South, and so was no longer truly national. The nation's apparent deviation from its own founding principles prompted an upsurge of nationalist sentiment predicated on the belief that only one section—the North—continued to hold to these principles.

The Mexican War was clearly a turning point for the construction of northern nationalism. Although the debate over the rights and wrongs of the conflict did not produce any new images of the South, it provided a focus for many of the most negative ideas about the South and encouraged the development of a nationalist sentiment that was, in virtually all aspects, sectional. The full impact of the conflict, however, was not felt until the 1850s. The concept of the South as a threat to American values intensified, but did not alter, the negative imagery surrounding the slave states and prompted a reaffirmation of sectional sentiment that had always been one aspect of the northern mind. By the 1850s, however, this sectional sentiment had in many cases been translated into national concerns. The image of the South as backward had been acceptable to northerners for much of the early nineteenth century. Indeed, as a suitable foil that highlighted the comparative success of the North, the image of the blighted South often said more about the North's self-image than it did about the reality of the South. It was expected that slavery, the supposed cause of much of the South's backwardness, would die a natural death in time, at which point the South would come to resemble the North in both the ideological and the practical sense. Until that time came, however, many northerners would have concurred with John Hale, who in 1850 declared himself willing to compare the free laboring of the North "with the population of the South, leaving the slaves out of the comparison altogether, and taking the masters; and then see on which side of the scale the intellect, the intelligence, and all the virtues which adorn the human character will be found." Hale's audience would have had no doubt that the northern laborer would come out best in such a comparison. The North's superiority was something that many northerners took for granted by 1850, even if they purported to believe that it would not necessarily last.

Once northerners understood that the South was prepared not only to defend its peculiar institution but also to attempt to extend it into the West, they became concerned. As Theodore Parker put it, "the North is like New England … essentially so. The West is our own daughter." Southern influence could not be permitted to dominate the new territories. In this context, southern society came to be perceived as increasingly antithetical to northern concepts of freedom and democracy, and when that society seemed to be imposing its values on the North and potentially the West, the problem became a national one. Essentially, this type of view was indicative of northern concerns about the future of the nation. How could America sustain the ideal of Manifest Destiny and be the nation of the future if the South, and its system of slave labor, held the country back not just economically but ideologically as well? Slavery was fast becoming an anachronism in the nineteenth century, and northerners were all too aware of that fact. Seen from this angle, the South was perceived as a moral and physical blight on the nation. This hostile image of the South drew its impulse from the same background as the benevolent image of the plantation South. Proponents of this negative view—even if they expressed concern over the economic development and increasing social mobility of the northern states—welcomed what they viewed as progress and resented what they perceived as southern attempts to restrict the nation's future potential.

This view was an intrinsic element in the Republican political outlook. As far as the Republicans were concerned, the South represented "a society which seemed to violate all the cherished values of the free labor ideology, and seemed to pose a threat to the very survival of what Republicans called their 'free-labor' civilization." This free-labor ideology not only defined the Republican model of the good society but also provided a standard against which to measure other social systems. However, it was in the 1850s, when the political upheavals that attended the passage of the revised Fugitive Slave Law, the repeal of the Missouri Compromise in the Kansas-Nebraska Act of 1854, and the *Dred Scott* decision of 1857 seemed to validate northern fears of southern unity and premeditation in the political arena, that the idea of the slave power conspiracy gained momentum. It was in this highly charged political climate that the most extreme image of the southerner-as-threat was defined.

FURTHER READING

Glenn C. Altschuler and Stuart M. Blumin, *Rude Republic: Americans and Their Politics in the Nineteenth Century* (2000).

John M. Belohlavek, *"Let the Eagle Soar!": The Foreign Policy of Andrew Jackson* (1985).

Thomas R. Hietala, *Manifest Design: Anxious Aggrandizement in Late Jacksonian America* (1985).

Daniel Walker Howe, *What Hath God Wrought: The Transformation of America, 1815–1846* (2007).

Michael Todd Landis, *Northern Men with Southern Loyalties: The Democratic Party and the Sectional Crisis* (2014).

Jon Meacham, *American Lion: Andrew Jackson in the White House* (2009).

Robert V. Remini, *Henry Clay: Statesman for the Union* (1991).

Mary Ryan, *Civic Wars: Democracy and Public Life in the American City during the Nineteenth Century* (1998).

Harry L. Watson, *Liberty and Power: The Politics of Jacksonian America* (1990).

Sean Wilentz, *The Rise of American Democracy: Jefferson to Lincoln* (2006).

Additional critical thinking activities and content are available in MindTap.

MindTap is a fully online, highly personalized learning experience built upon Cengage Learning content. MindTap combines student learning tools—readings, multimedia, activities, and assessments—into a singular Learning Path that guides students through the course.

CHAPTER 10

Reform and Religion

In his essay "Man the Reformer," Ralph Waldo Emerson observed in 1841 that "in the history of the world the doctrine of Reform had never such scope as the present hour." Although this was perhaps an overstatement, Emerson's ideas nonetheless point to a series of reform movements aimed at the betterment of humankind. As never before in American history, movements focused on temperance, women's rights, prison reform, educational reform, compassion for mentally and physically handicapped people, and abolitionism coursed across the American landscape. Led by charismatic leaders such as William Lloyd Garrison, David Walker, Horace Mann, Dorothea Dix, and Lucretia Mott, these movements profoundly influenced American society. Not coincidentally, this also was an era in which new religious doctrines found adherents who formed new faiths—such as those that would become known as the Church of Jesus Christ of Latter-day Saints and the Seventh-Day Adventists—that remain influential to the present day. This clearly was the era of "the Reformer."

We can attempt to explain the growth of reform movements in the early nineteenth century by considering four interlocking factors. First, this was a period of great change. Americans not only puzzled over changes in society but also questioned how old patterns of social organization might be reestablished in new forms. Religious belief and social reform were often cited as forces that might either recapture the old order or point to ways in which a new order could be created. Second, the early nineteenth century saw the growth of intellectual movements that rejected the rationalism of an earlier age. Americans were now fascinated with the gothic, with the sense of mystery, with romanticism and sentimentality. These ideas, which permeated society, are important for the purposes of this chapter because sentimentality could encourage the development of empathy for others. If Americans could "feel" the human costs of alcohol abuse or of slavery, for example, they could empathize with the victims and work to eradicate such evils. Third, many Americans continued to be imbued with a belief in progress. They continued to see the United States as a place of destiny, a nation with a mission of greatness. If conditions could improve, it followed that people should play an active role in bringing that improvement about.

Related to notions of progress and perfectibility is the fourth and perhaps the most important underlying factor: religious change. Between roughly 1795 and 1837, many Americans were roused by religious revivals that changed their views of the possibilities of the world. Known as the Second Great Awakening, this religious movement fostered the

*growth of Christian belief, particularly among those in denominations, such as the Metho-
dists and the Baptists, that saw humans as having a greater role in their own salvation. If
individuals could be saved, it followed that if all were delivered, the result might be a perfect
society. If individuals could choose good over evil, they could eradicate sin from the world.
Underlying these reform movements, then, was "millennialism," the belief that a
thousand-year era of peace, harmony, and Christian brotherhood on Earth would precede
the Second Coming of Christ. Given Americans' tendency to see their nation as having a
role in momentous events, it was not surprising that they saw the millennium as being set
in the United States.*

QUESTIONS TO THINK ABOUT

In this era, some religious movements developed that underscored the possibility
that everyone in society could achieve perfection and salvation. This differed
from the belief in earlier eras that salvation was limited to a few people who
were saved by a gracious God. How might these changing views be linked to
reform movements? How did religious change focus upon the family? Did religion liberate or inhibit the lives and freedom of women? Were reformers concerned more about improving society or about controlling it? How might people
in reform movements, such as abolitionism, view the government? Was it a positive or negative force?

DOCUMENTS

These documents detail the relationships among religion, reform, the family,
slavery, and women's rights. In document 1, Methodist evangelist Peter Cartwright describes his conversion and the revivals that spread throughout the
West. Finding some religious innovations too radical and outlandish, the author
of document 2 details and denounces the "Kingdom of Matthias," a small religious community that was known for the misogynistic and anti-business tirades
of its leader, Robert Matthews. In document 3, a speech and letter to the
"Christian women of the South," Angelina Grimké uses religious arguments to
call upon white women to act politically and rise against slavery. Document 4, as
was the case with Frederick Douglass in Chapter 9, emphasizes the international
elements of reform. James McCune Smith, an educated African American, calls
on Americans to end slavery by following the example of the French and British,
who had recently done so. Dorothea Dix's letter to the Massachusetts legislature
in document 5 is a chilling depiction of the treatment endured by the mentally
ill in jails and almshouses. The same year as Dix's letter, 1843, was the publication of Joseph Smith's revelation regarding plural marriage for the Church of
Jesus Christ of Latter-day Saints. In document 6, Smith recounts what God revealed to him about marriage and family life. Document 7 is the Declaration of
Rights and Sentiments that was adopted by the Seneca Falls Convention in

1848. Although modeled on the Declaration of Independence, notice how widely it critiques male supremacy. Sojourner Truth, in document 8, a former member of the Kingdom of Matthias, provides a powerful expression of the relationships between women's rights and abolitionism.

1. Peter Cartwright, a Methodist Itinerant Preacher, Marvels at the Power of Religious Revivals, 1801

In 1801, when I was in my sixteenth year, my father, my eldest half brother, and myself, attended a wedding about five miles from home, where there was a great deal of drinking and dancing, which was very common at marriages in those days. I drank little or nothing; my delight was in dancing. After a late hour in the night, we mounted our horses and started for home. I was riding my race-horse.

A few minutes after we had put up the horses, and were sitting by the fire, I began to reflect on the manner in which I had spent the day and evening. I felt guilty and condemned. I rose and walked the floor. My mother was in bed. It seemed to me, all of a sudden, my blood rushed to my head, my heart palpitated, in a few minutes I turned blind; an awful impression rested on my mind that death had come and I was unprepared to die. I fell on my knees and began to ask God to have mercy on me.

My mother sprang from her bed, and was soon on her knees by my side, praying for me, and exhorting me to look to Christ for mercy, and then and there I promised the Lord that if he would spare me, I would seek and serve him; and I never fully broke that promise. My mother prayed for me a long time. At length we lay down, but there was little sleep for me. Next morning I rose, feeling wretched beyond expression. I tried to read in the Testament, and retired many times to secret prayer through the day, but found no relief. I gave up my race-horse to my father, and requested him to sell him. I went and brought my pack of cards, and gave them to mother, who threw them into the fire, and they were consumed. I fasted, watched, and prayed, and engaged in regular reading of the Testament. I was so distressed and miserable, that I was incapable of any regular business.

My father was greatly distressed on my account, thinking I must die, and he would lose his only son. He bade me retire altogether from business, and take care of myself....

There were no camp-meetings in regular form at this time, but as there was a great waking up among the Churches, from the revival that had broken out at Cane Ridge, before mentioned, many flocked to those sacramental meetings. The church would not hold the tenth part of the congregation. Accordingly, the officers of the Church erected a stand in a contiguous shady grove, and prepared seats for a large congregation.

Peter Cartwright, *Autobiography of Peter Cartwright, the Backwoods Preacher,* ed. W. P. Strickland (New York: Phillips and Hunt, 1856), 34–35, 37–38, 45, 48–49.

The people crowded to this meeting from far and near. They came in their large wagons, with victuals mostly prepared. The women slept in the wagons, and the men under them. Many stayed on the ground night and day for a number of nights and days together. Others were provided for among the neighbors around. The power of God was wonderfully displayed; scores of sinners fell under the preaching, like men slain in mighty battle; Christians shouted aloud for joy.

To this meeting I repaired, a guilty, wretched sinner. On the Saturday evening of said meeting, I went, with weeping multitudes, and bowed before the stand, and earnestly prayed for mercy. In the midst of a solemn struggle of soul, an impression was made on my mind, as though a voice said to me, "Thy sins are all forgiven thee." Divine light flashed all round me, unspeakable joy sprung up in my soul. I rose to my feet, opened my eyes, and it really seemed as if I was in heaven; the trees, the leaves on them, and everything seemed, and I really thought were, praising God. My mother raised the shout, my Christian friends crowded around me and joined me in praising God; and though I have been since then, in many instances, unfaithful, yet I have never, for one moment, doubted that the Lord did, then and there, forgive my sins and give me religion....

[A] new exercise broke out among us, called the *jerks,* which was overwhelming in its effects upon the bodies and minds of the people. No matter whether they were saints or sinners, they would be taken under a warm song or sermon, and seized with a convulsive jerking all over, which they could not by any possibility avoid, and the more they resisted the more they jerked. If they would not strive against it and pray in good earnest, the jerking would usually abate. I have seen more than five hundred persons jerking at one time in my large congregations. Most usually persons taken with the jerks, to obtain relief, as they said, would rise up and dance. Some would run, but could not get away. Some would resist; on such the jerks were generally very severe.

To see those proud young gentlemen and young ladies, dressed in their silks, jewelry, and prunella, from top to toe, take the *jerks* would often excite my risibilities. The first jerk or so, you would see their fine bonnets, caps, and combs fly; and so sudden would be the jerking of the head that their long loose hair would crack almost as loud as a wagoners whip.

2. A Journalist Describes a City Prophet and His Attacks on Women, 1835

ROBERT MATTHEWS—for that is the real name of the subject of this history—is a native of Washington county, in the State of New-York, and of Scotch extraction. He is about forty-five years of age, and of respectable parentage, though a mental eccentricity has characterized several members of the family. He was left

---

William L. Stone, *Matthias and His Impostures* (1835).

an orphan at a tender age, and was brought up in the family of a respectable farmer....

At the age of about twenty years, Matthews came to the city of New-York, and worked at the business of a carpenter and house-joiner,...

Not succeeding to his wishes, however, he removed to Albany in 1827 or '28, and resumed the joiner's business as a journeyman, taking good care of his family, and attending constantly upon the public services in the sanctuary.... He very soon appeared to take an increasing interest in religious matters; attended church and social prayer meetings, and conversed frequently upon the subject.... [A] young clergyman from New-York, the Rev. Mr. Kirk, was to occupy the pulpit on a certain evening. Matthews went to hear him, and on his return home appeared to be in a state of great excitement, declaring that he had never heard any thing like preaching before, and sat up the greater part of the night repeating, expounding, and commending passages from the sermon. His enthusiasm was so great that Mrs. Matthews remarked to her daughter in the course of the night, "If your father goes to hear this man preach any more, he will go wild or crazy." He did go again to hear him a number of times—was always exceedingly pleased, and became more and more excited....

At about the same time, Matthews engaged actively in the temperance reform, in which he laboured with all his might; but he was ultra in his notions,— contending that the use of meats should be excluded, as well as of strong drinks....

In his street-preaching, consisting for the most part of more incoherent harangues than are often uttered by men in any condition of mind,...

[In one sermon, he preached] "The spirit that built the Tower of Babel is now in the world—it is the spirit of the devil. The spirit of man never goes upon the clouds—all who think so are Babylonians. The only heaven is on the earth. All who are ignorant of truth, are Ninevites. The Jews did not crucify Christ,—it was the Gentiles. Every Jew has his guardian angel attending him in this world. God don't speak through preachers, he speaks through me, his prophet."...

"All *real* men will be saved; all *mock* men will be damned. When a person has the Holy Ghost, then he is a man, and not till then. They who teach women are of the wicked. The communion is all nonsense: so is prayer. Eating a nip of bread and drinking a little wine won't do any good. All who admit members into their church and suffer them to hold their lands and houses—their sentence is, 'Depart yo wicked, I know you not.' All females who lecture their husbands, their sentence is the same. The sons of truth are to enjoy all the good things of this world, and must use their means to bring it about. Every thing that has the smell of woman will be destroyed. Woman is the capsheaf of the abomination of desolation—full of all deviltry. In a short time the world will take fire and dissolve—it is combustible already. All women, not obedient, had better become so as soon as possible, and let the wicked spirit depart, and become temples of truth."...

3. Angelina Grimké Appeals to Christian Women to Oppose Slavery, 1836

Now the Bible is my ultimate appeal in all matters of faith and practice, and it is to *this test* I am anxious to bring the subject at issue between us....

I have thus, I think, clearly proved to you seven propositions, viz.: First, that slavery is contrary to the declaration of our independence. Second, that it is contrary to the first charter of human rights given to Adam, and renewed to Noah. Third, that the fact of slavery having been the subject of prophecy, furnishes *no* excuse whatever to slavedealers. Fourth, that no such system existed under the patriarchal dispensation. Fifth, that *slavery never* existed under the Jewish dispensation; but so far otherwise, that every servant was placed under the *protection of law,* and care taken not only to prevent all *involuntary* servitude, but all *voluntary perpetual* bondage. Sixth, that slavery in America reduces a man to a *thing,* a "chattel personal," *robs him* of all his rights as a *human being,* fetters both his mind and body, and protects the *master* in the most unnatural and unreasonable power, whilst it *throws him out* of the protection of law. Seventh, that slavery is contrary to the example and precepts of our holy and merciful Redeemer, and *of* his apostles.

But perhaps you will be ready to query, why appeal to *women* on this subject? We do not make the laws which perpetuate slavery. No legislative power is vested in us; *we* can do nothing to overthrow the system, even if we wished to do so. To this I reply, I know you do not make the laws, but I also know that you *are the wives and mothers, the sisters and daughters of those who do;* and if you really suppose you can do nothing to overthrow slavery, you are greatly mistaken. You can do much in every way: four things I will name. 1st. You can read on this subject. 2d. You can pray over this subject. 3d. You can speak on this subject. 4th. You can *act* on this subject....

3. Speak on this subject. It is through the tongue, the pen, and the press, that truth is principally propagated. Speak then to your relatives, your friends, your acquaintances on the subject of slavery; be not afraid if you are conscientiously convinced it is *sinful,* to say so openly, but calmly, and to let your sentiments be known....

4. Act on this subject. Some of you own slaves yourselves. If you believe slavery is sinful, set them at liberty, "undo the heavy burdens and let the oppressed go free." If they wish to remain with you, pay them wages, if not let them leave you. Should they remain teach them, and have them taught the common branches of an English education; they have minds and those minds ought to be improved. So precious a talent as intellect, never was given to be wrapt in a napkin and buried in the earth. It is the duty of all, as far as they can, to improve their own menial faculties, because we are commanded to love God with all our minds, as well as with all our hearts, and we commit a great sin, if we forbid or prevent that cultivation of the mind in others, which would

---

Angelina Grimké, "Appeal to Christian Women of the South" (1836).

enable them to perform this duty. Teach your servants then to read &c, and encourage them to believe it is their duty to learn, if it were only that they might read the Bible....

The *women of the South can overthrow* this horrible system of oppression and cruelty, licentiousness and wrong. Such appeals to your legislatures would be irresistible, for there is something in the heart of man which *will bend under moral suasion.* There is a swift witness for truth in his bosom, which *will respond to truth* when it is uttered with calmness and dignity. If you could obtain but six signatures to such a petition in only one state, I would say, send up that petition, and be not in the least discouraged by the scoffs, and jeers of the heartless, or the resolution of the house to lay it on the table....

4. James McCune Smith Applauds the British and French for Ending of Slavery, 1838

On motion of JAMES McCUNE SMITH, M.D., (a native of New York, but a graduate of the University of Glasgow, whither, on account of his *color,* he was obliged to resort for his education,) it was

Resolved, That we contemplate, with heartfelt satisfaction, the noble efforts that are making by the abolitionists in Great Britain and France, for the total cessation of slavery, and its concomitant the *slave trade,* and pledge to them our co-operation until, by the blessing of God, both these cruel customs shall wholly cease.

Dr. Smith said—

Mr. President, Ladies and Gentlemen:—I rise to offer a resolution expressive of our high satisfaction in the noble efforts of the abolitionists of Great Britain and France, who, although they are separated from us by the width of an ocean, and by distinct political institutions, are nevertheless united with us in sentiment and exertion in the sacred cause of immediate and universal emancipation: and, Sir, whether we look at their position amongst the nations of the earth, the principles by which they seem actuated, or the measures which, in this cause, they have adopted, we have abundant reason to rejoice, and cannot but be thankful to Him who hath raised up for us in our time of need such devoted and efficient coadjutors....

Mr. President, the resolution which I hold in my hand, states that we not only rejoice in the efforts of the trans-atlantic Abolitionists, but also pledge them our co-operation in the cause. Sir, in order to co-operate with them, we must not only acknowledge their principles, we must also adopt their practice. If we look at the British example, we find that in their pursuit of the universal, they omit no one of the particulars of which that universal is made up. Their abolitionism is thorough. It began at home. They first consecrated their own soil to liberty—so that "slaves cannot breathe" thereon. They next purified their colonies from the stain of slavery. Their principles now compel them, before they can call upon other sovereign people for immediate emancipation, first to practice immediate

James McCune Smith *Applauds the British and French for Ending of Slavery,* 1838. Fifth Annual Report of the Executive Committee of the American Anti-Slavery Society (New York: William R. Dorr, 1838), 25–30.

emancipation themselves by abolishing the apprenticeship. Mr. President, are there no apprentices around you? Are there not five hundred thousand apprentices to liberty not for one year or six years, but for a time not yet defined, scattered throughout this and other states in which abolitionism almost reigns? How then can we co-operate with Great Britain, how can we emulate her example, unless we abolish the last vestiges of slavery in our own states before we send our remonstrances to other sovereign states? Or, how can we call upon the South for immediate and entire emancipation, whilst we permit gradual emancipation in the North? It may be said, Sir, that this Society is pursuing the great general object of the emancipation of all the slaves, and that when this is obtained, the elevation of the colored people of the North will follow of course. Sir, it was a similar train of reasoning and of conduct that has entailed upon the American people the necessity of forming an American Anti-Slavery Society. Our ancestors—for they were mine as well as yours—fought for and obtained the precious boon of republican liberty—of equal rights—but they omitted to extend the same to those who had been slaves at the South, believing that the great object being obtained for all, liberty would as a matter of course be given to these unfortunate bondsmen. Sir, we now behold the consequences of that omission. Let us beware of following so disastrous a precedent, else we shall entail on the present generation, or those who may come after us, the necessity of a still more radical Anti-Slavery movement. Let us then, Sir, thoroughly do the work. Let us begin at home. Let us first purify our own soil and then may we call upon the South to follow the example. An eloquent gentleman who addressed you this morning observed, that if the whole moral and intellectual power of the North be brought to bear upon the South, it must accomplish the abolition of slavery. Sir, the North cannot collect nor concentrate its moral and intellectual power whilst there is slavery at the North—for semi-emancipation is slavery still—and it is my firm belief, a belief which springs from the deepest and strongest conviction, that that which will tell most, and do most towards the abolition of southern slavery, will be the sight of freed colored men, elevated in these northern white communities to the dignities and privileges of citizens of the republic....

5. Reformer Dorothea Dix Depicts the Horrible Conditions Endured by the Mentally Ill, 1843

Gentlemen,—I respectfully ask to present this Memorial, believing that the cause, which actuates to and sanctions so unusual a movement, presents no equivocal claim to public consideration and sympathy. Surrendering to calm and deep convictions of duty my habitual views of what is womanly and becoming. I proceed briefly to explain what has conducted me before you unsolicited and unsustained, trusting, while I do so, that the memorialist will be speedily forgotten in the memorial....

Dorothea Dix, petition of the Massachusetts Legislature (1843). Also found in *Our Nation's Archive*. Erik Bruun and Jay Crosby (New York: Black Dog and Leventhal Publishers, 1999), 266–268.

... I have seen many who, part of the year, are chained or caged. The use of cages all but universal.... [C]hains are less common; negligences frequent, wilful abuse less frequent than sufferings proceeding from ignorance, or want of consideration. I encountered during the last three months many poor creatures wandering reckless and unprotected through the country.... I have heard that responsible persons, controlling the almshouses, have not thought themselves culpable in sending away from their shelter, to cast upon the chances of remote relief, insane men and women. These, left on the highways, unfriended and incompetent to control or direct their own movements, sometimes have found refuge in the hospital, and others have not been traced. But I cannot particularize. In traversing the State, I have found hundreds of insane persons in every variety of circumstance and condition, many whose situation could not and need not be improved; a less number, but that very large, whose lives are the saddest pictures of human suffering and degradation....

DANVERS. November. Visited the almshouse. A large building, much out of repair....

Long before reaching the house, wild shouts, snatches of rude songs, imprecations and obscene language, fell upon the ear, proceeding from the occupant of a low building, rather remote from the principal building to which my course was directed. Found the mistress, and was conducted to the place which was called "the home" of the forlorn maniac, a young woman, exhibiting a condition of neglect and misery blotting out the faintest idea of comfort, and outraging every sentiment of decency. She had been, I learnt, a respectable person, industrious and worthy. Disappointments and trials shook her mind, and, finally, laid prostrate reason and self-control.... She had passed from one degree of violence to another, in swift progress. There she stood, clinging to or beating upon the bars of her caged apartment, the contracted size of which afforded space only for increasing accumulations of filth, a loud spectacle. There she stood with naked arms and dishevelled hair, the unwashed frame invested with fragments of unclean garments, the air so extremely offensive, though ventilation was afforded on all sides save one, that it was not possible to remain beyond a few moments without retreating for recovery to the outward air. Irritation of body, produced by utter filth and exposure, incited her to the horrid process of tearing off her skin by inches. Her face, neck, and person were thus disfigured to hideousness. She held up a fragment just rent off. To my exclamation of horror, the mistress replied: "Oh, we can't help it. Half the skin is off sometimes. We can do nothing with her; and it makes no difference what she eats, for she consumes her own filth as readily as the food which is brought her."...

Men of Massachusetts, I beg, I implore, I demand pity and protection for these of my suffering, outraged sex. Fathers, husbands, brothers, I would supplicate you for this boon; but what do I say.... Here you will put away the cold, calculating spirit of selfishness and self-seeking; lay off the armor of local strife and political opposition; here and now, for once, forgetful of the earthly and perishable, come up to these halls and consecrate them with one heart and one mind to works of righteousness and just judgment. Become the benefactors of your race, the just guardians of the solemn rights you hold in trust....

6. Joseph Smith Records a Revelation
on Plural Marriage, 1843

1. Verify, thus saith the Lord unto you my servant Joseph, that inasmuch as you have inquired of my hand to know and understand wherein I, the Lord, justified my servants Abraham, Isaac, and Jacob, as also Moses, David and Solomon, my servants, as touching the *principle and doctrine of their having many wives* and concubines—…

4. For behold, I reveal unto you a new and an everlasting covenant; and if ye abide not that covenant, then are ye damned; for no one can reject this covenant and be permitted to enter into my glory.…

37. Abraham received concubines, and they bore him children; and it was accounted unto him for righteousness,…

38. David also received many wives and concubines, and also Solomon and Moses my servants, as also many others of my servants, from the beginning of creation until this time; and in nothing did they sin save in those things which they received not of me.…

61. And again, as pertaining to the law of the priesthood—if any man espouse a virgin, and desire to espouse another, and the first give her consent, and if he espouse the second, and they are virgins, and have vowed to no other man, then is he justified; he cannot commit adultery for they are given unto him; for he cannot commit adultery with that that belongeth unto him and to no one else.

62. And if he have ten virgins given unto him by this law, he cannot commit adultery, for they belong to him, and they are given unto him; therefore is he justified.

63. But if one or either of the ten virgins, after she is espoused, shall be with another man, she has committed adultery, and shall be destroyed; for they are given unto him to multiply and replenish the earth, according to my commandment, and to fulfil the promise which was given by my Father before the foundation of the world, and for their exaltation in the eternal worlds, that they may bear the souls of men; for herein is the work of my Father continued, that he may be glorified.

7. The Seneca Falls Convention
Declares Women's Rights, 1848

When in the course of human events it becomes necessary for one portion of the family of man to assume among the people of the earth a position different from that which the laws of nature and of nature's God entitle them, a decent respect to the opinions of mankind requires that they should declare the causes that impel them to such a course.

We hold these truths to be self-evident; that all men and women are created equal; that they are endowed by their Creator with certain inalienable

R. Marie Griffith, ed., *American Religions: A Documentary History* (2008), 165–172.

Lydia Sigourney, "Home" (1850).

rights; that among these are life, liberty, and the pursuit of happiness; that to secure these rights governments are instituted, deriving their just powers from the consent of the governed. Whenever any form of government becomes destructive of these ends, it is the right of those who suffer from it to refuse allegiance to it, and to insist upon the institution of a new government, laying its foundation on such principles, and organizing its powers in such form as to them shall seem most likely to effect their safety and happiness. Prudence, indeed, will dictate that governments long established should not be changed for light and transient causes; and accordingly, all experience hath shown that mankind are more disposed to suffer, while evils are sufferable, than to right themselves by abolishing the forms to which they are accustomed. But when a long train of abuses and usurpation, pursuing invariably the same object, evinces a design to reduce them under absolute despotism, it is their duty to throw off such government, and to provide new guards for their future security. Such has been the patient sufferance of the women under this government, and such is now the necessity which constrains them to demand the equal station to which they are entitled.

The history of mankind is a history of repeated injuries and usurpation on the part of man toward woman, having in direct object the establishment of an absolute tyranny over her. To prove this, let facts be submitted to a candid world.

He has never permitted her to exercise her inalienable right to the elective franchise.

He has compelled her to submit to laws, in the formation of which she has no voice.

He has withheld from her rights which are given to the most ignorant and degraded men—both natives and foreigners.

Having deprived her of this first right of a citizen, the elective franchise, thereby leaving her without representation in the halls of legislation, he has oppressed her on all sides.

He has made her, if married, in the eye of the law, civilly dead.

He has taken from her all right in property, even to the wages she earns.

He has made her, morally, an irresponsible being, as she can commit many crimes with impunity, provided they be done in the presence of her husband. In the covenant of marriage, she is compelled to promise obedience to her husband, he becoming, to all intents and purposes, her master—the law giving him power to deprive her of liberty, and to administer chastisements.

He has so framed the laws of divorce, as to what shall be the proper causes of divorce; in case of separation, to whom the guardianship of the children shall be given; as to be wholly regardless of the happiness of women—the law, in all cases, going upon the false supposition of the supremacy of man, and giving all powers into his hands.

After depriving her of all rights as a married woman, if single and the owner of property, he has taxed her to support a government which recognizes her only when her property can be made profitable to it.

He has monopolized nearly all the profitable employments, and from those she is permitted to follow, she receives but a scanty remuneration.

He closes against her all the avenues to wealth and distinction, which he considers most honorable to himself. As a teacher of theology, medicine, or law, she is not known.

He has denied her the facilities for obtaining a thorough education, all colleges being closed against her.

He allows her in Church, as well as State, but a subordinate position, claiming Apostolic authority for her exclusion from the ministry, and, with some exceptions, from any public participation in the affairs of the Church.

He has created a false public sentiment, by giving to the world a different code of morals for men and women, by which moral delinquencies which exclude women from society, are not only tolerated but deemed of little account in man.

He has usurped the prerogative of Jehovah himself, claiming it as his right to assign for her a sphere of action, when that belongs to her conscience and her God.

He has endeavored, in every way that he could to destroy her confidence in her own powers, to lessen her self-respect, and to make her willing to lead a dependent and abject life.

Now, in view of this entire disfranchisement of one-half the people of this country, their social and religious degradation—in view of the unjust laws above mentioned, and because women do feel themselves aggrieved, oppressed, and fraudulently deprived of their most sacred rights, we insist that they have immediate admission to all the rights and privileges which belong to them as citizens of these United States.

In entering upon the great work before us, we anticipate no small amount of misconception, misrepresentation, and ridicule; but we shall use every instrumentality within our power to effect our object. We shall employ agents, circulate tracts, petition the State and national Legislatures, and endeavor to enlist the pulpit and the press in our behalf. We hope this Convention will be followed by a series of Conventions embracing every part of the country.

8. Former Slave Sojourner Truth Links Women's Rights to Antislavery, 1851

Well, children, where there is so much racket there must be something out of kilter. I think that 'twixt the negroes of the South and the women at the North, all talking about rights, the white men will be in a fix pretty soon. But what's all this here talking about?

That man over there says that women need to be helped into carriages, and lifted over ditches, and to have the best place everywhere. Nobody ever helps me into carriages, or over mud-puddles, or gives me any best place! And ain't I a woman? Look at me! Look at my arm! I have ploughed and planted, and gathered into barns, and no man could head me! And ain't I a woman? I could work as much and eat as much as a man—when I could get it—and bear the lash as well! And ain't I a woman? I have borne thirteen children, and seen them

---

Sojourner Truth in a speech given at a women's convention in Akron, Ohio (1851).

most all sold off to slavery, and when I cried out with my mother's grief, none but Jesus heard me! And ain't I a woman?

Then they talk about this thing in the head; what's this they call it? [Intellect, someone whispers.] That's it, honey. What's that got to do with women's rights or negro's rights? If my cup won't hold but a pint, and yours holds a quart, wouldn't you be mean not to let me have my little half-measure full?

Then that little man in black there, he says women can't have as much rights as men, 'cause Christ wasn't a woman! Where did your Christ come from? Where did your Christ come from? From God and a woman! Man had nothing to do with Him.

If the first woman God ever made was strong enough to turn the world upside down all alone, these women together ought to be able to turn it back, and get it right side up again! And now they is asking to do it, the men better let them.

Obliged to you for hearing me, and now old Sojourner ain't got nothing more to say.

 # ESSAYS

Religious revivalism and reform organizations changed individuals and society. These essays ask you to consider which changed more and what the limits of change were. Nell Irvin Painter writes about the life and times of Sojourner Truth, a former slave from New York. Painter shows the power of religion in Truth's life as she moves from enslavement, through the Kingdom of Matthias, and ultimately to become an outspoken critic of slavery and a powerful proponent of women's rights. Religion in her life and relationships at times inhibited her and at other times liberated her. According to Painter, it was Truth's religious beliefs that carried her through each struggle and brought her to a life of amazing reform. W. Caleb McDaniel's essay showcases the limits of reform. By looking at the case of John L. Brown, a white man in South Carolina who was tried for allegedly helping an enslaved woman escape in the early 1840s, McDaniel exposes how certain individuals and events became international stories and others did not. Situating the event in terms of transatlantic reform, McDaniel emphasizes that even local and personal events could become almost global.

Religion as Inhibiting and Liberating: The Complicated Case of Sojourner Truth

NELL IRVIN PAINTER

SOJOURNER TRUTH, born Isabella, is one of the two most famous African-American women of the nineteenth century. The other, Harriet Tubman, the

"Moses" of her people, also came out of slavery. Many people confuse the two because both lived in an era shadowed by human bondage, but Truth and Tubman were contrasting figures. New York was Truth's Egypt: Tubman's was in Maryland, these respective places marking each woman with a regional identity that Truth, at least, later came very much to prize. Born in about 1797, Truth was a generation older than Tubman, born in about 1821....

A woman of remarkable intelligence despite her illiteracy, Truth had great presence. She was tall, some 5 feet 11 inches, of spare but solid frame. Her voice was low, so low that listeners sometimes termed it masculine, and her singing voice was beautifully powerful. Whenever she spoke in public, she also sang. No one ever forgot the power and pathos of Sojourner Truth's singing, just as her wit and originality of phrasing were also of lasting remembrance.

As an abolitionist and feminist, she put her body and her mind to a unique task, that of physically representing women who had been enslaved. At a time when most Americans thought of slaves as male and women as white, Truth embodied a fact that still bears repeating: Among the blacks are women; among the women, there are blacks....

Only Truth had the ability to go on speaking, year after year for thirty years, to make herself into a force in several American reform movements. Even though the aims of her missions became increasingly secular after midcentury, Truth was first and last an itinerant preacher, stressing both itinerancy and preaching. From the late 1840s through the late 1870s, she traveled the American land, denouncing slavery and slavers, advocating freedom, women's rights, woman suffrage, and temperance.

Pentecostal that she was, Truth would have explained that the force that brought her from the soul murder of slavery into the authority of public advocacy was the power of the Holy Spirit. Her ability to call upon a supernatural power gave her a resource claimed by millions of black women and by disempowered people the world over. Without doubt, it was Truth's religious faith that transformed her from Isabella, a domestic servant, into Sojourner Truth, a hero for three centuries—at least....

ISABELLA freed herself in several steps and in three dimensions: She left slavery with the Dumonts when *she* thought the time was right; she freed herself from fear through a discovery of Jesus, love; and, empowered by her new religious faith, she broke out of the passivity of slavery by using the law toward her own ends. In so complicated a process, no one date captures her passage out of bondage. Citing the moment in July 1827 when she became legally free may conveniently date her liberation, but focusing mainly on the aspects of slavery that affected owners—the legal and the economic—obscures much of emancipation's larger significance.

There is no denying that legal and economic status counted enormously in circumscribing slaves' chances in life; but the injuries of slavery went much deeper, into the bodies and into the psyches of the people who were its victims. In their experience, slavery meant a good deal more than lack of standing before the law and endless, unpaid labor, just as there would be a good deal more to freedom than being able to make a contract or earn a shilling.

In the North, the process of emancipation was made personal by the very gradualness of the laws of most states. Slaves surely preferred to be free sooner rather than later, but their desires were hardly uppermost in the minds of state legislators. Rather, northern abolition moved incrementally, seeing to it that owners were not deprived abruptly of their accustomed labor.

In New York, discussion of abolition began in earnest in the 1780s, and in 1799 the state began the process of gradual emancipation. Slavery would end on the Fourth of July 1827. For those born before 1799, emancipation would be unconditional; but those born after 1799 might have to serve a further period of indentured servitude: until they were twenty-eight, if male, or twenty-five, if female.

This legislation would have kept Isabella and Thomas slaves until 1827. Their children owed indentured servitude for much longer: Diana until about 1840, Peter until about 1849, Elizabeth until about 1850, and Sophia until about 1851. Requirements of law and work kept the family scattered. Indentured, the children could not follow Isabella into freedom, and as a live-in domestic servant, she lacked the home she had dreamed of as she mended by firelight with her children. When Sojourner Truth became an abolitionist, some of her children were still not free....

In 1826, Isabella heard the voice of her God instructing her when to set out on her own as a free woman. Just before dawn in the late fall, she left the Dumonts' carrying only her baby, Sophia, and a supply of food and clothing so meager that it fit in a cotton handkerchief. She intended only a short journey, so as to save John Dumont trouble when he came looking for her, which she knew he was bound to do, for she was depriving him of two servants—herself and her baby—whom, according to law, he still owned. About five miles away, she called upon an old friend, Levi Rowe, who welcomed her from his deathbed and directed her to Isaac and Maria Van Wagenen of Wagondale, whom she had also known for years. Like the Dumonts, the Van Wagenens were prominent members of the Klyn Esopus Dutch Reformed Church. Unlike the Dumonts, the Van Wagenens opposed slavery. When John Dumont came to fetch Isabella, the Van Wagenens paid him $25: $20 for Isabella for a year, $5 for baby Sophia. Taking the Van Wagenens' last name (often rendered "Van Wagner" outside Ulster County), she lived a "quiet, peaceful life" with "excellent people" there for about a year....

IN MAY 1832, Isabella and the widower Elijah Pierson received a visit from a resplendently dressed figure: Robert Matthews, a Scots-American calling himself "the Prophet Matthias," whose singular manifestations of perfectionism had already created consternation upstate. Sylvester Mills, Pierson's fellow perfectionist Pearl Street merchant, vouched for him. This attractive forty-four-year-old stranger combed his hair and beard to make himself look like the chromo pictures of Jesus. When Isabella met him at the door, she knew immediately from Matthew, Chapter 16, to ask. "Art thou the Christ?" When the visitor answered, "I am," she kissed his feet and burst into tears of joy. Pierson's welcome was equally ecstatic. In the parlor, Isabella, Pierson, and Matthias exchanged their experiences of visions and voices and agreed on everything.

For a while Pierson and Matthias alternated preaching in meeting at Pierson's house, but Pierson—whom Matthias now called John the Baptist—gave up preaching after Matthias said, and his followers believed, that "God don't speak through preachers; he speaks through me, his prophet."...

Supposedly everyone belonged to the community on a footing of equality and held everything in common (as in early Christianity), and everyone worked according to physical ability. Nonetheless, a hierarchy that was very reminiscent of the world of the "Gentiles" prevailed. Matthias, called "Father," gave all the orders and sat at the head of the table. He decided when to go to work and when to practice the rituals of the kingdom, such as the communal bathing that he called baptism. No matter when he preached to his followers or how angrily and how long, they were bound to listen. Isabella no longer preached, for Matthias set preaching out of bounds for women.

Matthias had long inflicted corporal punishment on those he controlled. As Robert Matthews he had beaten his wife and children, and as the Prophet Matthias he beat Isabella for the infraction he considered abominable in women: insubordination. On an occasion when she was not feeling well—already the apparent proof that she was possessed by a "sick devil"—she had intervened when Matthias was punishing one of his young sons. Matthias lashed her with his cowhide whip, shouting, "Shall a sick devil undertake to dictate to me?" While in the kingdom he also beat his eighteen-year-old daughter so severely that she bore marks from his whip six weeks later.

Matthias's instincts were patriarchal, literally and figuratively. He did not call the kingdom "the family," but he did insist on being called "Father," and, once he had taken Ann Folger as his "match spirit" (that is, his new wife), he called her "Mother." As Mother she was still a child, for he treated everyone in the household as children, lecturing them for hours, frequently in shrill, harsh anger. Ann Folger described Matthias's power: "We consider[ed] him as God the Father possessing the Holy Ghost, and the power of bestowing it on others; the power also of executing wrath on whom he would. We regarded him as the last trumpet, answering to all the angels of wrath spoken of in the Revelation; that is the executing angels." As the last trumpet, Matthias would bend down, fill his lungs, and shout in a voice loud enough to deafen his hearers temporarily. Ann Folger admitted that "we indeed thought he did cast evil spirits out of us. We were to obey all his commands, and we showed our obedience to him.... He had the command of all things in the house."...

Though not paid as a servant would be, Isabella was still a black woman with the diminished social stature that came from having been a slave. When the formerly wealthy were about to discuss delicate or weighty matters, it was their habit to send Isabella to do work that would take her out of the room—a practice she disregarded when the kingdom was dissolving and she felt that she must have a say in crucial decisions. Even more important, in a household that included Ann Folger as a pampered lady, was Isabella's ability to work. She was a strong woman who knew how to cook, clean, and launder....

In the fall of 1844, Truth gave her first antislavery speech in Northampton. In May 1845, she spoke to the annual meeting of the American Anti-Slavery

Society in New York City, identified in the *National Anti-Slavery Standard* only as "a colored woman who had been a slave, but more recently resident of Northampton, Mass." Truth's remarks, according to the *Standard,* were full of "good sense and strong feeling."

I cannot track completely Truth's antislavery and women's rights appearances, for reporters did not invariably consider her worth identifying by name, or even mentioning at all. She doubtless attended and addressed many meetings without notice between 1845 and 1850. I do know for certain that she attended and addressed a large women's rights meeting in Worcester, Massachusetts, in 1850—the first such meeting of national scope in the United States. This Worcester meeting was an immediate successor of the pioneering Seneca Falls, New York, women's convention of 1848 organized by Elizabeth Cady Stanton, Lucretia Mott, and others—including the Rochester abolitionist Amy Post, who would play so large a role in Truth's later life.

Women had been publicly vindicating their rights as women, as workers, and as blacks in the United States since the Scotswoman Frances Wright lectured in New York City in the late 1820s and the African American Maria Stewart spoke in Boston in the early 1830s. But women as speakers before mixed, or "promiscuous" audiences of women and men were rare, even when the subject was evangelical and the tradition—as in the case of women itinerant preachers—centuries older. Women lecturers like Angelina Grimké and Abby Kelley caused a sensation when they joined the anti-slavery circuit in the 1830s, since critics opposed women's right to advocate anything in public.

By 1840, the issue of women as leaders in abolitionism had split the American movement, with Garrisonians like Frederick Douglass and Abby Kelly defending women's rights, and less radical men, especially Arthur and Lewis Tappan, leaving the American Anti-slavery Society on this and other grounds. The Tappans' unwillingness to mix antislavery with other reforms, such as women's rights, is probably the main reason they do not appear in the *Narrative of Sojourner Truth.* The rival society set up by the Tappans and their supporters withered, while the Garrisonian American Anti-Slavery Society flourished. After 1840, in the fashion of excommunicators, the Garrisonians pretended that the Tappans did not exist, despite their crucial early role in abolitionism.

Garrison firmly supported the 1850 women's rights meeting in Worcester and may have suggested that Douglass and Truth speak. According to a newspaper report, Truth "uttered some truths that told well," although her skin was dark and her outward appearance "uncomely." Truth spoke primarily as a preacher: "She said Woman set the world wrong by eating the forbidden fruit, and now she was going to set it right. She said Goodness never had any beginning; it was from everlasting, and could never die. But Evil had a beginning, and must have an end. She expressed great reverence for God, and faith that he will bring about his own purposes and plans."

In her concluding remarks, Lucretia Mott, a leader of the convention, mentioned Truth by name as "the poor woman who had grown up under the curse of Slavery," and repeated Truth's formulation of the finite nature of evil and the everlasting quality of good. Truth's other early reported anti-slavery speech in 1850, at the annual meeting of the Rhode Island Anti-Slavery Society in Providence, in November, was also vague on antislavery politics. While the men, Frederick Douglass, Charles C. Burleigh, and Charles Lenox Remond, damned the Fugitive Slave Act for hours and demanded Garrison's version of disunion—"No union with slaveholders!"—Truth was reported as brief and hesitant: "she had been a slave, and was not now entirely free. She did not know anything about politics—could not read the newspaper—but thanked God that the law was made—that the worst had come to worst; but the best must come to best."

TRUTH'S first tour on the antislavery and women's rights circuit in the winter of 1851 came at Garrison's behest. He invited her to accompany him and his dear friend, the radical British Member of Parliament George Thompson, on a trip into western New York....

The Fourth of July 1854 found Truth back before white audiences, speaking at an Independence Day celebration in Framingham, Massachusetts. She spoke after a white abolitionist from Virginia described his ordeal in jail. This experience, he said, helped him appreciate the sufferings of blacks. Truth agreed. "White folks should sometimes feel the prick," she said, eliciting "laughter and cheers." Despite such merriment, her message, as recorded by the secretary of the meeting (her printer, George Brown Yerrinton), was severe and anguished:

> God would yet execute his judgments upon the white people for their oppression and cruelty. She had often asked white people why God should have more mercy on Anglo-Saxons than on Africans, but they had never given her any answer; the reason was, they [white people] hadn't got it to give. (Laughter.) Why did the white people hate the blacks? Were they [white people] not as good as they were brought up? They [black people] were a great deal better than the white people had brought them up. (Cheers.) The white people owed the colored race a big debt, and if they paid it all back, they wouldn't have anything left for seed. (Laughter.) All they could do was to repent, and have the debt forgiven them.

Abolitionists were fond of implicating orthodox Christianity in the moral economy of slavery. The regular ministry and conventional churches tolerated slavers and slavery, they said, and Truth picked up this theme. The proceeds of the sale of slave children, she says, paid for the training of ministers of the gospel....

According to [Harriet Beecher] Stowe ... Frederick Douglass once spoke emphatically at a meeting in Boston's Faneuil Hall of his lost faith that black Americans would ever gain justice from white Americans. Douglass had concluded that blacks must seize their freedom by force of arms: "It must come to blood; they must fight for themselves, and redeem themselves, or it would never be done."

Truth, sitting in the front row—so Stowe says—rejected Douglass's desperate logic:

> in the hush of deep feeling, after Douglas[s] sat down, she spoke out in her deep, peculiar voice, heard all over the house.—
> "Frederick, *is God dead?*"

Then Stowe adds a paragraph whose imagery would reappear time and again as generation after generation sought to capture Truth's essence in words:

> The effect was perfectly electrical, and thrilled through the whole house, changing as by a flash the whole feeling of the audience. Not another word she said or needed to say: it was enough....

"Frederick, *is God dead?*" made Truth an electrifying presence and a symbol of Christian faith and forbearance, a talisman of non-violent faith in God's ability to right the most heinous of wrongs. When Douglass had come to doubt, Stowe's Truth still believed in the power of God and the goodness of white people. To reinforce Truth's attachment to whites, Stowe quotes her revelation when she became a Christian: "'Dar's de white folks, that have abused you an' beat you an' abused your people.'" Jesus allows Truth to forgive them: " 'Lord, Lord, I can love *even de white folks!* "

Thanks to Stowe and the *Atlantic Monthly*, "Frederick, *is God dead?*" became the dominant symbol for Truth. For three-quarters of a century, the image of Stowe's faithful Christian delighted thousands of Americans, while the exasperated, vengeful Truth of the Book of Esther, the blood of Abel, and the taunting question, do you "wish to suck?" remained more obscure. "Sojourner Truth, the Libyan Sibyl" spread the gentleness of spiritualism over Truth's own millennial conviction that there surely would come a day of racial judgment....

Slavery, Sex, and Transatlantic Abolitionism

CALEB McDANIEL

Antebellum American abolitionists traveled overseas frequently and built complex transatlantic networks with British abolitionists. Their motive was simple: they believed that publicizing facts about American slavery abroad was the best way to pressure slaveholders at home. Frederick Douglass, for example, contended that his power as an activist increased with his distance from the United States, much like the force of a lever.

The mechanical metaphor would have appealed to other abolitionists as well. Nineteenth-century abolitionists often viewed their international networks like a Rube Goldberg machine in which a sequence of gears, levers, and bells were set in motion by a single marble released at the top: first, white southerners would commit some barbarity; next, abolitionists would bring it to light and inform their

Excerpt from Caleb McDaniel, "The Case of John L. Brown: Sex, Slavery, and the Trials of a Transatlantic Abolitionist Campaign," *American Nineteenth-Century History* 14, no. 2 (June 2013), 141–159. Reprinted by permission of the publisher (Taylor & Francis Ltd, http://www.tandfonline.com).

overseas allies; then, activists on both sides of the ocean would mobilize in protest; and finally, when the facts were sufficiently publicized, embarrassed southerners would relent. Pull, roll, whir, ding, and the domino would fall. Or, as Douglass put it while in England in 1846, "Expose slavery, and it dies."

Yet exposure did not kill slavery outright. Exposed slaveholders fought back, often by seizing opportunities created by the abolitionists' own methods of attack. Abolitionist publicity about the facts of slavery did pressure slaveholders by bringing specific charges before northern and international audiences. But by tying outrage to *particular* events and stories, abolitionist rhetoric also made it possible for slaveholders to contest specific facts and, in so doing, to suggest that the abolitionists' argument failed even on its own terms. Abolitionists imagined their fact-finding strategies as a one-directional force that would lead inexorably to slavery's demise, yet those strategies also enabled publicity-savvy opponents to throw wrenches into what one historian calls the abolitionists' "well-oiled... propaganda machine."

An early example of this dynamic process of exposure and reaction occurred in 1838, when an Alabama newspaper editor challenged the authenticity of the story of James Williams, author of the first fugitive slave narrative ever published by the American Anti-Slavery Society. Unable to disprove the editor's charges, abolitionists decided to withdraw Williams's narrative from circulation. Abolitionists more successfully rebutted later challenges to the facticity of *Uncle Tom's Cabin* by Harriet Beecher Stowe, who produced a *Key to Uncle Tom's Cabin* containing "Facts and Documents ... Together with Corroborative Statements Verifying the Truth of the Work." Yet, the challenges to both Williams's narrative and Stowe's novel underline that abolitionist exposures of slavery were themselves "vulnerable to exposure," as Ann Fabian notes.

This article argues that transatlantic activism created additional and special vulnerabilities for abolitionists. Unique challenges arose first from the still-considerable lag time between the reportage of news in the United States and its reception in Great Britain, which potentially allowed rumors or erroneous information to spread widely before they could be corrected or refuted. By the 1840s, ocean steamships were capable of crossing the Atlantic in two weeks, but as many as four weeks could pass between the publication of news by American abolitionists and the receipt of reactions from their British counterparts. Separating signal from noise—reconciling discrepant reports, clarifying rumors, and correcting errors—would be difficult enough in the age of the telegraph or Twitter. It was even harder in an age of sail and steam.

In addition to overcoming difficulties in transmission, abolitionists also confronted several challenges of cultural translation: it was not always easy to publicize antislavery arguments in ways that did not offend the sensibilities of transatlantic audiences. That problem was heightened by the fact that abolitionists themselves could not always agree on how stories about slavery should be told. A case in point was the ambivalence that many Anglo-American abolitionists felt about the propriety of publicizing the most sensitive information about slavery, particularly when it concerned interracial sex or a confusion of accepted gender roles. On the one hand, abolitionists' broadly evangelical worldview enabled powerful critiques of slavery and facilitated their cooperation across national and cultural lines. Christian ideas about the evils of passion and sexual licentiousness, for example, contributed to the international outrage over reports of "slave-breeders" or fictional characters like Stowe's abusive Simon Legree. Yet, the evangelical sensibilities of Anglo-American abolitionists also closed off some directions that the transatlantic movement might otherwise have taken.

In other words, abolitionists' own ideas about gender and public propriety both constrained as well as enabled transatlantic abolitionism. Few proofs of this are better known than the exclusion of American women from the 1840 "World's Convention" hosted by British abolitionists, whose political culture and religious views created more limited public roles for female reformers, thereby creating conflict with transatlantic allies. But Frederick Douglass also encountered the limits of British ideas about appropriate publicity in 1845 when one English patron—a Unitarian who actually supported women's inclusion at the "World's Convention"—objected to some of the "unnecessary and disgusting" passages in Douglass's autobiographical narrative. John B. Estlin warned Douglass especially about those passages alluding to sex on southern plantations and encouraged their excision. Estlin and many abolitionists on both sides of the Atlantic were still uncomfortable with public narratives of sexual license and violence and preferred to shroud accounts of illicit sex in euphemism or fiction.

Both of these episodes reveal how and why the very same religious, gendered, and racialized ideas about sex that powered abolitionists' appeals also complicated efforts at transatlantic cooperation and led to some unintended consequences. But less obvious—though equally important—were the potential vulnerabilities these ideas exposed to abolitionists' opponents. If and when slaveholders could exploit abolitionists' own ambivalence about interracial sex, gender roles, or the dangers of overexposing salacious details, they could disrupt the chain of events that abolitionists hoped would lead from the exposure of slavery to emancipation. To understand fully the nature of transatlantic abolitionism before the Civil War thus requires paying attention not only to those cases in which the abolitionists' propaganda machine functioned smoothly, but also to times like these when the machine broke down.

The understudied case of John L. Brown, a southern man who was accused of helping an enslaved woman to escape, illustrates with particular clarity both the challenges of communication and the vulnerabilities to exposure that transatlantic abolitionism often entailed. The case began in November 1843 when Brown was tried and convicted under a South Carolina state law that sentenced to death anyone who aided an escaping slave. Brown appealed his case in December but lost, and newspaper reports of the sentencing appeared the next month in New York City and Philadelphia. Abolitionists, who hoped to turn Brown's impending execution into an engine of international outrage over the horrors of southern slavery, quickly amplified these reports, ensuring that they were heard overseas as well.

In this particular case, the abolitionists' publicity campaign focused on an offensive speech addressed to Brown by his sentencing judge, John Bolton

O'Neall, after the failure of his appeal. Newspaper reports showed that O'Neall—a prominent jurist in South Carolina—had melodramatically addressed Brown as "the vilest sinner" before condemning him to death with words that soon echoed across the Atlantic. For his role in helping a slave to run away, O'Neall told Brown, "you are to die! Die a shameful ignominious death, the death upon the gallows." The Cincinnati *Weekly Herald* reprinted this speech from an unnamed New Orleans newspaper on 14 February under the headline "Judicial Murder!" And only two weeks later, leading Boston abolitionist William Lloyd Garrison reprinted that Cincinnati report in the *Liberator,* bringing the case to the attention of New England abolitionists for the first time.

O'Neall's sentencing of John L. Brown came at a pivotal juncture in the history of both American and transatlantic abolitionism. First, as historian Stanley Harrold has shown, the year 1843 marked the rise of an increasingly "aggressive abolitionism," as leaders across the movement began calling for direct action against southern slaveholders and started to issue addresses to southern slaves. For some, John L. Brown's sentencing only underlined the Slave Power's depravity and the need to attack it with more than simply arguments. And the rise of aggressive abolitionism primed many antislavery audiences to see a figure like John L. Brown, who had reportedly risked his life to free a slave, as a hero, paving the way for their later celebrations of another, more famous John Brown. Indeed, within a few weeks of the first coverage of the case in the North, public meetings in Pittsburgh, Pennsylvania, and Hallowell, Maine had passed resolutions censuring O'Neall, and some meetings even raised the possibility of sending delegations to northern legislatures or directly to South Carolina to seek Brown's release.

The John L. Brown case occurred at an equally crucial moment in the history of transatlantic abolitionist networks. The 1838 founding of the British and Foreign Anti-Slavery Society (BFASS), led by Quaker abolitionist Joseph Sturge, signaled British abolitionists' growing interest in forging links to antislavery movements elsewhere, as did two international conferences on slavery hosted by BFASS leaders in 1840 and 1843. But as transatlantic ties among abolitionists had thickened, so too had fears among anti-abolitionists in the United States about Britain's role in the antislavery movement.

In fact, as news of John L. Brown reached the North, Americans were already closely watching British public opinion about American slavery, thanks to several recent incidents: simmering tensions over the recent liberation of slaves aboard the *Creole* by British officials; the growing pressure on South Carolina from abolitionists and British diplomats to repeal its Negro Seamen's Acts; and new rumors about British interference with closeted negotiations then underway for the annexation of Texas. Anglophobia among anti-abolitionists was also growing in response to transatlantic abolitionist efforts like Daniel O'Connell's 1842 Irish Address on American slavery. Yet to abolitionists, even negative attention suggested the power of their new international networks to provoke discussion of slavery in the United States, encouraging them to widen the search for issues that could spark international outrage.

The current state of "aggressive abolitionism" and transatlantic abolitionism in 1843 virtually assured that Judge O'Neall's sentencing speech would sound like a thunderclap on both sides of the Atlantic. Abolitionists in the North were on the lookout for opportunities to attack slavery more directly and so latched onto the case quickly. And thanks to newspaper exchanges and personal correspondence between abolitionists, editors in London, Leeds, Bristol, and numerous other English cities received news of the speech quickly, too. Soon British editors were reporting breathlessly about the "hellish" crimes of slaveholders who had sentenced a man to death "under a conviction of aiding a slave to run away!!!" The London *Anti-Slavery Reporter,* for example, printed O'Neall's "revolting" speech on 21 February, a week after its appearance in a Cincinnati paper. Only a fortnight later the case had been mentioned in the House of Lords. And a month later it received a censure from veteran British abolitionist Thomas Clarkson in a public letter in the *Reporter.* Throughout March, British newspapers continued to editorialize about the case, and in the middle and final weeks of March, public meetings were held in Birmingham and Glasgow to protest Brown's sentence. Several British churches even prepared and forwarded to the United States a memorial bearing 1300 signatures....

Discussions of Brown's case had taken a more explosive turn within the United States, thanks to a letter from O'Neall published in the northern press. In mid-March, O'Neall wrote directly to a Pittsburgh newspaper to refute a clipping that had been sent to him in the mail. Defending his sentencing of Brown, the judge now suggested that "the proof [for Brown's conviction] created a strong belief that the woman [he helped to escape] had been his kept mistress for some time." According to O'Neall, in other words, Brown was not the disinterested abolitionist some northern papers were making him out to be; rather, the black woman he had aided was his lover.

In a concluding jab that pandered to prejudices about interracial sex that most white northerners shared, O'Neall invited the Pittsburgh editor who had attacked him to come to South Carolina after Brown had been whipped, so that he could escort him back to the West, "where he can soothe and cherish him as one of 'the young and ardent men' who *loved negro women."* In another letter addressed to his critics in Cincinnati, O'Neall added a more elaborate accusation that Brown:

> did not seek by aiding the woman to run away, to enable her to go to a free State, and there to be free; but his object either was to prolong an adulterous intercourse with the woman, or, taking advantage of the power which he thus had, to carry her off and sell her.

O'Neall made clear that Brown was no antislavery hero: "He is still in the world, and if he were today charged with being an abolitionist, he would regard it as a greater reproach than to be called a negro thief."

Determining the truth of any of these rumors was and is difficult. Even today, it is difficult to discern Brown's actual relationship with "the slave Hetty" (who was named only in the court records) from the public narratives of his case. Brown himself pled not guilty when he appealed his conviction and sentence, claiming that in helping Hetty to travel from Fairfield County to Columbia, South Carolina, he was under the impression that she was merely returning to the home of her owner, Charlotte Hinton. Hetty had been hired out for many years to Hinton's brother, John Taylor, who was Brown's employer.

It is difficult to determine if Brown knew Hetty was attempting to escape or sincerely assumed that she had permission to go to Columbia, given her past history of "coming and going at her own pleasure." It is equally impossible to cross-examine those white men who claimed that they had frequently seen Brown "in the morning, just before day, slipping out of the kitchen where the woman lodged." Viewed in retrospect, Brown's case may therefore be seen as one in which "Hetty"—not Brown—was the primary actor all along. While her own motives for trying to return to the city are unknown, she appears to have approached Brown, who claimed he was traveling to Columbia to look for work, about a ride to the city. She may well have convinced Brown that she went with Taylor's knowledge.

O'Neall's court, however, concluded that Hetty's powers of persuasion were ultimately sexual in nature. Indeed, allusions to an "adulterous" relationship with Brown made their way into the earliest reports of the case. While some of O'Neall's allegations may well have been responses to abolitionist pressure, his assertion that Hetty had seduced Brown also predated the abolitionists' publicity offensive. Even the sentencing speech itself referred elliptically to Hetty as Brown's mistress, referring to Brown as a "dissolute" young man who had been "snared" by "the 'strange woman'" an allusion to the biblical warnings of the Book of Proverbs against the temptations of lust. "She 'flattered with her words,'" O'Neall told Brown, "and you became her victim … led on by a desire to serve her." O'Neall's later letter to Cincinnati modified those claims by implying that Brown had desired to *sell* his mistress, but the gist of his accusation in the spring was already between the lines of his speech the previous winter. Instead of prompting O'Neall to invent new claims, abolitionist attack had mainly led O'Neall to make explicit and more public some charges that had earlier been swaddled in euphemism and allusion.

Whether true or false, these charges had an immediate and, for abolitionists, damaging impact on northern discussions of the case. Some northern newspapers, accepting O'Nell's construction of the facts, soon began to report that Brown was "enamored" of the slave in question. Many editors flatly dismissed Brown as "a scamp." "It is now proven," said one Maine paper on 3 May, that Brown "attempted to sell the being who reposed confidence in him, he having satisfied the only passion he felt—one of lust."…

Ultimately, most abolitionists simply decided that the entire case was too touchy; it was better to turn their searchlight onto other campaigns with less complicated heroes and villains. Indeed, transatlantic mobilization around the case died down rapidly almost as soon as the sexual innuendo surrounding Brown crossed the Atlantic.…

[T]he Brown case opened the floodgates for a new wave of proslavery publications in the late 1840s. Hammond's lengthy reply to the British petitions that he received about the Brown case was published in pamphlet form in December 1844 as the *Letter of His Excellency Governor Hammond, to the Free Church of Glasgow, on the Subject of Slavery,* a book that soon became a "proslavery classic," in the words of [historian] Drew Gilpin Faust. The next year, emboldened by the praise heaped on his first pamphlet by fellow slaveholders, Hammond engaged abolitionists in further debate by publishing two letters to Thomas Clarkson in a longer and even more influential proslavery tract. Both Hammond and O'Neall also decided, in the aftermath of the Brown protests, to open brief correspondences with the very northern and British abolitionists they had once wanted to "gag." After ending his gubernatorial term in a state where abolitionist newspapers and tracts had been burned in a bonfire in 1835, Hammond even purchased subscriptions to two major abolitionist newspapers, the New York *Emancipator* and the London *Anti-Slavery Reporter,* and had them sent to him at his home in Silver Bluff.

As these developments suggest, transatlantic abolitionists not only failed to pressure Hammond directly before his pardon of Brown, but they also unintentionally created opportunities that the governor could eagerly seize and turn to his own ends. In his pamphlets, Hammond clearly delighted in being able to correct the inaccurate or outdated reports about Brown's fate that had been broadcast on both sides of the Atlantic. Moreover, by highlighting what abolitionists had overlooked in the sentencing speech about Brown's alleged motives, writers like Hammond and O'Neall also claimed that abolitionist exaggeration on such matters was typical. In his 1845 letters to Clarkson, for example, Hammond said that "you have read and assisted to circulate a great deal about affrays, duels and murders occurring here, and all attributed to the terrible demoralization of slavery. Not a single event of this sort takes place among us, but is caught up by the Abolitionists and paraded over the world with endless comments, variations and exaggerations. You should not take what reaches you as a mere sample, and infer that there is a vast deal more you never hear. You hear all, and more than all the truth."

Attention to these easily overlooked points reveals that the long history of transnational activism was not a simple string of increasingly successful campaigns, beginning with the abolitionists and continuing to the present day. In fact, episodes like the John L. Brown case may well enable historians to see transatlantic abolitionism in the 1830s and 1840s not just as the origin of a new story but as the continuation of old ones stretching back into the eighteenth century. Many parts of this case's story—the efforts at abolitionist fact-finding that led to unintended expectations and consequences across the Atlantic Ocean; the efforts of proslavery planters to deflect abolitionist attacks with lurid stories and rumors of their own; and the difficulty of verifying reports from long distances about the details of slavery and emancipation—echo historians' recent accounts of the debates over slavery that ricocheted through the British Atlantic World in the Age of Revolutions, resulting simultaneously in more concerted antislavery and proslavery movements.

Situating cases like the Brown campaign within this longer history may well underline the factor that remained most constant throughout the struggle for

New World emancipation; the continuing efforts by enslaved actors like "Hetty" to control their own destinies, despite the different sets of circumstances presented by each historical moment. Though obscured and never named in abolitionist discussions of the case, though transformed in the rhetoric of abolitionists and slaveholders either into a "strange" seducer or into the passive object of Brown's help or exploitation, this one woman's short-lived escape in rural South Carolina was, in the final analysis, the real marble at the top of the abolitionists' Rube Goldberg machine. At a moment of heightened attention to southern slavery on two sides of an ocean, her local action triggered a transatlantic war of words that rattled abolitionists and slaveholders alike. For historians who look beyond the transatlantic campaigns that abolitionists touted as innovative victories and begin to analyze the forgotten campaigns that did not fully succeed, more stories like hers may be waiting, too.

 # FURTHER READING

Robert H. Abzug, *Cosmos Crumbling: American Reform and the Religious Imagination* (1994).

Catherine A. Brekus, *Strangers and Pilgrims: Female Preaching in America, 1740–1845* (1998).

Richard L. Bushman, *Joseph Smith: Rough Stone Rolling* (2007).

J. Spencer Fluhman, *"A Peculiar People": Anti-Mormonism and the Making of Religion in Nineteenth-Century America* (2012).

Paul Goodman, *Of One Blood: Abolitionism and the Origins of Racial Equality* (1998).

Peter P. Hinks, *To My Afflicted Brethren: David Walker and the Problem of Antebellum Slave Resistance* (1996).

Nancy Isenberg, *Sex and Citizenship in Antebellum America* (1998).

Paul E. Johnson and Sean Wilentz, *The Kingdom of Matthias* (1994).

Bruce Laurie, *Beyond Garrison: Antislavery and Social Reform* (2005).

W. Caleb McDaniel, *The Problem of Democracy in the Age of Slavery: Garrisonian Abolitionists and Transatlantic Reform* (2013).

Additional critical thinking activities and content are available in MindTap.

 **MindTap** is a fully online, highly personalized learning experience built upon Cengage Learning content. MindTap combines student learning tools—readings, multimedia, activities, and assessments—into a singular Learning Path that guides students through the course.

CHAPTER 11

Commercial Development
and Immigration

In the thirty years before the Civil War, society was transformed by massive commercial gains and immigration to the United States and migration within the nation. There was a huge migration westward, effectively redistributing the population of the nation. Between 1830 and 1860, the white population of the Old Northwest (the states of Ohio, Michigan, Indiana, Illinois, and Wisconsin) grew from 1.5 million to nearly 7 million. Agricultural innovations, including Cyrus McCormick's mechanical reaper and John Deere's self-polishing steel plow, enabled the fast and lucrative cultivation of the Midwest. By 1860, one-quarter of the nation's population, most of whom toiled on the land and lived in these northwestern states, provided much of the voting power for the new Republican Party of the 1850s. As millions of people moved westward, others migrated to the cities. By 1860, there were thirty-five cities in the United States with more than 25,000 inhabitants; New York City had more than one million inhabitants. Most of these cities were located in the northern states. Many city dwellers labored for wages in factories or mills, and many of these early workers were young women who left their rural homes to labor in the factories.

Cloth manufacturing changed radically when a factory in Waltham, Massachusetts, was built that mechanized all the stages in the production of cloth and brought the whole process under one roof. The evolution of cloth factories was complemented by innovations in the use of interchangeable parts that enabled manufacturers to develop complex assembly plants that produced clocks and guns, among other products. By 1860, nearly 300,000 workers toiled in northern industries, and population densities in the city reached up to 150 people per acre. As time went on, immigrants from Europe replaced many of the young female workers in the factories and also labored on western farms. Immigration, which was a mere 150,000 in the 1820s, swelled to over 1.5 million in the 1840s and 2.2 million in the 1850s. Mainly from the German states or Ireland, these immigrants often lived in poverty in cities and worshipped in Roman Catholic churches. They illustrated to many Americans the dangers of urbanization, commercialization, and mechanization in the North.

These vast changes created grave challenges for northern society, especially in its grow-ing cities. Densely settled neighborhoods became increasingly unhealthy. Workers strove to organize trade unions that would improve wages and working conditions. But wages often lagged and workers fell victim to the financial crashes in 1837 and 1857, which increased unemployment and uncertainty. Some northerners began to fear that they would become "wage slaves," people who would never be freed of their need to labor in order to stay alive. To make matters worse, the cultural differences within the cities created tensions that occa-sionally exploded in violence. Riots in New York, Boston, and Philadelphia, and in rural areas as well, pitted the native-born against the immigrant. Immigrants often were scape-goats, and their allegiance to Roman Catholicism only made them more suspect to citizens in a largely Protestant nation.

Despite these challenges, many northerners remained optimistic that their world of commerce, farming, and manufacturing was the direction in which the United States should head. In particular, they were certain that their society was superior to the slave society in the South. As a result, they developed ideologies that explained their predicament and celebrated their society. Although some northerners feared "wage slavery," others applauded the economic mobility that workers were offered. Free laborers, so the argument went, could improve their condition through their own hard work and could ultimately become economi-cally independent. As Abraham Lincoln observed, "The man who labored for another last year, this year labors for himself, and next year he will hire others to labor for him." The sum total of free individuals working to improve themselves created a mobile society and a growing economy. "The desire of bettering one's condition," wrote newspaper editor Horace Greeley, "is the mainspring of effort." A key element supporting the system of free labor was the availability of the vast tracts of land in the West. People could move up as they moved west. By forsaking an urban occupation, so the argument went, they relieved the pressures that built up in the city. The West was a necessary "safety valve." It is no coincidence that the Republican Party, a political organization founded in the 1850s whose membership came almost entirely from the northern states, would proclaim that it was the party of "Free Labor, Free Soil, and Free Men."

QUESTIONS TO THINK ABOUT

How were economic and geographical mobility central to the experience and ideologies of Americans before the Civil War? Why would immigrants move to the North if they experienced oppression there? In what ways did immigra-tion create a more volatile society when it increased dramatically in the decades after 1830? Was internal migration or external immigration more central in remaking the United States? What were the main reasons for American wealth?

DOCUMENTS

Alexis de Tocqueville, in document 1, observes that although early nineteenth-century Americans were among the "freest and best-educated" people in the world, they were unhappy. He attributes this oddity to the desire for mobility that stems from that very freeness. In document 2, Orestes Brownson offers a scathing critique of the status of workers in the North in 1840. He goes so far as to suggest that the plight of these "wage slaves" is worse than that of slaves in the South. In document 3, a Swedish immigrant reflects on life in Wisconsin in 1841 and 1842; he enjoys an independence not available in his homeland. Although he finds Americans different from his people, he does appreciate the republican form of government. In document 4, George Templeton Strong describes in his diary the impact of European immigrants on New York City. No friend to immigrants, Strong compares the Irish with the Chinese. Document 5 features the articulation of "manifest destiny" by John L. O'Sullivan and the call to Americans to move west. In document 6, naval officer Matthew C. Perry receives orders for exploring Japan and access to markets in Asia. One force propelling new movements of people and ideas was gold. The newly found massive loads in California and elsewhere throughout the world transformed the national and global economy, and document 7 is a magazine article wrestling with all of the changes. The final document is a song from the early 1860s, "No Irish Need Apply." In it, the singer details anti-Irish sentiment in the United States and how Irish Americans should take pride in their ethnic heritage.

1. Alexis de Tocqueville Marvels at the Mobile Northern Society, 1831

In certain remote corners of the Old World you may sometimes stumble upon little places which seem to have been forgotten among the general tumult and which have stayed still while all around them moves. The inhabitants are mostly very ignorant and very poor; they take no part in affairs of government, and often governments oppress them. But yet they seem serene and often have a jovial disposition.

In America I have seen the freest and best educated of men in circumstances the happiest to be found in the world; yet it seemed to me that a cloud habitually hung on their brow, and they seemed serious and almost sad even in their pleasures.

The chief reason for this is that the former do not give a moment's thought to the ills they endure, whereas the latter never stop thinking of the good things they have not got.

It is odd to watch with what feverish ardor the Americans pursue prosperity and how they are ever tormented by the shadowy suspicion that they may not have chosen the shortest route to get it.

Americans cleave to the things of this world as if assured that they will never die, and yet are in such a rush to snatch any that come within their reach, as if expecting to stop living before they have relished them. They clutch everything but hold nothing fast, and so lose grip as they hurry after some new delight.

Alexis de Tocqueville, *Democracy in America*, Volume II (Boston: Little and J. Brown, 1841), 536–538.

An American will build a house in which to pass his old age and sell it before the roof is on; he will plant a garden and rent it just as the trees are coming into bearing; he will clear a field and leave others to reap the harvest; he will take up a profession and leave it, settle in one place and soon go off elsewhere with his changing desires. If his private business allows him a moment's relaxation, he will plunge at once into the whirlpool of politics. Then, if at the end of a year crammed with work he has a little spare leisure, his restless curiosity goes with him traveling up and down the vast territories of the United States. Thus he will travel five hundred miles in a few days as a distraction from his happiness.

Death steps in in the end and stops him before he has grown tired of this futile pursuit of that complete felicity which always escapes him.

At first sight there is something astonishing in this spectacle of so many lucky men restless in the midst of abundance. But it is a spectacle as old as the world; all that is new is to see a whole people performing in it.

The taste for physical pleasures must be regarded as the first cause of this secret restlessness betrayed by the actions of the Americans, and of the inconstancy of which they give daily examples.

A man who has set his heart on nothing but the good things of this world is always in a hurry, for he has only a limited time in which to find them, get them, and enjoy them....

When all prerogatives of birth and fortune are abolished, when all professions are open to all and a man's own energies may bring him to the top of any of them, an ambitious man may think it easy to launch on a great career and feel that he is called to no common destiny. But that is a delusion which experience quickly corrects. The same equality which allows each man to entertain vast hopes makes each man by himself weak. His power is limited on every side, though his longings may wander where they will.

Not only are men powerless by themselves, but at every step they find immense obstacles which they had not at first noticed.

They have abolished the troublesome privileges of some of their fellows, but they come up against the competition of all....

No matter how a people strives for it, all the conditions of life can never be perfectly equal. Even if, by misfortune, such an absolute dead level were attained, there would still be inequalities of intelligence which, coming directly from God, will ever escape the laws of man....

Among democratic peoples men easily obtain a certain equality, but they will never get the sort of equality they long for. That is a quality which ever retreats before them without getting quite out of sight, and as it retreats it beckons them on to pursue. Every instant they think they will catch it, and each time it slips through their fingers. They see it close enough to know its charms, but they do not get near enough to enjoy it, and they will be dead before they have fully relished its delights.

2. Essayist Orestes Brownson Condemns the Plight of "Wage Slaves," 1840

No one can observe the signs of the times with much care, without perceiving that a crisis as to the relation of wealth and labor is approaching....

In this coming contest there is a deeper question at issue than is commonly imagined, a question which is but remotely touched in your controversies about United States Banks and Sub-Treasuries, chartered Banking and free Banking, free trade and corporations, although these controversies may be paving the way for it to come up....

What we would ask is, throughout the Christian world the actual condition of the laboring classes, viewed simply and exclusively in their capacity of laborers? They constitute at least a moiety of the human race. We exclude the nobility, we exclude also the middle class, and include only actual laborers, who are laborers and not proprietors, owners of none of the funds of production, neither houses, shops, nor lands, nor implements of labor, being therefore solely dependent on their hands....

... We are not ignorant of the fact, that the merchant, who is literally the common carrier and exchange dealer, performs a useful service, and is therefore entitled to a portion of the proceeds of labor. But make all necessary deductions on his account, and then ask what portion of the remainder is retained, either in kind or in its equivalent, in the hands of the original producer, the workingman? All over the world this fact stares us in the face, the workingman is poor and depressed, while a large portion of the non-workingmen, in the sense we now use the term, are wealthy. It may be laid down as a general rule, with but few exceptions, that men are rewarded in an inverse ratio to the amount of actual service they perform....

In regard to labor two systems obtain; one that of slave labor, the other that of free labor. Of the two, the first is, in our judgement, except so far as the feelings are concerned, decidedly the least oppressive. If the slave has never been a free man, we think, as a general rule, his sufferings are less than those of the free laborer at wages. As to actual freedom one has just about as much as the other. The laborer at wages has all the disadvantages of freedom and none of its blessings, while the slave, if denied the blessings, is freed from the disadvantages. We are no advocates of slavery, we are as heartily opposed to it as any modern abolitionist can be; but we say frankly that, if there must always be a laboring population distinct from proprietors and employers, we regard the slave system as decidedly preferable to the system at wages. It is no pleasant thing to go days without food, to lie idle for weeks, seeking work and finding none, to rise in the morning with a wife and children you love, and know not where to procure them a breakfast, and to see constantly before you no brighter prospect than the almshouse. Yet these are no unfrequent incidents in the lives of our laboring population.... It is said there is no want in this country. There may be less

Orestes Brownson, "The Laboring Classes," *Boston Quarterly Review*, 1840.

than in some other countries. But death by actual starvation in this country is we apprehend no uncommon occurrence. The sufferings of a quiet, unassuming but useful class of females in our cities, in general sempstresses, too proud to beg or to apply to the almshouse, are not easily told. They are industrious; they do all they can find to do; but yet the little there is for them to do, and the miserable pittance they receive for it, is hardly sufficient to keep soul and body together....

We pass through our manufacturing villages; most of them appear neat and flourishing. The operatives are well dressed, and we are told, well paid. They are said to be healthy, contented, and happy. This is the fair side of the picture; the side exhibited to distinguished visitors. There is a dark side, moral as well as physical. Of the common operatives, few, if any, by their wages, acquire a competence. A few of what Carlyle terms not inaptly the *body-servants* are well paid, and now and then an agent or an overseer rides in his coach. But the great mass wear out their health, spirits, and morals, without becoming one whit better off than when they commenced labor.... We know no sadder sight on earth than one of our factory villages presents, when the bell at break of day, or at the hour of breakfast, or dinner, calls out its hundreds or thousands of operatives. We stand and look at these hard working men and women hurrying in all directions, and ask ourselves, where go the proceeds of their labors? The man who employs them, and for whom they are willing as so many slaves, is one of our city nabobs, revelling in luxury; or he is a member of our legislature, enacting laws to put money in his own pocket; or he is a member of Congress, contending for a high Tariff to tax the poor for the benefit of the rich; or in these times he is shedding crocodile tears over the deplorable condition of the poor laborer, while he docks his wages twenty-five per cent; building miniature log cabins, shouting Harrison and "hard cider."—And this man too would fain pass for a Christian and a republican. He shouts for liberty, stickless [argues] for equality, and is horrified at a Southern planter who keeps slaves.

One thing is certain; that of the amount actually produced by the operative, he retains a less proportion than it costs the master to feed, clothe, and lodge his slave. Wages is a cunning device of the devil, for the benefit of tender consciences, who would retain all the advantages of the slave system, without the expense, trouble, and odium of being slave-holders.

Messrs. Thome and Kimball, in their account of the emancipation of slavery in the West Indies, establish the fact that the employer may have the same amount of labor done 25 per ct. cheaper than the master. What does this fact prove, if not that wages is a more successful method of taxing labor than slavery? We really believe our Northern system of labor is more oppressive, and even more mischievous to morals, than the Southern. We, however, war against both. We have no toleration for either system. We would see a slave a man, but a free man, not a mere operative at wages. This he would not be were he now emancipated. Could the abolitionists effect all they propose, they would do the slave no service. Should emancipation work as well as they say, still it would do the slave no good. He would be a slave still, although with the title and cares of a freeman. If then we had no constitutional objections to abolitionism, we could not, for the reason here implied, be abolitionists.

The slave system, however, in name and form, is gradually disappearing from Christendom. It will not subsist much longer. But its place is taken by the system of labor at wages, and this system, we hold, is no improvement upon the one it supplants. Nevertheless the system of wages will triumph. It is the system which in name sounds honester than slavery, and in substance is more profitable to the master. It yields the wages of iniquity, without its opprobrium. It will therefore supplant slavery, and be sustained—for a time.

3. Gustof Unonius, a Swedish Immigrant, Reflects on Life in the United States, 1841–1842

Milwaukee, Wisconsin, 13 October 1841

The soil here is the most fertile and wonderful that can be found and usually consists of rich black mold. Hunting and fishing will provide some food in the beginning, but they must be pursued sparingly, otherwise time which could more profitably be spent in cultivating the soil is wasted. I beg the emigrant to consider all these factors carefully and closely calculate his assets before he starts out.... [He] will have to suffer much in the beginning, limit himself considerably, and sacrifice much of what he was accustomed to in Europe.... I caution against all exaggerated hopes and golden air castles; cold reality will otherwise lame your arm and crush your courage; both must be fresh and active.

As far as we are concerned, we do not regret our undertaking. We are living a free and independent life in one of the most beautiful valleys the world can offer; and from the experiences of others we see that in a few years we can have a better livelihood and enjoy comforts that we must now deny ourselves. If we should be overcome by a longing for the fatherland (and this seems unlikely), we could sell our farm which in eight years will certainly bring ten or twelve dollars per acre.... But I believe that I will be satisfied in America.

I am partial to a republican form of government, and I have realized my youthful dream of social equality. Others may say what they will, but there are many attractive things about it. It is no disgrace to work here. Both the gentleman and the day laborer work. No epithets of degradation are applied to men of humble toil; only those whose conduct merits it are looked down upon.... Liberty is still stronger in my affections than the bright silver dollar that bears her image....

Pine Lake, Wisconsin, 25 January 1842

... I admit that I am no friend of the big city of New York. The shopkeeper's spirit is too prevalent, but to judge the American national character from that is incorrect. I have found the Americans entirely different. We live in an industrial era and it is true that the American is a better representative of that than any other nationality. Despite this fact, there is something kindly in his speculation for profit

Gustof Unonius, "Letters from a Swedish Man," in *Letters from the Promised Land: Swedes in America, 1840–1914,* ed. H. Arnold Barton (Minneapolis: University of Minnesota Press, 1975).

and wealth, and I find more to admire in his manner than in that of the European leaders. The merchant here is withal patriotic; in calculating his own gain he usually includes a share for his country.... [T]he universities and other educational institutions, homes for the poor, and other institutions of value to society are dependent on and supported by the American merchants. Canals, railroads, etc., are all financed by companies composed of a few individuals whose collective fortunes serve the public for its common benefit and profit. One must, therefore, overlook an avariciousness which sometimes goes to extremes.

It is true that the American is a braggart.... During the struggles which rend and agitate the countries of the Old World he sees in the progress of his peaceful fatherland the results of liberty and equality which he considers impossible to obtain under any other conditions. Even though I do not wish to blame him for this, yet I do not deny that his resulting self-satisfaction expresses itself in a highly ridiculous fashion in trivial matters.

4. New Yorker George Templeton Strong Berates the Immigrants in His Midst, 1838–1857

November 6 [1838]. It was enough to turn a man's stomach—to make a man adjure republicanism forever—to see the way they were naturalizing this morning at the *Hall*. Wretched, filthy, bestial-looking Italians and Irish, and creations [creatures] that looked as if they had risen from the lazarettos of Naples for this especial object; in short, the very scum and dregs of human nature filled the clerk of C[ommon] P[leas] office so completely that I was almost afraid of being poisoned by going in. A dirty Irishman is bad enough, but he's nothing comparable to a nasty French or Italian loafer....

April 28 [1848]. Orders given to commence excavating in Twenty-first Street Wednesday night.... Hibernia came to the rescue yesterday morning; twenty "sons of toil" with prehensile paws supplied them by nature with evident reference to the handling of the spade and the wielding of the pickaxe and congenital hollows on the shoulder wonderfully adapted to make the carrying of the hod a luxury instead of a labor....

November 13 [1854]. Met a prodigious Know-Nothing [nativist political party] procession moving uptown, as I omnibussed down Broadway to the vestry meeting; not many banners and little parade of any kind, but a most emphatic and truculent demonstration. Solid column, eight or ten abreast, and numbering some two or three thousand, mostly young men of the butcher-boy and *prentice* type ... marching in quick time, and occasionally indulging in a very earnest kind of hurrah. They looked as if they might have designs on St. Patrick's Cathedral, and I think the Celts of Prince and Mott Streets would have found them ugly customers....

Allan Nevins and Milton H. Thomas, eds., *The Diary of George Templeton Strong* (New York: Macmillan, 1952), I:94, 318 and II:197, 348.

July 7 [1857]. Yesterday morning I was spectator of a strange, weird, painful scene. Certain houses of John Watts DePeyster are to be erected on the northwest corner of this street and Fourth Avenue, and the deep excavations therefore are in progress. Seeing a crowd on the corner, I stopped and made my way to a front place. The earth had caved in a few minutes before and crushed the breath out of a pair of ill-starred Celtic laborers. They had just been dragged, or dug, out, and lay white and stark on the ground where they had been working, ten or twelve feet below the level of the street. Around them were a few men who had got them out, I suppose, and fifteen or twenty Irish women, wives, kinfolk or friends, who had got down there in some inexplicable way. The men were listless and inert enough, but not so the women. I suppose they were "keening"; all together were raising a wild, unearthly cry, half shriek and half song, wailing as a score of daylight Banshees, clapping their hands and gesticulating passionately. Now and then one of them would throw herself down on one of the corpses, or wipe some trace of defilement from the face of the dead man with her apron, slowly and carefully, and then resume her lament. It was an uncanny sound to hear…. Our Celtic fellow citizens are almost as remote from us in temperament and constitution as the Chinese.

5. John L. O'Sullivan, a Democratic Newspaperman, Defines "Manifest Destiny," 1845

Texas is now ours. Already, before these words are written, her Convention has undoubtedly ratified the acceptance, by her Congress, of our proffered invitation into the Union; and made the requisite changes in her already republican form of constitution to adapt it to its future federal relations. Her star and her stripe may already be said to have taken their place in the glorious blazon of our common nationality; and the sweep of our eagle's wing already includes within its circuit the wide extent of her fair and fertile land….

Why, were other reasoning wanting, in favor of now elevating this question of the reception of Texas into the Union, out of the lower region of our past party dissensions, up to its proper level of a high and broad nationality, it surely is to be found, found abundantly, in the manner in which other nations have undertaken to intrude themselves into it, between us and the proper parties to the case, in a spirit of hostile interference against us, for the avowed object of thwarting our policy and hampering our power, limiting our greatness and checking the fulfilment of our manifest destiny to overspread the continent allotted by Providence for the free development of our yearly multiplying millions. This we have seen done by England, our old rival and enemy; and by France, strangely coupled with her against us….

It is wholly untrue, and unjust to ourselves, the pretence that the Annexation has been a measure of spoliation, unrightful and unrighteous—of military

John L. O'Sullivan, editorial on Manifest Destiny and Texas Annexation, *United States Magazine and Democratic Review*, October 1837.

conquest under forms of peace and law—of territorial aggrandizement at the expense of justice, and justice due by a double sanctity to the weak.... If Texas became peopled with an American population, it was by no contrivance of our government, but on the express invitation of that of Mexico herself; accompanied with such guaranties of State independence, and the maintenance of a federal system analogous to our own, as constituted a compact fully justifying the strongest measures of redress on the part of those afterwards deceived in this guaranty, and sought to be enslaved under the yoke imposed by its violation. She was released, rightfully and absolutely released, from all Mexican allegiance, or duty of cohesion to the Mexican political body, by the acts and fault of Mexico herself, and Mexico alone. There never was a clearer case. It was not revolution; it was resistance to revolution....

Nor is there any just foundation for the charge that Annexation is a great pro-slavery measure—calculated to increase and perpetuate that institution. Slavery had nothing to do with it. Opinions were and are greatly divided, both at the North and South, as to the influence to be exerted by it on Slavery and the Slave States....

California will, probably, next fall away from the loose adhesion which, in such a country as Mexico, holds a remote province in a slight equivocal kind of dependence on the metropolis. Imbecile and distracted, Mexico never can exert any real governmental authority over such a country.... Already the advance guard of the irresistible army of Anglo-Saxon emigration has begun to pour down upon it, armed with the plough and the rifle, and marking its trail with schools and colleges, courts and representative halls, mills and meeting-houses. A population will soon be in actual occupation of California, over which it will be idle for Mexico to dream of dominion. They will necessarily become independent. All this without agency of our government, without responsibility of our people—in the natural flow of events, the spontaneous working of principles, and the adaptation of the tendencies and wants of the human race to the elemental circumstances in the midst of which they find themselves placed.

6. Commodore Matthew C. Perry Receives Instructions for His Expedition to Japan, 1852

Recent events—the navigation of the ocean by steam, the acquisition and rapid settlement by this country of a vast territory on the Pacific [California], the discovery of gold in that region, the rapid communication established across the isthmus which separates the two oceans—have practically brought the countries of the east in closer proximity to our own; although the consequences of these events have scarcely begun to be felt, the intercourse between

This document can be found in U.S. Congress, 33rd Congress, 2nd Session, Executive Documents Printed by Order of the Senate of the United States (Washington, D.C.: Beverly Tucker, Senate Printer, 1855), Ex. Doc. 34, pp. 4–9.

them has already greatly increased, and no limits can be assigned to its future extension....

The objects sought by this government are—

1. To effect some permanent arrangement for the protection of American sea-men and property wrecked on these islands, or driven into their ports by stress of weather.

2. The permission to American vessels to enter one or more of their ports in order to obtain supplies of provisions, water, fuel, &c., or, in case of disasters, to refit so as to enable them to prosecute their voyage.

    It is very desirable to have permission to establish a depot for coal, if not on one of the principal islands, at least on some small uninhabited one, of which, it is said, there are several in their vicinity.

3. The permission to our vessels to enter one or more of their ports for the purpose of disposing of their cargoes by sale or barter....

It is manifest, from past experience, that arguments or persuasion addressed to this people, unless they be seconded by some imposing manifestation of power, will be utterly unavailing.

You will, therefore, be pleased to direct the commander of the squadron [Perry] to proceed, with his whole force, to such point on the coast of Japan as he may deem most advisable, and there endeavor to open a communication with the government, and, if possible, to see the emperor in person, and deliver to him the letter of introduc-tion from the President with which he is charged. He will state that he has been sent across the ocean by the President to deliver that letter to the emperor, and to commu-nicate with his government on matters of importance to the two countries. That the President entertains the most friendly feeling towards Japan, but has been surprised and grieved to learn, that when any of the people of the United States go, of their own accord, or are thrown by the perils of the sea within the dominions of the emperor, they are treated as if they were his worst enemies....

He will inform him of the usages of this country, and of all Christian countries, in regard to shipwrecked persons and vessels, and will refer to the case of the Japanese subjects who were recently picked up at sea in distress and carried to California, from whence they have been sent to their own country; and will state that this government desires to obtain from that of Japan some positive assurance, that persons who may hereafter be shipwrecked on the coast of Japan, or driven by stress of weather into her ports, shall be treated with humanity; and to make arrangements for a more ex-tended commercial intercourse between the two countries. The establishment of this intercourse will be found a difficult, but, perhaps, not an impossible task.

The deep-seated aversion of this people to hold intercourse with Christian nations is said to be owing chiefly to the indiscreet zeal with which the early missionaries, particularly those of Portugal, endeavored to propagate their reli-gion. The commodore will therefore say, that the government of this country, unlike those of every other Christian country, does not interfere with the reli-gion of its own people, much less with that of other nations. It seems that the fears or the prejudices of the Japanese are very much excited against the English, of whose conquests in the east, and recent invasion of China, they have probably heard. As the Americans speak the same language as the English, it is natural that they should confound citizens of the United States with British subjects. Indeed, their barbarous treatment of the crews of the [U.S.] vessels ... was partly occasioned by the suspicion that they were really English....

Commodore Perry will, therefore, explain to them that the United States are connected with no government in Europe. That they inhabit a great country which lies directly between them and Europe, and which was discovered by the nations of Europe about the same time that Japan herself was first visited by them; that the portion of this continent lying nearest to Europe was first settled by emigrants from that country, but that its population has rapidly spread through the country until it has reached the Pacific ocean....

If, after having exhausted every argument and every means of persuasion, the commodore should fail to obtain from the government any relaxation of their system of exclusion, or even any assurance of humane treatment of our shipwrecked seamen, he will then change his tone, and inform them in the most unequivocal terms that it is the determination of this government to insist, that hereafter all citizens or vessels of the United States that may be wrecked on their coasts, or driven by stress of weather into their harbors shall, so long as they are compelled to remain there, be treated with humanity; and that if any acts of cruelty should hereafter be practised upon citizens of this country, whether by the government or by the inhabitants of Japan, they will be severely chastised. In case he should succeed in obtaining concessions on any of the points above mentioned, it is desirable that they should be reduced into the form of a treaty, for negotiating which he will be furnished with the requisite powers....

In his intercourse with this people, who are said to be proud and vindictive in their character, he should be courteous and conciliatory, but at the same time, firm and decided. He will, therefore, submit with patience and forbearance to acts of discourtesy to which he may be subjected, by a people to whose usages it will not do to test by our standard of propriety, but, at the same time, will be careful to do nothing that may compromit [compromise], in their eyes, his own dignity, or that of the country. He will, on the contrary, do everything to impress them with a just sense of the power and greatness of this country, and to satisfy them that its past forbearance has been the result, not of timidity, but of a desire to be on friendly terms with them.

7. A Magazine Author Reflects Upon the Impact of Gold and Silver from California and Elsewhere in the World, 1852

It is supposed that not less than $80,000,000 of gold will be raised from the mines of California in the year 1853. Before many years have passed, this yield, it is said, will be largely increased. Gold regions of vast extent, whose existence is known only to a few travellers and mineralogists, will soon be resorted to and

From *The Golden Trade; Or, A Discovery of the River Gambra, and the Golden Trade* by Richard Jobson, London: 1623.

opened in other parts of this continent. We speak advisedly in this matter. Already an incredible quantity of gold dust is washed in Australia. It is not improbable that $30,000,000 will be drawn within a year from the mines of Australia. New-Grenada and the Isthmus of Darien are also rich in gold. A very large yield may be expected from the river sands of New-Grenada, within two or three years. American enterprise is beginning already to move in that direction.

Previous to the discovery of gold in California, the most accurate English statistics computed the entire amount of gold *in circulation* at $240,000,000....

Enormous amounts of gold are known to be employed for ornamental purposes, more especially in Africa and Asia. This is thrown into circulation by very slow degrees; by European conquests and commercial enterprises, converting the luxuries of barbarous countries into the uses of trade....

The application of new machinery to the gold rocks and sands of California has proved to be an incredible advantage. It is within the limits of probability that California in the year 1855 will produce not less than $100,000,000 of gold....

If, between the present time and the period supposed [1855], an irruption of European and American emigrants should throw open the enormous gold deposits of New-Grenada and Central America, not to say of Mexico, whose richest gold regions lie within the grasp of the United States, it is possible another fifty may be added to the two hundred already estimated....

The wealth of California, like that of all other countries, though it is produced by the gold miners, is not retained by them. The law of social exchange compels them, by what is called rise of price, in provisions, clothing, and all the necessaries of life, to yield the largest share of their profits to those who supply their wants. In respect of all such enterprises, the entire community share the profits of the producers....

Gold has the advantage of being imperishable by rust or violence; even fire changes nothing but its shape. In all respects it seems to be the material intended by nature to serve as the embodied arithmetic of commerce, the counters of large exchange.

8. Irish Americans Sing About Their Struggles and Successes, c. 1860s

NO IRISH NEED APPLY. Written by JOHN F. POOLE, and sung, with immense success, by the great Comic-Vocalist of the age, TONY PASTOR.

I'm a dacint boy, just landed from the town of Ballyfad;
I want a situation: yis, I want it mighty bad.
I saw a place advertised. It's the thing for me, says I;

John F. Poole, "No Irish Need Apply" *American Memory*, Library of Congress, http://memory.loc.gov/rbc/amss/as1/as109730/001q.gif.

But the dirty spalpeen [rascal] ended with: No Irish need apply.
Whoo! says I; but that's an insult—though to get the place I'll try.
So, I wint to see the blaggar with: No Irish need apply.

I started off to find the house, I got it mighty soon;
There I found the ould chap saited: he was reading the TRIBUNE.
I tould him what I came for, whin he in a rage did fly:
No! says he, you are a Paddy, and no Irish need apply!
Thin I felt my dandher rising, and I'd like to black his eye—
To tell an Irish Gintleman: No Irish need apply!

I couldn't stand it longer: so, a hoult of him I took,
And I gave him such a welting as he'd get at Donnybrook.
He hollered: Millia murther! and to get away did try,
And swore he'd never write again: No Irish need apply.
He made a big apology; I bid him thin good-bye,
Saying: Whin next you want a bating, add: No Irish need apply!

Sure, I've heard that in America it always is the plan
That an Irishman is just as good as any other man;
A home and hospitality they never will deny
The stranger here, or ever say: No Irish need apply.
But some black sheep are in the flock: a dirty lot, say I;
A dacint man will never write: No Irish need apply!

Sure, Paddy's heart is in his hand, as all the world does know,
His praties and his whiskey he will share with friend or foe;
His door is always open to the stranger passing by;
He never thinks of saying: None but Irish may apply.
And, in Columbia's history, his name is ranking high;
Thin, the Divil take the knaves that write; No Irish need apply!

Ould Ireland on the battle-field a lasting fame has made;
We all have heard of Meagher's men, and Corcoran's brigade.
Though fools may flout and bigots rave, and fanatics may cry,
Yet when they want good fighting-men, the Irish may apply,
And when for freedom and the right they raise the battle-cry,
Then the Rebel ranks begin to think: No Irish need apply!

ESSAYS

The United States expanded dramatically during the first sixty years of the nineteenth century. This was the case not only territorially but also monetarily and
commercially. Historians have asked, in particular, where the rise of wealth originated. Did it come from meticulous planning or did it occur from happenstance
and geographical luck? For Sven Beckert, the concentration of capital in New
York City was pivotal to the emergence of a commercial United States. Set

beside a deep harbor, New York City became a hub of imports and exports. Trade helped create a class of aspiring and wealthy New Yorkers who found ways to leverage their various forms of capital—cash, networks, location, and abilities—to grow not only the city but also the nation itself. Edward Dolnick looks to the other side of the continent. By examining the California Gold Rush, Dolnick showcases how Americans and those from the world endeavored to "get rich quick" through gold. The infusion of gold and people was matched by an expectant spirit—that wealth was to be found and made in the United States.

Concentrating Capital and Power in New York City

SVEN BECKERT

Unlocking the history of upper-class Americans, the central social actors of the quintessential bourgeois century, provides one important key to understanding the dynamics of economic, social, and political change between 1850 and 1900 and with it the emergence of modern America.

It was in New York that these developments unfolded most dramatically and from there had the greatest impact on the rest of the nation. Capital and capitalists gather in cities, and nowhere did economic, social, and political power coalesce more than in New York City. New York's bourgeoisie dominated the nation's trade, production, and finance and served as the gatekeeper of America's most important outpost in the Atlantic economy. The city's merchants, bankers, and industrialists staged the most elaborate social events anywhere, setting the bourgeois standard for the nation. And their economic, social, and political power reverberated from California to South Carolina, from the factory to the farm, from City Hall to the White House. For these reasons, no other site of inquiry promises such rich insights into when, how, and why an upper class formed as a cohesive group with a shared identity, as well as the place of this emerging economic elite in the political, social, and economic context of the nation.

Throughout the Western world, the nineteenth century saw the rise of the bourgeoisie and bourgeois society. As a result of the unfolding of capitalist economies and the emancipation of society from the state, owners of capital decisively shaped economic change and the newly emerging societies. As the first elite not to derive its status from the accidents of birth and heritage, the rising bourgeoisie worked hard, lived in modest comfort, and celebrated individual accomplishment. Accumulating ever more capital and power, this new social class gained the upper hand over an older, feudal, social elite and eventually shaped the economy, ideology, and politics of all Western nations.

Sven Beckert, *Concentrating Capital and Power in New York City* [Excerpt, Sven Beckert, The Monied Metropolis, (Cambridge University Press, 2001). Reprinted with the permission of Cambridge University Press.

In the fall of 1857, August and Caroline Belmont sailed into New York harbor, his four-year assignment as United States ambassador to The Hague complete. As their boat passed the Narrows between Brooklyn and Staten Island, the steeples of Trinity Church appeared on the horizon, followed by the merchant houses of South Street and the banks just north of the Battery. On the calm waters before them, dozens of ships crisscrossed the port, ferry boats shuttling between lower Manhattan and Brooklyn, canal sloops loaded with wheat arriving from Albany via the Erie Canal, ocean-going clippers unloading barrels stamped "Liverpool," and coastal brigs lying low with their heavy load of cotton bales. As it unfolded before the Belmonts, New York radiated material bounty. Indeed, August himself had thrived in the city in the short twenty years after first setting foot on the North American continent as a representative of the banking house of Rothschild. Now, he was one of the richest and most powerful Americans. Within days of the Belmonts' return to their mansion on Fifth Avenue and 18th Street, they had exhibited their exquisite art collection, "containing paintings of most of the first living masters," and given lavish dinners that featured the delicacies of a chef brought back with them from Europe. By giving back to this nascent world capital some Old World culture, the Belmonts were reasserting their prominent position.

By the year of the Belmonts' return, New York and the nation had risen on a great, fast-moving swell of economic growth. In the course of this boom, the city, the nation, and the relationship between the two had changed radically. During the short span of seven years before 1857, American coal production had more than doubled, railroad mileage nearly tripled, and pig-iron shipments expanded fully thirteen times. At the helm of this expanding economy was New York. Already the most important port in the Americas, New York in these years saw exports—especially of cotton, wheat, and corn—increase by 139 percent and imports—especially of textiles and iron goods—rise by 97 percent. By 1860, a full two-thirds of the United States' imports and one-third of its exports went via New York. Its chief rivals, Boston, Philadelphia, and Baltimore, could not compete: Together they traded in goods only one-quarter the value of those which passed through the port of New York. Trade, in turn, supported the city's burgeoning factories, and during the decade of the 1850s, capital invested in manufacturing grew by 60 percent, making it the New World's most important manufacturing location.

Such rapid expansion reshaped the very face of the city: Returning citizens marveled at the growing number of docks and wharves, thickening forests of masts and steam pipes in the harbor, and sprawling warehouses and dry goods stores. A short walk from these powerful testimonies to the city's enormous trade they found evidence of New York's industry: Northward along the East River they encountered large iron factories, among them the Morgan, Allaire, and Novelty Works. Strolling through the streets of lower Manhattan they ran into workshops small and large, which churned out shirts, shoes, newspapers, and hundreds of other goods. At the tip of Manhattan, around Wall Street, new Renaissance-inspired palazzi ennobled the city's banks, insurance companies, and expanding financial and commodities markets—the fount of capital for the trade and manufacturing of the city and the nation. By midcentury the Western world knew few cities like it; its wealth dwarfed that of all but London and Paris.

New York outpaced its rivals through good fortune and determination. It was blessed by geography: A large, protected port that remained free of ice throughout most of the year, its closeness to the open sea, and a river that provided it with easy access to a vast hinterland gave it a privileged start. New York's merchants, capital rich and risk taking, used these endowments to good advantage by dredging shallow passages in the harbor, and by forging canals and railroads that enlarged the city's hinterland ever more. But more important in the story of New York's rise than geography or even infrastructure were the commercial enterprises that its merchants built. Here, where the Hudson meets the Atlantic, they fashioned trading houses that connected the British industrial economy to the cotton plantations in the American South. New Yorkers bought cotton in the South for transport to Liverpool, returning in their sailing vessels the bountiful goods of Britain's industry to equip and clothe western farmers, northern workers, and southern plantation owners. Once they drew this trade into their port, it was all but impossible for others to compete. Advantages in trade, in turn, could be translated into other enterprises. Drawing labor from the densely inhabited streets along the East River, manufacturers large and small produced ever more printing presses, carriages, books, and ready-made clothing, supplying not only New York's unrivaled urban market but also much of the rest of the nation. Along the fine boulevards of southern Manhattan just north of the Battery, bankers, insurance agents, and lawyers set up shop and lubricated the machinery of trade and production. Strategically placed at the center of a rapidly growing economy, New York's bankers, manufacturers, and merchants reaped proceeds from the cotton fields of Louisiana, the iron works of Pennsylvania, the sugar plantations of Cuba, and the railroads extended throughout the nation.

The merchants' activities, in turn, strengthened the city's position ever more, making it the center of the nation's trade, information, and transportation networks. Indeed, in contrast to all other urban areas in the United States, New York dominated not only its hinterland and the northeastern region but also the nation as a whole. Thanks to the merchants' resolve to take advantage of the privileged position of New York, the city sat like a spider in the web of the American economy, drawing resources into the metropolis, transforming them, and sending them to places near and far. Moreover, as a central outpost of the trading networks of the Atlantic world that stretched from the coasts of Europe and Western Africa to North and South America, the city connected the southern plantation economy to the factories of Great Britain. Few cities in the world owed as much to capitalists and capital than New York at midcentury, and in 1857, such capitalists as August Belmont were poised to reap the harvest of all their activity.

These capitalists stood out in dramatic relief against a city that was mostly artisanal and proletarian. In 1856, 9,000 individuals, about 1.4 percent of New York's inhabitants, or 5 percent of the city's economically active, owned assets exceeding $10,000 each—a sum that provided them well-furnished living quarters and the help of servants, and thus the essential attributes of respectability.

Though small in number, these capitalists, together with their families, controlled a significant share of the city's and nation's resources. At midcentury, they owned roughly 71 percent of the city's real and personal wealth. This was a concentration of assets made all the more remarkable considering that 84 percent of the city's economically active citizens owned no personal or real wealth of consequence at all.

These propertied New Yorkers represented the largest and most diverse segment of the nation's economic elite, surpassing in wealth, power, and diversity of their business undertakings the merchants of both Boston and Philadelphia. While Boston and Philadelphia had their long-established merchant elites, and Pittsburgh would eventually have a well-defined group of industrialists, New York City had all this and more. Already at midcentury, its economic elite was extraordinarily diverse. Most strikingly, in a city built by merchants, a full 20 percent of substantial taxpayers had accumulated their capital in an entirely different kind of undertaking, manufacturing. The city on the Hudson, so it seemed, was a springboard for capital and entrepteneurial vision of every kind. Indeed, by the 1850s, New York enjoyed an influx not just of trade but also of the merchants themselves, drawn, like August Belmont, by its seemingly unlimited opportunities. New York was different New York was the future.

Despite New York's almost unbridled growth and increasing diversity, its traditional mercantile elite still bestrode the core institutions of the city's economy. They were, for one, the oldest and most numerous segment of the city's economic elite. Ever since the arrival of the first settlers on Manhattan island in 1625, the city had prided itself on its trade. The merchant community thrived throughout the centuries, and by 1855, despite the rise of competing economic elites, they still constituted approximately 40 percent of all taxpayers assessed on personal and real wealth, above $10,000. They were not only the most numerous segment of the city's economic elite but also by far the wealthiest. This small group of about 3,600 merchant families owned roughly 28 percent of the city's total real and personal wealth. Even more dramatic was their concentration among the very richest New Yorkers: Merchants, auctioneers, brokers, and agents constituted an estimated 70 percent of the 300 wealthiest New Yorkers in 1845.

For these merchants, moreover, the 1850s were a golden age, a flowering of decades of intense investment and planning. By offering reliable shipping at competitive rates, by advancing credit to cash-hungry planters, by providing buyers with the greatest selection of goods available anywhere in the Americas, by supplying ready markets for huge quantities of agricultural commodities, by furnishing legal expertise, and by arranging insurance, these merchants had turned themselves into a vital link between producers and customers in a new nation building its transportation, communication, and banking facilities. The ships that regularly left New York for ports close and far, the canals and railroads that radiated from the city, and the market information that traveled through its newspapers and telegraphs further solidified their position. The ever-expanding cotton kingdom, and the slave-labor system that produced it, remained the primary engine of profits for merchants as it had since the early nineteenth century.

Indeed, it was, above all, New York's intense commitment to cotton that helped it decisively leave Philadelphia, Baltimore, and Boston behind.

Despite their long history in New York and their privileged position in the urban, national, and international economy, the world of these merchants remained challenging, risky, and volatile, demanding great vigilance. They constantly needed to adapt to the rapid expansion and growing complexities of trade. In response, many of New York's merchants specialized their lines of business and diversified their investments. And they intensely cultivated social, cultural, and personal networks that were the bone and sinew of their businesses. While the 1850s were a decade for harvesting huge gains, they were also a decade of rapid and sometimes unsettling change.

Merchants made the most dramatic and consequential changes to their ways of doing business. By the 1850s, few New York merchants remained the generalists of an earlier generation who had traded in a wide range of goods and provided an integrated array of services. The increased volume of trade and competition forced them to specialize—by either commodity or function. At midcentury, some houses exclusively traded certain commodities such as cotton, whereas others provided services such as shipping or financing. This specialization was imprinted on the face of the city. While most merchant activity was concentrated in the southernmost area of Manhattan, different lines of business clustered on specific streets. Importers and shipping merchants located next to the port on South Street, commission merchants and wholesale grocers set up shop on Water Street and Front Street, jobbers and auctioneers concentrated their activities on Pearl Street, and large retailers erected their shopping emporiums on the lower reaches of Broadway. Specialization not only segregated merchant businesses from one another but also began to loosen the ideological and political ties that once had reliably held the merchant community together. It set a small but growing number of traders free from the political economy of Atlantic trade and, thus, free of the powerful dependence on slavery and low tariffs.

For a majority of the city's merchants, however, specialization meant ever tighter embrace with New York's traditional strength: the cotton trade. Cotton, the fuel of the industrial revolution, remained at the center of the city's trade relationships, and a growing number of merchants committed themselves to this line of business. Many New York traders made their fortunes buying cotton in the South, advancing credit to planters, and shipping the raw material to Liverpool and a few other European ports. The Leverich Brothers, for example, bought cotton and sugar in the South and exported them to Great Britain. Charles Morgan covered another aspect of the trade, running numerous ships between New York City and Charleston, New Orleans, and Texas ports. These and other merchants earned remarkable profits because their capital was so desperately needed in the South and because they had a hand in each step of the trade, most notably a virtual stranglehold on the regularly scheduled ships shuttling between northern, southern, and European ports. Even if cotton was shipped directly from New Orleans or Charleston to Europe and did not touch

New York, the city's merchants still profited from commissions, interest on loans, shipping charges, insurance payments, and, ultimately, the import of manufactured goods to the South.

Often associated with the cotton trade but soon transcending it in importance was the dry goods and hardware commerce. Merchants specializing in this line of business acquired manufactured goods from Europe and the United States and sold them to retailers in the South, the Northeast, and the expanding West. Many cotton-bearing ships returned from Liverpool with the fruits of British industry, especially such materials as textiles and iron, for which Britain's advanced factories lacked serious competition in the North American market. In 1860 alone, fully 904 ships disgorged European goods to New York warehouses; that is, on any given day, an average of nearly three ships arrived from Europe loaded with Manchester cloth, Sheffield iron, or Lyon silk. Once stevedores landed these goods, New York merchants disposed of them in a variety of ways. Auctioneers usually put dry goods under the hammer, to be sold to the city's numerous jobbers. Jobbers, in turn, delivered them wholesale to retailers all over the United States. Commission merchants, who, in contrast to the jobbers, never took ownership of the goods they traded, specialized in bulkier products, such as machines and iron rails. They also at times marketed textiles to retailers or to New York wholesalers.

Wholesalers played a particularly important role in the distribution of imported and domestic manufactured products. Their presence in such great numbers was another factor that set New York apart from all other American cities. These jobbers received shopkeepers from the most remote parts of the United States in their stores on Pearl Street, especially during the retailers' annual summer sojourn to the city. They offered their visitors the opportunity to stock up their entire stores in Manhattan, stressing the vast array of goods available and the convenient transportation of them back home.

For decades, a steady stream of southern customers had lavishly spent their cotton money with these New York City jobbers, further solidifying the merchants' links to the plantation economy of the South. By the 1850s, however, a trickle of retailers from the trans-Appalachian West had become a flood at their stores. Western commerce began in the 1850s to challenge the exalted role of trade with the South, a slow-moving shift whose political repercussions were only just being felt on the eve of the Civil War. This change was partly the result of the merchants' own exertions: Since 1825, the Erie Canal, built on their urging, had connected New York to western hinterlands, and by 1857, the canal was moving goods worth $218 million to and from the city. Merchants had also financed new railroad connections to complement the canal, and by 1853, the New York Central stretched all the way to Buffalo. These new links led to a rapid expansion of capitalist agriculture in the West. Farms, in turn, became new markets for manufactured goods, markets served by a swelling stream of western retailers pouring into the city. During the 1850s, moreover, the California gold rush created new business opportunities in the Pacific West. Some merchants saw bright opportunities for profit in this western trade: The firm of Schuyler,

Hartley, and Graham, for example, bought sporting guns and small arms in Europe and sold them in the West. Similarly, Isaac Sherman, who had migrated in 1854 from Buffalo to New York City, traded barrel staves in the West.

This transformation of the West also gave rise to a group of merchants who would specialize in the trade in wheat and corn. They purchased grains from rural store owners who had accepted provisions as payment by farmers. These merchants transported the grains to New York City and then sold them to the Caribbean, and to Europe, as well as to other places in the United States itself. So rapid was the increase in their line of business, that in 1851, the provision merchants founded the Produce Exchange to rationale and organize their trade.

Another group of traders specialized in long-distance trade. They sent ships to the remotest corners of the world—from India they bought tea, from China silk, and from Brazil rubber, exchanging it for American flour, textiles, and manufactured products such as carriages and furniture, as well as furs. Prominent among them was Abiel Abbot Low, owner of a fleet of ships, who imported tea and silk from the Far East, and George Griswold, who exported flour to the West Indies, from whence he imported rum and sugar. The expanding economy provided an ever-larger number of Americans with the resources to purchase these luxury goods from faraway places. And with the growing volume of trade, specialization became possible for long-distance merchants, despite the fact that their ships were in transit for many weeks.

If Abiel Abbot Low and George Griswold made their fortunes in trading with distant places, New Yorkers such as Alexander T. Stewart and Rowland Macy understood that money was to be made by selling at retail to the new metropolis. They opened up gigantic shopping emporiums with an unmatched variety of goods, at a stroke capturing the imagination and pocketbooks of well-off consumers, who traditionally had shopped at a host of small retailers. Alexander T. Stewart launched this revolution in the city's retail culture when he opened A. T. Stewart's, his large "marble palace," in 1846. He was emulated twelve years later by Rowland Macy, whose store would eventually advertise itself as the largest department store in the world. In addition to New York's huge urban market, visitors flocked to their stores to acquire the goods that would make them look "smart" upon returning to their home towns.

Whereas in the 1850s some merchants specialized in a limited number of products such as tea or cotton, or concentrated on relationships that involved mostly one section of the United States, others sensed an opportunity to diversify into growing auxiliary segments of the merchant economy. The most important of these was banking, both the American branches of European houses and a growing number of domestic banks. This shift from the world of trading goods to the world of finance came easily since one of the central functions of merchants had always been to advance credit. Merchants' willingness to extend credit to farmers for crops not yet harvested and to traders for goods not yet sold was the keystone of New York's booming economy. The nation's hub for goods thus also became the nation's center for the trade in money. With the first commercial bank having been founded in 1784, New York dominated the nation's banking industry by 1830 and expanded rapidly, especially after the closure of the Second Bank of the United States in 1836.

Earlier in the century, general merchants had supplied the bulk of this credit. By the 1850s, however, banks had taken on this role. The most important innovation of banks was to allow merchants to discount promissory notes, and thereby considerably enlarge the pool of capital they could lend. If a merchant, for example, delivered dry goods to a South Carolina retailer and was paid with a ninety-days note, he could take this note to a bank and have it discounted, receiving the face value of the note, less interest for ninety days. As the flow of trade into New York surged to record levels, demand for capital and banking services expanded proportionately. In 1851 alone, twelve new banks opened their doors in Manhattan, and of the fifty-four banks conducting business in 1858, merchants had founded twenty-eight in the previous eight years. Together, these institutions controlled fully one-fifth of the banking capital in the United States.

A growing number of New York merchants found banking so profitable that they ceased merchandising. Six percent of those New Yorkers who paid taxes on assets of more than $10,000 in 1856 engaged primarily in banking and insurance. On average they were the richest New Yorkers, their real and personal wealth averaging $59,580, compared to the typical merchant's $39,350.

Although an unprecedented share of the capital fueling the growth of banking was generated domestically, during the 1850s New York's banks directed primarily British and Continental capital into American agriculture and trade. Fittingly, the two most important bankers of the city were the chief agents for European capital: George Cabot Ward of London's Baring Brothers and August Belmont of the house of Rothschild. They provided their respective houses access to American investment opportunities, as well as market information, shaping the immense flow of French, British, and to some degree German capital into the up-and-coming American economy.

The Hard Quest for Quick Riches in California

EDWARD DOLNICK

IN AMERICA IN THE mid-1800s, everyone knew that two laws governed the world. First, the path to success was long and difficult; the race was not to the swift but to the diligent, who collected their pennies day after day. Second, calamity came in countless guises and swooped down without warning. Jobs, savings, and homes could vanish overnight. In the Panic of 1837, a forerunner of the Great Depression, meat doubled in price; so did flour. Nearly half the banks in the country failed. President Martin Van Buren, who rejected any efforts by the government to ease the crisis as "effeminate indulgence," came to be known as Martin Van Ruin. In eastern cities, one man in three was unemployed, and crowds of rioters shouted, "Bread! Bread! Bread!" Tens of thousands of hungry, homeless New Yorkers wandered the city's streets.

What no one in the 1840s knew—because no one had ever experienced such a thing—was that life-changing, fantastic-as-a-fairytale good news could arrive just as suddenly as disaster. Then, in December, 1848, came the most startling message imaginable. In far-off California, the president of the United States proclaimed, *gold had fallen from the sky!* Hesitant to believe at first, Americans eventually gathered their nerve and gave way to hope.

Most people had heard of fortunes won and lost, in commercial investments or in real estate speculation, but only a handful of wheeler-dealers played those heady games. For ordinary Americans, the ecstatic talk of gold and sudden riches was new and shocking and overwhelmingly exciting. They had dreamed and fantasized, of course, but those dreams had always been refuges from real life, not genuine possibilities. Now this!

THE GOLD-SEEKERS AT THE jumping-off towns set out eagerly, shoving their way into line for a ferry across the Missouri. "The crowd at the ferry is a dense mass fighting for precedence to cross," Joseph Bruff wrote on May 5, 1849. "Two teamsters killed each other on one of these occasions, with pistols, at the head of their wagons."

Once they had made it across the river, the travelers looked around to get their bearings. With the United States and all its comforts now behind them, they confronted for the first time just what they had volunteered for. "Our first campfire was lighted in Indian Territory, which spread in one unbroken, unnamed waste from the Missouri River to the border line of California," Luzena Wilson wrote. "Here commenced my terrors."

Wilson's terrors, like those of nearly all the emigrants, had mostly to do with Indians, who would no doubt swoop down in the night, tomahawks clutched in their teeth. "I had read and heard whole volumes of their bloody deeds," Wilson wrote, "the massacre of harmless white men, torturing helpless women, carrying away captive innocent babes." Tales of Indian depravity had been a staple of American literature from the earliest colonial days, as popular as crime thrillers today or pulp novels a few generations ago. Readers shivered at first-person narratives of kidnaps, desperate escapes, and tortures. "Gracious God! What a scene presented itself to me! My child scalped and slaughtered ... my husband scalped and weltering in his blood," Mary Kinnan wrote in one of countless similar narratives, in 1795.

As the years passed, the tales grew less earnest and more lurid, the blood and gore ever more explicit. By the 1840s, readers across America put their work aside at day's end, sank into a favorite chair, and settled down with *Captivity and Sufferings of Mrs. Mason, with an Account of the Massacre of her Youngest Child* or perhaps *Indian Atrocities: Affecting and Thrilling Anecdotes.*

No sooner had Luzena Wilson begun her journey and crossed the Missouri River than she found herself surrounded by two hundred of the red fiends.

Darkness fell and she cowered in fear. "I felt my children the most precious in the wide world, and I lived in an agony of dread that first night.... I, in the most tragi-comic manner, sheltered my babies with my own body, and felt imaginary arrows pierce my flesh a hundred times during the night." Finally the sun rose, and the Wilson party set off through Indian country. "I strained my eyes with watching, held my breath in suspense, and all day long listened for the whiz of bullets or arrows."

The second night proved as harrowing as the first. Wilson saw a wagon train camped nearby and begged her husband to ask if they could all travel together, for protection. The train had a grand name—the Independence Company—and a splendid appearance, with sturdy, mule-drawn wagons, banners flapping in the wind, and a brass band tootling away.

Mason Wilson pleaded on his wife's behalf. No dice. "They sent back word they 'didn't want to be troubled with women and children; they were going to California,'" Luzena recalled years later, still indignant at the memory. "My anger at their insulting answer roused my courage, and my last fear of Indians died a sudden death. 'I am only a woman,' I said, 'but I am going to California, too, and without the help of the Independence Company!'"

Luzena and Mason and their small wagon train trudged along, on their own. The Independence Company raced ahead, their speedy mules vastly outpacing the Wilsons' oxen. Luzena watched them vanish in the distance.

They would meet again.

No attack came. The Indians turned out to be "friendly, of course," Luzena remarked later, and had nothing more dire in mind than trading ponies for liquor and tobacco. (This would not always be the case. In the 1840s, Indians could still look at the tiny trickle of westward-moving whites as more a novelty than a threat, and as a source of trade goods besides. By the 1850s, the trickle of outsiders had grown to a flood, and Indian indifference had shaded into hostility. Even so, the emigrants killed more Indians than the other way round. By the tally of the historian John Unruh, a renowned scholar of westward migration, Indians killed 362 emigrants in the years between 1840 and 1860, and emigrants killed 426 Indians.)

The emigrants' terror drained away when they saw they would not be attacked. No longer in a panic, they found themselves perplexed and intrigued instead, adrift in an unfamiliar landscape. The long, open, empty views lured them but spooked them, too. "The timber continued four or five miles," Alonzo Delano wrote, "when it ceased, and the eye rested on a broad expanse of rolling prairie, till the heavens and earth seemed to meet, on one vast carpet of green."

They had yet to reach the true prairie, but this blankness was dismaying enough. Delano scanned the horizon for something familiar to grab onto. Nothing. "In vain did the eye endeavor to catch a glimpse of some farmhouse, some cultivated field, some herd of cattle cropping the luxuriant grass in the distance; yet no sign of civilization met the eye. All was still and lonely, and I had an overwhelming feeling of wonder and surprise at the vastness and silence of the panorama."

Nearly all the emigrants, used to forests and fields, struck a similar bewildered note. "Now that we are over [the Missouri], and the wide expanse of the plains is before us," wrote a woman named Margaret Frink, "we feel like mere specks on the face of the earth." After another five days' travel, her awe began to shift toward distaste. Other eyes might have found the vista enticing—rolling hills, a dozen varieties of grass in countless shades of green, darting birds, flitting butterflies, wildflowers—but the emigrants saw only emptiness. "We left all forests behind us at the Missouri River," Frink went on. "Here the whole earth, as far as the eye can reach, is naked and bare except that a thin growth of grass partly hides the sandy ground."

The panorama soon grew oppressive. The worst feature of the trip's first several hundred miles was that the scenery scarcely changed, and the prospect of crossing that infinite expanse came to seem a mockery. The emigrants found themselves in the predicament of swimmers who had never seen the ocean but had nonetheless vowed to cross it.

Some lost heart and turned around. "Gobacks," as they were called, numbered perhaps several hundred altogether. Emigrants on their way west routinely ran into their discouraged, eastbound counterparts. Joseph Banks, part of an Ohio company of gold-seekers with the jaunty name Buckeye Rovers, noted in his diary that he had met a man who had decided to head back home. "Says he can't go all the way," Banks wrote. "Has money enough; loves his wife more than gold."

Still, considering the hordes heading west, the number of those retreating was minuscule. For most travelers, life at this early stage of the journey retained a quality of cheerful chaos that reality had not yet managed to undo. Wagons carried brash names like *Wild Yankee* or *Gold-Hunter* or *Helltown Greasers* painted on the canvas, or high-toned ones like *Pilgrim's Progress—California Edition.* So many wagons flew the Stars and Stripes that, in camp at night, the emigrants looked more like an army than a party of civilians.

But no army had this improvised, helter-skelter feel. "Every" mode of travel that ever was invented since the departure of the Israelites has been resorted to this year," one gold-seeker wrote, and the mood in the early days on the road was more akin to that of a parade than an expedition. "Some drive mules," Israel Lord wrote, "some oxen, some horses. All kinds of vehicles are en route for California—buggies, carts, boats on wheels, arks."

These misadventures would have delighted many stay-at-homes, who envied and mocked the gold-seekers in roughly equal measure. The genteel and hugely popular *Godey's Lady's Book*—the magazine's editor was the author of "Mary Had a Little Lamb"—spoke for many who could scarcely abide the '49ers. Thousands were going to California, scolded *Godey's,* "who have never dug a rood of garden in their lives, and never slept out of the home."

To spoof the gold rush greenhorns, *Godey's* created a character named Jeremiah Saddlebags and made him the star of one of the first comic strips. A city dweller to his core, Jeremiah has not the least notion of what life on the road and in the mines will demand. He prepares for the journey by carefully selecting the white gloves and silk tie that best set off his appearance. (He spoils the effect somewhat by shaving his head, to thwart any Indians who might be after his scalp.) His palms are soft, his muscles puny.

And, as if he were not already ludicrous enough to make *Godey's* readers roll their eyes, Jeremiah was a "low-paid clerk." So were a great many of his real-life counterparts on the road to California. Small wonder. In the mid-1800s, a clerk's work was excruciatingly dull. The most soul-sucking cubicle job in today's world hardly compares. Offices had no typewriters, no adding machines, and, worst of all, no carbon paper or copiers. What they had were clerks with quill pens. Men in the nineteenth century wore out their lives in paperwork, copying towers of wills and mortgages by hand in duplicate and triplicate. (In his great story "Bartleby, the Scrivener"—a scrivener was a human copying machine—Melville describes poor, forlorn Bartleby "copying by sunlight and by candlelight ... silently, palely, mechanically.")

Any spirited person sentenced to such a fate would yearn to break free. The main virtue of "the servile trade of quill driving," as one clerk described his job, was that most of the alternatives were just as bad. In Wisconsin, teen-aged Lucius Fairchild could hardly bear to think that he was stuck behind the counter of his father's store, "showing rags to the ladies of Madison." Rural life was no better. In Mark Twain's Hannibal and in countless towns like it, "the day was a dead and empty thing," despite all the era's talk of progress. The sun beat down, a fly buzzed against a window, the town drunk rolled over, life drowsed on.

Even without the lure of gold, countless young men would have filled their days with dreams of adventure and a change of scenery. But there *was* gold, and it proved almost irresistible. No one has ever matched Mark Twain in capturing his peers' desperation to get away. A few years too young to venture off to California himself, he watched, yearningly, as gold-seekers on their way west poured through Hannibal in 1849. More tantalizing still, eighty Hannibal residents joined the exodus and set off, too. For young Sam Clemens and thousands of young men like him, the notions of travel, and the West, and striking it rich set the head spinning.

"I was young, and I envied my brother," he wrote later, when Orion Clemens finagled a job as secretary to the governor of the newly created Nevada Territory. "He was going to travel! I never had been away from home, and that word 'travel' had a seductive charm for me. Pretty soon he would be hundreds and hundreds of miles away on the great plains and deserts, and among the mountains of the Far West, and would see buffaloes and Indians, and prairie dogs, and antelopes, and have all kind of adventures, and maybe get hanged or scalped, and have ever such a fine time, and write home and tell us all about it, and be a hero and he would see the gold mines and the silver mines, and maybe go about of an afternoon when his work was done, and pick up two or three pailfuls of shining slugs, and nuggets of gold and silver on the hillside. And by and by he would become very rich, and return home by sea, and be able to talk as calmly about San Francisco and the ocean, and 'the isthmus' as if it was nothing of any consequence to have seen those marvels face to face. What I suffered in contemplating his happiness, pen cannot describe."

There was no good way to travel to California, but there was a choice of bad ways. Those who lived inland immediately thought of wagons drawn by animals. Near the coast, thousands upon thousands opted for travel by ship. Newspaper editors and guidebook authors hurried to lay out the options. Maps showed the various sea routes from New York to San Francisco and explained their pros and cons.

To travel by way of Cape Horn, around South America, was fairly safe but maddeningly slow. The route covered nearly fifteen thousand miles—five times the overland distance—and took five months. Passengers suffered through a long, storm-racked passage around the Horn and then a mind-numbing stretch of motionless torpor in the tropical heat off the west coast of South America, where the sun beat down and the winds failed and ships wallowed in place.

To go by way of Panama was faster but riskier and more expensive. You sailed to Panama, then traveled some sixty miles overland, and completed your journey on a second ship. The land leg was the hardest. One mapmaker remarked matter-of-factly that "the swamps, stagnant waters, reptiles etc. render walking across next to impossible." To sail to Mexico instead, and then cross overland to the Pacific coast, was faster still but even less inviting, especially bearing in mind the lingering hostility from the just-concluded Mexican-American War. "To prevent danger of being attacked by robbers through Mexico," the same mapmaker advised, "persons should go in parties of 50 or more."

A journey by sea had considerable advantages over a trip by wagon, though both took about five months. A shipboard traveler could start at once, for one thing, rather than wait for spring to come to the prairie. In a race, this was no small factor. And, as a fare-paying passenger, you would have little to do for much of the journey but pass the time while someone else carried you toward your goal. The overland emigrants, trudging their way along step by weary step, could only dream of such luxury.

Shipbuilders and shipowners raced to capitalize on gold fever. With hordes of passengers thrusting their money at anyone who would carry them westward, California-bound ships jammed every port. A few were elegant affairs, like the new and roomy *Edward Everett* out of Boston, named for Harvard's president, which boasted a library and a troupe of musicians who performed each evening. Many were converted whalers whose opportunistic owners saw more profit in hauling gold-struck passengers than in hunting fifty-ton beasts with hand-flung harpoons. A fair number were ancient, barely seaworthy relics that had been built to carry cargo. Passengers shoved their way aboard these floating wrecks only to find themselves crammed into the dark, dank space between decks. There they slept in makeshift bunks and gulped for fresh air at hastily cut hatches.

From around the world, ships bound for California carried hordes of passengers every bit as hopeful, and as ignorant and frustrated, … The gold rush was primarily an American story, but no nation found itself indifferent to California's news. Gold-seekers from Australia, Chile, Mexico, France, England, and China swarmed to the diggings, pouring into California as though spilled from a giant scoop. The Americans and the foreigners had overlapping but not quite identical motives. By and large, Americans felt *pulled* to California, drawn by dreams of freedom and riches. Foreigners felt *pushed* from home, shoved out the door by war, hunger, and economic hardship.

In 1848 and 1849 the world was falling apart. Australia had been hit by a depression, China by famine and seething political unrest, Europe by a series of devastatingly bad harvests. Europeans had dubbed the decade the Hungry Forties, as they watched the price of bread and potatoes, the staple foods of the poor, soar out of reach. "The old year ended in scarcity," a Prussian minister wrote in January, 1847, "and the new one opens in starvation." Food riots broke out in France, Italy, Germany, and Holland. Angry peasants broke into granaries and attacked merchants, landowners, and tax collectors. As the cost of food shot ever upward, people had little or no money left to spend on nonessentials, and the economy spiraled farther and farther downward. Thousands upon thousands of workers and small craftsmen lost their jobs, in an era when government help for the poor scarcely existed.

For a brief time, it looked as if the grim story in Europe would have a glorious outcome. Democracy would supplant monarchy; freedom and equality would overcome feudalism and oppression. The year 1848 saw revolution break out in one European country after another, most dramatically in France. In February crowds of demonstrators barricaded the streets of Paris with cobblestones. Shouting "Vive la réforme!" and singing "La Marseillaise," they brandished looted rifles and waved shards of iron wrenched from gates and railings. The king's soldiers opened fire; the revolutionaries fought back. Within weeks, King Louis Philippe fled to England. Ecstatic crowds swarmed into the abandoned palace and jostled for a turn sitting on the throne. In the same month, February, 1848, Karl Marx published his *Communist Manifesto*. "Let the ruling classes tremble at a Communist revolution," he thundered.

It was not to be. The revolutions of 1848 first raised hopes and then dashed them, as if a brief, giddy spring had suddenly transformed itself into a long, gray autumn. Across Europe reformers and radicals found that they had succeeded mainly in shaking the old regime out of its complacency. The economy continued to stagger, the same tired leaders clung to power, and the heady talk of liberty and workers' rights vanished into memory. With few prospects at home—even worse, with yesterday's jubilant visions turned to ash—countless Europeans clutched at the news of gold and made their way to California.

 # FURTHER READING

Sven Beckert, *Empire of Cotton: A Global History* (2014).

Stuart W. Bruchey, *Enterprise: The Dynamic Economy of a Free People* (1990).

Jon Gjerde, *The Minds of the West: Ethnocultural Evolution in the Rural Middle West, 1830–1917* (1997).

Joan M. Jensen, *Loosening the Bonds: Mid-Atlantic Farm Women, 1750–1850* (1986).

Susan Lee Johnson, *Roaring Camp: The Social World of the California Gold Rush* (2000).

John F. Kasson, *Civilizing the Machine: Technology and Republican Values in America, 1776–1900* (1976).

Bruce Laurie, *Artisans into Workers: Labor in Nineteenth-Century America* (1997).

Kerby A. Miller, *Emigrants and Exiles: Ireland and the Irish Exodus to North America* (1985).

William Moran, *The Belles of New England: The Women of the Textile Mills and the Families Whose Wealth They Wove* (2004).

Jean Pfaelzer, *Driven Out: The Forgotten War against Chinese Americans* (2008).

Christine Stansell, *City of Women: Sex and Class in New York City, 1789–1860* (1986).

Peter Way, *Common Labour: Workers and the Digging of North American Canals 1780–1860* (1993).

Additional critical thinking activities and content are available in MindTap.

MindTap

MindTap is a fully online, highly personalized learning experience built upon Cengage Learning content. MindTap combines student learning tools—readings, multimedia, activities, and assessments—into a singular Learning Path that guides students through the course.

CHAPTER 12

Agriculture and Slavery

in the South

The cotton gin (short for "cotton engine") was a very simple device that had revolutionary implications. Patented by Eli Whitney in 1794, it was able to remove the seeds from short-staple cotton without damaging the fibers. Because short-staple cotton, unlike its long-staple counterpart, did not require wet, semitropical climates, it could be grown throughout much of the antebellum south. The cotton gin, then, played a central role in reinvigorating the southern economy and solidifying the slave system. Already by 1800, cotton and slavery together were spreading westward. Between 1815 and 1840, cotton output jumped from 200,000 to 1.35 million bales, each of which weighed four hundred pounds. Another cotton boom began in 1849, when output reached 2.85 million bales, and lasted until 1860, when 4.8 million bales were produced. Southern planters confidently proclaimed that "cotton was king."

By 1860, almost four million people lived and worked as slaves on a belt of land stretching from Virginia into Texas. Slavery and race, moreover, influenced almost every aspect of southern society. Although most white people considered slave owning a source of economic mobility and social status and gave political deference to the wealthy planters, more than two-thirds of white families in the region owned no slaves. These non-slaveowning whites often found themselves pushed off the better land by affluent cotton, sugar, or rice entrepreneurs. Thus slavery also had its costs for many white people. Although not all black people in the south were enslaved, the "free people of color," some quarter of a million people, found their position in southern society increasingly circumscribed. As the nineteenth century wore on and the status of slave increasingly came to be equated with African ancestry, "free people of color" faced growing legal disadvantages. The rise of the cotton south, in sum, created a curious combination of opulence and misery.

Southerners justified, condemned, and accommodated themselves to the slave system in a variety of ways. Many white southerners became increasingly aware that slavery was being criticized as a system of labor whose time had passed. As Americans in the north and Europeans worked to abolish the system, the white south both developed ideologies that justified slavery and increased its vigilance over enslaved people. The master class presented themselves as custodians of the welfare of a grateful and harmonious slave society. Some went so far as to argue that slavery was "a positive good" rather than simply a necessary evil. All societies contained a working class, they argued, and enslaved people were better off than the "wage slaves" of the north because the slaveowner truly cared for his people. As apologists for slavery made these arguments, however, the south also developed increasingly harsh "slave codes" that reflected a growing fear of slave revolts incited by abolitionists. The North Carolina law prohibiting slaves to read and write, for example, contended that literacy "has a tendency to excite dissatisfaction in their minds."

In fact, laws against literacy were one of many factors that excited dissatisfaction among slaves. After toiling from sunrise to sundown, slaves were nonetheless vulnerable to complaints—supplemented by physical punishment—that they had not worked well enough. If white women could object to slavery because of illicit relationships between their men and their slaves, slave women were obviously at even greater risk. Perhaps most disheartening was the fact that an imperious master might separate slaves from their loved ones through sale.

Slaves retaliated in their own way. They used the paternalist ideology to illustrate the inherent contradictions between the ideal of a benevolent master and the reality of cruelty in slave life. Slaves also developed strategies within their own community to temper the cruelties of enslavement. The family and local neighborhoods served as arenas in which children were socialized. Christian belief likewise was a powerful resource that simultaneously allowed slaves to look to a better life after death and criticize the system of slavery in which they were set. How one might be both a slaveowner and a Christian was a telling question that few could adequately answer.

QUESTIONS TO THINK ABOUT

How might southern apologists for slavery have used the northern "wage slave" discussed in the last chapter to justify slavery? To what extent do you agree with this argument? How did slaves use religious belief and kinship to temper their plight? Did this strategy play into the hands of slaveholders? Did white women benefit from slavery or suffer because of it? How were non-slaveholding whites and "free people of color" affected by the institution of slavery?

DOCUMENTS

These documents illustrate the deep imprint that slavery and plantation agriculture made on southern society. Document 1 is a North Carolina law that prohibits teaching slaves to read or write. Slave revolts and knowledge of the growing abolitionist movement in the north, many white southerners feared, would be furthered through literacy. The next two documents relate everyday life and labors for whites and blacks in the south. Document 2 recounts the experiences of a small farm owner, while document 3 focuses upon a much larger cotton plantation. Document 4 is an account by a physician that describes certain diseases that are peculiar to African Americans, such as running away. For many enslaved people, running away was in actuality both painful and liberating. In document 5, one woman writes to her husband of her distress in slavery and the pains of family separation. Document 6 is a celebration of the white yeoman farmer by a white southerner who argues that non-slaveholding whites nonetheless support slavery. In document 7, Harriet Jacobs describes her trials as a young woman living in slavery. Jacobs argues that female slaves were in particular jeopardy because of the actions of powerful male slaveowners. Whereas Jacobs scolds white mistresses who did not protect female slaves, Mary Boykin Chestnut's diary in document 8 provides us with the perspective of a slave mistress who comes close to blaming women slaves for making the plantation similar to a harem.

1. A North Carolina Law Prohibits Teaching Slaves to Read or Write, 1831

Whereas the teaching of slaves to read and write, has a tendency to excite dissatisfaction in their minds, and to produce insurrection and rebellion, to the manifest injury of the citizens of this State: Therefore, *Be it enacted by the General Assembly of the State of North Carolina, and it is hereby enacted by the authority of the same,* That any free person, who shall hereafter teach, or attempt to teach, any slave within the State to read or write, the use of figures excepted, or shall give or sell to such slave or slaves any books or pamphlets shall be liable to indictment in any court of record in this State having jurisdiction thereof, and upon conviction, shall, at the discretion of the court, if a white man or woman, be fined not less than one hundred dollars, nor more than two hundred dollars, or imprisoned; and if a free person of color, shall be fined, imprisoned, or whipped, at the discretion of the court, not exceeding thirty nine lashes, nor less than twenty lashes.

Be it further enacted, That if any slave shall hereafter teach, or attempt to teach, any other slave to read or write, the use of figures excepted, he or she may be carried before any justice of the peace and on conviction thereof, shall be sentenced to receive thirty nine lashes on his or her bare back.

2. Ferdinand L. Steel Records Daily Life as a Yeoman, 1838–1841

Sunday, June 3d, 1838
    Went to Meeting Mr. Fitzgerald preach a fine sermon.

Monday, June 4th, 1838
    We run around cotton with both ploughs.

"A North Carolina Law Forbidding the Teaching of Slaves to Read and Write" (1831), as reprinted in *A History of the U.S.: Sourcebook and Index*, Joy Hakim (New York: Oxford University Press, 1999), 108.

Excerpts from Ferdinand L. Steel Diary, in the Steel Family Papers, #4504. These documents can be found in the Southern Historical Collection, Wilson Library, The University of North Carolina at Chapel Hill.

Tuesday, June 5th, 1838

Finished running around cotton and commenced to work in corn. Sam'l chopped through cotton. We have been something like a month almost exclusively [in] the cotton. And I find it has hurt our corn very much. I do not think that it is a good plan to depend so much on cotton; it takes up all our time; we can find no time scarcely to do the smallest business. I at this time think that we had better raise corn and let cotton alone. We are to[o] weak handed; we had better raise small grain and corn and let cotton alone; raise corn and keep out of debt and we will have no necessity of raising cotton. Another thing it makes us work to excess as well as do many other things to excess. Look at this by and by.

Monday, September 17, 1838

We went to work on the road; rained very hard. I got very wet. This day is my birthday; this day closes my 25th year. My life is thus prolonged. Bless the Lord, may I set out afresh this coming year to love & serve the Lord more faithfully....

Tuesday, September 25, 1838

I picked out 103 lbs. of Cotton. Sam'l picked out 100 lbs. Fine weather....

Saturday, September 29, 1838

We gathered some corn, about 20 bushels; hauled wood. I went to Grenada & bought 2 pr. of fine shoes. One pair for Mar & the other for myself. Bought also 2 dols worth coffee, $ 1 worth nails....

Friday, March 22, 1839

A few Remarks on my Present manner of life, which will do for me to look at in after days. I arise regularly at 5 o'clock in the morning. After the rest of the family have arisen we have Prayers. I then feed 2 horses and with the assitance of m[y] Brother milk 3 cows. From then to Breakfast I jenerally do some little job about the house. After breakfast I go to my regular work which is cultivating the soil, and work untill 12 o'clock at which time I come into dinner. Rest jennerally 2 hours, during which time I dine, then Pray to God and endeavor to improve my mind by some useful study. At 2 o'clock I again repair to work, and work untill sun down. I then come in, feed horses, milk Cows, and the days work is done. I sup and then I have a few hours for study. At 9 o'clock we have Prayers, and then we all retire to Rest. This is the manner in which my time is spent. My life is one of toil, but blessed be God that it is as well with me as it is. I confess with shame, that when I look ahead, I am prone to give way to anxiety. But I truly desire and humbly Pray that I may be anxious for nothing. I cannot add one cubit to my statu[r] e by taking thought. When I look back on my past life I can see great cause of Gratitude to my heavenly father. He hath hitherto helped me, and I will endeavor hearafter to trust in him.

Wednesday, July 28, 1841

It is, undoubtedly, the Dryest time of any I have ever seen, Cotton suffering greatly for the want of rain, Corn crops will be cut short, in this neighborhood. What would now be my case, if I had no other Comfort, but that which is derived from the acquisition of Temporal good? It would be a pitiful case. But blessed be God, I am enabled to believe, that he does all things Well, and although I suffer loss in temporal things; I believe my soul prospers, & grows in the love of God.

Wednesday, August 4, 1841

Our Camp Meeting Commenced, and continued until Tuesday 10th. We had a Blessed Time from the presence of the Lord. The Merciful Giver of all Good, not only blessed us spiritually, But he also Blessed us temporily. During the time, the long needed showers of Rain, were poured out on our thirsty land. A goodly number of Persons proffessed Religion, among which was one Sullivan who was reported to have been the most ungodly man in Yalobusha County. He had (contrary to the Rules of the meeting), brought two bottles of ardent Spirits. After he obtained Religion, on Some of his Companions saying, now he had got Religion [he] give them the liquor. He declared (It is said) I will never touch it again.

3. Cotton Planter Bennett Barrow Describes Life in Louisiana, 1838, 1839, 1841

September 18 Cloudy damp morning—some rain at noon, picking cotten since Breakfast—went driving with James Leak Dr Desmont and Sidney Flower, started two Fawns in my field, ran some time, dogs quit them.

19 Clear pleasant morning—62 Bales pressed last night—Cotten bend down verry much from wind on Sunday—between 90 & 100 Bales out in No— Went hunting in my field started 3 Deer. Killed a fine young Buck—Several joined me afterwards—went driving on the swamp—started a Deer dogs ran off—in coming out of the drive started a Bear, only one dog—he became too much frightened to do any thing ...

21 Verry Foggy morning—Com'enced hauling Cotten this morning—1st shipment—Bales will avreage 470 lbs upwards of 100 out in No 100 & 15 of 400, this time last year had out 125—25 behind last year, owing to the season— cotten more backward in opening—at first picking—never had Cotten picked more trashy than yesterday. And to day by dinner—some few picked badly— 5 sick & 2 children

22 Considerable rain before Breakfast, Appearance of a bad day—pressing— 4 sick—Caught Darcas with dirt in cotton bag last night, weighed 15 pounds— Tom Beauf picked badly yesterday morning Whiped him. few Cuts—left the field some time in the evening without his Cotten and have not seen him since—He is in the habit of doing so yearly, except last year Heavy rains during the day women spinning—trashing Cotten men & children—Tom B. showed himself— "sick"—Cotten picked since the storm looks verry badly—Cotten market opened

From *Plantation Life in the Florida Parishes of Louisiana*, 1836–1846, edited by Edwin Adams Davis.

this year at 13 & 13¾ cts—Bagging & cordage 20 & 24 and 8½ & 9 cts—
Porke from $ 16 to $ 24 a Barrel—Never com'ence hauling Cotten that it did'ent
rain—...

[*October*] *12* Clear verry cold morning—hands picked worse yesterday than they
have done this year, lowest avreage 157—picked in the morning—in the bottom
on L creek—rotten open long time—the same this morning—Whiped near half
the hands to day for picking badly & trashy Tom Beauf came up and put his
Basket down at the scales and it is the last I've seen of him—will Whip him
more than I ever Whip one, I think he deserves more—the second time he has
done so this year—light Frost yesterday and to day...

27 Clear warm—picking Gns—Dennis ran off yesterday—& after I had Whiped
him—hands picked verry light weight by dinner—complaint picking in Rank &
Rotten Cotten—4 sick—have out 270 Bales or upward of 400. certain 250 or upwards out in No by 1st of November. Will [be] at least 30 Bales ahead of last year....

1839
[*August*] *13* Morning cloudy—Bartley was not to be found last night' till late,
was not seen after 12. taken sick at Gns found in the night—& never saw hands
in better spirits, worked finely—Ginny Jerry has not been seen since Friday
morning last—has been shirkin for some time came to me Friday morning
sick—suspecting him Examined him found nothing the matter complaining of
pains & c. told him to go & work it off—he has concluded to woods it off—
cotten in Lower part Gns place improved verry much new land still doing well
old Land past recovery—owing I am certain to its having been broke up wet—
both an injury to the land Horses & negros to work in the mud & wet...

15 Morning cloudy sprinkle of rain this evening, started 5 scrapers old Land
above

16 Cloudy morning—Finished the roade last night—well done—never finished
as soon part or most of it worse than usual—negroes ... at the rascal in giving
them Whiskey & c. 5 scrapers running—2 putting up scaffolds—all others picking
cotten—was taken yesterday with violent pain in my right side in going to swamp
—had to stop & get a blister at Ruffins & c. I Bennet H. Barrow do certify that I the
said Bennet have got the meanest crop in this neighborhood & the meanest by far I
ever had—been absent too often—would not care how mean it was if I was not in
Debt—& last accounts from England verry unfavorable—two thirds of the people
must be ruined—should the times continue beyond this season...

20 Damp cloudy morning started Gins at Home yesterday picking to day at
Gns avreaged yesterday 176—picking as clean cotten as I ever saw—
Dr Desmont an Englishman has left here, verry strangely a villian no doubt—&
left me to pay between 10.000 & 16.000 for him—his uncommonly gentle-manly
manners—modesty & chastity caused me to be discerned by him—I've allways been
opposed to Yankey speculators coming out here to seek their fortunes, by marrying
or any thing else that suits their purpose—particular the D——proffessional
Preachers—stragling foreigners, are no better—sister Eliza here to day...

23 Clear verry warm—hands picking well—Avreaged 201 day before yesterday—picked 3 days at Gns 15 Bales—most ever picked there in Augst—Want rain very much—ground as dry as can be—cotten com'enced forming in the last 8 days verry fast, rain now & a late fall would make a verry fair crop—attempting to Learn James & John their book—had rather drive a Team of Mules—James 8 years old John 6—Johns looks one way & thinks another—more sickness for week past than I've had this season, bowel complaints & c....

28 Clear cool morning—more sickness yesterday & to day than I've had this season—avreaged two day 203—never saw a better crop than Turnbulls Home crop—my crop injured as much "I think" from being too thick as the drought...

November 6 ... Mrs Joor owes me from the 1st of this month $14727.23 not paying me the interest yearly—& nothing' till the End of 5 years—I will loose $1500 thus—interest—Each year added to the principle for 5 yrs will make 21559.30—upon the Amount she owes me dated 29 Oct. 1838 $13387.73, I wish all young persons knew What I've learnt of this world in the last 3 years—one thing marry a Daughter against the mothers will—hatred or dislike remains with her forever, & 99 out of a 100 think of nothing but self—corruption appears the order of the day—a corrupt govement makes corrupt people—Gnl Jackson 1st destroying the United S. Bank & then distributing the revenue among the State Bank inducing them to over issue—& this creating a spirit of speculation—not with the people but by the Banks themselves—through their agents buying up large bodies of Land & he then issued his Specie circular—that nothing but Gold & Silver would be taken for dues to the Government, caused a rush for Metals—Banks having over issued people borrowed largely—everything rose to an enormous price—& altogether fictitious—the consequence was the Banks were forced to stop specie paying—curtail money greatly depreciating—has caused the Whole country to be Bankrupt. We are forced in buying any thing not to give What it is worth in Gold & Silver—or What our money is worth here—but What it is worth to the trader in his country—an Excuse for them to add from 25 to 100 pr. ct above the usual rates you cannot buy a decent horse for less $200. 5 yr ago $200 bought the finest saddle horse & c. turning verry cold...

1841

July 17 Clear verry warm Returned from Woodville this morning, Caroline B. Joor was Married on 15th to James Flower jur, Received a note from Ruffin stating that several of my negros were implicated in an intended insurection on the 1st of August next. It seems from What he writes me, it was to have taken place Last March—mine are O Fill O Ben Jack Dennis & Demps—will go up to Robert J. B. to have them examined & c. six negros were found guilty in the first degree, it appears they were to meet at jno: Towles Gate and at Mr Turnbulls inheritance place, Leaders one of Robert J. Barrow one Bennet J. B. one of Towles one of C. Perceys one W. J. Forts & one of D. Turnbulls, none of mine were implicated farther than one of Robert J. B boys said he heard the names of the above mentioned & c. intend having an examination of the Whole plantation & the neighbourhood

19 Clear Verry Hot—Examined Mrs Stirlings negros Courtneys & my own yesterday found none of them concerned in the Expected insurection, Went to Judge Wades this morning, found several of his men concerned it. Dave Bonner the most & he was the Leder, Sent to Jail for trial...

16 Cloudy warm—Several of my negro's in returning off of the road Saturday night came through Ruffins Quarter he having the measles forbid their Returning that way. had them staked down all yesterday, several of them had killed a hog, found out the right ones, gave them all a severe Whipping, Ginney Jerry has been sherking about ever since Began to pick cotten. after Whipping him yesterday told him if ever he dodged about from me again would certainly shoot him. this morning at Breakfast time Charles came & told me that Jerry was about to run off. took my Gun found him in the Bayou behind the Quarter, shot him in his thigh—& c. raining all around

4. Samuel Cartwright, a Southern Doctor, Theorizes About the Peculiar Diseases of Slaves, 1851

1.—DISEASES AND PECULIARITIES OF THE NEGRO RACE.
By Dr. Cartwright of New-Orleans—(Concluded.)
DRAPETOMANIA, OR THE DISEASE CAUSING NEGROES TO RUN AWAY.

Drapetomania is from δραπέτης, a runaway slave, and μανια, *mad* or *crazy*. It is unknown to our medical authorities, although its diagnostic symptom, the absconding from service, is ... well known to our planters and overseers.... The cause, in the most of cases, that induces the negro to run away from service, is as much a disease of the mind as any other species of mental alienation, and much more curable, as a general rule. With the advantages of proper medical advice, strictly followed, this troublesome practice that many negroes have of running away, can be almost entirely prevented, although the slaves be located on the borders of a free state, within a stone's throw of the abolitionists....

To ascertain the true method of governing negroes, so as to cure and prevent the disease under consideration, we must go back to the Pentateuch, and learn the true meaning of the untranslated term that represents the negro race. In the name there given to that race, is locked up the true art of governing negroes in such a manner that they cannot run away. The correct translation of that term declares the Creator's will in regard to the negro; it declares him to be the submissive kneebender. In the anatomical conformation of his knees we see "*genu flexit*" written in his physical structure, being more flexed or bent, than any other kind of man. If the white man attempts to oppose the Deity's will, by trying to make the negro anything else than "*the submissive knee-bender*," (which the

Dr. Cartwright, "Diseases and Peculiarities of the Negro Race," *De Bow's Review*, 2 (September 1851): 331–332, 334–336.

Almighty declared he should be,) by trying to raise him to a level with himself, or by putting himself on an equality with the negro; or if he abuses the power which God has given him over his fellow-man, by being cruel to him, or punishing him in anger, or by neglecting to protect him from wanton abuses of his fellow-servants and all others, or by denying him the usual comforts and necessaries of life, the negro will run away; but if he keeps him in the position that we learn from the Scriptures he was intended to occupy, that is, the position of submission; and if his master or overseer be kind and gracious in his bearing towards him, without condescension, and at the same time ministers to his physical wants, and protects him from abuses, the negro is spell-bound, and cannot run away....

When left to himself, the negro indulges in his natural disposition to idleness and sloth, and does not take exercise enough to expand his lungs and to vitalize his blood, but dozes out a miserable existence in the midst of filth and uncleanliness, being too indolent, and having too little energy of mind to provide for himself proper food and comfortable lodging and clothing. The consequence is, that the blood becomes so highly carbonized and deprived of oxygen, that it not only becomes unfit to stimulate the brain to energy, but unfit to stimulate the nerves of sensation distributed to the body. A torpor and insensibility pervades the system; the sentient nerves distributed to the skin lose their feeling in so great a degree, that he often burns his skin by the fire he hovers over without knowing it, and frequently has large holes in his clothes, and the shoes on his feet burnt to a crisp, without having been conscious of when it was done. This is the disease called dysæsthesia....

The complaint is easily curable, if treated on sound physiological principles.... Any kind of labor will do that will cause full and free respiration in its performance, as lifting or carrying heavy weights, or brisk walking; the object being to expand the lungs by full and deep inspiration and expirations, thereby to vitalize the impure circulating blood by introducing oxygen and expelling carbon....

According to unaltered physiological laws, negroes, as a general rule to which there are but few exceptions, can only have their intellectual faculties awakened in a sufficient degree to receive moral culture and to profit by religious or other instructions, when under the compulsatory authority of the white man; because, as a general rule to which there are but few exceptions, they will not take sufficient exercise, when removed from the white man's authority, to vitalize and decarbonize their blood by the process of full and free respiration, that active exercise of some kind alone can effect....

... The dysæsthesia æthiopica adds another to the many ten thousand evidences of the fallacy of the dogma that abolitionism is built on; for here, in a country where two races of men dwell together, both born on the same soil, breathing the same air, and surrounded by the same external agents—liberty, which is elevating the one race of people above all other nations, sinks the other into beastly sloth and torpidity; and the slavery, which the one would prefer death rather than endure, improves the other in body, mind and morals; thus proving the dogma false, and establishing the truth that there is a radical, internal or physical difference between the two races, so great in kind, as to make what is wholesome and beneficial for the white man, as liberty, republican or free institutions, etc., not only unsuitable to the negro race, but actually poisonous to its happiness.

5. A Virginia Slave Woman Articulates Her Distress to Her Enslaved Husband, 1852

Charlottesville [VA] Oct 7th 1852

Dear Husband I write you a letter to let you know of my distress my master has sold albert to a trader on monday court day and myself and other child is for sale also and I want you to let hear from you very soon before next cort if you can I don't know when I dont want you to wait till chrismas I want you to tell dr Hamilton your master if either will buy me they can attend to it know and then I can go after wards I don't want a trader to get me they asked me if I had got any person to buy me and I told them no they told [took] me to the court houste too they never put me up a man buy the name of brady bought albert and is gone I don't kow whare they say he lives in scottesville my things is in several places some is in stannton and if I sould be sold I don't know what will be come of them I don't expect to meet with the luck to get that way till I am quite heart sick nothing more I am an ever will be your kind Wife Maria Perkins To Richard Perkins

6. Southern Author Daniel Hundley Robinson Depicts the White Yeoman Farmer, 1860

And of all the hardy sons of toil, in all free lands the Yeomen are most deserving of our esteem. With hearts of oak and thews of steel, crouching to no man and fearing no danger, these are equally bold to handle a musket on the field of battle or to swing their reapers in times of peace among the waving stalks of yellow grain....

Know, then, that the Poor Whites of the South constitute a separate class to themselves; the Southern Yeomen are as distinct from them as the Southern Gentleman is from the Cotton Snob. Certainly the Southern Yeoman are nearly always poor, at least so for as this world's goods are to be taken into the account. As a general thing they own no slaves; and even in case they do, the wealthiest of them rarely possess more than from ten to fifteen. But even when they are slaveholders, they seem to exercise but few of the rights of ownership over their human chattels, making so little distinction between master and man, that their

A Virginia Slave Woman Articulates Her Distress to her Enslaved Husband [Maria Perkins to Richard Perkins, 7 Oct. 1852, folder 47, box 3, U.B. Phillips Papers, Manuscripts and Archives, Yale University Library.]

D. R. Hundley, Esq., *Social Relations in Our Southern States* (New York: Henry B. Price, 1860), 192–193, 197, 219.

negroes invariably become spoiled, like so many rude children who have been unwisely spared the rod by the foolish guardians....

Again, should you go among the hardy yeomanry of Tennessee, Kentucky, or Missouri, whenever or wherever they own slaves (which in these States is not often the case) you will invariably see the negroes and their masters ploughing side by side in the fields; or bared to the waist, and with old-fashioned scythe [vying] with one another who can cut down the broadest swatch of yellow wheat, or of the waving timothy; or bearing the tall stalks of maize and packing them into the stout-built barn, with ear and fodder on, ready for the winter's husking. And when the long winter evenings have come, you will see blacks and whites sing, and shout, and husk in company, to the music of Ole Virginny reels played on a greasy fiddle by some aged Uncle Edward....

[T]he Southern Yeomanry are almost unanimously pro-slavery in sentiment. Nor do we see how any honest, thoughtful person can reasonably find fault with them on this account. Only consider their circumstances, negrophilist of the North, and answer truthfully; were you so situated would you dare to advocate emancipation? Were you situated as the Southern Yeoman are—humble in worldly position, patient delvers in the soil, daily earning your bread by the toilsome sweat of your own brows—would you be pleased to see four millions of inferior blacks suddenly raised from a position of vassalage, and placed upon an equality with yourselves? made the sharers of your toil, the equals and associates of your wives and children? You know you would not. Despite your maudlin affectation of sympathy in behalf of the Negro, you are yet inwardly conscious that you heartily despise the sotty African, and that you deny to even the few living in your own midst an equality of rights and immunities with yourselves.

7. Harriet Jacobs Deplores Her Risks in Being a Female Slave, 1861

During the first years of my service in Dr. Flint's family, I was accustomed to share some indulgences with the children of my mistress. Though this seemed to me no more than right, I was grateful for it, and tried to merit the kindness by the faithful discharge of my duties. But I now entered on my fifteenth year— a sad epoch in the life of a slave girl. My master began to whisper foul words in my ear. Young as I was, I could not remain ignorant of their import. I tried to treat them with indifference or contempt. The master's age, my extreme youth, and the fear that his conduct would be reported to my grandmother, made him bear this treatment for many months. He was a crafty man, and resorted to many means to accomplish his purposes. Sometimes he had stormy, terrific ways, that made his victims tremble; sometimes he assumed a gentleness that he thought must surely subdue.... He peopled my young mind with unclean images, such as only a vile monster could think of. I turned from him with disgust and hatred.

Harriet Jacobs, *The Trials of Girlhood* (1861), as reprinted in *Our Nation's Archive*, ed. Erik Bruun and Jay Crosby (New York: Black Dog and Leventhal Publishers, 1999). 291–293.

But he was my master. I was compelled to live under the same roof with him—where I saw a man forty years my senior daily violating the most sacred commandments of nature. He told me I was his property; that I must be subject to his will in all things.... No matter whether the slave girl be as black as ebony or as fair as her mistress. In either case, there is no shadow of law to protect her from insult, from violence, or even from death.... The mistress, who ought to protect the helpless victim, has no other feelings towards her but those of jealousy and rage. The degradation, the wrongs, the vices that grow out of slavery, are more than I can describe. They are greater than you would willingly believe. Surely, if you credited one half the truths that are told you concerning the helpless millions suffering in this cruel bondage, you at the north would not help to tighten the yoke. You surely would refuse to do for the master, on your own soil, the mean and cruel work which trained bloodhounds and the lowest class of whites do for him at the south....

I once saw two beautiful children playing together. One was a fair white child; the other was her slave, and also her sister. When I saw them embracing each other, and heard their joyous laughter, I turned sadly away from the lovely sight. I foresaw the inevitable blight that would fall on the little slave's heart. I knew how soon her laughter would be changed to sighs. The fair child grew up to be a still fairer woman. From childhood to womanhood her pathway was blooming with flowers, and overarched by a sunny sky. Scarcely one day of her life had been clouded when the sun rose on her happy bridal morning.

How had those years dealt with her slave sister, the little playmate of her childhood? She, also, was very beautiful; but the flowers and sunshine of love were not for her. She drank the cup of sin, and shame, and misery, whereof her persecuted race are compelled to drink.

In view of these things, why are ye silent, ye free men and women of the north? Why do your tongues falter in maintenance of the right? Would that I had more ability! But my heart is so full, and my pen is so weak! There are noble men and women who plead for us, striving to help those who cannot help themselves. God bless them! God give them strength and courage to go on! God bless those, every where, who are laboring to advance the cause of humanity!

8. Southerner Mary Chestnut Describes Her Hatred of Slavery from a White Woman's View, 1861

I wonder if it be a sin to think slavery a curse to any land. Men and women are punished when their masters and mistresses are brutes, not when they do wrong. Under slavery, we live surrounded by prostitutes, yet an abandoned woman is sent out of any decent house. Who thinks any worse of a Negro or mulatto woman for being a thing we can't name? God forgive us, but ours is a monstrous system, a wrong and an iniquity! Like the patriarchs of old, our men live all in

Mary Boykin Chestnut, A Diary from Dixie (1861), ed. Ben Ames Williams (Boston: Houghton Mifflin, 1949), 21–22, 122–123, 162.

one house with their wives and their concubines; and the mulattoes one sees in every family partly resemble the white children. Any lady is ready to tell you who is the father of all the mulatto children in everybody's household but her own. Those, she seems to think, drop from the clouds. My disgust sometimes is boiling over. Thank God for my country women, but alas for the men! They are probably no worse than men everywhere, but the lower their mistresses, the more degraded they must be....

I hate slavery. You say there are no more fallen women on a plantation than in London, in proportion to numbers; but what do you say to this? A magnate who runs a hideous black harem with its consequences under the same roof with his lovely white wife, and his beautiful and accomplished daughters? He holds his head as high and poses as the model of all human virtues to these poor women whom God and the laws have given him. From the height of his awful majesty, he scolds and thunders at them, as if he never did wrong in his life. Fancy such a man finding his daughter reading "Don Juan." "You with that immoral book!" And he orders her out of his sight. You see, Mrs. Stowe did not hit the sorest spot. She makes Legree a bachelor.

Someone said: "Oh, I know half a Legree [villain in *Uncle Tom's Cabin*], a man said to be as cruel as Legree. But the other half of him did not correspond. He was a man of polished manners, and the best husband and father and church member in the world." "Can that be so?" "Yes, I know it. And I knew the dissolute half of Legree. He was high and mighty, but the kindest creature to his slaves; and the unfortunate results of his bad ways were not sold. They had not to jump over ice blocks. They were kept in full view, and were provided for, handsomely, in his will. His wife and daughters, in their purity and innocence, are supposed never to dream of what is as plain before their eyes as the sunlight. And they play their parts of unsuspecting angels to the letter. They profess to adore their father as the model of all earthly goodness."

"Well, yes. If he is rich, he is the fountain from whence all [blessings] flow."

"The one I have in my eye, my half of Legree, the dissolute half, was so furious in his temper, and so thundered his wrath at the poor women that they were glad to let him do as he pleased if they could only escape his everlasting fault-finding and noisy bluster."...

"... The make-believe angels were of the last century.... Women were brought up not to judge their fathers or their husbands. They took them as the Lord provided, and were thankful."...

"You wander from the question I asked. Are Southern men worse because of the slave system, and the facile black women?"

"Not a bit! They see too much of them. The barroom people don't drink, the confectionary people loathe candy. Our men are sick of the black sight of them!" ...

Martha Adamson is a beautiful mulattress, as good looking as they ever are to me. I have never seen a mule as handsome as a horse, and I know I never will; no matter how I lament and sympathize with its undeserved mule condition. She is a trained sempstress, and "hired" her own time, as they call it; that is, the owner pays doctor's bills, finds food and clothing, and the slave pays his master five dollars a month, more or less, and makes a dollar a day if he pleases. Martha, to the amazement of everybody, married a coal-black Negro, the son of Dick the Barber, who was set free fifty years ago for faithful services rendered Mr. Chestnut's grandfather. She was asked: How could she? She is so nearly white. How could she marry that horrid Negro? It is positively shocking! She answered that she inherits the taste of her white father, that her mother was black.

ESSAYS

The contradictions of a world of slaves and slaveholders in a nation that prided itself on individual freedom and rights have long occupied historians. Scholars have considered how white slaveholders reconciled their commitments to liberty with their commitments to slavery. Moreover, scholars have examined how slaves used these contradictions to carve out greater power in what by all accounts was a brutal institution. The two essays in this chapter illustrate how historians have stressed the incongruities of freedom and slavery. The first, by Anthony Kaye, examines how enslaved peoples created neighborhoods and families associated with particular geographical spaces. Kaye shows how slaves created space in their worlds in terms of neighborhoods, intimate relationships, and struggle. Alternatively, Susan Eva O'Donovan details how a group of slaves broke into a prison for their own freedom. O'Donovan shows how in the midst of one form of imprisonment (slavery), these men sought freedom creatively, counter-intuitively, and through the complicated, albeit poorly run, institutions of the south. In unison, O'Donovan and Kaye highlight the creativity of enslaved women and men. In disagreement, O'Donovan and Kaye offer distinct views of the powers of mobility and southern institutions.

The Neighborhoods and Intimate Lives of Slaves

ANTHONY E. KAYE

John Wade, a slave on the Terry plantation in Jefferson County, Mississippi, could claim many friends in his vicinity. Wade knew Aaron Barefield and his people on Poplar Hill well enough to take note when Barefield's son went to Natchez during the Civil War in the wake of a Union raid into the hinterland. And Barefield the younger knew his father's friend well enough to brighten at the mention of Wade's name years later: "I knew John Wade during the war and know him yet, too; in fact I knew him before the war; we lived on joining places." Wade also had other contacts on Polar Hill. "I have known Harriet Pierce all my life," he recalled; "we lived in the same neighborhood."

From *Joining Places: Slave Neighborhoods in the Old South* by Anthony E. Kaye. Copyright © 2007 by the University of North Carolina Press. Used by permission of the publisher. www.uncpress.unc.edu

"Neighborhood," this seemingly prosaic term, opens a window with a panoramic view of antebellum slave society.

Slave neighborhoods cut across Jefferson County, up and down the Natchez District in Mississippi, and throughout the South. They prevailed from the Chesapeake to the trans-Mississippi West and virtually everywhere in between in the Upper South and the Old Southwest. This is where Frederick Douglass grew up, Nat Turner launched his inspired revolt, men and women struggled in obscurity all their days. In some locales, neighborhoods marked the field of discipline or the terrain of marriage and family life, the dominion where a coterie of old folks held sway. In others, this was the circuit worked by slave preachers, where seekers repaired to their praying grounds and convened for religious meetings. In some precincts, neighborhoods were the quarters of every kind of fraternizing. The geography of kinship, work, sociability, and struggle overlapped with neighborhoods in different ways in different regions. Neighborhoods might encompass some of these social relations or all of them and more. Everywhere neighborhoods covered different geographic areas. In short, they were pervasive but not uniform. Neighborhoods in the Natchez District, then, were similar but not identical to those migrants had left in the Upper South....

Planters began turning this fertile soil during the eighteenth century, when the region was still a modest prize traded in diplomatic settlements among the French, English, and Spanish, who named it the Natchez District. Southwest Mississippi was an anchor in the Jeffersonian vision of a commercial farming republic during the 1790s. The Louisiana Purchase finally guaranteed American sovereignty over the length of the Mississippi and an outlet for exports from the cotton frontier. By then, Congress had already decided the slaves in the district would be mostly American born. The act organizing the Mississippi Territory in 1798 prohibited importing slaves from Africa or anywhere else abroad and authorized slaveholders to bring their chattels from anywhere in the United States. Many of those slaves had come from Africa by the trans-Atlantic trade before undertaking their second middle passage to Mississippi. Even after the United States dropped out of the international slave trade, Americans smuggled an untold number of Africans into the Deep South, Mississippi included.

Slaves were essential to local planters' hopes for the region. One coterie declared in a petition to Congress that without slavery, their farms would be merely "waste land." From their vantage point, the district still extended beyond the territory to include lands along the west bank of the Mississippi. The district also persisted as a regional identity among the planters, many of whom presided over plantations in Louisiana or Mississippi from a town seat in Natchez. By the time Mississippi joined the Union in 1817, settlers had already organized the district into five counties: Wilkinson, Adams, Jefferson, Claiborne, and Warren.

Here slaves carved out neighborhoods in one of the most princely domains in the Cotton Kingdom. Many arrived from the Upper South in a forced march accompanying owners, and most had been acquired via the slave trade. Throughout the antebellum period, most slaves were only a generation or two removed from the Upper South. Slaves outnumbered the rest of the population by a ratio of two to one in 1830 and three to one at the end of the antebellum period. By 1840, the Natchez District also included the three Mississippi counties that produced the most cotton in the state, which was now ensconsed among the first rank of the United States producing the staple. Wear and tear from all these strivings was already starting to show on the land, most dramatically where the soil collapsed into deep ravines. The district was home to only two of the state's five most productive counties in 1849, none ten years later. Yet these planters still had few peers for riches. Wilkinson, Jefferson, and Claiborne numbered among the dozen wealthiest counties in the country in 1860. The size of slave-holdings in the district though smaller than those in the Louisiana sugar country and the rice kingdom in the low country, were three times those of the South as a whole, on a par with the South Carolina Sea Islands.

In the Natchez District, slaves defined neighborhoods precisely, as adjoining plantations, because this was the domain of all the bonds that constituted their daily routine. Slaves worked and went visiting on adjoining plantations and attended dances, Christmas celebrations, and other big times there—weddings, religious services, and prayer meetings, too. Slaves courted, married, and formed families across plantation lines. Here slaves told their stories, conversed, gossiped, conspired, and collected intelligence about intimate relations, parties, and other affairs; about the staple, the livestock, and other goods; about newcomers to the neighborhood, drivers, overseers, and brutal owners; about harsh words, whippings, and other run-ins. Adjoining plantations were also where slaves lay out, purloined food, and otherwise contended with the powers that be. Neighborhoods encompassed the bonds of kinship, the practice of Christianity, the geography of sociability, the field of labor and discipline, the grounds of solidarity, the terrain of struggle. For slaves, neighborhoods served as the locus of all the bonds that shaped the contours of their society.

Neighborhoods were dynamic places. To endure, they could not be otherwise. Making places is always a process. Making places under the exactions of slavery and slave trading, which enabled owners to unmake neighborhood ties as readily as slaves make them, was a perpetual struggle. Slaves were continually sent out of the Natchez District after their forced migration from the Upper South. They were sold as punishment, mortgaged for debt, bequeathed to heirs, and pressed into caravans by owners migrating to distant parts along the rolling southern frontier. The planters' exchanges of human property reproduced the plantation household across generations, further into the Deep South, and created a steady traffic in and out of slave neighborhoods in the district. Slaves were forever giving up their neighbors and incorporating folks new to the place. This is not to say that individual people could be replaced exactly; rather, the social relations they had forged, broken by their departure, had to carry on. Men and women still had to keep up all the ties—intimate relations, work, trade, struggles, links to adjoining plantations—that bound neighborhoods together. Slave neighborhoods were in a constant state of making, remaking, and becoming....

Slaveholders were inextricable figures in slave neighborhoods. The planters had their own neighborhoods, too, bigger than those of the slaves. From the slaves' standpoint, their neighborhood was enclosed within the slaveholders' neighborhood and surrounded by it. Slaves in the Natchez District and/elsewhere in the

South mounted fewer revolts than their peers elsewhere in the Americas not because they loved master more but because they knew where power was located.

What is most remarkable about neighborhoods is not how little slaves achieved in struggle on these grounds but how much. They used the neighborhood to monitor intimate relations and gain recognition for permanent unions between men and women unrecognized by law. The slaves established the neighborhood as a field where runaways could find respite from increasingly exacting regimes of labor and discipline. The slaves' critical achievement, though, was the neighborhood itself. Despite planters' attempts to control mobility—by the whip, the law, the slave patrol, and the pass system—slaves forged enduring bonds to adjoining plantations. Men and women multiplied the possibilities of courtship, worship, amusement, struggle, and collective identity, of love, faith, pleasure, and solidarity; extended networks of kinfolk, friends, collaborators, and Christians; gave permanence to their neighborhoods by creating and recreating the bonds that held them together, even as slaveholders constantly sold people in and out of the place. By pressing social ties across plantation lines, in short, slaves attenuated the power relations of slavery and cleared some ground for themselves to stand on....

Mary Ann Helam was a reluctant bride, perhaps because she had endured a great many separations in her day. There were her parents and her daughter away off in Kentucky, and she had already lost two husbands. She buried one and was sold away from Robert Helam but kept his name anyhow. Now in 1845, her owner, Latham Brown, was asking her to marry William Madison. She refused, but Brown would not take no for an answer. "I was told to marry this man by my master," Helam recalled. "I got 50 lashes on my back to make me marry him," And so a pledge exacted at the whipping post was taken as a vow at Belle Grove Church, "a colored peoples church."

At the wedding, the bride, the groom, and their neighbors somehow made a start at consecrating the marriage, despite its unlovely beginnings. Among the slaves in attendance were two from the Brown place. The rest, she noted, were slaves "in the neighborhood." Over twenty years, Helam and Madison turned a forced concubinage into an enduring marriage, even if she maintained a certain distance and marked it by keeping the surname Helam. Her old friend, Rose Ballard, married at Belle Grove that day, too, and Helam and Madison named their first child a year later after Ballard's husband, Sidney. The boy died at just one month, but their two other children, Eli and his younger sister, Elizabeth, survived to adulthood. The baths Helam gave Madison were less a romantic interlude than a wifely service. "I done it to Keep him clean when he would come in from the field tired hot and dusty," she explained. Yet there was a touching intimacy to this chore as well, and she "washed him all *over many* times." When he enlisted in the Union army in 1863, he bought her some lumber, and she built a house in Natchez, where his regiment camped for a time. Madison returned to her from Vicksburg in May 1866, his face "hollow and sunken," with a feeling that told him he was "sick in his heart." He was only skin and bones: "He asked me to wash him. I washed him all over, and the next day he died."

Intimate relations were fraught with tension for slaves because the weight of mastery bore heavily on even the most personal bonds. In the absence of legal recognition for spouses, forever subject to separation and vulnerable to the sexual predations of owners and their agents, men and women sought order for their attachments by contriving a structure of intimate relations. Comprising that structure was a set of understandings about different types of conjugal relationships—how they were created, what a couple could expect of each other, and how these unions related to one another.

In the Natchez District, slaves made fine distinctions between "sweethearting," "taking up," "living together," and marriage. Sweethearting—neither permanent, nor monogamous, nor subject to the neighborhood's sanction—was an open-ended relationship for the young. Taking up was temporary, too, but was for mature couples prepared to submit to neighbors' informal recognition. Living together, by contrast, was a permanent bond, perhaps the most familiar to modern eyes, and entitled men and women to share a surname as well as a cabin. Marriage was permanent as well, yet distinguished from cohabitation by the formal recognition of weddings. The boundary between living together and marriage, slaves believed, was essential to the integrity of the bond between husband and wife. Rights and duties did not set unions apart. Sweethearting and taking up overlapped from that standpoint. So did living together and marriage. What distinguished them was how slaves and owners sanctioned these unions. The endless task of creating and re-creating this structure, of articulating its rules and enforcing them as norms, was a neighborhood undertaking. As neighbors fastened bonds between men and women, they clinched the most binding ties in the neighborhood....

Slaves fashioned the structure of intimate relations as they came to terms with the conflicting desires of men and women as well as the capricious interventions of owners. Planters as well as their drivers and overseers forced themselves sexually on bondwomen. Slaves knew all too well that no couple was master of their own fate when owners had the power to sell, bequeath, or hire out either party as an exercise in discipline, as a bequest to children upon marriage, to settle a debt, or to divide an estate among heirs. Some measure of the toll these transactions exacted can be reckoned from Union army registers of marriages performed in 1864 and 1865 at Natchez, Vicksburg, and Davis Bend. Among 3,846 men and women reporting previous spouses, nearly one of every six aged twenty or over reported a forced separation by an owner. The likelihood of separation increased over time. More than a third of all couples with one partner at least years old had come through at least one broken union—one in five women thirty years old and over, one in four men....

Indeed, no tie bound the neighborhoods of southwestern Mississippi more tightly than marriage. After the wedding, often a neighborhood event, the husband became a fixture over at his wife's quarters. The proximity of adjoining plantations facilitated more frequent visiting than was possible in an "abroad marriage," which typically permitted couples to spend weekends together. In the Natchez District, some married men had a standing pass to spend one night during the week, usually Wednesdays, as well as Saturdays and Sundays with their families. Edward Hicks beat the path every day between his cabin on Oak Ridge and his wife's, only three-quarters of a mile off on the adjoining Grant place. The relationship between spouses naturally created other bonds of kinship that crossed plantation lines. Henry Hunt, who was sold from Virginia to Warren County in his early teens during the mid-1830s, got around as a teamster but married a woman in his neighborhood in 1848. She already had a son, Jefferson, who was nine years old by then. Marriage thus made Hunt both a stepfather and a husband. As husbands and wives became mothers and fathers, they begat new connections in the neighborhood—among generations, among families, among kin of all kinds.

Men shouldered many burdens to bring together spouses and neighborhoods. The mandatory negotiations with owners, for example, were conducted by the groom. When it came time to request permission to live together or marry, he was obliged to do the asking. If a couple belonged to different owners, he talked to her white people as well. This diplomacy was no easy task. Couples had a lot riding on his words, and testy slaveholders could get unpleasant even about the best intentions. Henry Lewis's owners cast aspersions on his request to marry Tishne Price, although they eventually agreed. When "my husband asked my old master for me," she recalled, Lewis was dismissed as a neophyte. "You have only been here four years, and you want to marry your mistress' body servant." Lewis, who had nerve but not the cheek his owner implied, stood his ground. "Well, she loves me and I love her," he responded. Price was not spared the abuse, but it seemed to take her by surprise, particularly when master asked whether Lewis was the best she could do. "I might do worser," she ventured....

No one confounded the order slaves tried to impose on conjugal unions more than planter men. The ravages of the planters were too numerous to catalog. They turned a blind eye on drivers and overseers who had their way with slave women. They raped their people, seduced them, and imposed on them with a combination of force and cajolery that defies latter-day distinctions between consensual sex and sexual coercion. Some slaveholders were deterred by a husband's presence. Mary Ann Holmes had a husband belonging to another owner at the time she bore her daughter, Eliza, by Austin Williams. But neither the bond between spouses nor the proximity of husbands accorded much protection to women belonging to planters of Gabriel Shield's ilk. He gave his consent for two house servants, Eveline and James Perano, to live together but had her sleep in the big house. For Shields, the arrangement conveniently kept his nurse close by his children and preserved his own easy access to her for nearly a decade. Eveline Perano bore one child by Shields while she had two with her husband. Then in the late 1850s, Shields sent him to another plantation in Louisiana and broke up the Peranos' tenuous union for good....

Slaves made their structure of intimate relations prevail in many ways, all of which constituted victories, moral and practical, of a high order. This structure hissed and sputtered with contradictions, to be sure, and breaches opened up in the quarters. Drivers placed themselves outside it, and some unions were not incorporated into it. Nowhere in the Americas did slaves entirely protect conjugal life from the trespasses of owners and their agents, and the Natchez District was no exception. Slaves did not even have a tenable means of calling owners to account for the worst outrages. That slaves managed to give any structure at all to unions between men and women, considering the powers that bore down on them, was no mean feat. That they imposed this order, imperfect as it was, on their owners was an ingenious work of social engineering. That they obtained owners' cooperation was the most difficult maneuver of all, tactic slaves used to good effect in other struggles as well. Slaves achieved all of these ends by making the most personal bonds profoundly social. A wedding only gave formal, full-blown expression to the regulating of intimate relations that took place in every neighborhood. Sweethearting, taking up, living together, and marriage dispersed affinities throughout the neighborhood and grounded them there.

How Slaves Transformed Jails

SUSAN EVA O'DONOVAN

IN THE LAST DAYS OF SEPTEMBER 1854, a number of the enslaved workers on George Noble Jones's El Destino estate, a massive cotton plantation in west Florida, schemed their way into jail. Precisely what the details of the plot were and how many people were involved is not altogether clear from the record. What is clear is that at least four, maybe more, of the El Destino slaves, all "runaway [and] went rit Strait to Tallahassee and was put in jail." "I have been with Negroes for Sometime," the bemused overseer, D. M. Moxley, reminded the absentee owner, George Noble Jones. Yet "I never have knowe nor heard tell of thar running away to be put in Jail befor." "[T]har is Somthing rong about it but I am not able to See it yet, but I think that I have got on the rit track."

In reporting the events that had disrupted production on the El Destino plantation just as cotton harvest was reaching its peak, D. M. Moxley offered more than a puzzling and idiosyncratic story about slaves who had deliberately plotted their way into jail. He revealed something about jails too, and about the ways in which enslaved Americans understood and occasionally exploited public and private jails in the slaveholding states. While slaveholders and many subsequent scholars have generally represented such institutions as one of the more visible symbols of state power, many enslaved Americans saw something different. To be sure, jails were loathsome and often deadly places that most enslaved people appropriately feared. Jails were, after all, closely associated with some of the worst horrors that visited black people's lives while in bondage: sale, forced migration, family rupture, and brutal punishment. But at the same time and in one of those ironic twists that define so much of slavery's history, detention behind bars could sometimes be used by the enslaved to advance their own interests in a world in which power was otherwise stacked steeply against them.

The bondswomen and -men who so frustrated D. M. Moxley were not alone in this knowledge. Harriet Jacobs, for example, saw in jails sanctuaries of

Susan Eva O'Donovan, *How Slaves Transformed Jails*. Excerpt from "Universities of Social and Political Change: Slaves in Jail in Antebellum America," in *Buried Lives: Incarcerated in Early America*, ed. Michele Lise Tarter and Richard Bell (Athens, Ga.: University of Georgia Press, 2012).

a sort from the horrors daily visited on her by a lewd and lecherous owner. Likewise, the enslaved men who shared a crowded jail cell with a young abolitionist, George Thompson, used their time behind bars to develop their religious knowledge. They pressed white inmates to read aloud from the Bible, transforming first the jail in Palmyra, Missouri, and later the state penitentiary at Jefferson City into what one of the enslaved inmates described as "a House of God and a gate[way] to heaven." Most significantly, these communal cells returned to the enslaved precisely what owners wanted desperately to deny them: opportunities for the kind of comings and goings, contacts, and conversations that had, as Donna Haraway noted of a later revolution in technologies of knowledge, "serious potential for changing the rules of the game."

Slaves in Jail

Picked up on the lam, arrested for crime, sent in by owners for punishment, or simply locked behind bars for security purposes, slaves represented an ever-present and ever-more-predominant part of the South's inmate population. While judges sentenced increasing numbers of white people to reformative terms in the region's slowly growing penitentiary system, slaves typically endured stints in town and county jails. Mindful that long prison sentences would remove much-needed black labor from circulation, most southern lawmakers accepted and acted upon Georgian jurist Thomas R. R. Cobb's claim that the only way for the law (or, for that matter, a slaveowner) to reach a recalcitrant slave was "through his body." Though slaves appeared occasionally within the confines of southern prisons and penitentiaries, they dominated southern jails. Thus by the time Robert Everest visited New Orleans in the mid-1850s, he found the city's four police lockups filled with what he estimated were at least 240 enslaved inmates, all of whom he suspected had been sent in by their owners "for correction."

In many cases, the time slaves spent behind bars was fairly short. Slave traders, for instance, often locked their human wares into local jails for safekeeping during overnight stops. Tyre Glen, a North Carolinian who traded in slaves before he shifted his entrepreneurial attention to dry goods and groceries, would stash newly purchased slaves in local jails until he had accumulated a large enough number to make it worth his while to drive them further south for sale. Owners, too, occasionally tucked their slaves into jail for safekeeping. Fearful that their cook, Marie, might have become intoxicated by thoughts of freedom after having accompanied her owners to Europe, the Doussans of Baton Rouge made it a practice to consign Marie to that city's jail every night for eight years. Indeed, Marie's nocturnal incarcerations only came to an end when she petitioned successfully for manumission, basing her case, as a matter of fact, on the nine months she had spent with the Doussans in France. Alexander Farnsley of Kentucky briefly considered remanding one of his father's slaves to jail overnight so that Alexander might attend a dance with the woman who would soon be his wife. "Early this morning I had to go over on Clark Plank Road, to attend to some business for pa, and when I returned, I found a negro man drunk, who is really dangerous when he is so [and] Pa is afraid for me to leave the place,"

Alexander wrote as he explained why he had to miss the evening's entertainment. "It is true," he admitted, "I could put [the slave man] in gaol, and just avoid the necessity of my staying home to-night; but I though[t] if I were to put him in gaol, and let him out again, that it would only make him worse, because he might infer from it, that I was afraid of him too."

Given the value attached by free people to slaves' labor, those who were confined on suspicion of crime moved into and out of jail at an especially speedy rate. Most stayed in jail just long enough for their cases to be considered and, if so ordered, punishment inflicted. Thus while an enslaved North Carolinian named Isaac remained in the sheriff's custody for 306 days before the court dropped the murder charge against him, and a Kentucky slave named Frank waited "many months" behind bars before he received a gubernatorial pardon, most of those who landed in jail on criminal charges came and went in a matter of hours. More typical were those like ten-year-old Julia Ann of Delaware or William, who was arrested for "drinking rum" in one of New Orleans' cabarets. In the first case, not wanting to retain a person of "so dangerous a character" in the bosom of their community, the justices of the New Castle County court held Julia Ann three days before granting her owner permission to carry the child out of state for sale. In the second case, William remained in custody just long enough for the New Orleans court to hear his case and for the jailer to lay on a sentence of twenty lashes. An enslaved Mississippian named Jim did not stay behind bars for long, either. Arrested on February 17, 1838, for larceny, he was back on his owner's plantation five days later. Washington was in and out of jail just as quickly. Like Jim, he was arrested on a larceny charge, and like Jim, he was released into his owner's custody after just five days in jail.

While large numbers of slaves passed through jails at considerable speed, others lingered much longer behind bars. This was especially true of fugitives, who, depending on the state in which they were captured, could be held from four to twelve months while jailers advertised for owners to come forward to claim them. Even then, there was no guarantee that immediate release would follow. If the owner failed to appear in the allotted time, the same legislation usually directed local officials to dispose of the slave at "public outcry," a process that could add considerably to an inmate's stay. A fugitive named Henry, who made his way from west Mississippi to southern Alabama before being caught, spent at least seven months in confinement while the sheriff advertised for Henry's owner. When no one came forward, the sheriff arranged to sell the slave at auction "for cash." A man named Charles spent even more time behind bars. Arrested as a fugitive on September 23, 1847, he remained in jail at least through August of the following year, waiting for someone to claim him or buy him. Long stays were not necessarily reserved for black men, either; women and children who had managed by some means to give owners the slip also endured long periods of public confinement. Laura, a black woman who was picked up on suspicion of being a fugitive on July 1, 1854, remained behind bars a year and a half later, with no release in sight. Another Henry, this one just fifteen years old when arrested on May 11, 1848, by Habersham County, Georgia, officials, was still in that county's jail on October 30, 1849. He had gone unclaimed and unsold perhaps because of the scars that marked his hands: grisly reminders of self-inflicted wounds.

It was those who landed in jail for no other reason than being the property of quarreling slaveholders who often endured the longest stints in one squalid jail cell or another. Incarceration for this category of slaves could often be measured in years. Take Edmund, for example. The subject of a long and complicated pair of suits brought by two different parties against his owner, Edmund spent 591 days in jail in Russell County, Alabama. As the sheriff later reported to the court, he had taken custody of the slave "on the 22 day of November [1856] and Kept him Until the 5th day of July 1858." Swedish reformer Fredrika Bremer stumbled onto a similar situation while touring a jail in Louisville, Kentucky. Perplexed at finding among the female part of the population two young enslaved women who "bore so evidently the stamp of innocence" on their faces, Bremer could not help but ask what evil deed they had committed. None, replied her guide, who explained that the women had been lodged behind bars to prevent them from being seized and sold to cover their owner's debts. "How long will they remain here?" Bremer inquired. "Oh, at furthest, two or three weeks—quite a short time," came the reply. On hearing that, one of the young women "smiled, half sadly, half bitterly": "Two weeks!" "We have already been here two years!"

As terrible as they were, the conditions that brought the South's jails to reformers' and inspectors' attention imperiled the very control on which slavery and slaveowners depended. In a world in which social, political, and productive success hinged on a master's or mistress's ability to distance their laborers from competing—and almost by definition, subversive—influences, the custom of lumping miscreants with murderers, thugs with thieves, the innocent with the depraved, and above all slaves with each other seemed more than a little paradoxical. For as crowded as they were with all manner of people from all manner of places, the dreary, dank, and sometimes deadly cells contained within them the potential to destabilize what was always an unstable balance of power. "The prison," [historians] Marcus Rediker and Peter Linebaugh observe of an earlier age, "was something of a leveler." It was a truism that even slaveholders occasionally admitted. Fully aware that no inmate—male or female, enslaved or free, innocent or depraved—could be made to check their eyes, ears, minds, or mouths at the jailhouse door, an antebellum Natchez correspondent described the social and political potentials of his state's jails in language that could just as easily have come from a Boston reformer. They were, the writer groaned, nothing more than "school[s] of experimental villainy, in which each [inmate] is taught new lessons by the other."

Subverting what were meant to be frontline defenses against public disorder, jails promoted precisely what slaveholders by the late 1820s had come to fear most: free and unfettered conversation among and between slaves and all those with whom they might share a cell. Thus at the same historical moment that state lawmakers across the South were enacting increasingly draconian measures— quarantining black sailors, evicting enslaved workers from print shops, and prohibiting the unsupervised gatherings of slaves—in order to insulate slaves from outside influences and isolate them from each other, a steady stream of chatter emanated from southern jails as enslaved inmates struck up conversations with all manner of people. Cacophony, in fact, was what fugitive Henry Bibb remembered most about the day he was ordered by authorities to the workhouse in Louisville, Kentucky. Stepping through the door, it was not what he saw so much as what greeted his ears—inmates who filled the air with their prayers, their cries, and their curses—that made the deepest impression on a man who experienced some of slavery's most heinous abuses.

As Bibb soon came to learn, cacophony was a constant condition of the inmate experience. Words swirled freely and sometimes fiercely behind bars. But as was commonly the case among slaves—a people for whom talk was key to social survival—many of those words and the messages they conveyed were relatively innocuous, touching on the problems of slavery only lightly, if they touched on slavery at all. The enslaved inmates who circulated through Jonathan Walker's account of the months he spent in police custody in Pensacola, Florida, spoke, for example, about their homes, their families, and the distances that kept them apart. Benny, Harriet Jacobs's young son, talked with an inmate who would go on to be the boy's tutor. Before his two months were out, Benny had learned to count. Others talked about their criminal exploits and the deeds they had committed that had put them behind bars. The "gamblers, drunkards ... [and] harlots" with whom Henry Bibb shared his jail space took delight, for instance, in boasting about how they had "robbed houses, and persons on the highway, by knocking [their victims] down." Israel Campbell, his cellmate Barry, and a woman named Lucinda turned their eleven-day stay into a reunion of sorts. "We all had quite a lively time in prison," Israel later recalled, "laughing, talking and singing." In Mecklenburg, North Carolina, a slave named Jeff also spoke, but in his case, he chose both topic and audience imprudently. Arrested on suspicion of rape, Jeff allowed himself to be led by a stranger he met while in jail into admitting his guilt. The judge in Jeff's case later agreed, and ordered Jeff's reckless words about having "had his will" of a white woman to be entered into the records as a lawful confession. It was a decision that would cost Jeff his life, for the court eventually sentenced him to death.

Sooner or later, however, the words that swirled behind bars would gravitate toward slavery and its grave injustices. Indeed, cells provided an especially fertile environment for this kind of talk, for while much of the more innocuous thoughts could be safely released by speakers out in the open, the South's dimly lit, loosely supervised, and internally open jails invited a distinctly dissident brand of exchange. It was a phenomenon with which fugitive slave Anthony Burns was deeply familiar. Apprehended in Boston in 1854 and then sent by his owner to Richmond, Virginia, Burns was first secured in the city's public jail before being removed to a slave trader's pen. Distinguished primarily by its scale (it was not unusual for the larger of the privately owned slave pens to contain several hundred enslaved inmates at any one time), Burns settled into Robert Lumpkin's filthy dungeon to await his turn on the auction block. As was the case with countless other inmates across space and through time, Burns refused to settle silently. Using a spoon, he soon dug a hole in the floor that allowed him to open a channel of verbal "intercourse" with those confined in the cell directly below. According to his biographer, Burns then proceeded to occupy otherwise idle time by "fill[ing] their eager and wondering ears with the story of his escape from bondage, his free and happy life at the North, his capture, and the mighty effort that it cost the Government to restore him to Virginia." With his lips close to the floor, Burns relayed accounts of the places he had seen to the inmates below. He told his audience of the people he had met. He warned them of perils that must be avoided. He suggested the size of the prize that might even be won. He may even have told his listeners about the five hundred free black men who had staged a protest on his behalf after his capture in Boston. Burns performed, in short, as the slaves' "Columbus," the explorer home from foreign shores, eager to share what he had heard and learned and observed while living beyond the horizon.

Burns's relation was hardly unique. People who fulfilled similar roles could be found scattered throughout the commons that were the South's local jails, ready to expand the epistemological boundaries of enslaved inmates' minds and lives. In the process, these impromptu leaders, teachers, and guides helped transform the southern jail—one of the most ubiquitous and visible symbols of slaveholders' power—into what Stokely Carmichael would later describe as "university[ies] of social struggle and moral" change: sites that in the turbulence of the mid-twentieth century would give rise to a black power movement "For us," Carmichael explained, the carceral experience "would be life altering, a rite of passage, a turning point."

The time slaves spent in jail could change their lives, sometimes in profoundly political ways and sometimes in ways that could change the rules of the game. Powerful and potentially leveling ideas and dreams circulated throughout antebellum sites of confinement, carried along by inmates who talked. Thus just as George Thompson came to know something about the people he met during his imprisonment at Palmyra and later in Jefferson City, Missouri, so his enslaved cellmates came to know something about Thompson; a young theologian from Illinois who in 1841 launched his own assault on human bondage. Announcing themselves "eager for conversation" that would "enlighten their minds," the slaves who shared the white abolitionist's cells took advantage of the shabby and crowded surroundings to expand on their own bodies of knowledge. According to Thompson's later account, the slaves who occupied those Missouri jails learned, for example, about antislavery activities both near to home and further abroad. One of them, a man named Albert, learned how to write; someone else asked for and obtained a counterfeit pass while still in jail. On receiving much prized "directions to liberty" from Thompson, yet another enslaved inmate assured his abolitionist-adviser that "one word from you is better than gold."

And so it went in other jails and in other sites of confinement. John Parker recalled using his time behind bars in New Orleans to learn how to effectively "outwit men and [their] combinations," while Henry Bibb, though shocked by the depravity of the crooks and thieves with whom he was forced to share cells, appreciated the practical knowledge about the lay of the land and fugitive tactics that they freely shared with those around them. In Richmond, slaves confined in the same facility that would later contain Anthony Burns likewise took impromptu and informal instruction in geopolitical knowledge. But rather than teach one another about how to get out of the South and into the North—a topic that figured prominently in Bibb's recollections of jailhouse talk—the slaves who preceded Burns through the Richmond slave-trader's pen heard and learned about abolitionists' Atlantic outposts, about maritime life, and about how to take command of a ship from a hostile crew. In a demonstration of the tectonic forces that simmered inside the South's common and usually crowded jails, these were lessons that a cohort of those Richmond inmates would later put to good use when in November 1841 they hijacked the slave ship *Creole* and sailed her away to freedom in the British Bahamas.

Nor did the lessons stop there. Because of the practice of lumping inmates together regardless of age, sex, color, or crime, inmates frequently learned from and sometimes cooperated across racial and class lines. In the process, they challenged categories of control that had long been mainstays of American slavery. Much to the consternation of local authorities, this is what matured within the close confines of the Scott County, Mississippi, jail. Sneaking in an auger (a long flexible metal tool used for boring holes through wood), one black inmate, apprehended on suspicion of being a fugitive slave, used it to destroy the locks on the jail doors. He and two white inmates escaped to freedom, forging in the process a spontaneous and pragmatic bridge across a racialized gulf that slaveholders had opened centuries before in an effort to preempt precisely this kind of action: a class-based alliance against privilege and power. Strikingly similar jail breaks shocked other southern communities. In early 1855, for instance, a Savannah newspaper reported that four black men—one of whom "belongs in New Orleans"—had opened a hole in a wall and then returned to release the lone white man with whom they had shared their confinement, a convicted murderer named Charles Griffith. Not a month later, a slave named Bill slipped from the irons that held him in the Bibb County, Georgia, jail; freed six of his fellow inmates (at least two of whom were white men); and together they descended to the ground through a hole in a second-floor wall using their blankets as rope.

It is likely that the majority of slaves did not benefit immediately or even personally from what they heard and learned behind bars. For some, it was enough, or perhaps all they could do, to share the content of carceral conversations with others, taking "great pleasure," as Henry Bibb once did, in relaying to family, friends, and occasionally strangers the knowledge they had obtained while in jail. Many more alert and attentive inmates simply stored what they had heard and learned for future use, building a library of ideas, information, and inspiration that could be drawn on as conditions permitted. The enslaved who passed through Rebecca Crouch's cell during the three (or perhaps four) years she spent in jail in Warren County, Mississippi, probably fell into the latter category, committing to memory accounts about how Rebecca had been freed in Mobile, Alabama; about her subsequent life in Ohio; and about how a person who dreamed of freedom might purchase passage as Rebecca did, aboard one of the northbound vessels that plied the South's largest river. Likewise, those slaves who crossed paths with the suspected slave rebel John during his stint in a Louisiana jail may have tucked away images of a world upturned: one in which white Europeans allied themselves with enslaved black men and who, together, dared to mount an armed challenge to the South's masters. And who knows what John Pedro and Richard Coleman spoke of—or to whom—during the months they overlapped in the Vicksburg jail. One was a free-born black sailor from Venezuela who knew his way around the Caribbean and Atlantic littoral, and the other was a free man of color from Westmoreland County, Virginia, who had moved west to work on a railroad. Both had been wrongly arrested as fugitive slaves, and both were founts of geopolitical—and in Pedro's case for sure, transnational—knowledge.

The Politics of Talk

Denied the right to read and write by both custom and law, enslaved women and men evidently vested special importance in talk. It was in meeting and conversing with others, Henry "Box" Brown would freely admit, that he and his brother came to know something about "whatever was going on in the world." The Brown brothers received much of that instruction while shuttling between their owner's plantation and a local gristmill, a twenty-mile excursion the boys were ordered to take on a regular basis. Hundreds of thousands of other enslaved people received their news while traipsing along behind migrating slaveholders, waiting tables for gregarious white diners, or talking to one of the many northern or foreign visitors who frequented Deep South plantations. Moses came to understand something about the world around him while chalking up as he did close to 4,000 miles on the road every year while driving a wagon for his owner. So did Ben, who sometimes accompanied Moses, as well as Daniel, who went with his owner from Georgia to California and back again in the early 1850s. Still other slaves, particularly personal servants and nurses, claimed a share of their enlightenment by traveling to Philadelphia, New York, Boston, and occasionally abroad, bearing witness on their return to the sounds as well as the sights of full freedom.

But as we have seen, large numbers of enslaved Americans took at least some of their lessons while biding their time behind bars. As critics of the antebellum penal system kept pointing out, common jails and the unsupervised contacts and conversations that they fostered were indeed universities of a dank and fetid sort. Bearing more than a passing resemblance to the encampments of slaves who built the South's railroads, dug its canals, and mined its precious minerals, jails made possible precisely what the South's lawmakers had been desperately attempting to preempt ever since Nat Turner's 1831 insurrection had sent shock waves through the slaveholding states. Lapsing into language that accorded a striking degree of political power to slaves, Richard Lyon, a Georgia slaveholder, likened unsupervised gatherings such as those that unfolded in the South's county jails to "regular conventions" at which all slaves would be "abley represented." Fretting about exchanges of the kind that took place between an enslaved man named J. H. Banks and the six other inmates with whom he shared a Deep South cell, conversations that in this particular instance culminated in a mass escape, Richard Lyon warned that any slave who returned to his owner's estate after such an experience, if not rebellious himself, would surely "inform those who are of what he has seen & heard—and incalculable mischief ... [would] follow."

The vast majority of the meetings that Lyon granted the status of political convention yielded little of the mischief that made him so nervous. Only infrequently did enslaved inmates translate what they had learned while behind bars into immediate freedom. John Brown, who acquired his "useful and practical hints" about routes out of the South while penned up in New Orleans, was the exception, not the rule. So too were King and Jack, a pair of slaves who "came to the dungeon grates about the dead hour of night" to have a conversation with Henry Bibb "about Canada, and the facilities for getting there" and who, Bibb proudly remembered, successfully applied what they had heard and learned. Within a week of their conversation with Bibb, Jack and King had arrived at their Canadian destination. Nor did jailhouse talk always arrive at a *Creole* conclusion: such dramatic outcomes were the exception, not the rule, following on prisoners' shared conversations. Yet, in a nation that by the 1850s was splitting along sectional and ideological seams, for slaves to know who was a friend, who was a foe, and something of the world in which they existed was no mean or futile achievement.

Thus while the years leading up to Abraham Lincoln's election stand out for the absence of large-scale revolts, America's bound workers nonetheless spent much of those years accumulating a potent body of knowledge: about their surroundings, about their owners, and about a nation that was hurtling toward war. It was information that some were able to use to escape slavery altogether, actions that in calling northerners' attention to the horrors of human bondage helped to intensify sectional tensions. It was information that gave many more the means to deflect some of slavery's abuses—by introducing them to allies in unlikely places, by giving rise to new social connections, and by opening slaves' eyes and minds to a much larger political terrain. It was information that many of the nation's slaves accumulated in whole or in part while locked in a cell.

Most of all, it was information that slaves would draw on in the weeks and months following the Confederate secession. For it was then that the meetings Lyon so graphically imagined bore their most radical fruit. Acting under the cover of war, America's slaves were at last able to put into practice lessons that many had heard while confined to a cell, laying aside their tools, taking to their feet, and launching what has been recently described as the largest of New World rebellions. In the process, those four million people would accomplish a whole lot more. Perhaps Henry Bibb was right when, in reflecting back on his experience as a prisoner in southern jails, he noted that if slaveholders had understood what unfolded on a daily basis behind the bars, "they would never [have] let their slaves" do time.

FURTHER READING

Erskine Clarke, *Dwelling Place: A Plantation Epic* (2005).

Richard Follett, *The Sugar Masters: Planters and Slaves in Louisiana's Cane World, 1820–1860* (2007).

Elizabeth Fox-Genovese, *Within the Plantation Household: Black and White Women of the Old South* (1988).

Elizabeth Fox-Genovese and Eugene Genovese, *The Mind of the Master Class* (2005).

Michael A. Gomez, *Exchanging Our Country Marks: The Transformation of African Identities in the Colonial and Antebellum South* (1998).

James Oliver Horton and Lois E. Horton, *Slavery and the Making of America* (2004).

Charles F. Irons, *The Origins of Proslavery Christianity: White and Black Evangelicals in Colonial and Antebellum Virginia* (2008).

Walter Johnson, *Soul by Soul: Life inside the Slave Market* (1999).

Stephanie McCurry, *Masters of Small Worlds: Yeoman Households, Gender Relations, and the Political Culture of the Antebellum South Carolina Low Country* (1995).

Albert J. Raboteau, *Slave Religion: The "Invisible Institution" in the Antebellum South* (2004).

Marie Jenkins Schwartz, *Birthing a Slave: Motherhood and Medicine in the Antebellum South* (2010).

Brenda E. Stevenson, *Life in Black and White: Family and Community in the Slave South* (1997).

Gavin Wright, *The Political Economy of the Cotton South* (1978).

Additional critical thinking activities and content are available in MindTap.

MindTap

MindTap is a fully online, highly personalized learning experience built upon Cengage Learning content. MindTap combines student learning tools—readings, multimedia, activities, and assessments—into a singular Learning Path that guides students through the course.

CHAPTER 13

Toward Civil War

For many Americans, the signing of the Treaty of Guadalupe Hidalgo on February 2, 1848, was a moment of fulfillment and a cause for jubilation. The United States had just won a war against Mexico and had gained title to some 500,000 square miles of land. Although in retrospect we may see the Mexican-American War as a war of aggression by the United States, many Americans at the time saw it as the realization of manifest destiny. The nation now encompassed nearly three million square miles; in some seventy years, the United States had become a transcontinental colossus. Ironically, this national victory planted the seeds for civil war. As Americans celebrated, they had to determine politically the ways in which the newly acquired lands would be developed. For nearly thirty years, American politicians had attempted to create a balance between slave and free states. Now the issue of how or if slavery would be extended westward became the question of the day. As politicians endeavored to deal with the question, Americans of various stripes became actively engaged in the debate and drew attention to the fact that perhaps this was not an issue that had a political solution. Americans became increasingly violent in their political and economic opinions.

Both before the 1840s and afterward, politicians typically attempted to arrive at compromise. Because there were two strong national political parties vying for power, it was in their interests to maintain a spirit of compromise between the North and the South. Accordingly, after bitter debate, Congress passed the Compromise of 1850, which purportedly solved the problem. One part of the legislation admitted California as a free state, thus forever creating an imbalance between free and slave states. Another component of the compromise was the Fugitive Slave Act, which empowered slave owners to go to court to recapture people who had escaped northward. Alleged fugitives were denied the right of trial by jury, and white people in the North were required to abet efforts to recapture fugitive slaves. As Americans soon found out, however, this time compromise did not solve the problem; in fact, it may have worsened it.

Distrust among Americans multiplied in the 1850s, in part because of the failure of the attempts at compromise. The abolitionist movement grew in the North, in part because of the publication of Uncle Tom's Cabin, a novel by Harriet Beecher Stowe that powerfully indicted slavery and the Fugitive Slave Act. Many northerners contended that their region, with its growing population, flourishing industry, and "free labor," was the best model for America's future. They worried about a "slave power conspiracy" that seemingly controlled the national government and was intent on spreading slavery westward, to the detriment of white farmers who also wanted to farm the available western lands. With increased reliance on the economy of the slave trade, southern whites seemed to need more and more land. At the same time, white people in the South became increasingly distrustful of northerners. In the southern view, northerners were promoting abolitionism and thus endangering the system of plantation slavery, which from their perspective was what created an ordered and stable society.

As these divisions grew, the strains on the political party systems became so great that a political crisis developed in the 1850s. First the Whig Party, then the newly formed American Party, and finally the Democratic Party were unable to address the concerns of their constituents. These failures were compounded by further attempts to address the question of slavery. The Kansas-Nebraska Act in 1854 resulted in de facto civil war in Kansas Territory shortly after its passage; the Dred Scott decision in 1857 convinced many northerners that the Supreme Court was proslavery; and John Brown's raid in 1859 persuaded many white southerners that northern abolitionists were intent on fomenting slave rebellion. In 1860, when Abraham Lincoln became the first candidate of the Republican Party to be elected president, he received only 39 percent of the popular vote and only a little over 1 percent of the vote in slave states. Many white southerners considered Lincoln to represent not just the North but the incendiary abolitionist elements of northern society. Within five weeks of Lincoln's election, seven legislatures of the Lower South had called for elections to consider secession. By February 22, they had formed a new nation, written a constitution, and inaugurated their new president, Jefferson Davis. Ten days remained before Lincoln would take office. The United States was on the brink of its bloodiest war.

QUESTIONS TO THINK ABOUT

Was the Civil War inevitable? Can you think of ways in which compromises might have forestalled the division between the North and the South? Were economic or political issues at the base of the conflict? Of the documents you have read in this chapter, which is most conciliatory toward the other side? Which is most antagonistic?

DOCUMENTS

Before northerners and southerners waged war, many came to view members of the other section not only as different, but also as antagonistic. Document 1 is a description of a "Yankee" from a young Kentuckian who traveled to Yale University for college. Alternatively, Harriet Beecher Stowe, a northerner, described southern society dramatically in her best-selling *Uncle Tom's Cabin*. Reactions to the novel varied, as the two reviews included as document 2 illustrate. Whereas an abolitionist paper objects to the nonviolence of Uncle tom, a literary journal in the South considers Stowe's depiction of slavery to be too harsh. In document 3, a series of letters written in "bleeding Kansas" in 1856, a southerner recounts the violence between southerners and "Yankees" that existed in the territory following the Kansas-Nebraska Act. The violence in Kansas ultimately was duplicated on the floors of Congress. Senator Charles Sumner's speech, delivered in May of 1856, about the "crime against Kansas," document 4, was viewed by many white southerners as excessive. Sumner was attacked some days later by a relative of Senator Butler, who is vilified in the speech. Document 5 is Chief Justice Roger Taney's decision in *Dred Scott v. Sanford,* which was hailed by proslavery southerners and condemned by antislavery northerners. Among other things, Taney held that neither slaves nor free black people could sue in court because they were not citizens and that no law could be passed to prohibit slavery in the territories. In document 6, Senator William Seward celebrates the system of free labor and argues that conflict between societies based on free and slave labor is irrepressible. Document 7 features a southern politician praising the power of cotton and its international importance. After John Brown led a raid into the South in hopes of fostering a slave revolt, he became a hero, not only to many northerners but also to those throughout the world who wished to end slavery. Document 8 is a memorial from Haiti. Finally, in document 9, northern writer Frederick Law Olmsted describes slavery as a poor and backward economic system.

1. J. Stoddard Johnston Answers "What Is a Yankee," 1850

Since by choice I have come among this queer set of beings, it would seem decidedly out of place to record anything unfavorable to their good name, but then I was induced to make this choice from a wish to obtain a classical education and not from motives of affection for this hotbed of abolitionism. I shall not be so harshly judged, I hope, if I from time to time note in this book of heterogeneous collections their peculiarities, customs, and prejudices against the South. For fear whoever may read this has never seen a Yankee I will venture on a detail of the most prominent and peculiar characteristics by which they may distinguish one of them from any of the average Kentuckian. If my reader should be travelling and meets a man with light or red hair who talks as if his time on earth was limited and he didn't want to consume it by slow talking, he may set him down as a Yankee and more certainly if he says he is going out west to carry on business. He will perceive these peculiarities in his pronunciation. For 'whole' he says 'hull.' For 'home' 'hum.' 'Nothing' 'Naw-thing'. 'Does.' 'Dooze'....

The Yankees are the strangest people in the world perhaps. Since my arrival in Yankeedom, I have heard that quite a respectable and thriving family used the toasted ... of bread instead of coffee for the truth of which I will stand responsible.

J. Stoddard Johnston Answers "What is a Yankee", 1850 [Josiah Johnson Papers, Filson Historical Society, MSS A J 72 14, Folder 37, pages 35–37; Cengage-transcribed]

In buying from the Yankees they must always have the exact sum, and if in paying a man a debt of $600.00¼, the quarter of a cent would be demanded if 600.00 was paid....

Anecdotes

The Yankees are an ingenious race and turn their ingenuity into utility as may seem from the substance of an article which I saw in a newspaper, that a Yankee had invented a machine to gin cotton, hoe potatoes, grind corn, rock the cradle, feed the baby, make up the bed, and play checkers.

2. Reviewers Offer Differing Opinions About *Uncle Tom's Cabin*, 1852

I.

In the execution of her very difficult task, Mrs. Stowe has displayed rare descriptive powers, a familiar acquaintance with slavery under its best and its worst phases, uncommon moral and philosophical acumen, great facility of thought and expression, feelings and emotions of the strongest character....

The appalling liabilities which constantly impend over such slaves as have "kind and indulgent masters" are thrillingly illustrated in various personal narratives; especially in that of "Uncle Tom," over whose fate every reader will drop the scalding tear, and for whose character the highest reverence will be felt. No insult, no outrage, no suffering, could ruffle the Christ-like meekness of his spirit, or shake the steadfastness of his faith. Towards his merciless oppressors, he cherished no animosity, and breathed nothing of retaliation. Like his Lord and Master, he was willing to be "led as a lamb to the slaughter," returning blessing for cursing, and anxious only for the salvation of his enemies. His character is sketched with great power and rare religious perception. It triumphantly exemplifies the nature, tendency and results of CHRISTIAN NON-RESISTANCE. We are curious to know whether Mrs. Stowe is a believer in the duty of non-resistance for the white man, under all possible outrage and peril, as well as for the black man.... That all the slaves at the South ought, "if smitten on the one cheek, to turn the other also"—to repudiate all carnal weapons, shed no blood, "be obedient to their masters," wait for a peaceful deliverance, and abstain from all insurrectionary movements—is every where taken for granted, because the VICTIMS ARE BLACK. *They* cannot be animated by a Christian spirit, and yet return blow for blow, or conspire for the destruction of their oppressors. *They* are required by the Bible to put away all wrath, to submit to every conceivable outrage without resistance, to suffer with Christ if they would reign with him.... Is there one law of submission and non-resistance for the black man, and another law of rebellion and conflict for the white man? When it is the whites who are trodden in the

---

(I) William Lloyd Garrison, Review in *The Liberator*, March 26, 1852, 50.

dust, does Christ justify them in taking up arms to vindicate their rights? And when it is the blacks who are thus treated, does Christ require them to be patient, harmless, long-suffering, and forgiving? And are there two Christs?

II.

We have devoted a much larger space to the plot of "Uncle Tom's Cabin" than we designed...; it only remains for us to consider briefly those points upon which the authoress rests her abuse of the Southern States, in the book as a whole. These may be reduced to three—the cruel treatment of the slaves, their lack of religious instruction, and a wanton disregard of the sacred ties of consanguinity in selling members of the same family apart from each other.

... [M]any of the allegations of cruelty towards the slaves, brought forward by Mrs. Stowe, are absolutely and unqualifiedly false. As for the comfort of their daily lives and the almost parental care taken of them on well-regulated plantations, we may say that the picture of the Shelby estate, drawn by Mrs. Stowe herself, is no bad representation. The world may safely be challenged to produce a laboring class, whose regular toil is rewarded with more of the substantial conflicts of life than the negroes of the South. The "property interest" at which the authoress sneers so frequently in "Uncle Tom's Cabin," is quite sufficient to ensure for the negro a kindness and attention, which the day-laborer in New England might in vain endeavor to win from his employer....

The lack of religious instruction for slaves is a charge against the South, in great favor with Northern fanatics, many of whom are deplorably in want of "religious instruction" themselves, and vastly beneath the pious slave in that love for their neighbour which is the keystone of the Christian arch. Yet never was there a charge more extravagant. We can tell these worthies that throughout the Southern States a portion of every house of worship is set apart for the accommodation of slaves; that upon very many plantations, may be seen rude but comfortable buildings, dedicated to God, where stated preaching of His Holy Word is ordained; that Sabbath schools for negroes are established in several of the Southern cities; and that in every Southern family, almost without an exception, where morning and evening prayers are held, the domestics of the household are called together to unite in them.... Writers like Mrs. Stowe, in treating of this subject, assume that there can be no acquaintance with gospel truth among a class who are not permitted to learn to read. But how many of the early Christians were ignorant and illiterate persons? The fishermen of Galilee were men without instruction when they first followed the fortunes of the lowly Nazarene. As for Mrs. Stowe, she is answered upon this point in her own pages. Uncle Tom was no scholar, and after many years of diligent application could at last read his bible with difficulty. Yet where shall we find a nobler and purer exemplification of the "beauty of holiness" than in him? It is, indeed, a triumphant vindication of the institution of slavery against Mrs. Stowe's assaults, that in a slaveholding community, a character so perfect as "Uncle Tom" could be produced....

(II) Unsigned (probably John R. Thompson), Review in *Southern Literary Messenger*, October 1852, 637–638.

The sundering of family ties among the negroes is undoubtedly a dreadful thing as represented by Abolition pamphleteers. Nor have we any desire to close our eyes to the fact that occasionally there do occur instances of compulsory separation involving peculiar hardship. But ... in the very State which Mrs. Stowe has chosen for her most painful incident of this character, there are statutory regulations mitigating very much the severity of this condition of affairs, and we may add that every where the salutary influence of an enlightened public opinion enforces the sale of near relatives in such manner as that they may be kept as much as possible together. We are of opinion too that heart-rending separations are much less frequent under the institution of slavery than in countries where poverty rules the working classes with despotic sway. But admit the hardship to its full extent, and what does it prove? Evils are inseparable from all forms of society and this giant evil (if you will call it so) is more than counterbalanced by the advantages the negro enjoys.

3. Axalla John Hoole, a Southerner, Depicts "Bleeding Kansas," 1856

Kansas City, Missouri, Apl. 3d., 1856

My Dear Brother ...

The Missourians (all of whom I have conversed with, with the exception of one who, by the way, I found out to be an Abolitionist) are very sanguine about Kansas being a slave state & I have heard some of them say it *shall* be. I have met with warm reception from two or three, but generally speaking, I have not met with the reception which I expected. Everyone seems bent on the Almighty Dollar, and as a general thing that seems to be their only thought....

... Give my love to [the immediate family] and all the Negroes....

Your ever affectionate brother, Axalla.

Lecompton, K. T., Sept. 12, 1856

My dear Mother ...

You perceive from the heading of this that I am now in Lecompton, almost all of the Proslavery party between this place and Lawrence are here. We brought our families here, as we thought that we would be better able to defend ourselves when altogether than if we scattered over the country.

Lane came against us last Friday (a week ago to-day). As it happened we had almost 400 men with two cannon—we marched out to meet him, though we were under the impression at the time that we had 1,000 men. We came in gunshot of each other, but the regular soldiers came and interferred, but not before our party had shot some dozen guns, by which it is reported that five of the Abolitionists were killed or wounded. We had strict orders from our

William Stanley Hoole, ed., "A Southerner's Viewpoint of the Kansas Situation" (1856–1857), *Kansas Historical Quarterly*, Vol. 3 (1934).

commanding officer (Gen'l Marshall) not to fire until they made the attack, but some of our boys would not be restrained. I was a rifleman and one of the skirmishers, but did all that I could to restrain our men though I itched all over to shoot....

... I am more uneasy about making money than I am about being killed by the Yankees...

Your Affectionate Son.

Douglas, K. T., July the 5th., 1857

Dear Sister

I fear, Sister, that coming here will do no good at last, as I begin to think that this will be made a Free State at last. 'Tis true we have elected Proslavery men to draft a state constitution, but I feel pretty certain, if it is put to the vote of the people, it will be rejected, as I feel pretty confident they have a majority here at this time. The South has ceased all efforts, while the North is redoubling her exertions....

One of our most staunch Proslavery men was killed in Leavensworth a few days ago. It is hard to ascertain the facts in relation to the murder correctly, but as far as I can learn, there was an election for something. The man who was killed (Jas. Lyle) went up to the polls and asked for a ticket. An Abolitionist handed him one which he, Lyle, tore in two. The other asked him why he did that; he replied he did all such tickets that way. The Abolitionist told him he had better not do so again, when Lyle told him if he would give him another he would. It was given him, and he tore it also, at which the Abolitionist drew a bowie knife and stabbed Lyle to the heart, then ran a few paces, drew a revolver, and commenced firing at the dying man. The fellow was taken prisoner and eighty men were sent from Lawrence that night, by Jim Lane, to keep Lyle's friends from hanging him. Gov. Walker put out for Leavensworth on Friday to have the prisoner carried to the fort, in order to keep the Abolitionists from rescuing him, or prevent Lyle's friends from hanging him by mob law....

You must give my love to all.... Tell all the Negroes a hundred Howdies for us....

Your Affectionate Brother, Axalla.

4. Senator Charles Sumner Addresses the "Crime Against Kansas," 1856

MR. PRESIDENT:

You are now called to redress a great transgression. Seldom in the history of nations has such a question been presented....

Senator Charles Sumner, speech in the U.S. Senate on the "Crime Against Kansas," delivered May 19–20, 1856; reprinted in *Evening Journal* (Albany, N.Y.), May 22–23, 1856.

Take down your map, sir, and you will find that the Territory of Kansas, more than any other region, occupies the middle spot of North America.... A few short months only have passed since this spacious and mediterranean country was open only to the savage who ran wild in its woods and prairies; and now it has already drawn to its bosom a population of freemen larger than Athens....

Against this Territory, thus fortunate in position and population, a crime has been committed, which is without example in the records of the past....

... It is the rape of a virgin Territory, compelling it to the hateful embrace of Slavery; and it may be clearly traced to a depraved longing for a new slave State, the hideous offspring of such a crime, in the hope of adding to the power of slavery in the National Government....

... The strife is no longer local, but national. Even now, while I speak, portents hang on all the arches of the horizon threatening to darken the broad land, which already yawns with the mutterings of civil war. The fury of the propagandists of Slavery, and the calm determination of their opponents, are now diffused from the distant Territory over widespread communities, and the whole country....

... [A] madness for Slavery which would disregard the Constitution, the laws, and all the great examples of our history; also a consciousness of power such as comes from the habit of power; a combination of energies found only in a hundred arms directed by a hundred eyes; a control of public opinion through venal pens and a prostituted press; an ability to subsidize crowds in every vocation of life—the politician with his local importance, the lawyer with his subtle tongue, and even the authority of the judge on the bench; and a familiar use of men in places high and low, so that none, from the President to the lowest border postmaster, should decline to be its tool; all these things and more were needed, and they were found in the slave power of our Republic. There, sir, stands the criminal, all unmasked before you—heartless, grasping, and tyrannical....

... I must say something of a general character, particularly in response to what has fallen from Senators who have raised themselves to eminence on this floor in championship of human wrongs. I mean the Senator from South Carolina (Mr. Butler), and the Senator from Illinois (Mr. Douglas).... The Senator from South Carolina has read many books of chivalry, and believes himself a chivalrous knight, with sentiments of honor and courage. Of course he has chosen a mistress to whom he has made his vows, and who, though ugly to others, is always lovely to him: though polluted in the sight of the world; is chaste in his sight. I mean the harlot, Slavery. For her, his tongue is always profuse in words. Let her be impeached in character, or any proposition made to shut her out from the extension of her wantonness, and no extravagance of manner or hardihood of assertion is then too great for this Senator. The frenzy of Don Quixote, in behalf of his wench, Dulcinea del Toboso, is all surpassed. The asserted rights of Slavery, which shock equality of all kinds, are cloaked by a fantastic claim of equality. If the slave States cannot enjoy what, in mockery of the great fathers of the Republic, he misnames equality under the Constitution in other words, the full power in the National Territories to compel fellowmen to unpaid toil, to separate husband and wife, and to sell little children at the auction block then, sir, the chivalric Senator will conduct the State of South Carolina out of the

Union! Heroic knight! Exalted Senator! A second Moses come for a second exodus!

... [T]he Senator in the unrestrained chivalry of his nature, has undertaken to apply opprobrious words to those who differ from him on this floor. He calls them "sectional and fanatical"; and opposition to the usurpation in Kansas he denounces as "an uncalculating fanaticism."... He is the uncompromising, unblushing representative on this floor of a flagrant sectionalism, which now domineers over the Republic, and yet with a ludicrous ignorance of his own position unable to see himself as others see him..., he applies to those here who resist his sectionalism the very epithet which designates himself....

... [T]he Senator from Illinois (Mr. Douglas) is the Squire of Slavery, its very Sancho Panza, ready to do all its humiliating offices.... Standing on this floor, the Senator issued his rescript, requiring submission to the Usurped Power of Kansas; and this was accompanied by a manner—all his own—such as befits the tyrannical threat. Very well. Let the Senator try. I tell him now that he cannot enforce any such submission. The Senator, with the slave power at his back, is strong; but he is not strong enough for this purpose....

The Senator dreams that he can subdue the North. He disclaims the open threat, but his conduct still implies it. How little that Senator knows himself or the strength of the cause which he persecutes! He is but a mortal man; against him is an immortal principle. With finite power he wrestles with the infinite, and he must fall. Against him are stronger battalions than any marshalled by mortal arm[,] the inborn, ineradicable, invincible sentiments of the human heart[;] against him is nature in all her subtle forces; against him is God. Let him try to subdue these.

5. Chief Justice Roger Taney Determines the Legal Status of Slaves, 1857

The question is simply this: Can a negro, whose ancestors were imported into this country, and sold as slaves, become a member of the political community formed and brought into existence by the Constitution of the United States, and as such become entitled to all the rights, and privileges, and immunities, guarantied by [the Constitution] to the citizen? One of which rights is the privilege of suing in a court of the United States in the cases specified in the Constitution....

... We think they [negroes] are not, and that they are not included, and were not intended to be included, under the word "citizens" in the Constitution, and can therefore claim none of the rights and privileges which [it] ... secures to the citizens of the United States. On the contrary, they were at the time considered as a subordinate and inferior class of beings, who had been subjugated by the dominant race, and, whether emancipated or not, yet remained subject to their authority, and had no rights or privileges but such as those who held the power and the Government might choose to grant them....

Roger Taney, opinion in *Dred Scott v. Sanford* (1857).

In discussing this question, we must not confound the rights of citizenship which a State may confer within its own limits, and the rights of citizenship as a member of the Union. It does not by any means follow, because he has all the rights and privileges of a citizen of a State, that he must be a citizen of the United States....

The question then arises, whether the provisions of the Constitution, in relation to the personal rights and privileges to which the citizen of a State should be entitled, embraced the negro African race, at that time in this country, or who might afterwards be imported, who had then or should afterwards be made free in any State; and to put it in the power of a single State to make him a citizen of the United States....

The court think the affirmative of these propositions cannot be maintained. And if it cannot, the plaintiff in error could not be a citizen of the State of Missouri ... and consequently, was not entitled to sue in its courts....

It is difficult at this day to realize the state of public opinion in relation to that unfortunate race, which prevailed in the civilized and enlightened portions of the world at the time of the Declaration of Independence, and when the Constitution of the United States was framed and adopted. But the public history of every European nation displays it in a manner too plain to be mistaken.

They had for more than a century been regarded as beings of an inferior order, and altogether unfit to associate with the white race, either in social or political relations; and so far inferior, that they had no rights which the white man was bound to respect; and that the negro might justly and lawfully be reduced to slavery for his benefit....

And in no nation was this opinion more firmly fixed or more uniformly acted upon than by the English Government and English people....

The opinion thus entertained and acted upon in England was naturally impressed upon the colonies they founded on this side of the Atlantic. And accordingly, a negro of the African race was regarded by them as an article of property, and held, and bought and sold ... in every one of the thirteen colonies....

[Laws passed in the thirteen colonies] show that a perpetual and impassable barrier was intended to be erected between the white race and the one which they had reduced to slavery, and governed as subjects with absolute and despotic power....

[T]here are two clauses of the Constitution which point directly to the negro race as a separate class of persons, and show clearly that they were not regarded as a portion of the people or citizens of the Government then formed.

One of these clauses reserves to each of the thirteen States the right to import slaves until the year 1808.... And by the other provision the States pledge themselves to each other to maintain the right of property of the master, by delivering up to him any slave who may have escaped from his service, and be found within their respective territories....

The only two provisions [of the Constitution] which point to [slaves] and include them, treat them as property, and make it the duty of the Government to protect it; no other power, in relation to this race, is to be found in the Constitution....

[T]he court is of the opinion, that, upon the facts stated in the plea of abatement, Dred Scot was not a citizen of Missouri within the meaning of the Constitution of the United States, and not entitled as such to sue in its courts.

6. Republican William Seward Warns of an Irrepressible Conflict, 1858

Our country is a theatre, which exhibits, in full operation, two radically different political systems; the one resting on the basis of servile or slave labor, the other on the basis of voluntary labor of freemen.

The laborers who are enslaved are all negroes, or persons more or less purely of African derivation. But this is only accidental. The principle of the system is, that labor in every society, by whomsoever performed, is necessarily unintellectual, groveling and base; and that the laborer, equally for his own good and for the welfare of the state, ought to be enslaved. The white laboring man, whether native or foreigner, is not enslaved, only because he cannot, as yet, be reduced to bondage....

... One of the chief elements of the value of human life is freedom in the pursuit of happiness. The slave system is not only intolerable, unjust, and inhuman, towards the laborer, whom, only because he is a laborer, it loads down with chains and converts into merchandise, but is scarcely less severe upon the freeman, to whom, only because he is a laborer from necessity, it denies facilities for employment, and whom it expels from the community because it cannot enslave and convert him into merchandise also.... The free-labor system conforms to the divine law of equality, which is written in the hearts and consciences of man, and therefore is always and everywhere beneficent.

The slave system is one of constant danger, distrust, suspicion, and watchfulness. It debases those whose toil alone can produce wealth and resources for defense, to the lowest degree of which human nature is capable....

The free-labor system educates all alike, and by opening all the fields of industrial employment, and all the departments of authority, to the unchecked and equal rivalry of all classes of men, at once secures universal contentment, and brings into the highest possible activity all the physical, moral and social energies of the whole state....

Hitherto, the two systems have existed in different states, but side by side within the American Union. This has happened because the Union is a confederation of states. But in another aspect the United States constitute only one nation. Increase of population, which is filling the states out to their very borders, together with a new and extended net-work of railroads and other avenues, and an internal commerce which daily becomes more intimate, is rapidly bringing the states into a higher and more perfect social unity or consolidation. Thus, these antagonistic systems are continually coming into closer contact, and collision results....

William Seward, "The Irrepressible Conflict," speech given at Rochester, N.Y. (October 25, 1858), in *The Works of William H. Seward*, IV (new edition), ed. George Baker (Boston: Houghton, Mifflin, and Company, 1884), 289–302.

Shall I tell you what this collision means?... It is an irrepressible conflict between opposing and enduring forces, and it means that the United States must and will, sooner or later, become either entirely a slaveholding nation, or entirely a freelabor nation....

... In the field of federal politics, slavery, deriving unlooked-for advantages from commercial changes, and energies unforeseen from the facilities of combination between members of the slaveholding class and between that class and other property classes, early rallied, and has at length made a stand, not merely to retain its original defensive position, but to extend its sway throughout the whole Union.... The plan of operation is this: By continued appliances of patronage and threats of disunion, they will keep a majority favorable to these designs in the senate, where each state has an equal representation. Through that majority they will defeat, as they best can, the admission of free states and secure the admission of slave states. Under the protection of the judiciary, they will, on the principle of the Dred Scott case, carry slavery into all the territories of the United States now existing and hereafter to be organized. By the action of the president and the senate, using the treaty-making power, they will annex foreign slaveholding states. In a favorable conjecture they will induce congress to repeal the act of 1808, which prohibits the foreign slave trade, and so they will import from Africa, at the cost of only twenty dollars a head, slaves enough to fill up the interior of the continent.... When the free states shall be sufficiently demoralized to tolerate these designs, they reasonably conclude that slavery will be accepted by those states themselves....

I think, fellow citizens, that I have shown you that it is high time for the friends of freedom to rush to the rescue of the constitution, and that their very first duty is to dismiss the democratic party from the administration of the government.

7. James Henry Hammond Praises King Cotton, 1858

[W]ould any sane nation make war on cotton? Without firing a gun, without drawing a sword, should they make war on us we could bring the whole world to our feet. The South is perfectly competent to go on, one, two, or three years without planting a seed of cotton. I believe that if she was to plant but half her cotton, for three years to come, it would be an immense advantage to her. I am not so sure but that after three years' entire abstinence she would come out stronger than ever she was before, and better prepared to enter afresh upon her great career of enterprise. What would happen if no cotton was furnished for three years? I will not stop to depict what every one can imagine, but this is certain: England would topple headlong and carry the whole civilized world with her, save the South. No, you dare not make war on cotton. No power on earth dares to make war upon it. Cotton *is* king. Until lately the Bank of England was king; but she tried to put her screws as usual, the fall before the last, upon the cotton crop, and was utterly vanquished. The last power has

This document can be found in the Congressional Globe: 35th Congress, First session, speech given on March 4, 1858, quoted sections on pp. 961–62.

been conquered. Who can doubt, that has looked at recent events, that cotton is supreme? When the abuse of credit had destroyed credit and annihilated confidence; when thousands of the strongest commercial houses in the world were coming down, and hundreds of millions of dollars of supposed property evaporating in thin air; when you [Northerners] came to a dead lock, and revolutions were threatened, what brought you up? Fortunately for you it was the commencement of the cotton season, and we have poured in upon you one million six hundred thousand bales of cotton just at the crisis to save you from destruction. That cotton, but for the bursting of your speculative bubbles in the North, which produced the whole of this convulsion, would have brought us $100,000,000. We have sold it for $65,000,000, and saved you. Thirty-five million dollars we, the slaveholders of the South, have put into the charity box for your magnificent financiers, your "cotton lords," your "merchant princes."

But, sir, the greatest strength of the South arises from the harmony of her political and social institutions. This harmony gives her a frame of society, the best in the world, and an extent of political freedom, combined with entire security, such as no other people ever enjoyed upon the face of the earth. Society precedes government; creates it, and ought to control it; but as far as we can look back in historic times we find the case different; for government is no sooner created than it becomes too strong for society, and shapes and moulds, as well as controls it. In later centuries the progress of civilization and of intelligence has made the divergence so great as to produce civil wars and revolutions; and it is nothing now but the want of harmony between governments and societies which occasions all the uneasiness and trouble and terror that we see abroad. It was this that brought on the American Revolution. We threw off a Government not adapted to our social system, and made one for ourselves. The question is, how far have we succeeded? The South, so far as that is concerned, is satisfied, harmonious, and prosperous, but demands to be let alone.

In all social systems there must be a class to do the menial duties, to perform the drudgery of life. That is, a class requiring but a low order of intellect and but little skill. Its requisites are vigor, docility, fidelity. Such a class you must have, or you would not have that other class which leads progress, civilization, and refinement. It constitutes the very mud-sill of society and of political government; and you might as well attempt to build a house in the air, as to build either the one or the other, except on this mud-sill. Fortunately for the South, she found a race adapted to that purpose to her hand. A race inferior to her own, but eminently qualified in temper, in vigor, in docility, in capacity to stand the climate, to answer all her purposes. We use them for our purpose, and call them slaves. We found them slaves by the common "consent of mankind," which, according to Cicero, *"lex naturæ est."* The highest proof of what is Nature's law. We are old-fashioned at the South yet; slave is a word discarded now by "ears polite;" I will not characterize that class at the North by that term; but you have it; it is there; it is everywhere; it is eternal.

The Senator from New York [William H. Seward] said yesterday that the whole world had abolished slavery. Aye, the *name,* but not the *thing;* all the powers of the earth cannot abolish that. God only can do it when he repeals the *fiat,* "the poor ye always have with you;" for the man who lives by daily labor, and scarcely lives at that, and who has to put out his labor in the market, and take the best he can get for it; in short, your whole hireling class of manual laborers and "operatives," as you call them, are essentially slaves. The difference between us is, that our slaves are hired for life and well compensated; there is no starvation, no begging, no want of employment among our people, and scantily compensated, which may be proved in the most painful manner, at any hour in any street in any of your large towns. Why, you meet more beggars in one day, in any single street of the city of New York, than you would meet in a lifetime in the whole South. We do not think that whites should be slaves either by law or necessity. Our slaves are black, of another and inferior race.

8. Feuille du Commerce Eulogizes John Brown, January 21, 1860

In the Haitian capital, Port-au-Prince, flags flew at half-mast on the day of Brown's execution. Then on January 20, 1860, three days of mourning began with a mass and memorial service for Brown in the Port-au-Prince cathedral. Public officials were among the huge crowd, and Brown's name was displayed in gold on a large black cloth. The speeches described Brown as a Christian martyr to abolition, his heroic actions as a signal that slavery must be abolished, and his death as an affirmation of human brotherhood between black and white. A main boulevard in Port-au-Prince was eventually named for Brown. Ceremonies and tributes took place in several other Haitian cities as well, and Haitians collected thousands of dollars for Brown's family. The Haitian French-language newspapers, including *Le Progrès* and *Feuille du Commerce,* were filled with commentary during the days and weeks following the commemorations. *Le Progrès* published a letter from John Brown, Jr., to Haitian president Fabre Geffrard which thanked Geffrard and the Haitian citizens for their support, paid tribute to Toussaint-L'Ouverture, a leader of the Haitian revolution, and praised the fact of emancipation in Haiti. *Feuille du Commerce,* a four-page newspaper based in Port-au-Prince and edited by Joseph Courtois, printed Victor Hugo's famous letter of December 2, a public letter to Hugo from several citizens thanking him for that public letter and describing Brown as a "sublime figure of Christ," and the lyrics to a song about the "martyr" and "defender of our race" John Brown. It also published the editorial below.

The cause of the abolition of slavery has just counted another martyr. This fact, however indifferent it may be to others, cannot be so to us, descendants as we are of the persecuted race of Africa: this event must weigh upon our hearts as a public calamity. John Brown, with his noble co-workers, has been sent to an ignominious death on the gallows! And this in a country where liberty appears to have its grandest aspiration, where nothing is said or done but in the name of liberty; it is in this country, it is in the United States, in fact, that this man who demanded liberty for an unjustly oppressed and enslaved race, is shamefully dragged to the scaffold. John Brown and his friends perhaps too quickly

Feuille du Commerce, *John Brown Eulogy,* January 21, 1860.

abandoned themselves to despair. But shall we therefore say that the hour of emancipation for our unhappy brethren is not yet come? However it may be, the blood of John Brown guarantees that it is at hand. Despite all the demonstrations of interest on behalf of the condemned; despite the eloquent plea that civilization and the nineteenth century put into the sublime mouth of the guest of Jersey, the martyrdom was performed. Reassure yourselves, ye slaves; nothing is lost—liberty is immortal. New Ogés and Chavannes, Brown and his companions have sown this slave land with their glorious blood, and doubt not that consequently avengers will arise.

9. Northerner Frederick Law Olmsted Depicts the Economic Costs of Slavery, 1861

One of the grand errors out of which this rebellion has grown came from supposing that whatever nourishes wealth and gives power to an ordinary civilized community must command as much for a slaveholding community. The truth has been overlooked that the accumulation of wealth and the power of a nation are contingent not merely upon the primary value of the surplus of productions of which it has to dispose, but very largely also upon the way in which the income from its surplus is distributed and reinvested. Let a man be absent from almost any part of the North twenty years, and he is struck, on his return, by what we call the "improvements" which have been made: better buildings, churches, schoolhouses, mills, railroads, etc. In New York city alone, for instance, at least two hundred millions of dollars have been reinvested merely in an improved housing of the people; in labour-saving machinery, waterworks, gasworks, etc., and much more. It is not difficult to see where the profits of our manufacturers and merchants are. Again, go into the country, and there is no end of substantial proof of twenty years of agricultural prosperity, not alone in roads, canals, bridges, dwellings, barns and fences, but in books and furniture, and gardens, and pictures, and in the better dress and evidently higher education of the people. But where will the returning traveller see the accumulated cotton profits of twenty years in Mississippi? Ask the cotton-planter for them, and he will point in reply, not to dwellings, libraries, churches, schoolhouses, mills, railroads, or anything of the kind; he will point to his negroes—to almost nothing else. Negroes such as stood for five hundred dollars once, now represent a thousand dollars. We must look then in Virginia and those Northern Slave States which have the monopoly of supplying negroes for the real wealth which the sale of cotton has brought to the South. But where is the evidence of it? where anything to compare with the evidence of accumulated profits to be seen in any Free State? If certain portions of Virginia have been a little improving, others unquestionably have been deteriorating, growing shabbier, more comfortless, less convenient. The total increase in wealth of the population during the last twenty years shows for almost nothing. One year's improvements of a Free State exceed it all.

Frederick Law Olmsted, *The Cotton Kingdom: A Traveler's Observations on Cotton and Slavery in the American Slave States*, I (New York: Mason Brothers, 1861), 24–26.

It is obvious that to the community at large, even in Virginia, the profits of supplying negroes to meet the wants occasioned by the cotton demand have not compensated for the bar which the high cost of all sorts of human service, which the cotton demand has also occasioned, has placed upon all other means of ac-cumulating wealth; and this disadvantage of the cotton monopoly is fully expe-rienced by the negro-breeders themselves, in respect to everything else they have to produce or obtain.

 # ESSAYS

Historians have long debated the causes of the Civil War. Some scholars have argued that the war could have been avoided, that a generation of blundering politicians had ineptly maneuvered the nation into war. Other historians have agreed with William Seward, a statesman from New York who served in Presi-dent Lincoln's cabinet, that the war was an "irrepressible conflict." Some histor-ians focus on political differences between the North and the South, whereas others show greater attention to economic distinctions between "free" and "slave" labor. The following two essays reflect historical debates over the causes of the war. In the first, Bruce Levine asks why northerners voted for Abraham Lincoln. The Republican Party was less than a decade old and yet Lincoln won a significant majority of northern voters. While other scholars have emphasized the anti-immigrant, nativist leanings of the Republican Party, Levine finds that the central reason was opposition to slavery. A large number of northerners felt that slavery had expanded enough and Lincoln's candidacy reflected these feelings. In the second essay, Brian Schoen examines how southerners created their own co-alition around cotton. He shows how cotton production and sales not only bound many southern whites together but also fixed them into a transatlantic economic web. These southerners relied on cotton and the territorial and labor expansions it necessitated. The "cotton kingdom" not only led them to war but also led them to believe they could win.

Why Northerners Voted for Abraham Lincoln

BRUCE LEVINE

Abraham Lincoln's election to the presidency urgently posed a series of questions about both the man and his young party. Just who was Abraham Lincoln politi-cally? Precisely what did he and his allies truly stand for? What could be ex-pected from the new administration? And, since elections not only decide the identity of the future government but also take the electorate's political temper-ature, what did Lincoln's election reveal about the values and priorities of the majority of northern voters who had just given him their support?

From *Journal of the Civil War Era*, Volume 1, no. 4. Copyright © 2011 by the University of North Carolina Press. Used by permission of the publisher. www.uncpress.unc.edu

These were and are simple, straightforward questions, but the answers to some of them have long been hotly contested.

To many, what spawned and sustained Lincoln's party seemed obvious: a pre-occupation with slavery and its future. Lincoln had forcefully said as much on in-numerable occasions, as in his high-profile 1858 debates with Stephen A. Douglas. "The sentiment that contemplates the institution of slavery in this country as a wrong is the sentiment of the Republican party," Lincoln emphasized in Alton, Illinois. And it was that sentiment, he added, "around which all their actions, all their arguments, circle, from which all their propositions radiate. They look upon it as being a moral, social, and political wrong."

The abolitionist Frederick Douglass, who could be very critical of Lincoln's party, nonetheless agreed with Lincoln both about the focus of that party's argument with the Democrats and about how rank-and-file Republi-cans viewed that clash. "Slavery," Douglass observed in August 1860, "is the real issue—the single bone of contention between all parties and sections," and "the anti-slavery sentiment in the Northern States is the vital element of the Republican party."

Many observers more hostile to the Republicans bitterly agreed. "The great point upon which the political parties of the country are at variance, is that of slav-ery," declared the Democratic *Illinois State Register*. The *New York Herald* de-nounced the Republicans in 1860 exactly because they "were founded on and animated by the antislavery idea." The *Charleston Mercury* warned a few months earlier that in the North now "a party predominates whose vital principle is hostil-ity to African slavery in the South." One secession advocate after another made the same point in 1860–61. Over the years, many scholars have seen things similarly, and today this constitutes a broadly based consensus among historians of the subject.

At the time, however, some steadfastly denied that the desire to contain and ultimately destroy bondage was the essence of the Republican creed or appeal. During the mid-1850s, Stephen Douglas asserted that the Republicans were a party of ethnic hatred and cultural tyranny. Much of the Republicans' support came, according to Douglas and many of his party colleagues in the North, from anti-immigrant bigots. In making that case, such opponents depicted the Re-publican Party as the virtual clone of another organization that emerged during that decade—the anti-immigrant, anti-Catholic American party, better known as the Know-Nothings, which notoriously aimed to exclude the foreign born from political life in the United States. "Abolitionism, Know Nothingism, and all other isms are akin to each other and are in alliance," declared Douglas. The Republi-cans, critics charged, have "no objection to Know-Nothingism and its distinctive and proscriptive doctrines." Both of those parties "combine against the political rights and religious freedom" of those "who were born on European soil." The growth of Republicanism, these northern Democrats concluded, thus reflected "the powerful influence" of sheer "bigotry" in much of the northern electorate.

During the past few decades, some scholars have revived the notion that Re-publicans secured much of their support by endorsing nativist sentiments and mea-sures. In 1856, they point out, the Know-Nothing presidential candidate, Millard Fillmore, received 22 percent of the popular vote, in the process depriving the

Republicans of the crucial electoral votes of Illinois, Indiana, Pennsylvania, and New Jersey ... and, thereby, of the White House. Four years later, however, Lincoln obtained nearly all the electoral votes of those same states, in no small part by winning the support of a great many former Fillmore supporters.

The Republicans accomplished this feat, according to Joel Silbey, William E. Gienapp, and others, by adapting to the prejudices of the Know-Nothings. Their "blatant solicitation of nativist support" involved adding a big admixture of nativism, especially anti-Catholicism, to their message and program, thereby "making themselves attractive to the Know Nothings on the latter's terms." By the time this makeover was completed, they hold, "Know Nothings had ... every reason to be satisfied" with the result.

Just a year before being elected president, Abraham Lincoln famously stated that he had been "always a Whig in politics." What Lincoln left unsaid, however, was that for most of its life the Whig Party's politics was the subject of vigorous internal dispute.

Uniting Whigs generally was a devotion to economic development and the government support that such development seemed to require. Other issues, however, tended to divide their party. At the two poles of that debate stood conservatives and liberal democrats. Differentiating these two camps were their contrasting reactions to the development of political democracy and calls to expand the scope of democratic rights and increase the number of those who enjoyed them. These differences, in turn, revealed themselves in disputes about two major questions of the day—what to do about chattel slavery and how to cope with the era's massive immigration from Europe.

Whig conservatives, like Federalists before them, considered republics to be fragile structures. A broad franchise and open political conflict seemed to threaten social order and private wealth. An electorate that included men with little or no property, formal education, or cultural refinement, they were sure, was susceptible to dangerous manipulation by demagogues and therefore quite incapable of assuring the social peace and calm so essential to national prosperity.

In many urban centers, these fears and suspicions of mass-based political democracy expressed themselves most openly and forcefully in hostility toward an expanding and enfranchised immigrant population, an especially large proportion of which owned little or no property. Irish- and German-born working people proved to conservative Whig observers that they were poor citizen material. They proved that in part by rallying to Democratic politicians who professed sympathy for the plight of the man of small means who was oppressed by the power of "concentrated capital."

Such northern Whig conservatives therefore gravitated toward nativist politicians and policies, especially the attempt to deny immigrants the right to vote, either permanently or at least for some extended period following federal naturalization. Nativism, wrote Philadelphia Whig attorney Sidney George Fisher in his diary in 1844, "is decidedly conservative, because by excluding foreigners so much democracy is excluded, so much of the rabble, so much ignorance & brutality from political power." Nativism therefore "harmonizes with the instincts & secret wishes & opinions of the Whigs."

Conservative northern Whigs also brought their distinctive fusion of enthusiasm for economic development and distrust of democratic politics into the escalating controversy over slavery's future. Although critical of slavery, they generally strove to muffle controversies about that institution for fear of polarizing political life, endangering transregional political parties, and dissolving national cohesion.

Whig liberals took their distance from more conservative party colleagues in regard to both immigration and slavery. They were more devoted to the principles of civic equality and political democracy. They believed, with New York's William H. Seward, that history was moving away from legal inequality and physical coercion, that "the democratic principle is leading the way to universal liberty." Although few of them stood for full racial equality, Whig liberals were more convinced than Whig conservatives that slavery was not only economically stunting but also morally repugnant and politically toxic. The perfect embodiment of aristocratic, antidemocratic principles, it endangered the republic as a whole.

Liberal-democratic Whigs also differed with conservatives concerning the proper political status of immigrants. To be sure, they were not modern multiculturalists. They shared with conservatives an Anglo-American cultural tradition that associated Catholicism with moral laxity, economic stagnation, and antirepublican politics. And here again social realities—the large contingent of immigrants who were poor, working-class, Catholic, and pro-Democratic—reinforced those associations and inflamed those longstanding prejudices. Many politicians and journalists of liberal Whig antecedents continued to express suspicion of and hostility to such immigrants down through 1860 and beyond.

But those sentiments led few Whig liberals to favor aggressive anti-immigrant policies. Charles Sumner, George Julian, and Joshua Giddings were especially vocal in their repudiation of nativism on principle. So was William H. Seward, in whose opinion northern economic development and a welcoming attitude toward immigrants went hand in hand....

That popular anti-immigrant animosity proved a godsend for Whiggish conservatives, giving them much of the traction they needed to break with the by-now virtually paralyzed Whig organization and launch a new party defined by their own principles. And so the Americans (or Know-Nothings) came into existence, pledged both to restrict the rights of immigrants and to muffle and defuse the explosive slavery issue.

In the event, however, the slavery issue refused to be defused. On the contrary: it reemerged with a vengeance within the Know-Nothing Party itself, eventually unmaking it. And as that party disintegrated, it cast adrift a growing number of Whiggish northern voters and politicians, some of whom gravitated, either sooner or later, toward that other party born of the national Whig organization's demise—the Republicans—a party in which liberal-democratic Whigs featured prominently.

The future political allegiance of the rest of those ex-Know-Nothing voters was a matter of great interest to Republicans generally during the second half of the 1850s. If those voters could be won over, the Republicans might well look forward to victory in the next presidential election. But opinions varied about how that task was to be accomplished.

Some Republicans did try to reshape their party's program to accommodate the politics of Whiggish conservatism between 1856 and 1860. Those who did that included some ex-Know-Nothings who had already joined the Republican Party, who had decided that with the nativist party's decline "the only reasonable course" left to them was "to Americanize" the Republican organization. Working with them were other Republicans (such as Horace Greeley) who, while not themselves nativists or "soft" on slavery, were quite willing to woo voters who were by bending in that direction, attempting to soften the Republican Party's adamant opposition to slavery's expansion or to infuse nativist themes into its platform and rhetoric.

But this campaign to temper the Republican opposition to slavery's expansion and to court nativist-minded voters aroused strong resistance within the Republican Party. The result was a major, protracted struggle over Republicanism's basic tenets and public stance. In that struggle, Republican conservatives ultimately failed to impose their will.

A variety of forces and factors strengthened the resistance to them. One of those was the adhesion to the Republican Party of some groups that were both militantly antislavery and antinativist that had initially kept their distance, notably German American liberals and radicals. But perhaps even more important to the Republican conservatives' ultimate failure was the national political dynamic that had so badly damaged the Democrats in 1854 and that had then precipitated the decline of the Know-Nothing Party—the deepening intransigence (indeed, aggressiveness) of proslavery forces that was, reciprocally, convincing more and more northerners that all attempts to conciliate the "Slave Power" were hopeless, that only firmness could meet the southern challenge.

Resistance to the conservative campaign within the national Republican Party helped induce the Massachusetts legislature to sharply reduce the waiting period imposed in that state on naturalized voters from the twenty-one years originally stipulated by the Know-Nothings to two years—a reduction carried out over the protest of the Know-Nothings themselves. Just as telling, the ratification in 1859 of even a "Two-Year Amendment" to the state constitution brought down upon the Massachusetts party a barrage of criticism by Republicans elsewhere. And no other Republican-controlled state legislature in the country approved a measure like the one passed in the Bay State.

This intraparty struggle between conservatives and liberal democrats over the Republicans' program came to a head in May 1860 at the Chicago national convention. Republican notables of Know-Nothing antecedents (along with others seeking to appease nativist voters) tried to bestow the Republican presidential nomination upon a man with nativist credentials. They also tried to weaken both the Republican Party's condemnation of slavery and its determination to block slavery's expansion through federal action.

The Chicago platform reaffirmed the defining Republican doctrine on slavery, which held that bondage was inherently unconstitutional in any and all federal territories and that federal power should be used to prevent its establishment there. Second, the platform took solid antinativist ground. At the behest of German-born members of the platform committee, the convention explicitly repudiated any federal or state laws "by which the rights of citizens hitherto accorded to immigrants from foreign lands shall be abridged or impaired."

Nativists recognized in these words a slap at themselves and their pet measures. Republican conservatives objected to that plank precisely for that reason. It "is a bad thing for our cause here," fretted one Bostonian, "and in Pennsylvania and New Jersey." For that matter, grieved a Connecticut party leader, New Englanders generally "have been, and are now, strong in Americanism, and believe in just what that 'sec' [section] condemns."

Which brings us back to the question of Lincoln's political identity generally and his stand on immigration and immigrant rights in particular.

Lincoln did not begin his career in the Whig Party as a member of its liberal wing. In those early years, he had instead taken the rather conservative Henry Clay as his model. As late as 1858, indeed, Lincoln was still referring to Clay as "my beau ideal of a statesman." But in truth he had by then come to champion a brand of Whiggery different in crucial ways from that of his supposed "beau ideal." The difference is especially apparent in the case of nativism and slavery.

Lincoln had since boyhood felt a strong revulsion toward slavery. He believed it was an institution grounded in "injustice." He believed, as he would later put it, that if slavery was not wrong, nothing was. In 1845, he declared it a northerner's duty to "never knowingly lend ourselves directly or indirectly, to prevent that slavery from dying a natural death," never to help it "to find new places for it to live in, when it can no longer exist in the old." And when, a few years later, supporters of the Wilmot proviso attempted to bar slavery from the lands taken from Mexico, Lincoln stood with them.

In 1850, fears for the Union led Lincoln and many other like-minded Whigs to backtrack and applaud Clay's 1850 Compromise, which not only failed to exclude slavery by federal law from the Utah and New Mexico territories but also included a new and stronger fugitive slave law. But in 1854 the Kansas-Nebraska law convinced Lincoln that slaveholders and their allies were determined to reinforce slavery and extend its domain as widely as possible. Lincoln concluded that the systems of free and slave labor could not indefinitely and peacefully coexist within the borders of the United States. One of them would have to subdue the other, and it would do so through the deliberate, organized efforts of its champions. Antislavery citizens in the North would have to take control of the federal government in order to block the further extension of bondage and thereby "put it in the course of ultimate extinction." That conclusion led Lincoln into the leadership of the Illinois Republican Party.

To strengthen his new party, Lincoln did very much wish to attract ex-Know-Nothing voters to it. He wished (as he later put it) to fuse with as many people as possible. But he insisted on doing so without departing from Republican principles. So he warned Republicans against "the temptation to lower the Republican Standard in order to gather recruits" from various quarters. He was "against letting down the [R]epublican standard [of 1856] a hair's breadth." He was adamantly opposed to any concession that would "surrender the o[b]ject of the Republican organization—of preventing the spread and nationalization of Slavery."

The Lincoln whom convention delegates picked to head their national ticket was a firm and publicly-identified opponent of both slavery's expansion and nativism.

The national Republican Party's refusal, as the 1860 elections approached, to alter its stands on either immigrant rights or slavery in the territories angered many Whiggish conservatives, including those who had become Republicans in an attempt to "Americanize that party." Missouri's Edward Bates gave vent to his frustration in his diary. Bates was proud to have been the favorite candidate at the Chicago convention of "the most moderate and prudent" Republicans, those who had sought to "secure the alliance of the remnants of the Whig and American parties." The failure of his candidacy and the convention's rejection of the political program for which it stood was all too evident to him. The platform adopted in Chicago, thought Bates, was too "exclusive and defiant," calculated "only to gratify a handful of extreme abolitionists." Excessively radical on the slavery issue, it was also far too generous toward immigrants. "To please the Germans unreasonably," Bates complained, "it galls (not to say insults) the Americans [Know-Nothings] and all the Republicans who came in through the American party." (The Missourian was no more enthusiastic about the selection as the party's national standard-bearer of Abraham Lincoln—a man who, Bates wrote, "is as fully committed as Mr. Seward is, to the extremest doctrines of the Republican party.")

Illinois's own Orville H. Browning saw things in the same light. Bates counted Browning as a political friend, and Browning had favored Bates for the presidential nomination precisely "to give some check to the ultra tendencies of the Republican party" and "to bring to our support the old whigs in the free states, who have not yet fraternized with us." In passing over Bates and nominating Lincoln, Browning therefore fretted, the party had made "a mistake."

Sentiments like these were, of course, a far cry from the expressions of satisfaction with the outcome of the Republican convention that some modern writers have attributed to the nativists in 1860. It was the foreign-born and more militantly antislavery members of the Republican Party, rather than those anxious to accommodate nativism or sectional conciliators, who had reason to cheer Lincoln's nomination. One German-language newspaper in New York, although originally aligned with Seward, happily observed after the convention, "The struggle [against] a corrupt clique ... which had smuggled a narrow-minded Know-Nothingism into the very bosom of free and honest Republican principles" has now been successfully "fought out upon the field of the Republican nomination."

But in the convention's aftermath, some Republican notables called upon the party and its candidate to change course and "repudiate" the Chicago platform's antinativist plank. Others urged that when Lincoln publicly accepted the party's nomination he at least take care to "say nothing about the platform."

That was not the course that Lincoln chose. His letter of acceptance made a point, in fact, not only of endorsing the Chicago platform but also of specifically and pointedly pledging "not to violate, or disregard it, in any part." And during the campaign proper, both that platform and Lincoln's position on immigrant rights were laid squarely before the electorate. An important and widely distributed piece of Republican campaign literature was Horace Greeley's *Political Text-Book for 1860,* an anthology of documents (including, of course, the Chicago platform) offered as essential reading for the informed voter. By the time of the fall election, that volume had gone through fourteen editions and had circulated throughout the free states. Lincoln's antinativist letter to Theodore Canisius occupied a place of honor in that widely read book, one of only six samples of the candidate's writings included therein. Another of those six samples was Lincoln's aforementioned public acceptance of the presidential nomination and his emphatic endorsement of the party platform.

How was it, then, that in 1860's fall elections so many northerners who four years earlier had voted for Millard Fillmore now cast ballots for Abraham Lincoln? No doubt some who did so believed that even a Lincoln administration would prove more sympathetic to nativism than would one led by a Democrat. And some Republican officials and journalists were happy to encourage such hopes.

But attentive nativists and proponents of a weakened stand against slavery could hardly mistake Lincoln for one of their own. Most of the conservative Whigs and former Know-Nothings who voted for Lincoln did that not because he or his national party had made major concessions to their views about either of those subjects. They threw in with the Republicans as the sharpening terms of the sectional conflict demonstrated to them the urgency of stopping "the slave power," thereby undermining the appeal and prospects of the parties of the political center. Lincoln, in short, had not moved toward those voters; it was they who had moved toward him.

A case in point was the conservative New York Whig George Templeton Strong, a patrician attorney whose diary had earlier overflowed with denunciations of both antislavery militants and foreign-born voters. But Strong's resentment of slaveholder bullying was driving him toward the Republicans even in 1856. In 1860, because "the crack of the plantation whip" had again grown "too audible" to tolerate in national politics, he once more concluded that "the North must assert its rights, now, and take the consequences."

How Cotton Wove Together a Secession Coalition

BRIAN SCHOEN

The debate over slavery's expansion, along with concerns over its political and economic security in the Union, propelled the Cotton States toward secession. Early advocates of secession urged that the drastic step needed to be taken at the first sign of defeat: California's entrance as a free state. That event led William

---

Schoen, Brian. The Fragile Fabric of Union: Cotton, Federal Politics, and the Global Origins of the Civil War. pp. 197–201, 213, 219, 237–338, 246, 258–259. © 2009 The Johns Hopkins University Press. Reprinted with permission of Johns Hopkins University Press.

Trescot to declare in 1850 that a "political revolution" had been inaugurated and "the only safety of the South is the establishment of a political centre within itself; in simpler words, the formation of an independent nation." Others in the Deep South agreed, as southern rights associations sprang up throughout the Lower South, many threatening secession unless Congress protected southern interests. In the spirit of John C. Calhoun and at the behest of Governor John Quitman, the Mississippi legislature called for a southern convention to ensure the return of fugitive slaves and to guarantee slaveholders' access to new lands. Observers braced for a possible secessionist triumph when delegates elected vocal South Carolina secessionist, Robert Barnwell Rhett, president. This first secession crisis, and particularly Trescot's arguments, disseminated as a pamphlet entitled "The Position and Course of the South," provide insights into Cotton South secessionist thought and a template, albeit a premature one, for future action. It exhibited some of the defensiveness and irrationality historians have typically attributed to alleged "fire-eaters." Yet early secessionists also used domestic and international developments to provide a surprisingly pragmatic, and material-driven, argument for southern independence.

In explaining the origins of domestic conflict, Trescot prioritized allegedly universal laws of political economy, proposing that slavery had given the struggle between labor and capital (modernity's "vital principle of political organization") an ominous sectional tone. "At the North," he explained, "labour and capital are equal; at the South, labour is inferior to capital. At the North labour and capital strive; the one, to get all it can; the other, to give as little as it may—they are enemies. At the South, labour is dependent on capital, and having ceased to be rivals, they have ceased to be enemies." Race-based slavery had permanently subordinated the South's primary labor force and thus, according to Trescot, muted class conflict and left slaveholding capitalists to dominate southern politics. By contrast, northern working-class whites composed the Democratic Party's rank and file, especially in eastern cities and western farms. "Can a more violent contrast be imagined?" he retorted. "Free labour hates slave labour—capital, at the mercy of labour is jealous of capital owning labour—where are their points of sympathy?" There were none, Trescot concluded: "The North and the South are irreconceivably hostile ... their social and political systems cannot co-exist ... the one in the nature of things wages internecine war against the other." Contrasting social systems impacted almost every aspect of politics, creating "competing systems of representation and taxation" and even divergent foreign policies.

Proponents for secession drew richly from international developments and converted earlier free traders' calls for U.S. and British global cooperation into an imagined alliance between the South and Europe. As events suggested that the North was "in fact, a foreign, power," Trescot placed almost infinite faith in cotton's power to ensure cooperation from allegedly more natural allies abroad. Quoting a September 1850 *London Times* article that highlighted the significance of the cotton trade, Trescot noted that Britain's trade "with America transcends all others." "Does it not follow," he arrogantly claimed, "that the industrial economy and the system of foreign relations of the nation, so far as based on commercial principles, should spring from, and be controlled by the cotton growing States?" A southern Confederacy, "cultivated by a slave population—supplying the staple of the world's manufacture, and ranged in imposing strength around the Gulf of Mexico, so as to command the trade of the Isthmus connection," would have "a close alliance with the few great manufacturing nations" and possess an "unchangeable resolution to leave the interior affairs of other nations to their own discussion." Trescot predicted that "the most selfish interests of the foreign world" would prompt "a speedy recognition of [the South's] national independence" while perpetuating selfish northern merchants' and manufacturers' "active diplomatic rivalry with Great Britain." "Out of the union," another South Carolinian commented, "there may be some hope of safety for our institution, in it there is none." According to Trescot, the "destructive energy" emanating from antislavery forces in the federal government made it "as wise, as safe, as honourable, to trust our domestic institutions and foreign interests to the Parliament of Great Britain as to a Congress with a northern majority. Nay, wiser and safer, for her colonial experience has taught England never again to sacrifice her profits to her philanthropy." Only half jesting, Robert Barnwell Rhett presented just such a possibility. If other states refused to join South Carolina in seceding, then, he suggested, she could revitalize her commerce by embracing complete free trade and becoming in effect a British protectorate.

Secessionists in 1850 drew extensively from the previous tirades against northern exploitation levied by free trade cosmopolitans like George McDuffie but repudiated the pacifist utopianism often underlying such arguments. John Quitman, a prominent general during the Mexican-American War and future filibusterer, accepted war as a way of life and in 1850 ordered an inventory of military supplies in the event of another one. Even for the future diplomat, Trescot, "the marked characteristic of political life is the violent and uncompromising antagonism of great interests." Like future Marxist and Progressive historians and their intellectual heirs, Trescot and late antebellum secessionists assumed that conflict, rather than peace, reflected the natural state of political affairs.

Unlike later interpretations that pitted a mighty capitalist and modernizing North against a traditional agrarian society, contemporaries like Trescot, one of the nation's first historians, assumed slaveholders to be a superior type of "capitalist." Having used slavery to win the historic class struggle, he saw them as operating from a position of political and economic strength. Once "mature" the Lower South's "command of the Gulf and the cotton trade" would make them "the guardian of the world's commerce." "The formation of an independent Southern confederacy would," in Trescot's view, not only defend against real or perceived northern antislavery gestures but also "give to the South the control of its industrial policy and its commercial connection; thus arming it, at the very outset of its national career, with diplomatic power, and at the same time, from the character of those interests propitiating all foreign jealousy, and inviting the cordial alliance of European powers." More than honor was at stake for Quitman, who proclaimed that the South must not "quietly submit to be robbed of her share in the broad harbours of the Pacific coast, and the vast territories," which they had helped win. For these men sectional conflict had become inevitable because both the North and the South sought progress and were determined to pursue their respective interests within a rapidly changing and increasingly interconnected world.

After much thought, majorities in the Cotton South rejected the secessionist appeals of Trescot, Rhett, and Quitman. They accepted instead the contentions of self-proclaimed "unionists" that northern allies remained numerous and powerful enough to serve Lower South interests. Their evidence came from the actions of western Democrats and "Cotton Whigs" who joined just enough southern Whigs and procompromise Democrats to secure a stronger federal Fugitive Slave Act, an acceptable western boundary to Texas, and nonrestriction of slavery into the remaining former Mexican provinces. Though the loss of California kept many Cotton South politicians yearning for secession, the compromise, as affirmed by Georgia voters in November 1850, blunted the independence movement. A Georgia platform, later endorsed by Mississippi and Alabama legislators, asserted the right to secede but promised to "abide by" the compromise "as a permanent adjustment of this sectional controversy" only so long as fugitive slaves were returned and slavery permitted to extend into new territories. Southern protonationalists had gained more adherents than when Thomas Cooper first proposed disunion two decades earlier, but by spring 1851 Mississippian Albert Gallatin Brown declared that "the Southern movement was dead."

In reality it had helped redefine regional politics before going into hibernation, only to emerge with vengeance after domestic and foreign developments provided secessionists a more convincing case that regional interests would be better served outside of the Union. This need not have been so. Slaveowners seeking merely to preserve a traditional society might have sacrificed free trade or economic development, saving political capital to cultivate stronger northern alliances capable of protecting slavery. They might have dropped the question of slavery's expansion westward, threatening and compromising their way to a stronger Fugitive Slave Act and amendments protecting slavery in the states. Future efforts suggest that a majority of northerners, perhaps even Free Soil Republicans, would have accommodated such demands. Yet, constituencies in the Cotton States did not merely seek to hold on to the old. They sought the economic and political progress so closely identified with the modern experience. In fact, they firmly believed their central place in the global cotton business entitled them to it. Consequently, they aggressively fought to develop local and regional economies and to preserve their perceived rights in the federal territories.

Slaveholders' ambitions during the 1850s placed them squarely at odds with previous northern allies over major policy areas, including western homesteading, the meaning of popular sovereignty, long-cherished navigation acts, the Pacific railroad, and to a fax lesser extent, the tariff. As fierce debates and eventual gridlock ensued over these substantive issues, antislavery Republicans in the North grew stronger after each battle. A majority of Cotton South politicians came to the conclusion—first offered by Turnbull in the 1820s, then by secessionists in 1850, and repeatedly by Free Soil Republicans—that free labor and slave capitalists represented separate civilizations incapable of peaceful coexistence. Reports of actual bloodshed, from the Kansas plain to the Senate floor to the streets of Harper's Ferry, provided tangible evidence. In the meantime, careful and successful diplomacy over potentially catastrophic disagreements (the arrest of American and British sailors, expansion into the Caribbean rim, and the illicit slave trade) along with the perceived centrality of King Cotton, kept hope alive for an imagined partnership with European nations, a development central to secessionist aspirations. While solid majorities in the Upper South, sugar planters in the Mississippi Delta, and many yeoman farmers outside of the black belt hesitated before secession, residents of the Cotton South generally welcomed it with a mixture of concern, relief, and optimism. Though certainly not all cotton planters and farmers supported secession, systematic voting studies suggest they disproportionately did so. This was no mere coincidence.

Converting Friends to Enemies and Enemies to Friends: The Search for Natural Allies

The quest for slavery's expansion into either the Great Plains or the Caribbean rim and the related need for more labor threatened to destroy domestic political alliances that were decades in the making. They also heightened the possibility of conflict with European partners. Recognizing these potentialities, many former Whigs and some South Carolina pragmatists tried to blunt their neighbors' enthusiasm. They fought an uphill battle, however, as regional political economy, honor, and rights had been redefined around grander economic ambitions and the ability to take slaves south and west. Triangulating between perceived regional interests, a domestic situation seen as increasingly hostile, and foreign developments they interpreted as favorable, many Cotton South politicians and commentators came to Trescot's 1850 conclusion: the region possessed more clout internationally than domestically. Its true allies were to be found not at home but abroad....

Proponents of slavery's expansion sometimes joined others who believed that international circumstances might even allow the South to meet another critical need: African labor. The movement for reopening the international slave trade had supporters as early as the 1830s but gained new impetus when Governor Adams, having just successfully resolved the Negro Seaman's controversy, used a November 1856 address to ask South Carolina legislators to repeal state laws that closed the trade. Developments in the British West Indies and the perception of European accommodation appear to have been foremost in Edward B. Bryan's mind as he drafted the state's 1857 majority committee report that recommended going forward with Adams's proposal. After the proposal narrowly failed, Bryan took his appeal to the broader public, highlighting the wider economic and geopolitical context for a movement mistakenly seen by historians as delusional or motivated by disunionist motives. Bryan opened each of his twelve "Letters to the Southern People" with quotations from the *London Times* and *Paris Constitutionalist* that characterized emancipation as misguided "philanthropy." Believing that slaves were necessary for southern and global economic development, Bryan argued that a "COTTON PARLIAMENT" would not let "abolitionist influence"' stand in the way of further profits and would concede to economic interest: "Commerce now rules. *It* is king; cotton is heir-apparent, and slavery is queen-dowager." Subsequent quotes cherry-picked from the European press and parliaments to highlight the political and economic weakness of the West Indies compared to slave economies in Cuba, Brazil, and the United States.

Realists Decide: Election and Secession

Unlike Rhett and Yancey, most voters in the Cotton South did not approach the election of 1860 believing secession was inevitable or desirable. They did, however, enter the contest celebrating politicians who confidently asserted "southern" rights and interests on the national and international stage. The Panic of 1857, mutinies in India, the turn to African and coolie labor in the West Indies, and Europe's seemingly malleable foreign policy elevated faith in cotton and, by extension, slavery's power abroad. A bumper crop at relatively high prices created significant economic optimism, leading Godfrey Barnsley, a British-born New Orleans factor-turned-slaveowning-planter, to exclaim that "the receipts of cotton are astounding, I hardly know what to think." Yet a bleak political forecast at home clouded any bright economic forecast. The rejection of the Lecompton Constitution, John Brown's raid at Harper's Ferry, and Stephen Douglas's Freeport Doctrine had eroded faith that northerners, Democrats or Republicans, would continue to serve the diverse and ambitious interests of the Cotton South.

As Congress convened in early 1860, Jefferson Davis brought the debate over slavery in the territories to a head by proposing a resolution that would make it the "duty of Congress" to intervene if "the judiciary does not possess power to insure adequate protection" for slaveowners. Opportunistic South Carolinians rallied behind Davis's proposal for congressional intervention. The most forceful advocates, though, came from newer cotton states, including Mississippian Albert Gallatin Brown and Alabamians C. C. Clay and William Yancey, whose constituents would be more directly affected by exclusion from the West. Newer but still insecure planters and slaveholding farmers in the southwest cotton areas had great expectations but also grave concerns about their future and that of their children should slave territory not spread. Though many fervently denied it, backers of so-called positive protection lacked faith in popular sovereignty. Their new demands promised to fracture the Democratic Party.

Northern Democrats, still stinging from defeat at the polls and the selection of a Republican speaker of the House, rightly perceived the proposed legislation as a betrayal of congressional nonintervention. The issue ground congressional politics to a halt, leading recently returned representative James Hammond to tell a relative in April that "no two nations on earth are or ever were more distinctly separated and hostile than we are. Not Carthage and Rome, England and France at any period. How can the thing go on?" After blocking Davis's bill, which Stephen Douglas compared to the "doctrine of the Tories of the Revolution," northern Democrats prepared for the national party convention, ready to reaffirm congressional noninterference and nominate Douglas, its chief proponent. Some noteworthy politicians in the Lower South, including Alexander

Stephens and Douglas's eventual running mate Georgian Herschel Johnson, angrily blamed Davis and others for manufacturing a controversy that threatened to undermine the Union. They did not, however, have the sway to stop more aggressive majorities from composing the slate delegations headed to Charleston in May.

Instead, slave expansionists played to regional pride and interest, claiming that the region's economic, political, and social viability necessitated access to new lands and arguing that northern Democrats could no longer be trusted. "Python" raised the pointed question in the March issue of *De Bow's Review*: "Of what advantage is it to the South to be destroyed by Mr. Douglas through territorial sovereignty to the exclusion of Southern institutions, rather than by Mr. Seward through congressional sovereignty to the same end? What difference is there to the South whether they are forcibly led to immolation by Seward, or accorded, in the alternative, the Roman privilege of selecting their own mode of death, by Douglas? Die they must in either event." South Carolina's Alfred Huger agreed, emphasising that at least Republican policy framed the matter honestly; "If there be any difference so far as the South is concerned between the Squatter Sovereignty of Mr. Douglas and the 'irrepressible conflict' of Mr. Seward, *that* 'difference' is in my poor judgment, in favour of the latter! It is more natural, & it is farther off—the one is abolition *eo nomine* the other is abolition in an offensive disguise! and therefore the more alarming."

Secessionists used Lincoln's resounding victory to highlight for Cotton South residents the weakness of potential political allies in the North and to suggest that the Union had devolved into two irrevocably hostile sections. "Why has the election of Lincoln so altered the opinion of conservative Southerners in favor of Secession?" the *New Orleans Bee* rhetorically asked and then answered: because, even with Democratic successes in some key congressional races, "the result ... showed the tremendous power and popularity of Black Republicanism ... With what shadow of reason could Southern men be advised to submit and await the possible events of the future when abolitionism had swept every Northern Commonwealth?" Editors for Augusta, Georgia's, *Daily Constitutionalist* agreed that the "'ties of Union,' if by the term is meant ties of fraternal sympathy, can never again be strengthened, for they no longer exist to bind the two sections together. They are broken—utterly sundered between portions of the South, and portions of the North." Not even the most conservative Republican or northern Democrat, the paper continued, could change that.

The events culminating in the secessionist winter of 1860 and 1861 have been often told and much debated. Contradictory histories attribute the Lower South's motivation to various impulses: "a crisis of fear" or an abundance of arrogance; a grand "honor" affair to save public face or a paranoid minority's "dishonorable" overthrow of a supposedly unionist public; the culmination of a slaveholding "counterrevolution" or the climax of a second American Revolution. Yet secession represented much more than simply the hasty reactions of an insecure people. The decision reflected a strongly held conviction, based on years of political calculation—or rather miscalculation—that the federal Union no longer served regional interests. This conclusion derived largely from the belief that northern partners were unable or unwilling to continue protecting slave-holders' rights. Those in the Cotton South had also concluded, however, that international economic and political developments afforded them considerable opportunities for advancement outside of the Union. Assisted by high cotton prices and growing European markets, Lower South elites looked across the Atlantic and saw reason for optimism. Secessionists in the Lower South were not simply fleeing a system they believed would fail their slave society; they were also creating a new one that they believed would have powerful partners abroad.

The trajectory of Lower South self-perception from 1787 to 1860 demonstrates how far regional perspective had come. South Carolinians and Georgians had embraced the federal Union from a position of weakness because they believed it provided the best option for their interests in stabilizing a society reeling from the aftershocks of revolution. Pierce Butler, the Rutledges, the Pinckneys, Joseph Clay, and Joseph Habersham all believed that a stronger national government would protect a slave society and assist regional commercial interests. These hopes had found new life in a diverse Jeffersonian majority which cotton planters had thought would organize the nation's interests into harmony under a decentralized political system. By 1860, however, the decades-old debates over slavery and political economy led all but the most strident unionists to conclude that the federal Union had become an unnatural and unequal partnership. The prediction of Rawlins Lowndes, that the "sun, of the Southern States, would set never to rise again," reverberated throughout the region. The political struggles of the 1850s suggested to most whites in the region, some more reluctantly than others, that the Union had outlived its usefulness and become a, perhaps *the*, major obstacle to protecting slavery and enhancing economic profitability. Driven by these calculations, aided by a reservoir of real and perceived grievances, and burgeoning with confidence from the commercial leverage they felt they had, the Cotton States helped inaugurate a devastating war that eventually destroyed the very society and economic hopes they desired to protect and expand.

The region's commitment to cotton permeated nearly every aspect of this aggressive drive toward secession and, by consequence, the war that followed. Cotton had deepened and broadened the region's commitment to slavery and its extension, which was the overriding issue that politically fragmented the second party system and the Union. Cotton inspired in planters and politicians an abiding faith in international commerce and free trade, the defense of which alienated them from otherwise sympathetic northern merchants and manufacturers. Cotton hindered regional industrial development in some areas, though few contemporaries admitted it, and led to a deep (and generally misplaced) frustration over an allegedly exploitative federal Union that the Cotton South blamed for fostering regional dependence on a more populous and rapidly advancing North.

Finally, cotton's central place within the global economy drove planters and farmers, merchants and manufacturers, politicians and writers to imagine a better future outside the Union and gave them the confidence for bold action. Whereas many grain producers, artisans, and even hemp and tobacco planters in the Upper South hesitated and even rejected the call to secede, the Deep South seized the language of revolution and masculine honor, convincing regional majorities to create a nation founded "on the cornerstone" of slavery and protected, they assumed, by King Cotton. Rather than lightening the bonds of union, as Tench Coxe had hoped it would in 1787, cotton's internationally driven political economy had weakened the bonds by limiting the degree to which its growers would invest intellectually, politically, and financially, in the idea of *a* United States. It is perhaps not too much of a stretch to say that, without cotton and the international demand for it, there would not have been secession or a Civil War.

 # FURTHER READING

Tyler G. Anbinder, *Nativism and Slavery* (1994).

Eric Foner, *The Fiery Trial: Abraham Lincoln and American Slavery* (2011).

Lacy K. Ford, Jr., *Origins of Southern Radicalism: The South Carolina Upcountry, 1800–1860* (1988).

William W. Freehling, *The Road to Disunion: Secessionists Triumphant, 1854–1861* (2007).

William E. Gienapp, *The Origins of the Republican Party, 1852–1856* (1986).

James L. Huston, *Calculating the Value of the Union: Slavery, Property Rights, and the Economic Origins of the Civil War* (2003).

Bruce Levine, *Half Slave and Half Free: The Roots of the Civil War* (1992).

James Oakes, *The Scorpion's Sting: Antislavery and the Coming of the Civil War* (2014).

Manisha Sinha, *The Counterrevolution of Slavery: Politics and Ideology in Antebellum South Carolina* (2000).

Elizabeth R. Varon, *Disunion: The Coming of the American Civil War* (2008).

Additional critical thinking activities and content are available in MindTap.

 **MindTap** is a fully online, highly personalized learning experience built upon Cengage Learning content. MindTap combines student learning tools—readings, multimedia, activities, and assessments—into a singular Learning Path that guides students through the course.

CHAPTER 14

The Civil War

Events moved quickly after Abraham Lincoln assumed the presidency on March 4, 1861. When Lincoln attempted to resupply Fort Sumter, an outpost in the harbor of Charleston, South Carolina, that was still controlled by Union forces, the Confederate army shelled the fort; the federal troops surrendered on April 13, 1861. This brief bombardment began a long civil war from which a second revolution would be forged.

When the war began, few expected that it would last four horrifying years. Confederate leaders believed that the world's need for cotton would lead other nations to support their cause. They realized that the Union armies would have to conquer the Confederacy, and they expected that most northerners would tire of war before this could be achieved. Strategists for the Union advocated the "anaconda plan," which coupled a blockade of southern port cities with a military thrust down the Mississippi River valley to divide the Confederacy. In theory, this plan would squeeze the economic life out of the Confederacy, causing its citizenry to sue for peace.

The war went badly for the Union in the early campaigns, particularly in the eastern theater. Indecisive Union generals failed to take advantage of their superior military strength, while able Confederate military leaders, such as Robert E. Lee and "Stonewall" Jackson, befuddled the Union armies. The tide turned in mid-1863 when the Union won two battles in rapid succession, at Vicksburg in the western theater and at Gettysburg in the east. Under the leadership of Ulysses S. Grant and William Tecumseh Sherman, the Union forces took advantage of their numerical strength. These two formerly obscure generals utilized an idea of "total war," which meant that they were willing to wage war against the civilian population as well as against the army and government of their enemy. Shortly after Lincoln's reelection in 1864, Sherman began his "march to the sea," which devastated Georgia. By December 21, 1864, his army had reached the sea at Savannah. Within four months, General Lee surrendered.

The war was revolutionary on many levels. In some ways it might be called the world's first modern war. For the first time, armies engaged in trench warfare. Using rifles that could fire up to five hundred yards, soldiers killed people they could not see. Railroads were used to transfer armies; ironclad ships faced one another in naval combat. As a result, the loss of life suffered by the armies was frightening. In all, 620,000 men died as a result of battle and disease. One out of every six white males in the southern states aged thirteen to forty-three in 1860 was dead five years later. An additional half million men were *maimed during the war, and yet another half million spent some time in overcrowded and unsanitary prison camps. People throughout the world observed the war with wonderment and horror. This was what future wars would be like.*

In part because of these horrors, American society was transformed. Northern society was not unified behind the war effort, and dissent grew when the government suspended the right of habeas corpus and introduced a draft. The result was riots in northern cities and a heightened distrust of Lincoln's leadership. Basic questions of rights during war thus plagued society. Women's roles expanded as well, in part because men were at war, but also because women actively sought ways, such as participation in the Sanitary Commission, to support the war effort. In the Confederacy, the exigencies of war forced its leader to consider measures that had been unthinkable prior to the war. A confederacy formed on the rights of states found that it needed to centralize its government during war. A culture based on the splendor of a rural world had to foster industrialization in order to fight a war. And a society based on slavery ultimately considered arming slaves to fight in the Confederate army. As the war destroyed southern society, all Americans had to ponder how that society would be reconstructed following the war's conclusion.

One monumental change became clear by 1863: the Emancipation Proclamation signaled the end of slavery in the South. African Americans throughout the United States mobilized to end slavery. Whether fighting for the Union army or fleeing their plantation homes to provide aid to invading forces, black people were instrumental in turning the war into a conflict to end slavery. With the end of slavery, Americans joined several other nations who had or were in the process of ending their own systems of unfreedom. In the 1850s, Peru, Venezuela, and Argentina abolished slavery, while in 1860 Russia ended serfdom. For these nations and Americans, they would continue to ponder how much their national cleansings would alter the trajectory of their nations and the world.

QUESTIONS TO THINK ABOUT

What advantages did the Confederacy have at the outset of the Civil War? What were the Union's advantages? Why did the Union ultimately win the war? How did war strain and change the societies in both the North and South? What freedoms would former slaves most anticipate and desire? Which questions about the future of the United States were answered by the Civil War? Which questions were not?

DOCUMENTS

Southern secession was deeply contested, and there were many white southerners who opposed it. Document 1 comes from debates in Virginia over whether to leave the Union or not. In it, this Virginian maintains that separation will be impossible because the northern states will never allow the South to leave without a fight. The war itself transformed nearly every element of society. In document 2, northern women instruct one another how they can support the Union cause. The war also affected the lives of Native Americans, as is shown in documents 3 and 5. In the South, those who had been moved so that slavery could advance, such as the Cherokee, had to take sides even if they did not want to do so. Document 5 relates to white-Native American battles in the northern Midwest. In this case, Abraham Lincoln calls for the execution of Dakota Indians. Document 4 contains excerpts from the diary of a southern white woman where she discusses her fears and deprivations. Document 6 is a letter to President Lincoln from James Henry Gooding, a black soldier. Gooding pleads to be treated—and paid—like a real soldier rather than a mere laborer. Document 7, Tally Simpson, a Confederate soldier, in a letter home, describes the battle of Gettysburg and the devastation of the Confederate troops as a result. Document 8 contains two political cartoons representing emancipation. The first, by a pro-southern author, suggests that demonic forces led Lincoln when writing the Emancipation Proclamation and that it would unleash chaos. The second, by northern artist Thomas Nast, portrays how African Americans experienced the shift from slavery to freedom. In document 9, Karl Marx writes from Europe to applaud Lincoln for the Emancipation Proclamation. Document 10 also highlights the international elements of the Civil War with a memorial from Liberia for Abraham Lincoln after his assassination at the end of the war.

1. A White Virginian Argues Against Secession, 1861

The first argument in favor of secession alleged, I believe, by the gentleman from Orange [Mr. MORTON], were the bitterness and acrimony with which Southern institutions are constantly assailed by the Northern press, Northern schools, and by the Northern pulpit. I would inquire of the gentleman from Orange and of this Convention, how do they expect that the mere act of secession will silence the Northern press, school-house and pulpit? I want to know how the mere act of secession—when we have thrown off all allegiance to the common Government, when we have left our brethren, if it may be proper to call them so, with a bitter hatred rankling in the bosom, to be still more intensified by a direct antagonism; when we have thrown off all the obligations of a common Government, common country—and a common nationality—will advance us one inch towards the silence of the Northern press, pulpit or school-house? It will only aggravate the evil; it will only add poison to the virulence and acrimony of which they now complain, and will give vigor and effect to the very objections which these gentlemen are urging as a cause for Virginia seceding from the Union.

Again—another argument in favor of secession, urged by these gentlemen, was to be found in. the efforts made by the Northern Abolitionists to induce our slaves to abscond, in the operations of the Underground Railroad, in the Personal Liberty Bills and the inefficiency of the Fugitive Slave Law for the recovery of fugitives. Now, sir, secession is proposed as a remedy to cure these evils. How will it accomplish this object? As I told you, I am not going into a legal argument here. From the fact that I am recognized as a kind of outside barbarian, and as

A White Virginian Argues Against Secession, George H. Reese, ed., Proceedings of the Virginia State Convention of 1861 (Richmond: Virginia State Library, 1965).

living away up in Northern Virginia, amongst the Abolitionists there, of course, you cannot expect me to be very acute in logic; I come here as a plain man from the mountains, looking to common sense as my guide. As I said, secession, for the evils of which we complain, is proposed as the remedy. How will it work, for instance, in reference to the recovery of our slaves? Let us look at this matter. You dissolve the Union. What then? The common national obligation is destroyed. Will not the negro find it out? The motives to flee across the line would be increased, because the negro would know that whenever he crosses that line, he will be free. There will be no fugitive slave law for his recovery, and he will know it. There will be no *posse comitatus* to aid in the delivery of the slave to his master; there will be no federal arm to enforce the recovery of Anthony Burns at the point of the Northern bayonet. There will be none of the power of the law, the power of the Constitution and the power of a common nationality to do this. How, then, will secession remedy the evils of which gentlemen complain? As I have shown you, it will only increase and aggravate them.

2. The Detroit Soldiers' Aid Society President Calls on Women to Assist the War Effort, 1861

The Ladies Aid Society of Detroit has been formed and now they look to the ladies of the city to help them carry on. The ladies of our State have done and are doing nobly. Boxes after boxes have been sent in and still they come.... Do not let any one damp your zeal, by telling you there are enough hospital supplies.... All things go safely, but remember thousands need them. Arouse then dear ladies; do not act from impulse, but let working for the soldiers be your steady purpose and aim till the war is at an end. Do not fold your hands and discuss the questions whether you think the North is right. If you will not work for your country, work for humanity sake. God does not designate who is to be the recipient when he says, "It is more blessed to give than to receive." Mittens knit out of good yarn, are needed, with the thumb and forefinger knit to enable them to fire their muskets. Let that thought strike deep in your heart, that it is for those who are fighting. Warm night-caps are needed. Sick men in tents want their heads covered. Make them any shape that you please, only let them be large enough. Flannel hospital shirts, blankets, and bed sacks are needed; mustard, barley, cocoa, anything that you would provide for your dear ones, were they invalids. How many mothers and sisters pillows are wet with tears for "the loved ones far away." "Women feel where men act" is a common saying. Let us, then carry out our noble mission, and feel for the troops and then we will act also.... Our troops who have gone from Michigan are taken from our "hearts and homes"—and shall we not work for them? The rich may need a bed-sack or a hospital shirt as well as the poor. The Lord is maker of them all; let us then be almoners of Him who "came to bind up the broken-hearted," and he will bless us. Respond quickly to the call of our ladies....

From *Detroit Free Pass*, November 12, 1861, in *Michigan Women in the Civil War* (Michigan Civil War Centennial Observance Commission, 1963), 128.

3. Cherokee Declare Their Support for the Confederacy, 1861

FRIENDS AND FELLOW CITIZENS: It affords me great pleasure to see so many of you on the present occasion. The invitation to you to meet here went from the executive department, in compliance with the wishes of many citizens who desired to make stronger the cords that bind us together and to advance the common welfare. The circumstances under which you have assembled are full of import. You have precious rights at stake, and your posterity, it may be, will be affected by the sentiments you may express. You need not be told that evil times have befallen the great Government with which we have been connected. Rent by dissensions, its component parts stand in hostile array. They have marshaled powerful armies, who have already engaged in deadly conflicts. The United States claim to contend for the integrity of their Government; the Confederates for their independence and a government of their own. Gigantic preparations are made by both sides to carry on the war. The calamities, the length, and the result of that war cannot be fore-told. The Cherokees will be concerned in its issue, which in all probability, it now appears, will be the establishment of the new government. The attention of your authorities was early directed to the subject from their position and by correspondence with officers of the Confederate States, and the delicate and responsible duty devolved upon them of deciding to some extent the course to be pursued by the Cherokee Nation in the conflict between the whites, to whom she was equally bound in peace and friendship by existing treaties. Our situation is peculiar. Our political relations had long been established with the United States Government, and which embraces the seceding as well as the adhering States. Those relations still exist. The United States have not asked us to engage in the war, and we could not do so without coming into collision with our friends and neighbors, with whom we are identified by location and similar institutions. Nor, on the other hand, had we any cause to take up arms against the United States, and prematurely and wantonly stake our lives and all our rights upon the hazards of the conflict. I felt it to be my duty, therefore, then to advise the Cherokee people to remain neutral, and issued a proclamation to that effect. I am gratified to know that this course has met the approbation of the great mass of the Cherokee people, and been respected by the officers of both Governments in a manner that commands our highest gratitude. Our soil has not been invaded, our peace has not been molested, nor our rights interfered with by either Government. On the contrary, the people have remained at home, cultivated their farms in security, and are reaping fruitful returns for their labors. But for false fabrications, we should have pursued our ordinary vocations without any excitement at home, or misrepresentations and consequent misapprehensions abroad, as to the real sentiments and purposes of the Cherokee people. Alarming reports, however, have been pertinaciously circulated at home and unjust imputations among the people of the States. The object seems to have been to create strife and conflict, instead of

"Cherokee Declare their Support for the Confederacy, 1861" *The War of the Rebellion: A Compilation of the Official Records of the Union and Confederate Armies*, Series 1, Volume 3, Part 1 (Washington: Government Printing Office, 1861)

harmony and good will, among the people themselves and to engender prejudice and distrust, instead of kindness and confidence, towards them by the officers and citizens of the Confederate States.

...The great object with me has been to have the Cherokee people harmonious and united in the full and free exercise and enjoyment of all their rights of person and property. Union is strength, dissension is weakness, misery, ruin. In time of peace, enjoy peace together; in time of war, if war must come, fight together. As brothers live, as brothers die.... The preservation of our rights and of our existence are above every other consideration. And in view of all the circumstances of our situation I do say to you frankly that in my opinion the time has now come when you should signify your consent for the authorities of the nation to adopt preliminary steps for an alliance with the Confederate States upon terms honorable and advantageous to the Cherokee Nation.

4. Margaret Junkin Preston Describes Southern Suffering in Her Diary, 1862

April 3d, 1862: ...

Darkness seems gathering over the Southern land; disaster follows disaster; where is it all to end? My very soul is sick of carnage. I loathe the word—*War*. It is destroying and paralyzing all before it. Our Schools are closed—all the able-bodied men gone—stores shut up, or only here and there one open; goods not to be bought, or so exorbitant that we are obliged to do without. I actually dressed my baby all winter in calico dresses made out of the lining of an old dressing-gown; and G. in clothes concocted out of old castaways. As to myself, I rigidly abstained from getting a single article of dress in the entire past year, except shoes and stockings. Calico is not to be had; a few pieces had been offered at 40 cents per yard. Coarse, unbleached cottons are very occasionally to be met with, and are caught up eagerly at 40 cents per yard. Such material as we used to give ninepence for (common blue twill) is a bargain now at 40 cents, and then of a very inferior quality. Soda, if to be had at all, is 75 cents per lb. Coffee is not to be bought. We have some on hand, and for eight month have drunk a poor mixture, half wheat, half coffee. Many persons have nothing but wheat or rye.

These are some of the *very trifling* effects of this horrid and senseless war. Just now I am bound down under the apprehension of having my husband again enter the service; and if he goes, he says he will not return until the war closes, if indeed he come back alive. May God's providence interpose to prevent his going! His presence is surely needed at home; his hands are taken away by the militia draught, and he has almost despaired of having his farms cultivated this year. His overseer is draughted, and will have to go, unless the plea of sickness will avail to release him, as he has been seriously unwell. The [Virginia Military] Institute is full, two hundred and fifty cadets being in it; but they may disperse at any time, so uncertain is the tenure of everything now. The College [Washington College] has five students; boys too young to enter the army....

Elizabeth Preston Allan, *The Life and Letters of Margaret Junkin Preston*, (Boston: Houghton Mifflin, 1903).

August 2d: ... What straits war reduces us to! I carried a lb. or so of sugar and coffee to Sister Agnes lest she should not have any, and she gave me a great treasure—a *pound of soda!* When it can be had, it is $1.25 per lb....

Sept. 3d: ... Yesterday asked the price of a calico dress; "Fifteen dollars and sixty cents!" Tea is $20, per lb. A merchant told me he gave $50. for a pound of sewing silk! The other day our sister, Mrs. Cocke, purchased 5 gallons of whiskey, for which, by way of favor, she only paid $50.! It is selling for $15. per gallon. Very coarse unbleached cotton (ten cent cotton) I was asked 75 cts. for yesterday. Eight dollars a pair for servants' coarse shoes. Mr. P. paid $11. for a pair for Willy. These prices will do to wonder over after a while.

10 *o'clock* P.M. Little did I think, when I wrote the above, that such sorrow would overtake this family so soon! News came this afternoon of the late fearful fight on Manassas Plains, and of Willy Preston *being mortally wounded*—in the opinion of the surgeons! His Father was not at home, and did not hear the news for some time. Oh! the anguish of the father-heart! This evening he has gone to Staunton; will travel all night in order to take the cars tomorrow morning. I am afraid to go to bed, lest I be roused by some messenger of evil tidings, or (terrible to dread) the possible arrival of the dear boy—dead! Father in Heaven! Be merciful to us, and spare us this bitterness!

Sept. 4th: The worst has happened—our fearful suspense is over: Willy, the gentle, tender-hearted, brave boy, lies in a soldier's grave on the Plains of Manassas! This has been a day of weeping and of woe to this household. I did not know how I loved the dear boy. My heart is wrung with grief to think that his sweet face, his genial smile, his sympathetic heart are gone. My eyes ache with weeping. But what is the loss to me, compared to the loss to his Father, his sisters, his brothers! Oh! his precious stricken Father! God support him to bear the blow! The carriage has returned, bringing me a note from Mr. P. saying he had heard there was faint hope. Alas! the beloved son has been five days in his grave. My poor husband! Oh! if he were only here, to groan out his anguish on my bosom. I can't write more.

5. President Abraham Lincoln Orders the Execution of 39 Dakotas Involved in the 1862 Minnesota War

To Henry H. Sibley

Brigadier General H.H. Sibley Executive Mansion,

St. Paul Washington,

Minnesota. December 6th. 1862.

Ordered that of the Indians and Half-breeds sentenced to be hanged by the Military Commission, composed of Colonel [William] Crooks [of the Sixth Minnesota Volunteers], Lt. Colonel [William] Marshall [of the Seventh Minnesota Volunteers], Captain [Hiram] Grant, Captain [Hiram] Bailey [both of the Sixth Minnesota Volunteers] and Lieutenant [Rollin] Olin [assistant adjutant general on

Abraham Lincoln to General Henry H. Sibley, December 6, 1862, *Collected Works of Abraham Lincoln, 1809-1865*, 8 volumes, (Ann Arbor: University of Michigan Digital Library Production Services, 2001), 5:543–44.

Sibley's staff] and lately sitting in Minnesota, you cause to be executed on Friday the nineteenth day of December, instant, the following named, towit

"Te-he-hdo-ne-cha." No. 2. by the record.

"Tazoo" alias "Plan-doo-ta." No. 4. by the record.

"Wy-a-tah-to-wah" No. 5 by the record.

"Hin-han-shoon-ko-yag." No. 6 by the record.

"Muz-za-bom-a-du." No. 10. by the record.

"Wah-pay-du-ta." No. 11. by the record.

"Wa-he-hud." No. 12. by the record.

"Sna-ma-ni." No. 14. by the record.

"Ta-te-mi-na." No. 15. by the record.

"Rda-in-yan-kna." No. 19. by the record.

"Do-wan-sa." No. 22. by the record.

"Ha-pan." No. 24. by the record.

"Shoon-ka-ska." (White Dog). No. 35. by the record.

"Toon-kan-e-chah-tay-mane." No. 67. by the record.

"E-tay-hoo-tay." No. 68. by the record.

"Am-da-cha." No. 69. by the record.

"Hay-pee-don—or, Wamne-omne-ho-ta." No. 70. by the record.

"Mahpe-o-ke-na-ji." No. 96. by the record.

"Henry Milord"—a Half-breed. No. 115. by the record.

"Chaskay-don"—or Chaskayetay." No. 121. by the record.

"Baptiste Campbell" a Halfbreed. No. 138. by the record.

"Tah-ta-kay-gay." No. 155. by the record.

"Ha-pink-pa." No. 170 by the record.

"Hypolite Ange" a Half-breed. No. 175 by the record.

"Na-pay-Shue." No. 178. by the record.

"Wa-kan-tan-ka." No. 210. by the record.

"Toon-kan-ka-yag-e-na-jin." No. 225. by the record.

"Ma-kat-e-na-jin." No. 254. by the record.

"Pa-zee-koo-tay-ma-ne." No. 264. by the record.

"Ta-tay-hde-don." No. 279. by the record.

"Wa-She-choon," or "Toon-kan-shkan-shkan-mene-hay." No. 318. by the record.

"A-e-cha-ga." No. 327. by the record.

"Ha-tan-in-koo." No. 333. by the record.

"Chay-ton-hoon-ka." No. 342. by the record.

"Chan-ka-hda." No. 359. by the record.

"Hda-hin-hday." No. 373. by the record.

"O-ya-tay-a-koo." No. 377. by the record.

"May-hoo-way-wa." No. 382. by the record.

"Wa-kin-yan-na." No. 383 by the record

The other condemned prisoners you will hold subject to further orders, taking care that they neither escape, nor are subjected to any unlawful violence.

ABRAHAM LINCOLN,
President of the United States.

6. James Henry Gooding, an African American Soldier, Pleads for Equal Treatment, 1863

MORRIS ISLAND, S.C.

SEPTEMBER 28, 1863

YOUR EXCELLENCY, ABRAHAM LINCOLN:

Your Excellency will pardon the presumption of an humble individual like myself, in addressing you, but the earnest solicitation of my comrades in arms besides the genuine interest felt by myself in the matter is my excuse, for placing before the Executive head of the Nation our Common Grievance.

On the 6th of the last Month, the Paymaster of the Department informed us, that if we would decide to receive the sum of $10 (ten dollars) per month, he would come and pay us that sum, but that, on the sitting of Congress, the Regt. [regiment] would, in his opinion, be allowed the other 3 (three). He did not give us any guarantee that this would be, as he hoped; certainly he had no authority for making any such guarantee, and we cannot suppose him acting in any way interested.

Now the main question is, are we Soldiers, or are we Laborers? We are fully armed, and equipped, have done all the various duties pertaining to a Soldier's life, have conducted ourselves to the complete satisfaction of General Officers, who were, if anything, prejudiced against us, but who now accord us all the encouragement and honors due us; have shared the perils and labor of reducing the first strong-hold that flaunted a Traitor Flag; and more, Mr. President, to-day the Anglo-Saxon Mother, Wife, or Sister are not alone in tears for departed Sons, Husbands and Brothers. The patient, trusting descendant of Afric's Clime have dyed the ground with blood, in defence of the Union, and Democracy. Men, too, your Excellency, who know in a measure the cruelties of the iron heel of oppression, which in years gone by, the very power their blood is now being spilled to maintain, ever ground them in the dust.

But when the war trumpet sounded o'er the land, when men knew not the Friend from the Traitor, the Black man laid his life at the altar of the Nation—and he was refused. When the arms of the Union were beaten, in the first year of the war, and the Executive called for more food for its ravenous maw, again the black man begged the privilege of aiding his country in her need, to be again refused.

James Henry Gooding to Abraham Lincoln, in *A Documentary History of the Negro People in the U.S.*, ed. Herbert Aptheker (New York: Citadel Press, 1951), 482–484.

And now he is in the War, and how has he conducted himself? … Obedient and patient and solid as a wall are they. All we lack is a paler hue and a better acquaintance with the alphabet.

Now your Excellency, we have done a Soldier's duty. Why can't we have a Soldier's pay? You caution the Rebel chieftain, that the United States knows no distinction in her soldiers. She insists on having all her soldiers of whatever creed or color, to be treated according to the usages of War. Now if the United States exacts uniformity of treatment of her soldiers from the insurgents, would it not be well and consistent to set the example herself by paying all her soldiers alike?

We of this Regt. were not enlisted under any "contraband" act. But we do not wish to be understood as rating our service of more value to the Government than the service of the ex-slave. Their service is undoubtedly worth much to the Nation, but Congress made express provision touching their case, as slaves freed by military necessity, and assuming the Government to be their temporary Guardian. Not so with us. Freemen by birth and consequently having the advantage of thinking and acting for ourselves so far as the Laws would allow us, we do not consider ourselves fit subjects for the Contraband act.

We appeal to you, Sir, as the Executive of the Nation, to have us justly dealt with. The Regt. do pray that they be assured their service will be fairly appreciated by paying them as American Soldiers, not as menial hirelings. Black men, you may well know, are poor; three dollars per month, for a year, will supply their needy wives and little ones with fuel. If you, as Chief Magistrate of the Nation, will assure us of our whole pay, we are content. Our Patriotism, our enthusiasm will have a new impetus, to exert our energy more and more to aid our Country. Not that our hearts ever flagged in devotion, spite the evident apathy displayed in our behalf, but we feel as though our Country spurned us, now we are sworn to serve her. Please give this a moment's attention.

7. Tally Simpson, a Confederate Soldier, Recounts the Battle of Gettysburg, 1863

Bunker's Hill Va

Saturday, July 18th /63

My dear Carrie

It had been a very long time since I received a letter from you when your last arrived, and I'll assure you it afforded me much pleasure.

Ere this reaches its destination you will have heard of the terrible battle of Gettysburg and the fate of a portion of our noble Army. I am a good deal of Pa's nature—extremely hopeful. But I must confess that this is a gloomy period for the Confederacy. One month ago our prospects were as bright as could well be conceived. Gallant Vicksburg, the Gibraltar of the West and the pride of the South, has fallen the victim to a merciless foe. Port Hudson has surrendered unconditionally,

Guy R. Everson and Edward H. Simpson, Jr., eds., *"Far, Far from Home": The Wartime Letters of Dick and Tally Simpson, Third South Carolina Volunteers* (New York: Oxford University Press, 1994), 256–259.

and it is now reduced to a fact that cannot be disputed that the Mississippi is already or must very soon be in the possession of the Yankees from its source to its mouth. And what good will the Trans Mississippi be to the Confederacy thus cut off?

A few weeks ago Genl Lee had the finest Army that ever was raised in ancient or modern times—and commanded by as patriotic and heroic officers as ever drew a sword in defence of liberty. But in an unfortunate hour and under disadvantageous circumstances, he attacked the enemy, and tho he gained the advantage and held possession of the battlefield and even destroyed more of the foe than he lost himself, still the Army of the Potomac lost heavily and is now in a poor condition for offensive operations. I venture to assert that one third of the men are barefooted or almost destitute of necessary clothing. There is one company in this regt which has fifteen men entirely without shoes and consequently unfit for duty. This is at least half of the company alluded to. The night we recrossed the river into Virginia, Harry's shoes gave out, and he suffered a great deal marching over rough turnpikes. But when he reached Martinsburg, he purchased a pair of old ones and did very well afterwards.

Tis estimated by some that this Army has been reduced to at least one fifth its original strength. Charleston is closely beset, and I think must surely fall sooner or later. The fall of Vicksburg has caused me to lose confidence in something or somebody, I can't say exactly which. And now that gunboats from the Mississippi can be transferred to Charleston and that a portion of Morris Island has been taken and can be used to advantage by the enemy, I fear greatly the result of the attack. I trust however, if it does fall, its gallant defenders will raze it to the ground that the enemy cannot find a single spot to pitch a tent upon the site where so magnificent a city once raised, so excitingly, its towering head. Savannah will follow, and then Mobile, and finally Richmond.

These cities will be a loss to the Confederacy. But their fall is no reason why we should despair. It is certainly calculated to cast a gloom over our entire land. But we profess to be a Christian people, and we should put our trust in God. He holds the destiny of our nation, as it were, in the palm of his hand. He it is that directs the counsel of our leaders, both civil and military, and if we place implicit confidence in Him and go to work in good earnest, never for a moment losing sight of Heaven's goodness and protection, it is my firm belief that we shall be victorious in the end. Let the South lose what it may at present, God's hand is certainly in this contest, and He is working for the accomplishment of some grand result, and so soon as it is accomplished, He will roll the sun of peace up the skies and cause its rays to shine over our whole land. We were a wicked, proud, ambitious nation, and God has brought upon us this war to crush and humble our pride and make us a better people generally. And the sooner this happens the better for us....

Your ever affec cousin
T. N. Simpson

James is quite well and stands these marches finely. He sends his love to his family and to all the negros generally. He likewise wishes to be remembered to his master and all the white family.

8. Two Artistic Representation of Emancipation, 1863, 1864

LINCOLN SIGNING THE EMANCIPATION PROCLAMATION.—FROM A SOUTHERN WAR ETCHING.

EMANCIPATION CARTOON. Abraham Lincoln signing the Emancipation Proclamation—a pro-Confederate point of view. Reproduction of an etching from Adalbert J. Volck's *Confederate War Etchings*.

This *Harper's Weekly* cartoon by Thomas Nast celebrates the Emancipation Proclamation by President Abraham Lincoln on January 1, 1863.

9. Karl Marx Applauds Abraham Lincoln, 1864

To Abraham Lincoln,
President of the United States of America.

Sir,

We congratulate the American people upon your reelection by a large majority.

If resistance to the Slave Power was the reserved watchword of your first election, the triumphant war cry of your reelection is Death to Slavery.

From the commencement of the titanic American strife the workingmen of Europe felt instinctively that the star-spangled banner carried the destiny of their class. The contest for the territories which opened the dire *epopée*, was it not to decide whether the virgin soil of immense tracts should be wedded to the labor of the immigrant or prostituted by the tramp of the slave driver?

When an oligarchy of 300,000 slaveholders dared to inscribe, for the first time in the annals of the world, "slavery" on the banner of armed revolt; when on the very spots where hardly a century ago the idea of one great democratic republic had first sprung up, whence the first Declaration of the Rights of Man was issued, and the first impulse given to the European revolution of the eighteenth century; when on those very spots counterrevolution, with systematic thoroughness, gloried in rescinding "the ideas entertained at the time of the formation of the old Constitution" and maintained "slavery to be a beneficent institution, indeed the only solution of the great problem of the relation of labor to capital," and cynically proclaimed property in man "the cornerstone of the new edifice," then the working classes of Europe understood at once, even before the fanatic partisanship of the upper classes for the Confederate gentry had given its dismal warning, that the slaveholders' rebellion was to sound the tocsin for a general holy crusade of property against labor, and that for the men of labor, with their hopes for the future, even their past conquests were at stake in that tremendous conflict on the other side of the Atlantic. Everywhere they bore therefore patiently the hardships imposed upon them by the cotton crisis, opposed enthusiastically the proslavery intervention, importunities of their "betters," and from most parts of Europe contributed their quota of blood to the good cause.

While the workingmen, the true political power of the North, allowed slavery to defile their own republic, while before the Negro, mastered and sold without his concurrence, they boasted it the highest prerogative of the white-skinned laborer to sell himself and choose his own master, they were unable to attain the true freedom of labor or to support their European brethren in their struggle for emancipation, but this barrier to progress has been swept off by the red sea of civil war.

The workingmen of Europe feel sure that as the American War of Independence initiated a new era of ascendancy for the middle class, so the American antislavery war will do for the working classes. They consider it an earnest of

---

Karl Marx, "Address of the International Working Men's Association to Abraham Lincoln, President of the United States of America", *The Bee-Hive Newspaper*, No. 169, November 7, 1865.

the epoch to come, that it fell to the lot of Abraham Lincoln, the single-minded son of the working class, to lead his country through the matchless struggle for the rescue of an enchained race and the reconstruction of a social world.

Signed on behalf of the International Workingmen's Association, the Central Council...

Bee-Hive (London), January 7, 1865

10. Liberian Secretary of State Hilary Johnson Responds to the Assassination of Abraham Lincoln, 1866

Whereas the honorable Abraham Lincoln, late President of the United States of America, a ruler ordained of Heaven, has, by the ruthless hand of the assassin, been removed from his sphere of usefulness in this life; and

Whereas in the death of that great chief of the American nation has sustained a severe loss, in which the interests of nations, as well as those of mankind generally, have participated; and

Whereas the government and people of the republic of Liberia, which is legitimately an offspring of the great American republic, fostered during the period of its colonial growth by a society of American citizens, and recently greatly favored and sustained by the United States government, recognized in the late President of the United States one who utterly abhorred slavery—a friend of the negro race and a promoter of the interests of Liberia; and

Whereas, by the sudden and lamentable death of this great ruler, not only has a nation been deprived of its head, but a home and a hearth are desolate, and kindred hearts are broken, and tears of grief are shedding by those there who, by reason of a foul murder, have been deprived of a companion, a father, a friend: Therefore,

Resolved by the President of the republic of Liberia and his cabinet in council, That it is with sincere regret and pain, as well as with feelings of horror and indignation, the government of Liberia has heard of the foul assassination of the honorable Abraham Lincoln, late President of the United States.

Resolved, That the government and people of Liberia deeply sympathize with the government and people of the United States in the sad loss they have sustained by the death of so wise, so just, so efficient, so vigorous, and yet so merciful a ruler.

Resolved, That while with due sorrow the government and people of Liberia weep with those that mourn the loss of so great and good a chief, they are, nevertheless, mindful of the loss they themselves have experienced in the death of the great philanthropist whose virtues can never cease to be told so long as the republic of Liberia shall endure; as long as there survives a member of the negro race to tell of the chains that have been broken; of the griefs that have been

Liberian Secretary of State Hilary Johnson Responds to the Assassination of Abraham Lincoln *The Assassination of Abraham Lincoln.* (Washington, DC: Government Printing Office, 1866), 472–473 http://digicoll.library.wisc.edu/cgi-bin/FRUS/FRUS-idx?idFRUS.FRUS186566p4

allayed; of the broken hearts that have been bound up by him who, as it were a new creation, breathed life into four millions of that race whom he found oppressed and degraded.

By order of the President:

H. B. W. Johnson,
Secretary of State

ESSAYS

When historians consider the Civil War, they have tended to address several key questions: How did the North win? Why did the Confederacy lose? How did slavery come to an end and who was primarily responsible? In these two essays, historians Drew Gilpin Faust and David Williams offer alternative central meanings of the war. For Faust, death was the defining feature of the struggle. The ravages of war transformed how Americans experienced and related to death. The central element of the struggle, she suggests, was how it transformed American thinking about the end of life and what lies beyond. David Williams hones in on what Abraham Lincoln called the "new birth of freedom." By emphasizing emancipation as the central theme of the war, and in particular how African Americans ended slavery, Williams enters a long-standing debate over who brought emancipation. While other scholars have claimed that Abraham Lincoln was responsible or that the Union army was, Williams follows the lead of several other scholars to emphasize the role of African Americans both in the South and the North.

The Good Death in the Civil War

DREW GILPIN FAUST

MORTALITY DEFINES THE HUMAN CONDITION, "WE ALL HAVE OUR Dead—we all have our Graves," Stephen Elliott, a Confederate Episcopal bishop, observed in an 1862 sermon. Every age, he explained, must confront "like miseries"; every age must search for "like consolation." Yet in spite of the continuities that Elliott identified in human history, death has its discontinuities as well. Men and women fashion the way they approach the end of life out of their understandings of who they are and what matters to them. And inevitably these understandings are shaped by historical and cultural circumstances, by how others around them regard death, by conditions that vary over time and place. Even though "we all have our Dead" and even though we all die, we are likely to do so quite differently from century to century or even generation to generation, from continent to continent and from nation to nation.

In the middle of the nineteenth century the United States embarked on a new relationship with death, entering into a civil war that proved bloodier than any other conflict in American history, a war that would presage the slaughter of World War I's

Western Front and the global carnage of the twentieth century. The number of soldiers who died between 1861 and 1865 is approximately equal to American fatalities in the Revolution, the War of 1812, the Mexican War, the Spanish American War, World War I, World War II, and the Korean War combined. The Civil War's rate of death, its incidence in comparison with the size of the American population, was six times that of World War II; a similar rate of death, about 2 percent, in the United States today would mean almost five million fatalities. Although mortality rates differed North and South, with the percentage of Confederate men who died in the war three times greater than the proportion of Yankees, death seemed omnipresent throughout Civil War America. As the *Daily South Carolinian* observed in 1864, "Carnage floods our once happy land."

But the impact and meaning of the war's casualties were not simply a consequence of scale, of the sheer numbers of Union and Confederate soldiers who died. Death's significance for the Civil War generation derived as well from the way it violated prevailing assumptions about life's proper end—about who should die, when and where, and under what circumstances. As a newly appointed chaplain explained to his Connecticut regiment in the middle of the war, "neither he nor they had ever lived and faced death in such a time, with its peculiar conditions and necessities...." Civil War soldiers and civilians alike distinguished what many referred to as "ordinary death," as it had occurred in prewar years, from the way in which so many men were now dying in Civil War battlefields and camps. Historians have only recently begun to consider the social and cultural meanings of Civil War death, perhaps because the war was so long seen as the all-but-exclusive province of military historians, who regarded casualties chiefly as an index to an army's continuing strength and effectiveness. Burgeoning recent interest in the war by social historians, however, has begun to raise questions about the wider impact of battlefield slaughter and to suggest that such mortality, even in a society far more accustomed to death than our own, must have exerted a profound influence on Americans' perceptions of the world around them as well as their hopes for a world to come, Like the Connecticut chaplain, these scholars see Civil War death as representing a new departure—in its scale, in its brutality, in its seeming endlessness as the war continued on and on. The Mexican War had yielded a total of 1,800 American military deaths over a period of two years; the Revolution killed approximately 4,000. More than 4,800 soldiers died on a single day at Antietam in September 1862, and 7,000 more would die from wounds received there. Death was no longer just encountered individually; mortality rates were so high that nearly every American family was touched. Death's threat, its proximity, its actuality became the most widely shared of war's experiences. As Emily Dickinson wrote from western Massachusetts during the conflict, "Sorrow seems to me more general [than] it did, and not the estate of a few persons, since the war began; and if the anguish of others helped one with one's own, now would be many medicines." At war's end, this shared suffering would override persisting differences about the meanings of race, citizenship, and nationhood to establish sacrifice and its memorialization as the common ground on which North and South would ultimately reunite. Even in our own time, this fundamentally elegiac understanding of the Civil War retains its powerful hold.

Our understanding of the impact and influence of Civil War mortality must necessarily begin with an exploration of the deaths themselves, with how they were managed emotionally, spiritually, and ideologically by soldiers and their families. Americans North and South would be compelled to confront—and resist—the war's assault on their conceptions of how life should end, an assault that challenged their most fundamental assumptions about life's value and meaning. As they faced horrors that forced them to question their ability to cope, their commitment to the war, even their faith in a righteous God, soldiers and civilians alike struggled to retain their most cherished beliefs, to make them work in the dramatically altered world that war had introduced. Civil War death would transform America and Americans in ways that new scholarship is just beginning to explore. But this change would emerge only slowly and only out of the often desperate efforts of Yankees and Confederates to mobilize traditional religious and intellectual resources to operate in the dramatically changed circumstances of what has often been called the first modern and the last old-fashioned war. In the experiences of soldiers and their families, we can see this conflict between old and new cast into sharp relief as Americans endeavored to reconstruct conventional consolations to serve new times and a new kind of slaughter. Civil War death must thus be understood as at once old and new, for the effort of Americans to hold on to cherished beliefs and assumptions indelibly shaped the necessarily transformed world that war made.

Mid-nineteenth-century American culture treated dying as an art and the "Good Death" as a goal that all men and women should struggle to achieve. From the fifteenth century onward, texts describing the *Ars Moriendi* ["art of dying"] had provided readers with rules of conduct for the moribund and their attendants: how to give up one's soul "gladlye and wilfully"; how to meet the devil's temptations of unbelief, despair, impatience, and worldly attachment; how to pattern one's dying on that of Christ; how to pray. With the spread of vernacular printing, such texts multiplied in number, culminating in the mid-seventeenth century with Jeremy Taylor's *The Rule and Exercise of Holy Dying* (1651). Taylor, an Anglican divine, has been called a "prose Shakespeare." His revision of the originally Catholic *Ars Moriendi* was not just an example of literary art, however, but an intellectual triumph that succeeded in firmly establishing the genre within Protestantism. Taylor, who had already published a volume on holy living, placed deathbed conduct within the context of the whole life that served as its preparation.

By the nineteenth century Taylor's books had become classics, and the tradition of the *Ars Moriendi* spread both through reprints of earlier texts and through more contemporary considerations of the Good Death. Often these more modern renditions appeared in new contexts and genres; in sermons that focused on one or two aspects of the larger subject; in American Sunday School Union tracts distributed to youth across the nation; in popular health books that combined the expanding insights of medical science with older religious conventions about dying well; or in popular literature, with the exemplary deaths of Dickens's Little Nell, Thackeray's Colonel Newcome, or Harriet Beecher Stowe's Eva. So diverse and numerous were these representations of the Good

Death that they reached a wide spectrum of the American population at mid-century, and they would become a central aspect of the popular culture, the songs, stories, and poetry of the Civil War itself. By the 1860s many elements of the Good Death had been to a considerable degree separated from their explicitly theological roots and had become as much a part of respectable middle-class behavior and expectation in both North and South as they were the product or emblem of any particular religious affiliation. Assumptions about the way to die remained central within both Catholic and Protestant faiths but had spread beyond formal religion to become a part of more general systems of belief held across the nation about life's meaning and life's appropriate end.

But perhaps the most distressing aspect of death for many Civil War–era Americans was that thousands of young men were dying away from home. As one group of Confederate prisoners of war observed in a resolution commemorating a comrade's death in 1865, "we ... deplore that he should die ... in an enemys land far from home and friends." Most soldiers would have shared the wishes of the Georgia man whose brother sadly wrote after his death in Virginia in 1864, "he always did desire ... to die at home." As a South Carolina woman observed in 1863, it was "much more painful" to give up a "loved one [who] is a stranger in a strange land."

Civil War soldiers experienced an isolation from relatives uncommon among the free white population. Civil War armies, moreover, segregated men from women, who in the nineteenth century bore such a significant part of the responsibility for care of both the living and the dead. As a Sanitary Commission observer remarked of the Army of the Potomac, "Of this hundred thousand men, I suppose not ten thousand were ever entirely without a mother's, a sister's, or a wife's domestic care before."

Family was central to the *Ars Moriendi* tradition, for kin performed its essential rituals. Victorian ideals of domesticity further reinforced these assumptions about death's appropriate familial setting. As a British social historian has explained in an observation that would apply equally well to nineteenth-century America, "the family was the primary Victorian and Edwardian social institution in which the meaning of individual deaths was constructed and transmitted across the generations." One should die amidst family assembled around the deathbed. Relatives would of course be most likely to show concern about the comfort and needs of their dying loved one, but this was ultimately a secondary consideration. Far more important, family members needed to witness a death in order to assess the state of the dying person's soul, for these critical last moments of life would epitomize his or her spiritual condition. Kin would use their observations of the deathbed to evaluate the family's chances for a reunion in heaven. A life was a narrative that could only be incomplete without this final chapter, without the life-defining last words.

No effective system of reporting casualties operated on either side during the war. Families most often learned of the deaths of loved ones by scrutinizing unreliable newspaper lists of killed and wounded, lists that were often inaccurate as well as painfully incomplete in their mere enumeration of names with no attempt to explain attendant circumstances. To compensate for the inadequacy of such arrangements, it became customary for a slain soldier's closest companions at the time of his death to write a letter to his next of kin, not just offering sympathy and discussing the disposition of clothes and back pay but providing the kind of information a relative would have looked for in a conventional peacetime death-bed scene. These were condolence letters intended to offer the comfort implicit in the narratives of the *Ars Moriendi* that most of them contained. News of a Good Death represented the ultimate solace—the consoling promise of life everlasting.

Some soldiers tried to establish formal arrangements to ensure the transmission of such information, to make certain that not just the fact but a description of their death would be communicated to their families. In 1862 Williamson D. Ward of the Thirty-Ninth Indiana made a pact with several members of his company to provide this assurance for one another. In the Union prison at Fort Delaware, captured Confederate officers formed a Christian Association with a similar purpose. The group's minute book recorded their resolution, passed on January 6, 1865, "making it the duty" of the organization "to ascertain the name of every Confederate off[icer] dying in this prison and the attendant circumstances, and to transmit the same to their nearest friends or relatives."

But even without the formality of such resolutions, soldiers performed this obligation. After Gettysburg, W. J. O'Daniel informed Sarah Torrence of her husband Leonidas's death, explaining that the two of them "went into battle side by side," promising each other "if one go[t] hurt to do all we could for him." This letter represented the final fulfillment of that obligation. William Fields wrote to Amanda Fitzpatrick about how her husband passed his last hours in a Richmond hospital at the very end of the war: "As you in all probability have not heard of the death of your husband and as I was a witness to his death I consider it my duty to write to you although I am a stranger to you." Duty similarly motivated I. G. Patten of Alabama to respond with "Aufaul knuse" to a letter that arrived in camp from I. B. Cadenhead's wife almost two weeks after his battlefield death. Another Confederate castigated himself for not stopping in the aftermath of an 1863 battle to record an enemy soldier's last words and transmit them to his family. In retrospect, this seemed to the young rebel a far more egregious failure than not providing water to the thirsty man.

Remarkably similar North and South, condolence letters constitute a genre that emerged from the combination of the assumptions of *Ars Moriendi* with the "peculiar conditions and necessities" of the Civil War. These letters sought to make absent loved ones virtual witnesses to the dying moments they had been denied, to mend the fissures war had introduced into the fabric of the Good Death. In camp hospitals, nurses and doctors often took on this responsibility, sending the bereaved detailed descriptions not just of illnesses and wounds, but of last moments and last words. Clara Barton kept a notebook filled with such declarations to be forwarded to kin. Some hospital personnel even assumed the role of instructors in the art of dying, eliciting final statements and cueing their patients through the enactment of the Good Death. When Jerry Luther lay wounded after the Battle of Yorktown in 1862, a physician urged him to send a message to his mother. Another soldier, asked by a doctor for his last words to send home, responded by requesting the doctor to provide them. "I do not know what to say. You ought to know what I want to say. Well, tell them only just such a message as you would like to send if you were dying." The expiring soldier obviously regarded the doctor as an expert in the art of dying as well as in medicine. The soldier comprehended that this was a ritual the physician understood far better than he. The Civil War provided a context not just for the performance of the traditions of *Ars Moriendi*, but for their dissemination. Chaplains North and South in fact saw this instruction as perhaps their most important duty toward the soldiers in their spiritual charge, a duty Catholic father William Corby of a New York regiment described as "the sad consolation of helping them ... to die well."

Sometimes soldiers would attempt to eliminate the need for intermediaries in order to narrate their deaths directly. Many carried letters to be forwarded to loved ones if they were killed, but these did not, of course, provide descriptions of final moments or hours. Some men, however, managed to write home as they lay dying, speaking through their pens instead of from the domestic deathbeds that war had denied them. These letters are particularly wrenching, in part because the last words of more than a century ago appear seemingly unmediated on the page, speaking across the years, serving as a startling representation of immortality for a twenty-first-century reader. Jeremiah Gage of the Eleventh Mississippi wrote his mother after Gettysburg, "This is the last you may ever hear from me. I have time to tell you I died like a man," James R. Montgomery's 1864 letter to his father in Mississippi is rendered all the more immediate by the bloodstains that cover the page. But if the reality of his wounds seems almost present and even tangible, his assumptions about death emphasize the years that distance him from our own time. "This is my last letter to you," he explains. "I write to you because I know you would be delighted to read a word from your dying son." His choice of the word "delight" here—a term that seems strikingly inappropriate within the context of our modern understanding—underlines the importance accorded the words of the dying. Even as his father faced the terrible news of his son's death, Montgomery expected him to have the capacity to be delighted by the delivery of his son's last thoughts. And even *in extremis*, Montgomery followed the generic form of the Civil War death letter. By the middle of the 1864 Wilderness campaign, Montgomery may well have had a good deal of practice at writing such letters to other families. Now he could use this proficiency in composing his own.

Letters describing soldiers' last moments on earth are so similar, it seems almost as if their authors had a checklist in mind, enumerating the necessary details....

The Hard Freedom of the Civil War

DAVID WILLIAMS

Duncan Winslow escaped from slavery in Tennessee during the Civil War and eventually joined the Union army. April of 1864 found him along the Mississippi River with the Sixth U.S. Heavy Artillery defending Fort Pillow, Tennessee, from attack by General Nathan Bedford Forrest and his Confederate cavalry.

David Williams, "The Hard Freedom of the Civil War" Excerpt, David Williams, *I Freed Myself: African American Self-Emancipation in the Civil War Era* (New York: Cambridge University Press, 2014). Reprinted with the permission of Cambridge University Press.

Outnumbered nearly four to one, the defenders were quickly overwhelmed. As rebel troops overran the fort, Winslow and his comrades threw down their arms and tried to surrender, but Forrest's men took few prisoners. In what came to be known as the Fort Pillow Massacre, Confederates slaughtered nearly 300 of their captives, most of them former slaves. To rebel officers' shouts of "Kill the God damned nigger," Winslow was shot in his arm and thigh. In the confusion, he managed to escape by crawling among logs and brush, hiding there until the enemy moved on. When darkness fell, Winslow made his way down to the riverbank and boarded a federal gunboat.

After his release from a military hospital in Mound City, Illinois, Winslow settled on a farm three miles west of town, where he raised garden vegetables and sold them house to house. One day a candidate for local office asked Winslow for his support in an upcoming election. As if to seal the deal, the candidate remarked, "Don't forget. We freed you people." In response, Winslow raised his wounded arm and said, "See this? Looks to me like I freed myself."

Generations of Americans have grown up believing that Abraham Lincoln freed the slaves with a stroke of his pen by signing the Emancipation Proclamation. Lost in this simple portrayal is the role that African Americans such as Duncan Winslow played in forcing the issue. At the war's outset, knowing that most white northerners were hardly abolitionists, Lincoln made clear that his intent was to save the Union, not to free the slaves. Although Lincoln personally disliked slavery, he claimed no authority to interfere with the institution. On the contrary, he promised to enforce all laws upholding slavery, including the Fugitive Slave Act. Desperate to appease slaveholders, Lincoln even supported a thirteenth amendment to the Constitution, the Corwin Amendment, which would have guaranteed slavery forever. Said Lincoln of the amendment in his first inaugural address, "I have no objection to its being made express and irrevocable."

Nevertheless, enslaved men and women escaped to Union lines by the tens of thousands and could not or would not be forced back into slavery. The actions of those many self-emancipated refugees eventually compelled Lincoln and Congress to modify their war aims and formulate a policy that reflected a slave-initiated reality. To say, as the government at first did, that escapees within Union lines technically remained slaves was problematic. If escapees were neither free nor actually held in slavery, then what was their legal status? The label "contraband" imposed upon them in 1861 satisfied few and settled nothing. Lincoln and Congress wrestled with the issue of refugee status for more than a year before finally deciding with the Second Confiscation Act, then the Emancipation Proclamation, that the refugees had been right all along. They had effectively freed themselves. Lincoln practically admitted as much. Writing of slavery's demise in April 1864, he stressed, "I claim not to have controlled events, but confess plainly that events have controlled me."

Others knew that as well. Union General John Logan, speaking to a crowd of potential recruits, echoed Lincoln's assertion that saving the Union, not ending slavery, was the war's prime objective. "Yet," he acknowledged, "the negroes are getting free pretty fast. It is not done by the army, but they are freeing themselves; and if this war continues long, not a slave will be left in the whole South." Years after the war, the formerly enslaved Betty Guwn told how her husband "ran away early and helped Grant to take Fort [Donelson]. He said he would free himself, which he did."

Roughly 200,000 blacks, most of them refugees from slavery, served in the Union armed forces. Hundreds of thousands more were employed as laborers. Without their efforts, and those of increasingly resistant slaves, the Union would likely not have survived. Freedom was what they struggled for, but that freedom is often viewed as dependent on, almost a by-product of, a war to preserve the Union. Considering the invaluable contributions of black folk toward Union victory, one could as easily say the opposite—that preserving the Union was dependent on ending slavery.

For most northerners who backed the war, it remained primarily—and for many exclusively—a war to save the Union. Slavery was almost beside the point. "If I could save the Union without freeing *any* slave," Lincoln wrote in August 1862, "I would do it, and if I could save it by freeing *all* the slaves I would do it; and if I could save it by freeing some and leaving others alone I would also do that. What I do about slavery, and the colored race, I do because I believe it helps to save the Union."

Lincoln meant what he said. Of course he felt that slavery was wrong, knew it was a source of conflict, and wished it to end sooner or later. But, like most whites who thought slavery wrong, he was deeply conflicted regarding when, how, and to what extent. He led no drumbeat for abolition. He could hardly have been elected had he done so. The Union was Lincoln's priority, and he frequently said so in public and private. When Lincoln moved against slavery, he did so cautiously, even reluctantly, fearing that it might do more harm than good to the Union war effort. But by the summer of 1862, although still hesitant, he came to see that the issues of Union and slavery could not be separated. Blacks would not allow it. Every refugee who entered federal camps, by the act of escape and refusal to be reenslaved, issued a personal statement that slavery was over. Arriving in such numbers that they could hardly be ignored, the government had little choice but to recognize their claim to freedom. Thus it was, as W. E. B. Du Bois observed, that "with perplexed and laggard steps, the United States Government followed the footsteps of the black slave."

By the war's second year, the government badly needed black support. White recruits were difficult to come by. Lincoln and Congress had at first refused to enlist black volunteers, but the war was not going well for Union armies, and there was no end in sight. They now wanted blacks to fight, and they knew that blacks would fight only for liberty. That was the price of their service, a service that Lincoln knew was indispensable to the Union's survival. "Any different policy in regard to the colored man," Lincoln wrote in 1864, "deprives us of his help, and this is more than we can bear.... This is not a question of sentiment or taste, but one of physical force which may be measured and estimated as horse-power and Steam-power are measured and estimated. Keep it and you can save the Union. Throw it away, and the Union goes with it." Lincoln finally came to realize, although he did not always make it so clear, that the Union was as dependent on freedom as the other way around.

Blacks had known that from the start. They publicly and repeatedly stressed that Lincoln's initial notion of preserving the Union without reference to slavery was self-defeating. Slavery and slave resistance had brought on the war. There could be no Union victory without slavery's defeat. With a foresight born of experience, Frederick Douglass warned in May 1861 that the war against secession "bound up the fate of the Republic and that of the slave in the same bundle."

> Any attempt now to separate the freedom of the slave from the victory of the Government over slaveholding rebels and traitors; any attempt to secure peace to the whites while leaving the blacks in chains; any attempt to heal the wounds of the Republic, while the deadly virus of slavery is left to poison the blood, will be labor lost."

Less than a year later, with the war going badly for Lincoln, Harriet Tubman made much the same point in her own direct way. "They may send the flower of their young men down South.... They may send them one year, two years, three years, till they are tired of sending, or till they use up all the young men. All no use! God's ahead of Master Lincoln. God won't let Master Lincoln beat the South till he do the right thing." Decades after the war, former slave Marshall Mack remembered that the war's tide began to turn only after Lincoln committed the Union to emancipation. The Confederacy was whipping the Union "two battles to one," he said. "Then Grant whipped Lee two battles to one 'cause he had Negroes in the Union Army."

Northern blacks volunteered for the army early on and sometimes served despite Lincoln's refusal to accept them. Nicholas Biddle, a former slave, went to war with Pennsylvania's Washington Artillerists in May 1861 and became perhaps the first man wounded in the conflict. When the army officially allowed blacks to enlist, they came forward by the tens of thousands. On the civilian side, northern blacks organized to aid southern refugees. Others went south to render assistance. Many became politically involved, demanding not only freedom for slaves but equal rights for themselves.

Blacks in the South contributed mightily to the freedom war as well. They helped refugees, black and white, escape to federal lines. They helped Confederate deserters make their way back home. And they served as spies, guides, and informants to Union forces. As one escaped Union prisoner of war later wrote, "They were always ready to help anybody opposed to the Rebels. Union refugees, Confederate deserters, escaped prisoners—all received from them the same prompt and invariable kindness."

Slave resistance took many forms during the war. In what W. E. B. Du Bois called a "general strike" against the Confederacy, southern blacks staged work slow-downs, refused instruction, resisted punishment, demanded pay for their work, gathered freely, traveled at will, and took freedom for themselves in various other ways long before the Union army arrived. In doing so, they forced the Confederacy to divert tens of thousands of men who might otherwise have been put on the front lines, engaging them in a vain effort to maintain control.

Enslaved blacks also struck out violently against slaveholders and local authorities, sometimes cooperating with anti-Confederate whites in the effort. Two slaves in Dale County, Alabama, helped John Ward, leader of a local deserter gang, kill their owner in his bed. In the spring of 1862, authorities arrested three white citizens of Calhoun County, Georgia, for supplying area slaves with firearms in preparation for a rebellion. Two years later, slaves in nearby Brooks County conspired with a local white man, John Vickery, to take the county and hold it for the Union.

A Story Too Long in the Shadows

Although the Union, to a large extent, owed its survival to blacks both on and off the battlefield, white America quickly forgot black contributions in the post-war years. It became the martyred Lincoln, and by extension magnanimous white northerners, who had removed the nation's stain of slavery and granted an unearned freedom to the slaves. In his 1928 biography of Ulysses S. Grant, W. E. Woodward expressed white America's prevailing view that "negroes are the only people in the history of the world, so far as I know, that ever became free without any effort of their own.... They twanged banjos around the railroad stations, sang melodious spirituals, and believed that some Yankee would soon come along and give each of them forty acres of land and a mule."

Sadly, the public's general view of blacks during the Civil War has changed little despite decades of scholarly attention. Pop culture media has been far more influential. The 1939 film *Gone with the Wind*, which shapes public views of the war to this day, presents blacks as hardly fit for anything but slavery and perfectly content to remain enslaved. Even the 1989 film *Glory*, which focuses on the white Colonel Robert Gould Shaw and an assortment of fictional black characters, portrays enslaved people of the southeastern lowcountry as hapless "raga-muffins" who simply waited to be freed.

More recently, Steven Spielberg's 2012 film *Lincoln* has done perhaps the most damage in robbing blacks of their slavery-ending role in the popular mind. With help from historical advisors Doris Kearns Goodwin and Harold Holzer, Spielberg, America's greatest myth-maker, takes Lincoln, America's most mythical figure, and simply perpetuates the image of Lincoln as the Great Emancipator handing freedom to slaves as a gift. Nowhere does Spielberg credit blacks with having much to do with ending slavery. For Spielberg and his associates, it is as if the past few decades of scholarship on blacks in the Civil War era never happened.

When, on occasion, the public does become briefly aware that black freedom was hard-earned, it seems to come as a revelation. As recently as 2012, an article appeared in a Lancaster, Pennsylvania, news outlet entitled "Black Role in Civil War Among the Best Kept Secrets." An editorial in Virginia's *Roanoke Times* wrote of the "untold" part that blacks played in the state's Civil War history. "Theirs is a story that has too long been in the shadows." It is to me astounding, and more than a little depressing, that we must use words such as "secrets," "untold," and "shadows" to describe modern America's public awareness when it comes to the role of blacks in gaining freedom.

In our history textbooks, the active and essential part blacks played, which should be a central focus, still tends to be mentioned only in passing, treated as secondary, or ignored completely. In a survey of major high school and college texts, one finds scant explanation of how a Union war moved toward being a freedom war as well, and little sense that blacks were involved in the movement at all. The effect of that omission is predictable. I recently asked my incoming freshmen to compose a brief essay on their impressions of how slavery ended. Fewer than 10 percent credited blacks in any way with contributing to the process. Most were sure that Lincoln, nearly single-handedly and of his own volition, had freed the slaves.

That mis-impression is so widely ingrained as almost to be a presumption that every U.S. citizen, or anyone hoping to become one, ought to affirm it. A sample question from the current Immigration and Naturalization Service (INS) citizenship test asks "What was *one* important thing that Abraham Lincoln did?" Among three acceptable answers is "Freed the slaves." A word of warning to potential new citizens who may know that the answer is more complex. This is not an essay question. The INS is not looking for a debate. Simply answer as expected. Do not try to educate the INS.

Inadequate as our schools have been at emphasizing black self-agency during the Civil War, fairly well-educated Americans do tend to have some sense that Lincoln's Great Emancipator image has shortcomings. In 2005, then-Senator Barack Obama wrote in a *Time Magazine* editorial that although he admired Lincoln's "moral compass," he could not "swallow whole the view of Lincoln as the Great Emancipator." Not surprisingly, Obama was lambasted in the blogosphere. He had his defenders, to be sure, but they were largely drowned out by people who accused Obama of everything from being uneducated to un-American. Surely some of the criticism was politically motivated, but much of it was born of pure ignorance.

Among scholars of the Civil War era as well, the Great Emancipator icon has lost some of its luster in recent years. Still, the image has its champions, although some tend to come to its defense from nontraditional angles. Gary Gallagher readily acknowledges in his recent book *The Union War* that Lincoln's Great Emancipator star does not shine as brightly among scholars as it once did. He stresses the fairly obvious point that for war-supporting white northerners, including Lincoln, preserving the Union, not ending slavery, was the prime objective. At the same time, he short-changes black contributions to the freedom side of the war, giving credit for black liberation mainly to the Union military, specifically the *white* Union military. "Without the United States Army," says Gallagher, "none of the other actors could have succeeded." Gallagher might have added, as Lincoln himself recognized, that the army succeeded only with the help of many hundreds of thousands of blacks—North and South, soldier and civilian. But Gallagher does the opposite, narrowly arguing that blacks featured in none of the war's "biggest battles," that they were relegated to "supporting tasks," and that they performed no "decisive service." In a series of speculative scenarios, he even imagines that "the United States might have achieved victory with slavery intact and no African American units in its armies." Such speculation is astonishing in light of Lincoln's early—and failed—efforts to do precisely that. The supporting tasks and nondecisive service Gallagher dismisses would have diverted hundreds of thousands of whites had blacks not been there to fill those roles. Black efforts were far broader in scope and more significant in impact than Gallagher appears to recognize.

Gallagher is particularly critical of Professor Steven Hahn's view, outlined in *The Political Worlds of Slavery and Freedom*, that the Civil War involved a "massive rebellion of southern slaves." Gallagher complains that "Hahn relies on an expansive definition of 'rebellion,' finessing the fact that approximately 3 million slaves remained under Confederate control at the time of Appomattox." One might as easily argue that Gallagher relies on an expansive definition of "control," ignoring the internal resistance and liberties taken by so many blacks whose enslavement was little more than "presumptive," as Hahn puts it, long before Appomattox.

Implicit in Gallagher's argument is that Lincoln, as the Union army's commander-in-chief, largely retains his popular title of Great Emancipator even if emancipation was not his prime motive. This sort of sideways approach to preserving the Great Emancipator image is hardly uncommon. Some take an even more direct route. Historian James McPherson, a leading defender of the image, argues in *Drawn with the Sword: Reflections on the American Civil War* that without Lincoln there would have been no war and, hence, no opportunity for freedom. With regard to emancipation, it was Lincoln's determination to maintain the Union—it was the war itself—that was "the essential condition, the one thing without which it would not have happened." Without Lincoln, there would have been no Emancipation Proclamation and no Thirteenth Amendment. Therefore, says McPherson, "Lincoln freed the slaves."

Arguments such as those of Gallagher, McPherson, and others have some validity as far as they go. To my knowledge, no reputable scholar denies that Lincoln and the Union military played a significant part in the emancipation process. But following their lines of reasoning more deeply, we cannot help but see the efforts of black folk at their core.

Lincoln's insistence on the Union's survival was a reaction to the South's secession, a movement engineered by slaveholders who feared not only Lincoln but, more immediately, their own slaves. Controlling slaves had been increasingly difficult for years. It could only be more difficult, perhaps impossible, with slaves believing that Lincoln's election meant their freedom. How could they believe otherwise? Although Lincoln was no threat to slavery where it existed, and said so often during the 1860 presidential campaign, fire-eating secessionists railed against him as a radical abolitionist with a secret agenda to foment slave rebellion. Such overheated rhetoric was intended to stir up support for secession among southern whites, but southern blacks heard the message too. Resistance and rumors of resistance pervaded the South that year and drove slaveholder fears to a fever pitch. Most significantly, underlying their fear was the certain knowledge that slaves wanted freedom. It was that certainty, born of many decades of slave resistance, that led to secession, war, and slavery's downfall.

Slaveholders' doubts about their ability to maintain slavery indefinitely had a long history. The need to justify slavery had for decades occupied their brightest minds. The need to keep southern whites, three-quarters of whom owned no slaves, supporting slavery made fomenting fear of blacks a political priority. Most threatening to slaveholders were the slaves themselves. Blacks had never submitted to slavery willingly or completely. They did little more than what they had to do and took liberties where they could. They resisted in so many ways that the slaveholders' need to exercise control was constant and all-consuming. Had blacks been content to remain enslaved, slaveholders would have had no cause for alarm. Nor would abolitionist arguments have inspired such panic among them. As it was, slaveholder fears of threats to slavery, as much from within as from without, led them to insist on guarantees for slavery's future and the means to control that future. And that fear led them to secede when those guarantees and their means of control seemed at risk. There was, as historian John Ashworth reminds us, a direct causal link between the slaves' desire for freedom and slaveholder politics. "Behind every event in the history of the sectional controversy," Ashworth points out, "lurked the consequences of black resistance to slavery."

That resistance was not confined to the South. Escaping slaves saw to that. By the tens of thousands they headed north, undermining northern efforts to keep the slave's war south of the Mason-Dixon Line. In so doing, as historian Scott Hancock stresses, black folk "maintained an unrelenting pressure on the sectional fault lines of identity, law, and space." That pressure expanded those fault lines and increasingly drew northerners into the conflict. Time and again, northern failures to keep blacks and slavery locked in the South put them at odds with slaveholders' expansionist demands. Hancock concludes, and rightly so, that "not simply slavery, but slaves—black people!—caused the Civil War."

It was, then, at the heart of it all, the unrelenting resistance to slavery among slaves themselves that was the essential condition, the one thing without which the sectional crisis, secession, the Civil War, the Emancipation Proclamation, and the Thirteenth Amendment would not have happened.

Of course, it did not happen overnight. For more than two centuries before the Civil War, millions of African Americans lived in bondage all their lives. But it was a resisted bondage, an ongoing struggle, that would eventually reach its consummation. Some whites recognized that early on. "Freedom must be as dear to them as to us," wrote settlers at Darien, Georgia, in 1739 as they petitioned the colony's trustees to maintain their ban on slavery. One passage was especially prophetic. "It is shocking to human Nature, that any Race of Mankind and their Posterity should be sentence'd to perpetual Slavery; nor in Justice can we think otherwise of it, than that they are thrown amongst us to be our Scourge one Day or other for our Sins." In June 1863, black Union soldiers, many of them formerly enslaved along the Georgia-Carolina coast, ransacked Darien and set the town afire.

The internal pressures against slavery—rebellion, resistance, escape—were always there and became ever greater as slavery spread. Slaveholders clamped down with more slave codes, more slave patrols, and increasingly brutal control. But the more they tried to tighten their grip on slaves, the more slaves slipped through their fingers. By the late 1850s, there were perhaps 50,000 escapes annually, temporary and permanent. Such resistance fueled a desperation reflected in slaveholder politics and the secession crisis. The resulting freedom war was neither an isolated event nor an endpoint in itself. It was part of a massive black resistance movement that had been going on for generations, finally becoming so intense that whites could not help but be drawn into it whether they wanted to or not.

Even so, both sides, Union and Confederate, insisted in the war's early months that the conflict was a white man's war. But blacks knew it was theirs and quickly took ownership of it. They struggled for freedom not only as a political right but also seized what liberties they could for themselves, individually and collectively. Blacks knew that freedom was not a single thing, granted from on high by an act of Congress, a presidential proclamation, or even a Constitutional amendment. Nor was freedom simply the absence of slavery. Black northerners of the antebellum era repeatedly testified to that. Segregated, disenfranchised, discriminated against, and denied opportunity, "northern freedom" was, as one disgusted man put it, "nothing but a nickname for northern slavery." For northern blacks, the freedom war was as much a struggle against prejudice as a struggle against slavery.

In the experience of black Americans, freedom was little more than a set of possibilities surrounding a space that had to be carved out and occupied. They had been carving out those spaces for more than two centuries, ever since they were brought to the continent as forced labor. The boundaries of those spaces were rarely obvious, so there was always poking and prodding to discover their edges and push them a little further. Setbacks there were, and plenty of them. Long after emancipation, the struggle for freedom went on. That continual pressure from black folk had always been, and would continue to be, the driving force behind their expanding freedoms.

 # FURTHER READING

Drew Gilpin Faust, *This Republic of Suffering: Death and the American Civil War* (2009).

Joseph T. Glatthaar, *Forged in Battle: The Civil War Alliance of Black Soldiers and White Officers* (1989).

Harold Holzer, Edna Greene Medford, and Frank Williams, *The Emancipation Proclamation: Three Views* (2006).

James Oakes, *Freedom National: The Destruction of Slavery in the United States, 1861–1865* (2014).

Bruce Levine, *Confederate Emancipation* (2007).

Chandra Manning, *What This Cruel War Was Over: Soldiers, Slavery, and the Civil War* (2008).

Stephanie McCurry, *Confederate Reckoning* (2012).

James M. McPherson, *Battle Cry of Freedom: The Civil War Era* (1988).

Phillip S. Paludan, *"A People's Contest": The Union and the Civil War, 1861–1865* (1989).

Charles Royster, *The Destructive War: William Tecumseh Sherman, Stonewall Jackson, and the Americans* (1991).

Nina Silber, *Daughters of the Union* (2005).

Additional critical thinking activities and content are available in MindTap.

   **MindTap** is a fully online, highly personalized learning experience built upon Cengage Learning content. MindTap combines student learning tools—readings, multimedia, activities, and assessments—into a singular Learning Path that guides students through the course.

CHAPTER 15

Reconstruction

Many nations that have a civil war end up having more civil wars. The reasons for the originating conflict are often unresolved. In the case of the United States, the epic struggle from 1861 to 1865 did not lead to another full-blown military encounter. Instead, the states that had seceded were quickly reincorporated into the legal fold of the nation; Confederate leaders and civilians were reconstituted as citizens; and the key political problems that caused the war—slavery and its future in the territories and states—were resolved. Three new constitutional amendments transformed the nation's founding document to make certain of this final point. The questions for Reconstruction were many, but the central ones were how would the United States avoid another violent war? What would be the status of people formerly owned by other people? What would be the status of those who had committed treason against the government? How would the nation develop economically and territorially into the West now that slavery was not an option?

Even before the Civil War ended, President Lincoln and congressional leaders puzzled over how best to reintegrate the people of the South into the Union. Before he was assassinated, President Lincoln proposed a "10 percent plan," which would have allowed a state government to reestablish itself once one-tenth of those who had voted in 1860 took an oath of loyalty to the United States. Radicals in Congress were appalled by the seemingly lenient plan and pushed through their own bill, which increased the proportion to one-half of the voters who were required to swear that they had never supported secession. Lincoln's assassination cut short this increasingly scathing debate and drastically altered the mood of Reconstruction.

Political disagreements over Reconstruction policy were vast, and the strategies advocated were so varied that Reconstruction took a crooked road. As approaches to rebuilding the South shifted, the hopes among some to transform Southern society grew and then were dashed. Despite important legal precedents that were made in the era, many of the social, political, and economic conventions that had characterized antebellum society endured after Reconstruction ended. Eventually, the racial system of segregation came to replace the system of slavery.

Although people differed on what was the best policy for Reconstruction, everyone agreed that the Confederate states were in dire straits and the primary goal of

Reconstruction was to reincorporate those states politically and socially into the Union. The war had devastated the South: cities lay in ruins; two-thirds of Southern railroads had been destroyed; and at least one-third of its livestock had disappeared. Likewise, the abolition of slavery unalterably transformed Southern society at the same time that it gave hope to people freed from their bondage. With Andrew Johnson, a Democrat before the war, becoming president after Lincoln's assassination, congressional Republicans struggled to determine how Reconstruction would function. Johnson looked to placate Southern whites, which infuriated many Republicans. After the Republican Party won a resounding victory in the elections of 1866, Congress reconvened in 1867 and set out to punish rebellious Southern whites while offering more rights and freedoms to African Americans.

While politicians in Washington engineered Reconstruction, Southerners forged new social conventions that would also be extremely important in the future. The lives of former slaves changed dramatically changed, and freed women and men expressed their under-standing of freedom in a variety of ways. Significantly, many African Americans played important roles in the new Republican Party of the South, and by 1868 black men were seated for the first time in Southern state legislatures. These political gains, however, were short-lived. In spite of the electoral successes of African Americans, the Democratic Party enjoyed increasing political success in the South as former Confederates eventually had their political rights restored. Changes in the electorate in conjunction with intimidation shifted the trajectory of Reconstruction once again as radical transformation was replaced with a movement toward the white South's goals for reclaiming the world they had known before the Civil War.

When Reconstruction ended is hard to say. Perhaps it was when the last Southern states reentered the union in 1870. Perhaps it was after the 1876 presidential election. Perhaps it was not until 1898 when former foes fought together in the Spanish-American War. If Reconstruction meant finding an equitable solution to the tragedy of slavery, then perhaps Reconstruction is not yet over. In any event, interest in Southern problems waned considerably in the North in 1873, when the nation was rocked by a financial panic that led Americans into a depression lasting six years. Scandal and depression weakened the Republican Party. Then the Supreme Court gutted much of the civil rights legislation. In many ways, Americans of the twentieth century lived in the shadow of Reconstruction, and it was for that reason that D.W. Griffith's cinematic marvel The Birth of a Nation *(1915) was not a story of the American Revolution. It was a tale of American Reconstruction.*

 # QUESTIONS TO THINK ABOUT

What were the failures of Reconstruction and what were its successes? Why did it collapse, to the extent that it did? How successful was the Union in reincorporating the Southern states and people? Did Reconstruction come to an end primarily because the North abandoned it or because it was opposed by the white South? How did African Americans feel about the possibilities and the terrors of Reconstruction?

DOCUMENTS

The first three documents represent the diversity of feelings at the end of the war regarding the federal government and rights for African Americans. Document 1 is an oration given by William Howard Day, an African American minister, in 1865. Notice how—unlike African Americans before the Civil War—he now celebrated the federal government. Day proclaimed the Fourth of July as "our day," the United States as "our nation," and Washington, D.C., as "our capital." In the South, though, many whites opposed the federal government and wanted to keep former slaves as second-class citizens. Document 2 is a song from the South where the white vocalist proclaims his hatred for the federal government. In law, many Southern states enacted "black codes" immediately after the war, one of which is given in document 3. This example from Louisiana in 1865 illustrates the many ways in which the rights of "freedom" were abridged. The next four documents show contrasting agendas in the North. In document 4 Thaddeus Stevens, a Radical representative in Congress, argues for passage of the Reconstruction Act of 1867 because he believes that only an unfaltering federal presence will prevent "traitors" from ruling the South. Document 5 provides pictorial views of Reconstruction. On one hand, there is Andrew Johnson's embrace of Southern whites; on another, there is federal endorsement of difference and diversity. Note in the Thanksgiving depiction how women and men of various backgrounds share a moment of social equality. In document 6, however, Elizabeth Cady Stanton draws attention to rights that went largely overlooked during the era: women's rights. The next two documents show frustrations with the civil rights agendas of Reconstruction. Documents 7 and 8 show the possibilities and perils of Reconstruction. The first showcases how efforts to educate former slaves after the war brought some northern African American women to the South and how the experience altered their perspectives. Document 8 is the testimony of a freed woman about the violence of the Ku Klux Klan. The final document details sectional feelings at the end of the century. Document 9, "The Blue and the Gray," expresses the hopes for North–South reconciliation in the form of mutual love and respect for white Union and Confederate soldiers.

1. William Howard Day, an African American Minister, Salutes the Nation and a Monument to Abraham Lincoln, 1865

... We meet under new and ominous circumstances to-day. We come to the National Capital—our Capital—with new hopes, new prospects, new joys, in view of the future and past of the people; and yet with that joy fringed, tinged,

Celebration by the Colored People's Educational Monument Association (1865).

permeated by a sorrow unlike any, nationally, we have ever known. A few weeks since all that was mortal of Abraham Lincoln was laid away to rest. And to-day, after the funeral cortege has passed, weeping thoughts march through our hearts— when the muffled drum has ceased to beat in a procession five hundred, aye, two thousand miles long, the chambers of your souls are still echoing the murmur—and though the coffin has been lowered into its place, "dust to dust," there ever falls across our way the coffin's shadow, and, standing in it, we come to-day to rear a monument to his blessed memory, and again to pledge our untiring resistance to the tyranny by which he fell, whether it be in the iron manacles of the slave, or in the unjust written manacles for the free....

Up to now our nation,... [t]he shout of the freeman and the wail of the bondman have, I repeat, always been heard together, making "harsh discords." Hitherto a damning crime has run riot over the whole land. North and South alike were inoculated with its virus. It has lain like a gangrene upon the national life, until the nation, mortified, broke in twain. The hand of slavery ever moulded the Christianity of the nation, and wrote the national songs. What hand wrote the laws of the nation and marked this National District all over with scars? What hand went into the Capitol and half murdered Charles Sumner, nature's nobleman?...

All the heroes of all the ages, bond and free, have labored to secure for us the right we rejoice in to-day. To the white and colored soldiers of this war, led on as they were by our noble President and other officers, in the presence of some of whom I rejoice to-day, are we indebted, in the providence of God, for our present position. For want of time, I pass by any more detailed mention of the noble men and their noble deeds. Together they nobly labored—together they threw themselves into the breach which rebellion had made across the land, and thus closed up that breach forever. And now, in their presence, living and dead, as over the prostrate form of our leader, Abraham Lincoln—by the edge of blood-red waves, still surging, we pledge our resistance to tyranny, (I repeat,) whether in the iron manacles of the slave, or in the unjust written manacles of the free....

It is related in the diary of one of the writers of old that when the slave trade was at its height, a certain vessel loaded with its human freight started under the frown of God and came over the billows of the ocean. Defying God and man alike, in the open daylight, the slave was brought up from the hold and chained to the foot of the mast. The eye of the Omnipotent saw it, and bye and bye the thunders muttered and the lightnings played over the devoted vessel. At length the lightning leaped upon the mast and shivered it, and, as it did this, also melted the fetter which fastened the black slave to it; and he arising unhurt, for the first time walked the deck a free man.

Our ship of state, the Union, has for eighty years gone careering over the billows; our slave has been chained to our mast in the open daylight, and in the focal blaze of the eighteen centuries gone by, and we have hurried on in our crime regardless alike of the muttering of the thunder and the flashes of the lightning, until in one devoted hour the thunderbolt was sped from the hand of God. The mast was shivered; the ship was saved; but, thank God, the slave was free....

2. A Southern Songwriter Opposes Reconstruction, c. 1860s

O, I'm a good old Rebel,
Now that's just what I am,
For this "Fair Land of Freedom"
I do not care at all;

I'm glad I fit against it–
I only wish we'd won,
And I don't want no pardon
For anything I done.

I hates the Constitution,
This Great Republic too,
I hates the Freedman's Buro,
In uniforms of blue;

I hates the nasty eagle,
With all his brags and fuss,
The lyin', thievin' Yankees,
I hates 'em wuss and wuss.

I hates the Yankee nation
And everything they do,
I hates the Declaration
Of Independence too;

I hates the glorious Union –
'Tis dripping with our blood –
I hates their striped banner,
I fit it all I could....

Three hundred thousand Yankees
Is stiff in Southern dust;
We got three hundred thousand
Before they conquered us;

They died of Southern fever
And Southern steel and shot,
I wish they was three million
Instead of what we got.

"O, I'm a Good Old Rebel," c. 1860s.

I can't take up my musket
And fight 'em now no more,
But I ain't going to love 'em,
Now that is sarten sure;

And I don't want no pardon
For what I was and am,
I won't be reconstructed
And I don't care a damn.

3. Louisiana Black Codes Reinstate Provisions of the Slave Era, 1865

Section 1. *Be it therefore ordained by the board of police of the town of Opelousas.* That no negro or freedman shall be allowed to come within the limits of the town of Opelousas without special permission from his employers, specifying the object of his visit and the time necessary for the accomplishment of the same....

Section 2. *Be it further ordained,* That every negro freedman who shall be found on the streets of Opelousas after 10 o'clock at night without a written pass or permit from his employer shall be imprisoned and compelled to work five days on the public streets, or pay a fine of five dollars.

Section 3. No negro or freedman shall be permitted to rent or keep a house within the limits of the town under any circumstances, and any one thus offending shall be ejected and compelled to find an employer or leave the town within twenty-four hours....

Section 4. No negro or freedman shall reside within the limits of the town of Opelousas who is not in the regular service of some white person or former owner, who shall be held responsible for the conduct of said freedman....

Section 5. No public meetings or congregations of negroes or freedmen shall be allowed within the limits of the town of Opelousas under any circumstances or for any purpose without the permission of the mayor or president of the board....

Section 6. No negro or freedman shall be permitted to preach, exhort, or otherwise declaim to congregations of colored people without a special permission from the mayor or president of the board of police....

Section 7. No freedman who is not in the military service shall be allowed to carry firearms, or any kind of weapons, within the limits of the town of Opelousas without the special permission of his employer, in writing, and approved by the mayor or president of the board of police....

Condition of the South, Senate Executive Document No. 2, 39 Cong., 1 Sess., pp. 92–93.

Section 8. No freedman shall sell, barter, or exchange any articles of merchandise or traffic within the limits of Opelousas without permission in writing from his employer or the mayor or president of the board....

Section 9. Any freedman found drunk within the limits of the town shall be imprisoned and made to labor five days on the public streets, or pay five dollars in lieu of said labor.

Section 10. Any freedman not residing in Opelousas who shall be found within the corporate limits after the hour of 3 P.M. on Sunday without a special permission from his employer or the mayor shall be arrested and imprisoned and made to work....

Section 11. All the foregoing provisions apply to freedmen and freedwomen....

E. D. ESTILLETTE,
President of the Board of Police.
JOS. D. RICHARDS, *Clerk.*

Official copy:

J. LOVELL,
Captain and Assistant Adjutant General.

4. Congressman Thaddeus Stevens Demands a Radical Reconstruction, 1867

.... It is to be regretted that inconsiderate and incautious Republicans should ever have supposed that the slight amendments [embodied in the pending Fourteenth Amendment] already proposed to the Constitution, even when incorporated into that instrument, would satisfy the reforms necessary for the security of the Government. Unless the rebel States, before admission, should be made republican in spirit, and placed under the guardianship of loyal men, all our blood and treasure will have been spent in vain. I waive now the question of punishment which, if we are wise, will still be inflicted by moderate confiscations, both as a reproof and example. Having these States, as we all agree, entirely within the power of Congress, it is our duty to take care that no injustice shall remain in their organic laws. Holding them "like clay in the hands of the potter," we must see that no vessel is made for destruction. Having now no governments, they must have enabling acts. The law of last session with regard to Territories settled the principles of such acts. Impartial suffrage, both in electing the delegates and ratifying their proceedings, is now the fixed rule. There is more reason why colored voters should be admitted in the rebel States

Thaddeus Stevens, speech in the House (January 3, 1867), *Congressional Globe*, 39 Cong., 2 Sess., Vol. 37, pt. 1, 251–253. This document can also be found in *Radical Republicans and Reconstruction*, ed. Harold M. Hyman (Indianapolis, Ind., and New York: Bobbs-Merrill, 1967), 373–375.

than in the Territories. In the States they form the great mass of the loyal men. Possibly with their aid loyal governments may be established in most of those States. Without it all are sure to be ruled by traitors; and loyal men, black and white, will be oppressed, exiled, or murdered. There are several good reasons for the passage of this bill. In the first place, it is just. I am now confining my argument to negro suffrage in the rebel States. Have not loyal blacks quite as good a right to choose rulers and make laws as rebel whites? In the second place, it is a necessity in order to protect the loyal white men in the seceded States. The white Union men are in a great minority in each of those States. With them the blacks would act in a body; and it is believed that in each of said States, except one, the two united would form a majority, control the States, and protect themselves. Now they are the victims of daily murder. They must suffer constant persecution or be exiled. The convention of Southern loyalists, lately held in Philadelphia, almost unanimously agreed to such a bill as an absolute necessity.

Another good reason is, it would insure the ascendancy of the Union party. Do you avow the party purpose? exclaims some horror-stricken demagogue. I do. For I believe, on my conscience, that on the continued ascendancy of that party depends the safety of this great nation. If impartial suffrage is excluded in rebel States then every one of them is sure to send a solid rebel representative delegation to Congress, and cast a solid rebel electoral vote. They, with their kindred Copperheads of the North, would always elect the President and control Congress. While slavery sat upon her defiant throne, and insulted and intimidated the trembling North, the South frequently divided on questions of policy between Whigs and Democrats, and gave victory alternately to the sections. Now, you must divide them between loyalists, without regard to color, and disloyalists, or you will be the perpetual vassals of the free-trade, irritated, revengeful South. For these, among other reasons, I am for negro suffrage in every rebel State. If it be just, it should not be denied; if it be necessary, it should be adopted; if it be a punishment to traitors, they deserve it.

But it will be said, as it has been said, "This is negro equality!" What is negro equality, about which so much is said by knaves, and some of which is believed by men who are not fools? It means, as understood by honest Republicans, just this much, and no more: every man, no matter what his race or color; every earthly being who has an immortal soul, has an equal right to justice, honesty, and fair play with every other man; and the law should secure him those rights. The same law which condemns or acquits an African should condemn or acquit a white man. The same law which gives a verdict in a white man's favor should give a verdict in a black man's favor on the same state of facts. Such is the law of God and such ought to be the law of man. This doctrine does not mean that a negro shall sit on the same seat or eat at the same table with a white man. That is a matter of taste which every man must decide for himself. The law has nothing to do with it.

5. Thomas Nast Depicts Contrasting Views of Reconstruction, 1866, 1869

UNCLE SAM'S THANKSGIVING DINNER.

6. Elizabeth Cady Stanton Questions Abolitionist Support for Female Enfranchisement, 1868

To what a depth of degradation must the women of this nation have fallen to be willing to stand aside, silent and indifferent spectators in the reconstruction of the nation, while all the lower stratas of manhood are to legislate in their interests, political, religious, educational, social and sanitary, moulding to their untutored will the institutions of a mighty continent....

While leading Democrats have been thus favorably disposed, what have our best friends said when, for the first time since the agitation of the question [the enfranchisement of women], they have had an opportunity to frame their ideas into statutes to amend the constitutions of two States in the Union?

Charles Sumner, Horace Greeley, Gerrit Smith and Wendell Phillips, with one consent, bid the women of the nation stand aside and behold the salvation of the negro. Wendell Phillips says, "one idea for a generation," to come up in the order of their importance. First negro suffrage, then temperance, then the eight hour movement, then woman's suffrage. In 1958, three generations hence, thirty years to a generation, Phillips and Providence permitting, woman's suffrage will be in order. What an insult to the women who have labored thirty years for the emancipation of the slave, now when he is their political equal, to propose to lift him above their heads. Gerrit Smith, forgetting that our great American idea is "individual rights," in which abolitionists have ever based their strongest

Elizabeth Cady Stanton, "Who Are Our Friends?" *The Revolution*, 15 (January 1868).

arguments for emancipation, says, this is the time to settle the rights of races; unless we do justice to the negro we shall bring down on ourselves another bloody revolution, another four years' war, but we have nothing to fear from woman, she will not revenge herself!...

Horace Greeley has advocated this cause for the last twenty years, but to-day it is too new, revolutionary for practical consideration. The enfranchisement of woman, revolutionizing, as it will, our political, religious and social condition, is not a measure too radical and all-pervading to meet the moral necessities of this day and generation.

Why fear new things; all old things were once new.... We live to do new things! When Abraham Lincoln issued the proclamation of emancipation, it was a new thing. When the Republican party gave the ballot to the negro, it was a new thing, startling too, to the people of the South, very revolutionary to their institutions, but Mr. Greeley did not object to all this because it was new....

And now, while men like these have used all their influence for the last four years, to paralyze every effort we have put forth to rouse the women of the nation, to demand their true position in the reconstruction, they triumphantly turn to us, and say the greatest barrier in the way of your demand is that "the women themselves do not wish to vote." What a libel on the intelligence of the women of the nineteenth century. What means the 12,000 petitions presented by John Stuart Mill in the British Parliament from the first women in England, demanding household suffrage? What means the late action in Kansas, 10,000 women petitioned there for the right of suffrage, and 9,000 votes at the last election was the answer. What means the agitation in every State in the Union? In the very hour when Horace Greeley brought in his adverse report in the Constitutional Convention of New York, at least twenty members rose in their places and presented petitions from every part of the State, demanding woman's suffrage. What means that eloquent speech of George W. Curtis in the Convention, but to show that the ablest minds in the State are ready for this onward step.

7. Charlotte Forten Reflects on Teaching Among Southern African Americans, 1863

Thursday, New Year's Day, 1863. The most glorious day this nation has yet seen, *I* think. I rose early—an event here—and early we started, with an old borrowed carriage and a remarkably slow horse. Whither were we going? thou wilt ask, dearest A. To the ferry; thence to Camp Saxton, to the celebration. From the ferry to the camp the "Flora" took us. How pleasant it was on board! A crowd of people, whites and blacks, and a band of music—to the

---

Excerpt from "States" (Washington, 1872), printed in Dorothy Sterling. ed., *Trouble They Seen: The Story of Reconstruction in the Words of African Americans.*

great delight of the negroes. Met on board Dr. [Solomon] and Mrs. Peck and their daughters, who greeted me most kindly. Also Gen. S. [axton]'s father whom I like much, and several other acquaintances whom I was glad to see. We stopped at Beaufort, and then proceeded to Camp Saxton, the camp of the 1st Reg. [iment] S. [outh] C. [arolina] Vol [unteer]s. The "Flora" c'ld not get up to the landing, so we were rowed ashore in a row boat. Just as my foot touched the plank, on landing, a hand grasped mine and a well known voice spoke my name. It was my dear and noble friend, Dr. [Seth] Rogers. I cannot tell you, dear A., how delighted I was to see him; how *good* it was to see the face of a friend from the North, and *such* a friend. I think myself particularly blessed to have him for a friend. Walking on a little distance I found myself being presented to Col. Higginson, whereat I was so much overwhelmed, that I had no reply to make to the very kind and courteous little speech with which he met me. I believe I mumbled something, and grinned like a simpleton, that was all. Provoking, isn't it? that when one is most in need of sensible words, one finds them not. I *cannot* give a regular chronicle of the day. It is impossible. I was in such a state of excitement. It all seemed, and seems still, like a brilliant dream. Dr. R. [ogers] and I talked all the time, I know, while he showed me the camp and all the arrangements. They have a beautiful situation, on the grounds once occupied by a very old fort, "De La Ribanchine," built in 1629 or 30. Some of the walls are still standing. Dr. R. [ogers] has made quite a good hospital out of an old gin house. I went over it. There are only a few invalids in it, at present. I saw everything; the kitchens, cooking arrangements, and all. Then we took seats on the platform. The meeting was held in a beautiful grove, a live-oak grove, adjoining the camp. It is the largest one I have yet seen; but I don't think the moss pendants are quite as beautiful as they are on St. Helena. As I sat on the stand and looked around on the various groups, I thought I had never seen a sight so beautiful. There were the black soldiers, in their blue coats and scarlet pants, the officers of this and other regiments in their handsome uniforms, and crowds of lookers-on, men, women and children, grouped in various attitudes, under the trees. The faces of all wore a happy, eager, expectant look. The exercises commenced by a prayer from Rev. Mr. [James H.] Fowler, Chaplain of the Reg. An ode written for the occasion by Prof. [John] Zachos, originally a Greek, now Sup. [erintendent] of Paris Island, was read by himself, and then sung by the whites. Col. H. [igginson] introduced Dr. [William] Brisbane in a few elegant and graceful words. He (Dr. B. [risbane]) read the President's Proclamation, which was warmly cheered. Then the beautiful flags presented by Dr. [George] Cheever's Church were presented to Col. H. [igginson] for the Reg. in an excellent and enthusiastic speech, by Rev. Mr. [Mansfield] French. Immediately at the conclusion, some of the colored people—of their own accord sang "My Country Tis of Thee." It was a touching and beautiful incident, and Col. Higginson, in accepting the flags made it the occasion of some happy remarks. He said that *that* tribute was far more effecting than any speech he c'ld make. He spoke for some time, and all that he said was grand, glorious. He seemed inspired. Nothing c'ld have been better, more perfect. And Dr. R. [ogers] told me afterward that the Col. was much affected. That tears were in his eyes.

8. Lucy McMillan, a Former Slave in South Carolina, Testifies About White Violence, 1871

SPARTANBURGH, SOUTH CAROLINA, July 10, 1871.

LUCY McMILLAN (colored) sworn and examined.

By the CHAIRMAN:

QUESTION. Where do you live?

ANSWER. Up in the country. I live on McMillan's place, right at the foot of the road.

QUESTION. How far is it?

ANSWER. Twelve miles.

QUESTION. Are you married?

ANSWER. I am not married. I am single now. I was married. My husband was taken away from me and carried off twelve years ago....

QUESTION. How old are you now?

ANSWER. I am called forty-six. I am forty-five or six.

QUESTION. Did the Ku-Klux come where you live at any time?

ANSWER. They came there once before they burned my house down. The way it was was this: John Hunter's wife came to my house on Saturday morning, and told they were going to whip me. I was afraid of them; there was so much talk of Ku-Klux drowning people, and whipping people, and killing them. My house was only a little piece from the river, so I laid out at night in the woods. The Sunday evening after Isham McCrary was whipped I went up, and a white man, John McMillan, came along and says to me, "Lucy, you had better stay at home, for they will whip you anyhow." I said if they have to, they might whip me in the woods, for I am afraid to stay there. Monday night they came in and burned my house down; I dodged out alongside of the road not far off, and saw them. I was sitting right not far off, and as they came along the river I know some of them. I know John McMillan, and Kennedy McMillan, and Billy Bush, and John Hunter. They were all together. I was not far off, and I saw them. They went right on to my house. When they passed me I run further

Excerpt from "Testimony Taken by the Joint Select Committee to Inquire into the Condition of Affairs in the Late Insurrectionary States" (Washington, 1872), printed in Dorothy Sterling. ed., *Trouble They Seen: The Story of Reconstruction in the Words of African Americans* (New York: Da Capo Press, 1994).

up on the hill to get out of the way of them. They went there and knocked down and beat my house a right smart while. And then they all got still, and directly I saw the fire rise.

QUESTION. How many of these men were there?

ANSWER. A good many; I couldn't tell how many, but these I knew. The others I didn't.

QUESTION. Were these on foot or on horseback?

ANSWER. These were walking that I could call the names of, but the others were riding. I work with these boys everyday. One of them I raised from a child, and I knew them. I have lived with them twelve years.

QUESTION. How were they dressed?

ANSWER. They had just such cloth as this white cotton frock made into old gowns; and some had black faces, and some red, and some had horns on their heads before, and they came a-talking by me and I knew their voices.

QUESTION. How far were you from where they were?

ANSWER. Not very far. I was in the woods, squatted down, and staid still until they passed; but then I run further up the hill.

QUESTION. Have you any family with you there?

ANSWER. I had one little daughter with me. I had one grown daughter, but my grown daughter had been up the country to my mother's staying, and my little girl was staying there with me.

QUESTION. Had you your little girl out with you?

ANSWER. Yes, sir; I could not leave her there.

QUESTION. What was the reason given for burning your house?

ANSWER. There was speaking down there last year and I came to it. They all kept at me to go. I went home and they quizzed me to hear what was said, and I told them as far as my senses allowed me.

QUESTION. Where was the speaking?

ANSWER. Here in this town. I went on and told them, and then they all said I was making laws; or going to have the land, and the Ku-Klux were going to beat me for bragging that I would have land. John Hunter told them on me, I suppose, that I said I was going to have land....

9. Francis Miles Finch Mourns and Celebrates Civil War Soldiers from the South and North, 1867

The Blue and the Gray

By the flow of the inland river,
Whence the fleets of iron have fled,

Frances M. Finch, *The Blue and the Gray: And Other Verses* (New York: Henry Holt and Company, 1909), 1–3.

Where the blades of the grave-grass quiver,
Asleep are the ranks of the dead:
Under the sod and the dew,
Waiting the judgment-day;
Under the one, the Blue,
Under the other, the Gray....

From the silence of sorrowful hours
The desolate mourners go,
Lovingly laden with flowers
Alike for the friend and the foe;
Under the sod and the dew,
Waiting the judgment-day;
Under the roses, the Blue,
Under the lilies, the Gray.

So with an equal splendor,
The morning sun-rays fall,
With a touch impartially tender,
On the blossoms blooming for all:
Under the sod and the dew,
Waiting the judgment-day;
Broidered with gold, the Blue,
Mellowed with gold, the Gray.

So, when the summer calleth,
On forest and field of grain,
With an equal murmur falleth
The cooling drip of the rain:
Under the sod and the dew,
Waiting the judgment-day,
Wet with the rain, the Blue
Wet with the rain, the Gray.

Sadly, but not with upbraiding,
The generous deed was done,
In the storm of the years that are fading
No braver battle was won:
Under the sod and the dew,
Waiting the judgment-day;
Under the blossoms, the Blue,
Under the garlands, the Gray

No more shall the war cry sever,
Or the winding rivers be red;
They banish our anger forever

When they laurel the graves of our dead!
Under the sod and the dew,
Waiting the judgment-day,
Love and tears for the Blue,
Tears and love for the Gray.

ESSAYS

Of all the struggles and complexities of Reconstruction, one main discussion among historians has been how much did life change for African Americans. With the end of slavery, did freedom come? What did freedom mean? How, if at all, did they relate differently with one another, the legal system, and white Americans? These essays offer stark contrasts. The first, by Douglas Blackmon, fixates upon the ways Southern whites reinstituted new forms of control. Blackmon claims that economic interests and white supremacy worked together for Southern whites to create new forms of slavery, which they simply did not call slavery. Alternatively, Edward J. Blum, emphasizes the radical social and personal possibilities of Reconstruction. By looking closely at interactions among former slaves and missionaries from the North, Blum maintains that Reconstruction made possible new forms of close and intimate contact among whites and blacks that had the potential to transform the United States. Where Blackmon finds continuity with the antebellum era, Blum finds rupture and possibility. Where Blackmon finds an unyielding white supremacy, Blum finds racial perspectives transformable.

Slavery by Another Name: The Re-enslavement of Black Americans from the Civil War to World War II

DOUGLAS A. BLACKMON

In the immediate wake of emancipation, the Alabama legislature swiftly passed a measure under which the orphans of freed slaves, or the children of blacks deemed inadequate parents, were to be "apprenticed" to their former masters. The South Carolina planter Henry William Ravenel wrote in September 1865: "There must ... be stringent laws to control the negroes, & require them to fulfill their contracts of labour on the farms."

With the Southern economy in ruins, state officials limited to the barest resources, and county governments with even fewer, the concept of reintroducing the forced labor of blacks as a means of funding government services was viewed by whites as an inherently practical method of eliminating the cost of building prisons and returning blacks to their appropriate position in society. Forcing convicts to work as part of punishment for an ostensible crime was clearly legal too; the Thirteenth Amendment to the Constitution, adopted in 1865 to formally abolish slavery, specifically permitted involuntary servitude as a punishment for "duly convicted" criminals.

Beginning in the late 1860s, and accelerating after the return of white political control in 1877, every Southern state enacted an array of interlocking laws essentially intended to criminalize black life. Many such laws were struck down in court appeals or through federal interventions, but new statutes embracing the same strictures on black life quickly appeared to replace them. Few laws specifically enunciated their applicability only to blacks, but it was widely understood that these provisions would rarely if ever be enforced on whites. Every Southern state except Arkansas and Tennessee had passed laws by the end of 1865 outlawing vagrancy and so vaguely defining it that virtually any freed slave not under the protection of a white man could be arrested for the crime. An 1865 Mississippi statute required African American workers to enter into labor contracts with white farmers by January 1 of every year or risk arrest. Four other states legislated that African Americans could not legally be hired for work without a discharge paper from their previous employer—effectively preventing them from leaving the plantation of the white man they worked for. In the 1880s, Alabama, North Carolina, and Florida enacted laws making it a criminal act for a black man to change employers without permission.

In nearly all cases, the potential penalty awaiting black men, and a small number of women, snared by those laws was the prospect of being sold into forced labor. Many states in the South and the North attempted to place their prisoners in private hands during the eighteenth and early nineteenth centuries. The state of Alabama was long predisposed to the idea, rather than taking on the cost of housing and feeding prisoners itself. It experimented with turning over convicts to private "wardens" during the 1840s and 1850s but was ultimately unsatisfied with the results. The state saved some expense but gathered no revenue. Moreover, the physical abuse that came to be almost synonymous with privatized incarceration always was eventually unacceptable in an era when virtually every convict was white. The punishment of slaves for misdeeds rested with their owners.

Hardly a year after the end of the war, in 1866, Alabama governor Robert M. Patton, in return for the total sum of $5, leased for six years his state's 374 state prisoners to a company calling itself "Smith and McMillen." The transaction was in fact a sham, as the partnership was actually controlled by the Alabama and Chattanooga Railroad. Governor Patton became president of the railroad three years later. Such duplicity would be endemic to convict leasing. For the next eighty years, in every Southern state, the questions of who controlled the fates of black prisoners, which few black men and women among armies of defendants had committed true crimes, and who was receiving the financial benefits of their re-enslavement would almost always never be answered.

Later in 1866, Texas leased 250 convicts to two railroads at the rate of $12.50 a month. In May 1868, ... the state of Georgia signed a lease under which the Georgia and Alabama Railroad acquired one hundred convicts, all of them black, for $2,500. Later that year, the state sold 134 prisoners to the Selma, Rome and Dalton Railroad and sent 109 others to the line being constructed between the towns of Macon and Brunswick, Georgia.

Arkansas began contracting out its state convicts in 1867, selling the rights to prisoners convicted of both state crimes and federal offenses. Mississippi turned over its 241 prisoners to the state's largest cotton planter, Edmund Richardson, in 1868. Three years later, the convicts were transferred to Nathan Bedford Forrest, the former Confederate general, who in civilian life already was a major planter and railroad developer. In 1866, he and five other former rebel officers had founded the Ku Klux Klan. Florida leased out half of the one hundred prisoners in its Chattahoochee penitentiary in 1869.

North Carolina began "farming out" its convicts in 1872. After white South Carolinians led by Democrat Wade Hampton violently ousted the last black government of the state in 1877, the legislature promptly passed a law allowing for the sale of the state's four hundred black and thirty white prisoners.

Six years earlier, in 1871, Tennessee leased its nearly eight hundred prisoners, nearly all of them black, to Thomas O'Connèr, a founding partner along with Arthur Colyar of Tennessee Coal, Iron & Railroad Co. In the four decades after the war, as Colyar built his company into an industrial behemoth, its center of operations gradually shifted to Alabama, where it was increasingly apparent that truly vast reserves of coal and iron ore lay beneath the surface.

Prominent Southern businessmen bridged the era of slavery and the distinct new economic opportunities of the region at the end of the nineteenth century. They were true slavers, raised in the old traditions of bondage, but also men who believed that African Americans under the lash were the key to building an industrial sector in the South to fend off the growing influence of northern capitalists.

Already, whites realized that the combination of trumped-up legal charges and forced labor as punishment created both a desirable business proposition and an incredibly effective tool for intimidating rank-and-file emancipated African Americans and doing away with their most effective leaders.

The newly installed white government of Hale County—deep in the majority-black cotton growing sections of Alabama—began leasing prisoners to private parties in August 1875. A local grand jury said the new practice was "contributing much to the revenues of the county, instead of being an expense." The money derived from selling convicts was placed in the Fine and Forfeiture Fund, which was used to pay fees to judges, sheriffs, other low officials, and witnesses who helped convict defendants.

The prior year, during a violent campaign by Ku Klux Klansmen and other white reactionaries to break up black Republican political meetings across Alabama, a white raiding party confronted a meeting of African Americans in Hale County. Shots were fired in the dark and two men died— one white and one black. No charges were brought in the killing of the African American, but despite any evidence they caused the shooting, leading black Republicans R. H. Skinner and Woodville Hardy were charged and convicted of murder. They were sent to the Eureka mines south of Birmingham in the spring of 1876.

By the end of 1877, fifty convict laborers were at work in Newcastle Coal Company mine outside Birmingham. An additional fifty-eight men had been forced into the Eureka mines he founded near Helena. A total of 557 prisoners had been turned over that year to private corporations by the state of Alabama.

By the end of Reconstruction in 1877, every formerly Confederate state except Virginia had adopted the practice of leasing black prisoners into commercial hands. There were variations among the states, but all shared the same basic formula. Nearly all the penal functions of government were turned over to the companies purchasing convicts. In return for what they paid each state, the companies received absolute control of the prisoners. They were ostensibly required to provide their own prisons, clothing, and food, and bore responsibility for keeping the convicts incarcerated. Company guards were empowered to chain prisoners, shoot those attempting to flee, torture any who wouldn't submit, and whip the disobedient—naked or clothed—almost without limit. Over eight decades, almost never were there penalties to any acquirer of these slaves for their mistreatment or deaths.

On paper, the regulations governing convict conditions required that prisoners receive adequate food, be provided with clean living quarters, and be protected from "cruel" or "excessive punishment." All floggings were to be recorded in logbooks, and indeed hundreds were. But the only regularly enforced laws on the new slave enterprises were those designed primarily to ensure that no black worker received freedom or experienced anything other than racially segregated conditions. In Alabama, companies were fined $150 a head if they allowed a prisoner to escape. For a time, state law mandated that if a convict got free while being transported to the mines, the sheriff or deputy responsible had to serve out the prisoner's sentence. Companies often faced their strongest criticism for allowing black and white prisoners to share the same cells. "White convicts and colored convicts shall not be chained together," read Alabama law.

In almost every respect—the acquisition of workers, the lease arrangements, the responsibilities of the leaseholder to detain and care for them, the incentives for good behavior—convict leasing adopted practices almost identical to those emerging in slavery in the 1850s.

By the late 1870s, the defining characteristics of the new involuntary servitude were clearly apparent. It would be obsessed with ensuring disparate treatment of blacks, who at all times in the ensuing fifty years would constitute 90 percent or more of those sold into labor. They were routinely starved and brutalized by corporations, farmers, government officials, and small-town businessmen intent on achieving the most lucrative balance between the productivity of captive labor and the cost of sustaining them. The consequences for African Americans were grim. In the first two years that Alabama leased its prisoners, nearly 20 percent of them died. In the following year, mortality rose to 35 percent. In the fourth, nearly 45 percent were killed.

The system of leasing convicts soon radically altered the implications of the debt enforcement process and the significance of each official involved in it. County sheriffs and judges had dabbled with leasing black convicts out to local farmers, or to contractors under hire to repair roads and bridges, beginning almost immediately after the Civil War. But as the state turned ever larger blocs of African Americans over to private companies, an organized market for prisoners began to evolve. Soon, labor agents for the mining and timber companies were scouring the countryside to make arrangements for acquiring able-bodied black laborers....

Instead of slave owners, the men who now controlled squads of black laborers available to the highest bidder were sheriffs. The key distinction, however, between the sheriff and the old slave masters was that since these African Americans were not his or anyone else's permanent property, he had no reason for concern about how they were treated by their new keepers or whether they survived at all. By the early 1880s, twenty-nine of Alabama's sixty-seven counties were leasing their prisoners. The trade in black workers continued to swell. Because of the financial benefits of leasing convicts rather than sending them to state officials, some counties opted to prosecute men accused of felonies on misdemeanor charges—solely so the sheriff and other locals could receive the proceeds of the prisoner's lease. County prisoners eventually far surpassed the number of men pressed into forced labor by the state.

Control of those county convicts was lucrative, for both the companies who acquired them and the sheriffs who supplied them. In addition to the fees they received from defendants, sheriffs also kept any amount left over from daily feeding fees paid for each prisoner by the state. As a result, Alabama's sheriffs were financially motivated to arrest and convict as many people as possible, and simultaneously to feed them as little as they could get away with.

In counties where large numbers of convicts were sold to the mining companies, such as Jefferson County, where Birmingham was located, a speculative trade in convict contracts developed. The witnesses and public officials who were owed portions of the lease payments earned by the convicts received paper receipts—usually called scrips—from the county that could be redeemed only after a convict had generated enough money to pay them off. Rather than wait for the full amount, holders of the scrips would sell their notes for cash to speculators at a lower than face amount. In return, the buyers were to receive the full lease payments—profiting handsomely on those convicts who survived, losing money on the short-lived. In Jefferson County, the financial arrangements on each convict were recorded in ledger books showing earnings due to each official and then a subsequent calculation of the final rate of return on each prisoner after his release, escape, or death.

The job of a county sheriff became a heady enterprise, often more akin to the business of trading in mules than law enforcement. Sheriffs and their local judges developed special relationships with local companies and preferred acquirers of their prisoners. Arrests surged and fell, not as acts of crime increased or receded, but in tandem to the varying needs of the buyers of labor. Companies, commissioners, justices of the peace, probate judges, and sheriffs issued offers of rewards for escapees. Constables arrested men on speculation that they might be wanted elsewhere, seizing them on the basis of rumors, and then inquiring whether there might be reward money available in the county from which they hailed....

Swift, uncomplicated adjudication was the key to the system. Trials were discouraged; lawyers for black misdemeanor defendants were scant. Indeed, the fee system—with its additional charge for each act in the judicial process or appearance of another witness or official—was a built-in disincentive to prisoners who knew that each added dollar of their final fine and costs would ultimately equate to additional days held in forced labor. The span of time from arrest to conviction and judgment to delivery at a slave mine or mill was often no more than seventy-two hours. The most common penalty was nine months to a year in a slave mine or lumber camp.

All of this was predicated on the absolute defenselessness of black men to the legal system, and the near certainty that most would be unable to bond themselves out of jail or pay fines imposed upon them. Across Alabama, northern Florida, and Georgia, a bewildering world of casual judicial process emerged in which affidavits were scribbled on scraps of notebook paper, half-official judges and strongmen assuming the authority to arrest resided every few miles, men were identified and arrested on the basis of meaningless physical descriptions, and hardly anyone could sign their own name. Increasingly, it was a system driven not by any goal of enforcement or public protection against serious offenses, but purely to generate fees and claim bounties.

Reforging the White Republic: Race, Religion, and American Nationalism, 1865–1898

EDWARD J. BLUM

After serving as a doctor among African American soldiers during the Civil War, Esther Hawks was teaching black children in Charleston, South Carolina, when news of Lincoln's assassination arrived. She agreed with the northern ministers who proposed a "fatalistic theory" of Lincoln's murder, believing that his "work was accomplished and he is removed." Even in her despair, Hawks was certain that "God has other men and means, to finish what is yet undone!" But missionaries like Hawks had much more to accomplish than to simply make theological sense of the president's assassination for themselves. They also had to break the news to their African American pupils. Confused, angered, and saddened, these northern whites and Southern blacks grieved together. After she

Excerpt from Edward J. Blum, "On the Verge of Heaven: Religious Missions, Interracial Contact, and the Radicalism of Radical Reconstruction," chap. 2 in *Reforging the White Republic: Race, Religion, and American Nationalism, 1865–1898* (Baton Rouge: Louisiana State University Press, 2005). Reprinted with permission.

and the school's principal informed the students of the tragic event, "many of the older children cried aloud.... several of the large girls who are in classes.... came to me, weeping bitterly." The sadness of the freedpeople was almost too much to bear. "The colord [*sic*] people express their sorrow and sense of loss in many cases, with sobs and loud lamentations."

Hawks was one of thousands of northern whites who traveled south during and after the war in a massive movement to aid the freedpeople, and emotional encounters similar to those she described helped further tie northern radicals and African Americans together. By the war's end, at least seventy "freedmen's aid societies" were collecting and distributing a host of goods to send to the South, while men and women from a variety of theological and racial backgrounds rallied to the cause. The American Missionary Association (AMA), principally led by Congregationalists, received the endorsement of the Dutch Reformed Church, the New School Presbyterians, the United Brethren, the Free Methodist Church, and even the Church of Scotland. Other denominations, including the African Methodist Episcopal Church, the African Methodist Episcopal Zion Church, the Methodist Episcopal Church, the United Presbyterians, the Northern Baptists, and the New and Old School Presbyterians, formed their own societies and sent their own missionaries. Several associations eschewed particular denominational labels and allowed thousands of other northerners to contribute as well. These nonsectarian groups, principally composed of Quakers and Unitarians and misidentified by some historians as "secular," banded together after the war to form the American Freedmen's Union Commission (AFUC). Together, these organizations and their missionaries were the hands and feet of the radical northern Protestant quest to transform former slaves into Christian and Republican citizens.

For the most part, historians have found much more to criticize than to compliment in the Reconstruction-education crusade and "radical" Reconstruction. While white scholars in the early twentieth century denounced the missionaries as blind fanatics who had little understanding of Southern racial dynamics, historians in the late twentieth century have portrayed them as bourgeois moralists who merely wanted to inculcate notions of time–management and thrift into Southern blacks so that they would become contented wage laborers. Even more sympathetic accounts of the crusaders, such as those by Jacqueline Jones and Joe Richardson, have maintained that while the teachers endeavored to help African Americans, they could never overcome their paternalistic and prejudicial attitudes. Their chauvinism created a cultural "chasm" between northern whites and Southern blacks that could not be bridged.

But the image of Esther Hawks and countless other white northerners weeping with Southern freedpeople complicates these scholarly appraisals. There was something powerful and precious occurring during the 1860s and early 1870s as whites and blacks sought to work together in new ways and under new conditions. As W. E. B. Du Bois first recognized in his magisterial *The Souls of Black Folk* in 1903, interracial contact was one of the most critical aspects of post–Civil War Reconstruction. He considered the northerners who ventured south "saintly souls" who initiated "the finest thing in American history." He waxed poetic about them: "This was the gift of New England to the freed Negro, not alms, but a friend; not cash, but character. It was and is not money that these seething millions want, but love and sympathy…. In actual formal content their curriculum was doubtless old-fashioned, but in educational power it was supreme, for it was the contact of living souls."

Taken from the perspective of white and black Americans in the 1860s, the Reconstruction-education crusade was a dramatic moment of interracial fraternity that had the power to alter Southern and American society. It was part of a widespread effort among northern Protestants and radical Republicans to restructure the nature of national citizenship. In addition to the missions, Congress passed a number of bills, laws, and constitutional amendments that overturned much of the legislation that had previously upheld the white republic. The years of radical Reconstruction were loaded with revolutionary potential as politicians, religious leaders, and the relief associations envisioned a nation in which race and freed people's former status as slaves no longer determined citizenship and civil rights. Through their publishing, their reports to the federal government, their letters and diaries, and their actions, organizational leaders and missionaries imagined and endeavored to create an integrated nation where whites and blacks learned, worked, and lived together. Although they did not represent the attitudes of the majority of northern whites, the extremity and intensity of their radicalism suggests that the tenets of the white republic were being fully and systematically challenged.

The drive to provide humanitarian relief and education to Southern freedpeople was an interdenominational and interracial crusade that brought thousands of northerners into a common cause and generated massive amounts of concern for African American rights and privileges. Compassion for the physical and spiritual well-being of freedpeople was part of a long history of Protestant missionary involvement in conveying the gospel and bringing western-style education to peoples of various cultures. Although many historians have focused on single denominations or organizations, the crusade to aid Southern blacks was a mass movement of northerners, especially Protestants. As one missionary recalled, "Almost every Church in the North has contributed to educational purposes in the South." Another claimed that "freedman's aid societies were started in churches of all denominations. Members of families and neighbors joined themselves into independent clubs,—all to help on this great work amongst the negroes." Missionary Elizabeth Botome perhaps summed up the need for relief best when she claimed: "A common cause made all friends."

Northerners and Southern freedpeople demonstrated their commitments to transforming Southern society and the nation's identity by donating an impressive amount of capital and goods to racial uplift. By the end of the war, northern organizations had sent over thirty thousand books and pamphlets, ninety thousand garments, and fifty-eight hundred yards of cloth to the South, In 1866, the AMA alone garnered over $250,000 in cash donations, a five-fold increase from the amount it had received in 1862. The federal government and Southern blacks also chipped in large amounts. In 1869, the Freedmen's Bureau reported over $500,000 in expenditures on Southern education, while freedpeople supplied roughly $180,000 for their schools during that year. Donations continued to pour in throughout the late 1860s. In 1870, the AMA's receipts had risen to over $430,000. Northern Presbyterians gave $77,000 to aid the freedpeople in 1871. All in all, between 1861 and 1889 northerners contributed an estimated $20 million in cash to the relief associations. Compared to spending on political campaigns during the same years, the donation amounts were remarkable. For the presidential campaign of 1868, for instance, the Republican Party spent only around $200,000.

Money, supplies, and books were not the heart and soul of this crusade, however. The thousands of missionaries who flocked to the South served as the lifeblood of the movement. They embodied radicalism, endeavoring to put ideas of equal citizenship into practice. As W. E. B. Du Bois noted at the turn of the century, contact was more powerful than capital; handshakes were more meaningful than handouts....

As they spent more time with local blacks in classrooms and Sabbath schools, the missionaries were amazed by the intelligence of the freedpeople and their earnest desire for education. Before, during, and after the Civil War, Southern blacks went to extraordinary lengths to learn to read and write, and teachers recognized and applauded these strivings. Laura Haviland, for instance, marveled at one African American woman "who had taught a midnight school for years" before the war. "It was opened at eleven or twelve o'clock at night, and closed at two o'clock A. M. Every window and door was carefully closed to prevent discovery. In that little school hundreds of slaves learned to read and write a legible hand. After toiling all day for their masters they crept stealthily into this back alley, each with a bundle of pitch-pine splinters for lights." Upon talking with Will Capers, a local black who had received an education before the war, Laura Towne recorded, "He is very intelligent and self-respecting. He is in hopes he will be paid for teaching." In a later entry, she referred to him as "a fine fellow in every respect."

Countless missionary-teachers wrote to their supporters in the North that African American children learned just as quickly as white students and were equally capable. The reports of the teachers influenced broader northern opinions. According to John W. Alvord, the general superintendent of education for the Freedmen's Bureau, the teachers' findings thoroughly destroyed the "charge that the negro is 'too stupid too learn.'" This stereotype, he concluded, "has passed away."

Along with the classroom experiences, Christian worship services provided numerous moments for northern missionaries and Southern blacks to interact with one another spiritually and to experience new feelings of community. Although most religious historians have focused on why Southern African Americans left white churches en masse after the Civil War and further solidified the segregation of the churches, these scholars have overlooked the scores of examples of integrated religious services during radical Reconstruction. Moreover, few historians have recognized the importance of integrated worship on the minds and spirits of nineteenth-century whites. Missionary accounts were filled with descriptions of black worship services, prayers, and sermons. During church meetings northerners sang and prayed alongside blacks, and several missionary-teachers preached to these congregations. Some were even invited to "secret" church services like those African Americans had held during the antebellum period in order to worship outside of their masters' or mistresses' gaze.

Church services, along with weddings, baptisms, and funerals, provided powerful moments of interracial socializing and had a marked effect on several missionaries. Some recorded being emotionally and spiritually moved by the prayers of freedpeople. Lucy Chase was struck when one freedman "prayed for black and white, for rich and poor, for bond and free." "A prayer-meeting" of fifty African Americans deeply stirred Marie Waterbury. Some of the participants, she recalled, "were stolen from Africa when they were infants; some whose mothers had been sold and run off to the sugar plantations, before they were a year old. Ah! how such had learned to pray." Laura Towne was equally touched when a local elder "prayed that 'the little white sisters who came to give learning to the children might be blessed.' " A missionary in Mississippi probably put the impact of interracial worship most poignantly. "As I walked home in the beautiful moonlight" from attending and preaching at a worship service with local blacks, "I could but think that perhaps God was as well pleased with that lowly group in the humble cabin, as with many a gilded throng in splendid cathedrals."

Several teachers expressed a new respect for African American religious practices as they spent more spiritual time with freedpeople. After speaking with an elderly black woman and her family, Reverend W. J. Richardson wrote from South Carolina, "Such interviews, even in the *lowly cabin*—seem *quite* on the *verge of Heaven*." "This aged mother cannot read a word," he continued, "and yet she seemed to possess the life experience of a mature Christian." In July 1862, Towne described one local minister as "looking like Jupiter himself, grave, powerful, and awfully dignified." Historian Kurt Wolfe has shown that with time Towne stopped using words like "superstitious" or "backward" to describe black religion in her diary. Even more, she began to seek out African American elders to learn about African customs. "I went to-day to see Maum Katie, an old African woman, who remembers worshipping her own gods in Africa," Towne wrote in her journal. She was deeply impressed by Katie: "She is very bright and talkative, and is a great 'spiritual mother,' a fortune-teller, or rather prophetess, and a woman of tremendous influence." Katie so captivated Towne, in fact, that she determined to "cultivate her acquaintance." African American religious services thoroughly enthralled one missionary in Mississippi. "The religion of these people is not a cold abstraction," she asserted. "Its life giving influence lightens the eye, quickens the step, gives tone and vigor to the whole man." Several teachers expressed sincere fondness for the slave spirituals. The Chase sisters lauded African American hymns and songs as "poetic and picturesque." Elizabeth Botome concurred, writing years later, "One who has not heard these spirituals under such circumstances cannot understand their power and pathos. I can never hear them, even at this date, without emotion."

Ultimately, interracial interaction transformed the ways in which missionaries viewed themselves and their relationships to the black community. When most northerners first ventured south, they tended to characterize blacks as "they" and "them." But as these teachers attended worship services, cooked dinners, and taught schools alongside freedpeople, the pronouns "we" and "us" slowly crept into their writings. Martha Johnson was a case in point. In her initial letters home from Port Royal, she regularly referred to local African Americans as "they" or "them." But with time, her viewpoint shifted. "If I do my duty by my school and visit among my people I have very little time or strength for household work," she wrote to her sisters in Vermont. Likewise, when leaving Virginia's Fort Magruder for the summer, Margaret Newbold Thorpe recalled that "[i]t was very painful to leave our people." When Thorpe returned to the school in the early fall, she recorded that "[o]ur people are now taking up letter writing." Lucy Chase recognized that something new was happening to her. "I can truly say," she wrote in March 1863, "white-man though I am, that I have, with the Negro, 'a feeling sense' of this state of transition. Lo! an episode! Every hour of my life here is strange; it is not the past; it is not the future, and, with all the chances and changes of war it does not seem to be the present either." By 1866, Lucy's sister Sarah had cast off identification as a "white-man." She now characterized herself as part of the African American community, "*If* I live, I must work *among* my people again," she wrote. In a study of missionary letters, one modern historian has found that northern missionaries so often employed idioms like "my people" in reference to African Americans that "one could be easily led astray by thinking that the writer who used such phrases.... was black."

Surprisingly, at least one missionary even sought to pass as black so that Southern whites would leave her alone. In West Virginia, Sarah Jane Foster forged close relationships with several African American men, and they regularly escorted her home in the evenings. Her interactions with these black men led some local whites to wonder about her race. "Out there it has been told that I was part colored and was *married to Geo. Brown*," Foster noted in February 1866. One neighbor even asked if Foster was "half nigger." These assertions and queries, which would have infuriated most other northern whites, did not enrage Foster. Instead, she actually preferred that local whites consider her "part black" so that she could work with the freedpeople without interference. "I hope they will believe it," Foster wrote to *Zion's Advocate*, "for then surely they could not complain of my teaching the people of my own race." To Foster, becoming "part colored" was an effective strategy to continue her great work.

Social contact, emerging friendships, and the blurring of racial lines reinforced a larger political and social radicalism enacted by these missionary teachers. Their personal encounters generated larger social and political awareness. Many became staunch and life-long advocates of political and civil rights for people of color, striving for a new American republic that would look beyond race as the key determinant of civic inclusion. Not only did they express a hope that blacks would obtain equal rights, but they also actively championed that cause. Methodist teachers in New Orleans, for example, asserted that "[t]he question ... of equal rights ... among men, irrespective of ... race, is not one to be argued, but accepted by those who believe in the Bible." Sounding much like Thaddeus

Stevens when he repeatedly called on the federal government to give confiscated lands to freedpeople, Cornelia Hancock thought that "the best plan would be to put all the secesh in the poor house and let the negroes have the land." Connecting her experiences with African American soldiers at church to her growing feeling that God demanded universal manhood suffrage, a missionary in Baltimore professed, "As I watched their coming into church on their crutches, as I saw their earnest and devout attention, the intelligence manifested in their engaging in the different parts of worship, ... I thought, can there be found a man who would dare deny these men the right of suffrage or any other privilege which freemen have? If so, God will by some *other* judgment teach us *His* will." Linda Slaughter dearly expressed the belief that American citizenship and identity should not be premised upon racial categories when she referred to freedpeople as America's "true home-born sons."

Some missionary-teachers and their northern advocates even challenged whites' phobias surrounding interracial marriage and sexuality. In the North, prominent abolitionist and Christian reformer Lewis Tappan, one of the vice presidents of the AMA, claimed that since the Bible made no declaration against interracial marriage, then humans ought not to either. There were, moreover, several instances of interracial marriages among those who took part in the education crusade, and some missionaries adamantly defended the rights of whites and blacks to marry whomever they wished. In 1869, Gilbert Haven predicted that interracial marriage would become the norm in the near future. "The hour is not far off when the white hued husband shall boast of the dusky beauty of his wife," he claimed, "and the Caucasian wife shall admire the sun-kissed countenance of her husband as deeply and as unconsciously of the present ruling abhorrence as is his admiration for her lighter tint." When a chaplain in Florida refused to wed a black soldier and his white fiancée, a Southern woman who had formerly owned him, Esther Hawks vigorously disputed his decision. "I took the ground that he had no right to refuse to perform the ceremony *simply* on account of color," she wrote in her journal: "If a white woman *chooses* to marry a black man who can say her nay.... The discussion grew quite animated but I do not think we made the Chaplin see the *foolishness* of his position."

Hawks went far beyond accepting social interaction and equality between whites and blacks. She helped foster it. In July 1865, she threw a party for African American members of the Massachusetts 54th Regiment and white Yankee schoolteachers and nurses. The party was a smashing success in Hawks's estimation, because it overcame notions of racial difference if only for the moment. She wrote triumphantly: "[F]or *one* evening, at least, a company of ladies and gentlemen treated each other as such without regard to *color*." To Hawks, "the most observing critic could not have noticed the least prejudice—or unpleasant feeling of any kind towards each other." She considered these soldiers "gentlemen" regardless of their skin color, and she saw no reason for northern women not to enjoy their company.

Regular holiday celebrations were occasions for whites and blacks to reflect upon and enact changes in their racial and national imaginations. Northern missionaries regularly observed Christmas, Thanksgiving, New Year's Day, and the

Fourth of July with Southern blacks, often commenting that these interracial celebrations seemed to prove that a new and integrated nation was being forged. On New Year's Day, 1863—the day Lincoln signed the Emancipation Proclamation—a massive celebration took place on the Sea Islands of South Carolina. Thousands of whites and blacks prayed, sang, and cheered together. Charlotte Forten penned a powerful description of the event, which was later published in the *Atlantic Monthly* and reprinted in Lydia Marie Child's *The Freedmen's Book*. "New-Year's Day, Emancipation Day, was a glorious one to us," she claimed. It was "[t]he greatest day in the nation's history." Local blacks believed that emancipation had made the country their own. After Colonel Thomas Wentworth Higginson, the white leader of the 2nd Regiment of the U.S. Colored Troops, had finished speaking, "some of the colored people, of their own accord, began to sing, 'My country 'tis of thee/Sweet land of liberty,/Of thee we sing.'" Forten and the local freedpeople were ecstatic. "'Forever free! forever free!'—those magical words in the President's Proclamation were constantly singing themselves in my soul."

Some Southerners took to openly denouncing and threatening the teachers, sometimes rhetorically associating the missionaries with demonic forces. A writer for the *Norfolk Virginian* described the teachers as "a lot of ignorant, narrow-minded, bigoted fanatics." The epithet "nigger teacher" became widely employed. "From one set of students, whose boarding-house I was compelled constantly to pass, I habitually received the polite salutation of 'damned Yankee bitch of a nigger teacher,' with the occasional admonition to take up my abode in the infernal regions," said one missionary. Another teacher heard local whites proclaiming, "Here comes Hell," every time she came near. Lucy and Sarah Chase recounted similar episodes. "One of our main-land neighbors," Lucy wrote in March 1863, "is disgusted at the very thought that any-body could be found so silly as to come out here to teach the negroes! 'I'd poison a Yankee in a moment, if I could get a chance,' she says." Another Southern woman told one of Lucy's friends, "I wish I had a pistol, and I would shoot you." At least one opponent of the teachers explicitly denounced them for defying the chief tenets of the white republic. "The Radicals are [the] flail of Deity," a white supremacist theologian asserted, "they have turned traitors to their race, their religion and their God."

But verbal barbs and church ostracism were perhaps the least of northerners' worries. During Reconstruction the symbols of blacks' empowerment and interracial fraternity—schools, churches, teachers, and politicians—became objects of such hatred that former Confederates often resorted to violence. Guns, arson, and intimidation became the chief tools of opposition to the new nation that the radicals envisioned. Examples of violence committed against teachers and African Americans littered John Alvord's reports for the Freedmen's Bureau. The Bureau superintendent in Louisiana, for instance, wrote in 1866, "The hostility to colored schools was so great that many acts of violence and insult were committed on the teachers; school-houses were burned, and pupils beaten and frightened." Scores of churches and schools were set ablaze, while white and black teachers were brutalized. The tale of Alonzo B. Corliss, a partially crippled teacher at a Quaker-sponsored school, revealed the extent to which Southern whites would go to rid their land of northern missionaries. On November 26, 1869, several disguised men dragged Corliss from his house and gave him about thirty lashes with a rawhide and hickory sticks, shaved one side of his head, painted it black, and warned him to leave. Corliss eventually did vacate the South, but only after his landlord forced him out. Local authorities did nothing to arrest or prosecute the attackers.

For all of the violence and mayhem, Southern whites could not obliterate the dramatic changes that the educational crusade imposed upon Southern society. Nor could white supremacists destroy the commitments of the teachers who re-mained in the South. Klan members could burn schoolhouses, but they could never get to all of the books, primers, and Bibles. Southern whites could whip northern teachers, but they could not drive out the friendships forged between white teachers and black students. African Americans could be terrorized, but that would not stop them from seeking to provide a better future for their chil-dren. The Reconstruction-education crusade drastically and radically altered the landscape of Southern society and the lives of African Americans. It provided the funds, schools, and teachers that led to one of the most remarkable increases in literacy in the modern world and the creation of an African American middle class that would continue to battle for social and civil rights long after Recon-struction ended. The missions also offered a historical legacy of white radicalism and friendship that African Americans drew upon for courage and hope. In short, the mission of the northern schoolteacher had a powerful and long-lasting influ-ence that white terror could rage against with all of its might, but never fully defeat.

Missionary groups and Southern blacks created a host of schools, colleges, and universities for the educational advancement of African Americans that proved critical to the fight against white supremacy in the late nineteenth and twentieth centuries. Atlanta University, Fisk University, Clark University, More-house College, Scotia Seminary, Howard University, and Lincoln University were only the most prominent. By 1892, there were more than twenty-five thousand schools for African Americans in the South, with more than twenty thousand Southern blacks teaching in them. Thirteen thousand of these teachers had themselves been educated in schools created during radical Reconstruction, Over 2 million Southern blacks had learned to read by the early 1890s, and many of them could write as well. These schools, moreover, did not collapse when Southern whites put an end to Reconstruction. Schools for Southern blacks continued to persevere throughout the nineteenth and twentieth centu-ries. The educational crusade also provided theological seminaries for African American religious leaders and fuel for the rise of the African American press. By the early 1890s, there were more than 150 newspapers edited in the South by African Americans, several of which were published at black colleges. This black press was crucial in creating a counter public sphere in which African Americans could resist the derogatory reports of their lives and qualities that per-meated the white press. Furthermore, the press provided opportunities for

African Americans to hone their literary skills and their arguments against racial exploitation.

The growth of black schools and newspapers was matched by an amazing rise in African American literacy, which the Reconstruction-education crusade had helped to bring about. As of 1865, less than 10 percent of Southern blacks were literate. By 1870, that percentage had only advanced to 18.6 percent, but only two decades later it was more than 55 percent. By 1940, African American literacy stood at 89 percent. Put in international perspective, this increase was particularly impressive. African American educational improvements far outstripped similar gains in other nations. In post-emancipation societies, including Trinidad, Haiti, and British Guiana, literacy rates of freedpeople and their descendants remained well behind those in the United States. As late as the 1930s, Haiti's Afro-Caribbean literacy rate stood under 20 percent, while literacy in Trinidad was under 60 percent. But even compared to more economically sound European nations, such as Spain and Italy, the advance of African American education was astonishing. In 1860 about 25 percent of Spain's citizens were literate. By 1900, that rate had increased only to 37 percent. Furthermore, in Italy, literacy rates stood at about 31 percent in 1871. By 1901, they had increased to 52 percent. The improvement in African American literacy was nothing short of remarkable. It stood as a testament to the desire of people of color within the United States to obtain educational advancement and to the commitment of northern relief organizations and missionaries.

During the high-water mark of radical Reconstruction, a young African American scholar at Trinity School in Athens, Alabama, asked a poignant question in a letter to the white students of a northern Sunday school class: "[W]ould you speak to a black boy?" During and after the Civil War, thousands of northerners answered this rhetorical question by traveling south, working on behalf of African American education, and joining black men and women in a struggle for racial uplift. Although cultural chauvinism and deep-seated prejudices marred many of their missions, some schoolteachers had their racial views altered. Their opinions and beliefs about race were not static, but dynamic, and contact led them to new planes of human brotherhood and solidarity. These teachers stood as the arm of the post–Civil War Protestant and radical plan for a new American republic constructed around loyalty to the Union, rather than racial classification. They sought nothing less than to dismantle the chief bulwarks of the white republic and construct in their place a new country of brotherhood and fraternity.

 # FURTHER READING

David W. Blight, *Race and Reunion: The Civil War in American Memory* (2001).

Laura Edwards, *Gendered Strife and Confusion: The Political Culture of Reconstruction* (1997).

Eric Foner, *A Short History of Reconstruction, 1863–1877* (1990).

Steven Hahn, *A Nation under Our Feet: Black Political Struggles in the Rural South from Slavery to the Great Migration* (2003).

Moon-Ho Jung, *Coolies and Cane: Race, Labor, and Sugar in the Age of Emancipation* (2008).

Ari Kelman, *A Misplaced Massacre: Struggling over the Memory of Sand Creek* (2013).

Charles Lane, *The Day Freedom Died: The Colfax Massacre, the Supreme Court, and the Betrayal of Reconstruction* (2008).

Heather Cox Richardson, *West from Appomattox: The Reconstruction of America after the Civil War* (2008).

Heather Andrea Williams, *Self-Taught: African American Education in Slavery and Freedom* (2005).

Gavin Wright, *Old South, New South: Revolutions in the Southern Economy since the Civil War* (1986).

Additional critical thinking activities and content are available in MindTap.

MindTap

MindTap is a fully online, highly personalized learning experience built upon Cengage Learning content. MindTap combines student learning tools—readings, multimedia, activities, and assessments—into a singular Learning Path that guides students through the course.